Classical Approaches to the Study of Religion

Classical Approaches to the Study of Religion

Aims, Methods and Theories of Research

Introduction and Anthology

by
Jacques Waardenburg

Walter de Gruyter
New York · Berlin 1999

♾ Printed on acid-free paper which falls within the guidelines of the ANSI to ensure permanence and durability.

This paperback edition contains the original clothbound edition of *Classical Approaches to the Study of Religion. Aims, Methods and Theories of Research*, 1: Introduction and Anthology by Jacques Waardenburg (Religion and Reason 3).

Library of Congress Cataloging-in-Publication Data

Classical approaches to the study of religion : aims, methods, and
   theories of research / [compiled] by Jacques Waardenburg.
       p.   cm. — (Religion and reason ; 3)
    Originally published: The Hague : Mouton, [1973–. (Religion and
reason ; 3). With new pref.
    Includes bibliographical references and index.
    Contents: 1. Introduction and anthology.
    ISBN 3-11-016328-4 (pbk.)
    1. Religion—Study and teaching.   I. Waardenburg, Jacques.
II. Series.
BL41.C53   1999
200'.71—dc21   98-52538
                                                   CIP

Die Deutsche Bibliothek–CIP–Einheitsaufnahme

Waardenburg, Jacques:
Classical approaches to the study of religion : aims, methods and
theories of research / introduction and anthology by Jacques
Waardenburg. - Berlin ; New York : de Gruyter, 1999
    ISBN 3-11-016328-4

DBN: 95.524438.2
SG: 13

Preface to the Paperback Edition

I conceived the idea of the *Classical Approaches* in the early seventies when new generations of students and perhaps also researchers had to familiarize themselves with the history of the scholarly study of religions. My main concern, however, was less to offer a history of the discipline than to open up some underlying questions which turn out to be fundamental in this area of research.

These questions touched what may be called the epistemology of the study of religions. In trying to answer them, various theories have been developed to make religion a subject of scholarly research and various methodologies devised to study religious data sometimes of the most intricate nature. By incorporating scholarship from very different disciplines I wanted to make clear how much research into religious data can gain by learning from disciplines that may not necessarily be focussing on religion but concentrate on the cultures, societies, communal and individual lives in which religious expressions may appear.

Behind this idea there were other intentions as well. First, I wanted to make clear that for the study of religions to be recognized as a distinct field of research – and not just a matter of personal taste or gifts – questions of theory and method had to be discussed. As a platform for such discussions I created the series *Religion and Reason*, the first volume of which appeared in 1971. In this series the *Classical Approaches* was intended as a flash back to the most important texts in which scholars of reknown had expressed themselves on matters of method and theory.

Second, I was looking for a theoretical renewal of the academic study of religions. Such a renewal requires knowledge of previous theoretical approaches. And since true renewal, as I see it, lies on the level of fundamental research, we have to familiarize ourselves with this level of inquiry.

Third, the focus of research on this fundamental level should address the logic underlying approaches which at first sight seem to be mutually exclusive. The best course then is to address the work of those scholars who are most representative of these approaches. What did they do exactly? What were they aiming at? How did they envisage the scholarly nature of the study of religious data and religions?

Fourth, while loking for innovation I trusted that as a result of the study of fundamental, that is, theoretical issues treated by scholars of the past, space would come free to develop new theoretical starting points. They should help, specifically, to treat research problems which show up in the study of present-day "living" religions, an activity which should not remain confined to sociology or anthropology alone.

In order to achieve these various aims, I decided to make a presentation in three parts. In the Introduction I would summarize the history of the scholarly study of religion, roughly between 1850 and 1950, mentioning the names of some 170 chosen prominent scholars in the field. Then I would present relevant texts by some 40 scholars selected from this group, in which they write about their own theoretical and methodological procedures. Finally I would offer a bibliography of works by and about the 170 scholars treated in the introduction; this Bibliography would appear as Volume Two of the *Classical Approaches*, but could not be included in the paperback edition.

One may well ask: who can be considered representative of the "classical" approaches in our field, supposing that such approaches can be identified according to disciplines? On first sight the answer seems to be easy. Historically, they are those scholars who must be considered as the Founding Fathers of the scholarly study of religion. More systematically, they are those who are still viewed and quoted as reference figures. In terms of research, they are those who may be considered to constitute the backbone of the research tradition of the study of religion until the mid-20th century. How did they define the procedures of research and what did they see as the basic problems of this field of research in their time? Of course, they do not enjoy unconditional authority, but they may be extremely helpful in stimulating our own questioning of what the study of religions and religion is like.

I readily admit that the very concept of "classical" approaches is a construct, useful though it is to distinguish the most important perspectives in the scholarly study of religion. The choice of the 170 scholars, and the selection of 40 who were theoretically interested among them, has not been as arbitrary as it may seem. As a basic rule, I only took scholars who did innovating empirical research in the first place and I left aside the many philosophical attempts to deal with religion. I also left out those theoreticians in scholarship who sharpened their knives but could not find materials to use them on.

Another kind of selection came about simply because of dating. When I conceived of the book I saw reason to decide that no living scholars should be included yet, even if they had expressed themselves more or less extensively in their researches on matters of method and theory. Consequently, and probably to his or her dismay, the reader will not find here names like Jan van Baal, Georges Dumézil, Mircea Eliade, Edward Evan Evans-Pritchard, Claude Lévi-Strauss, Wilfred Cantwell Smith, Victor Turner and others. Readers will also miss certain names of other well-known scholars such as Ernst Benz, Ugo Bianchi, Karl Kerényi, Henri-Charles Puech, Gilles Quispel, Gershom Scholem, Marcel Simon, Geo Widengren. The original book was thick enough to make additions in the paperback edition prohibitive.

I admit that, consequently, there is an arbitrary element in my construction of "classical approaches" as well as in the choice of representative scholars for them. Moreover, the precise place and role of these scholars in the scholarly tradition have not been treated. In the meantime some precious historical work has been carried out on this subject but much still has to be done. Even the historical rise of the scholarly study of religion in different countries has been much more gradual, varied and complex than the glorification of largely symbolic figures like Max Müller and Cornelis Petrus Tiele suggests. And throughout the history of the field there have been not only many hard-working scholars known through their publications rather than reputation; sometimes their work was not even published. There have also been most original minds doing scholarly research into religion and religions but suffering institutional marginalization by those who were recognized as representing the study of religions in their same time.

19TH CENTURY EUROPE AND THE INTEREST IN RELIGION

Nineteenth century Europe underwent powerful technological, social and political transformations, with movements of both emancipation and restoration together with strong nationalistic overtones and a powerful drive toward imperialism and expansion outside the continent. All of this affected religion in European societies as well as the study of religion; it led both to a secularization of society and to intellectual inquiries in the field of religion.

On the one hand intense spiritual searches were carried out about the nature and destiny of the universe and the human race. In certain quarters it was felt that Oriental religions had something to say about the nature and destiny of man, and that religions of the past and those of the East had achieved insights that should not be lost and ought to be retrieved.

On the other hand a feverish scholarly activity developed to study the distinctive features and facts of foreign cultures and religions and to arrive at a more comprehensive view of them. For Europe, the nineteenth century was a peak period of new discoveries of the world in both its geographical and historical and its intellectual and more spiritual dimensions.

It was not, of course, the whole of Europe or all Europeans that participated in this venture of exploration and discovery. Where the study of religions is concerned, scholarly research and the underlying spiritual quests were located in specific educated and liberal minded groups and they were stimulated by ideological tendencies which acknowledged tolerance, knowledge and insight to be precious goods. Thanks to them private initiatives developed together with new institutions like scholarly societies, academies and universities, working under the protection of the civil authorities. All of this favored the emergence of new views of religion, based on new ideas about history, society and the human species as a whole.

Who were the various groups contributing to the rise of the scholarly study of religion? Apart from the leading scholars who knew the relevant languages and explored unknown fields, there were a number of what may be called amateur or volunteer researchers who worked on materials from foreign or ancient religions in their spare time. And they were surrounded by a cultivated general public, both Christians and humanists, who wanted to be informed, read their books and attended their public lectures. These people did not engage in research but they read religious texts in translation and followed up what travellers and literary men, missionaries and preachers, explorers and scholars had to tell about religions other than Christianity. Without the support of the amateurs and the educated public the study of religions could not have developed as it did.

An essential feature of researchers at the time was the élan and thirst for making new discoveries and the pursuit of scholarship for the sake of truth and to correct or unmask current wrong opinions and prejudices. Among these more or less passionate researchers the founding fathers of Religionswissenschaft distinguished themselves by the fact that they boldly took *religion* as their focus of research. That is to say, they set out to objectify religious data, whole religions, and even religion as such. As soon as this research was recognized institutionally – which was not only a matter of scholarly but also of ideological and political debate – the field could develop further. It supposed, however, on one hand that in society at the time religion was a matter not only of religious but also of cultural interest. A society that did not care about religion or was interested only in its own particular religion, had difficulty in developing a science of religion. On the other hand, scholarly research had to work at a distance from the immediate religious concerns existing in society.

Among the motivations of these early scholars two extreme positions should be mentioned. On the one hand there were those who, for lack of a better expression, may be called the idealists. They had a fundamentally positive appreciation of religion and they held certain ideas about its historical development and its crucial role in society and culture. These scholars were keen to discover the truths, norms and values by which other peoples had lived or were living, especially if such truths were neglected in the modern West. This could even lead to an individual or communal recuperation of other cultures' values, sometimes with important ideological and even political consequences. An interest in the spiritual values of other peoples in past and present may have developed as a reaction to the decline or virtual absence of such values in modernizing western societies undergoing a process of secularization. In any case, the idealists made constructs of the meaning and significance of other religions or religion in general. Their constructs were not deduced from facts alone. On closer consideration they show a curious and fascinating relation between given "objective" facts and the highly personal and "subjective" insights, experiences and tastes or preferences of certain researchers. Without doubt both the cultural frustrations and the spiritual ideals that were alive in certain circles in Europe at the time contributed much to such idealistic research trends. One can argue that this kind of research, tending to "construct" the spirituality of other religions under the general heading of "religion", opened a way for other societies and cultures to be dominated by western spiritual constructs being imposed on them.

The other extreme motivation was represented by those researchers who, on the contrary, were suspicious of religion as a phenomenon and denied the claims to truth not only of the different religions but also of the idealists' constructs. On the contrary, they were keen to discover the "real" factors operative behind religious behavior and representations. These could be ascribed to impersonal social, political or psychological forces, or to the wilful manipulation of religions by self-interested political and religious factions and their leaders. These critical scholars could not but be irritated by what could be called the naive constructs of credulous idealists. The idealistically oriented researchers, for their part, were daunted by those critical minds who subordinated the sincere beliefs and customs of other people to the methodological and theoretical constructs of western scholarship.

The majority of scholars, however, could be found between these two extreme motivations. They avoided constructs and did not want to say more than what the results of empirical factual research allowed them to say. In the humanities they kept to strict philology, textual research and history, in the social sciences to sociological and anthropological description. Instead of spiritualizing or demonizing religion, they restricted themselves to working on verifiable facts and cecking hypotheses. For them, scholarship had its own strict discipline and rules which had to be obeyed. At worst it could deteriorate into a more or less anonymous technical activity where any researcher could be replaced by any other one. And at best it could pursue rational explorations in a field which was generally considered to be avowedly irrational. Most classical scholars in the field represent this empirical orientation. It did not prevent them from having other views, convictions and commitments too, but these remained within each one's personal domain. It was the scholar as an individual and not the discipline as such that was responsible for them. The empirical approach and the distinction made between scholarship and private views succeeded in gaining the upper hand and gave the study of religion a degree of respectability in academics.

THE CLASSICAL SCHOLARS: THEIR VIRTUES AND LIMITATIONS

Looking back at the forty scholars chosen here to represent Classical Approaches in the study of religions, I would like to mention some characteristic features. All of them had put their faith in scholarship, sometimes expressing what may be called a true belief in the scientific enterprise as such. To all of them, religion was a fairly clear notion, even if they assigned to it very different kinds of reality, social functions, psychological roots or spiritual dimensions. Some of these scholars seem to have been literally absorbed by religion, and not only as a subject of scholarly research. All of them regarded religion as something that could be observed and empirically studied.

As to their research, these forty distinguished themselves by a particular combination of factual research and theoretical concerns; in this sense they were accomplished scholars. I would contend that in the final analysis they founded or constructed the scholarly study of religion less on the basis of facts than on that of certain ideas and theoretical postulates of what religion was, what the scientific enterprise was, and how the latter could be applied to the former. A dialectic between religion as something given, an object, and the rational activity of man as a subject, is characteristic of all their scholarly approaches. Besides their more theoretical postulates we often find an ingenious questioning about the right technical procedure for solving a given scholarly problem. The search for method and the conviction that a generally valid method would lead to generally valid conclusions were common to all.

These forty scholars attracted followers, institutionally through university teaching or more personally; this of course was a condition for obtaining scholarly authority. There are no women among them although names like Ruth Benedict, Jane Harrison and Evelyn Underhill figure on the longer list and will be remembered. There were hardly any non-Europeans among them at the time.

Most scholars concentrated on history or on what were seen as remnants of bygone times, such as primitive religions or contemporary popular religion and folklore. Only a few worked on the world of the larger living religions and only a few related religious behavior to non-religious interests, contexts and structures. In the discussions between philologists and historians, historians and comparativists, comparativists and social scientists, and between all of them and the phenomenologists of the time, the attentive reader will recognize the roots of so many repetitious and stale debates on method and theory which have characterized 20th century academic studies of religion.

On the other hand, when looking back at these Classical figures, one cannot but acknowledge some fundamental limitations to which their work was subject – apart from the technological progress which has been made from card indexes and typewriters to xerox machines, computers, E-mail and Internet communication.

First and foremost, from any theoretical point of view, these scholars worked with what may be called a "realistic" concept of religion. That is to say, they took what people considered or consider as religious data and as religions, according to the prevailing judgment of specific authorities and institutions, as their object of research. Moreover, with a few exceptions they considered the existence itself of the "Reality" or the "Realities" to which religious data or religions refer, again according to given authorities and institutions, either as true or as a fundamental illusion. Debate concerned the existence or non-existence of these realities as a postulate for research; there was not yet a third, scholarly, position. In short, though these scholars offered definitions of religion, they did not really examine and problematize the notion of religion itself. They were not yet able to apply what may be called a "nominalistic" concept of religion in their scholarship. One especially pernicious consequence of this state of affairs was that they apparently did not see the full implications of the fact that the notion of religion is not only "constructed" (in this case defined) in research and scholarship but that religion is also and continuously constructed in the cultures and societies studied. In the present state of theoretical reflection, the ways in which different kinds of authorities ("religious", political, social, charismatic), institutions and popular orientations delimit and prescribe what is religiously normative and what is not, should be investigated. It is what different groups of people in fact consider to be "religion" or "religious", and how they act on this premise, which should now be a focus of interest. The scholar's own opinion, conviction or belief about what religion really is or should be has to be resolutely discarded in research nowadays. If all depends on how you define things, the consequence for serious research is that it is not so much the scholarly definition of religion that counts as the different ways in which religious and other actors themselves construct and define it. Such a nominalist theoretical position, however, seems to have been reached only exceptionally in the time of the classical approaches.

A second characteristic limitation of the period of the "Classical" Approaches, although most scholars said little on the subject, was that many of them held personal convictions about religion and were encouraged by their own group or by society at large to do so. This must have been one of the reasons why it was difficult for them to reach a more theoretical position. For a variety of reasons, a number of scholars took an apologetic stand in favor of either religion in general or one religion, religious view, or faith in particular. Such a position could not but affect the way in which they perceived religions, especially those of other people. The other way round, quite a few scholars in their heart of hearts viewed particular forms of religion or religion in general hostilely, critically or disdainfully. They often adhered to the idea of the struggle of reason and modernity with religion and tradition. Such a position, too, could not but affect fundamentally the way in which these scholars perceived religions. In short, neither the apologists nor the polemicists were able fully to recognize given religious data or religions without reacting to them on a fundamental, not to say instinctive, level. It seems to me that, from any scholarly point of view, such deeply personal reactions for or against are precisely what militates against an open scholarly inquiry about other people and their religions in the past or at present. In fact, such fundamental reactions have mostly led to the adoption of firm positions which have then been elaborated intellectually into rather rigid theological or philosophical stands. Such scholars were then ultimately working in the framework of a particular theology or philosophy. In extreme cases of dependence – which do not concern our scholars – they were subservient to religious or other authorities, institutions or ideologies, which influenced their research for the worse. But a humanist position was possible as well. This was probably held by the majority of the scholars of religion of the period who combined a certain humanism in their own lives with a more or less critical scholarship. This position, however, could also lead to resolutely anti-theological positions. In extreme cases – which again our scholars do not represent – they could also become anti-philosophical and ideological, constructing the scholarly study of religions not as independent from but as basically opposed to theology, in fact as a kind of anti-theology.

The third limitation to which the scholars of the "Classical" Approaches were subjected was not due to a lack of theoretical reflection or to a fixed existential position but was given with the world in which they lived and worked at the time. It may be true that the study of past or foreign religions offered an escape from the ever more rationalizing European society and culture, but at the same time nearly all of them lived in Europe which, up to World War II, had a dominant position in the world. This position affected not only the socio-political as well as cultural and scholarly discourse among Europeans about the rest of the world. It also affected the very relationships between Europeans and especially people from Asia and Africa not only in political, economic and social matters but also in the field of culture and religion. Asians and Africans, generally speaking, could not yet give their own accounts of their individual and social life and they could not yet present themselves as equal to Europeans. Is it not a remarkable fact that hardly any of the scholars considered here lived for any time in Asia or Africa, at least not on expeditions for which local people had to be recruited but in situations of encounter in which one had to learn from others and relativize the knowledge one had acquired back at home? And is it not also remarkable that, though some of these scholars were intent on a dialogue of religions and, later, of cultures, they were unable to take into account those structures of domination and movements of liberation or emancipation that largely determine hopes and expectations of people and to a large extent condition their mental orientation? Those who are in power or simply in a dominant position always run the risk of having a distorted view of the world, not seeing what is real for those who are the have-nots or the dominated ones.

As far as the study of religions and its relation to European dominance are concerned, one should acknowledge the fact that both the classificatory and the interpretative "classical" categories of the scholarly study of religion were coined in Europe at a time when Europeans looked at the religions of mankind in very particular ways. It should also be realized that Europeans, and not people of the cultures concerned, elaborated what was considered knowledge of mankind's spiritual life. In short, everything "religious" in the world was perceived through particular French, German, British or other European glasses and colored by the cultural and religious orientations which prevailed in Europe at the time. European scholars of religions were working in a civilization which perceived and judged the surrounding cultures and civilizations of past and present through its particular concepts (for instance that of religion) and its particular readings (for instance that of spirituality). If one were in a bitter mood, one might say that the existence of these Others allowed Europeans to build their Scholarship, their encompassing Theories, and their World Views over those Others' heads.

Looking back, I cannot help thinking that, because of the very dominance of Europe in the world, Europeans inevitably lived in a rather closed civilization. They now give the impression of having been isolated and almost blind to the possibility of a constructive dialogue with others. In this light the position of scholars of other religions was not enviable and could in fact be rather ambiguous. Were they prisoners of European civilization or were they bridgeheads toward other civilizations of past or present? Those scholars who, under the circumstances just described, while working with discipline, committed themselves to such daring positions as recognizing other religions, entering into interreligious dialogue, or even pleading for interreligious ecumenism, are all the more admirable. They stand out as singular voices in a self-confident but monological and ever more rigidified world which in the end destroyed itself in the two World Wars it had brought about. But the voices like those of so many thinkers were drowned by political, economic and other forces for which no one wanted to take responsibility.

As mentioned earlier, none of these scholars adopted a nominalist concept of religion. Apparently each one fundamentally knew what he was doing when he was studying religions, taking a western concept of religion for granted and universalizing it. In their work they perceived and studied religions first according to their historical origin and early development, and second according to their forms in full bloom. Comparative research tended to concentrate on timeless structures and truths. That is to say, these scholars perceived religions and religion according to what may be called their "classical" forms. It is only at the end of this Classical period that elements of religions other than the classical ones began to attract attention. At that time the living religions themselves underwent manifest changes in their responding to Western influences, the nationalist movements and modernization generally. And when religions lose their classical forms, the same happens to the study of them if it wants to be adequate.

BYGONES ARE BYGONES

The period of the classical approaches treated in this book is now over, even if much research is still done along the same lines. One cannot fail to respect the scholars who accomplished the difficult tasks they had set themselves, at a time when there was little communication between scholars in different countries or even within the countries themselves, apart from correspondence and a single international congress every four years.

Looking at our list of 170 names we see a striking diversity among the scholars represented. This was not only due to the many different kinds of source materials they studied, or to the variety of disciplines in which they were trained, or to the diversity of their views of religion. Some of them would not even have identified themselves as scholars of religion but as philologists or historians, sociologists or anthropologists. Others, on the contrary, wanted to serve the cause of a real Science of Religion. Some of them had ambivalent feelings about religion, took it for granted or were prepared to further it. Others, more critically, saw it as out of date and unmasked its ignorance or pointed out its ill effects. It is only when looking from a distance that one recognizes that each of them in his own way contributed significantly to our multiform present-day scholarly knowledge of religion. At the time, tensions may have existed between those working, for instance, in history and phenomenology, or in anthropology and history – but again, from a distance, one sees that these perspectives were not mutually exclusive.

Even in the time of the classical approaches, the study of religion turns out to have been not one discipline but rather a field of research requiring multi-disciplinary cooperation. And nowadays research on religions is carried out increasingly in different disciplines, each demanding their proper training. In this kind of interdisciplinary research on religions there must be a fundamental openness for how each researcher formulates his questions and pursues the quest for answers, and how he or she carries out his or her research.

The logical conclusion of the points made earlier is that it is just as difficult to give one rigorous definition of the study of religion as it is to give one rigorous definition of religion. Beware of any system claiming to be the "best way of studying religion". Such claims tend to develop a kind of scholasticism that hinders fruitful research rather than promoting it, whatever source materials it is based on.

The link between the scholars represented in this book is their empirical attitude, their concern with the data studied rather than with their own ideas, and their fundamentally open approach. They refused to make a priori value judgments, to look at material through confessional glasses, or to synthesize their findings within a given ideological, philosophical or theological system.

Most of all, and this was one of the reasons to include them in this anthology, they were aware of the methodological rules and the theoretical assumptions and implications of the work they carried out. The study of religion as they conceived it, be it with significant nuances, follows the general rules of the humanities and social sciences. It is not determined by a theological, philosophical or ideological discourse. Consequently, this field of research and teaching could receive a legitimate place in any university that defends scholarship for its own sake.

If specific interests seek to give the study of religion a particular political bias or religious orientation, a problem arises. For the humble but noble task of this kind of scholarship is to search for empirical and verifiable truth on the basis of the available data and reason alone. In order to do so, it should not be subjected to other claims to truth. In fact, it has its own empirical demands. In order to study Islam one should know Arabic and know it well. In order to carry out research on the history of a religion one should be a good historian. In order to do research on a given religious community in its context one should be familiar with sociology or anthropology. And no comparative study of religions can be pursued without a good knowledge of at least two religions from the sources.

The basis of the scholarly study of religion which emerges from a reading of these texts is the critical and self-critical research into very different kinds of data considered to be religious, a research carried out in terms of well-defined methods and well-chosen theoretical assumptions. The study of religion, even if it works on the best possible theoretical basis and with the smartest methods imaginable, still justifies its existence, however, through the truly new discoveries it makes to improve our knowledge. And if there is progress on a theoretical level, it should subsequently be supported through a new and better study of facts.

A NEW OUTLOOK

It is not only the time of the classical approaches, as said earlier, that is over now but also that of the founding fathers as individual giants. At present individuals can hardly engage in creative scholarship without communication. The future of research seems to lie with small research groups of competent researchers working together. In the scholarly study of religion the cooperation of open-minded specialists representing different approaches seems to be most promising. The rather monological attitude of isolated researchers in the past may yield to a more dialogical attitude among the researchers of the future.

This implies that the classical approaches have become relativized, not only as to their assumptions and presuppositions but also as to their practice. There is now room for new approaches. These may be interdisciplinary, as suggested above. They may also become intercultural, in particular as far as the study of still living religions is concerned. That is to say, researchers with a background not only of different scholarly approaches but also of different social, cultural and spiritual traditions may work together. What is self-evident for one, may not be for another, and this should be brought into the open. The results cannot be foreseen. On a planetary scale and seen in the long-term, the future not only of the religions but also of the study of them is fortunately unpredictable.

Our aim and purpose, then, is to bring the study of religions to greater maturity. One way to do this is to achieve an internal scholarly criticism of the study of religions in particular contexts, especially its postulates, methods and theories and their adequacy to the materials under investigation. Such an operation is not the same thing as a wholesale criticism of religion in general or of certain religions in particular, although realism forces us to acknowledge the profoundly ambiguous character of all things religious. The study of religions aims not at destroying them but at knowing them better. How much knowledge and insight are reached, and what fruits they may bear on a human level, will depend not only on what facts are brought together but also on the deciphering of their meaning and the values they represent for given persons and communities.

Whereas religious people may show a certain naivety in their concern with religion in private and communal life, the study of religions offers a more critical knowledge about religion in its context and serves rationality. And over against the use of religion, whether by social and political or by religious authorities and institutions, studying religion has a revealing and disclosing function.

At present and in the near future the study of religion, as I see it, has a scholarly and human task. It should continue to acquire and spread reliable knowledge about religions and their implications in social and individual life while being as conscious as possible of its own postulates. As for its human task, this is up to each individual researcher to decide. I myself would call it acquiring insight into the meanings and values by which mankind has survived in situations of profound challenges, existential or otherwise. The less the study of religions is confessionalized or politicized, the better it can perform its tasks.

I am profoundly disturbed by the prevailing lack of good information and degree of ignorance in matters of religion(s) at the end of this century, perhaps comparable with the ignorance of the unconscious in Europe a century ago. Ignorance has to give way to knowledge and in so far as possible insight. The current praiseworthy attempts, for instance, at dialogue between people coming from different cultural and religious backgrounds, should be strengthened by knowledge. This knowledge should bear both on the culture of the other party and on the various social, political and other forces which constitute the context in which such dialogue takes place. This is only one example of the way in which a better knowledge of religions in their contexts can have visible fruits.

Like anthropologists and political scientists, students of religions are aware of the plurality of systems, the adherents of each of which tend to believe that their own is the best one. It seems to me that, unlike our knowledge of cultural and political systems, our knowledge of the realities and potentialities of religious systems and how people can relate to them, is still only elementary. In the so-called irrational field of religion rational inquiry should push forward with explorations inspired but not determined by the scholars of the Classical Approaches who started the venture.

Lausanne, 9 September 1998   Jacques Waardenburg

Contents

INTRODUCTION

View of a Hundred Years' Study of Religion

ANTHOLOGY

PART 1: *The Study of Religion established as an Autonomous Discipline*

PART 2: *Connections with Other Disciplines*

PART 3: *Religion as a Special Subject of Research*

PART 5: *Perspectives of a Phenomenological Study of Religion*

View of a Hundred Years' Study of Religion

Preliminary

To take 'religion' as a subject of empirical inquiry and to begin investigating it as a human reality must have demanded not only great effort but also considerable courage. The confidence thereby put in man's intellectual capacities was such that one of the major fields traditionally held to be 'irrational' was opened not only to philosophical inquiry but also to rational research. And although the discussion on the rationality, both of scholarly research and of the religious phenomenon, may still be going on, it is important to note that the frontiers of research were moved ahead and that, like nature and history, art and morality, religion too became susceptible of being studied.

It would appear that basic to the study of such subjects, and especially to that of religion, is man's very capacity to objectify his involvements, social and psychological as well as religious. Although this objectifying process may start through the category of 'the others', it actually implies that man is objectifying part of himself. No intelligent person could study other people, their culture and religion, without establishing at the same time a distance also to himself, his past, his surroundings, and his involvements up to now. The really interesting question, however, is what kind of distance he establishes and what he has in view when doing so. Intelligence often rises against given involvements, and wants to get rid of them in a movement of liberation. And since an involvement in anything considered to be sacred is particularly strong, and mostly sanctioned in unreasonable ways, reason, if moved at all, is propelled here with extraordinary power. It may destroy anything held to be sacred, it may restrain immediate judgment and come to critical verification, and it may also begin investigating what others hold to be sacred. Though religion, by being studied, does not necessarily disappear, it certainly changes through the very fact that man can objectify it and thereby establish his freedom with regard to it. In the final analysis, by using his intelligence to study his religion man can attain not only to more knowledge but also to better insight.

As students of religion we should remain aware of the fact that the very concept of 'religion' is part of us. Throughout their work, scholars like those treated here arrived at a certain idea or image of the religion they studied and, partly by force of generalization and partly by the notions of religion which they acquired through their own life experiences, they arrived at a notion of religion in general. It cannot be stressed enough that such ideas, images, or even notions, as soon as they have been conceived, are not only slightly different from the actual facts which were subject of inquiry, but also tend to persist and to pursue their own life during this inquiry, although they are only products of our minds. And this hang towards 'reification' tends to make us think that, when we speak of religions or religion, we have to do with things in themselves; whereas these 'things' really are our images and ideas. Throughout the history of scholarship on religion one can trace such ideas and images taken for granted and passing on from scholar to scholar, until someone became conscious of this traditional transmission and could start looking at the facts before him in a new way, developing a new hypothesis or theory, so that he could arrive at new knowledge. Just as there is an external history of scholarship through the growth of the materials that were studied, there is an internal history through the ideas, changing from time to time, that the scholars had about these materials. And scholarship on religion has benefited not only by the discovery of new religious facts but also by the change of the notion, image, or idea of religion itself.

There is here a massive problem: that the results of a scholar's work in the field of religion depend not only on his precise scholarly findings and on the immediate research problems which have given rise to them, but also on his notion of religion and the way in which he has arrived at this notion. And here not only his own thought and experience, but also the ideas on religion current in his time and environment are important factors in his conceptualization of religion, which is affected equally by the results of his scholarly research.

Now it is our contention that in a scholar's work his methodological statements are of utmost importance for our understanding not only of the concepts he used, but also of the perspective from which he worked and the very intentions of his investigations. To put it briefly, we do not understand a scholar's work unless we understand his methodology, and we cannot work in a discipline unless we can practice its methodology.

So we must be concerned with methodology in the study of religion too. When I was a student it was not too well considered for one to propose methodological questions; instead of sharpening one's knife one had to use it. This rule probably still applies in a number of established disciplines where methodology largely coincides with finding the right technical device to solve a given problem. But real methodological questions are raised when established ways of learning and research begin to lose something of their self-evidence, that is of their status as unquestioned truth. This may happen because new aspects of reality are seen whereby new techniques, theories, or even disciplines arise in order to solve problems that were unknown before. It may also happen because of a sheer passion for objective truth, with the search for a new hypothesis, model, or theory with regard to a particular set of facts. It may also be because of the simple need for clarity with regard to what one is doing or in view of scholarly communication. In many cases there is an underlying debate between different trends of thought or a conflict between different approaches to the same subject. A psychology and sociology of knowledge would certainly be able to mention a number of conditions under which methodological issues are raised in scholarly research. In the study of religion, for instance, there is a strong impulse coming from systems of thought — theological or philosophical — and from ideologies — religious or anti-religious — which affect the research. This may happen directly by formulating or even imposing certain problems to be solved, or indirectly by providing axiomatic premises in order to ensure that certain problems are not even raised. The conditions under which a scholar works are therefore of utmost importance, and the personality of the scholar with his commitments and involvements is of course the nerve center of this all. They affect both the way in which he formulates intellectual problems and the way in which he tackles the concrete research problems before him.

At present a number of important methodological issues are being reconsidered in the field of the study of religion, and here and there new approaches are being broached. So there is now all the more reason to bring together the different approaches which have become classical, and to pass in review their most important representatives, in a historical survey.

Several considerations have led to the present arrangement of the material, that is to say according to authors. First of all, in the more specialized literature, the methodological considerations are mostly arranged according to certain basic problems or themes of research; there is no need, therefore, to do this here. Secondly, the methodology formulated by a prominent scholar is usually closely connected with his own research work, so that the consequence of his method can be seen with the help of his further scholarly work; thus, the statements are part of the total work of a particular scholar. Thirdly, one of the purposes of this anthology has been to show the variety of disciplines, methods, and viewpoints which, in one way or another, have to do with religious materials. The biographical arrangement, then, brings this variety out in a clear manner, and protects editor and reader against the temptation to round off the differences in a scheme that does not do complete justice to the work of each scholar.

Also, certain rules have guided us in our selection and presentation. In the first place, all methodology which concerns literary, historical, sociological, anthropological, and psychological research as such, has been left out. Our choice has been made only from those methodological texts which have to do with religious subjects. In the second place, stress has been laid upon presenting a panorama of the most divergent viewpoints, so that we have chosen from each branch of research some representative but divergent scholars. In order to know the different approaches which exist within the disciplines of the history of religions, the sociology of religion, etc., the reader will have to consult existing methodological handbooks on these disciplines. In an anthology like this one, we had to renounce from the beginning all striving after completeness. In the third place, and this is most important, only such scholars could be treated here, as have left us texts from their own hands on the methods and theories used and upheld by them during their lives. Now it is worthwhile to note that a considerable number of scholars, amongst whom are some of the most eminent, never made such statements; so this group automatically falls out of our range. These scholars created their handiwork and left us the results, and only through teaching did they hand over their techniques and methods to their pupils. In the fourth place, though a number of people already had carried out individual critical research and thought in regard to their own or other people's religion, it is only about a century ago that the study of religion came to be regarded as an autonomous discipline. We decided, consequently, to start around 1870, when the first chairs of the discipline were established at university institutions.

The major publications of the scholars mentioned in the *Historical Survey**, as well as studies made about them, are given in the Bibliography which constitutes a second volume. The names of the scholars represented in the Anthology are printed here in capital letters, and in the Bibliography in Volume Two with an asterisk, whereas the names of the other scholars are printed in italics.

---

* The *Historical Survey* does *not* include scholars who at present are alive and active. It may be of interest to note that, besides this *Historical Survey*, some texts of the Anthology itself provide historical accounts of the study of religion, for instance by W. Smidt (pp. 267—273) and B. Malinowski (pp. 546—551).

Historical Survey

INTRODUCTION: UP TO THE MIDDLE OF THE 19th CENTURY

Beginnings. After the Reformation and the Contra-reformation in the 16th
and 17th centuries had forged the religious scene in Europe, it was the
century of Enlightenment which changed the intellectual outlook. In the
18th century, indeed, at least among a certain elite, there was great interest
in natural religion as guided by reason, in order that religion in all times and
places might be traced back to the three postulates of the existence of God,
the soul, and immortality. Reason had the highest place on the scale and
any conflict between reason and religion was usually decided in enlightened
circles in favor of the first.

During this period several philosophers worked on the problem of a natural
religion extending beyond Christianity proper. These thinkers departed
from the theological doctrine of the *religio naturalis*, and took into account
the plurality of religions existing among mankind, these being considered
as outgrowths of a natural reasonable religion or as the natural outcome of
the general manifestation of Divine grace. This thought represented in
a way a reflective response to the discoveries of new continents and peoples,
in present and past, with religions that had been practically unknown to
the West before. A growing knowledge of religions like Islam, Hinduism
and Buddhism, of Chinese religion and of non-literate beliefs and customs
had been the result. The interest in these non-Western religions had been
awakened, and to a certain extent their existence had to be justified philosophically. The same held true for Western religion which also had to be
reconsidered and justified. We can think here of philosophers as different
as Gottfried W. Leibniz (1646–1716), David A. Hume (1711–1776), and
Immanuel Kant (1724–1804).

Travel accounts often made mention of religious customs which impressed
the Western observers, and the 18th century witnessed the first more objective descriptions of various religions partly based on such travel accounts.
An example is the description of North American Indians given in 1724 by
Joseph-François Lafitau (1681–1746). The literate and non-literate people
who were discovered were first identified by means of their religions. Only

a few studies, however, tried to present the religious data not only in a general but also in a systematic way. Three of these works may be mentioned here.

The study by *Charles de Brosses* (1709–1777) on fetishism as it was found in West Africa and elsewhere, points to the parallelism between this fetishism as the worship of animals and inanimate objects, and similar phenomena from the ancient Egyptian and Greek religions. The book appeared in 1760. The author declares fetishism to be a primordial form of religion in which man, because of his fear and weakness, imagines that things are animated and worships them as he does animals. Fetishism serves here as an explanation of paganism which is considered to be the result of the development of fetishism as an earlier religion still extant among non-literate people, which was thought to have been practically universal. Rather than Hume's theory of polytheism as being at the origin of religion, de Brosses puts forth a theory of fetishism. In both cases, the problem was to find one elementary form of religion from which other forms have developed.

The study by *Christopher Meiners* (1747–1810), published in 1806–07 as a general history of religions, accepts the theory of fetishism as being the earliest form of religion and equally stresses the role of human imagination in the development of religious worship. The material is richer here than in the earlier book by de Brosses. The study by *Benjamin Constant y de Rebeque* (1767–1830), published between 1824 and 1831, equally offers a survey of religious phenomena. For Constant, religion is essentially a feeling which is the very foundation of man's nature. Through a mass of material the problem is raised not only of the origin but also of the psychological nature of religion.

Side by side with the travel accounts of living people, it was the discovery and decipherment of ancient texts that opened a field of research on as yet largely unknown religions. Two famous names, among others, may be mentioned here:

William Jones (1746–1794), by his intense study of Sanskrit which was already known at the time, and by comparing Sanskrit to certain classical European languages, discovered structural similarities between the two groups of languages and concluded that they belong to one linguistic family. This discovery was broadened by that of similarities between Indian myths on one hand, and Greek, Roman and even Biblical myths on the other hand. Indian culture and religion now not only became accessible to a wider public, but the road was also opened to further research on Indo-European linguistics and mythology through comparative studies.

Jean François Champollion (1790–1832) is to be mentioned here as the decipherer of the ancient Egyptian hieroglyphic script in a publication of 1822, using these texts immediately to describe the main lines of Egyptian religion in a study of 1830. The discovery of this and other ancient languages and literatures drew great public attention in the West; this interest was enhanced by the fact that reference to these civilizations was made in the Bible and that from them further information could be expected to emerge from the material itself.

On the European continent an important influence on the study of the history of religion in general has been exercised by some German philosophers who reflected on a global world history in which the different civilizations and religions could be brought together in a historical and logical sequence. Although religion could be understood by these thinkers in very different ways — e.g., as a way in which man gives shape to his relation to nature, as man's orientation to the infinite, as man's awareness of absolute dependence, as the self-realization of an absolute idea —, and although the concept of history too differed greatly among thinkers like Johann G. von Herder (1744–1803), Friedrich von Schlegel (1772–1829), Friedrich D. E. Schleiermacher (1768–1834) and Georg W. F. Hegel (1770–1831), it was stated once and for all that religions have a historical existence and that religion cannot be studied apart from history.

Mythology. The first half of the 19th century in particular was very much concerned with the phenomenon of myth; for some authors the history of religion was practically identical with the study of myth, and comparative religion with comparative mythology. It seems as if the age of romanticism rediscovered, after the age of rationalism, a deeper dimension to religion which was most apparent in myth and symbolism. One of the main problems of the time was how to find the deeper meaning hidden in these expressions, or in the absence of such a meaning to explain their occurrence.

The first scholar to be mentioned in this connection is *Georg F. Creuzer* (1771–1858), who published between 1810 and 1822 a famous study on the symbolism and mythology of the ancient peoples, especially the Greeks, which may be called both a phenomenology and a history of religion. Creuzer suspected that there was a mysterious revelation or wisdom in Greek mythology, in the imagery of which missionary priests from the Orient had conveyed a primeval wisdom or insight to the ignorant older people of Greece. The myths were supposed to be figurative expressions of ideas pertaining to higher reality and truth. But such reality and truth can be grasped by man only indirectly, through signs. Thus, there is an intrinsic relation between the gods and their signs, as the divine can only be revealed through symbols. Consequently, through symbolism, and through the study of it, one has access to expressions of divine reality. By comparing Indian myths and cults with their Greek counterparts, Creuzer hoped to be able to trace the elements of Oriental teachings which were conveyed to the barbarian Pelasgian Greeks. Creuzer took the problem of religious meaning deeply serious by holding that, in the absence of philosophy with its general concepts, such a meaning had to be expressed in ritual, symbol and myth. But this meaning can be rediscovered by the dedicated scholar who searches this wisdom through studying the symbols in which it was communicated.

Gottfried Hermann (1772–1848) worked along the same lines as Creuzer, but he placed the wisdom supposed to have originated from the East not in the general Greek mythology, but in the mystery religions which existed in Greece and Egypt under the surface of the official religion. This significance attached to mystery religion would still be apparent in the work of a scholar like W. B. Kristensen nearly a century later. In his work on the history of myths in Asia, which appeared in 1810, *Joseph von Görres* (1776–1848) stated, under the impact of the newly discovered Indian texts, that India had been the cradle of humanity and civilization, and that here a perfectly harmonious priestly state had existed where the people had not yet been in need of images and temples. The Indo-Europeans would have constituted a unity and originated from India where the primeval pure religion had to be sought.

A critical reaction against these interpretations of myth and symbol was not long in appearing. Already *Christian G. Heyne* (1729–1812) had observed that myths changed in the course of time, and were poetically embellished. Consequently, we do not know them in their original form and have no direct access to an original wisdom contained in them. For Heyne, the problem of scholarly research on mythology was not to find some hidden wisdom or revelation, but to reconstitute the process of myth formation through man's imagination, and to investigate its development in history through historical and archeological research anxious to spot local differences in mythical tradition and cult. Myth itself is a re-creation, through emotion-charged imagination, of what man perceives of the phenomena of nature. This happens because in his relation to nature man tends to personify the divine power which manifests itself in nature in various ways, and which man perceives and venerates because of his innate idea of God.

In a similar vein *Carl O. Müller* (1797–1840) stressed the fact that all mythology has reached us after a long historical development and with considerable changes. What is needed is a careful historical study of the development of the different mythological traditions, rather than an intuitive study of the basic ideas of the myths. Furthermore, he says, mythology is not the creation of a priestly class expressing a primeval wisdom in imaginery forms; it is, rather, a product of the popular emotion and understanding of the experience of life and of nature. It is a particular way in which the people's experience of reality is expressed. So in myths there are reminiscences of ancient ways of life of human society, when natural phenomena and historical events were interpreted as divine interventions. At the moment, however, that man developed a sense of history and a more abstract thought, he stopped creating myths. Carl O. Müller also denied that all myths would be of a religious nature. It is interesting to compare C. O. Müller's more rational but popular views on myth to F. Creuzer's more elitist but religious interpretation.

Still more philosophical was the interpretation that *Friedrich W. J. von Schelling* (1775–1854) gave of mythology in his lectures which were published posthumously in 1856. According to him, only the philosopher is able to discover the meaning of seemingly incoherent stories; that is to say, the significance which these myths held and still hold for man. Mythology reflects the evolution of man, and it represents man's 'mental' world. Revelation, on the contrary, which is the other form of religion, expresses man's 'practical' world. As an idealist philosopher, von Schelling, then, submits a hypothetical scheme for the dialectical development of mythology.

Mention should be made of a number of attempts to explain mythological data as a response to impressive natural phenomena which were expressed in language. By means of etymological research and using the comparative linguistics of the time, several scholars tried to discern in certain names of gods and spirits certain phenomena of nature which would have had a religious significance, especially for the Indo-European people. *F. F. Adalbert Kuhn* (1812–1881) and *Wilhelm Schwartz* (1821–1899), for instance, stressed the importance of lightning and thunder. Schwartz contended, moreover, that popular belief does not represent the decay of an ancient higher religion, but rather that it was the basis from which higher mythology had developed. Thus, he called the representations of such popular belief the lower mythology. All people in all times have believed in supernatural beings and forces; one should, therefore, take into account this basic ground layer of lower mythology, if one wants to understand the higher mythology and religiosity with their figures of the gods, which are born out of this lower mythology.

In the study of mythology mention should be made, finally, of *Friederich G. Welcker* (1784–1868) who published between 1857 and 1863 a study on the Greek gods. Welcker concentrated on the 'higher' mythology of the Greeks, and recognized there an original coherent representation of nature: the names of the gods express the various objects that exist in the religions of nature all over the world, and they indicate the main qualities of these gods. In course of time this coherent system went into decay, not only through the rise of polytheism and superstition but also through the poetic phantasy which elaborated mythology. Welcker contends that religion and myth have their origin in a particular layer of the soul which is situated beneath the conscious mind. Consequently, in order to understand them, more is needed than a purely intellectual approach. The Greek view of the gods, for instance, is neither the result of perceptions of nature nor something borrowed from elsewhere; it is rather a product of the Greek mind which projects its notion of the divine upon the outside world. Against the views of his time, Welcker contends that religion is not impression but expression. He then seeks to penetrate into the ideational contents of myth on a deeper level than had his contemporaries, and thus he may be called a forerunner of a scholar like Walter F. Otto, nearly a century later.

The image of mythology that arises from the investigations of the scholars mentioned above turns out to be, schematically speaking, threefold. First there is the 'higher mythology', with divine figures, studied either for its content — as a hidden wisdom or as an expression of the people's soul — or in its historical development, or in its 'outward' origin through sense perception of striking natural phenomena or historical events, followed by imaginative expression. Second there is the 'lower mythology' as it lives in the folkloric beliefs and customs of the people, viewed either as a decay of higher mythology or as the basis of mankind's mental life at a beginning stage of its development from which here and there a higher development could proceed. This lower mythology could also be studied as a phenomenon in itself, as 'folklore', whereby its relation to higher mythology remains open to discussion. And thirdly there is the view on mythology on a level of mental or psychic reality which may express itself on higher or lower levels, but which has its source in the soul's power to recognize the divine precisely by expressing itself in myth. It is interesting to note that a number of trends in the history and comparative study of religion appear to have had their precursors in the history and comparative study of mythology. Not without reason, comparative religion has been called a child of comparative mythology; for at this time the history of religion still largely coincided with the study of mythology.

Folklore. When speaking of research on 'lower mythology' we should mention the work of the brothers *Jacob* (1785–1863) and *Wilhelm* (1786–1859) *Grimm:* the famous Grimm brothers. Under the impact of the romantic movement, the Grimms recognized in living popular traditions, fairy tales, and sagas the remains of ancient myths and stories of pagan gods, and they wanted to understand them accordingly. With a vivid interest in what touches the soul of the people, they collected a great number of current oral traditions, studied their motives and tendencies, and concluded that a great number of parallels existed among them. This held true in particular for the Indo-European peoples, where a common ancient source had to be assumed. With these folkloristic-mythological concerns they combined linguistic interests, a substantial number of excellent publications being the result. In their line, an intense interest in the study of folklore arose in which this was seen as the remains of a presumed national past as well as an expression of a deeper felt unity of the Indo-European peoples and of mankind as a whole, such as became evident through comparative studies.

The most prominent among the scholars of European folklore, however, was *Wilhelm Mannhardt* (1831–1880) who collected on a large scale data from all over the continent. Mannhardt could indeed show the survival of parts of ancient religion in his own life-time. He found and investigated living and meaningful popular religion, especially in the countryside, where, for instance, there prevailed beliefs in fertility spirits and in the correspondence of plant-life with human life, whereby he was able to prove interesting parallels with similar elements of ancient Greek religion. Mannhardt has been called one of the pioneers of modern scholarship, both in folklore and in history of religions. Actually it appeared that a number of agrarian ideas and customs were not confined to the Indo-European peoples who would go back to a common source, but that they even referred to still more ancient strata in the history of mankind. Mannhardt contended that part of the earliest myths would owe its origin to a poetry of nature which is strikingly similar to certain forms of poetry of present-day non-literate people, an opinion which had great influence on the study of these people by later scholars. The significance of Mannhardt's laborious researches is that he put higher mythologies with their gods and lower mythologies with their spirits side by side, and that in his folklore research he made a serious and substantial study of the latter without necessarily reducing them to the former; rather, he viewed them as remains of more ancient times of which we have no written sources. History of religion could now use not only mythology but also folklore to its advantage; in this sense Mannhardt had much influence on a scholar like James G. Frazer.

1. THE STUDY OF RELIGION ESTABLISHED AS AN AUTONOMOUS DISCIPLINE

We should turn here to the first scholar whose work is represented in our anthology: FRIEDRICH MAX MÜLLER (1823–1900). Max Müller stands in the tradition of mythological research of which we have given a general outline, and he is famous for his statement that myths as poetry and phantasy are to be explained by striking natural phenomena like, for instance, the rising and setting of the sun; and further, that the names of the divinities basically are due to a 'disease of language' which substitutes *numina* for *nomina*, i.e. inflating ordinary names to religious powers, or poetic to religious language. But Müller rises head and shoulders above his contemporaries, if not so much any more through his etymological theories and comparative linguistics which have been proved to be wrong, then certainly by his great qualities as a sanskritist, by his theory that religion is a mental faculty to apprehend the infinite through nature apart from the senses and reason, and by his fervent call to found comparative mythology and comparative religion according to the model of comparative linguistics. Müller's application of these ideas in his work makes him of particular interest to us. For because of this work, Max Müller may be called the first scholar who lucidly and imperatively envisaged and proclaimed an autonomous 'science of religion'.

The texts reproduced (pp. 86 ff.) bear witness to the courage it required at the time to launch such a venture. Still now, it is fascinating to read the justification he gives of a science of religion before the general public. To be sure, no one likes to see his own religion being treated as a member of a general class, but actually Christianity is one of many religions and can be compared with religious aspirations found all over the world. Against those adversaries who deny the possibility of a scientific treatment of religions, the author firmly asserts his purpose: '. . . to find out what Religion is, what foundation it has in the soul of man, and what laws it follows in its historical growth' (p. 90). Man has not to surrender what he holds to be the truth; but still less the right of testing truth! The second text contains a fervent plea for the comparative method — 'he who knows one (religion), knows none' (p. 93) —, for applying the rules of critical scholarship, and for determining the most ancient forms of every religion before determining its value and comparing it with other forms of religious faith. We would like to see Max Müller as one of the founding fathers to whom the discipline itself owes its existence, even if from within that discipline manifold criticisms were levelled against his theory of language, his reduction of gods to names, his explanation of myths through the analysis of names, his view of polytheism as a nature cult, and his tendency to see the phenomenon of daybreak as a key to the understanding of nearly every myth.

Mention should be made here of a group of scholars for whom the study of language and its relation to religion and mythology was paramount, like *Moritz Lazarus* (1824–1903) and especially *Heymann Steinthal* (1823–1899).

As another founder CORNELIS P. TIELE (1830–1902) should be mentioned. More historically oriented than Max Müller, Tiele worked on the historical religions of Antiquity and was the first to offer a historical survey of a number of religions, based on the study of source materials in the original languages for Iran, Mesopotamia, Egypt, Israel and Greece. Tiele would later combine this historical approach with a systematic interest, and follow up the evolution of what he called the 'religious idea' through its various historical forms from 'nature' religions to 'ethical' religions.

The text reproduced (pp. 96 ff.) gives an interesting definition of religion, which is of a descriptive phenomenological nature. Religion is '. . . the aggregate of all those phenomena which are invariably termed religious',

... those manifestations of the human mind in words, deeds, customs, and institutions which testify to man's belief in the superhuman, and serve to bring him into relation with it' (p. 97). Like Müller, Tiele pleads for an over-all investigation of religion in its manifold aspects, and he indicates the importance and practical benefits of the new discipline, the degree in which it can pass judgment or exercise criticism. Characteristic of Tiele and a whole school after him is his appeal for an objective attitude to all forms of religion, which forms should be distinguished, however, from religion itself. Tiele distinguishes himself from other scholars in the historical field when he passes on to what he calls the 'philosophical' part of the investigation of religious phenomena. After having outlined the stages and directions of development, he openly proclaims the philosophical character of the science of religion, of which 'phenomenology' is the first stage and 'ontology' the second. Its final aim is to inquire what is permanent in the changing forms and what elements these forms all have in common. For Tiele's own view on religion, it is important to know his saying: 'Our religion is ourselves, in so far as we raise ourselves above the finite and transient' (p. 103). A following generation would reproach Tiele for his being too philosophical and not enough historical.

By the end of the 19th century history of religions had become a recognized discipline at several universities, either in the Faculty of Arts or in that of Theology. Although specialization was incumbent here, particularly because of the necessary knowledge of a chosen group of languages, the ideal was to remain informed about the progress of research in the discipline as a whole. Of the historians of religion who succeeded in doing so, the names of *Albert Réville* (1826–1906) and *Eugène Goblet d'Alviella* (1846–1925) deserve to be mentioned. The latter is also known for his division of the study of religion into three parts: hierography as the description of the religious data and of their geographical location, hierology as the grouping of data from their origin onwards according to their time sequence, and hierosophy as the inquiry of the truth, value, and metaphysical character of the religions. Similar divisions were made by other scholars distinguishing descriptive, historical, and philosophical investigations.

A third scholar who may be counted among the founders of the study of religion as an autonomous discipline, though less knowledgeable of the original sources, is PIERRE D. CHANTEPIE DE LA SAUSSAYE (1848–1920). He did not adhere to any one of the particular schools which were current during his lifetime, but considered the various theories merely as 'preliminary classifications'. Later he was more interested in philosophy of religion and ethics and more or less left the discipline, in part also because of his lack of the necessary knowledge of languages. De La Saussaye, himself of an irenical temperament, kept himself somewhat at a distance and, more than in concrete historical research, was interested in a classification of the religious data apart from time and space into classes and groups. So this scholar founded phenomenology of religion as a discipline of classification.

In the first text reproduced (pp.105 ff.), de La Saussaye enumerates three necessary conditions which made the foundation of the science of religion possible: an increasing knowledge of empirical data on religion, the concept of a world history in which the different religions have a historical existence, and the rise of one unifying philosophical concept of 'religion'. Writing somewhat later than Max Müller and Tiele, he does not so much make a plea for the new discipline or defend it against its adversaries. Instead, he simply gives an account of its object, which is '. . . the study of religion, of its essence and manifestations', and of its subdivision into philosophy and history of religion, which he considers to be closely connected. Between history and philosophy de La Saussaye puts as a transition the '. . . collecting and grouping of various religious phenomena', phenomenology of religion being intermediary between history and philosophy. Theology proper, as the science of the Christian religion, differs for de La Saussaye fundamentally from the science of religion in general. De La Saussaye's model of the science of religion would influence that of Van der Leeuw who was a pupil of his; but Van der Leeuw would consider phenomenology as an intermediary discipline between history and theology rather than philosophy.

For de La Saussaye the science of religion presupposes the unity of its subject: the unity of religion in its various forms. As stated in the second text reproduced (p. 109), phenomenology of religion was for him closely connected with psychology, since it deals with facts of human consciousness and since the outward forms of religion can only be explained from what de La Saussaye calls 'inward processes'. He defined thereby the difference between 'religious' and 'non-religious' by the presence, or absence respectively, of what he calls 'a certain inward relation'. In his stress on psychology and his conceiving religion in terms of an inward relation to something absolute, de La Saussaye would be followed again by Van der Leeuw. Of influence has been de La Saussaye's idea that it is philosophy of religion which is concerned with the definitions of things, and that its primary task thereby is to indicate the essence of things; this position has been taken by succeeding scholars of religion in the Netherlands. It is interesting to note, finally, that, for de La Saussaye, the study of religious acts, cult, and customs, where often written texts are lacking, is particularly incumbent on phenomenology of religion, insofar as their meaning is concerned.

It is clear from the text that religion for Chantepie de la Saussaye is finally a theological category since the only real object of religion is God. In history, however, religion has many objects, and the study of these objects is the concern of phenomenology.

The three founders, Max Müller, Cornelis Tiele, and Chantepie de la Saussaye, all had a historical interest, and were inclined to philosophical interpretations and thought. It would be unfair to exclude from the picture the role of anthropologists and sociologists doing research on religion as a specific subject. Their contributions are treated, however, in the next part as contributions to the study of religion by existing disciplines.

2. CONNECTIONS WITH OTHER DISCIPLINES

Although the establishment of the study of religion, in particular the history of religions, as an autonomous discipline at universities in the last quarter of the 19th century was an important event, the actual study had started already much earlier. Besides the students of mythology mentioned above, some prominent scholars of the 19th and the beginning of the 20th century should be mentioned here, since they are in fact at the start of an objective study of religion, a pursuit not always accepted by society at the time.

Early cases. A unique figure was JOHANN J. BACHOFEN (1815–1887), more generally known for his theory of a matriarchal stage which would have occurred in the development of human society, culture, and religion. Not without the influence of a romantic feeling of the experience of life and nature, Bachofen came to original and sometimes profound interpretations of myth and symbolism, and he made an effort to trace the development of mankind through the historical succession of its self-expressions in religious symbols. Himself a jurist and a classical scholar, Bachofen arrived in his inquiries at the discovery of an older cultural stage of Greek civilization than that of the classical period which was held to be exemplary. Bachofen discovered another world, a world of unbound matriarchy, containing religious views and practices that had been unsuspected by respectable classical scholarship. Consequently, his findings were judged to be extravagant and, had it not been for his personal fortune, he would have been unable to continue his work after having been practically ostracized by classical scholars.

The first text given (pp. 117 ff.) shows the way in which Bachofen viewed the relation between myth and symbol when they were alive, and their degradation to a tomb and death cult. The second text (pp. 119 ff.), typically, shows Bachofen's high opinion about woman's religious capacities, especially in maintaining the sense of the mysterious which for him was essential to religion. Further it shows his insistence on respecting all historical manifestations of religion, and his assertion that the ancients' concern for the supernatural, the transcendent and the mystical found its roots in the profoundest needs of the human soul. Bachofen boldly declared the historians to be wrong in relegating mystery to times of decadence.

Bachofen developed a new outlook on the evolution of society, an evolution which would have passed from a state of promiscuity through one of matriarchy to that of patriarchy. Each stage had its own particular religious forms, the second distinguishing itself by the element of mystery which Bachofen considered to be the true essence of all religion. In his interpretations of myths, Bachofen showed a vital interest in religion, looking for eternal values in the mythical structures. As a romantic, this scholar became very involved in his discoveries which he made his own experience; and it is perhaps thanks to this condition of his that he could notice elements in Greek culture which had escaped the attention of earlier and contemporary scholars. He discovered the phenomenon of matriarchy, but stressed the religious rather than the social or psychological side of it. Like the other romantic scholars, Bachofen possessed a strong sensitivity to religious significance which feeling enabled him to intuit, in various forms of symbolism, a new and religious dimension.

Where a number of philosophers showed a religious tolerance or indifference, several philosophers during the 19th century, on the other hand, came to an implicit or explicit critique of the religion of their time, and of religion in general. They opposed the pretension of absolute validity of the given beliefs and institutions, against which the use of reason in historical and comparative research was a powerful weapon. Indirectly, this trend of thought encouraged the critical study, historical or otherwise, of religion in general and of Christianity in particular. The name of Voltaire (1694–1778) may be mentioned here as that of a forerunner. For the 19th century, one thinks in France of Auguste Comte (1798–1857), and in Germany of thinkers like Ludwig Feuerbach (1804–1872), Karl H. Marx (1818–1883) and Friedrich Engels (1820–1895). Somewhat later would be the impact of Friedrich W. Nietzsche (1844–1900). In England one may think of the influence of a thinker like John Stuart Mill (1806–1873). In the case of Christianity the critical concern of the scholars is particularly with what was considered to be sacred: the Bible, the life of Jesus, and the history of the Church and of Christian dogma.

One of the first great critical minds in these fields was the founder of the so-called 'School of Tübingen', *Ferdinand Christian Baur* (1792–1860). In a number of critical learned studies he expounded what he considered to be the historical truth on the 'sacred origins' of Christianity, as opposed to the current religious truth.

In France it was JOSEPH-ERNEST RENAN (1823–1892) who came into conflict with his church when he applied critical methods to the study of the Bible, the life of Jesus, and the history of the Church. With its sensitivity and literary expression, his earlier work in particular is an outstanding example of the strength and courage needed to make the transition, within traditional Christian society, from a religious to a historical and critical consideration of the documents, doctrines, and history of one's own religion. It was not only his technical scholarly work or his literary gifts which gave Renan the glory of his later years in late-19th century Paris; it was also his personality, symbolizing a profound cultural and spiritual change which was felt to take place at the time.

The text reproduced (pp. 127 ff.) dates back to the very beginning of Renan's public scholarly career, before his famous *Vie de Jésus* [Life of Jesus]; it has been taken from his first book with essays on the history of religion. Like Max Müller and Tiele, Renan makes a fervent plea for the modern science of religion. Behind the elegant French the tension between imposed and received doctrines on one hand, and a critical spirit of inquiry on the other hand still is apparent. In the background there remains, however, an esthetic respect for religion as representing the highest aspirations and manifestations of human nature, and being by its very nature always disproportionate to its divine object. Perhaps more than in the work of other scholars one feels here the life experience of religion claiming absoluteness and supremacy, and that in a fixed form, demanding absolute obedience. It is important to note in this connection that Renan considers the life of the learned man as a vocation of being called and devoted to the honest search for truth. The student of religion is not a reformer of religion, but he requires the freedom to study religion, and to do it with an '... inflexible research after truth ...' (p. 133).

A third scholar studying religion independently, and with an eye open for the institutional setting, was NUMA DENIS FUSTEL DE COULANGES (1830–1889). As a classical scholar, historian and archeologist, he published his famous study on the ancient city in 1864, where he stressed the importance, for the understanding of ancient Greek and Roman civilization, of appreciating the role of religion therein. The major changes in Greek and Roman cultural history, according to this scholar, were mainly due to changes in the religious life. Consequently, the historian has the task of finding the roots of religious customs and ideas in the society during the period which is under investigation, and to assess their real function in that society.

In the text reproduced (pp. 134 ff.), Fustel de Coulanges reminds the reader of the difficulty in the study of the ancient peoples, in that we are inclined, through the values adopted by our own society, to idealize them and to see them as examples. He invites one, to see them as 'foreign' nations, and to appreciate the radical differences which distinguish these ancient peoples from modern societies. Fustel de Coulanges perhaps more than others consciously avows how difficult it is to study the religion which touches, positively or negatively, an ideal. And it is significant that he justifies such a critical examination, by arguing that our intelligence is developing and must continue to progress.

Insisting on the intimate relation that exists between the ideas of man and his social situation, Fustel de Coulanges was one of the first scholars to interpret religious ideas as part of their social setting and, the reverse, saying that a number of institutions of the ancients are inexplicable unless we look at their religious ideas. This scholar combined here the social science perspective with the historical dimension.

If Fustel de Coulanges was particularly interested in the *manes*-cult, professional classical scholars too became interested in the problem of the religion of the Greeks. We mentioned the name of Bachofen, and should add here that of *Erwin Rohde* (1845–1898) who wrote a famous study on the belief in immortality among the Greeks. Somewhat later *Jane Ellen Harrison* (1850–1928) devoted considerable attention to the much neglected ancient Greek folk religion. Miss Harrison applied sociological categories, interpreting group religion in terms of collective thought and feeling, social structure, and collective conscience and action. Besides myth and theology, she gave thereby particular attention to ritual and custom. It would be interesting to trace similar interests in the study of other religions at the time; such interests represented scholarly views and approaches that were elaborated in various theories on the elements which constitute religion, and in different methodologies, discussing ways and means to find these elements.

It is, however, to the study of the Christian religion that we want to look now, and in particular to the study of Christian Scriptures and the environment in which these documents originated.

Biblical scholarship. A capital name in Old Testament scholarship is that of JULIUS WELLHAUSEN (1844–1918), a representative of the historical critical school who worked in the three fields of Old Testament, New Testament, and early Islamic history. Besides his analysis of texts on their different sources with their respective tendencies, Wellhausen also was a master in his ability to reconstruct historical developments after his analytical and critical work.

The text presented here (pp. 139 ff.) is of an intricate nature. It shows, however, clearly and in an instructive way, how the author formulates the problem of the historical origin of the first five or six books of the Bible, and how he tackles this problem. Wellhausen destroys the traditional explanation, and then builds his own theory with a logical elimination of possible alternative hypotheses. The conclusion is that the so-called Priestly Code formulating the Law was written not only after the Jehovist recension, but also after the redaction of Deuteronomy; thus, its "ancient" appearance is fictitious. The text is interesting not only for Old Testament specialists but for literary historians in general; and the German original has its own stylistic beauty. Needless to say, it required considerable courage at the time first to doubt current views, and then to ascertain not only that the Torah cannot actually have been given by Moses, but also to assign a precise date to it which changes the pretended pristine document into a piece having a relatively late date.

Another scholar, though somewhat younger, who largely worked along the same lines on the Old Testament was *Abraham Kuenen* (1828–1891), known for his history of the books of the Old Testament.

An Old Testament scholar also working in a critical spirit deserves to be mentioned somewhat more elaborately, since his work extended beyond the Scriptures and even the written documents altogether and led to some much-discussed hypotheses for the history of religion in general and for religious anthropology in particular. This is WILLIAM ROBERTSON SMITH (1846–1894) who, like Renan, had to quit his professorship at a given moment, for giving in his teaching alleged offense to religious feelings and established order.

Robertson Smith was not only a good biblical scholar, for he also placed the religion of the Hebrews within the context of the religious customs and views of Semitic nomads in general. He elaborated thereby a theory of totemism and sacrifice, and he argued for the primacy of ritual over belief and even over the interpretation of ritual itself, at least for the area and time considered. Important also was the way in which he showed for a number of cases the equation of tribal with religious identity.

The text presented (pp. 151 ff.) is a plea, now that the historical order of the Old Testament books had been ascertained, for the understanding of the Old Testament against the background of Hebrew religion, and not vice versa. In its turn, this Hebrew religion has to be compared with other Semitic tribal religions as far as these are known; and then it has to be profiled against Semitic religion as a whole, as a particular type of religion, of which the concrete Semitic religions are variations. And if there are not yet sufficient materials for a complete comparative history of the Semitic religions, there is at least enough to arrive at a view of the general features that are widespread and permanent throughout Semitic religion taken as a whole. It is this Semitic religion as a body of traditional usage and belief, from which Judaism, Christianity and Islam have originated. Robertson Smith elaborates on the persistence of old religious institutions and on the resistance offered against any religious innovation, like for instance against that of the Hebrew prophets: 'Nothing appeals so strongly as religion to the conservative instincts'. The old religion consisted entirely of institutions and practices with practically no creed, so that the oldest religious and political institutions must be seen as being parts of a whole of social custom; religion was a part of the organized social life to which man could not but conform. The study of religions like the Semitic, consequently, is the study of the working religious institutions and of the way in which they shaped or still shape the lives of the people. The inquiry should not be directed towards the metaphysical nature of the gods about which so little was expressed, but rather towards knowing what place these gods held in the social setting of Antiquity. The history of ancient religion is that of religious institutions. And the religious history of mankind as such is to be compared with the geological history of the crust of the earth: instead of destroying completely what was before, the different layers simply cover one another.

This approach to religion meant a great innovation at the time. It was a break through the confines of traditional scholarship and it opened a completely new view on Semitic religion and on the religions of Antiquity in general. They were now interpreted in the functional terms of social institutions and customs, whereby full credit was given to their 'traditional' character, while ritual and not doctrine was taken as a primary datum. It meant also that a number of religions could be studied as variants of one specific type, and that the scholar might concentrate on this basic type as well as on the concrete variants. We leave aside now Robertson Smith's theory of the development of sacrifice out of a sacrificial meal which ultimately would go back to an original totem-meal; although the theory as such has been proved to be invalid, the stress which Robertson Smith laid on the element of communion was correct and was a departure from the current view on religion as being an affair of individuals. Religion as seen by Robertson Smith is basically a social reality that centers around certain basic institutions which are considered by the community to be sacred. The hypotheses inspired further research; what is more important still, is that hypothesizing was introduced into a field of studies traditionally considered to be completed when the contents of a text were correctly understood, in order to be translated.

A number of Old Testament scholars would continue to see the Old Testament in the context of Semitic religions; an outstanding scholar in this respect too would be *Arent Jan Wensinck* (1882–1939). But if, with Robertson Smith, they put Hebrew religion in the context of nomadic tribal religion, another group of Old Testament scholars would put it against the background of earlier Mesopotamian religion and civilization, and interpret it accordingly. They were the so-called panbabylonians. A scholar like *Hugo Winckler* (1863–1913), for instance, made a study of ancient Babylonian astrology and astronomy, and showed the influence of these Babylonian ideas in the subsequent centuries over the whole Mediterranean world including part of Europe. Winckler, moreover, held a new view of the nature of mythology for according to him, all myths are basically astral myths, originating historically from the country known for its special studies of the heavenly bodies, Babylonia. The attentive reader will surmise that, just as after the discovery of Sanskrit literature the origin of all civilization was ascribed to India, so according to the same mechanism the surprising discovery of ancient Babylonian civilization brought about the panbabylonian hypothesis, which equally developed into an ideology. *Alfred Jeremias* (1864–1935), another Old Testament scholar, who studied the surrounding ancient civilizations not only through the texts but also by means of archeology, had similar views on mythology and worked along the same lines as Winckler. He developed the hypothesis of certain patterns of myth and ritual originating in Mesopotamia but then spreading out into the world of Antiquity including Israel; the scholarly discussion of this issue still continues. Speaking about research on myth, we should also mention the classical scholar *Otto Gruppe* (1815–1919) who tried to explain numerous myths and cultic forms of ancient Greece and also of later time as borrowings from the Near East. Scholars like those mentioned here had an historical way of tackling the problem of similarities of religious phenomena at different places and times: the only hypothesis accepted was that of historical borrowing. This has been a school not only in myth research, but the same tendency can be found in the history of religions when comparative research is judged to be meaningless, and in anthropology when the diffusionists want to explain anthropological similarities exclusively by the hypothesis of worldwide wanderings.

The discovery of Mesopotamian civilization and the ideas of the panbabylonians made a great impact, especially on German speaking Europe at the beginning of this century. This is partly due to the fact that the Old Testament was submitted to historical research, not only with regard to its internal composition but also with regard to the outside influences which played a role in its formation and can be recognized in it. The baffling fact was that the Old Testament as a literary document was not as unique as had been supposed, or at least that its uniqueness apparently was not in what it had been thought to be. The simple fact that many traits of it could be shown to have existed earlier, and often on a larger scale, in Babylonia, meant that in a particular way the Scriptures were 'desacralized'.

A nice example of the effect of these discoveries not only in scholarly and cultural but also in religious respects at the time is the text from FRIEDRICH C. G. DELITZSCH's (1850–1922) first two lectures on Babel and Bible of 1900–01, which has been reproduced (pp. 161 ff.). Delitzsch was an eminent philologist in Sanskrit, Akkadian, Sumerian, Hebrew and Arabic; his reputation as an Assyriologist is undisputed. He could not but see the many parallels between Mesopotamian and Old Testament data, and concluded that the Old Testament was largely inspired by the earlier Babylonian materials; thus, Semitic monotheism turned out to have developed itself gradually in the course of history, and the doctrine of the verbal inspiration of the Old Testament had to be thrown overboard. The text in question, though written in simple and even pleasant language, is of methodological interest too, since it shows perfectly on an aggrandized scale the way in which the panbabylonians, and later the New Testament scholars of the 'religionsgeschichtliche Schule', reasoned. There is always the surprise of finding an element of the Scriptures outside the sacred text, and there is the attempt to explain the one by the other, without nuancing too much the forms of historical relationship. So Delitzsch introduces us into an atmosphere of discovery: that of the all-persuasive influence of Babylonian culture and literature from 2200 to beyond 1400 B. C. And we follow the range of Babylonian prototypes of Old Testament data such as the sabbath institution, the deluge, the patriarchs, the creation story, the story of the Fall, the occurrence of monotheism — and the consequences of this all for religious faith around 1900 A. D. Nice as it may read, one cannot but sense a bitter revolt against all religious authority obliging man to believe what goes against the results of scholarly research. In this time the conflict between traditional religion and modern science could be cruel, with sad consequences for social and personal human relations. Delitzsch's enthusiasm about Babylonia's religion has its counterpart in the touching note on his learned father's being threatened by churchmen on his deathbed. The resistance from religious quarters which the Lutheran Delitzsch experienced stands on one line with the resistance experienced by the Presbyterian Robertson Smith and the Roman Catholic Renan.

The panbabylonian ideas receded in the time of World War I, and so did the astral mythological school. We might mention the name of a scholar like *Heinrich Leszmann* (1873–1916) who derived myths from the moon as a basic nature phenomenon. Important is the name of *Paul Ehrenreich* (1855–1914) who also did anthropological work. Ehrenreich stated that all principal myths, not only in higher civilizations but also in non-literate societies, are always nature-myths referring especially to the moon and the sun. Ehrenreich developed also a theory on the various beings that are intermediary between the divinity and mankind.

From the foregoing, it appears that a number of scholars interpreted religion in terms of man's relation to nature. This underlying theme is especially clear in the work of the scholars on mythology, but is also present among historians of religion and anthropologists.

Still more than in the case of the Old Testament, critical historical and literary scholarship on the New Testament has meant a reversal of traditional raligious views on the Scripture. It brought about a crisis leading either to a modernist position or to a defensive attitude on the side of the orthodox; new religious views and theological approaches would then try to overcome the stiffling dilemma of the sacred text being either of human or of Divine origin. What Wellhausen did with the Old Testament, Baur and his 'School of Tübingen' would do with the New Testament: analyzing it critically on its literary and historical sources, mainly according to criteria of internal evidence.

In the case of the New Testament, however, more was at stake than objectifying the sacred texts and putting them under the norms of literary and historical truth. It implied the same procedure with regard to the very founder of the religion of the West: the question was raised of the historical truth and even reality of Jesus of Nazareth. A scholar like *David F. Strauss* (1808–1874) had concluded that the whole life of Jesus was a myth: that, as a historical person, he never existed.

The study made by ALBERT SCHWEITZER (1875–1965) on the subject in 1906, on the history of research on the historical personality of Jesus made an important mark. Though Schweitzer has been most known through his medical work in Africa, his significance extends beyond his founding and practising a consequent ethic of 'reverence for life'. As a New Testament scholar he redefined the problem of the historicity of Jesus by asking not only about the historical reality of the events, miraculous and otherwise, reported in the text, but also what concept of history the text itself presents. He then put full light on the eschatological expectation which pervades Jesus' preaching and acting, an expectation that coloured his notion of the "Kingdom of God" and the idea of it which was subsequently held by the early Christian community. Schweitzer also gave a reinterpretation of the work and teaching of Paul.

The text presented (pp. 174 ff.) is the first chapter of Schweitzer's book on the history of historical research on the person of Jesus. Not without reason, the critical investigation, on a historical basis, of the life of Jesus is called '... the most tremendous thing which the religious consciousness has ever dared and done' (p. 175). After explaining why for centuries there has been relative indifference towards the earthly life of the historical Jesus, he suggests then the deeper reason why the present historical interest could arise: '... it turned to the Jesus of history as an ally in the struggle against the tyranny of dogma' (p. 177). Schweitzer furthermore indicates not only the personal character of each study of the historical Jesus, but also the methodological difficulties due to antinomies in the text itself: 'The historical study of the life of Jesus has had to create its own methods for itself' (p. 179). For the non-specialist, too, it is fascinating to follow the way in which Schweitzer elucidates one of the fundamental problems of this study: '... to conjecture what kind of Messianic consciousness His must have been, if it left His conduct and His discourses unaffected' (p. 181). The method of hypothesizing that Schweitzer proposes for the treatment of this problem gave to the philological work a new inspiration, and led to further discoveries.

Similar to the way of the panbabylonians who had tried to assess the role of part of the environment in the formation of the Old Testament, a number of scholars of the so-called 'Religionsgeschichtliche Schule' made a sustained and serious effort to understand the New Testament and a number of religious phenomena described therein, in terms of the Hellenistic world in which the early Christian communities lived. The study of the terminology, ideas and cultic forms, for instance, of the Hellenistic religious world would lead, they hoped, to a better understanding of certain letters of Paul. Comparisons could perhaps be made and possible borrowings ascertained. As in the case of the Old Testament, here too, the enlargement of the scope of the world of the New Testament, the discovery of the civilization in which the new religion of the Christians had started to grow, gave a new orientation to research done on the New Testament and early Church history. Some leading scholars of this school in Germany were *Wilhelm Bousset* (1865–1920), *Hermann Gunkel* (1862–1932), and *Richard Reitzenstein* (1861–1931). At a later stage scholars like *Hans Heinrich Schaeder* (1896–1957), who had worked together with Reitzenstein, became more careful in attempting to ascertain historical determinations than the first scholars of the 'Religionsgeschichtliche Schule'. One of the important contributions of this school has been to study the beginnings of Christianity within a historical context and to interpret it from the viewpoint of general religious history. The resistance to this approach led to a debate between theology and history of religions whereby different solutions have been proposed but none definitely accepted by both parties.

Not only were the Old and New Testament and the religious communities described in them, subject to critical inquiry. The same thing happened with regard to the history of the Christian Church and of the Christian doctrines. And as in the other cases, here too, under the impact of the results of historical scholarship, the history of Christian doctrines and institutions also had to be rewritten. After *Ferdinand Christian Baur* (1792–1860), who in this field too was an initiator, two names of scholars may be mentioned as prominent ones in the subject: *Adolf von Harnack* (1851–1930) and *Alfred Loisy* (1857–1940).

We have now reviewed some disciplines and scholars who coped with the religious data which they met in the course of their research, trying to treat this material in a scholarly way. Bachofen discovered an ancient matriarchal culture and explored the religious dimension of it. Fustel de Coulanges found a correlation between ancient Greek social institutions and the prevailing religious ancestor cult. Such scholars discovered and studied religious data that were unknown before. On the other hand, those scholars who had to do with data which in the West precisely were viewed as being "religious" and consequently were interpreted religiously, took pains in order to study such data historically, i.e. divested from the current religious interpretations and evaluations. In other words, it appears that the study of religion in this period implied for 'foreign' religions in the first place a recognition of their religious side, and for one's 'own' religion first of all the recognition of its non-religious side. Moreover, it is to be noted that in the historical disciplines the research was directed to texts, and to a lesser extent to monuments and archeological remains. It is evident that disciplines like psychology, anthropology, and sociology, which are not in the first place dealing with the past and with objects that have reached us from this past, will view religion from other perspectives, and arrive at rather different approaches and interpretations.

Psychology. The name of WILLIAM JAMES (1842–1910) is reputed in psychology of religion for his study on the 'varieties of religious experience', of 1902, which was intended to contribute to a better understanding of human nature. James was trained in medicine, in the sciences and in psychology, and would develop a pragmatic philosophy. In the *Varieties* he gives an empirical treatment of man's religious experiences, and then draws some philosophical conclusions from it. A projected second series, for instance, would have treated 'man's religious appetites' and 'their satisfaction through philosophy'. It was indeed his lucidity which gave to this and other of his works its particular weight.

In the text presented here (pp. 186 ff.), James describes his method of studying religious experience. He wants to address himself to original experiences, and especially those that distinguish themselves by their more extreme expressions of feelings and impulses as they are recorded in religious treatises and autobiographies; he leaves aside, then, all institutional religion. James makes a fundamental distinction between the so-called existential on one hand and value judgments on the other hand, the latter to be left out of consideration in scholarly work. It is important to notice what James understands here by 'religion', 'religious sentiment', 'religious object' and 'religious act'. Equally important is his denial of the religious sentiment as being something of a psychologically specific nature; it is in his view rather a natural emotion or feeling that is directed to a 'religious object' of whatever kind. He intends then to analyze that particular quality of 'religious' experience which is constitutive of it and which cannot be found elsewhere.

It has been observed that what James understood by 'religious experience' actually remained restricted to particular individual experiences of a specific type, found among a number of Christians and specifically protestants, largely in America. He interpreted his cases apart from their socio-cultural context and hardly went into religious history or anthropology. Interestingly enough, James came to a positive appreciation of certain queer religious expressions, considering them in terms of a self-regenerating organic life and its mental reorientation and adaptation. On the other hand he assumed the existence of a subconscious dimension in man's life, which has some relation to deeper layers of reality.

A number of other psychologists of religion worked along similar lines. They were empirically oriented, often went about with questionnaires, and distinguished themselves by rational views, locating religion largely in the domain of emotions. Prominent names in America are those of *James Henry Leuba* (1868–1946), *Edwin Diller Starbuck* (1866–1947) and *James Bissett Pratt* (1875–1944). In England the theologian *Clement C. J. Webb* (1865–1954) worked from the perspective of religious philosophy. These psychologists came to some interesting results, for example with regard to the phenomenon of conversion. What was lacking, however, was a fundamental theory and a critical methodology of the discipline in this time. A scholar like *Alfred G. L. Lehmann* (1858–1921) gave considerable, though very critical, attention to parapsychological research, and published in 1893 a major study on occultism and spiritism as forms of superstition in Europe, while among some anthropologists too there was interest in parapsychology. The contribution by depth psychology is treated here separately (p. 50).

Anthropology. A fundamentally new approach is that of anthropology as the science of man in different cultures and civilizations. Most often the attention is directed to non-literate societies, and much research work has to be carried out in the field, in the societies which are under study. Among the forerunners of anthropology may be mentioned *Lewis H. Morgan* (1818–1881) in America, who did fundamental research on kinship organization, but did not work on religion. In Scotland *John F. MacLennan* (1827–1881) was the discoverer of the rules of exogamy and one of the first to describe totemism as a form of religion; while in England should be mentioned *John Lubbock*, since 1900 Lord Avebury (1843–1913) who, besides his manifold public duties, presented in 1870 a general theory of the cultural and religious evolution of man, beginning with a stage of religionlessness. The idea of evolution itself was a fertile idea in the second half of the 19th century, and its influence on the study of religion both in history and in anthropology has been quite considerable. What Charles R. Darwin (1809–1882) proved to have happened on the level of biology, anthropologists tried to show on the level of anthropology, and historians of religion on the religious level. Most scholars at the time did not see evolution as an hypothesis to be verified, but indeed as a self-evident assumption. It gave, however, a strong stimulus to the study of other civilizations and religions, in the past as well as in the present, since their plurality could now be interpreted within a meaningful framework. Another thinker whose philosophy had a great impact on research in the second half of the 19th century, was Auguste Comte (1798–1857). His influence was strong in the sciences and then in sociology, where he developed methodical norms for the study of reality in terms of objective facts. Religion, to Comte, represented only the first stage of man's mental development, followed by that of metaphysics and that of science.

An important spokesman for and representative of evolutionary thought was HERBERT SPENCER (1820–1903) whose work of 'Synthetic Philosophy' was wholly based upon the principle of evolution, through the cooperation of inner and outer forces. For Spencer, continuous progress is a necessary process consisting in the transformation of the homogeneous into the heterogeneous, i.e., as a process of differentiation. His own investigations dealt with nearly all disciplines related to man. In his studies on religion Spencer gave an important sociological treatment of religious institutions too. For Spencer, religion started with the cult of ancestral spirits (manism), with the assumption that, just as fear of the living is at the root of political control, fear of the dead is at the root of religious control.

The text presented (pp.199 ff.) shows the way in which Spencer deduces ancestor worship from a belief in the survival of the dead: once the conception of a ghost has arisen as the surviving duplicate of the dead, the desire arises to propitiate this ghost. The funeral rites, meant to effect this propitiation, then develop into a worship of the dead which becomes in its turn a religious worship when the worshipped ancestors develop into deities, as Spencer had contended. He then proceeds to show the wide spread of ancestor worship and its degrees of intensity, and hypothesizes '. . . that from the ghost, once uniformly conceived, have arisen the variously-conceived supernatural beings' (p. 208).

Spencer's general idea of religion is that, per definition, the unknowable is the domain of religion, while science has as its task to search for knowledge, thus subtracting things from the field of the unknown. The evolution of religions takes place according to the degree to which man develops intellectually and increases his knowledge. This view of knowledge as being itself an important factor in the process of evolution or development of mankind has been a powerful force in the development of scholarship and scholarly research.

The actual founder of anthropology as the science of man and his culture was EDWARD B. TYLOR (1832–1917). Like Spencer, he traced the evolution of civilization from primeval man, whom he saw represented to a large extent by present-day primitive man, up to the civilized man of his time.

But unlike Spencer, Tylor took his departure not in a preconceived scheme into which the data were classified, but in a careful arrangement of an immense number of data of all kinds, which he assembled in kind or about which he collected reports. On an evolutionist basis, Tylor used a comparative method and applied his theory of the recurrence and survival of elements of an older cultural stage in a later stage but without properly functioning in the setting of that stage. The result was that he could indeed present a survey of the total history of man and his culture, going back from the present to the past. Most influential on the study of religion, however, would be his theory of animism: that the belief in the soul, and not that in the ghost, is at the origin of the belief in spirits, which belief then developed with the necessary variations into higher religious conceptions and actions.

The text presented (pp. 209 ff.) shows Tylor's argumentation. He begins by denying that there are real non-religious tribes, saying that the reports in this sense are untrustworthy. Travelers could attribute irreligion to tribes whose doctrines were different from their own, in the same way as theologians could attribute atheism to those whose deities differed from their own: '... for the most part the "religious world" is so occupied in hating and despising the beliefs of the heathen ... that they have little time or capacity left to understand them' (p. 211). The implication is clear; the author has cleared the terrain for a more scholarly study of religion.

Tylor then gives a minimum definition of religion as 'the belief in spiritual beings' (p. 214), and wants to base his inquiry not on speculation but on observation; he proceeds then to investigate the forms and development of this doctrine of spiritual beings. It appears from the text that Tylor opposes animism, as the doctrine of spiritual beings and embodying 'spiritualistic philosophy' to 'materialistic philosophy', and that he sees in this doctrine '... the groundwork of the Philosophy of Religion, from that of savages up to that of civilized men' (p. 215). From his statement at the end that the deepest of all religious schisms is '... that which divides Animism from materialism' (p. 218) it at once becomes clear that Tylor, with his doctrine of animism, had in mind an apologetic of religion against the non-religious views existing in his lifetime: it is indeed a philosophy of religion. And this may explain, at least in part, the approval which Tylor's theory enjoyed among scholars of religion, comparable to the reception of Rudolf Otto's philosophy fifty years later.

For Tylor animism implies two types of belief: that in the souls of individual creatures which are capable of continued existence after the death or destruction of the body, and that in spirits graded upwards to the rank of deities. It constitutes altogether '... an ancient and world-wide philosophy, of which belief is the theory and worship is the practice' (p. 216).

The 'animism of savages' cannot be derived from elsewhere: it '. . . stands for and by itself; it explains its own origin' (p. 217). The 'animism of civilized men' should be explained largely as a developed product of it. Tylor then shows the presence of animism among non-literate people and traces its course in the development of higher civilizations.

Throughout his work, Tylor wants to study religious doctrines and practices not as resulting from a supernatural source or from revelation, but '. . . as belonging to theological systems devised by human reason, without supernatural aid or revelation; in other words, as being developments of Natural Religion' (p. 216); he does not want to work out '. . . the problems thus suggested among the philosophies and creeds of Christendom' (p. 216). The argument closes with the perceptive remark that though present-day civilization no longer attributes souls to plants and animals, still there is the religious doctrine of the human soul. And where this too disappears, there remains psychology as its intellectual product.

The work of Tylor is the product of a creative scholar who in his approach saw the totality of mankind as a field of study, just as J. G. Herder a century earlier had seen world history as such a field. For Tylor, all cultures could be studied according to their similarities and differences, and according to their greater or lesser degree of development. Given the time in which he lived, his study was carried out with a maximum of objective research of the available data and a minimum of prejudice. Parallel to the historians of religion, Tylor explicitly formulated the notion that religious ideas may be studied not for their revelationary contents and value, but as human ideas which are part of man's natural evolution. The very doctrine of evolution functioned, so to say, as a basis for the rejection of any supernaturalism, thereby rendering possible a scholarly study of religion. In Tylor's time this was a revolutionary idea.

On the other hand, it is interesting to note that, though Tylor's point of departure compelled him to remove the study of religious ideas from '. . . . the philosophies and creeds of Christendom', yet these philosophies and creeds themselves were not taken as subject to anthropological study. The separation of the study of non-Christian civilizations from that of Western civilization itself, in this phase of the development of anthropology, runs parallel to the separation of the study of non-Christian religions from that of Christian religion itself, in the first phases of the development of the history of religions. At most, phenomena of the non-Christian religions were shown to exist also within the orbit of Christianity, just as 'non-Western' cultural traits were shown to exist within Western civilization. Paradoxically enough, the same idea of evolution which served to study religious ideas and practices apart from the judgment of (Western) theology and philosophy, ensured that this very philosophy and theology was not studied in the same way in which the religious thought of non-Christian cultures and societies was studied. Western religion and civilization were not yet ripe for such an enterprise. But, thanks to the notion of evolution, one could see at least a continuity between all expressions of primitive cultures on one hand and those of modern civilization on the other hand.

Since Tylor's theory is discussed in nearly all handbooks of anthropology, we simply refer to some points of its critical discussion. Tylor did not accept a linear evolution as Spencer had done, but both scholars considered primitive culture as a beginning of development and not as a product of degeneration. Typically, Tylor and others after him considered the state of mind of primitive man, tending to personify nature, things and events, as more or less 'childlike'; it has been observed that for Tylor, as for others of his time, religion is fundamentally based on an error.

From various sides the rationalistic bent of Tylor, holding that souls and spirits are personified causes, has been stressed. Tylor considered primitive man as a philosopher looking for causation on an elementary level. Others have made clear that he was too much of an individualist himself to account for the social context in which religion functions, including animistic beliefs and practices. The fact that Tylor considered anthropology as a reformer's science may also partly account for its quickly spreading popularity. Tylor's anthropology was not yet the study in depth of one particular culture or society, for it moved on the level of general comparative studies, bringing together numerous similar data from different cultures, in order to compare them and to draw general conclusions. Only later anthropology would develop in the direction of an analysis of such cultures as units in themselves; an enterprise which would require intensive fieldwork.

A number of scholars, not only in anthropology, but also in history of religions, in folklore, and in cultural history, wanted to see to what extent the animist hypothesis would apply to their materials. Such investigations were not necessarily a check on the hypothesis itself, but could be an inquiry about the degree of its application or they could just interpret the data in the light of animism and consequently were a search for proof of it. In this respect we might mention the names of four anthropologists working in Indonesia, all having a central interest in the belief in souls: *George A. Wilken* (1847–1894), *Anton W. Nieuwenhuis* (1864–1953), *Nicolaus Adriani* (1865–1926) and *Albert C. Kruyt* (1869–1949). The latter two developed in a major study the concept of 'soul-substance' besides that of 'soul'.

A serious blow to the general validity of the doctrine of animism was given on the basis of field research as carried out by *Alfred W. Howitt* (1830–1908) in Australia. This research showed the existence of high gods among people whose level of development, according to Tylor's theory, rather required a lower animism. These facts could be established with certainty.

It is one of the virtues of the critical mind of ANDREW LANG (1844–1912) to have seen the implications of the discovery of the existence of "Supreme Beings" which cannot be explained by the theory of animism. Against Max Müller he gave an interpretation of mythology which opens more room for an understanding of its possible meaning than was done in Müller's linguistic-etymological approach. Lang himself also did much research on folklore, and pleaded very much for the study of parapsychology, with the argument that paranormal phenomena which are part of the life of certain people could perhaps furnish a possible clue to the understanding of animistic and also other kinds of religious beliefs. Generally speaking, Lang was a critic of nearly all theories current in his time, for he always pointed to those facts which could not be explained by the theories. Even contrariwise to the evolutionist trend, Lang does not speak of a unilateral development of religion. In brief, Lang was sensitive to the specifically religious and moral elements contained in the sources, and not willing to neglect them or to reduce them to other causes. And apart from all this, Andrew Lang was one of the most prolific literary authors of his time.

The text presented (pp. 220 ff.) is Lang's great polemic against Tylor. Its reading may be somewhat tiresome, but the author's way of arguing is striking. The questions are pertinent. First: what is the nature of the visions and hallucinations which, according to Tylor, are at the basis of the ideas of soul and spirit? Second: given the existence of Supreme Beings in primitive societies, can they be considered to be mere developments from the belief in ghosts of the dead? It is important to note that Lang in his turn, when rebutting theories, protests against the '... purely materialistic system of the universe' (p. 221) on which those theories rest which explain religion as the result of fallacious reasonings. One of his arguments is precisely the existence of an 'X-region' of human nature, which is ignored by these theories but recognized by parapsychological research. Lang then makes a long plea to incorporate 'psychical research' within anthropology and to study '... the savage and modern phenomena' in their factual reality side by side. He thereby suggests that parapsychology has more to say about the nature and origin of religion than rationalistic anthropological theories.

Without wanting to summarize his argument, we must note that Lang speaks at length about what to understand by religion, about the possible speculations of early man, about the possible differences and similarities between early man, present-day primitive men, and modern Westerners, indicating throughout the large distance in psychical condition and experience between the first two. One thread pervades the whole argument: the question whether a supernatural acquisition of knowledge in trance really exists. Lang discusses also extensively the implications of the belief in

'Supreme Beings', distinguishing, under all reserves, four stages in the development of this belief. In concluding, Lang explains what he intends: an anthropological — animistic or any other — theory of religion should not be accepted as a foregone conclusion, and science should never make dogmatic decisions about the origin of religion. His own hypothesis assumes two main sources of religion: the belief in a powerful Supreme Being, maker of things, moral Father and Judge of men, and the belief — based on paranormal phenomena — in something like a soul of man which may survive after death.

The work of Lang reflects the theories and concerns of his contemporaries in a particular way, for he took theories of scholars like Max Müller, Tylor and Frazer most seriously but subsequently escaped from their spell by pointing at the 'inexplicable' facts. On the other hand, he was much concerned with the comparison of phenomena in the primitive and the modern world, especially those of a paranormal nature. This issue was apparently for Lang much more involved than for others; for Lang did not ask only about beliefs and customs of other people out of curiosity, but he actually asked for the trustworthiness, the reality, the relevance, and the significance of their experiences. Lang was not looking for a theory, but for the reality and truth of strange matters reported by primitive people and by sensitive Westerners. Such a quest was not a dominant concern in the study of religion at the time.

One of the most prolific scholars on religion, a founder of comparative religion and a pioneer in folklore and anthropology, was JAMES GEORGE FRAZER (1854–1941). In all his publications, materials from all over the world, of different places and times, were brought together and used in treating problems of religion and magic largely through adducing parallels and using the comparative method to arrive at a solution. Frazer presented several theories of totemism, magic, dying gods, and other phenomena, but never united them to make one coherent theory or hypothesis. Three of Frazer's working principles were those of evolutionary development, the psychic unity of mankind, and the fundamental opposition between superstition on one hand and rationality on the other. He had in mind a mental anthropology, a history of the evolution of the religious mind.

The text presented (pp. 245 ff.) consists of the prefaces of the three successive and considerably expanded editions of his main work: *The Golden Bough*. These prefaces, in effect, constitute the official story of the book from the author's point of view. In the first preface, Frazer describes his work as a theory to solve the problem of the role of the Arician priesthood of Nemi. He pleads for using existing folklore of the peasantry with its characteristic continuity as potential evidence for the primitive religion of the ancient Aryans. He concedes that he derives the conception of the slain god directly from Robertson Smith. In the second edition, the author establishes that the theory given in the first edition — that the divine king-priest embodies the fertility of the land and should be slain when growing old — has been strengthened by new evidence. Frazer revises his earlier ideas on the relations between magic and religion, and states that these two are fundamentally opposed, with magic preceding religion historically.

Frazer then summarizes the problem of the book and his method of work: to bring together, in view of the given problem, parallel materials from cultures all over the world, and to develop certain general principles or laws. He admits that religion is too complex a structure to be explained as the product of one single factor. He here disputes Robertson Smith's theories and revokes his own earlier work on totemism. Frazer then gives a eulogy for to-day's anthropology — the first edition rather marks his work as comparative religion — and compares its discovery of the '... panorama of humanity's march from savagery to civilization' with the rediscovery of the Ancients by classical scholars in the Renaissance. Frazer also stresses the reformer's side of this discipline, claiming that the comparative study of the beliefs and institutions of mankind is an instrument of progress. Actually, the discipline strikes at the foundations of beliefs, since it shows much superstition also in Western society.

In his preface to the third edition, Frazer admits that his research on the priesthood of Nemi opened up many other questions in the field of primitive thought that he wanted to tackle. It is striking to see Frazer stating here as his conclusion that the human pretenders to divinity and their credulous worshippers turn out to have been much more numerous than had been suspected until now, and that the establishment of monarchy may have different causes, but that one of them at any rate is the development of magicians into sacred kings. He closes by saying that the study presents a theory of evolution of primitive religion and society.

Frazer's particular interest was in human thought and institutions, magic and religion, in prehistoric times, for it was to that era before history proper that he traced back the basic problems of the religious and the magic mind. The 'general principles' which he discovers are flexible enough to be replaced by others if the evidence should make this necessary. Frazer's theory of magic as a primitive science and his 'dualism' of magic and religion have given rise to much discussion and their eventual rejection. Magic was for Frazer to some extent what animism was for Tylor in that both outlooks would have been, in the primitive mind, the result of a wrong use of reason, but both provided rational devices to explain the world and to act upon it. Like Tylor, Frazer with his individualistic approach neglected the social context of the phenomena he studied and the structural unity of each culture. Another criticism is that Frazer, more than Tylor, accepted a mono-linear evolution, not taking into account historical influences or side-branches of development. Given his concept of religion, whereby man knows himself to be dependent on the gods he worships, which may be implored and even persuaded, Frazer considered neither totemism nor magic as religion. For magic, in Frazer's terms, is an elementary way of thinking while religion, on the other hand, is the acceptance of superhuman conscious and personal powers. Magic precedes religion; religion arises when magic fails. In such pronouncements Frazer subordinated the facts to his own evaluative categories, within an evolutionary scheme. It is most interesting to see how both Lang and Frazer expressed, each in his own way, the problems of religion, magic, and reason as these issues existed in their time, and treated them within the context of prehistoric times.

Scholarly discussion of the relation between religion and magic has been going on ever since, in direct or indirect connection with Frazer's scheme. A number of anthropologists have stressed the importance of magic as one of the sources of religion. We mention here only the names *John Henry King* (1843–after 1905) in the U.S.A, and *Konrad Theodor Preusz* (1869–1939) in Germany. The latter scholar was a specialist on Mexican and other American primitive religions and cultures, who also made important contributions to the theoretical issues of the discipline.

As with the case of Andrew Lang's theory of the Supreme Beings, it was again to be a discovery of someone in the field, that would lead to a new theory. *Robert H. Codrington* (1830–1922), during his stay on Norfolk Island, Melanesia, found the concept of 'mana' to be basic in the religion of the Melanesians. He wrote this in a letter to Max Müller, quoted by the latter in 1878, and established it in a study on 'the Melanesians' that appeared in 1891. He states there that mana '. . . is a power or influence, not physical, and in a way supernatural, but it shows itself in physical force, or in any kind of power or excellence which a man possesses . . . All Melanesian religion consists, in fact, in getting this mana for one's self or getting it used for one's benefit . . .' (repr. ed. 1957, p. 119). This concept of mana, its personal or impersonal, religious or not necessarily religious character, as well as its parallels in other religions and their development to a particular sort of religious category have all been the subject of much scholarly discussion. Careful research on the concept of mana was later carried out by *Friedrich Rudolf Lehmann* (1887–1969).

The theoretical importance of the concept of 'mana', as different from that of 'soul' or 'supreme being', was seen by ROBERT R. MARETT (1866–1943). Marett assumed a 'supernaturalistic stage' to have existed at the beginning of man's religious development. At this stage man recognized the existence of an impersonal religious force, which was felt rather than reasoned. The discovery of 'mana' belief helped Marett in developing his theory of 'pre-animism', referring to a stage preceding the belief in souls. This theory would later be known under the name of 'dynamism'. Marett's theory was less rationalistic than the theories of Max Müller, Tylor, Frazer, and even Lang, for Marett had a psychological approach based on the individual's experience, with much attention given to the affective and emotional side of it.

The text presented here (pp. 258 ff.) is a short communication originally presented at a congress. Without much polishing it shows what the author is looking for when he proposes a new 'minimum definition' of religion against those of Tylor — discussed elaborately by Lang as mentioned earlier — and Frazer. Apart from its contents, it is a nice example of the way in which Marett and others at the time tackled the problem of definition, as it helps us to understand why those scholars developed and used concepts in the way they did. For Marett the virtue of the definition of the '(negative) tabu— (positive) mana formula' is that it is descriptive, and that it expresses the universal nature of the supernatural, representing both its negative and positive aspects for man. Marett's general category is that of the 'supernatural', and in his definition he is concerned to leave room for all possible manifestations of this supernatural, be it negative as tabu (prohibition), or be it positive as mana (mystic power). Another advantage of the mana-tabu definition of religion is that both terms are coextensive with the supernatural, that they are homogeneous, and that the distinction between the personal and impersonal remains suspended. More consciously than others, Marett is throughout concerned with classificatory categories to be applied to 'rudimentary' religion. The paper closes with the wish that in the history of religion an 'orthogenic' line of human evolution may be traced which makes, however, allowance for lateral developments. Important is Marett's remark that the key to religious evolution is to be sought in social evolution, for this means a break-through against the individualistic views of his predecessors. He observes the fundamental ambiguity of 'personal' and 'impersonal' which is implicit in the notion of 'mana', and states that this ambiguity persists throughout the history of religion.

Marett's work deals perhaps less with the historical than with the psychological origin of religion, that is to say the rise of the notion of something 'religious' itself.

In his analysis of the feelings and emotions involved in religion, the author calls attention to the feeling of 'awe' as being most striking. Religious emotion somehow 'feels' the supernatural and subsequently shapes the intellectual conceptions of it. There are here interesting parallels with the theories of Nathan Söderblom and especially Rudolf Otto, as will become evident later. Like religion, magic also has a large emotional content.

For Marett magic and religion are not absolutely opposed to each other, as they are for Frazer, since both have the notion of 'mana' in common; thus both should be understood in terms of inner emotions. Further, for Marett the particular interest of the concept of 'mana', in the last analysis, would be that this concept refers to the supernatural experienced as the 'awful': wherever it reveals itself there is a power that inspires awe. The term 'dynamism' refers to this notion of 'power', which would become the basis of G. van der Leeuw's phenomenology of religion.

On the basis of Marett's theory the theoretical discussion of the origin of religion and the relation of magic and religion, which were current themes before World War I, took a new direction. Three scholars should be mentioned in this respect. *E. Sidney Hartland* (1848–1927) who also gave much credit to the notion of 'awe' and paid equal attention to the emotional side of religion. *Edward Washburn Hopkins* (1857–1932) who in 1924 developed the theory that for the primitives each thing has its own particular 'mana', without being differentiated into mind or matter, or even religious or non-religious. The German scholar *Karl Beth* (1872–after 1952) finally, who in an important study published in 1914, opposed magic and religion to each other as reliance on the efficacy of strict procedure, and as reliance on the actions of superhuman beings respectively. He held, however, that both were preceded by one common undifferentiated pre-magical and pre-religious stage. When man in this stage experienced the limitation of his own power he could react in two possible ways, developing either an egocentric sense of power which leads to magic, or a sense of a higher power which leads to religion.

A Finnish scholar who worked independently, but who was specifically in touch with the British schools, was *Edward A. Westermarck* (1862–1939). Actually Westermarck was one of the few scholars thoroughly interested in ethical precepts and moral ideas in different cultures and religions, and on this basis he hoped to establish what could be called man's natural morality — as the search for man's natural religion was an important motivation among other scholars. Westermarck also was one of the few who combined a systematic treatment of the materials with actual fieldwork, which he did in Morocco.

In the United States anthropology received a powerful stimulus through the work of *Franz Boas* (1858–1942) and his insistence on methodical fieldwork under the highest demands of critical anthropological scholarship. Rather than developing some new coherent theory, he analyzed, discussed critically and verified existing theories and doctrines on an empirical basis. Although Boas' theoretical work on religion and mythology, consequently, is relatively small, Boas gave in his numerous publications much attention to tracing historical connections between similar elements in the mythoogies and rituals of different Indian tribes. At this stage, his attention was directed more towards making an inventory of such elements than towards research on their meaning and function. Boas with his iron discipline had a great influence on nearly all American anthropologists of the following generations.

A student of Boas who was readily interested in methodological questions was *Alexander A. Goldenweiser* (1880–1940). Refraining from looking for an absolute beginning of religion or magic, Goldenweiser could study a phenomenon like totemism with more detachment than could other scholars of his time. So he arrived in 1910 at a thorough critique of the then current concept of totemism as religion. Goldenweiser rather brought totemism into relation with particular social groups and their different social structures, wanting to distinguish themselves in this way from other groups; he understood totemism on the basis of its emotional value, especially in the relation of man to nature. He denied that all totemic groups would have one common historical or even psychological origin. An American anthropologist who worked on religious data was *Roland B. Dixon* (1875–1934), who discovered, for instance, 'Supreme Beings' in Californian Indian tribes. The name of *Edward Sapir* (1884–1939) should be mentioned as one who did much research on North American Indian languages, and who could use linguistics as a means to analyze religious representations. In 1916 Sapir published a fundamental study of the historical dimension in anthropological research.

In Germany, the approach to religion as part of man's various cultures was quite different. First of all, two names should be mentioned of scholars who had a psychological approach to anthropological data including the religious ones. The first is that of the indefatigable *Adolf Bastian* (1826–1905) who visited a number of countries. Bastian interpreted the psychic unity of mankind in a way such that, when human nature is fundamentally one, the products of the human mind also have to be basically uniform. Anthropological research should therefore pay more attention to similarities than to differences, and should interpret the similarities between elements of different cultures not necessarily in terms of historical influences but rather as expressions of innate common tendencies. He hypothesizes then to the existence of so-called 'elementary ideas', which are certain forms of thought that are part and parcel of all men, and so-called 'ethnic or collective ideas', which are different in various regions because of the different interaction between elementary ideas and environmental stimuli. In his study of religion, for instance, Bastian analyzes it into its elements in each region, and then tries to explain the occurrence of certain elements in the concrete religions on the basis of the relative 'success' of given implements: those implements which bring 'luck' in a given culture will be considered there to have supernatural power. Bastian, stressing psychology, considered anthropology to be primarily ethno-psychology or folk psychology.

The second name is that of the well-known experimental psychologist *Wilhelm Wundt* (1832–1920), who between 1900 and 1920 wrote a ten-volume work on this ethno-psychology, in which he treated systematically an immense amount of anthropological data. His starting point was that phenomena that have a long duration and are of a complex nature — like religion, morality, art and language — cannot be understood in terms of the individual human existence, but only in terms of the life of communities which have a distinct reality of their own. Wundt, for his study of such phenomena, concentrated largely on non-literate peoples, his aim being to find and study the rules that govern such phenomena of a 'social' nature. Wundt moreover developed a psychological view of myth and imagination through which he saw the origin of religion in a specific 'religious' perception of reality.

Perhaps partly as a reaction to Bastian's theory of the independent origin of similar cultural traits in different cultures, and partly also in connection with its tradition of historical thought, there arose in Germany an anthropological school which was historically oriented. This school tried to explain such similarities by the hypothesis of historical movements of cultural diffusion due to perpetual migrations already in prehistoric times. The following names are representative of this school. *Friedrich Ratzel* (1844–1904) explicitly rejected Bastian's theory and called for research on possible early migrations. He did not deny, however, in principle, the possibility of repeated inventions at different times and places, and of independent developments of parallel cultural traits in different cultures. He also had an open eye for the intrinsic relation between a given people, their natural setting, and their own past: between land, people and history. Ratzel was an adversary of the evolutionist view, as the criterium according to which Ratzel and his school would conclude to a historical connection was basically a criterium of form: parallels that were not related to the essence of the artifact, or its natural purpose, or the material used for its construction, were to be explained as the result of historical borrowing.

A prominent student of Ratzel was *Leo Frobenius* (1873–1938), who worked out a view on civilizations as structural wholes — which include religion — in a particular geographical setting of time and place. Frobenius was the first to formulate the theory of 'culture cycles', according to which he tried to determine the different areas of civilization by mapping out similar cultural elements which are spread in different parts of the world. The coherence of such a culture cycle or area of civilization is more than a belonging together of disparate elements; rather, it is an inner whole, with material, social and religious aspects. The theorist of the school, however.

was *Fritz Graebner* (1877–1934), who — assuming that a discovery cannot be made more than once — proclaimed as a principle that similarities among cultures and religions are only to be explained by migration or diffusion. It is the migrations of small groups of people, each with its own culture, which account for the spread of certain cultural elements along certain tracks on the earth. Once given this starting point, the basic problems are how to ascertain the right sequence of the cultural layers which can be found together in one given cultural area, and what are the criteria by which diffusion is satisfactorily proved? It has rightly been observed that Graebner's is rather a geological than an historical method. With Graebner in Cologne worked *Bernhard Ankermann* (1859–1943), whose work was less speculative than Graebner's.

WILHELM SCHMIDT (1868–1954) applied the theory of culture cycles or areas of civilization in his study of religion. Moreover, he based himself on the assumption that the history of religion started with a primeval monotheism and morality. Schmidt thereby reversed the evolutionist idea that religion had to start with the least complex, the most simple constellation, as the theories of manism, animism and dynamism had tried to demonstrate. Following the line of Andrew Lang, Schmidt made large-scale investigations of the existing notions of Supreme Beings — all-fathers and skygods — among non-literate peoples. And following the line of Fritz Graebner, he reconstructed a hypothetical history of religion starting with an original pure monotheism by means of the theory of culture cycles or areas of civilization. Animism, polytheism, mana belief, and magic were explained as later accretions through imagination, which imposed themselves on the original monotheism, and spread according to the laws of the culture cycles. The high god beliefs found among non-literate people were considered to be survivals of mankind's primeval belief in a supreme personal deity.

The first text presented (pp. 265 ff.) gives Schmidt's account of the history of the discipline. The reader finds his definition of subjective and objective religion, his understanding of a comparative history of religions, and his idea of history. A useful survey is given under four headings: succession of religions and of cultures; succession of theories; succession of methods; and succession of attitudes. The second text (pp. 274 ff.) deals with the method which Graebner and Schmidt use in their anthropological work. It is stated that this method provides the definite proof that the 'High Gods' or 'Supreme Beings' are the oldest element known of religion. The author formulates the rule according to which one can arrive from 'culture cycles' or 'areas of civilization' to 'layers of culture', i.e. from juxtaposition in space to succession in time. Schmidt concludes with the present state of high god research at the time in North America.

Many discussions have been the result of Wilhelm Schmidt's theory of a primeval monotheism, of the methods he used to investigate cultural complexes, of the so-called proofs which he gave of his theory, and also of his distinction of primal, primary, secondary and tertiary degrees of civilization. These discussions often became debates wherein the opponents were unable to analyze not only the other party's but also their own assumptions and presuppositions. It was observed that the theory of culture cycles could be used to prove anything or nothing, and that the hypothesis of a primeval monotheism at the beginning of mankind's religious history is completely arbitrary. On the other hand, everyone could not but have respect for the masses of material which Schmidt gathered and the perseverance with which he worked his way through them. However, if there is any argument from experience, that a scholar in the field of the study of religion must be schooled not only technically but also methodologically and to some extent philosophically, it is an argument from the case of Wilhelm Schmidt. For Schmidt desperately tried to prove that primeval monotheism had to have existed, and that its survivals had to be found among present-day primitive peoples, since this was implied by his very definition of religion which to him was a value-charged subject.

It has, however, not always been sufficiently appreciated that, after all, Wilhelm Schmidt belongs to a group of scholars who concentrated their research on one particular type of god or gods. Actually, the discovery of a new type of god was all the more fascinating, since such a representation, evidently of the highest scholarly significance, could not possibly be found within the orbit of Christianity. It is in the nature of the case that the discovery of a god, more than other discoveries, evokes profound reactions. Such discoveries or at least studies, were made by different scholars, e.g., *Hermann Usener* (1834–1905) for the Roman 'special' deities; *Kurt Breysig* (1866–1940) for the mediators between god(s) and man; and *Jean Przyluski* (1885–1944) for the so-called 'great goddess'. Besides several studies on Indian religious history, the latter scholar wrote an article in 1936 asking in what sense one can speak of the science of religions as a discipline.

Important in a number of respects is the work of ARNOLD VAN GENNEP (1873–1957). This scholar saw the importance of minute and detailed investigations of facts as they present themselves in myth, ritual, folklore, and similar phenomena. Van Gennep worked outside the general theories of anthropology and sociology current at his time, which he knew well and which he criticized, and against which he preferred to work with small-range working-hypotheses that could be proved or disproved by concrete empirical research. Van Gennep was one of the first scholars to recognize the importance of non-periodic rituals not related to nature as it was understood in his time. The result was his classical work in 1909 on the rites of passage, which is a study of life crisis rites which facilitate individual and especially social transition. Later he would give much effort to the description of folklore existing in different parts of France. Van Gennep was particularly critical of Emile Durkheim's theories, and subjected in 1920 the whole research on religious totemism to a critical and methodical analysis, as Goldenweiser did in America.

The text presented (pp. 287 ff.) is a careful methodological account of the science of religion, of great subtlety and typical of Van Gennep's way of working. The science of religion must aim at a refined classification of religious facts. In order to do this, the general comparative method should be used, but it should be transposed to the 'ethnographical' method which deals with the study of concrete human groups. For its further application, the 'ethnographical' method is then adapted to the needs of the science of religion. Van Gennep studies religious data as an ethnographer; thus, he systematically uses the comparative method, as distinct from the historical method used in the history of religions. Van Gennep describes the process of generalization used in this research, treating extensively three different technical procedures: (1) the 'method of the fact coming-into-being'; (2) the 'ethnological' method or method of the natural environment, and (3) the so-called 'sequential' method. The essay closes with the emphatic assertion that the science of religion is not only 'history' of religion, for there is also 'present-day' religion: as a matter of fact, religion originates right now. Van Gennep then pleads that all newly acquired knowledge be linked to what we learn by daily experience. The aim of the science of religion is not simply to make scientific analyses and abstractions for themselves, but rather as technical expedients used to arrive at generalizing judgments, when one is moved by the desire to build syntheses.

The pursuit of historical and anthropological research on religion — to mention only the two most important approaches, which were not always on peaceful terms with each other — would lead to further thought on the nature of these disciplines, and on the methods and techniques to be used in them. Discussions of this kind have been going on ever since, and it may be assumed that most scholars have taken a position in these discussions, if not always theoretically, then at least by the very way in which they carried out their research. Two scholars working in the history of religions before World War I may be cited for their publications on methodology: the sanskritist *Edmund Hardy* (1852–1904) and the egyptologist *George Foucart* (1866–1943).

Sociology. One of the great sociologists and indeed one of the founders of sociology as a scholarly discipline was EMILE DURKHEIM (1853–1917). Durkheim was concerned with social reality as an entity and a force in itself, of a collective nature and with its particular institutionalizations. The discipline studying this social reality and establishing its laws is sociology. Social facts have to be objectified and understood in their connection with other social facts according to scientific laws; such facts can in turn be internalized by the individuals who belong to the collectivity. Durkheim gave great attention to the sociology of religion, for, sociologically speaking, he holds, religion 'is' society in a projected and symbolized form, and the reality symbolized by religion is a social reality. Religion then should be studied as a response to specific social needs. In the final analysis not only religion, but also other institutions and also representations and intellectual categories all have a social origin. Durkheim's great significance is that he developed a strict methodology for the study of social reality as he defined it. He wanted thereby to describe the social facts without prejudice, as objectively as possible, classifying them according to formal characteristics which are scientifically verifiable and which should explain the internal coherence among the facts.

The text reproduced (pp. 301 ff.) is from the beginning of Durkheim's study on 'the elementary forms of the religious life' of 1912, which is an example of clear methodological reasoning. The author states as his aim to study the most primitive and simple known religion, to analyze it, and to explain it without making use of any possible element borrowed from a previous religion. This should be done for a society, the organization of which has the greatest simplicity. Durkheim then discusses sociology and the ways in which it is different from ethnography and history, saying that the aim of sociological research on religion is to lead to an understanding of the religious nature of man, i.e. to show an essential and permanent aspect of humanity. Durkheim proclaims emphatically that human institutions including religion can, as such, not possibly rest upon 'errors'; for religious and other institutions are embedded in the nature of things and of man, and also that primitive religions hold fast to reality and express it. All religions, then, '. . . answer, though in different ways, to the given conditions of human existence' (p. 303). Thereupon Durkheim explains why he concentrates on a primitive religion; how he wants to establish the elements that constitute what is permanent and human in religion in general; and in which way he takes up again the old problem of the origin of religion, now under new conditions and looking for '. . . the ever-present causes upon which the most essential forms of religious thought and practice depend' (p. 308). Durkheim then discusses the problem of defining religion, and gives his own well-known definition in terms of the division of the world into a sacred and a profane domain, with sacred and profane things which are distinguished from each other. Furthermore, says Durkheim, religion is an eminently collective matter. Having refuted the 'naturist' theory of religion by Müller and the 'animist' theory by Tylor, and distinguishing carefully his sociology from the 'anthropological' school of Frazer, Durkheim then develops in this book his own theory of religion, based on totemism in Australia with references to the same phenomenon in North America.

There is a small library of publications devoted to Durkheim's work or to particular aspects thereof, and any fair discussion of this critical work is out of the question here. Durkheim wanted an objective sociology treating social facts as objective facts, like the objective facts of the sciences. Religion should be studied as a social fact in its own right; if it is as universal as it appears to be, it has a positive social basis. Religion distinguishes itself from other human institutions through its fundamental opposition between the profane and the sacred, and the absolute separateness of the latter from the former. The conceptualization carried out by Durkheim is of a formal nature, the definitions being based on external, observable characteristics: typical features of sets of facts that have been classified accordingly. In this way Durkheim and his school could analyze the typically formal structure of the phenomena under study. For Durkheim as a sociologist, nature is not the primary source of religion, as nature only provides the symbols, religious and otherwise, that are needed to enhance the identity of the group. And it is this identity which expresses itself religiously.

Durkheim was indeed the founder of a sociological school, in the way Tylor had been the founder of an anthropological school. Both scholars had an immense impact on the study of religion in their time. One of Durkheim's pupils was *Robert Hertz* (1882–1915) who gave a sociological explanation of mortuary rites, and of man's preference for the right over the left hand side. Close to Durkheim, also, was the historian *Henri Hubert* (1872–1927) who made a number of sociological investigations along with another pupil of Durkheim, Marcel Mauss.

MARCEL MAUSS (1873–1950) would carry on the work of Durkheim, and move more into the field of anthropology. Both Mauss and Lévy-Bruhl could be treated under anthropology as well, but since they have a theoretical approach comparable to that of Durkheim, and since they developed certain aspects of problems which had been formulated by Durkheim, we treat them here right after Durkheim. Mauss wanted to study religion and other social facts as 'total social phenomena'. The starting point is the indissoluble link which exists underneath all expressions of a society at a given time. If Durkheim had already said farewell to the individualistic approach to religion, Mauss went even further and held that there is no real opposition between the individual and his society; rather, there is interconnection, since it is society which allows someone to behave as an individual. Mauss was against an evolutionist view of religion, and actually may be seen as an important precursor of present-day structural research.

There was a close collaboration between Mauss and Hubert, both publishing studies together. The team of 'L'Année Sociologique' itself was based on solid collaboration.

The text reproduced (pp. 325 ff.) is from a book written by Durkheim and Mauss in collaboration and published in 1903. This book is concerned with the different classification systems, religious and otherwise, which can be found in the numerous civilizations and societies. Such systems, according to Durkheim's and Mauss' theory, have a social origin notwithstanding their utterly theoretical, religious, or metaphysical formulation. In this text are treated successively classifications given with divination, with mythology, and with philosophy. Primitive as well as scientific classifications have in common that they are systems of hierarchized notions, that they are meant to make intelligible the relations that exist between things, and that they connect ideas and unify knowledge as such. Now it is Mauss' hypothesis that divisions of society themselves serve as divisions for the system of classification adopted by that society, all abstract categories and classes being derived from social categories and classes, as are the relations between and among these categories and classes similarly socially derived. Where in social ties the sentimental and affective states of mind play an important role, it can actually be shown that a classification of things evokes sentimental affinities; ideas can in part be seen as products of sentiments and it is religious emotions in particular which convey to a representation its essential properties. The capacity to see 'differences' and 'resemblances', which determines the way in which phenomena are grouped together, is itself more of an affective than an intellectual nature. Mauss shows this phenomenon concretely in the divisions of space, in logical classification, and in the indisputable 'sacred' character which the collective representations have for the members of the group entertaining such representations. In course of time, however, social affectivity makes place for reflective thought.

When reading this piece which was written at the very beginning of this century, one cannot refrain from feeling that there is something particularly 'modern' in Mauss. His students would discuss the implications of studying social systems including religion from the perspective of 'total social phenomena' and of the invisible but existing social and affective origin of systems of thought and representation; and this sort of talk would lead straight into the present discussions of structuralist scholars.

Another French scholar who worked on collective representations, but who stressed their link with mental processes rather than with social structures, was LUCIEN LÉVY-BRUHL (1857–1939). Lévy-Bruhl had published a number of studies in philosophy and on the history of social thought before he turned to the problem of so-called 'primitive thought', thereby contrasting a primitive or archaic mentality to a modern mentality which cultivates abstract thought. This scholar's investigations of primitive ways of thinking had a significance not only for specialists in anthropology, but they were philosophically relevant in view of the problem of the unity of the human mind, and they were important for the problem how to interpret, as a matter of principle, fundamentally different forms of religious behavior and expression. These problems, as put by a philosopher, touched not only the non-literate societies under review, but human society in general. By the end of his life Lévy-Bruhl considered the difference between 'primitive' and 'modern' mentality to be one of nuance and not of principle, thus revoking his former theory of 'pre-logical' reasoning. But until his death he kept on considering 'participation' to be a fundamental human datum, though it manifests itself more clearly in primitive than in modern society. As a philosopher, Lévy-Bruhl was constantly searching for a clear conceptualization of the problems presented to the Western thinker by the very existence of 'primitive' ways of thought. Thus, he looked for a methodology based on description rather than on value judgments. Lévy-Bruhl had considerable influence on Van der Leeuw who put the theory of the former into a phenomenological perspective.

The text reproduced (pp. 335 ff.) describes what Lévy-Bruhl considered to be typical features of 'primitive' perception and thought. Here he stresses the concern with 'mystical' qualities of given objects and of objective reality, and the existence of collective representations which imply 'mystic' possibilities and which are held together on the basis of certain 'pre-connections'. Lévy-Bruhl tries to explain the classification systems, as analyzed by Durkheim and Mauss, by means of the concept of 'mystical participation', where he supposes that classifications refer back to participations of which the social ones are only a particular case. He proceeds to treat myths as substitutes for a real participation, holding that those who live in actual participation do not yet create mythology. Subsequently, Lévy-Bruhl analyzes the realities expressed by the words used in mythical language when he asserts that just as the perception of beings and objects in nature is 'mystical', so is their presentation in the form of myth, so that here it is the 'mystical' element which counts rather then the 'positive' content of the story. What is 'interpreted' is the feeling of communion with the 'mystical' reality. The author touches here the central problem of the correct understanding of myths as they live in non-literate societies.

If Lévy-Bruhl did not succeed in treating his materials correctly according to present-day standards, his work on the problem of so-called primitive thought can still be seen in another light: for it is the document of a confrontation between the rational mind of a Western philosopher and another type of mind as found among non-literate peoples. The basic problem remains indeed that of the existence of different modes of thought, in whatever terms this difference may be described. Where Durkheim, followed by Mauss, had already spoken of collective representations, Lévy-Bruhl connected the use of such collective representations with a particular mentality. This mentality occurs predominantly in primitive societies, and there is a correlation between the way of participating-synthetic thinking of this mentality on one hand, and the strong socialization of primitive societies on the other hand. Participation, therefore, becomes a key-concept for the understanding of both social relationships and collective representations; participating forms of thought on the basis of emotional participation would be the opposite of abstract thought with a minimum of emotional content. It has been observed that Lévy-Bruhl, speaking on primitive mentality, nearly always restricts himself to religious representations and actions, and that his theory does not apply to the daily life of non-literate societies and its non-religious aspects. On the other hand, for the interpretation of religious views and actions as such, inasfar as they are of a collective character and occur in literate as well as in non-literate societies, Lévy-Bruhl formulated problems that are still alive in present-day discussions.

Lévy-Bruhl met with much opposition from the side of anthropologists and sociologists. One of his loyal opponents with whom Lévy Bruhl has been in continuing dialogue, and who after his death published the 'Carnets', was *Maurice Leenhardt* (1878–1954).

In Germany, the sociological study of religion arose at about the same time as in France, but it was oriented in a different way. A scholar who came to do sociological research starting from theology was *Ernst Troeltsch* (1865–1923) who finally combined a historical, a systematic, and a sociological approach to religion. Troeltsch belonged to a generation of German scholars raised in the tradition of 'historicism' and discovering its limitations. Troeltsch carefully distinguished theology on the one hand from the historical study of religion on the other, pleading for the autonomy of the latter. As a church historian, Troeltsch became specifically interested in the social teachings of the Christian churches and sects, and the way in which these teachings were implemented. A scholar like *Georg Simmel* (1858–1918) came to sociology through his cultural studies, and from this perspective also put forth a sociology of religion. *Heinrich Schurtz* (1863–1903) had drawn attention to special classes and groups existing in 'primitive' societies.

The outstanding figure in Germany, however, was MAX WEBER (1864–1920). Weber, in the course of his work in the social sciences, of which he may be considered one of the founders, became concerned with the impact of a religious view, Christian and otherwise, on society. He was thereby in particular interested in the relationship of religion to other cultural institutions, especially economics. He succeeded in combining a historical and what could be called a 'functional' approach, using comparative studies for which he developed a classification through ideal types. Weber may be called, with Durkheim, a founder of sociology of religion as a discipline. It is interesting to note that Weber held religion to have been purposive at first and that it only later had become symbolic; this was a new view of religion which worked against a German tradition stressing the mythological and symbolic aspects of religion. Perhaps even more than in the case of Durkheim, the significance of Weber lies in his thorough methodological concerns; in a number of theoretical studies he laid the foundation of the social sciences, since his work introduces a number of issues that are under discussion at the present time.

The text reproduced (pp. 353 ff.) gives a succinct view of Weber's approach to religion. From the beginning Weber refuses to give a definition of religion, saying that he is not concerned with its essence but only with '. . . the conditions and effects of a particular type of social behavior' (p. 353). He calls for an understanding of religious behavior through its meaning for the individuals concerned. He affirms then that both religious and magical behavior and thought are basically oriented to the world in which they occur, and that, consequently, they ought not to be set apart from everyday purposive conduct. Weber then discusses his basic concept of 'charisma', and analyzes the different relationships which are possible between a religious phenomenon and the spiritual being — soul, demon, god — which lurks behind it, as viewed by the believer. Weber distinguishes successive stages of abstraction: the more this relationship tends to symbolization, the more the spiritual being becomes 'shadowy transcendental', up to the point that real events are experienced only as symbols of something spiritual. Weber elaborates on the consequences of the supplanting of the original 'naturalism' by an ever growing magical symbolism, into the circle of which more and more areas of human activity are drawn. One result is a growing stereotyping of the conduct of life, and a view of the sacred as 'the uniquely unalterable'. This transition from pre-animistic naturalism to symbolism would be a basic pattern of religious development.

As in the case of Durkheim, for Weber too there is a small library of publications on his work. Weber's investigations of the structural relationship between calvinistic views of life and the motive forces of early capitalism in particular, have led to profound discussions and numerous investigations, including studies in other parts of the world in connection with the motivations of economic development. Weber's studies on the social consequences of Chinese, Buddhist, and Hindu religious views on the societies concerned opened new perspectives for the understanding of the data of the history of religions, as did his similar interpretation of ancient Judaism; unfortunately, a planned parallel study of Islam could not be carried out because of Weber's death. Like Mauss, Weber appears to the present reader to be a 'modern' mind. Weber observes in the course of history an increasing degree of rationalization in all aspects of life, which has particularly interesting consequences for religion.

Depth psychology. Although William James alluded to a subconscious realm in man's soul, the psychologists of religion mentioned earlier did not investigate this realm empirically, while in parapsychology or 'psychical research' attention was directed more to para-normal phenomena. So for this reason, and because its approach to religion is distinctive, one must treat depth psychology separately. SIGMUND FREUD (1856–1939) was the founder of the new discipline. Freud discovered the existence of an unconscious realm in man, related to his personal history, and he was able to analyze the major forces within this realm and their influence on consciousness. Freud discovered thereby the negative, but in one sense positive role which religion, mythology, art, and literature play as repression or sublimation of psychological conflicts. This discovery opened the way to analysis and interpretation of religious motivations and expressions in terms of depth psychology. For Freud religion appeared to be, fundamentally, a projection of infantile dependencies upon imagined superhuman beings; the history of religion is as such the history of a collective neurosis through which mankind apparently had to go but from which it has to free itself through the use of reason. Thus, for Freud there is a basic antagonism between the religious *Weltanschauung* on one hand and the scientific spirit or scientific *Weltanschauung* on the other.

The three texts reproduced (pp. 361 ff.) contain some views at which Freud has arrived by the end of his life with regard to religion. The first text, of 1928, explains what is meant by calling religious ideas 'illusions': '. . . fulfilments of the oldest, strongest and most urgent wishes of mankind' (p. 361), whereas the strength of these ideas lies precisely in the strength of those wishes. Freud makes a distinction between an illusion and an error: something is an error when it is contrary to a truth that can be proved. As to religious doctrines, '. . . all of them are illusions and insusceptible of proof' (p. 362). Opposite to such illusions is scientific research, which is the only road that can lead us to a knowledge of reality outside ourselves. Since we know nowadays approximately who created religious doctrines, when, where, and with what motives, our attitude to the problem of religion has changed fundamentally compared to that of our ancestors.

In the second text, of 1933 (pp. 364 ff.), the problem is discussed whether psychoanalysis leads to a particular *Weltanschauung*. The answer is that it is not able to do so and that it accepts the scientific *Weltanschauung* which is in search of an explanation of the universe as a program for the future. The particular contribution of psychoanalysis thereby is to investigate the mind and the emotions and to study the emotional sources of the very demands upon a *Weltanschauung*. Freud then describes sympathetically the rise of the scientific spirit and its continuous struggle against the religious *Weltanschauung*, whereby psychoanalysis could lay bare the psychological origin of this religious *Weltanschauung*. When it is objected that religion is made subject to scientific investigation, Freud retorts that religion has no right to restrict thought or to exclude itself from having thought applied to it; the proper quality of thought is its endeavor to arrive at 'truth', i.e. correspondence with reality. This truth religion cannot give as religion actually issues a prohibition against thought in order to preserve itself. However, in the course of time the intellect should guide the mental life of man, and the very dominance of reason will prove to be the strongest uniting bond among men. Whatever opposes such a development — and were it religion — is a danger for the future of mankind.

The third text (pp. 371 ff.) dates from 1937–39; it summarizes Freud's theory on the origin and development of religion, and explains what he meant with his earlier publication of 1912 on "Totem and tabu". It gives an explanation of the rise of Judaic monotheism and of Pauline Christianity in terms of the 'murder' of Moses and Jesus and the subsequent guilt complex leading to the religions of Judaism and Christianity respectively.

The work of Freud cast a negative light on religion, at least according to the values of the time. It shows religious man to be immature and the victim of unresolved psychological problems, and it declares war on any religious *Weltanschauung* in the name of reason. It is interesting to see how the study of religion here, in the last analysis, became a struggle against religion: and in this case not in history or in prehistorical times or in the study of primitive cultures, but with regard to religion as Freud actually found it in his own environment. Freud could actually prove that a number of religious aspirations were to be explained by as many non-religious motivations which he was able to bring to light through psychoanalytic research. The psychoanalytic method disclosed a hitherto scientifically unknown realm of man's life: the dimension of the soul which had largely been the prerogative of religion. It was probably Freud's relentless involvement in psychoanalysis, both as subject and as object, which, through his unconditional faith in reason, led to discoveries on the role of religion in man's psychic life which were shocking to his contemporaries, but which put the whole religious venture of mankind within a bio-anthropological perspective.

Two of the scholars who, using the psychoanalytical method, came to interesting discoveries in their study of religion are to be mentioned here. In the first place *Herbert Silberer* (1882–1922) who worked on the symbolism used by mystics, and who differentiated various layers of meaning in such symbols on the basis of depth psychology. In the second place *William H. Rivers* (1864–1922) who applied psychoanalytical theory in his interpretation of anthropological data. The discussion of the way in which psychoanalysis can be applied in the study of religion has continued down to the present day.

3. RELIGION AS A SPECIAL SUBJECT OF RESEARCH

In the beginning of the 20th century more general handbooks or introductions to the history of religions came into existence. From a wider group three authors deserve to be mentioned in particular in this respect: *Frank B. Jevons* (1858–1936) in England, *Salomon Reinach* (1858–1932) in France, and *George Foot Moore* (1851–1931) in the United States. Once the science of religion had taken off, an ever growing number of handbooks, introductions, surveys, and popularizations of its results would follow. Since their writing required more a vast than an innovating knowledge, we will not deal with them in particular. The large number of publications on religion which lie outside the norms of scholarship must be passed by in silence, in any case.

Just as anthropologists were pursuing comparative studies on primitive societies with references to historical data, historians since Max Müller and Chantepie de la Saussaye had developed comparative studies in the history of religions, with references to anthropological data. There was an obvious need to classify the numerous religious data under general categories, classes, and subclasses, were it only for identifying and giving names to new data. In the treatment of a particular literary or historical problem the comparison with analogous data or situations could be helpful. Moreover, the better knowledge of other religions in the past or at present led to comparisons with the religion of the West, with Christianity, and research had to be done on the proper nature of the parallels and differences that could be observed. But also apart from one's own religion, it was interesting to compare different religions with each other in the way that earlier scholars had compared different mythologies; and it has been observed that comparative religion may be called a child of comparative mythology. Like historical research, comparative studies also could indirectly be used against the absolutist pretensions of one given religion. All in all, the comparative method became a more valuable instrument in the study of religion to the extent that the number of data increased, and that questions were raised which could not be answered by the study of only one or a few facts in their precise historical context. It was indeed the nature of the questions that were put to the religious data, which brought about the study of religion in general, or the systematic study of religion using the comparative method.

There were, however, also deeper motivations for taking religion as a special subject of research and for distinguishing the 'science of religion' from history, psychology, anthropology or sociology. There was, for instance, in Germany a stress on 'understanding' *(verstehen)* in the humanities and social sciences and an acceptance of 'religion' as a value category in itself. In the field of cultural history, partly because of the nature of the discipline and partly also as a delimitation of it against the sciences, much stress was laid on the fact that the aim of the cultural historian is not so much to explain, but rather to understand the materials on which he is working. Opinions differed greatly about the nature of this understanding and a number of hermeneutical theories were developed during the 19th century, but a group of scholars from different disciplines could meet each other in a common effort of 'understanding'. A prominent name among them was that of *Wilhelm Dilthey* (1833–1911) who both theoretically and in his own historical research made a clear distinction between the 'sciences of the mind' *(Geisteswissenschaften)* and the 'sciences of nature' *(Naturwissenschaften)*. Those historians of religion who wanted to apply this 'understanding' in their field, felt that the rationalistic approaches of their time were not only explaining religion, but were explaining it away, reducing it to something of a non-religious nature. They wanted, instead, to push forward where the rationalists stopped; to seize the essence of religion instead of its surface and periphery; to have access to the irrational life and inspiration that had given birth to the religious phenomena; and to break through the philosophical schemes that interposed themselves between the student of religion and the reality of religion itself. In general, these scholars sought to avoid the extremes of an objectivistic study of religion whereby all research is directed towards the objective side of religion, and of a subjectivistic study of religion whereby all research is directed towards the religious subject and his psychological make-up: the 'understanding' referred itself to something beyond the opposition of subject and object, i.e. the 'meaning'. This orientation can be found also in other disciplines where certain scholars gave priority to 'understanding' above 'explaining', e.g. Max Weber (1864–1920) in sociology, and Eduard Spranger (1882–1963) in psychology. In the study of religion, however, the aim of 'understanding' was applied specifically to the 'religious element' in the religious phenomena, i.e. that which constitutes these phenomena as being indeed 'religious', and which constitutes the unity of all that is religious.

We come here to a third motivation for taking religion as a special subject of research and for distinguishing the 'science of religion' from other disciplines. Thinkers like Friedrich Schleiermacher (1768–1834) and Georg W. F. Hegel (1770–1831), each in his own way, had tried to establish once and for all religion as a reality in itself, and subsequent philosophers had stressed the autonomy of religious values and of religion. In the hierarchy of values, religion was considered to be highest; in a way, the absoluteness that had been attributed to Christianity was here transferred to religion as such. In this way, all religious phenomena could be considered to be part of one whole, i.e. religion, which was not a descriptive but a value category. Consequently, the study of such phenomena had to interpret them in terms of their religious quality, and such a study separated itself fundamentally from other disciplines. Since several historians of religions were themselves accomplished theologians, the decisive step could be made not only to postulate religion as a special value-category, but also to qualify this value-category as such theologically. It was held, moreover, that an understanding of religious experience presupposed religious experience by the scholar himself.

NATHAN SÖDERBLOM (1866–1931), himself a specialist in Mazdaism, was also a distinguished historian of religions, in general. Not accepting any of the different theories on the origin of religion which had been proposed, Söderblom reformulated the problem and applied a typological approach. The question, as he put it, was that of the origin of man's belief in God, and with his typological method Söderblom was able to juxtapose three different ways in which this belief had originated: (1) by the notion of 'soul'; (2) by that of 'power'; and (3) by that of 'Supreme Being' or 'Originator'. In other words, the three theories of animism, dynamism, and high god belief were deprived of their pretended absolute validity; rather, they had to be accepted as three independent ways in which man had taken cognizance of God's existence. Söderblom used the same method to come to a typology of religion as a whole, in which were distinguished ethnic religion, mysticism of infinity, and prophetic revelation. The category of religion distinguishes itself from other categories through its characteristic quality of 'holiness', a notion that was more value-charged and 'irrational' than Durkheim's concept of 'the sacred', and less rationalized philosophically than Rudolf Otto's later concept of 'the Holy'. Throughout his work, Söderblom stressed the common religious searching and striving of mankind, and the common Ground of the different revelations which mankind had enjoyed. Actually, among the various scholars treated here, Söderblom may be called one of the most deeply religious.

The texts reproduced (pp. 382 ff.) throw some light on the view at which Söderblom arrived with regard to man's religious history. The first treats the discoveries, after the theory of animism, of the Supreme Beings or Originators, and of 'mana', and indicates that these three disoveries corresponded with as many ways in which the idea of the Deity began to take shape. Most interesting is the end where the author describes these different ways of man's becoming conscious of a Divine Being, and where he views the realization of God — from a spiritual process fermented by the Christian mission — as emerging as the common possession of mankind which '... is now propelling it towards perfection' (p. 385). Söderblom speaks here — differing in this respect too from the authors treated until now — with an ecumenical concern of a universal character. His concrete action, however, would be directed primarily to ecumenism of the churches.

The second text (pp. 386ff.) contains a number of points Söderblom wanted to make at the end of his life. Thus, he pleads for a view of religion in the first place as a matter of individual consciences, at least always when somewhere a new start has taken place. Söderblom distinguishes, further, the scholarly study of religion from Christian theology. The first leaves the question of Divine Revelation open, and does not even suggest a possible answer; the second implies for Söderblom a view of the history of religions as the field of Divine Self-communication whereby in religious sincerity, independent of place and time, a measure of Revelation must be recognized. On the other hand, the author states that the scholarly study of religion will distinguish 'the religion of revelation' as a particular type of religion within the whole history of religions. As it appears at the end of the text, Söderblom himself was convinced that Revelation extended beyond the confines of the Bible, and that it is palpable in the three forms of 'genius', 'history', and 'spiritual personality'.

Among the historians of religions who worked on the religions of Antiquity must be mentioned for the period until World War II *Albrecht Dieterich* (1866–1908), especially for classical religions; *Morris Jastrow* (1861–1921), especially for Mesopotamian religions; and *Franz Cumont* (1868–1947), especially for the religions of the Hellenistic period.

A distinct place was taken by WILLIAM BREDE KRISTENSEN (1867–1953) as a student of the historical religions of Antiquity. Kristensen's significance may be said to lie in his constant effort to grasp the religious values of these traditions, especially in the domain of an underlying mystery religion. Kristensen tried, on the basis of such values, to come to an understanding of the texts which he studied and he located these values in what he called 'the belief of the believers' which was at the same time subject and norm of scholarly research. A specific sensitivity of this scholar accounts for his attention to all symbolic expressions related to the problem of life and death, and to the idea of totality. Kristensen's views on the religions of Antiquity were opposed both to positivistic interpretations and to evolutionary judgments as were current in his time. Kristensen preferred to study the texts apart from their time sequence and hardly ever spoke of any 'historical' development of the religions he studied, their ideal contents presumably referring to one and the same eternal religious truth.

The text reproduced (pp. 390 ff.) gives a survey of the main statements of this scholar in matters of method and theory. The historian faced with his documents may arrive at a relative understanding, but an absolute understanding is impossible since he cannot have the experience of the believers themselves; comparisons and generalizations are useful only insofar as they help one to understand the particular data. For Kristensen there was a mutual fruition of historical and phenomenological research, bringing to light the religious idea or value contained in the text to which the scholar ought to have access. Though less clearly expressed, there is also the notion of a similar mutual fruition between phenomenological and philosophical research: so Kristensen distinguishes history, phenomenology or 'typology', and philosophy as the three subdivisions of one general 'science of religion'. Kristensen very much stresses the importance of the scholar's own religious experience for his understanding of the experience of others and as a basis for the required sympathy for the subject; actually, the devoted scholar is himself growing religiously in the course of his study of religious reality, and his intuitive power increases thereby. The author elaborates then on phenomenology of religion, by which he understands a 'descriptive' as opposed to a 'normative' comparative religion. Although he himself rejects an historical or an idealistic evolutionism, Kristensen typically recognizes that on philosophical — which is for Kristensen mainly Hegelian — grounds both can be defended and studied, but only in the abstract. The historian, indeed, distinguishes himself radically from the philosopher in that he refuses a particular pattern of development prescribed by the philosophical mind to be forced upon history. Over and against the philosopher, the historian and phenomenologist must investigate what the believers themselves said about their faith and what religion meant to them. They '. . . must therefore be able to forget themselves, to be able to surrender themselves to others' (p. 396). Understanding actually implies the recognition that: '. . . the believers were completely right !' (p. 396).

Around the time of World War I, partly as a reaction to historicism, quite a few students of religion held psychology to be a useful instrument in order to understand religion; such understanding would take place in an experiential way whereby the religious data do not remain imprisoned within their historical and geographical coordinates. This tendency to use 'experience' in a psychological approach in order to arrive at an understanding made itself felt methodologically among German scholars. The contents of this 'psychology' of religion could vary tremendously from author to author, if one compares for instance the philosopher *Traugott K. Österreich* (1880–1949) with his interest for parapsychology, and the theologian *Georg Wobbermin* (1869–1943) with his theory of the 'hermeneutical circle' in understanding.

A scholar of religion who consciously used psychology as an 'experiential' method to guide intuition and to arrive at an immediate understanding was GERARDUS VAN DER LEEUW (1890–1950). Speaking in 1928 of his 'phenomenological' method, Van der Leeuw states that it could also be called 'psychological'; he wants to call it 'phenomenological' only in the broad sense of the word, as it is used in modern psychiatry, consequently in the psychological sphere (p. 406). It is in this sense that Van der Leeuw developed a methodology for the 'understanding' of religious phenomena. Basic thereto is the classification of religious phenomena by means of ideal types that are constituted again by a psychological technique of re-experiencing religious meanings. In this way Van der Leeuw developed a phenomenology of religion which was methodically based on the experience of 'understanding'. He contended, however, that proper historical and exegetical studies have to precede such a phenomenological understanding, and thus he gave considerable attention to the history of religions where his own fields were the ancient Egyptian and Greek religions. In his broader interpretations of religion, Van der Leeuw became interested in the problem of anthropological structures, in the relationship between religion and art, and in the interpretation and theological appreciation of man's being a 'religious man' *(homo religiosus)*. Phenomenology of religion, for this scholar, led both to anthropology and to theology.

The texts that have been translated or reproduced here (pp. 399 ff.) present various methodological statements and elucidations of the author's phenomenological work.

The first text in translation (pp. 399 ff.) draws a parallel between certain trends in psychology and in the history of religions after World War I, which gave primary importance to 'understanding' as different from 'explaining'. Van der Leeuw reviews here in his first methodological account the work to be done under different headings: psychology and history of religions, empathy, structural relations, ideal types. At the end the author speaks of the psychological self-education necessary for the phenomenologist.

The second text in translation (pp. 406 ff.) begins by summarizing what Van der Leeuw means by his 'phenomenological-psychological' method, and continues to expound the way in which this method can be applied to theology. This application would result in a 'phenomenological theology' dealing with the 'understanding' of the religious data; it would be the intermediary stage between historical and systematic theology. Typically, Van der Leeuw identifies this 'theological phenomenology' with the 'science of religion': it is concerned with the context of meaning of the religious phenomena and not with empirical or ultimate realities.

The third text (pp. 408 ff.) is concerned with the notion of 'understanding' itself. This requires, along the lines of Wilhelm Dilthey and Eduard Spranger, the all-embracing ideal structure of the 'objective mind', a given circle of communication, and an existential involvement on the side of the researcher. Using Martin Heidegger's expression, Van der Leeuw identifies someone's 'understanding' with his 'being within the world', then discusses the concept of structure, the plurality of methods, and the three 'spheres of cognition'.

The fourth text (pp. 412 ff.) is a reproduction of part of the 'Epilegomena' of the author's *Religion in Essence and Manifestation* (1938). It defines the main concepts and assumptions, and describes the six levels or stages of phenomenological work. It then gives Van der Leeuw's double view of religion: religion as man's seeking power in life, and religion as God's revealing Himself to man. Subsequently, the problem is discussed, whether a phenomenology of religion is not a contradiction in itself. The answer is negative, with an appeal to the ultimately religious nature of all understanding. Phenomenology of religion is then delimited with regard to art (poetry), history, psychology, and philosophy of religion; nor would it be theology. Finally, a short description is given of the personal state of the phenomenologist.

The fifth text (pp. 425 ff.) is part of the Introduction of *Sacred and Profane Beauty*, in which Van der Leeuw gives an historical, phenomenological, and theological view of each of the seven Arts. It proposes the problem of how religion and art, the holy and the beautiful, have been related to each other in the course of Western cultural and religious history. Here it is the aesthete Van der Leeuw who speaks with his double the theologian in phenomenological language.

It has frequently been observed that Van der Leeuw's phenomenology of religion has numerous theological and philosophical assumptions, and this is evident from what precedes. It has been observed, too, that it neglects the cultural context of the phenomena as well as their empirical aspects, and this may be clear from the given methodology. In the final analysis, Van der Leeuw's phenomenology may perhaps best be called an 'experiential liturgy' presenting man's religion religiously.

The study of the Eastern world religions, interestingly enough, has been assigned traditionally in the first place to the orientalists, since they were specialized in the literature of the larger Eastern languages. The professional historians of religion before World War II were mostly working — often in connection with biblical studies — on religions that had disappeared. They made comparative studies or were interested in general problems that, characteristically, were more related to the religions of non-literate societies than to the present-day world religions. It was relatively rare that a historian of religions would devote himself to the study of one of the world religions. Their study was entrusted to those scholars among the orientalists who happened to be interested in the religious aspects of the civilization they studied. Some prominent names of German speaking orientalists who were historians of religions at the same time, are for the period before and shortly after World War I for instance: *Ignácz Goldziher* (Hungarian, 1850–1921) for Islam; *Richard Wilhelm* (1873–1930) for Chinese religion; *Hans Haas* (1868–1935) for Japanese religion; *Hermann Oldenberg* (1854–1920) for Vedic religion and Buddhism; *Heinrich Zimmer* (1890–1943) for Vedic religion and Hinduism; and combining this with comparative studies on Indo-European religion the Austrian scholar *Leopold von Schröder* (1851–1920) and the German scholar *Hermann Lommel* (1885–1967).

A place apart among the scholars of Eastern religions was taken by RUDOLF OTTO (1869–1937) who was at the same time an indologist and a systematic theologian. This made Otto approach the religious data and the phenomenon of religion as such with the questions of a systematic thinker. Otto is best known for his taking 'the holy' as an autonomous category of meaning and value, a category *a priori* which constitutes religion. On this basis he could postulate, against the naturalist and historicist trends of his time, the autonomy of religion as different from other spheres of life, a theme that gave to his work, which in the last analysis is of a theological nature, an apologetic tendency. This postulate allowed him, however, to give an epistemological foundation to — and a justification of — religious knowledge, by means of man's inborn 'sensus numinis'. Otto carried out number of studies on Indian religion, several of which made comparisons between religious themes and phenomena taken from the Indian and the Western religious traditions. In his philosophy of religion Otto developed a methodology, with a conscious use of intuition, to analyze religious experiences, in which he tried to do justice to the 'subjective' as well as to the 'objective' side of such experiences.

Two texts of Rudolf Otto are presented here (pp. 432 ff.). The first treats the category of 'the holy'. It sets forth the unbreakable connection between the rational and the non-rational aspects of the deity; these aspects are, however, bound to be separated by the quality of man's religious life which either pursues rationalization or is sensitive to non-rational experiences. Otto stresses throughout his work the non-rational aspects of religious experience and of the representation of the deity. The 'holy' as conceived by Otto is a complex category: rationalizations of it may take place but still the awareness of something unfathomable prevails, and it is just this non-rational 'moment' that gives to the holy that surplus which is its religious dimension. In treating the holy as an *a priori* category, Otto contends that the non-rational elements of this category refer to what is called in mysticism the 'ground of the soul'. This sparkle in man is predisposed to the experience of the numinous, and it has objective and valid *a priori* cognitive elements with regard to the holy through the experience of the numinous. Finally, Otto discusses the religious *a priori*, its internal polarity, and realm of validity, and gives examples thereof. He repeatedly pleads for the recognition of this non-rational dimension of religion, claiming that the faculty through which man is able to cognize and to recognize the holy in its different manifestations is that of divination.

The second text (pp. 447 ff.) treats systematically certain data of the history of religions. The reader sees here an application of Otto's approach in the notion of the 'wholly other' and the 'absolute', and in his discussion of parallels and convergences in religious developments in East and West.

One of the reasons for the particular attraction of Rudolf Otto's work for a number of historians of religions must have been his conception of the 'religious *a priori*'. This notion guaranteed religion to be an autonomous province of reality, and allowed one to interpret religious phenomena in view of the *a priori* religious reality of the holy and the experiential reality of the numinous. In this way, also, the study of religion as an autonomous discipline with a subject of its own was theologically justified. Another reason for the appeal of Otto's work must have been his attempt to do justice to the non-rational dimension of things religious, and so to defend religion against rationalizing theories of it. It also left room among the students of religion to use their intuitive as well as their rational faculties.

Otto's theory represents a typical systematization of a particular religious tradition in the West, in the line of which such names as F. Schleiermacher and N. Söderblom must be seen. Religion is here interpreted as the feeling of absolute dependence, as the presence of the holy, as the experience of the numinous. This does not disclaim the stature of Rudolf Otto as a religious thinker, specifically as a philosopher of religion. But it draws attention to the fact that a number of religious experiences can hardly be described in the terms coined by Otto on the model of one specific religious tradition. On the other hand, by using a normative concept of religion which ultimately goes back to a theological intention, Otto somehow alienated the scholars working on a strictly empirical basis from the history of religions as he conceived it.

The study of religious life and piety, of religiousness and mysticism, had been remarkably absent in the early history of the discipline. The scholars working in this field stressed the historical and rational character of the scholarly study of religion, as distinct from the 'religious' study performed within the particular religious traditions. Moreover, scholars from the protestant traditions could not but have an unclear picture of the religious experience in other traditions. It is no accident that the three names of serious students of mysticism in this period are those of Roman Catholics: *Friedrich von Hügel* (1852–1925); *Evelyn Underhill* (1875–1941); and *Jean Baruzi* (1881–1953). The same holds true for a student of Islamic mysticism, *Louis Massignon* (1883–1962).

An outstanding figure in this field was FRIEDRICH HEILER (1892–1967). In his studies on prayer, on certain religious personalities, and on ecumenical convergences of the different religions, Heiler made a continuous effort to do justice to the experiential value of the subject, and to the religious truth of which the text or the living person gives evidence. As becomes apparent from his comparative studies, Heiler's own religious consciousness made him see all religions as constituting, basically, a unity. Consequently, Heiler wanted to evolve a phenomenology of religion which would be oriented along theological lines, with the tension between *deus absconditus* and *deus revelatus* as its focus.

The texts presented in translation (pp. 461 ff.) date from the beginning and, respectively, the end of Heiler's scholarly career. The first has been taken from his major study *Prayer*, of 1918. It shows not only the personal religious involvement of this scholar and his appreciation of prayer as '... the elementary and necessary expression of the religious life' (p. 464), but also his demands on the scholarly study of religion. Prominent in Heiler's approach here is his preference and search for 'pure naive religion' as a focus of interest, at its origins and peaks '... where it spontaneously and freely, with creative force, breaks out of strong inner experiences ...' (p. 466). One notices also his preference for the great religious personalities '... whose spiritual values merge with or culminate in religious experience, and who have great creative significance in religious history' (p. 468). Heiler was one of the few classical historians of religion who was aware of the forces of religion among the less educated. He stressed the values of living folk religion, not only as opposed to rationalized religion but also as being in actual touch with the real needs in people's lives. Significant, furthermore, is Heiler's call for introspection on the part of the scholar of religion as indispensable for any religious psychological understanding, and his explicit demand for a scholar's personal religious experience as a precondition to having access to the world of religion.

The second text, of 1961, presents the demands on the study of religion as Heiler formulated them at the end of his life. He enumerates here five general scholarly requirements — among which is a personal formulation of what he calls the 'phenomenological method' —, and three requirements that are specific for the study of religion. The fragment closes with the formulation of a projected phenomenology of religion which is based on the *analogia entis* between created being and the non-created Divine Being, and which has a definite theological intention. For Heiler, who through his studies tried to accede to religious reality, this was an evidence given by religious experience itself.

A quite different approach is that which stresses the need of formal categories of universal validity, which are clearly defined and do not include the ideational or experiential contents of religion. Among several examples one may think of the work of the Swedish scholar *Edvard Lehmann* (1862–1930), who gave a clear and detached classificatory scheme of religious phenomena.

Important for this approach is the work, though of limited size, of HEINRICH FRICK (1893–1952). Frick outlined a typology of religion, and stressed in particular the systematic character of the study of religion. For this purpose, he coined some key concepts like 'stage', 'habitus' and 'basic phenomena'. On the other hand, as a theologian Frick was quite involved in a problem that occupied many minds at the time: how to think of Christianity both in its uniqueness and as being one among the many religions. Fundamentally, Frick viewed the study of religion as a theological discipline, and wanted to connect it with missiology.

The text given here in translation (pp. 480ff.) presents the project of a typology of religion. Frick discusses here the concept of 'type', the way in which the problem of typology arises, and different ways of understanding typology. The author's concern for clear concepts then appears from his discussion of the concept of *habitus*. Frick finally suggests paths to an exact method for the comparison of religions, and tackles the basic problem of the principle of comparison in the study of religion.

Apart from such few systematic studies on religion, the history of religions developed itself along the lines of ever greater specialization. This, of course, holds particularly true for the study of individual religions, and some names come to mind for the period until World War II: *Theodor Mommsen* (1817–1903) and *Georg Wissowa* (1859–1931) for the religion of the Romans; *Ulrich von Wilamowitz-Moellendorf* (1848–1931) for the religion of the Greeks; *Tor Andrae* (1885–1947) for Islam; *Arthur Christensen* (1875–1945) for ancient Persian religion; and *Arthur D. Nock* (1902–1963) for the Hellenistic religions.

On the other hand there were some historians of religion who, notwithstanding an intensive specialization on one religion in particular, kept an eye open both with regard to developments in the history of religions in general, and with regard to the general problems of the discipline and the questions put to the materials. Some representative names are those of the Danish scholar *Vilhelm Grönbech* (1873–1948), concentrating on Germanic religion; the Dutchman *Arent Jan Wensinck* (1882–1939), concentrating on West-Semitic religion and Islam; and the German scholars *Alfred Bertholet* (1868–1951), branching out his Old Testament studies; *Hans Heinrich Schaeder* (1896–1957), concentrating on Iranian and late Hellenistic religions; and *Carl Clemen* (1865–1940) with many-sided interests.

An outstanding place among the scholars able to follow the results of progressive research in the whole field of the study of religion, and someone able to contribute methodically to it, was JOACHIM WACH (1898–1955). Wach may be called one of the most universal minds in the field. The fact that he had to move in 1935 made his scholarly life fall into two halves, twenty years in Germany and twenty years in the United States. The main significance of Wach in our perspective is his constant methodological concern. In 1924 Wach published a basic methodological work on the study of religion as a systematic discipline, on the level of the humanities and the social sciences. Intent on the problem of interpretation and understanding — hermeneutics in the line of Wilhelm Dilthey — Wach wrote a three-volume work on theories on the subject in the 19th century. His period in the United States gave Wach the opportunity to practise this, and to form a group of scholars along these lines. Besides his theoretical work and a number of comparative studies, Wach worked intensely on sociology of religion, both in the German and the American tradition, whereby he advocated a typological approach. In his own approach to religious phenomena, too, Wach strove for a systematic typological understanding. He thereby took religious experience as his point of departure, and made the attempt to interpret the religious data as expressions of such religious experience: in thought, action, or human fellowship. Wach distinguished himself, also, by keeping an eye open for the philosophical problems raised by the results of the discipline and by the fact of man's apparent religiousness.

The five texts reproduced (pp. 487 ff.) present a good introduction to Wach's approach to religion. The first, from *Sociology of Religion*, has been taken from his study on sociology of religion, in which he treats the interrelation and the forms of interaction between religion and society. In the line of Ernst Troeltsch and Max Weber, Wach protests against the assumptions of a complete social and economic materialism, as found in Marxian doctrine. He then devotes considerable space to the preliminaries, philosophical and otherwise, of the sociology of religion as he wants to study it, listing thereby a number of prominent thinkers who studied and reflected on religion. This way of opening is typical of Wach's scholarship, and it permits the reader to situate Wach among the many others with whom he was in intellectual discourse.

The second text, from *The Comparative Study of Religions*, written shortly before Wach's death, gives similar preliminaries to the comparative study of religion. This text contains a useful historical appraisal of the work done until now, which serves as an introduction to the treatment of what was for Wach always a fundamental problem: whether and to what extent can one arrive at an understanding of a religion other than one's own, and what is to be 'understood' by such an 'understanding'? Wach then explicates the requirements to be put to the scholar of religion, and finally broaches the problem of the method to be followed which, he says, should be unified and should be adequate to the subject matter.

The third text, taken from an essay on what is universal in religion (pp. 498 ff.), deals mainly with religious experience. Wach formulates four formal criteria there which an experience must meet in order to be called 'religious', and in this connection he stresses the notion of religion as something distinct and *sui generis*. The author then expounds on the three lines along which religious experience finds its expression: the theoretical, the practical, and the sociological. Wach also explains a central theme in his thought, that of religious experience, as '. . . the total response of man's total being to what he experiences as ultimate reality' (p. 502).

The fourth text (pp. 504 ff.) treats of the concept of 'classical' as a possible relatively normative category to be used for a systematic presentation of religious phenomena. This category allows one to concentrate on what is essential and necessary, and distinguishes itself from the formal classifications which give a structural order of the elements of religion. The term 'classical' has an historical aspect as well as a systematic one.

The fifth text, finally, (pp. 508 ff.) is what has become Joachim Wach's own 'classical' statement on the meaning and task of the study of religion. It is one great plea for the recognition and further elaboration of this field of studies. It could be considered as a founding act of the discipline which he, some seventy-five years after its foundation, re-founded as a fully autonomous systematic discipline in America.

4. LATER CONTRIBUTIONS FROM OTHER DISCIPLINES

We come now, as we did two sections back, to some contributions that were made to the study of religions in the specialized disciplines. For this later period, which stretches into the 1960's, our selection, based again on scholars of the past, had to be more rigid. Out of the many disciplines and fields in which not only factual but also fundamental progress has been made for the study of religion, we chose the three of depth psychology, anthropology, and history of religions, on the basis of the work of some prominent representatives. The work of many other scholars still writing could not be considered.

CARL GUSTAV JUNG (1875–1961), after some years of collaboration with Freud, pursued his research in psychology in a direction that led to a new view of religion. Departing, like Freud, from what he called 'psychic reality', Jung proposed the theory of the existence of a 'collective' unconscious, besides that of the personal unconscious, proper to mankind as such. On the basis of this hypothesis, Jung could explain the existence and function of archetypes as centers of psychical energy situated in the collective unconscious. Such archetypes account for the occurrence of parallel motifs in myths at different places and times all over the world, and of similar sets of symbols with parallel patterns of meaning. Of particular interest is the fact that such motifs and symbols were proved to exist also in the life or dream world of some of Jung's patients who were being treated with the methods of his analytical psychology; this implied that the corresponding archetypes would have been activated again. On the basis of these discoveries, Jung gave — by studying religious phenomena on the level of psychic reality — a psychological interpretation of mythology, religious symbolism, and religious speculation, taking into account both a psychic origin and a psychic finality. A third fact to be mentioned is that Jung stressed the importance of man's religious expressions, interpreting the religious needs of his patients as authentic, at least on a psychological level. The archetypes then would provide possible solutions to life problems, and would hint at the necessary realization of man's 'Self'. Concerning the nature of this process of 'individuation' Jung would develop a more elaborate theory.

The texts presented (pp. 528 ff.) give an introduction to Jung's approach. The first text, from *Psychology of Religion*, shows the way in which Jung explains his view on, and practice of psychology, and '. ... the way in which practical psychology becomes confronted with the problem of religion' (p. 529). Jung calls his methodological standpoint 'exclusively phenomenological' (p. 529), since it is concerned with facts and not with a judgment as to their truth or falsity, except with regard to their sheer existence. 'Its truth is a fact and not a judgement' (p. 529). After explaining what he means by the term 'religion', Jung repeats that he studies religious phenomena from the standpoint of psychology; he does not look for explanations according to historical sequences or anthropological parallels. An application is then given in his discussion of the quaternity which would be, psychologically speaking, a more or less direct representation of the god manifested in his creation. At the end, Jung hints at the idea of the identity of god and man.

The second text, from *Introduction to a Science of Religion*, deals with the psychological interpretation of mythological motifs. This is based on the observation that myth formation is still a living function in the psychic life of 'civilized' man, and on the understanding of mythological motifs as archetypal structural elements of the psyche. Jung elaborates his hypothesis '. . . that the archetypes appear in myths and fairy-tales just as they do in dreams and in the products of psychotic fantasy' (p. 536), and explains the basic concepts of his psychology and psychological framework of interpretation. It is important to note that '. . . contents of an archetypical character' refer to something essentially unconscious, an unconscious core of meaning which lends itself per definition to multiple interpretations. Psychologically speaking, mankind's religious history is the rise, continuous interpretation and reinterpretation, and the possible disappearance of manifestations of certain archetypes of the collective unconscious. The author then gives a concrete example in his interpretation of the child-motif. Jung concludes by saying that, in the present state of research, a purely phenomenological point of view is necessary, permitting the classification of regularly occurring religious phenomena, figures, and situations in the form of images and types.

Various pupils of Jung have tried to apply his theory to data of the history of religions and to show its relevance for cultural history in general. Here may be mentioned the name of *Erich Neumann* (1905–1960) who wrote, among other books on expressions of the unconscious, a study on the archetype of the 'great mother' as it can be found through actual cults of this goddess in the course of religious history. The discussion on the importance of Jung's findings for the study of religion is still going on.

In anthropology BRONISLAW K. MALINOWSKI (1884–1942) inaugurated a functional approach in the study of the elements of a given society or culture, including the religious ones. On the basis of actual fieldwork, Malinowski developed a methodology according to which the anthropologist has to be for a certain period a participant observer in the society he studies. Malinowski wanted to interpret the problems of a given culture in terms of fundamental human situations. Such starting points are of great significance for the experience and interpretation of 'foreign' cultures by Western anthropologists. Malinowski's main significance, however, is his continuous concern with the function a particular element of a culture performs within the whole of that culture. Malinowski came to a functional interpretation of religion as well as other social institutions, considering religion to be, basically, an emotional response to the needs of 'cultural survival' of a given community.

The text reproduced, from *Magic, Science and Religion,* (pp. 546 ff.) starts by giving a useful survey of the history of anthropology through the work of Tylor, Frazer, Marett, Durkheim and others on subjects like magic, totemism, fertility cults, the idea of one god, and the place of morality. Malinowski then shows how anthropology has recognized an ever growing range of religious phenomena in primitive societies. He proceeds in summarizing his views on religion and magic '. . . as a mode of action as well as a system of belief, and a sociological phenomenon as well as a personal experience' (p. 551). Subsequently he touches on the subjects of primitive knowledge, of the distinction between sacred and profane in primitive religious ceremonies, and of the function of these ceremonies. Malinowski wants to distinguish magic and religion according to their function in a culture.

We have already dealt briefly with the rise of anthropology in the United States, especially through the work of Franz Boas and his pupils. The names of three of them come immediately to mind: *Ruth F. Benedict* (1887–1948) is known for her study on 'patterns of culture' of 1934 in which she studies three non-literate cultures as socio-psychological units with specific behavior patterns. Such patterns use selected human purposes and motivations within their cultures, and equally selected material techniques or objects for the realization of those purposes. *Ralph Linton* (1893–1953) as an anthropologist developed a new approach to personality development on the basis of cultural background. The model of a 'basic personality' within a particular cultural context can serve as an instrument to determine individual variations. *Clyde Kluckhohn* (1905–1960), in his turn, after having done much research on the Navaho Indians, also came to a theory on myth and ritual understood within their cultural context. One may submit that out of the social sciences, particularly in America, a new view of human personality and behavior was born. Man's religious beliefs and actions came to be treated no more as an isolated reality, but as part of the larger whole which is his 'culture'.

Robert H. Lowie (1883–1957), through careful fieldwork done among a number of North American tribes, could put an end to certain accepted theories of religion as they had been developed by earlier anthropologists who lacked sufficient empirical data. Lowie's fieldwork also brought to light the realization that religious data, to be understood, should not be isolated from either the total cultural constellation or from the total history of the society or culture under study. Psychology showed, moreover, that what made a particular object 'religious' was a subjective attitude rather than any external factor. Lowie's significance lies in his strictly empirical descriptive approach, with a minimum of preliminary theory and with a careful terminology that avoids generalizations as much as possible.

The text reproduced, from *Primitive Religion*, (pp. 560 ff.) may serve as an example of this approach in Lowie's discussion of the key-term 'religion' in anthropological research. Lowie shows how the term is used in current language and in various philosophies. After analyzing the terms used by Tylor and Söderblom, Lowie concludes that the only legitimate use of the concept in anthropological research is that whereby each 'religion' is considered from the point of view of its votaries.

PAUL RADIN (1883–1959), on the other hand, used a more theoretical approach to his material and did research on North American Indians with definite questions in mind. Radin wanted to study specifically the degrees of 'religious-mindedness' of different people in a given community, and he was able to differentiate this trait according to certain groups or persons within the community. Those who were more religious-minded constituted a minority, but could constitute a potential or actual religious leadership as so-called 'religious formulators'. Radin convincingly established that, contrary to current views, a great variety of religious thought, imagination, and morality exists within non-literate societies; the idea of the religious homogeneity of such societies was proved to be wrong. On religion itself, Radin had a psychological view: its psychological origin would be fear due to a lack of security. Radin therefore stressed in particular the role of economic insecurity and the rise, accordingly, of religion as a compensatory phantasy; and he was thus able to indicate neurotic features in a religious elite. Radin contended with force that, again contrary to current views, there is no specific 'religious' behavior or thought. On the other hand, there is no reason to deny rational thought to 'primitive' people, for the religious elite itself deals quite rationally with the problems of life and tries to find solutions in very much the same way as theologians do in the Western world. Radin distinguishes himself by a social psychological approach, making sharp distinctions between 'thinkers' and 'pragmatists', between 'religious' and 'irreligious' men. In his theory he uses findings of depth psychology.

The three texts reproduced (pp. 568 ff.) illustrate Radin's approach to religion in primitive societies. The first text, from *Primitive Religion*, discusses what is called the nature and substance of religion. Radin views this as a 'religious feeling' with which specific acts, customs, beliefs, and conceptions are associated. Basic to the relation between this 'religious feeling' and the belief in spirits outside of man is the physical and the social-economic background; for it is this background which conditions both the 'religious feeling' and the nature of the spirits which are believed in. Consequently, the specific quality of the religious feeling is '. . . the emotional correlate of the struggle for existence in an insecure physical and social environment' (p. 569). The resulting 'social precipitates of fear' — as represented in customs and beliefs — revolve around three given data: man's physical life, man's contact with the external world, and 'the collision of man with man'. Radin subsequently develops the argument that man originally postulated the supernatural in an attempt to adjust the ego to the external world. This would have happened in a hypothetical development from magic to religion as '... a progressive disentanglement of the ego from an infantile subjectivism' (p. 571). Once brought into existence, religion became part of man's permanent social-economic struggle for existence. 'Man thus postulated the supernatural in order primarily to validate his workaday reality' (p. 572). Finally, the author describes three types of people according to their degree of religiousness; in times of crises of life the 'religious feeling' would break through also among the normally 'indifferently religious' people. Actually, in primitive societies non-religious persons also can be found.

The second text, from *Primitive Man as Philosopher* (1927), enumerates some of the conditions under which 'primitive man' should be studied and some of the demands to be put on the anthropologist who carries out this research. In his 'Preface' Radin suggests some of the reasons why in the West a quite wrong image arose of the world of the non-literate people, which continued into the Western theories about them. In his 'Introduction' Radin pleads for a more scholarly anthropology in which the data will be acquired in their original form without rearrangement and interpretation. Another requirement is that the data be related to the specific group to which they belong, because they are not necessarily representative for the whole society under study. In the book itself, Radin wants to treat the cultures being studied from the viewpoint of their own priest-thinkers whose thought makes them 'religious formulators'.

In the third text, from *The World of Primitive Man*, Radin again makes the distinction between religious and non-religious man, and stresses the role of religion as means of adjustment to the natural world. The nature of religious feeling and attitude is discussed in terms of a psychical unbalance that heightens the sensitivity to 'something' outside of man.

Among the anthropologists, those who studied the religious aspects of cultures and civilizations were, however, a minority. Along with the two anthropologists just treated, two prominent names should be mentioned: *Alfred Kroeber* (1876–1960) who did much work on North American Indians, and may be considered as one of the most universally-minded anthropologists. And in Germany there was the outstanding work of *Adolf E. Jensen* (1899–1965), a specialist on Indonesian primitive religion who gave much attention to the theory of culture and the methodology of the disciplines studying it. Jensen discovered a new kind of gods, the so-called dema-deities who were active in primeval times and from whose sacrifice the world and man arose.

ALFRED R. RADCLIFFE-BROWN (1881–1955) was the theoretician of the functionalist approach in anthropology, and the father of social anthropology as a distinctive branch of anthropology. While it is the task of 'ethnology' to study the growth of social institutions, it is incumbent on social anthropology to study their function and to explore the laws that govern human social behavior. Radcliffe-Brown developed a theory and a systematic scientific method to study the problem of social structures in the light of the function that such structures perform within society.

The text reproduced (pp. 589 ff.) shows Radcliffe-Brown's approach not to religions as belief systems, but to '. . . the social functions of religions, i.e. the contribution that they make to the formation and maintenance of a social order (p. 590). Radcliffe-Brown concentrates thereby more on the social functions of rites than of beliefs, and he discusses examples in connection with the work of Fustel de Coulanges, Durkheim, and Tylor, with a reference to A. Loisy. Religion is one of the ways of controlling human conduct, the other two being morality and law. Where each coercive system has its own sanctions, religion develops a particular sense of dependence which is necessary for man's socialization. The lecture in question, of 1945, concludes with a call for further research with regard to the theory of the social function of religion. Needed are systematic studies of various types of religion 'in action', in relation to the social systems within which they occur. The author then gives some suggestions for particular problems to be investigated.

The change of perspective on and in the study of religion through the rise of the social sciences has been illustrated by the work of some prominent anthropologists. A similar illustration could be given through the work done in the field of sociology of religion since World War II, in particular its theoretical development. Here, it was the West's own religion which was subject of inquiry. We mention here the names of two scholars, both theologians, but of different confession, who introduced sociological viewpoints in their analysis of the present situation of the Christian churches. This is on one hand in the United States *H. Richard Niebuhr* (1894–1962), the brother of *Reinhold Niebuhr* (1892–1971), who considered the Protestant denominations in their social context. On the other hand there is the work of *Gabriel Le Bras* (1891–1970), who did much research on the actual religious practice of Roman Catholics in France.

In the field of the history of religions, progressive specialization on one particular religion made original work on general issues more and more difficult, and complete information on the progress of research in the discipline as a whole impossible. Nevertheless, the names of some scholars may be mentioned who consciously tried to maintain a general view on the history of at least a particular group of religions: *Johannes Leipoldt* (1880–1965) for the religions of the Hellenistic period; *Jan de Vries* (1890–1964) for the Germanic and Celtic religions; *Louis Massignon* (1883–1962) for Islam; and *Helmuth von Glasenapp* (1891–1963) for the religions that originated in India. The latter also published historical and comparative studies on the history of religions in general, whereas Jan de Vries paid much attention to myth research and wrote a history of it as well as a history of the history of religions. A distinguished name also is that of *Henri Frankfort* (1897–1954), who concentrated on ancient Near Eastern civilization and religion, and who supplemented literary research with extensive archeological investigations, bringing together the results of both approaches in a happy synthesis.

How different, however, within the history of religions, the approaches to one and the same religion can be, becomes clear if one puts side by side the work of two outstanding scholars on the history of ancient Greek religion: M. P. Nilsson and W. F. Otto.

MARTIN P. NILSSON (1874–1967), on one hand, did extensive research on the historical origins and on the development of the historical forms of Greek religion. He laid open the so-called Mycenaean civilization and religion, and showed many traces of it persisting, together with 'primitive' religion, in the religion of the Greeks.

In the texts reproduced (pp. 606 ff.), Nilsson discusses first the three types of religious intensity found among men, along the same lines as Paul Radin. Then he gives his opinion about the successive theories of religion, including phenomenology, which are finally all brought back to their relative proportions. Important is his account of what are in his view the advancements made in the study of Greek religion in the first half of the 20th century; the specialists will probably recognize certain 'parallel developments' in the study of other religions. Illuminating is the last text presented, where Nilsson gives his personal estimate of religion as man's 'protest against the meaninglessness of events'. Very clearly, the problem of religion is shown to be basically a problem of meaning, partly imposed upon man through the reality of death.

WALTER F. OTTO (1874–1958), on the other hand, in his study of Greek religion, focussed on what could be called its spiritual contents. Otto succeeded in achieving a sort of rehabilitation of ancient Greek religiosity, with its polytheism and mythology, in his own time, where his views met, however, with much resistance both from religious quarters and from specialists in the field who judged his interpretations to be too spiritual.

The texts reproduced (pp. 619 ff.) may give some idea of Walter Otto's approach. The first text, from *The Homeric Gods*, gives a scholarly apologetic for Greek religion, its gods, naturalness, and feeling for the mysteries in nature, and its fundamental religious ideas: in short, the Greek conception of the divine. The second text, from *Theophania*, is a passionate discussion of the ways in which the religious values of the Greeks ought and ought not to be studied by contemporary scholarship. The author observes that only a few of the classical scholars have tried to find out what was peculiar to ancient Greek religious thought, and he analyzes the reasons for this lapse. Subsequently, Otto adresses himself vehemently against the depth-psychological interpretations of myth which to his mind have no feeling for the revelationary character of original myth and its being the manifestation of the sacred character of the deity. The text concludes by pointing to three forms — gesture, act, and word — in which the divine in Greek religion manifested itself and became human. Here too, as in the words of Nilsson, the problem of meaning is raised; but here in the sense that 'meaning' manifests itself.

5. PERSPECTIVES OF A PHENOMENOLOGICAL STUDY OF RELIGION

The last part of the anthology contains some fragments taken from the work of four scholars who probably would have been surprised to find themselves together. Just as in the first part some founders of the study of religion were associated with each other, here the same is done with some scholars whose work opened up a perspective on the study of religion, in which the first concern is to grasp in religion as human reality certain significant structures, quests for meaning, and expressed intentions. All four looked at religion from a phenomenological perspective, without absolutizing it however, and in each case transcending the phenomenological approach in view of something else, be it history, theology, ontology, or existential awareness.

RAFFAELE PETTAZZONI (1883–1959) was an accomplished scholar in the history of religions, who was still able to survey and to follow the discipline as a whole. In the text reproduced, of 1954 (pp. 639 ff.), he warns against too great a distance between phenomenological and historical research, and calls for the study of religious structures in their actual historical context. The study of religion should be one unified discipline.

HENDRIK KRAEMER (1888–1965) was an interpreter and scholar of religion, fundamentally with a theological starting point that he called 'biblical realism'. In accordance with a scheme prevailing at the time, Kraemer assigns to the historical and comparative study of religion, as well as to philosophy of religion, a relative autonomy: these disciplines can move freely within the particular realm to which they are assigned. In the text reproduced, from *Religion and the Christian Faith* (pp. 664 ff.), Kraemer points at the presuppositions and limits which would be proper to the scholarly study of religion, and argues that the fact of religious consciousness as such leads to questions that can be treated in philosophy, but which finally refer to theological issues to be discussed in a mutual discourse of religions.

MAX SCHELER (1874–1928) was an accomplished philosopher within the German philosophical tradition, and was inspired by Edmund Husserl's phenomenology. The text reproduced, from *On the Eternal in Man* (pp. 654 ff.) shows Scheler's plea for a phenomenology of religion as different from psychology of religion. Scheler subsequently wants to distinguish a more empirical "concrete" phenomenology from a more philosophical "essential" phenomenology of religion. The latter is the aim of phenomenological research on religion and finally results in ontology.

GASTON BERGER (1896–1960), finally, was a distinguished philosopher within the French philosophical tradition, equally inspired by Edmund Husserl's phenomenology. The text translated, of 1957, (pp. 664 ff.) makes clear in what way the phenomenological approach may help defendants and adversaries of religion '. . . to take the right attitude and to understand religious life'. Berger pleads for an 'intentional description' of religion, using a certain point of view and a certain perspective from which to approach religion. Berger stresses thereby the permanent tension in religion between the spiritual and the historical elements, and points, with regard to the first, to '. . . an essential characteristic of all spiritual life, namely that it is a force, a march, a movement towards being, towards light, towards salvation' (p. 666). According to its intention, the venture of man's religion would be that of a wandering, a travel, or a pilgrimage. As would be the venture of studying this.

Looking Back

At the end of this bird's-eye view of more than a century of scholarly study of religion the question arises: how do we interpret this history? The history of a scholarly discipline can be written according to various standards: the increase of the available materials, the increase of the actual knowledge, the development of its theories, the succession of its major problems, the generations of the scholars. If we chose the latter approach, with a selection of a number of representative personalities arranged according to the various disciplines in the field of the study of religion, it is because we view the study in this field as the confrontation of persons with materials. The history of this study, then, is basically the succession of these persons and their work.

To be sure, still other approaches to the history of a discipline are possible, and certainly to that of a whole field of studies. One can depart from the different kinds of evidence on which knowledge is based — isolated artifacts of all kinds, texts, observed facts, provoked responses, experimental situations —, or from the different kinds of interpretation which were applied to such evidence. One can also take one's point of departure in the basic intentions that opened up new fields of research or even whole segments of reality to scholarly investigation. One can make a systematic survey of the manifold assumptions with which the scholars approached their subject matter: the explicit ones formulated in doctrines, convictions, or theories and the implicit ones that are given with one's attitude, character, situation, cultural background, and so on. And for the history of the study of religion it would be particularly important to know the attitude, in the largest sense of the word, taken by a given scholar with regard to religious or ideological issues of his time or to know what kinds of religion it were that he happened to encounter and to which he reacted. By its very nature, such an attitude or such a reaction, tends to reflect itself in the scholar's interpretation of other religions and of religion in general.

We would like to interpret the development of the study of religion — the interest in and study of other people's religion, the objectifying of and inquiring into one's own people's religion, the attempt to come to an insight into the phenomenon of religion on the basis of the 'own' and the 'other' religions —

we would like to interpret all this as breaking through a culture's or a religion's self-absolutization. In this interpretation, it would be the very ability to see someone else's strange thought and behavior in the light of what must be absolute for him — and the same holds true for societies —, which is the basic achievement in the study of religion over the last hundred years. That is to say, it is less the result of that study, but rather something that made that study possible. It implied breaking through the West's absolute position. We can give here only some hints as to the way in which this break-through manifested itself, within the study of religion, as a gradual opening of perspective on other religions and on religion as a human phenomenon.

It has been said often enough that the Enlightenment of the 18th century, with its stress on reason and tolerance, led to an initial openness toward other religious traditions than the Western one. And it has been affirmed equally that the Romantic movement of the beginning of the 19th century, with its stress on feeling and on nature, led to an openness to the dimension of religious experience and to the reality of experience in general. So there could develop a sense for deeper meanings than the rational ones, and there could arise a nostalgia toward times in which human existence would have had access to its sources in a deeper and more immediate way than was possible in the industrializing West. This attitude has indeed been an inspiration to much research in the field of religions of the past, and also in that of 'primitive' religion.

Some other discoveries, too, were conducive to self-relativization. On one hand, the openness to historical reality led not only to a certain relativizing of the present condition of the West in view of its past, but it also led to the idea of a common history of mankind, including its religions. The fascination with the Past could even become so strong as to identify the whole study of religion essentially with that of its history. On the other hand, the openness to the plurality of cultures and religions also could not but lead to a certain relativizing of the West in view of other civilizations and religions in past and present. The stream of publications at the time, in which the other religions were compared with Christianity, and *vice versa*, means that this plurality was actually felt as a problem. The very interest in anthropology, the call of Eastern and African countries to be discovered, studied, appreciated, suggests, however, that this plurality could also be felt as an enrichment. A third form of openness was that to social reality and in particular to the role of religion in the political, social, and economic life of society. Attention was given to the structure of society, to the natural evolution and the technical development of that society, to its social institutions, and the role of religion in all this became a question. Slowly the inner side of society became a subject of research, which would be accelerated by the quick development of the social sciences in the 20th century. The interest in the social side of religion could lead to new approaches in the study of it.

Such a widening perspective on man's religion — in the past, in its varieties and in society — cannot be seen, of course, independently from changing attitudes toward religion in the West itself. The West's transcending of its own feelings of absoluteness was not a completely painless operation for it implied a change in the attitude toward what was most sacred to the West, its own religion. The 19th century, with its growing openness, was also the time of a most absolute criticism of values until then held to be absolute. Christianity itself, its origins, history, and practice became the subject of assiduous examination, more often than not against the explicit and powerful will of the religious leaders. Against the supernatural origin or essence of religion an appeal was made on reason and experience as sole criteria of truth; religious phenomena needed no longer to be interpreted in supernaturalistic terms, but could be seen as natural expressions of man, of which an inventory and further examination would be possible. As to Christianity itself, the historical and literary critical study of the Bible, of the relationship between the Bible and its environment, of the historical reality of the sacred history, all amounted to a radical reinterpretation of traditional religion, with 'historical truth' as a new criterion. Similar attacks on traditional religion came from the side of the sciences, including biology and psychology which, after all, led to a thorough reorientation with regard to the nature and possibilities of man. It would indeed be impossible to separate the rise of the study of religion from deeper cultural and religious turbulences within the West at the time of its birth, of which it was a reasonable outcome. The fact that a powerful civilization which identifies itself with a world religion starts to be interested in other religions is too striking than that the rise and course of its interest should not demand attention.

Once the study of religion had established itself and developed its own methods according to the specialized disciplines, it could follow its own course. Since its main concerns were other religions than that of the West, and since many studies were devoted to the past, the immediate involvement with the issues that stirred the West itself remained limited. Such issues had their influence nevertheless. We can think of various currents of Western philosophical and theological thought which affected the interest and the attitude in the study of religions. A thorough study could certainly show to what extent the scholarly images which the West has developed of other religions or of religion in general have been determined by particular trends in its own cultural and intellectual history. In the same way, certain blind spots as well as certain pertinent interests of the scholars of this period in their study of religion can be traced back to the culture in which these scholars were rooted. One pertinent question, for instance, which may be asked, is that concerning the scope of attention given to the present-day world religions. Strange as it may sound, apart from some significant exceptions, the study of contemporary developments in the larger religions seems to have been relatively neglected, for those scholars of religion who worked on the major world religions nearly always studied them in their classical periods and gave only minor attention to the modern and contemporary period.

Looking back on the scholars mentioned above, one may make a distinction between two types, a distinction that goes right across the different disciplines of history, comparative studies, anthropology, sociology, and psychology. On one hand there are those scholars aiming at 'explaining', trying to determine causal or anyhow precisely verifiable relationships. Of those figuring in the anthology one may think of scholars as different as Wellhausen, Tylor, Durkheim, Freud, Lowie, Radin, and Radcliffe-Brown. On the other hand there are those scholars aiming at 'understanding', which goes beyond the explanations given by the first group. This understanding is aimed at the meaning of the phenomena studied, and eventually it may become an understanding of some message felt to be conveyed. Here one may think of scholars like Bachofen, William James, Lévy-Bruhl, Max Weber, Kristensen, Van der Leeuw, Jung, and Walter Otto. If such an understanding moves in the direction of an 'interpretation', methodology moves over to make a place for philosophy. One may think here of scholars like Tiele, James, and Wach. Such an interpretation may also have a clear theological inspiration; one may think here of scholars like Chantepie de la Saussaye, Van der Leeuw, Rudolf Otto, and Kraemer — to mention only some names which occur in the anthology.

It is not the place here to discuss methodological issues themselves; suffice it to observe that the division between scholars aiming at explaining and those aiming at understanding, possibly amounting to interpretation, is as old as scholarship itself. Throughout the history of the scholarly study of religion such fundamental philosophical problems of approach make themselves palpable, as they do in other disciplines.

This is not the place either to discuss the tremendous consequences which the different approaches had for the way in which scholars would interpret or reinterpret their own religious tradition. This holds true not only for the interpretation of Christianity but also, for example, for the *Wissenschaft des Judentums*. It would affect in its turn the religious communities in the West as a whole, which underwent profound changes during the last century and a half.

In conclusion we may say that, for a study of the history of scholarly research on religion, it will be necessary to take into account, besides the history of research actually done, also its cultural background, i.e., the intellectual history of Europe and of North America, in its context, and a series of what may be called perennial problems of thought, manifesting themselves in this as in other disciplines. The study of religion finds itself, like other disciplines, rooted both in the history of a culture and in the continuity of philosophical thought. The differentiation of scholarly approaches which developed over the last hundred years, and which are complementary to each other, may be seen again as a break-through: this time not through the self-absolutization of the West but through that of *Religionswissenschaft* itself.

Anthology

Introductory Note

In the Preface and Introduction some arguments were put forward for a renewed interest in the different approaches to the scholarly study of religion over the last hundred years or so. This interest pertains in particular to the methodology and theory of these approaches. Our purpose here is to offer a number of authentic texts in which scholars of religion who are no longer alive discuss the significance, the objectives and methods of the work they were doing. In other words, what follows is meant to be a methodological sourcebook.* While short references were made to these texts in the Introduction, we do not discuss these texts here; rather, it is up to the reader — scholar, teacher, student — who feels fit, to comment, interpret, refute, or adhere to these methodologies according to his own judgment. We want simply to let the methodological sources speak. In view of this purpose, only short introductions with the main biographical and bibliographical data of these forty-one scholars are given. It is through the bibliographies given in Volume Two that the interested reader will have to pursue his own research and find his own way.

The Anthology is divided into five parts:

Part One, *The Study of Religion established as an Autonomous Discipline,* gives some account of how the "founding fathers of the science of religion" considered this discipline, its scope, and its method. Their special fields were different, but they had in common the ideal of a new science: the scholarly study of religion. This ideal which moved them was explicitly written down, and it is heartening to see the enthusiasm and force with which they threw themselves upon the new field which they opened. Theirs was a spirit of discovery and endeavour, of which the chosen texts give ample evidence.

Part Two, *Connections with Other Disciplines,* intends to demonstrate that, in principle and practice, nearly all actual research in the field took place in existing and developing specialized disciplines, insofar as these encountered subjects of a religious nature. Attention is given to classical and biblical studies, to psychology, to anthropology and sociology, and to

---

* For the criteria of selection and arrangement, see pp. 5—6.

depth-psychology. It is shown that not only in these disciplines had the interpretation of religious materials become a matter of concern, but also that the newly hailed 'science of religion' could only neglect such 'connections with other disciplines' at its own expense. These texts were all written before World War II.

Part Three, *Religion as a Special Subject of Research*, deals with a group of scholars who, in one way or another, defended the autonomy of religion as a reality and a value in itself. They represent what we call 'classical' phenomenology of religion, in the first half of the 20th century.

Part Four, *Later Contributions from Other Disciplines*, is a continuation of Part Two for a period stretching largely beyond World War II. Although there is, evidently, an abundance of material, only a few scholars could be considered, even among those who are no longer with us. They are restricted to the fields of depth psychology, anthropology, and the history of Greek religion.

Part Five, *Perspectives of a Phenomenological Study of Religion*, is meant as a provisional 'perspective' and had to be short. Our idea was to bring together a few significant texts in which the whole enterprise of the study of religion is at stake. For the authors whom we finally chose, the study of religion as an autonomous discipline was an established fact which could be assessed now on its validity, on its relative significance, and on the perspectives for further thought which it opened. The problem of the meaning of religious phenomena is here considered to be central.

The titles of translated or reproduced texts are put between quotation marks if they correspond with the titles as given by the original authors. In all other cases the titles have been given by the editor of this Anthology. If English translations existed, these have been used even if the English was somewhat old-fashioned for present-day taste. Only in exceptional cases notes which lost their interest have been omitted.

The bio-bibliographical introductions only mention books published in English; the years of these books refer to the date of the first English edition or translation. For the bibliographies of these scholars, see Volume Two, in the 'General Bibliography' under the names with an asterisk.

PART ONE

The Study of Religion established as an Autonomous Discipline

F. Max Müller

Friedrich Max Müller was born in 1823 in Dessau, Germany, and received his primary and secondary school education in Dessau and in 1836 in Leipzig. In 1841 he enrolled at the University of Leipzig to study classical and other languages, psychology and anthropology. He then chose Sanskrit as his field, worked with Hermann Brockhaus, and obtained his Ph. D. in 1843. In 1844 he continued his studies in Berlin, working under Franz Bopp at comparative philology, and under Schelling at philosophy. After having spent a year in Paris, where he worked with E. Burnouf at Sanskrit and comparative religion, he went to England in 1846, lived in London for two years and went to Oxford in 1848. Here Müller became deputy Taylorian professor of modern European languages in 1850, and in 1854 full professor receiving the M. A. degree by decree of convocation. Having been a member of Christ Church since 1851, he obtained a life fellowship at All Souls College in 1858. In 1868 Müller became professor of comparative philology, but he retired from active duties in 1875 in order to devote himself entirely to the edition of the *Sacred Books of the East*. He died at Oxford in 1900.

Of Müller's numerous publications the following may be mentioned here: 1849—1873 edition and translation of the *Rigveda-Samhitā with Sāyanākārya's commentary* (6 vol.); 1856 *Comparative Mythology*; 1867–1875 *Chips from a German Workshop* (4 vol.); 1873 *Introduction to the Science of Religion*; 1878 *Lectures on the Origin and Growth of Religion as illustrated by the Religions of India*; 1881 *Selected Essays on Language, Mythology and Religion* (2 vol.); 1889 *Natural Religion*; 1891 *Physical Religion*; 1892 *Anthropological Religion*; 1893 *Theosophy or Psychological Religion*; 1897 *Contributions to the Science of Mythology* (2 vol.); 1899 *The Six Systems of Indian Philosophy*.

Müller may be considered a pioneer of the new 'science of religion'. As a scholar of Sanskrit he also worked on comparative linguistics and wanted to found comparative mythology and comparative religion on that as basis. He held that philological and etymological research can discover the meaning of religion for early man by restoring the original sense to the names of the gods and the stories told about them. Myths being in his view primarily poetry and phantasy Müller tried to explain their substance by means of natural phenomena, and their terminology by what he called a 'disease of language'. Religion proper would have started with an 'immediate perception of the infinite' through nature, apart from the senses and reason.

The following fragments have been chosen from *Chips from a German Workshop* and from *Introduction to the Science of Religion* in order to show what Max Müller considered the new science of religion to be, and what expectations he had of it.

PLEA FOR A SCIENCE OF RELIGION

I do not wish to disguise these difficulties which are inherent in a comparative study of the religions of the world. I rather dwell on them strongly, in order to show how much care and caution is required in so difficult a subject, and how much indulgence should be shown in judging of the shortcomings and errors that are unavoidable in so comprehensive a study. It was supposed at one time that a comparative analysis of the languages of mankind must transcend the powers of man: and yet by the combined and well directed efforts of many scholars, great results have here been obtained, and the principles that must guide the student of the Science of Language are now firmly established. It will be the same with the Science of Religion. By a proper division of labour, the materials that are still wanting, will be collected and published and translated, and when that is done, surely man will never rest till he has discovered the purpose that runs through the religions of mankind, and till he has reconstructed the true *Civitas Dei* on foundations as wide as the ends of the world. The Science of Religion may be the last of the sciences which man is destined to elaborate; but when it is elaborated, it will change the aspect of the world, and give a new life to Christianity itself.

The Fathers of the Church, though living in much more dangerous proximity to the ancient religions of the Gentiles, admitted freely that a comparison of Christianity and other religions was useful. 'If there is any agreement', Basilius remarked, 'between their (the Greeks) doctrines and our own, it may benefit us to know them: if not, then to compare them and to learn how they differ, will help not a little towards confirming that which is the better of the two'.[1]

But this is not the only advantage of a comparative study of religions. The Science of Religion will for the first time assign to Christianity its right place among the religions of the world; it will show for the first time fully what was meant by the fulness of time; it will restore to the whole history of the world, in its unconscious progress towards Christianity, its true and sacred character.

Not many years ago great offence was given by an eminent writer who remarked that the time had come when the history of Christianity should be treated in a truly historical spirit, in the same spirit in which we treat the history of other religions, such as Brahmanism, Buddhism, or Mohammedanism. And yet what can be truer? He must be a man of little faith, who would fear to subject his own religion to the same critical tests to which the historian subjects all other religions. We need not surely crave a tender or merciful treatment for that faith which we hold to be the only true one. We should rather challenge for it the severest tests and trials, as the sailor would for the good ship to which he entrusts his own life, and the lives of those who are most dear to him. In the Science of Religion, we can decline no comparisons, nor claim any immunities for Christianity, as little as the missionary can, when wrestling with the subtle Brahman, or the fanatical Mussulman, or the plain speaking Zulu. And if we send out our missionaries to every part of the world to face every kind of religion, to shrink from no contest, to be appalled by no objections, we must not give way at home or within our own hearts to any misgivings, that a comparative study of the religions of the world could shake the firm foundations on which we must stand or fall.

To the missionary more particularly a comparative study of the religions of mankind will be, I believe, of the greatest assistance. Missionaries are apt to look upon all other religions as something totally distinct from their own, as formerly they used to describe the languages of barbarous nations as something more like the twittering of birds than the articulate speech of men. The Science of Language has taught us that there is order and wisdom in all languages, and that even the most degraded jargons contain the ruins of former greatness and beauty. The Science of Religion, I hope, will produce a similar change in our views of barbarous forms of faith and worship; and missionaries, instead of looking only for points of difference, will look out more anxiously for any common ground, any spark of the true light that may still be revived, any altar that may be dedicated afresh to the true God.

And even to us at home, a wider view of the religious life of the world may teach many a useful lesson. Immense as is the difference between our own and all other religions of the world – and few can know that difference who have not honestly examined the foundations of their own as well as of other religions – the position which believers and unbelievers occupy with regard to their various forms of faith is very much the same all over the world. The difficulties which trouble us, have troubled the hearts and minds of men as far back as we can trace the beginnings of religious life. The great problems touching the relation of the Finite to the Infinite, of the human mind as the recipient, and of the Divine Spirit as the source of truth, are old problems indeed; and while watching their appearance in different countries, and their treatment under varying circumstances, we shall be able, I believe, to profit ourselves, both by the errors which others committed before us, and by the truth which they discovered. We shall know the rocks that threaten every religion in this changing and shifting world of ours, and having watched many a storm of religious controversy and many a shipwreck in distant seas, we shall face with greater calmness and prudence the troubled waters at home.

If there is one thing which a comparative study of religions places in the clearest light, it is the inevitable decay to which every religion is exposed.

It may seem almost like a truism, that no religion can continue to be what it was during the lifetime of its founder and its first apostles. Yet it is but seldom borne in mind that without constant reformation, i.e. without a constant return to its fountainhead, every religion, even the most perfect, nay the most perfect on account of its very perfection, more even than others, suffers from its contact with the world, as the purest air suffers from the mere fact of its being breathed.

Whenever we can trace back a religion to its first beginnings, we find it free from many of the blemishes that offend us in its later phases. The founders of the ancient religions of the world, as far as we can judge, were minds of a high stamp, full of noble aspirations, yearning for truth, devoted to the welfare of their neighbours, examples of purity and unselfishness. What they desired to found upon earth was but seldom realised, and their sayings, if preserved in their original form, offer often a strange contrast to the practice of those who profess to be their disciples. As soon as a religion is established, and more particularly when it has become the religion of a powerful state, the foreign and worldly elements encroach more and more on the original foundation, and human interests mar the simplicity and purity of the plan which the founder had conceived in his own heart, and matured in his communings with his God. Even those who lived with Buddha, misunderstood his words, and at the Great Council which had to settle the Buddhist canon, Asoka, the Indian Constantine, had to remind the assembled priests that 'what had been said by Buddha, that alone was well said'; and that certain works ascribed to Buddha, as, for instance, the instruction given to his son, Râhula, were apocryphal, if not heretical.[2] With every century, Buddhism, when it was accepted by nations, differing as widely as Mongols and Hindus, when its sacred writings were translated into languages as wide apart as Sanskrit and Chinese, assumed widely different aspects, till at last the Buddhism of the Shamans in the steppes of Tatary is as different from the teaching of the original *Samana*, as the Christianity of the leader of the Chinese rebels is from the teaching of Christ.

[...]

There is a strong feeling, I know, in the minds of all people against any attempt to treat their own religion as a member of a class, and, in one sense, that feeling is perfectly justified. To each individual, his own religion, if he really believes in it, is something quite inseparable from himself, something unique, that cannot be compared to anything else, or replaced by anything else. Our own religion is, in that respect, something like our own language. In its form it may be like other languages; in its essence and in its relation to ourselves, it stands alone and admits of no peer or rival.

But in the history of the world, our religion, like our own language, is but one out of many; and in order to understand fully the position of Christianity in the history of the world, and its true place among the religions of mankind, we must compare it, not with Judaeism only, but with the religious aspirations of the whole world, with all, in fact, that Christianity came either to destroy or to fulfil. From this point of view Christianity forms part, no doubt, of what people call profane history, but by that very fact, profane history ceases to be profane, and regains throughout that sacred character of which it had been deprived by a false distinction. [...].

THE COMPARATIVE STUDY OF RELIGIONS

In beginning to-day a course of lectures on the *Science of Religion*, - or I should rather say on some preliminary points that have to be settled before we can enter upon a truly scientific study of the religions of the world, – I feel as I felt when first pleading in this very place for the Science of Language.

I know that I shall have to meet determined antagonists who will deny the possibility of a scientific treatment of religions as they denied the possibility of a scientific treatment of languages. I foresee even a far more serious conflict with familiar prejudices and deep-rooted convictions; but I feel at the same time that I am prepared to meet my antagonists, and I have such faith in their honesty and love of truth, that I doubt not of a patient and impartial hearing on their part, and of a verdict influenced by nothing but by the evidence that I shall have to place before them.

In these our days it is almost impossible to speak of religion without giving offence either on the right or on the left. With some, religion seems too sacred a subject for scientific treatment; with others it stands on a level with alchemy and astrology, as a mere tissue of errors or halucinations, far beneath the notice of the man of science.

In a certain sense, I accept both these views. Religion *is* a sacred subject, and whether in its most perfect or in its most imperfect form, it has a right to our highest reverence. In this respect we might learn something from those whom we are so ready to teach. I quote from the Declaration of Principles by which the church founded by Keshub Chunder Sen professes to be guided. After stating that no created object shall ever be worshipped, nor any man or inferior being or material object be treated as identical with God, or like unto God, or as an incarnation of God, and that no prayer or hymn shall be said unto or in the name of any one except God, the declaration continues:

'No created being or object that has been or may hereafter be worshipped by any sect shall be ridiculed or contemned in the course of the divine service to be conducted here.'

'No book shall be acknowledged or received as the infallible Word of God: yet no book which has been or may hereafter be acknowledged by any sect to be infallible shall be ridiculed or contemned.'

'No sect shall be vilified, ridiculed, or hated.'

No one – this I can promise – who attends these lectures, be he Christian or Jew, Hindu or Mohammedan, shall hear his own way of serving God spoken of irreverently. But true reverence does not consist in declaring a subject, because it is dear to us, to be unfit for free and honest inquiry: far from it! True reverence is shown in treating every subject, however sacred, however dear to us, with perfect confidence; without fear and without favour; with tenderness and love, by all means, but, before all, with an unflinching and uncompromising loyalty to truth.

On the other hand, I fully admit that religion has stood in former ages, and stands also in our own age, if we look abroad, and if we look into some of the highest and some of the lowest places at home, on a level with alchemy and astrology. There exist superstitions, little short of fetishism; and, what is worse, there exists hypocrisy, as bad as that of the Roman augurs.

In practical life it would be wrong to assume a neutral position between such conflicting views. Where we see that the reverence due to religion is violated, we are bound to protest; where we see that superstition saps the roots of faith, and hypocrisy poisons the springs of morality, we must take sides. But as students of the Science of Religion we move in a higher and more serene atmosphere. We study error, as the physiologist studies a disease, looking for its causes, tracing its influence, speculating on possible remedies, but leaving the application of such remedies to a different class of men, to the surgeon and the practical physician. *Diversos diversa juvant* applies here as everywhere else, and a division of labour, according to the peculiar abilities and tastes of different individuals, promises always the best results. The student of the history of the physical sciences is not angry with the alchemists, nor does he argue with the astrologists; he rather tries to enter into their view of things, and to discover in the errors of alchemy the seeds of chemistry, and in the halucinations of astronomy a yearning and groping after a true knowledge of the heavenly bodies. It is the same with the student of the Science of Religion. He wants to find out what Religion is, what foundation it has in the soul of man, and what laws it follows in its historical growth. For that purpose the study of errors is to him more instructive than the study of truth, and the smiling augur as interesting a subject as the Roman suppliant who veiled his face in prayer, that he might be alone with his God.

The very title of the Science of Religion will jar, I know, on the ears of many persons, and a comparison of all the religions of the world, in which none can claim a privileged position, will no doubt seem to many dangerous and reprehensible, because ignoring that peculiar reverence which every-body, down to the mere fetish worshipper, feels for his *own* religion and for his *own* God. Let me say then at once that I myself have shared these mis-givings, but that I have tried to overcome them, because I would not and could not allow myself to surrender either what I hold to be the truth, or what I hold still dearer than truth, the right of testing truth. Nor do I regret it. I do not say that the Science of Religion is all gain. No, it entails losses, and losses of many things which we hold dear. But this I will say, that, as far as my humble judgment goes, it does not entail the loss of anything that is essential to true religion, and that if we strike the balance honestly, the gain is immeasurably greater than the loss.

One of the first questions that was asked by classical scholars when invited to consider the value of the Science of Language, was, 'What shall we gain by a comparative study of languages?' Languages, it was said, are wanted for practical purposes, for speaking and reading; and by studying too many languages at once, we run the risk of losing the firm grasp which we ought to have on the few that are really important. Our knowledge, by becoming wider, must needs, it was thought, become shallower, and the gain, if there is any, in knowing the structure of dialects which have never produced any literature at all, would certainly be outweighed by the loss in accurate and practical scholarship.

If this could be said of a comparative study of languages, with how much greater force will it be urged against a comparative study of religions! Though I do not expect that those who study the religious books of Brah-mans and Buddhists, of Confucius and Laotse, of Mohammed and Nānak, will be accused of cherishing in their secret heart the doctrines of those ancient masters, or of having lost the firm hold on their own religious con-victions, yet I doubt whether the practical utility of wider studies in the vast field of the religions of the world will be admitted with greater readiness by professed theologians than the value of a knowledge of Sanskrit, Zend, Gothic, or Celtic for a thorough mastery of Greek and Latin, and for a real appreciation of the nature, the purpose, the laws, the growth and decay of language was admitted, or is even now admitted, by some of our most eminent professors and teachers.

People ask, What is gained by comparison? – Why, all higher knowledge is acquired by comparison, and rests on comparison. If it is said that the character of scientific research in our age is pre-eminently comparative, this really means that our researches are now based on the widest evidence that can be obtained, on the broadest inductions that can be grasped by the human mind.

What can be gained by comparison? – Why, look at the study of languages. If you go back but a hundred years and examine the folios of the most learned writers on questions connected with language, and then open a book written by the merest tiro in Comparative Philology, you will see what can be gained, what has been gained, by the comparative method. A few hundred years ago, the idea that Hebrew was the original language of mankind was accepted as a matter of course, even as a matter of faith, the only problem being to find out by what process Greek, or Latin, or any other language could have been developed out of Hebrew. The idea, too, that language was revealed, in the scholastic sense of the word, was generally accepted, although, as early as the fourth century, St. Gregory, the learned bishop of Nyssa, had strongly protested against it.[3] The grammatical framework of a language was either considered as the result of a conventional agreement, or the terminations of nouns and verbs were supposed to have sprouted forth like buds from the roots and stems of language; and the vaguest similarity in the sound and meaning of words was taken to be a sufficient criterion for testing their origin and their relationship. Of all this philological somnambulism we hardly find a trace in works published since the days of Humboldt, Bopp, and Grimm.

Has there been any loss here? Has it not been pure gain? Does language excite our admiration less, because we know that, though the faculty of speaking is the work of Him who works in all things, the invention of words for naming each object was left to man, and was achieved through the working of the human mind? Is Hebrew less carefully studied, because it is no longer believed to be a revealed language, sent down from heaven, but a language closely allied to Arabic, Syriac and ancient Babylonian, and receiving light from these cognate, and in some respects more primitive, languages, for the explanation of many of its grammatical forms, and for the exact interpretation of many of its obscure and difficult words? Is the grammatical articulation of Greek and Latin less instructive because instead of seeing in the terminations of nouns and verbs merely arbitrary signs to distinguish the plural from the singular, or the future from the present, we can now perceive an intelligible principle in the gradual production of formal out of the material elements of language? And are our etymologies less important, because, instead of being suggested by superficial similarities, they are now based on honest historical and physiological research? Lastly, has our own language ceased to hold its own peculiar place? Is our love for our own native tongue at all impaired? Do men speak less boldly or pray less fervently in their own mother tongue, because they know its true origin and its unadorned history; because they know that everything in language that goes beyond the objects of sense, is and must be pure metaphor? Or does any one deplore the fact that there is in all languages, even in the jargons of the lowest savages, order and wisdom; nay, something that makes the world akin?

Why, then, should we hesitate to apply the comparative method, which has produced such great results in other spheres of knowledge, to a study of religion ? That it will change many of the views commonly held about the origin, the character, the growth, and decay of the religions of the world, I do not deny; but unless we hold that fearless progression in new inquiries, which is our bounden duty and our honest pride in all other branches of knowledge, is dangerous in the study of religions, unless we allow ourselves to be frightened by the once famous dictum, that whatever is new in theology is false, this ought to be the very reason why a comparative study of religions should no longer be neglected or delayed.

When the students of Comparative Philology boldly adapted Goethe's paradox, '*He who knows one language, knows none*', people were startled at first; but they soon began to feel the truth which was hidden beneath the paradox. Could Goethe have meant that Homer did not know Greek, or that Shakespeare did not know English, because neither of them knew more than his own mother tongue ? No ! what was meant was that neither Homer nor Shakespeare knew what that language really was which he handled with so much power and cunning. Unfortunately the old verb 'to can', from which 'canny' and 'cunning', is lost in English, otherwise we should be able in two words to express our meaning, and to keep apart the two kinds of knowledge of which we are here speaking. As we say in German *können* is not *kennen*, we might say in English, *to can*, that is to be cunning, is not *to ken*, that is to know; and it would then become clear at once, that the most eloquent speaker and the most gifted poet, with all their cunning of words and skilful mastery of expression, would have but little to say if asked, what language really is ? The same applies to religion. *He who knows one, knows none.* There are thousands of people whose faith is such that it could move mountains, and who yet, if they were asked what religion really is, would remain silent, or would speak of outward tokens rather than of the inward nature, or of the faculty of faith.

[. . .]

Lastly, and this, I believe, is the most important advantage which we enjoy as students of the history of religion, we have been taught the rules of critical scholarship. No one would venture, now-a-days, to quote from any book, whether sacred or profane, without having asked these simple and yet momentous questions: When was it written ? Where ? and by whom ? Was the author an eye-witness, or does he only relate what he has heard from others ? And if the latter, were his authorities at least contemporaneous with the events which they relate, and were they under the sway of party feeling or any other disturbing influence ? Was the whole book written at once, or does it contain portions of an earlier date; and if so, is it possible for us to separate these earlier documents from the body of the book ?

A study of the original documents on which the principal religions of the world profess to be founded, carried on in this spirit, has enabled some of our best living scholars to distinguish in each religion between what is really ancient and what is comparatively modern; between what was the doctrine of the founders and their immediate disciples, and what were the afterthoughts and, generally, the corruptions of later ages. A study of these later developments, of these later corruptions, or, it may be, improvements, is not without its own peculiar charm, and full of practical lessons; yet, as it is essential that we should know the most ancient forms of every language, before we proceed to any comparisons, it is indispensable also that we should have a clear conception of the most primitive form of every religion, before we proceed to determine its own value, and to compare it with other forms of religious faith. Many an orthodox Mohammedan, for instance, will relate miracles wrought by Mohammed; but in the Koran Mohammed says distinctly, that he is a man like other men. He disdains to work miracles, and appeals to the great works of Allah, the rising and setting of the sun, the rain that fructifies the earth, the plants that grow, and the living souls that are born into the world – who can tell whence? – as the real signs and wonders in the eyes of a true believer.

The Buddhist legends teem with miserable miracles attributed to Buddha and his disciples – miracles which in wonderfulness certainly surpass the miracles of any other religion: yet in their own sacred canon a saying of Buddha's is recorded, prohibiting his disciples from working miracles, though challenged by the multitudes, who required a sign that they might believe. And what is the miracle that Buddha commands his disciples to perform? 'Hide your good deeds', he says, 'and confess before the world the sins you have committed'. That is the true miracle.

Modern Hinduism rests on the system of caste as on a rock which no arguments can shake: but in the Veda, the highest authority of the religious belief of the Hindus, no mention occurs of the complicated system of castes, such as we find it in Manu: nay, in one place, where the ordinary classes of the Indian, or any other society, are alluded to, viz. the priests, the warriors, the citizens, and the slaves, all are represented as sprung alike from Brahman, the source of all being.

It would be too much to say that the critical sifting of the authorities for a study of each religion has been already fully carried out. There is work enough still to be done. But a beginning, and a very successful beginning, has been made, and the results thus brought to light will serve as a wholesome caution to everybody who is engaged in religious researches.

[...]

A Science of Religion, based on an impartial and truly scientific comparison of all, or at all events, of the most important, religions of mankind, is now only a question of time. It is demanded by those whose voice cannot be disregarded. Its title, though implying as yet a promise rather than a fulfilment, has become more or less familiar in Germany, France, and America; its great problems have attracted the eyes of many inquirers, and its results have been anticipated either with fear or with delight. It becomes therefore the duty of those who have devoted their life to the study of the principal religions of the world in their original documents, and who value religion and reverence it in whatever form it may present itself, to take possession of this new territory in the name of true science, and thus to protect its sacred precincts from the inroads of those who think that they have a right to speak on the ancient religions of mankind, whether those of the Brahmans, the Zoroastrians, or Buddhists, or those of the Jews and Christians, without ever having taken the trouble of learning the languages in which their sacred books are written. What should we think of philosophers writing on the religion of Homer, without knowing Greek, or on the religion of Moses, without knowing Hebrew?[. . .]

NOTES

1. Basilius, *De legendis Graecorum libris*, c. v. Εἰ μὲν οὖν ἐστί τις οἰκειότης πρὸς ἀλλήλους τοῖς λόγοις, προὖργον ἂν ἡμῖν αὐτῶν ἡ γνῶσις γένοιτο. εἰ δὲ μὴ, ἀλλὰ τό γε παράλληλα θέντας καταμαθεῖν τὸ διάφορον οὐ μικρὸν εἰς βεβαίωσιν βελτίονος.
2. E. Burnouf, *Lotus de la bonne Loi*, Appendice, No. x, § 4.
3. Max Müller, *Lectures on the Science of Language*, Vol. I, p. 32.

Cornelis P. Tiele

Cornelis Petrus Tiele was born in 1830 in Leiden, Holland, where he received his primary and secondary school education. He studied theology at the University of Amsterdam and at the Remonstrants' Seminary which then was established there. For his degree he wrote a dissertation concerning the Gospel of St. John. In 1853 Tiele became a Remonstrant minister, which he remained for twenty years, the last seventeen of which he had a parish in Rotterdam. During this time he applied himself to the study of ancient religions and taught himself the Avesta language, Akkadian and Egyptian. In 1872 he obtained the Th. D. *honoris causa* at the University of Leiden. The next year he became a professor at the Remonstrants' Seminary which then was transferred to Leiden, where he taught the history of religions. In 1877 Tiele occupied the new chair of the History of Religions and Philosophy of Religion at the University of Leiden, Faculty of Theology. He retired in 1900 and died at Leiden in 1902.

Tiele's main publications in English are: 1877 *Outlines of the History of Religion, to the Spread of the Universal Religions;* 1882 *History of the Egyptian Religion* (as Part One of the 'Comparative History of the Egyptian and Mesopotamian Religions'); 1894 *Western Asia, according to the most recent discoveries (the Tell el-Amarna tablets)* (Rectorial Address); 1897—1899 *Elements of the Science of Religion, Morphological and Ontological* (2 vol.); 1912 *The Religion of the Iranian People, Part One;* art. 'Religions' in *Encyclopaedia Britannica, 9th Edition.*

Tiele may be considered a pioneer of the 'science of religion', and it is largely due to his activity that the history of religions became a recognized discipline in the theological faculties in his country. He was one of the first to offer a historical survey of a number of religions based on study of source materials. In his general view of religion he stressed the evolution of the 'religious idea' through the historical forms of religion which represented different stages. Tiele looked for the 'laws' of this evolution, passing from nature religions to ethical religions. In his studies he combined a historical with a systematic interest.

The following fragments have been chosen from *Elements of the Science of Religion* and give some idea of Tiele's view and expectations of the new discipline.

'ELEMENTS OF THE SCIENCE OF RELIGION'—I

First of all, it is necessary to state what we understand by science of religion, and what right we have to call it a science. We shall not begin, as is so often done, by formulating a preconceived ideal of religion; if we attempted to do so, we should move in a circle. What religion really is in its essence can only be ascertained as the result of our whole investigation. By religion we mean for the present nothing different from what is generally understood by that term – that is to say, the aggregate of all those phenomena which are invariably termed religious, in contradistinction to ethical, aesthetical, political, and others. I mean those manifestations of the human mind in words, deeds, customs, and institutions which testify to man's belief in the superhuman, and serve to bring him into relation with it. Our investigation will itself reveal the foundation of those phenomena which are generally called religious. If it is maintained that the superhuman falls beyond the range of the perceptible, and that its existence cannot be proved by scientific or philosophical reasoning, we have our answer ready. The question whether philosophy or metaphysics has any right to judge as to the reality of the objects of faith does not concern us here. We therefore leave the question open. The object of our science is not the superhuman itself, but religion based on belief in the superhuman; and the task of investigating religion as a historical-psychological, social, and wholly human phenomenon undoubtedly belongs to the domain of science.

But whilst admitting this, some writers have felt an insuperable dislike to the term 'science of religion', and have attempted to substitute some more modest term. For my part I see nothing presumptuous in the word science. It does not mean that we know everything about a subject, but simply that we investigate it in order to learn something about it, in accordance with a sound and critical method, appropriate to each department. It cannot therefore be doubted that such an investigation of religion can claim the name of science, and that the science of religion has a right to rank as an independent study, and not merely as one of a group. What, then, are the characteristics that constitute a science? I cannot answer this question better than in the words of Whitney when he is vindicating the rights of the science of language. The characteristics are – a wide extent of domain; a unity which embraces the multiplicity of facts belonging to that domain; an inward connection of these facts which enables us to subject them to careful classification, and to draw fruitful inferences from them; and lastly, the importance of the results attained, and of the truth which reasoning has brought to light from the ascertained facts. Now, if the science of language can stand this test, and need not fear comparison with any other recognised science, the same holds true of the science of religion. This surely requires no lengthy demonstration. It is obvious to every one. The province of our investigation is sufficiently extensive – all religions of the civilised and uncivilised world, dead and living, and all the religious phenomena which present themselves to our observation. The unity which combines the multiplicity of these phenomena is the human mind, which reveals itself nowhere so completely as in these, and whose manifestations, however different the forms they assume on different planes of development, always spring from the same source. This unity renders a scientific classification of religions quite as justifiable as that of language. And it is self-evident that the results of such a science must be of the utmost importance in the study of man and his history, of his individual, social, and, above all, his religious life.

[...]

It may perhaps be thought that the votary of our science cannot be restrained in his criticisms and judgments, and that the science is therefore fraught with danger. But here again we must carefully distinguish. He judges, in so far as his task is to compare the different manifestations of religious belief and life, and the different religious communities, in order to classify them in accordance with the stage and direction of their development. He criticises, in so far as he points out where there has been retrogression from a higher to a lower plane, in so far as he scrutinises so-called religious facts which really belong to a different domain (such as that of art, philosophy, or politics), and pathological phenomena (such as intellectualism, sentimentalism, or moralism), and distinguishes all these from sound and living religion. He takes up, if we may use the favourite philosophical term, an entirely objective position towards all *forms* of religion, but distinguishes them carefully from religion itself. Religion reveals itself in every one of these forms more or less imperfectly – and so he studies them all. No religion is beneath his notice: on the contrary, the deeper he digs the nearer he gets to religion's source. He follows the example of the philologist, who does not despise the language of Mlecchas or barbarians, or whatever other nickname be given to people speaking a language one does not understand, and who takes as great an interest in the Hottentot or Australian dialects as in Sanscrit or Arabic. He knows nothing of heretics, schismatics, or heathens; to him, as a man of science, all religious forms are simply objects of investigation, different languages in which the religious spirit expresses itself, means which enable him to penetrate to a knowledge of religion itself, supreme above all. It is not his vocation to champion any of these forms as the best, or perhaps the only true form – he leaves that to the apologists. Nor does he attempt to purify, reform, or develop religion itself – that is the task of the divine and the prophet. And this scientific investigation is certainly not without practical benefit. It may bring to light the superiority of one cult to another; it may have a powerful influence on the purification and development of religion itself; it may, by showing religion to be rooted in man's inmost nature, vindicate its right to exist better than any long philosophical arguments; and such testimony is all the more valuable because unsought, unbiassed, and undesigned. For this neither is nor can be the goal of the science of religion. If such were its practical aim, the fruits which it now yields for practice, and for religious thought and life, would lose their value. For genuine science, which seeks nothing but the truth, is a light by which truth is made manifest; and therefore all that is good and true, genuine and beautiful, all that supplies actual wants and is therefore wholesome for humanity, need never fear the light. The rights of the religious conscience must not be limited; but science, too, vindicates her right to extend her investigations over everything human, and therefore over so important and mighty a manifestation of man's inmost nature as religion has ever been and ever will be.

It is an error to suppose that one cannot take up such an impartial scientific position without being a sceptic; that one is disqualified for an impartial investigation if one possesses fixed and earnest religious convictions of one's own; that a man is incapable of appreciating other forms of religion if he is warmly attached to the Church or religious community in which he has been brought up. Do we love our parents, to whom we owe so much, the less because, when we have come to years of discretion, we have discovered some of their faults and foibles? Does our mother-tongue sound less pleasantly in our ears because we have made acquaintance with the beauty and vigour of other languages? I, at least, do not love the religious community to which I belong the less because I strive to appreciate, by the light of our science, what is truly religious in other forms.

[...]

We have thus defined the character of our science. It is a special science or branch of study, and does not belong to general philosophy; but it is the philosophical part of the investigation of religious phenomena – a study which seeks to penetrate to their foundations. It is not a philosophic creed, or a dogmatic system of what is commonly called natural theology, or a philosophy with a religious tinge, and still less a philosophy regarding God Himself. All this is beyond its province. It leaves these matters to theologians and metaphysicians. It is in fact literally the philosophy of religion, according to the present use of that term, which is deservedly gaining ground: a philosophy which we must have the courage to reform, in accordance with the demands of science in its present state of development.

I cannot, therefore, include it among the natural sciences, however high be the authority of those who assign it such a position. We should in that case be obliged to stretch the conception of natural science so far as to deprive it of all precise meaning. Religion is certainly rooted in man's nature – that is, it springs from his inmost soul. But we may truly say of religion, as it has been said of language, that it is neither entirely a natural nor an artificial product. It would be idle to attempt to apply the exact methods of the natural sciences to our science; such an attempt would only expose one to self-deception and grievous disappointment.

Nor is our science historical in the usual sense of the term. A good deal of the material that it uses is historical, for it must strive to understand religion, as it now exists, by studying what it formerly was. We shall soon see that its first task is to trace the evolution of religion, and it is needless to say that this cannot be done without historical research. The time has long since passed when people fancied they could philosophise about religion without caring for its history. The relation between the philosophy and the history of religion was eloquently and cogently expounded some years ago in this very city of Edinburgh by Principal John Caird in the last of his Croall Lectures.[1] In Germany, the home of speculative philosophy, Hegel endeavoured, in his own way, to make the history of religion the handmaid of philosophy, but the materials at his command were necessarily scanty. With ampler materials Pfleiderer has built his philosophy of religion on historical foundations. And how vigorously Professor Max Müller, in his recent Gifford Lectures, has emphasised the importance and the absolute indispensability of historical studies, I need not remind you. I should be the last to dispute this, as I should then have to disavow my own past. I have been engaged in historical inquiries more than anything else, and all the more considerable works I have published have been of a historical kind. My late friend Kuenen used to say, 'I am nothing if not critical'. I would venture to say of myself, 'I am nothing if not historical'. Yet I believe that the science of religion requires a broader foundation than history in the ordinary sense of the word. Historical research must precede and pave the way for our science; but it does not belong to it. If I have minutely described all the religions in existence, their doctrines, myths, customs, the observances they inculcate, and the organisation of their adherents, besides tracing the different religious forms, their origin, bloom, and decay, I have merely collected the materials with which the science of religion works. And, indispensable as this is, it is not enough. Anthropology or the science of our social relations, psychology or the science of man's inmost being, and perhaps other sciences besides, must yield their contributions in order to help us to learn the true nature and origin of religion, and thus to reach our goal.

I have said that the exact method of natural science is not applicable to the science of religion; nor do I think that the historical method will suffice. I agree with Professor Flint that by the historical method we obtain only history. But we want more than that; we wish to understand and to explain. The strict historians have no right to ridicule what is called philosophic history, as they are fond of doing; but they are right in maintaining that this is not proper history, but a chapter in philosophy, and they are quite right in repudiating any obligation to add philosophical speculation to what we demand of them.

I therefore think that we need not hesitate openly to proclaim the philosophical character of our science, and to apply to it the method adapted to all philosophical branches of science – namely, the deductive. Not the one-sided empirical method, which culminates in positivism and only ascertains and classifies facts, but is powerless to explain them. Nor the one-sided historical method, which yields exclusively historical results. Nor again the so-called genetic-speculative method, a mixture of history and philosophy, which lacks all unity. Still less, I must hasten to add, the warped speculative method which has no foothold on earth, but floats in the clouds. For when I speak of the deductive method, I mean this speculative method least of all. On the contrary, our deductive reasoning must start from the results yielded by induction, by empirical, historical, and comparative methods. What religion is, and whence it arises, we can only ascertain from religious phenomena. Our inmost being can only be known by its outward manifestations. To wander in our speculations away from what has been discovered and established by anthropological and historical research, is to enter on a false path. To start from any *a priori* position, and to erect a system upon it, is a waste of time and leads to nothing. There must of course be a division of labour. None of us can do everything. One can hardly be at once an anthropologist, a historian, a psychologist, and a philosopher. Even in a single branch of science it is but few who are entirely at home. He who wishes to study the science of religion must survey the whole region, and must have traversed it in every direction; he must know what the researches of anthropologists and historians, and the discoveries of archaeologists, have yielded for the history of religion, what is merely probable, and what still uncertain or positively false. In short, he must be master of the material with which he has to work, although others have discovered it for him. And it is not only desirable, but I believe indispensable, that he should have taken part himself, for a time at least, in exploring and clearing the ground, and have studied at least two religions in the original sources. It is a long process, but it is the only way to achieve lasting results.

[...]

In order to make acquaintance with religion itself, which is a frame of mind adapted to the relation between man and his God, and thus becomes a definite sentiment towards God, we must attend to everything in which this frame of mind finds vent and this sentiment utters itself – to words as well as deeds, which together constitute the language of religion. But it is evident that observances have value for our research only where we know the conception attached to them by believers, and thus learn their significance. If that conception has not been handed down, either in the doctrine in general or in special records, or if it does not appear in the prayers and hymns associated with the observance, or in the attendant ceremonies, we then are confronted with a riddle the solution of which we can only guess. The old axiom that when two or more persons do the same thing, yet it is not the same thing, is here verified.

'ELEMENTS OF THE SCIENCE OF RELIGION'-II

In my previous course I endeavoured to explain my views regarding the development of religion. We investigated the stages and the directions of its development; we attempted to establish several laws or conditions which that development obeys; and lastly we tried to determine wherein that development essentially consists. We were concerned, in short, with an introduction to the morphological part of the science of religion. A different task now awaits us. We have hitherto been occupied with the ever-changing forms and varying manifestations of religion throughout human history, but we must now inquire as to what is permanent in the forms arising out of each other, and superseding each other, and as to the elements they all possess in common. This alone will enable us, so far as our limited knowledge permits, to determine the essence of religion and ascend to its origin. The subject of this second course will therefore be an introduction to the onto-logical part of the science of religion.

I am fully aware that this part of my task is more difficult than the first. To classify and explain phenomena, and to trace the development which they indicate, is not so easy a task as simply to describe them or to study them within a particular period of development, as for example in the history of a single religion or a single important epoch. But it is a still more difficult task to penetrate to the source whence they all spring, and to discover the Unity in their multiplicity and diversity. I will not, however, dogmatically formulate my conclusions. I shall confine myself to the task of investigation, or merely to that of initiating an investigation, and shall attempt nothing more ambitious. Adhering to the same method as before, we shall start from the solid ground of anthropology and history, the well-ascertained results of which can alone enable us to understand the essence of religion and trace it to its source.

We therefore again take our stand upon established facts. And the first question we have to answer is – Can we discover, among religious phenomena, any that recur so invariably that we are justified in regarding them as necessary manifestations of religious consciousness, whatever stage of development the religion may have attained? Or, in other words, Does religion contain any constant elements, none of which it can lack without injuring it and rendering it imperfect, and which therefore belong to every sound and normal religion?

[...]

There are, in short, three essential and inseparable requisites for the genuine and vigorous growth of religion: emotion, conception, and sentiment. All the morbid symptoms in religious life are probably due to the narrow-mindedness which attaches exclusive value to one of these, or neglects one of the three. If religion be sought in emotion alone, there is imminent danger of its degenerating into sentimental or mystical fanaticism. If the importance of conceptions be overrated, doctrine is very apt to be confounded with faith, creed with religion, and form with substance, an error which inevitably leads to the sad spectacle of religious hate, ostracism, and persecution. Those again who take account of sentiment alone regard every act done in the name of religion, however cruel and inhuman, as justifiable on the ground that they are acts of faith *(autos da fé)* – of what kind of faith, they do not inquire – while others would care nothing if religion were entirely swallowed up by a dreary moralism.

But, important as it is, the indissoluble union of these three elements does not of itself ensure the completeness of religion. They must also be in equilibrium. In this respect religion differs from other manifestations of the human mind. In the domain of art the feelings and the imagination predominate, and in that of philosophy abstract thought is paramount. The main object of science is to know accurately, imagination playing but a subordinate part; while ethics are chiefly concerned with the emotions and the fruit they yield. In religion, on the other hand, all these factors operate alike, and if their equilibrium be disturbed, a morbid condition of religion is the result.

And why is this? The answer is to be found in the fact already pointed out, that religion constitutes the deepest foundation, or rather the very centre, of our spiritual life. Or, as it is sometimes expressed, 'religion embraces the whole man'. If this means that religion, once awakened and quickened within our souls, sways our whole lives, nothing can be more certain. For the object I adore, and to which I have dedicated myself, occupies my thoughts and governs my actions. But, if understood too literally, the expression would hardly be accurate, and might easily lead to fanaticism. Human life has other and perfectly justifiable aspects besides the religious. Yet one thing is certain, religion dwells in the inmost depths of our souls. Of all that we possess it is our veriest own. Our religion is ourselves, in so far as we raise ourselves above the finite and transient. Hence the enormous power it confers upon its interpreters and prophets, a power which has been a curse when abused by selfishness and ambition, but a blessing when guided by love — a power against which the assaults of the adversaries of religion, with the keenest shafts of their wit, with all their learning and eloquence, their cunning statecraft, and their cruel violence, are in the long-run unavailing and impotent.

NOTE

1. John Caird, *Introduction to the Philosophy of Religion*, Glasgow, 1880, Chap. X.

Pierre D. Chantepie de la Saussaye

Pierre Daniel Chantepie de la Saussaye was born in 1848 in Leeuwarden, Nether-
lands, and received his primary and secondary school education in Leiden and
Rotterdam. He studied theology at the University of Utrecht. He obtained the
Th. D. degree in 1871 with a dissertation meant to be a methodological contribution to the search for the origin of religion. After a short stay in Bonn and
Tübingen where he worked with J. T. Beck, he became in 1872 a minister in the
Dutch Reformed Church but continued to pursue his interests in theology and
the history of religions. In 1878 Chantepie de la Saussaye occupied the new chair
of the History of Religions at the University of Amsterdam, Faculty of Theology.
He stayed there until 1899, keeping an open eye for the religious problems of
his time. From 1899 until 1916 Chantepie de la Saussaye occupied the chair of
Theological Encyclopaedia, Doctrine of God and Ethics in the Faculty of Theology at the University of Leiden. Though he presided the International Congress
for the History of Religions in Leiden in 1912, he did not pursue his work in the
field of his earlier interest. He died at Bilthoven in 1920.

Two publications of Chantepie de la Saussaye exist in English: 1891 *Manual
of the Science of Religion;* 1902 *The Religion of the Teutons.*

Chantepie de la Saussaye had a sharp eye for methodological issues. Besides
historical work in his field, he was primarily interested in systematic classification. So he considered the different schools of interpretation of religion which
were current at his time only as theories and as preliminary classifications of
the available material. In his view such theories could not solve the problem of
the essence and manifestations of religion, but they only could offer viewpoints
for the treatment of religion. His own research remained restricted to Greek and
Germanic religion. It is perhaps interesting to note that Chantepie de la Saussaye
left out the section 'Phenomenology of Religion' which occurred in the first
edition of his *Manual,* in its second and third edition, stating that it is a border-
discipline between history and philosophy and that, consequently, it had to be
treated separately *(Lehrbuch der Religionsgeschichte,* 2nd edition, 1897, Vol. II,
p. V.) He is one of the first scholars to speak of phenomenology of religion as a
special branch of the study of religion.

The following fragments have been chosen from the *Manual* (first edition)
because they give an idea of Chantepie de la Saussaye's concept of the science
of religion and of the way in which he conceived of phenomenology of religion.

'THE SCIENCE OF RELIGION'

The Science of Religion is a new science which has assumed an independent
existence during the last decades only. It has hardly reached as yet its full

growth, and is still fighting for the recognition of its rights. People like to consider men such as the Indian emperor Akbar or the Mohammedan philosopher Averroes as the forerunners of this science, because they recognized the relative merits of different religions; but their comparative treatment of religions was too restricted and their interest in the work too unscientific for us to regard them even as real precursors. It is only during the last half of our century that the essential conditions for founding a true science of religion existed. These conditions are three in number. The first is, that religion, as such, should become an object of philosophical knowledge. It is true that a dogmatic study of the Christian religion contained already the elements of such knowledge. We may speak of a philosophy of religion of the reformers; but it was nevertheless modern philosophy that first recognised religion as an object of philosophical study, without taking Christian revelation into account. The fundamental principles of Kant's and Schleiermacher's systems supplied some foundation stones on which to erect a philosophy of religion. But we must recognize Hegel as its true founder, because he first carried out the vast idea of realising, as a whole, the various modes for studying religion, (metaphysical, psychological, and historical), and made us see the harmony between the idea and the realisation of religion. No one approaches him in this respect. Hegel thus gave an aim and object to the science of religion, and on this account we may well forget the many errors in his lectures on the philosophy of religion, given from 1821—1831.

The second condition for a science of religion is the philosophy of history. This philosophy tries to realise the life of mankind as a whole, and not merely to study the concatenation of outward events. In the place, or rather by the side of political history, we have now the history of civilisation, which teaches us not only the fates of nations, but also their social systems, their material advancement, the development of arts and sciences, and the history of opinions.

During the last century a few men interested themselves in these studies. In 1725 Vico brought out in Italy a book on a 'Scienzia nuova', by which he meant much the same as what we call the philosophy of history, or the psychology of nations. In 1756 appeared Voltaire's *Essai sur les moeurs et l'esprit des nations*. In 1780 we find Lessing's *Erziehung des Menschengeschlechts*, which was followed in 1784 by Herder's *Ideen zur Geschichte der Menschheit*. These are all important dates in the development of studies to which in our century scholars pay an almost exaggerated and too exclusive attention. Particularly since the publication of Buckle's great work (*History of Civilisation in England*) in 1858, many students of the history of civilisation have run into wild extremes, and such masters of historiography as Ranke were perfectly right therefore when they laid particular stress on the importance of political history. Nevertheless the history of civilisation is a priceless acquisition; and it is essential to the science of religion because it reveals to us the connection of religion with other sides of life.

This framework, however, would be quite useless if there were no materials to fill it. The great work of the present age has been the collecting and studying of new materials, of the extent of which people had formerly no idea. The science of religion owes its steady growth to the discoveries and advances that have been made in the science of language, in archaeology, philology, ethnography, psychology of nations, mythology, and folk-lore. It was the comparative study of language which threw light on the real relationship of nations, and thus supplied the principal means for a proper classification of mankind.

Philology has deciphered monuments written in languages that were hitherto unknown, and has advanced so far as to give us trustworthy translations and classical editions of the writings of the ancient nations of the east.

The remains of ancient civilisations, not only on the Nile and in Mesopotamia, buried and forgotten under the débris of centuries, have been brought to light, and inscriptions have been collected and translated almost everywhere. We can now gain a clear idea of many savage races from the information brought home by intelligent travellers and missionaries. Political history totally ignored these savage tribes, and some of them had literally never been heard of.

The life of ancient and modern civilised nations is studied, not only in its higher strata and its literary productions, but in its popular manifestations, in customs, manners, and superstitions. All these studies furnish the materials necessary for the science of religion.

Nobody has a greater claim to be called the founder of that science than F. Max Müller, who besides being a recognised master in one branch of these studies, possesses also a wide knowledge of other branches, and joins sound learning to brilliant literary gifts. In his 'Introduction' he pointed out the direction that must be followed in a study of the science of religion; and though his method of explaining myths and religions by the study of language has roused much opposition, his merits as a teacher of the science of religion cannot be contested. He was the first who succeeded in convincing a larger public of the importance of the subject, and was able to persuade the best oriental scholars of Europe to combine in a translation of 'The Sacred Books of the East', so that the general public might be able to read them. His call for a study of the science of religion has been obeyed by almost every nation, nowhere more quickly than in Holland, where Tiele devoted his great powers to this subject, and among many other works published the first compendium, in which he gathered together the results of the study of the history of religion. In Holland the science of religion has now taken its recognized place amongst academic studies.

In Paris, Brussels, and lately in Rome also, chairs for the science of religion have been founded. Of course this has met with some opposition, partly from philologists and specialists who fancy that such a general study will lead to empty dilettantism, and partly in the interest of Christianity, since people are afraid that these studies will only increase scepticism and indifference. An honest, conscientious study of the subject alone can refute these objections. These studies have been carried the furthest in England, and the results are placed before the public in annual lectures delivered in various towns (for instance, the Hibbert Lectures in London and Oxford, the Muir Lectures and the Gifford Lectures). In Germany the single branches of the science of religion are well represented, but courses of lectures on the science of religion as a whole, like those, for instance, by R. Roth at Tübingen, have but seldom been delivered. It is only quite within the last few years that the great importance of the subject has been generally recognised.

The object of the science of religion is the study of religion, of its essence and its manifestations. It divides itself naturally into the philosophy and the history of religion. These two divisions are most closely connected. The philosophy of religion would be useless and empty if, whilst defining the idea of religion, it disregarded the actual facts that lie before us; and the history of religion cannot prosper without the philosophy of religion. Not only the order and the criticism of religious phenomena, but even the determining whether such phenomena are of a religious nature, depends on some, if only a preliminary definition of religion. The history of religion falls naturally into two divisions, the ethnographical, and, in a narrower sense, the historical. The ethnographical gives us details of the religions of savage tribes, the so-called children of nature *(Naturvölker)*, or that part of mankind that has no history. The second division gives us the historical development of the religions of civilised nations. The collecting and grouping of various religious phenomena forms the transition from the history to the philosophy of religion. The latter treats religion according to its subjective and objective sides, and therefore consists of a psychological and a metaphysical part. The present manual deals with the historical side only. But the limits of this work must not be too restricted; and although we shall not discuss the actual philosophical difficulties, yet we feel bound to give an outline of religious phenomena. We shall best succeed in dividing our subject if, after discussing some more general preliminary questions, we proceed to treat the phenomenological, the ethnographical, and lastly, in a narrower sense, the historical facts.

This last division will embrace all religions which have had an historical development, with the exception of Judaism and Christianity. Not that we would place these two outside the pale of the science of religion; on the contrary, they will be considered in the phenomenological section; for a philosophy of religion that did not take these two religions into account would indeed be defective. The unity of religion in the variety of its forms is what is presupposed by the science of religion. For merely practical reasons, however, it will be better not to include, in a still larger circle, the very comprehensive studies which have for their object the Christian religion and its forerunner, Judaism.

It is desirable also to use different forms of treatment for the science of religion and for theology, properly so-called. Lately, especially among Dutch savants, the question as to the relations between these two have been discussed in various encyclopaedic sketches, and methodological treatises.

Some wish to assign to the general science of religion a subordinate place in the Encyclopaedia of Theology, as being only an introduction to the historical or systematic section of the same. But this would only lead to a kind of *Theologia gentilis,* or a modification of the dogmatic *Locus de Religione,* even if it did not place the whole of the science of religion (as a science of false gods) in opposition to theology, which has for its object true religion only.

Others reverse this relation, and look upon Christian theology as a subdivision only of the science of religion. Although this is perfectly right in form, still theology can hardly submit to it; for even when it is not reactionary, but works with protestant freedom, it cannot surrender, without self-destruction, the character of its biblical and ecclesiastical teachings, which constitute the greatest part of its encyclopaedia. The science of religion, and the science of the Christian religion must follow, therefore, separate paths, and have separate objects in view. Of course they must mutually help one another. It is most important for theologians to study the science of religion. The wellknown saying which Max Müller has applied to religions: 'He who knows one, knows none', may rather exaggerate its value, but it is certainly true that the eye which has been sharpened, through a comparative study of religions, can better realise the religious idea of Christianity, and that the history of Christianity can only be rightly understood when one has studied the non-Christian religions from which Christianity borrows so much, or to which it stands in sharp opposition. Finally, missionaries cannot possibly do good work without having studied this subject.

PHENOMENOLOGY OF RELIGION

The phenomenology of religion is most closely connected with psychology, in so far as it deals with facts of human consciousness. Even the outward forms of religion can only be explained from inward processes: religious acts, ideas, and sentiments are not distinguished from non-religious acts, ideas and sentiments by any outward mark, but only by a certain inward relation. We must leave the accurate definition of the character of religious phenomena to philosophy, and content ourselves with classifying the most important ethnographic and historical material connected with the phenomena of religion. We shall not therefore attempt here an analysis of religious consciousness, but only discuss the meaning of the most important classes of religious phenomena. Pünjer has fixed on four such groups of homogeneous phenomena, namely, religious doctrines, acts, benefits, and sentiments. It is clear however that these four cannot be co-ordinated: the benefits which man possesses or desires in religion are ground or object, the religious states and sentiments are the efficient causes and forces of the external phenomena of religious life. There remain therefore the cult and the religious doctrine, or, to put it more generally, religious acting and thinking. But these cannot be separated from the benefits which man desires by them, nor from the sentiments that give rise to them. We shall therefore deal with the most important sides of cult and forms of doctrine, without attempting a strictly systematic order, or a theoretic division which does not correspond to actual facts. I speak intentionally of the forms of doctrine, for we cannot dwell in detail on the rich contents of religious consciousness, such as they are divided into seven principal articles, by Pfleiderer for instance.

The question whether religious acting or religious thinking comes first is easily settled. Every religious act must be preceded by a thought, however crude. On the other hand, many religious doctrines are much less primitive than the ritual act, and owe their origin to an attempt to explain them. In general, therefore, neither the act nor the doctrine can claim priority, and both are preceded by religious impressions, sentiments, and states. It may be admitted, however, that among the materials of which we dispose, those which are connected with ritual are the most original. Among the elements of religious life, those connected with ritual are most permanent. Ritual customs last for centuries, are differently combined and joined with other ideas, cease to be officially ritual, and become popular, but remain for all that the most stable elements of religion, carrying us back to the most distant time. Religious doctrines, on the contrary, develop, and without throwing away what is old they tend to adapt themselves to new requirements. There is here also a kind of tradition, which warrants a certain continuity, but not an unchanging permanence. Lastly, with regard to religious sentiment, every period, every group, every person, is more or less independent. In describing the religious history of any period we find that we have collected at the same time documents with regard to primitive times in cult and customs, documents with regard to a nearer past in the religious doctrines, and documents of the present in religious sentiment. In addition to this, the materials concerning the cult are not only the most primitive, but also the most generally accessible. Among all peoples and races known to us, acts, manners, and customs are immediately taken cognizance of. With many, these are almost the only thing known to us. Of all so-called savages we really know nothing but what they do, and we have to deduce their ideas from it, and from communications which generally lead to very little. It is only nations standing on a higher stage of civilisation, historical nations in the proper sense of the word, that yield us religious doctrines, while with regard to religious sentiments we can only form an opinion during periods which are represented by the large and many-sided literature left to us. The richest material therefore for the phenomenology of religion is supplied by religious acts, cult, and customs; with regard to many nations and periods, it is the only mirror that reflects something of their religious ideas and sentiments. This throws quite a new light on the history of cult, and leaves it no longer simply as a part of archaeology. It is no doubt of importance that we should not lose sight of the bond which connects ritual with other sides of public life, but ritual should first of all be understood as a religious act, and in that sense belongs essentially to the science of religion.

Ritual acts have to be considered from different points of view. They have a symbolical meaning, they are the 'sign-language of theology' (Tylor). Rites consist of symbols which reflect the object of worship, or the subjective sentiments, and give a dramatic expression to religious thoughts. Many, as for instance Schleiermacher, have laid too much stress on the aesthetic side of the cult as a representative action. In reality it can never be severed from the other more important side of the cult, namely the practical. What man most desires in his religion is, not first of all a symbolical representation of his ideas and sentiments, but an attainment of certain benefits which he hopes to gain by means of his representative acts. The practical objects of these ritual acts are very various. Sometimes the interest centres exclusively in certain objects which satisfy material wants, sometimes what is desired consists in more general and spiritual objects, as when for instance a ceremony is meant to preserve a certain cosmic order, or to gain for man certain powers and superhuman faculties. On a higher stage, what is looked for in a sacrificial act is not so much the gift as the giver, and what is desired is the favour of the gods, or communion with them. These different points of view lead to different ideas about the gods for whom the sacrifice is intended, and to different kinds and stages of piety, for it is said that 'man grows with the growth of his object'. The history of ritual displays the greatest variety in these objects, and in the means used for their realisation. It is of great importance to find out whether the desired communion with the gods is to be taken in a moral or in a material sense. In the former greater importance is attached to man as acting, and in the latter to the communication made by God. The ritual act is therefore considered either as a human performance, or as a divine blessing (sacrament), and this forms the deepest line of demarcation between the ethical and mystical sides of religious life and action. From an ethical point of view the difference between the subject and object of religion, between man and God, is carefully preserved; from a mystical point of view that difference vanishes, and communion changes into identification. There is still one more side of the cult which must be mentioned, namely, the pedagogic. Cult is the form in which religion manifests, maintains, and extends itself. Rites are the bond of the unity of religion, by which individuals enter into communion with their brothers in the faith, however distant from them in time and space. Lastly, by means of rites, laymen, half-believers, and children are educated so as to become fit to participate in the benefits of religion.

The objects of worship. As the most general definition of religion, Tylor has proposed a belief in spiritual beings. It would be more correct however, and more complete, to define religion as a belief in superhuman powers combined with their worship. At all events, the phenomenology of religion must begin with the consideration of the different objects of belief and of worship, therefore a few general considerations will be useful by way of introduction.

Religion has in reality but one object, the living God who manifests Himself among all nations as the only real God. Though by many He is but partially known, or not known at all, because divine honour is paid to His works and His powers rather than to Himself, yet in the end all worship is meant for Him, and man cannot conceive anything divine that is not really derived from Him. Considered from this point of view, the many gods worshipped by the heathen become either empty, meaningless, and even hostile beings, no-gods, false gods; or real divine powers, and qualities, only separated from their subject and represented singly. The former point of view was more common among the prophets of Israel, while so-called heathen thinkers in India, Egypt, and Greece were often led to look upon the many gods as manifestations of the one divine power.

At present we are concerned not with the one, but with the many objects of religion. It is not easy to say how we can define these objects in general. We saw before that the fetish is considered by some as an object of worship, by others as a means of magic, while in reality it is both, in inseparable unity. But even when the question is differently put, as for instance with regard to the worship of nature, it is still difficult to say definitely what constitutes the real object of worship. Is it the material object itself, or an indwelling spirit, or the divine power revealed in it? We shall be met by these questions again when we examine the various objects of religion, and we shall discover that there is no answer that applies equally to all. The worship of nature is so differently interpreted that it is impossible to discover a universal formula for its meaning. It is impossible on this account to devise a satisfactory division between the different objects of worship. The frontier line between the visible and invisible, the sensuous and the supersensuous, cannot but be wavering. Max Müller has divided the sensuous objects to which worship has been addressed into tangible, such as stones and shells, semi-tangible, such as trees, rivers, mountains, sea and earth, and intangible, such as sky, stars, sun and moon. Perhaps a division into earthly and heavenly objects would be better, but there is no division which would suffice for an exhaustive treatment.

It is clear from all this, how close is the bond which unites belief and worship with one another, and both with their objects. These rules however are never without exceptions; there are religious ideas which are never manifested by acts. Some savages, for instance, believe indeed in good gods, but worship always the evil gods, because the good ones cannot by their nature do anything but good, and need not therefore be feared. It is still more curious that there should be ritual acts of different kinds which have no relation to any object, or in which that relation has been completely lost sight of. This is often the case in magical practices. Though the gods were often invoked in them, yet their success does not depend on the gods, but on the formulas recited and the practices performed.

PART TWO

Connections with Other Disciplines

Johann J. Bachofen

Johann Jakob Bachofen was born in 1815 in Basel, where he received his primary education at a private school, and his secondary school education at the *Gymnasium* (1825—31) and the *Pädagogikum* (1831—33). In 1833 he enrolled in the University of Basel, and in 1834 in the University of Berlin. Here he first studied philology and history, but then decided to continue with law, working under F. K. von Savigny on the history of Roman law. In 1837 he continued his law studies at the University of Göttingen, and he returned to Basel in 1839, where he obtained the doctor's degree in law that same year. Having spent the next two years in England and France, Bachofen was appointed professor of Roman Law at the University of Basel in 1841. He became a judge in 1842 and a member of the *Groszer Rat* two years later. However, Bachofen resigned from his professorship in 1844 and shortly afterwards also left his judicial positions in order to devote himself completely to his studies. From then onwards, he worked as a private scholar, with regular travels to Italy and occasional visits to Greece and Spain. He died in Basel in 1887.

Only a selection from Bachofen's writings, which had appeared in German in 1926, has been translated into English: 1967 *Myth, Religion and Mother Right*.

Besides his work on Roman law and his many studies on Roman and Greek Antiquity, Bachofen is known for his historical investigations on matriarchy. He elaborated the hypothesis of a matriarchal stage in the development of human society, culture and religion. His interest for the study of religions is also great because of his interpretations of mythology and symbolism, and because of his tracing of the development of mankind through its expression in religious symbols.

The following fragments have been taken from *Myth, Religion and Mother Right* in order to show Bachofen's approach to the study of symbols and his ideas on early matriarchy.

'SYMBOL AND MYTH'

Myth is the exegesis of the symbol. It unfolds in a series of outwardly connected actions what the symbol embodies in a unity. It resembles a discursive philosophical treatise in so far as it splits the idea into a number of connected images and then leaves it to the reader to draw the ultimate inference. The combination of the symbol with the explanatory myth is a highly remarkable phenomenon. In the Pamphilian grave painting the symbol in itself sufficed but not on the sarcophagus,* where it seemed to require the support of the myth. In this combination the symbol finds the guarantee of its permanence. The myth restores the ancient dignity of the Orphic symbolism. To expound the mystery doctrine in words would be a sacrilege against the supreme law; it can only be represented in terms of myth. That is why mythology is the language of the tombs. As a rule the inscriptions are only statements of lesser importance; higher ideas inspired by death and tomb are expressed in the form of myth, aided by art. More and more the pure symbol is relegated to the background, while the myth becomes dominant. Gradually the entire mythology of the ancients enters into their tombs, so creating a drama that deserves our utmost attention. The treasury of myths, in which the ancients had set forth the earliest memories of their history, the entire sum of their physical knowledge, the recollection of earlier periods of creation and great tellurian transformations, is here employed to expound religious truths, to embody laws of nature, to express ethical and moral truths, and to awaken comforting intimations extending beyond the melancholy limits of the material *fatum*. Cloaked in mythical images, the content of the mysteries with their twofold physical and metaphysical significance is brought home to the beholder. Whereas heaven has descended to earth through the anthropomorphic vision of the divine, earth once more becomes heaven now that the myths have entered into the mystery and the human is traced back to the divine; in the lives of heroes valor and virtue are represented as the only means of transcending matter and achieving the ultimate reward: immortality. No longer an object of faith, the myth regains its highest dignity through its connection with mystery and tomb. The simple old symbolic faith, in part created and in part transmitted by Orpheus and the great religious teachers of the earliest times, is resurrected in new forms in the mythology of the tombs. The later period created no new symbols and no new myths: it lacked the necessary freshness of youth. But with its more inward attitude it was able to give the traditional representations a new and transfigured meaning. Thus the myths, as Plutarch said, became images and shadows of higher ideas, and by their mysterious character inculcated a profounder veneration. They resemble those mimetic καταδείξεις, representations in which the initiate beheld, as in a mirror, the more sublime truths of the mysteries. The whole composition suggests dramatized myth, and certain details are clearly modeled on performances of tragic works.

---

* The sarcophagus of Santa Chiara in Napels, which depicts the myth of Protesilaus and Laodamia; its discussion is omitted from this selection (J. J. Bachofen).

The static symbol and its mythical unfolding are the speech and writing the language of the tombs. The higher meditations inspired by the riddle of death, the grief and consolation, the hope and fear, the foreboding and joyful anticipation, are expressed only in art. There is a profound reason for this. Human language is too feeble to convey all the thoughts aroused. by the alternation of life and death and the sublime hopes of the initiate· Only the symbol and the related myth can meet this higher need. The symbol awakens intimations; speech can only explain. The symbol plucks all the strings of the human spirit at once; speech is compelled to take up a single thought at a time. The symbol strikes its roots in the most secret depths of the soul; language skims over the surface oí the understanding like a soft breeze. The symbol aims inward; language outward. Only the symbol can combine the most disparate elements into a unitary impression. Language deals in successive particulars; it expresses bit by bit what must be brought home to the soul at a single glance if it is to affect us profoundly. Words make the infinite finite, symbols carry the spirit beyond the finite world of becoming into the realm of infinite being. Intimating the ineffable, they are mysterious as all religion by its very nature must be, a silent discourse appropriate to the quiet of the tomb, beyond the reach of mockery and doubt, those unripe fruits of wisdom. Therein lies the mysterious dignity of the symbol, which so eminently enhances the solemnity of the ancient tombs. Therein lies the spell of the mythical representations, which show us the great deeds of the primordial age in the muted light of distant melancholy recollection, and that is what lends them the aura of conecration characteristic of the ancient necropolises.

MATRIARCHY AND RELIGION

I hope that the foregoing remarks have thrown new light on the method by which I am seeking to investigate an era hitherto relegated to the shadows of poetic fancy. In resuming my interrupted exposition of the matrisarchal world, I shall endeavor not to lose myself in the mass of variegated and always surprising details, but to concentrate on its most important manifestation, which may be regarded as the culmination and substrate of all others.

The religious foundation of matriarchy discloses this system in its noblest form, links it with the highest aspects of life, and gives a profound insight into the dignity of that primordial era which Hellenism excelled only in outward radiance, not in depth and loftiness of conception. Here more than ever I am aware of the broad gulf dividing my view of antiquity from current theories and the modern view of history based upon them. The idea of treating religion as a profound influence on the life of nations, of ranking it first among the creative forces which mold man's whole existence, of consulting it for illumination of the obscurest aspects of ancient thought, strikes present-day historians as indicative of an unnatural penchant toward theocracy, as narrow-minded incompetence, as a deplorable relapse into the Dark Ages.

I have heard all these accusations, and yet I remain faithful to the old conservative spirit. I should still rather be ancient than modern when investigating antiquity; I should still rather seek the truth than cater to the opinions of my time. There is only one mighty lever of all civilization, and that is religion. Every rise and every decline of human existence springs from a movement that originates in this supreme sphere. Without it no aspect of ancient life is intelligible, and earliest times in particular remain an impenetrable riddle. Wholly dominated by its faith, mankind in this stage links every form of existence, every historical tradition, to the basic religious idea, sees every event in a religious light, and identifies itself completely with its gods. If especially matriarchate must bear this hieratic imprint, it is because of the essential feminine nature, that profound sense of the divine presence which, merging with the feeling of love, lends woman, and particularly the mother, a religious devotion that is most active in the most barbarous times. The elevation of woman over man arouses our amazement most especially by its contradiction to the relation of physical strength. The law of nature confers the scepter of power on the stronger. If it is torn away from him by feebler hands, other aspects of human nature must have been at work, deeper powers must have made their influence felt. [...]

We have numerous indications of the intimate connection between matriarchy and woman's religious character. Among the Locrians only a maiden could enact the rite of the φιαληφορία (bearing of the sacrificial bowl). In citing this custom as the proof that mother right prevailed among the Epizephyrians, Polybius recognized its connection with the basic matriarchal idea. Moreover, the Locrians sacrificed a maiden in expiation of Ajax's sacrilege. This confirms the same relation and indicates the basis of the widespread belief that female sacrifices are more pleasing to the godhead. And this line of thought carries us to the deepest foundation and meaning of the matriarchal idea. Traced back to the prototype of Demeter, the earthly mother becomes the mortal representative of the primordial tellurian mother, her priestess and hierophant, entrusted with the administration of her mystery. All these phenomena are of a piece, manifestations of one and the same cultural stage. This religious primacy of motherhood leads to a primacy of the mortal woman; Demeter's exclusive bond with Kore leads to the no less exclusive relation of succession between mother and daughter; and finally, the inner link between the mystery and the chthonian-feminine cults leads to the priesthood of the mother, who here achieves the highest degree of religious consecration.

These considerations bring new insight into the cultural stage characterized by matriarchy. We are faced with the essential greatness of the pre-Hellenic culture: in the Demetrian mystery and the religious and civil primacy of womanhood it possessed the seed of noble achievement which was suppressed and often destroyed by later developments. The barbarity of the Pelasgian world, the incompatibility of matriarchy with a noble way of life, the late origin of the mysterious element in religion–such traditional opinions are dethroned once and for all. It has long been a hobby with students of antiquity to impute the noblest historical manifestations to the basest motives. Could they be expected to spare religion, to acknowledge that what was noblest in it–its concern with the supernatural, the transcendent, the mystical–was rooted in the profoundest needs of the human soul? In the opinion of these scholars only self-seeking false prophets could have darkened the limpid sky of the Hellenic world with such ugly clouds, only an era of decadence could have gone so far astray. But mystery is the true essence of every religion, and wherever woman dominates religion or life, she will cultivate the mysterious. Mystery is rooted in her very nature, with its close alliance between the material and the supersensory; mystery springs from her kinship with material nature, whose eternal death creates a need for comforting thoughts and awakens hope through pain; and mystery is inherent in the law of Demetrian motherhood, manifested to woman in the transformations of the seed grain and in the reciprocal relation between perishing and coming into being, disclosing death as the indispensable forerunner of higher rebirth, as prerequisite to the ἐπίκτησις τῆς τελετῆς (higher good of consecration).

All these implications of the maternal are fully confirmed by history. Wherever we encounter matriarchy, it is bound up with the mystery of the chthonian religion, whether it invokes Demeter or is embodied by an equivalent goddess. The relation between the two phenomena is clearly exemplified in the lives of the Lycians and Epizephyrians, whose high development of the mystery–revealed by a number of remarkable phenomena that have hitherto been misunderstood–accounts for the unusual survival of mother right among them. This historical fact leads us to an inescapable conclusion. If we acknowledge the primordial character of mother right and its connection with an older cultural stage, we must say the same of the mystery, for the two phenomena are merely different aspects of the same cultural form; they are inseparable twins. And this is all the more certain when we consider that the religious aspect of matriarchy is at the root of its social manifestations. The cultic conceptions are the source, the social forms are their consequence and expression. Kore's bond with Demeter **was** the source of the primacy of mother over father, of daughter over son, and was not abstracted from the social relationship. Or, in ancient terms: the cultic-religious meaning of the maternal κτείς (weaver's shuttle, comb, weaving woman) is primary and dominant; while the social, juridical sense *pudenda* (shame) is derivative. The feminine *sporium* (womb) is seen primarily as a representation of the Demetrian mystery, both in its lower physical sense and in its higher transcendent implication, and only by derivation becomes an expression of the social matriarchy, as in the Lycian myth of Sarpedon. This refutes the assertion of modern historians that mystery is appropriate only to times of decadence and is a late degeneration of Hellenism. History reveals exactly the opposite relationship: the maternal mystery is the old element, and the classic age represents a late stage of religious development; the later age, and not the mystery, may be regarded as a degeneration, as a religious leveling that sacrificed transcendence to immanence and the mysterious obscurity of higher hope to clarity of form.

Hellenism is hostile to such a world. The primacy of motherhood vanishes, and its consequences with it. The patriarchal development stresses a completely different aspect of human nature, which is reflected in entirely different social forms and ideas. In Egypt Herodotus finds the direct antithesis to Greek, and particularly Attic, civilization. Compared to his Hellenic surroundings, Egypt struck him as a world upside down. If the father of history had subjected the great two periods of Greek development to a similar comparison, he would have been equally amazed at the contrast between them. For Egypt is the land of stereotyped matriarchy, its whole culture is built essentially on the mother cult, on the primacy of Isis over Osiris; it offers striking parallels to countless matriarchal phenomena presented by the life of the pre-Hellenic peoples. And history has provided still another striking example of this same contrast between the two civilizations. In the midst of the Hellenic world Pythagoras restored religion and life to the old foundations, he attempted to give a new consecration to existence and to satisfy man's profounder religious needs by reviving the mystery of the chthonian-maternal cults. Essentially Pythagoreanism does not develop Hellenism but combats it. As one of our sources says, a breath of the hoariest antiquity blows through it. Its origins lie, not in the wisdom of the Greeks, but in the more ancient lore of the Orient, of the static African and Asian world. Pythagoras sought his followers chiefly among those peoples whose adherence to ancient tradition seemed to present the closest affinity to his doctrine, particularly among the tribes and cities of Hesperia (Italy), a land which would seem to have preserved down to our own day religious stages that have disappeared elsewhere.

This preference for an older view of life brought with it a decided recognition of the Demetrian mother principle, a distinct leaning toward the mysterious, transcendent, supersensory element in religion, and above all the appearance of sublime priestess figures: can we fail to recognize the inner unity of these phenomena and their bond with the pre-Hellenic culture? An earlier world rises from the grave; life strives back toward its beginnings. The long intervening years vanish, and late generations merge with those of the primordial era as though there had been no change in times and ideas. Only the chthonian-maternal mystery of the Pelasgian religion can account for the Pythagorean women; their acts and spiritual attitude cannot be explained by the concepts of Greek classicism. Separated from that cultic foundation, the religious character of Theano, the 'daughter of Pythagorean wisdom,' is a mere anomaly, a puzzle which we shall not get rid of merely by referring to the mythical origin of Pythagoreanism. The ancients confirm this connection by grouping Theano, Diotima, and Sappho together. Wherein consists the similarity of these three figures belonging to different times and nations? Where else than in the mystery of the maternal-chthonian religion? It is in these three outstanding figures that the religious vocation of Pelasgian womanhood achieves its richest and loftiest unfolding. Sappho's home was one of the great centers of the Orphic mystery religion, Diotima dwelt in Arcadian Mantinea, famous for its archaic way of life and its cult of the Samothracian Demeter; one is Aeolian, the other Pelasgian; both belonged to nations whose religion and culture had remained faithful to the pre-Hellenic foundations. In a woman of unknown name living among an archaic people untouched by Hellenism, one of the greatest of philosophers discerned a religious illumination not to be found amid the brilliant culture of Attica.

The central idea that I have emphasized from the outset, the relationship between the primacy of women and the pre-Hellenic culture and religion, is eminently confirmed by the very phenomena which, when viewed superficially and out of context, seem to argue most against it. Wherever the older mystery religion is preserved or revived, woman emerges from the obscurity and servitude to which she was condemned amid the splendor of Ionian Greece and restored to all her pristine dignity. Is there any further room for doubt as to wherein lay the foundation of early matriarchy and the source of all the benefits it conferred on the peoples it encompassed? Socrates at the feet of Diotima, hardly able to follow the flight of her mysterious revelation, freely admitting his need for the woman's wisdom: can there be any nobler expression of matriarchy, any more moving evidence of the inner kinship between the Pelasgian-maternal mystery and the feminine nature? Where shall we find a more perfect lyrical expression of the ethical principle of matriarchal culture, of love, this sanctification of mother-

hood? All epochs have admired this image, but our admiration is further
enhanced if we regard it not merely as the creation of a great mind but also
as a picture of matriarchal religion, of the feminine priesthood. Here again
history rises above poetic fancy.

I shall pursue the religious basis of matriarchy no further; it is most
deeply rooted in woman's vocation for the religious life. Who will continue
to ask why devotion, justice, and all the qualities that embellish man's life
are known by feminine names, why τελετή (initiation) is personified by a
woman? This choice is no free invention or accident, but is an expression
of historical truth. We find the matriarchal peoples distinguished by
εὐνομία, εὐσέβεια, παιδεία (rectitude, piety, and culture); we see women
serving as conscientious guardians of the mystery, of justice and peace, and
the accord between the historical facts and the linguistic phenomenon is
evident. Seen in this light, matriarchy becomes a sign of cultural progress,
a source and guarantee of its benefits, a necessary period in the education
of mankind, and hence the fulfillment of a natural law which governs
peoples as well as individuals.

Here we are carried back to our starting point. We began by showing
matriarchy to be a universal phenomenon, independent of any special
dogma or legislation. Now we can go further in our characterization and
establish its quality of natural truth. Like childbearing motherhood, which
is its physical image, matriarchy is entirely subservient to matter and to
the phenomena of natural life, from which it derives the laws of its inner and
outward existence; more strongly than later generations, the matriarchal
peoples feel the unity of all life, the harmony of the universe, which they
have not yet outgrown; they are more keenly aware of the pain of death
and the fragility of tellurian existence, lamented by woman and particularly
the mother. They yearn more fervently for higher consolation, which they
find in the phenomena of natural life, and they relate this consolation
to the generative womb, to conceiving, sheltering, nurturing mother love.
Obedient in all things to the laws of physical existence, they fasten their
eyes upon the earth, setting the chthonian powers over the powers of
uranian light. They identify the male principle chiefly with the tellurian
waters and subordinate the generative moisture to the *gremium matris*
(maternal womb), the ocean to the earth. In a wholly material sense they
devote themselves to the embellishment of material existence, to the
πρακτικὴ ἀρετή (practical virtues). Both in agriculture, which was first
fostered by women, and in the erection of walls, which the ancients identified
with the chthonian cult, they achieved a perfection which astonished later
generations. No era has attached so much importance to outward form, to
the sanctity of the body, and so little to the inner spiritual factor; in juridical life no other era has so consistently advocated maternal dualism and

the principle of actual possession; and none has been so given to lyrical enthusiasm, this eminently feminine sentiment, rooted in the feeling of nature. In a word, matriarchal existence is regulated naturalism, its thinking is material, its development predominantly physical. Mother right is just as essential to this cultural stage as it is alien and unintelligible to the era of patriarchy.

Ernest Renan

Joseph-Ernest Renan was born in 1823 at Tréguier, Britanny, where he received his primary and part of his secondary school education. He continued his studies in Paris in 1838 at the ecclesiastical college of Saint-Nicolas du Chardonnet, in 1841 at the seminary of Issy, which was a branch of the seminary of St Sulpice, and in 1843 at the latter itself. He also attended lectures at the Collège de France where he was a student of E. Burnouf. Renouncing the ecclesiastical career in 1845, he was for a short time at the lay college Stanislas of the Oratorians, but then went on to study for himself Semitic philology and to pursue his readings, while working as a tutor at a private school. In 1848 he passed the *agrégation* examination and wrote in a short time 'L'avenir de la science', which would be published only much later. In 1849 Renan went on a scientific mission to Italy; on his return he found a post at the Bibliothèque Nationale where he worked until 1862. In 1852 he obtained his doctorate with a thesis on Averroes and one on Aristotle in Syriac translations. Renan accomplished an archeological mission to Syria in 1860–61 and was on his return appointed to the chair of Hebrew, Chaldaic and Syriac Languages at the Collège de France in 1862. However, he was suspended four days after having delivered his inaugural address, since his lectures were thought to lead to a disturbance of the public peace. In 1864 he was formally dismissed, and in 1864–65 he travelled once more to the Near East. Renan was rehabilitated by an appointment at the Collège de France in 1870, and he became its *administrateur* in 1883. From 1881 onwards Renan directed the publication of the *Corpus Inscriptionum Semiticarum*. During those years Renan was one of the leading figures in French cultural intellectual and literary life. He died in Paris in 1892.

Of the books by Renan which have been translated into English the following may be mentioned: 1859 *Translation and Introductory Essay of the Book of Job;* 1860 *Translation and Introductory Essay of the Song of Songs;* 1863 *The Life of Jesus;* 1864 *Studies of Religious History and Criticism;* 1884 *Lectures on the Influence of the Institutions, Thought and Culture of Rome on Christianity and the Development of the Catholic Church;* 1886 *Studies in Religious History (second series);* 1888–1890 *History of the Origins of Christianity* (7 vol.); 1888–1891 *History of the People of Israel* (3 vol.); 1891 *The Future of Science, ideas of 1848.* . .

Apart from his work in Semitic philology proper and his literary and philosophical oeuvre, Renan studied problems of Islamic philosophy and of the origins of Islam, was a biblical scholar both for the Old and the New Testament, and worked as a historian on the history of Israel and on the early history of Christianity. The results of these studies were presented with the literary gifts of the author. The work of Renan as a whole demonstrates the transition from a religious to a historical and critical consideration of the documents, doctrines

and history of Christianity. It had profound repercussions both on his persona
career and on the religious and cultural life of his lifetime.

The following fragment has been taken from Renan's Preface to his *Studies
of Religious History*, published in French in 1857. It shows the way in which
the author vindicates the right of critical historical scholarship on religion
including Christianity.

VINDICATION OF A CRITICAL MIND

The fragments which compose the present volume all relate to the history
of religions, and will be found to embrace the principal forms with which
religious sentiment has been clothed in ancient times, in the Middle Ages,
and in modern days. These subjects have for me an attraction which I
cannot conceal, and which I know not how to resist. Religion is certainly
the highest and most interesting of the manifestations of human nature.
Among all kinds of poetry, it is the one that best reaches the end essential
to art, which is to raise man above the vulgar life and awaken in him the
sense of his celestial origin. No part of the great instincts of the heart shows
itself with better evidence. Even when one adopts in particular, the teaching
of any of the great religious systems, they divide themselves, or they divide
the world; from the whole of these systems results one fact, which constitutes to my mind the most consolatory guarantee of a mysterious future,
where the race and the individual will find again their works and the fruit
of their sacrifices.

A grave difficulty, I know, attaches to these studies, and causes timid
people to impute to the authors that they occupy themselves with tendencies and objects to which they are strangers. The essence of all religions is
to exact absolute belief, and consequently to place themselves above
common right, and to deny to the impartial historian all competence when
he seeks to judge them. Religions, in effect, in order to sustain the pretension
of being beyond reproach, are obliged to have recourse to a particular
system of philosophic history, founded upon the belief of a miraculous
intervention of the Deity in human affairs — an intervention made solely
for their profit. Religions otherwise are not able to dispose freely of their
past; the past must bend to the necessities of the present, and furnish
a foundation for institutions more evidently brought about by the course
of time. The critic, on the contrary, whose rule is to follow only sight, and
fair deduction, without any political after-thought; the critic, whose first
principle is that the miracle has no part in the course of human affairs,
any more than in the series of natural facts; the critic, who begins by
proclaiming that everything in history is capable of human explanation,
even when that explanation escapes us by reason of insufficient teaching,

would evidently not agree with the schools of theology, who employ a
method opposed to his, and follow it with a different purpose. Susceptible,
like all powers attributed to a divine source, religions naturally regard the
expression, however respectful, of a difference of opinion as hostility, and
look upon those as enemies, who place before themselves the most simple
duties of reason.

This unfortunate misunderstanding, which will endure eternally between
the critical spirit and the habitual doctrines imposed all of a piece, ought it
to obstruct the human mind in the track of free research? We think not.
Firstly, human nature never consents to mutilate itself; however one may
conceive, perhaps, that reason consents to its own sacrifice, if it finds itself
in the face of a doctrine which is unique, and adopted by all mankind.
But one set of systems claims the absolute truth, which all can possess at
the same time; any one of these systems, showing a title by which it says
it can reduce to nothing the pretensions of the others, the abdication of
the critic will contribute nothing towards giving the world the benefit, so
desirable, of peace and unanimity. In default of a conflict between religions
and criticism, religions fight among themselves for the supremacy. If all
the religions were reduced to a single one, the different fractions of that
religion would each curse the other; and even supposing that all the sects
came to recognize a sort of catholicity, the internal dissensions — twenty
times more active and more hateful than those which separate religions
and rival Churches — would serve to supply the eternal need which individual thought has to create, according to its fancy, the divine world.
What are we to conclude from this? That in suppressing criticism we shall
not suppress the cause, but we shall suppress perhaps the only judge who
can clear up the difficulty. The right which each religion insists on as absolute truth is a perfectly respectable right, which no one ought to dream
of contesting; but it does not exclude a parallel right in other religions,
nor the right of the critic, who regards himself as outside the sects. The duty
of civil society is to maintain itself in the face of all these contradictory
rights, without seeking to reconcile them. That would be to attempt the
impossible, and, without permitting them to be absorbed, nullify, which
could not be done without detriment to the general interests of civilisation.
It is as well to remark, that in effect the critic, in exercising, with regard
to the history of religions, the right which belongs to him, does not encroach,
so that one might complain, I do not say only from the point of view as
to equality of rights (that is too clear, since religious controversialists daily
permit themselves to deliver against independent science attacks full of
violence), but even in making concessions as large as possible to propriety
and the majesty of established worship. Religion, at the same time that it
reaches in its height the pure heaven of the ideal, stands for its base upon

the unstable ground of human affairs, and participates in things which are fleeting and defective. Every work of which men furnish the matter being but a compromise between the opposing necessities which make up this transitory life, necessarily provides matter for the critic, and one has said nothing against an institution so much that one is limited to this inoffensive remark, that she has not completely escaped from the fragile nature which belongs to all structures here below. Religion must be of one manner and not of another: that condition, essential to all existence, implies a limit — something excluded, a defect. Art, which, like religion, aspires to render the infinite under finite forms, does it renounce its mission because it knows of no image to represent the ideal? Does it not disappear in the vague and the intangible, whenever it would be as boundless in its forms as it is in its conceptions?

Religion, in the same way, only exists on the condition of its being a decided opinion, a fixed idea, very clear, very finite, and consequently very much liable to criticism. The narrow and peculiar side of each religion, which constitutes its weakness, constitutes also its strength; for men are drawn together by their narrow thoughts rather than by their enlarged ideas. It would be a small matter to have shown that every religious form is enormously disproportionate to its divine object, if one did not hasten to add that it could not be otherwise, and that every symbol must appear insufficient and coarse when compared with the extreme delicacy of the truths which it represents. The glory of religion is precisely this: it provides a programme beyond human power for one to pursue the realisation with boldness, and to nobly make the attempt to give a determinate form to the infinite aspirations of the heart of man.

[...]

I protest once for all against the false interpretation which will be given to my works if the different essays upon the history of religions which I have published, or which I may in future publish, are taken as polemical works. Considered as polemical works, these essays (and I am the first to recognise the fact) are very unskillfully prepared. Polemics require a degree of strategy to which I am a stranger: one ought to know how to select the weak side of one's adversary; to keep there, and never to touch upon any uncertain question; to keep every concession — that is to say, to renounce that which constitutes the very essence of the scientific spirit. Such is not my method. The fundamental question upon which religious discussion ought to turn — that is to say, the question of the fact of revelation and of the supernatural — I never touch; not but that these questions may not be solved for me with complete certainty, but because the discussion of such questions is not scientific, or rather because independent science supposes them to have been previously settled. Certainly if I should pursue an end, whether of

polemics or of proselytism, this would be a leading fault: it would be to bring upon the ground of delicate and obscure problems a question to be dealt with on much more evidence in the common terms which controversialists and apologists usually lay down. Far from regretting these advantages which I have given as against myself, I rejoice at it, if it will convince theologians that my writings are of another order to theirs; that they are the pure researches of erudition, assailable, as such, where one endeavours to apply those principles of criticism, equally to the Jewish religion as to the Christian, which one observes in the other branches of history and philology. As to the discussion of questions properly theological, I never enter upon it any more than MM. Burnouf, Creuzer, Guigniaut, and other critical historians of the religions of antiquity, who do not consider themselves obliged to undertake the refutation or the apology of the worships on which they employ themselves. The history of humanity is to me a vast entirety, where everything is unequal and diverse, but where all is of the same order, arises out of the same causes, and obeys the same laws. These laws I search out with no other intention than to discover the exact shade or degree of that which is. Nothing will make me exchange a part so obscure, but productive to science, for the part of controversialist — an easy part in this, that it gains for the writer an assured favour from those who believe in the duty of opposing war to war. This polemic, of which I am far from disputing the necessity, but which is neither to my taste nor my ability, satisfied Voltaire. One cannot be at the same time a good controversialist and a good historian.
     [...]
The regrettable but necessary difference of opinion which will always exist upon the history of a religion between the partisans of that religion and disinterested science, ought not, then, to give occasion to accuse science of anti-religious proselytism. That if in a moment of passing impulse, a man devoted to critical research evinces something of the desire of St. Paul *Cupio omnes fieri qualis et ego sum*, there is a sentiment which effaces itself before a truer judgment of the limits and common range of the human spirit. Each person makes of religion a shelter to his measure and according to his needs. To dare to place hands upon this particular work of the faculties of each person is dangerous and rash, for no one has a right to penetrate deep enough into the conscience of another to distinguish the accessory from the principal. In seeking to extirpate beliefs which may be thought superfluous, one risks the injury of the organs essential to religious life and morality. Propagandism is out of its element when it undertakes high scientific culture or philosophy, and the most excellent intellectual discipline imposed upon persons who have not been prepared for it, cannot but have an evil effect. The duty of the learned man, then, is to express with frankness the result of his study, without seeking to trouble the conscience of

persons who have not been called to the same life as himself, but also without regarding the interested motives and pretended proprieties which so often assume the expression of truth.

[. . .]

We may understand now what distance separates the controversialist, who aspires to change existing religious forms, from the learned man who only proposes a speculative end, without any direct reference to the order of contemporaneous facts. Strangers to the causes which produce these abrupt varieties of opinion, which belong rightfully to the circle of men of the world, but which ought not to extend beyond the learned, they are not obliged to perform acts of faith according to the caprices of fashion, nor condemn themselves to silence because they have not brought their studies to bear upon ideas which such parties think most suitable to their views at the time. The government of affairs here below belongs, in fact, to other forces than science and reason; the thinker believes himself to have but a small right to the direction of affairs in his planet, and, satisfied with the share allotted to him, he accepts his impotence without regret. A spectator in the universe, he knows that the world only belongs to him as a subject of study, and that the part of reformer requires almost always in those who undertake it, defects and qualities which he does not possess.

Let us keep, then, each of the elements in their place, though often contradictory, yet without which the development of humanity remains incomplete. Let us leave the religions to proclaim themselves unassailable, since without that they will not obtain from their adherents the respect of which they are in need; but do not let us compel science to pass under the censure of a power which has nothing scientific about it. Do not let us confound legend with history; but let us not endeavour to get rid of legend, since that is the form in which the faith of humanity is necessarily clothed. Humanity is not composed of the learned and the philologist. She deceives herself frequently, or, we should rather say, she deceives herself of necessity, upon questions of facts and persons: she often renders homage and bestows sympathy in the wrong place; more often still she exaggerates the position of individuals, and heaps on the heads of her favourites, merits which belong to the entire generation; but to see the truth of all this, one ought to have a delicacy of mind and a knowledge which is utterly wanting in her. But she does not deceive herself on the particular object of her worship: that which she adores is really adorable; for what she adores in characters, what she has idealised, are the goodness and beauty she has put there. It may be affirmed that if a new religious phenomenon were to appear, the myth would find its place in the timid disposition which characterises our age of reflection. Whatever care may be taken at first to repress everything which emanates from the purest rationalism, the second generation would doubtless be less puritanical than the first, and the third less still. Thus we should introduce successive complications where the great imaginative instincts of humanity would give themselves full scope, and then the critic would find, again at the end of several ages, that he would have to undertake his work of analysis and research.

Persons more influenced towards sentiment than towards science, and more richly endowed for action than for thought, understand with difficulty (I know it) the opportunity of like researches, and receive them generally with displeasure. This is a respectable sentiment, which we ought to be slow to blame. To those who entertain it I would venture to advise not to read works composed from the point of view of the modern critic; these writings can only provoke, as far as they are concerned, disagreeable feelings, and even the trouble that they feel in reading them proves that such reading is not good for them.

[...]

I had at first resolved to answer here the recent criticisms which, by distortions of fact, mixed with strange reasoning, rather than by their own value, seemed to require rectification. But the attack regulates the defence, and it would have been difficult for me to answer sophism and subtlety without being myself somewhat fastidious and subtle. The silence which I have kept until now, which has enabled my adversaries to triumph as for a victory, I desire still to keep. However, I am ready to receive with gratitude; to discuss, and adopt, if need be, any observations truly scientific which may be addressed to me. Moreover, I shall be firm in resisting the declamations of the sectarian spirit, and avoiding at any price those pitiable debates which too often make learning ridiculous in substituting personal questions for pure researches after truth. If it be thought that by injuries, by falsified citations, anonymous denials which none dare avow, equivocations skilfully calculated to delude people unacquainted with science, I shall be hindered in the object of research and reflection on which I am engaged, they deceive themselves. These researches have always had for me a supreme interest; they will remain, under a form more and more enlarged the principal object of my curiosity. If I was, like many others, the slave of my desire, of self-interest or vanity guided me in the conduct of my works, they would by such means doubtless succeed in making me abandon my studies, which are generally recompensed by injury. But desiring nothing, if this is not to do good, not demanding for study other reward than itself, I venture to affirm that no human motive has the power to make me say one word more or less than I have resolved to say. The liberty of which I have need, being that of science, it ought not to be wanting; if the seventeenth century had its Holland, it is difficult that, in the diminution of souls of our day, we cannot find a corner of the world where we can think at our ease. Nothing, consequently, will make me deviate from the plan I have laid down, and which seems to me to be the line of duty: inflexible research after truth, according to the measure of my strength, by all the means of legitimate investigation which are at the disposal of the human mind; firm and frank expression of the results which seem to me probable or certain, without any after-thought of application and all expedient formulas; open to the correction which the criticism of competent persons or the progress of science may bring to bear upon me. The attacks of ignorance as well as fanaticism afflict me, without moving me when I think they are sincere. In the case where I cannot consider them as such, I hope to arrive by familiarity to the time when they will not even trouble me.

N. D. Fustel de Coulanges

Numa Denis Fustel de Coulanges was born in 1830 in Paris, where he received his primary and secondary school education. From 1850 until 1853 he was a student at the *Ecole Normale Supérieure* in Paris, from 1853 until 1855 he worked as an archeologist and historian at the *Ecole Française* in Athens. He then carried out excavations on the island of Chios. In 1857 he passed the *agrégation* examination, and in 1858 he received his doctorate with a dissertation on 'Polyby or Greece conquered by the Romans'. He was a historian, first of all interested in classical antiquity. In 1860 Fustel de Coulanges became professor of history at the University of Strasbourg. He left this city in 1870 and became *maître de conférences* of history at the *Ecole Normale Supérieure* (1870—1875). From 1875 until 1878 he was *professeur suppléant*, and from 1875 until 1879 full professor of history at the Sorbonne. After having been director of the *Ecole Normale Supérieure* from 1880 until 1883, Fustel de Coulanges resumed his professorship at the Sorbonne from 1884 until 1888. He died at Massy in 1889.

Of particular interest for the study of religion is a book published in French in 1864, which appeared in English translation in 1873 as *The Ancient City: a Study on the Religion, Laws and Institutions of Greece and Rome*. In his later publications he deals more with French history.

As a classical historian Fustel de Coulanges recognized the importance of religion in ancient Greek and Roman civilization. He tried then to find the roots of the prevailing religious customs and ideas and to assess their function in society. He contended that major changes in Greek and Roman cultural history were mainly due to changes in religious beliefs.

The following text is the Introduction to *The Ancient City*, in which he states the purpose and method of his research.

'THE NECESSITY OF STUDYING THE EARLIEST BELIEFS OF
THE ANCIENTS IN ORDER TO UNDERSTAND THEIR INSTITUTIONS'

It is proposed here to show upon what principles and by what rules Greek and Roman society was governed. We unite in the same study both the Greeks and the Romans, because these two peoples, who were two branches of a single race, and who spoke two idioms of a single language, also had the same institutions and the same principles of government, and passed through a series of similar revolutions.

We shall attempt to set in a clear light the radical and essential differences which at all times distinguished these ancient peoples from modern societies.

In our system of education, we live from infancy in the midst of the Greeks and Romans, and become accustomed continually to compare them with ourselves, to judge of their history by our own, and to explain our revolutions by theirs. What we have received from them leads us to believe that we resemble them. We have some difficulty in considering them as foreign nations; it is almost always ourselves that we see in them. Hence spring many errors. We rarely fail to deceive ourselves regarding these ancient nations when we see them through the opinions and facts of our own time.

Now, errors of this kind are not without danger. The ideas which the moderns have had of Greece and Rome have often been in their way. Having imperfectly observed the institutions of the ancient city, men have dreamed of reviving them among us. They have deceived themselves about the liberty of the ancients, and on this very account liberty among the moderns has been put in peril. The last eighty years have clearly shown that one of the great difficulties which impede the march of modern society is the habit which it has of always keeping Greek and Roman antiquity before its eyes.

To understand the truth about the Greeks and Romans, it is wise to study them without thinking of ourselves, as if they were entirely foreign to us; with the same disinterestedness, and with the mind as free, as if we were studying ancient India or Arabia.

Thus observed, Greece and Rome appear to us in a character absolutely inimitable; nothing in modern times resembles them; nothing in the future can resemble them. We shall attempt to show by what rules these societies were regulated, and it will be freely admitted that the same rules can never govern humanity again.

Whence comes this? Why are the conditions of human government no longer the same as in earlier times? The great changes which appear from time to time in the constitution of society can be the effect neither of chance nor of force alone.

The cause which produces them must be powerful, and must be found in man himself. If the laws of human association are no longer the same as in antiquity, it is because there has been a change in man. There is, in fact, a part of our being which is modified from age to age; this is our intelligence. It is always in movement; almost always progressing; and on this account, our institutions and our laws are subject to change. Man has not, in our day, the way of thinking that he had twenty-five centuries ago; and this is why he is no longer governed as he was governed then.

The history of Greece and Rome is a witness and an example of the intimate relation which always exists between men's ideas and their social state. Examine the institutions of the ancients without thinking of their religious notions, and you find them obscure, whimsical, and inexplicable.

Why were there patricians and plebeians, patrons and clients, eupatrids
and thetes; and whence came the native and ineffaceable differences which
we find between these classes? What was the meaning of those Lacedae-
monian institutions which appear to us so contrary to nature? How are
we to explain those unjust caprices of ancient private law; at Corinth and
at Thebes, the sale of land prohibited; at Athens and at Rome, an inequality
in the succession between brother and sister? What did the jurists understand by *agnation*, and by *gens*? Why those revolutions in the laws, those
political revolutions? What was that singular patriotism which sometimes
effaced every natural sentiment? What did they understand by that liberty
of which they were always talking? How did it happen that institutions
so very different from anything of which we have an idea to-day, could
become established and reign for so long a time? What is the superior
principle which gave them authority over the minds of men?

But by the side of these institutions and laws place the religious ideas
of those times, and the facts at once become clear, and their explanation
is no longer doubtful. If, on going back to the first ages of this race – that
is to say, to the time when its institutions were founded – we observe the
idea which it had of human existence, of life, of death, of a second life, oᵗ
the divine principle, we perceive a close relation between these opinions
and the ancient rules of private law; between the rites which spring from
these opinions and their political institutions.

A comparison of beliefs and laws shows that a primitive religion constituted the Greek and Roman family, established marriage and paternal
authority, fixed the order of relationship, and consecrated the right of
property, and the right of inheritance. This same religion, after having
enlarged and extended the family, formed a still larger association, the city,
and reigned in that as it had reigned in the family. From it came all the
institutions, as well as all the private law, of the ancients. It was from this
that the city received all its principles, its rules, its usages, and its magistracies. But, in the course of time, this ancient religion became modified or
effaced, and private law and political institutions were modified with it.
Then came a series of revolutions, and social changes regularly followed
the development of knowledge.

It is of the first importance, therefore, to study the religious ideas of
these peoples, and the oldest are the most important for us to know. For
the institutions and beliefs which we find at the flourishing periods of Greece
and Rome are only the development of those of an earlier age; we must
seek the roots of them in the very distant past. The Greek and Italian
populations are many centuries older than Romulus and Homer. It was at
an epoch more ancient, in an antiquity without date, that their beliefs were
formed, and that their institutions were either established or prepared.

But what hope is there of arriving at a knowledge of this distant past? Who can tell us what men thought ten or fifteen centuries before our era? Can we recover what is so intangible and fugitive — beliefs and opinions? We know what the Aryas of the East thought thirty-five centuries ago: we learn this from the hymns of the Vedas, which are certainly very ancient, and from the laws of Manu, in which we can distinguish passages that are of an extemely early date. But where are the hymns of the ancient Hellenes? They, as well as the Italians, had ancient hymns, and old sacred books; but nothing of these has come down to us. What tradition can remain to us of those generations that have not left us a single written line?

Fortunately, the past never completely dies for man. Man may forget it, but he always preserves it within him. For, take him at any epoch, and he is the product, the epitome, of all the earlier epochs. Let him look into his own soul, and he can find and distinguish these different epochs by what each of them has left within him.

Let us observe the Greeks of the age of Pericles, and the Romans of Cicero's time; they carry within them the authentic marks and the unmistakable vestiges of the most remote ages. The contemporary of Cicero (I speak especially of the man of the people) has an imagination full of legends; these legends come to him from a very early time, and they bear witness to the manner of thinking of that time. The contemporary of Cicero speaks a language whose roots are very ancient; this language, in expressing the thoughts of ancient ages, has been modelled upon them, and it has kept the impression, and transmits it from century to century. The primary sense of a root will sometimes reveal an ancient opinion or an ancient usage; ideas have been transformed, and the recollections of them have vanished; but the words have remained, immutable witnesses of beliefs that have disappeared.

The contemporary of Cicero practised rites in the sacrifices, at funerals, and in the ceremony of marriage; these rites were older than his time, and what proves it is that they did not correspond to his religious belief. But if we examine the rites which he observed, or the formulas which he recited, we find the marks of what men believed fifteen or twenty centuries earlier.

Julius Wellhausen

Julius Wellhausen was born in 1844 in Hameln, Germany, and received his primary and secondary school education there and in 1859 in Hannover. In 1862 he enrolled in the University of Göttingen, in the Faculty of Theology. He did his Old Testament studies with H. Ewald and obtained his degree in 1865. Between 1865 and 1867 he was a house teacher at Hannover, and from 1867 until 1870 he pursued his studies at Göttingen, again with H. Ewald, concentrating on oriental languages. In 1870 he obtained his *Lizenziat* with a dissertation on the names figuring in I Chronicles 2:4. In the same year he passed his *Habilitation* and became *Privatdozent* for Old Testament at the University of Göttingen. In 1872 Wellhausen became full professor of Old Testament in the Faculty of Theology at the University of Greifswald. In 1882, at his request, he was transferred and became *Extraordinarius* for Semitic Languages in the Faculty of Philosophy at the University of Halle. Subsequently Wellhausen became professor for the Old Testament at the University of Marburg in 1885, and in 1892 the same at the University of Göttingen. He died at Göttingen in 1918.

Of the many publications of Wellhausen the following have been translated into English and should be mentioned here: 1881 article 'Israel' in the *Encyclopaedia Britannica*, 9th edition (later published as a separate volume: *Sketch of the History of Israel and Judah*); 1885 *Prolegomena to the History of Israel, with a reprint of the article 'Israel' from the 'Encyclopaedia Britannica'*; 1927 *The Arab Kingdom and its Fall*.

Wellhausen devoted himself to historical critical scholarship in various fields. In his Old Testament studies he analyzed the Pentateuch and the historical books, making them available as sources for the writing of a history of ancient Israel. In his New Testament studies he analyzed the gospels and ascertained the historical development of their writing. In his Arabic studies he analyzed existing historical texts with regard to the early history of Islam, and was able to reconstruct the political and religious history of its first two centuries. Throughout his work Wellhausen made an attempt to reconstruct historical developments through a rigorous literary and historical analysis and criticism of the available literary sources.

The following fragment is the Introduction of the *Prolegomena to the History of Ancient Israel*. The author explains the way in which the Torah presents a historical problem and the procedure which he follows in order to come to a historical dating of the first five books of the Bible.

HISTORICAL RESEARCH ON THE PENTATEUCH

In the following pages it is proposed to discuss the place in history of the 'law of Moses'; more precisely, the question to be considered is whether that law is the starting-point for the history of ancient Israel, or not rather for that of Judaism, *i.e.*, of the religious communion which survived the destruction of the nation by the Assyrians and Chaldaeans.

I. It is an opinion very extensively held that the great mass of the books of the Old Testament not only relate to the pre-exilic period, but date from it. According to this view, they are remnants of the literature of ancient Israel which the Jews rescued as a heritage from the past, and on which they continued to subsist in the decay of independent intellectual life. In dogmatic theology Judaism is a mere empty chasm over which one springs from the Old Testament to the New; and even where this estimate is modified, the belief still prevails in a general way that the Judaism which received the books of Scripture into the canon had, as a rule, nothing to do with their production. But the exceptions to this principle which are conceded as regards the second and third divisions of the Hebrew canon cannot be called so very slight. Of the Hagiographa, by far the larger portion is demonstrably post-exilic, and no part demonstrably older than the exile. Daniel comes as far down as the Maccabaean wars, and Esther is perhaps even later. Of the prophetical literature a very appreciable fraction is later than the fall of the Hebrew kingdom; and the associated historical books (the 'earlier prophets' of the Hebrew canon) date, in the form in which we now possess them, from a period subsequent to the death of Jeconiah, who must have survived the year 560 B. C. for some time. Making all allowance for the older sources utilised, and to a large extent transcribed word for word, in Judges, Samuel, and Kings, we find that apart from the Pentateuch the pre-exilic portion of the Old Testament amounts in bulk to little more than the half of the entire volume. All the rest belongs to the later period, and it includes not merely the feeble after-growths of a failing vegetation, but also productions of the vigour and originality of Isa. 40–66 and Ps. 73.

We come then to the Law. Here, as for most parts of the Old Testament, we have no express information as to the author and date of composition, and to get even approximately at the truth we are shut up to the use of such data as can be derived from an analysis of the contents, taken in con unction with what we may happen to know from other sources as to the course of Israel's history. But the habit has been to assume that the historical period to be considered in this connection ends with the Babylonian exile as certainly as it begins with the exodus from Egypt. At first sight this assumption seems to be justified by the history of the canon; it was the Law that first became canonical through the influence of Ezra and Nehemiah; the Prophets became so considerably later, and the Hagiographa last of all. Now it is not unnatural, from the chronological order in which these writings were received into the canon, to proceed to an inference as to their approximate relative age, and so not only to place the Prophets before the Hagiographa, but also the five books of Moses before the Prophets. If the Prophets are for the most part older than the exile, how much more so the Law ! But however trustworthy such a mode of comparison may be when applied to the middle as contrasted with the latest portion of the canon, it is not at all to be relied on when the first part is contrasted with the other two. The very idea of canonicity was originally associated with the Torah, and was only afterwards extended to the other books, which slowly and by a gradual process acquired a certain measure of the validity given to the Torah by a single public and formal act, through which it was introduced at once as the Magna Charta of the Jewish communion (Neh. 8 – 10). In their case the canonical – that is, legal – character was not intrinsic, but was only subsequently acquired; there must therefore have been some interval, and there may have been a very long one, between the date of their origin and that of their receiving public sanction. To the Law, on the other hand, the canonical character is much more essential, and serious difficulties beset the assumption that the Law of Moses came into existence at a period long before the exile, and did not attain the force of law until many centuries afterwards, and in totally different circumstances from those under which it had arisen. At least the fact that a collection claiming public recognition as an ecclesiastical book should have attained such recognition earlier than other writings which make no such claim is no proof of superior antiquity.

We cannot, then, peremptorily refuse to regard it as possible that what was the law of Judaism may also have been its product; and there are urgent reasons for taking the suggestion into very careful consideration. It may not be out of place here to refer to personal experience. In my early student days I was attracted by the stories of Saul and David, Ahab and Elijah; the discourses of Amos and Isaiah laid strong hold on me, and I read myself well into the prophetic and historical books of the Old Testament. Thanks to such aids as were accessible to me, I even considered that I understood them tolerably, but at the same time was troubled with a bad conscience, as if I were beginning with the roof instead of the foundation; for I had no thorough acquaintance with the Law, of which I was accustomed to be told that it was the basis and postulate of the whole literature. At last I took courage and made my way through Exodus, Leviticus, Numbers, and even through Knobel's *Commentary* to these books. But it was in vain that I looked for the light which was to be shed from this source on the historical and prophetical books. On the contrary, my enjoyment of the latter was marred by the Law; it did not bring them any nearer me, but intruded itself uneasily, like a ghost that makes a noise indeed, but is not visible and really effects nothing. Even where there were points of contact between it and them differences also made themselves felt, and I found it impossible to give a candid decision in favour of the priority of the Law. Dimly I began to perceive that throughout there was between them all the difference that separates two wholly distinct worlds. Yet, so far from attaining clear conceptions, I only fell into deeper confusion, which was worse confounded by the explanations of Ewald in the second volume of his *History of Israel*. At last, in the course of a casual visit in Göttingen in the summer of 1867, I learned through Ritschl that Karl Heinrich Graf placed the Law later than the Prophets, and, almost without knowing his reasons for the hypothesis, I was prepared to accept it; I readily acknowledged to myself the possibility of understanding Hebrew antiquity without the book of the Torah.

The hypothesis usually associated with Graf's name is really not his, but that of his teacher, Eduard Reuss. It would be still more correct to call it after Leopold George and Wilhelm Vatke, who, independent alike of Reuss and of each other, were the first to give it literary currency. All three, again, are disciples of Martin Lebrecht de Wette, the epoch-making pioneer of historical criticism in this field.[1] He indeed did not himself succeed in reaching a sure position, but he was the first clearly to perceive and point out how disconnected are the alleged starting-point of Israel's history and that history itself. The religious community set up on so broad a basis in the wilderness, with its sacred centre and uniform organisation, disappears and leaves no trace as soon as Israel settles in a land of its own, and becomes, in any proper sense, a nation. The period of the Judges presents itself to us as a confused chaos, out of which order and coherence are gradually evolved under the pressure of external circumstances, but perfectly naturally and without the faintest reminiscence of a sacred unifying constitution that had formerly existed. Hebrew antiquity shows absolutely no tendencies towards a hierocracy; power is wielded solely by the heads of families and of tribes, and by the kings, who exercise control over religious worship also, and appoint and depose its priests. The influence possessed by the latter is purely moral; the Torah of God is not a document in their hands which guarantees their own position, but merely an instruction for others in their mouths; like the word of the prophets, it has divine authority but not political sanction, and has validity only in so far as it is voluntarily accepted. And as for the literature which has come down to us from the period of the Kings, it would puzzle the very best intentions to beat up so many as two or three unambiguous allusions to the Law, and these cannot be held to prove anything when one considers, by way of contrast, what Homer was to the Greeks.

To complete the marvel, in post-exile Judaism the Mosaism which until then had been only latent suddenly emerges into prominence everywhere. We now find the Book regarded as the foundation of all higher life, and the Jews, to borrow the phrase of the Koran, are 'the people of the Book;' we have the sanctuary with its priests and Levites occupying the central position, and the people as a congregation encamped around it; the cultus, with its burnt-offerings and sin-offerings, its purifications and its abstinences, its feasts and Sabbaths, strictly observed as prescribed by the Law, is now the principal business of life. When we take the community of the second temple and compare it with the ancient people of Israel, we are at once able to realise how far removed was the latter from so-called Mosaism. The Jews themselves were thoroughly conscious of the distance. The revision of the Books of Judges, Samuel, and Kings, undertaken towards the end of the Babylonian exile, a revision much more thorough than is commonly assumed, condemns as heretical the whole age of the Kings. At a later date, as the past became more and more invested with a certain nimbus of sanctity, men preferred to clothe it with the characters of legitimacy rather than sit in judgment upon it. The Book of Chronicles shows in what manner it was necessary to deal with the history of bygone times when it was assumed that the Mosaic hierocracy was their fundamental institution.

II. The foregoing remarks are designed merely to make it plain that the problem we have set before us is not an imaginary one, but actual and urgent. They are intended to introduce it; but to solve it is by no means so easy. The question what is the historical place of the Law does not even admit of being put in these simple terms. For the Law, if by that word we understand the entire Pentateuch, is no literary unity, and no simple historical quantity.[2] Since the days of Peyrerius and Spinoza, criticism has acknowledged the complex character of that remarkable literary production, and from Jean Astruc onwards has laboured, not without success, at disentangling its original elements. At present there are a number of results that can be regarded as settled. The following are some of them. The five Books of Moses and the Book of Joshua constitute one whole, the conquest of the Promised Land rather than the death of Moses forming the true conclusion of the patriarchal history, the exodus, and the wandering in the wilderness. From a literary point of view, accordingly, it is more accurate to speak of the Hexateuch than of the Pentateuch. Out of this whole, the Book of Deuteronomy, as essentially an independent law-book, admits of being separated most easily. Of what remains, the parts most easily distinguished belong to the so-called 'main stock' *(Grundschrift)*, formerly also called the Elohistic document, on account of the use it makes of the divine name *Elohim* up to the time of Moses, and designated by Ewald, with reference to the regularly recurring superscriptions in Genesis, as the Book of Origins. It is distinguished by its liking for number, and measure, and formula generally, by its stiff pedantic style, by its constant use of certain phrases and turns of expression which do not occur elsewhere in the older Hebrew; its characteristics are more strongly marked than those of any of the others, and make it accordingly the easiest to recognise with certainty. Its basis is the Book of Leviticus and the allied portions of the adjoining books, – Exod. 25–40 with the exception of chaps. 32–34 and Num. 1–10; 15–19; 25–36, with trifling exceptions. It thus contains legislation chiefly, and, in point of fact, relates substantially to the worship of the tabernacle and cognate matters. It is historical only in form; the history serves merely as a framework on which to arrange the legislative material, or as a mask to disguise it. For the most part, the thread of the narrative is extremely thin, and often serves merely to carry out the chronology, which is kept up without a hiatus from the Creation to the Exodus; it becomes fuller only on the occasions in which other interests come into play, as, for example, in Genesis, with regard to the three preludes to the Mosaic covenant which are connected with the names of Adam, Noah, and Abraham respectively. When this fundamental document is also separated out as well as Deuteronomy, there remains the Jehovistic history-book, which, in contrast with the two others, is essentially of a narrative character, and sets forth with full sympathy and enjoyment the materials handed down by tradition. The story of the patriarchs, which belongs to this document almost entirely, is what best marks its character; that story is not here dealt with merely as a summary introduction to something of greater importance which is to follow, but as a subject of primary importance, deserving the fullest treatment possible. Legislative elements have been taken into it only at one point, where they fit into the historical connection, namely, when the giving of the Law at Sinai is spoken of (Exod. 20–23; 34).

Scholars long rested satisfied with this twofold division of the non-Deuteronomic Hexateuch, until Hupfeld demonstrated in certain parts of Genesis, which until then had been assigned partly to the 'main stock' and partly to the Jehovist, the existence of a third continuous source, the work of the so-called younger Elohist. The choice of this name was due to the circumstance that in this document also Elohim is the ordinary name of the Deity, as it is in the 'main stock' up to Exod. 6; the epithet 'younger', however, is better left out, as it involves an unproved assumption, and besides, is no longer required for distinction's sake, now that the 'main stock' is no longer referred to under so unsuitable a name as that of Elohist. Hupfeld further assumed that all the three sources continued to exist

separately until some one at a later date brought them together simultaneously into a single whole. But this is a view that cannot be maintained:
not merely is the Elohist in his matter and in his manner of looking at
things most closely akin to the Jehovist; his document has come down to us,
as Nöldeke was the first to perceive, only in extracts embodied in the Jehovist
narrative.[3] Thus, notwithstanding Hupfeld's discovery, the old division
into two great sections continues to hold good, and there is every reason
for adhering to this primary distinction as the basis of further historical
research, in spite of the fact, which is coming to be more and more clearly
perceived, that not only the Jehovistic document, but the 'main stock' as
well, are complex products, and that alongside of them occur hybrid or
posthumous elements which do not admit of being simply referred to either
the one or the other formation.[4]

Now the Law, whose historical position we have to determine, is the so-
called 'main stock', which, both by its contents and by its origin, is entitled
to be called the Priestly Code, and will accordingly be so designated. The
Priestly Code preponderates over the rest of the legislation in force, as well
as in bulk; in all matters of primary importance it is the normal and final
authority. It was according to the model furnished by it that the Jews
under Ezra ordered their sacred community, and upon it are formed our
conceptions of the Mosaic theocracy, with the tabernacle at its centre,
the high priest at its head, the priests and Levites as its organs, the legitimate cultus as its regular function. It is precisely this Law, so called *par
excellence*, that creates the difficulties out of which our problem rises, and
it is only in connection with it that the great difference of opinion exists
as to date. With regard to the Jehovistic document, all are happily agreed
that, substantially at all events, in language, horizon, and other features,
it dates from the golden age of Hebrew literature, to which the finest parts
of Judges, Samuel, and Kings, and the oldest extant prophetical writings
also belong – the period of the kings and prophets which preceded the
dissolution of the two Israelite kingdoms by the Assyrians. About the
origin of Deuteronomy there is still less dispute; in all circles where appreciation of scientific results can be looked for at all, it is recognised that it was
composed in the same age as that in which it was discovered, and that it
was made the rule of Josiah's reformation, which took place about a generation before the destruction of Jerusalem by the Chaldaeans. It is only in
the case of the Priestly Code that opinions differ widely; for it tries hard to
imitate the costume of the Mosaic period, and, with whatever success, to
disguise its own. This is not nearly so much the case with Deuteronomy,
which, in fact, allows the real situation (that of the period during which,
Samaria having been destroyed, only the kingdom of Judah continued to
subsist) to reveal itself very plainly through that which is assumed (12 : 8,

19 : 8). And the Jehovist does not even pretend to being a Mosaic law of any kind; it aims at being a simple book of history; the distance between the present and the past spoken of is not concealed in the very least. It is here that all the remarks are found which attracted the attention of Aben-ezra and afterwards of Spinoza, such as Gen. 12 : 6 ('And the Canaanite was then in the land'), Gen. 36 : 31 ('These are the kings who reigned in Edom before the children of Israel had a king'), Num. 12 : 6, 7, Deut. 34 : 10 ('There arose not a prophet since in Israel like unto Moses'). The Priestly Code, on the other hand, guards itself against all reference to later times and settled life in Canaan, which both in the Jehovistic Book of the Covenant (Exod. 21—23) and in Deuteronomy are the express basis of the legislation: it keeps itself carefully and strictly within the limits of the situation in the wilderness, for which in all seriousness it seeks to give the law. It has actually been successful, with its movable tabernacle, its wandering camp, and other archaic details, in so concealing the true date of its composition that its many serious inconsistencies with what we know, from other sources, of Hebrew antiquity previous to the exile, are only taken as proving that it lies far beyond all known history, and on account of its enormous antiquity can hardly be brought into any connection with it. It is the Priestly Code, then, that presents us with our problem.

III. The instinct was a sound one which led criticism for the time being to turn aside from the historical problem which had originally presented itself to De Wette, and afterwards had been more distinctly apprehended by George and Vatke, in order, in the first instance, to come to some sort of clear understanding as to the composition of the Pentateuch. But a mistake was committed when it was supposed that by a separation of the sources (in which operation attention was quite properly directed chiefly to Genesis) that great historical question had been incidentally answered. The fact was, that it had been merely put to sleep, and Graf has the credit of having, after a considerable interval, awakened it again. In doing so, indeed, he in turn laboured under the disadvantage of not knowing what success had been achieved in separating the sources, and thereby he became involved in a desperate and utterly untenable assumption. This assumption, however, had no necessary connection with his own hypothesis, and at once fell to the ground when the level to which Hupfeld brought the criticism of the text had been reached. Graf originally followed the older view, espoused by Tuch in particular, that in Genesis the Priestly Code, with its so obtrusively bare skeleton, is the 'main stock', and that it is the Jehovist who supplements, and is therefore of course the later. But since, on the other hand, he regarded the ritual legislature of the middle books as much more recent than the work of the Jehovist, he was compelled to tear it asunder as best he could from its introduction in Genesis, and to separate the two halves of the Priestly Code by half a millennium. But Hupfeld had long before made it quite clear that the Jehovist is no mere supplementer, but the author of a perfectly independent work, and that the passages, such as Gen. 20—22, usually cited as examples of the way in which the Jehovist worked over the 'main stock', really proceed from quite another source, – the Elohist. Thus the stumbling-block of Graf had already been taken out of the way, and his path had been made clear by an unlooked-for ally. Following Kuenen's suggestion, he did not hesitate to take the helping-hand extended to him; he gave up his violent division of the Priestly Code, and then had no difficulty in deducing from the results which he had obtained with respect to the main legal portion similar consequences with regard to the narrative part in Genesis.[5]

The foundations were now laid; it is Kuenen who has since done most for the further development of the hypothesis.[6] The defenders of the prevailing opinion maintained their ground as well as they could, but from long possession had got somewhat settled on their lees. They raised against the assailants a series of objections, all of which, however, laboured more or less under the disadvantage that they rested upon the foundation which had already been shattered. Passages were quoted from Amos and Hosea as implying an acquaintance with the Priestly Code, but they were not such as could make any impression on those who were already persuaded that the latter was the more recent. Again it was asserted, and almost with violence, that the Priestly Code could not be later than Deuteronomy, and that the Deuteronomist actually had it before him. But the evidences of this proved extremely problematical, while, on the other hand, the dependence of Deuteronomy, as a whole, on the Jehovist came out with the utmost clearness. Appeal was made to the latest redaction of the entire Hexateuch, a redaction which was assumed to be Deuteronomistic; but this yielded the result that the Deuteronomistic redaction could nowhere be traced in any of the parts belonging to the Priestly Code. Even the history of the language itself was forced to render service against Graf: it had already been too much the custom to deal with that as if it were soft wax. To say all in a word, the arguments which were brought into play as a rule derived all their force from a moral conviction that the ritual legislation *must* be old, and *could* not possibly have been committed to writing for the first time within the period of Judaism; that it was not operative before then, that it did not even admit of being carried into effect in the conditions that prevailed previous to the exile, could not shake the conviction – all the firmer because it did not rest on arguments – that at least it existed previously.

The firemen never came near the spot where the conflagration raged; for it is only within the region of religious antiquities and dominant religious ideas, – the region which Vatke in his *Biblische Theologie* had occupied in its full breadth, and where the real battle first kindled – that the contro- versy can be brought to a definite issue. In making the following attempt in this direction, I start from the comparison of the three constituents of the Pentateuch, – the Priestly Code, Deuteronomy, and the work of the Jehovist. The contents of the first two are, of course, legislation, as we have seen; those of the third are narrative; but, as the Decalogue (Exod. 20), the Law of the Two Tables (Exod. 34), and the Book of the Covenant (Exod. 21–23) show, the legislative element is not wholly absent from the Jehovist, and much less is the historical absent from the Priestly Code or Deuteronomy. Further, each writer's legal standpoint is mirrored in his account of the history, and conversely; thus there is no lack either of indirect or of direct points of comparison. Now it is admitted that the three constituent elements are separated from each other by wide intervals; the question then arises, In what order? Deuteronomy stands in a relation of comparative nearness both to the Jehovist and to the Priestly Code; the distance between the last two is by far the greatest, – so great that on this ground alone Ewald as early as the year 1831 *(Studien und Kritiken* p. 604) declared it impossible that the one could have been written to supplement the other. Combining this observation with the undisputed priority of the Jehovist over Deuteronomy, it will follow that the Priestly Code stands last in the series. But such a consideration, although, so far as I know, proceeding upon admitted data, has no value as long as it confines itself to such mere generalities. It is necessary to trace the succession of the three elements in detail, and at once to test and to fix each by reference to an independent standard, namely, the inner development of the history of Israel so far as that is known to us by trustworthy testimonies, from inde- pendent sources.

The literary and historical investigation on which we thus enter is both wide and difficult. It falls into three parts. In the *first*, which lays the foundations, the data relating to sacred archaeology are brought together and arranged in such a way as to show that in the Pentateuch the elements follow upon one another and from one another precisely as the steps of the development demonstrably do in the history. Almost involuntarily this argument has taken the shape of a sort of history of the ordinances of worship. Rude and colourless that history must be confessed to be, – a fault due to the materials, which hardly allow us to do more than mark the contrast between pre-exilic and post-exilic, and, in a secondary measure, that between Deuteronomic and pre-Deuteronomic. At the same time there is this advantage arising out of the breadth of the periods treated: they cannot fail to distinguish themselves from each other in a tangible manner; it must be possible in the case of historical, and even of legal works, to recognise whether they were written before or after the exile. The *second* part, in many respects dependent on the first, traces the influence of the successively prevailing ideas and tendencies upon the shaping of historical tradition, and follows the various phases in which that was conceived and set forth. It contains, so to speak, a history of tradition. The *third* part sums up the critical results of the preceding two, with some further determining considerations, and concludes with a more general survey.

The assumptions I make will find an ever-recurring justification in the course of the investigation; the two principal are, that the work of the Jehovist, so far as the nucleus of it is concerned, belongs to the course of the Assyrian period, and that Deuteronomy belongs to its close. Moreover, however strongly I am convinced that the latter is to be dated in accordance with II Kings 22, I do not, like Graf, so use this position as to make it the fulcrum for my lever. Deuteronomy is the starting-point, not in the sense that without it it would be impossible to accomplish anything, but only because, when its position has been historically ascertained, we cannot decline to go on, but must demand that the position of the Priestly Code should also be fixed by reference to history. My inquiry proceeds on a broader basis than that of Graf, and comes nearer to that of Vatke, from whom indeed I gratefully acknowledge myself to have learnt best and most.

NOTES

1. M. W. L. de Wette, *Beiträge zur Einleitung in das A. T.* (Bd. I. *Kritischer Versuch über die Glaubwürdigkeit der Bücher der Chronik;* Bd. II. *Kritik der Mosaischen Geschichte*, Halle, 1806/7); J. F. L. George, *Die älteren Jüdischen Feste mit einer Kritik der Gesetzgebung des Pentateuch* (Berlin, 1835; Preface dated 12th October); W. Vatke, *Die biblische Theologie wissenschaftlich dargestellt* (Berlin, 1835; Preface dated 18th October; publication did not get beyond first part of the first volume); K. H. Graf, *Die geschichtlichen Bücher des Alten Testaments* (Leipsic, 1866). That Graf as well as J. Orth *(Nouv. Rev. de Théol.*, iii. 84 sqq., iv. 350 sqq., Paris, 1859/60) owed the impulse to his critical labours to his Strassburg master was not unknown; but how great must have been the share of Reuss in the hypothesis of Graf has only been revealed in 1879, by the publication of certain theses which he had formulated as early as 1833, but had hesitated to lay in print before the general theological public.

2. Compare the article 'Pentateuch' in the 9 th edition of the *Encylopaedia Britannica*, vol. xviii.

3. Hermann Hupfeld, *Die Quellen der Genesis und die Art ihrer Zusammensetzung*, Berlin, 1853; Theodor Nöldeke, *Die sogenannte Grundschrift des Pentateuch*, in *Untersuchungen zur Kritik des Alten Testaments*, Kiel, 1869.

4. J. Wellhausen, *Die Composition des Hexateuchs*, in *Jahrb. f. Deutsche Theologie*, 1876, p. 392—450, 531—602; 1877, p. 407—479. I do not insist on all the details, but, as regards the way in which the literary process which resulted in the formation of the Pentateuch is to be looked at in general, I believe I had indicated the proper line of investigation. Hitherto the only important correc-

tions I have received have been those of Kuenen in his *Contributions to the Criticism of the Pentateuch and Joshua,* published in the Leyden *Theologisch Tijdschrift;* but these are altogether welcome, inasmuch as they only free my own fundamental view from some relics of the old leaven of a mechanical separation of sources which had continued to adhere to it. For what Kuenen points out is, that certain elements assigned by me to the Elohist are not fragments of a once independent whole, but interpolated and parasitic additions. What effect this demonstration may have on the judgment we form of the Elohist himself is as yet uncertain. [. . .].

5. K. H. Graf, *Die sogenannte Grundschrift des Pentateuchs,* in Merx's *Archiv* (1869), p. 466—477. As early as 1866 he had already expressed himself in a letter to Kuenen (November 12) as follows: — 'Vous me faites pressentir une solution de cette énigme . . . c'est que les parties élohistiques de la Genèse seraient postérieures aux parties jéhovistiques.' [. . .].

6. A. Kuenen, *De Godsdienst van Israel,* Haarlem, 1869-70 (Eng. transl. *Religion of Israel,* 1874-5), and *De priesterlijke Bestanddeelen van Pentateuch en Josua* in *Theologisch Tijdschrift* (1870), p. 391-426.

William Robertson Smith

William Robertson Smith was born in 1846 at New Farm, Keig, Scotland, and received his primary and secondary school education completely from his father at the manse. He enrolled in Aberdeen University in 1861 and graduated with the B. A. degree in 1865. Having done some work on German and mathematics, he decided to study theology and in 1866 he entered New College, the theological hall of the Free Church in Edinburgh. He studied the Old Testament with A. B. Davidson. In Edinburgh he met and became befriended with J. F. MacLennan who worked on the problem of totemism. The summers of 1867 and 1869 he spent in Bonn and Göttingen respectively. In 1870 Robertson Smith was ordained a minister of the Free Church and appointed to the chair of Oriental Languages and Exegesis of the Old Testament in the Free Church College of Aberdeen. In view of his scholarly publications, he was accused of heresy in 1876 and had to cease his teaching activity in 1878. In 1880 he was permitted to take up his post again, but he was definitely fired in 1881. During these years Robertson Smith visited Europe and made extensive travels in North Africa, Egypt and Arabia. On his return he became editor of the ninth edition of the Encyclopaedia Britannica and lived in Edinburgh for some time. He then moved to Cambridge where he became a fellow of Trinity College, and in 1885 of Christ's College. In Cambridge Robertson Smith was successively Lord Almoner Reader of Arabic in 1883, University Librarian in 1886, and Professor of Arabic in 1889. He developed, among many other things, the project of the later Encyclopaedia of Islam. He died at Cambridge in 1894.

The following publications of Robertson Smith are to be mentioned here: 1875 art. 'Bible' for the *Encyclopaedia Britannica*, 9th edition, vol. III.; 1881 *The Old Testament in the Jewish Church. A Course of Lectures on Biblical Criticism;* 1882 *The Prophets of Israel and their Place in History to the Close of the Eighth Century B. C.;* 1885 *Kinship and Marriage in Early Arabia;* 1889 *Lectures on the Religion of the Semites.*

As an Old Testament scholar, Robertson Smith wanted to place the religion of the Hebrews within the context of the religious customs and views of the semitic nomads in general. He developed hereby a theory on totemism and on the nature of sacrifice among these people; he stressed the primacy of ritual over its interpretation and the equation of tribal with religious identity. In this way he developed from an Old Testament scholar to a student of religion in a wider context.

The following fragment has been taken from the *Lectures on the Religion of the Semites.* The author contends here that the religion in question should be studied as part of a social order

THE STUDY OF THE RELIGION OF THE SEMITES

'Preface'

[. . .] In Scotland, at least, no words need be wasted to prove that a right understanding of the religion of the Old Testament is the only way to a right understanding of the Christian faith; but it is not so fully recognised, except in the circle of professed scholars, that the doctrines and ordinances of the Old Testament cannot be thoroughly comprehended until they are put into comparison with the religions of the nations akin to the Israelites.
   [. . .]
In modern times Comparative Religion has become in some degree a popular subject, and in our own country has been treated from various points of view by men of eminence who have the ear of the public; but nothing considerable has been done since Spencer's time, either in England or on the Continent, whether in learned or in popular form, towards a systematic comparison of the religion of the Hebrews, as a whole, with the beliefs and ritual practices of the other Semitic peoples. In matters of detail valuable work has been done; but this work has been too special, and for the most part too technical, to help the circle to whom the Burnett Lectures are addressed; which I take to be a circle of cultivated and thinking men and women who have no special acquaintance with Semitic lore, but are interested in everything that throws light on their own religion, and are prepared to follow a sustained or even a severe argument, if the speaker on his part will remember that historical research can always be made intelligible to thinking people, when it is set forth with orderly method and in plain language.
   There is a particular reason why some attempt in this direction should be made now. The first conditions of an effective comparison of Hebrew religion, as a whole, with the religion of the other Semites, were lacking so long as the historical order of the Old Testament documents, and especially of the documents of which the Pentateuch is made up, was unascertained or wrongly apprehended; but, thanks to the labours of a series of scholars (of whom it is sufficient to name Kuenen and Wellhausen, as the men whose acumen and research have carried this inquiry to a point where nothing of vital importance for the historical study of the Old Testament religion still remains uncertain), the growth of the Old Testament religion can now be followed from stage to stage, in a way that is hardly possible with any other religion of antiquity. And so it is now not only possible, but most necessary for further progress, to make a fair comparison between Hebrew religion in its various stages and the religions of the races with which the Hebrews were cognate by natural descent, and with which also they were historically in constant touch. [. . .]

'The subject and the method of inquiry'

The subject before us is the religion of the Semitic peoples, that is, of the group of kindred nations, including the Arabs, the Hebrews and Phoenicians, the Aramaeans, the Babylonians and Assyrians, which in ancient times occupied the great Arabian Peninsula, with the more fertile lands of Syria, Mesopotamia and Irac, from the Mediterranean coast to the base of the mountains of Iran and Armenia. Among these peoples three of the great faiths of the world had their origin, so that the Semites must always have a peculiar interest for the student of the history of religion. Our subject, however, is not the history of the several religions that have a Semitic origin, but Semitic religion as a whole in its common features and general type. Judaism, Christianity and Islam are *positive* religions, that is, they did not grow up like the system of ancient heathenism, under the action of unconscious forces operating silently from age to age, but trace their origin to the teaching of great religious innovators, who spoke as the organs of a divine revelation, and deliberately departed from the traditions of the past. Behind these positive religions lies the old unconscious religious tradition, the body of religious usage and belief which cannot be traced to the influence of individual minds, and was not propagated on individual authority, but formed part of that inheritance from the past into which successive generations of the Semitic race grew up as it were instinctively, taking it as a matter of course that they should believe and act as their fathers had done before them. The positive Semitic religions had to establish themselves on ground already occupied by these older beliefs and usages; they had to displace what they could not assimilate, and whether they rejected or absorbed the elements of the older religion, they had at every point to reckon with them and take up a definite attitude towards them. No positive religion that has moved men has been able to start with a *tabula rasa*, and express itself as if religion were beginning for the first time; in form, if not in substance, the new system must be in contact all along the line with the older ideas and practices which it finds in possession. A new scheme of faith can find a hearing only by appealing to religious instincts and susceptibilities that already exist in its audience, and it cannot reach these without taking account of the traditional forms in which all religious feeling is embodied, and without speaking a language which men accustomed to these old forms can understand. Thus to comprehend a system of positive religion thoroughly, to understand it in its historical origin and form as well as in its abstract principles, we must know the traditional religion that preceded it. It is from this point of view that I invite you to take an interest in the ancient religion of the Semitic peoples; the matter is not one of mere antiquarian curiosity, but has a direct and important bearing on the great problem of the origins of the spiritual religion of the Bible. Let me illustrate this by an example. You know how large a part of the teaching of the New Testament and of all Christian theology turns on the ideas of sacrifice and priesthood. In what they have to say on these heads the New Testament writers presuppose, as the basis of their argument, the notion of sacrifice and priesthood current among the Jews and embodied in the ordinances of the Temple. But, again, the ritual of the Temple was not in its origin an entirely novel thing; the precepts of the Pentateuch did not create a priesthood and a sacrificial service on an altogether independent basis, but only reshaped and remodelled, in accordance with a more spiritual doctrine, institutions of an older type, which in many particulars were common to the Hebrews with their heathen neighbours. Every one who reads the Old Testament with attention is struck with the fact that the origin and *rationale* of sacrifice are nowhere fully explained; that sacrifice is an essential part of religion is taken for granted, as something which is not a doctrine peculiar to Israel but is universally admitted and acted on without as well as within the limits of the chosen people. Thus, when we wish thoroughly to study the New Testament doctrine of sacrifice, we are carried back step by step till we reach a point where we have to ask what sacrifice meant, not to the old Hebrews alone, but to the whole circle of nations of which they formed a part. By considerations of this sort we are led to the conclusion that no one of the religions of Semitic origin which still exercise so great an influence on the lives of men can be completely understood without enquiry into the older traditional religion of the Semitic race.

You observe that in this argument I take it for granted that, when we go back to the most ancient religious conceptions and usages of the Hebrews, we shall find them to be the common property of a group of kindred peoples, and not the exclusive possession of the tribes of Israel. The proof that this is so will appear more clearly in the sequel; but, indeed, the thing will hardly be denied by any one who has read the Bible with care. In the history of old Israel before the captivity, nothing comes out more clearly than that the mass of the people found the greatest difficulty in keeping their national religion distinct from that of the surrounding nations. Those who had no grasp of spiritual principles, and knew the religion of Jehovah only as an affair of inherited usage, were not conscious of any great difference between themselves and their heathen neighbours, and fell into Canaanite and other foreign practices with the greatest facility. The significance of this fact is manifest if we consider how deeply the most untutored religious sensibilities are shocked by any kind of innovation. Nothing appeals so strongly as religion to the conservative instincts; and conservatism is the habitual attitude of Orientals. The whole history of Israel is unintelligible if we suppose that the heathenism against which the prophets contended was a thing altogether alien to the religious traditions of the Hebrews. In principle there was all the difference in the world between the faith of Isaiah and that of an idolater. But the difference in principle, which seems so clear to us, was not clear to the average Judaean, and the reason of this was that it was obscured by the great similarity in many important points of religious tradition and ritual practice. The conservatism which refuses to look at principles, and has an eye only for tradition and usage, was against the prophets, and had no sympathy with their efforts to draw a sharp line between the religion of Jehovah and that of the foreign gods. This is a proof that what I may call the natural basis of Israel's worship was very closely akin to that of the neighbouring cults.

The conclusion on this point which is suggested by the facts of Old Testament history, may be accepted the more readily because it is confirmed by presumptive arguments of another kind. Traditional religion is handed down from father to child, and therefore is in great measure an affair of race. Nations sprung from a common stock will have a common inheritance of traditional belief and usage in things sacred as well as profane, and thus the evidence that the Hebrews and their neighbours had a large common stock of religious tradition falls in with the evidence which we have from other sources, that in point of race the people of Israel were nearly akin to the heathen nations of Syria and Arabia. The populations of this whole region constitute a well-marked ethnic unity, a fact which is usually expressed by giving to them the common name of Semites.[...]

[...]

The Semitic nations are classed together on the ground of similarity of language; but we have every reason to recognise their linguistic kinship as only one manifestation of a very marked general unity of type. The unity is not perfect; it would not, for example, be safe to make generalisations about the Semitic character from the Arabian nomads, and to apply them to the ancient Babylonians. And for this there are probably two reasons. On the one hand, the Semite of the Arabian desert and the Semite of the Babylonian alluvium lived under altogether different physical and moral conditions; the difference of environment is as complete as possible. And, on the other hand, it is pretty certain that the Arabs of the desert have been from time immemorial a race practically unmixed, while the Babylonians, and other members of the same family settled on the fringes of the Semitic land, were in all probability largely mingled with the blood of other races, and underwent a corresponding modification of type.

But when every allowance is made for demonstrable or possible variations of type within the Semitic field, it still remains true that the Semites form a singularly well marked and relatively speaking a very homogeneous group.

So far as language goes the evidence to this effect is particularly strong.
[...]
Let it be understood from the outset that we have not the materials for
anything like a complete comparative history of Semitic religions, and that
nothing of the sort will be attempted in these Lectures. But a careful study
and comparison of the various sources is sufficient to furnish a tolerably
accurate view of a series of general features, which recur with striking
uniformity in all parts of the Semitic field, and govern the evolution of
faith and worship down to a late date. These widespread and permanent
features form the real interest of Semitic religion to the philosophical
student; it was in them, and not in the things that vary from place to place
and from time to time, that the strength of Semitic religion lay, and it is
to them therefore that we must look for help in the most important practical
application of our studies, for light on the great question of the relation
of the positive Semitic religions to the earlier faith of the race.

Before entering upon the particulars of our enquiry, I must still detain
you with a few words about the method and order of investigation that
seem to be prescribed by the nature of the subject. To get a true and well-
defined picture of the type of Semitic religion, we must not only study the
parts separately, but must have clear views of the place and proportion of
each part in its relation to the whole. And here we shall go very far wrong
if we take it for granted that what is the most important and prominent
side of religion to us was equally important in the ancient society with
which we are to deal. In connection with every religion, whether ancient
or modern, we find on the one hand certain beliefs, and on the other certain
institutions, ritual practices and rules of conduct. Our modern habit is to
look at religion from the side of belief rather than of practice; for, down
to comparatively recent times, almost the only forms of religion seriously
studied in Europe have been those of the various Christian Churches, and
all parts of Christendom are agreed that ritual is important only in connection with its interpretation. Thus the study of religion has meant mainly
the study of Christian beliefs, and instruction in religion has habitually
begun with the creed, religious duties being presented to the learner as
flowing from the dogmatic truths he is taught to accept. All this seems to
us so much a matter of course that, when we approach some strange or
antique religion, we naturally assume that here also our first business is to
search for a creed, and find in it the key to ritual and practice. But the
antique religions had for the most part no creed; they consisted entirely of
institutions and practices. No doubt men will not habitually follow certain
practices without attaching a meaning to them; but as a rule we find that
while the practice was rigorously fixed, the meaning attached to it was
extremely vague, and the same rite was explained by different people in

different ways, without any question of orthodoxy or heterodoxy arising in consequence. In ancient Greece, for example, certain things were done at a temple, and people were agreed that it would be impious not to do them. But if you had asked why they were done, you would probably have had several mutually contradictory explanations from different persons, and no one would have thought it a matter of the least religious importance which of these you chose to adopt. Indeed, the explanations offered would not have been of a kind to stir any strong feeling; for in most cases they would have been merely different stories as to the circumstances under which the rite first came to be established, by the command or by the direct example of the god. The rite, in short, was connected not with a dogma but with a myth.

[...]

Strictly speaking, indeed, I understate the case when I say that the oldest religious and political institutions present a close analogy. It would be more correct to say that they were parts of one whole of social custom. Religion was a part of the organised social life into which a man was born, and to which he conformed through life in the same unconscious way in which men fall into any habitual practice of the society in which they live. Men took the gods and their worship for granted, just as they took the other usages of the state for granted, and if they reasoned or speculated about them, they did so on the presupposition that the traditional usages were fixed things, behind which their reasonings must not go, and which no reasoning could be allowed to overturn. To us moderns religion is above all a matter of individual conviction and reasoned belief, but to the ancients it was a part of the citizen's public life, reduced to fixed forms, which he was not bound to understand and was not at liberty to criticise or to neglect. Religious nonconformity was an offence against the state; for if sacred tradition was tampered with the bases of society were undermined, and the favour of the gods was forfeited. But so long as the prescribed forms were duly observed, a man was recognised as truly pious, and no one asked how his religion was rooted in his heart or affected his reason. Like political duty, of which indeed it was a part, religion was entirely comprehended in the observance of certain fixed rules of outward conduct.

The conclusion from all this as to the method of our investigation is obvious. When we study the political structure of an early society, we do not begin by asking what is recorded of the first legislators, or what theory men advanced as to the reason of their institutions; we try to understand what the institutions were, and how they shaped men's lives. In like manner, in the study of Semitic religion, we must not begin by asking what was told about the gods, but what the working religious institutions were, and how they shaped the lives of the worshippers. Our enquiry, therefore, will

be directed to the religious institutions which governed the lives of men-
of Semitic race.

In following out this plan, however, we shall do well not to throw ourselves
at once upon the multitudinous details of rite and ceremony, but to devote
our attention to certain broad features of the sacred institutions which are
sufficiently well marked to be realised at once. If we were called upon to
examine the political institutions of antiquity, we should find it convenient
to carry with us some general notion of the several types of government
under which the multifarious institutions of ancient states arrange themselves. And in like manner it will be useful for us, when we examine the
religious institutions of the Semites, to have first some general knowledge
of the types of divine governance, the various ruling conceptions of the
relations of the gods to man, which underlie the rites and ordinances of
religion in different places and at different times. Such knowledge we can
obtain in a provisional form, before entering on a mass of ritual details,
mainly by considering the titles of honour by which men addressed their
gods, and the language in which they expressed their dependence on them.
From these we can see at once, in a broad, general way, what place the
gods held in the social system of antiquity, and under what general categories their relations to their worshippers fell. The broad results thus
reached must then be developed, and at the same time controlled and
rendered more precise, by an examination in detail of the working institutions of religion.

The question of the metaphysical nature of the gods, as distinct from their
social office and function, must be left in the background till this whole
investigation is completed. It is vain to ask what the gods are in themselves
till we have studied them in what I may call their public life, that is, in
the stated intercourse between them and their worshippers which was kept
up by means of the prescribed forms of cultus. From the antique point of
view, indeed, the question what the gods are in themselves is not a religious
but a speculative one; what is requisite to religion is a practical acquaintance
with the rules on which the deity acts and on which he expects his worshippers to frame their conduct – what in II Kings 18 : 26 is called the 'manner' or rather the 'customary law' *(mishpat)* of the god of the land. This is
true even of the religion of Israel. When the prophets speak of the knowledge
of God, they always mean a practical knowledge of the laws and principles
of His government in Israel,[1] and a summary expression for religion as
a whole is 'the knowledge and fear of Jehovah,'[2] *i.e.* the knowledge of what
Jehovah prescribes, combined with a reverent obedience. An extreme scepticism towards all religious speculation is recommended in the Book of
Ecclesiastes as the proper attitude of piety, for no amount of discussion
can carry a man beyond the plain rule of 'fear God and keep His command-

ments'.[3] This counsel the author puts into the mouth of Solomon, and so
represents it, not unjustly, as summing up the old view of religion, which
in more modern days had unfortunately begun to be undermined.

The propriety of keeping back all metaphysical questions as to the nature
of the gods till we have studied the practices of religion in detail, becomes
very apparent if we consider for a moment what befell the later philosophers
and theosophists of heathenism in their attempts to construct a theory
of the traditional religion. None of these thinkers succeeded in giving an
account of the nature of the gods from which all the received practices
of worship could be rationally deduced, and those who had any pretensions
to orthodoxy had recourse to violent allegorical interpretations in order to
bring the established ritual into accordance with their theories.[4] The reason
for this is obvious. The traditional usages of religion had grown up gradually
in the course of many centuries, and reflected habits of thought characteristic of very diverse stages of man's intellectual and moral development.
No one conception of the nature of the gods could possibly afford the clue
to all parts of that motley complex of rites and ceremonies which the later
paganism had received by inheritance, from a series of ancestors in every
state of culture from pure savagery upwards. The record of the religious
thought of mankind, as it is embodied in religious institutions, resembles
the geological record of the history of the earth's crust; the new and the
old are preserved side by side, or rather layer upon layer. The classification
of ritual formations in their proper sequence is the first step towards their
explanation, and that explanation itself must take the form, not of a speculative theory, but of a rational life-history.

I have already explained that, in attempting such a life-history of religious
institutions, we must begin by forming some preliminary ideas of the
practical relation in which the gods of antiquity stood to their worshipp rs.
I have now to add, that we shall also find it necessary to have beforeeus
from the outset some elementary notions of the relations which early races
of mankind conceived to subsist between gods and men on the one hand,
and the material universe on the other. All acts of ancient worship have
a material embodiment, the form of which is determined by the consideration that gods and men alike stand in certain fixed relations to particular
parts or aspects of physical nature. Certain places, certain things, even
certain animal kinds are conceived as holy, *i.e.* as standing in a near relation
to the gods, and claiming special reverence from men, and this conception
plays a very large part in the development of religious institutions. Here
again we have a problem that cannot be solved by *a priori* methods; it is
only as we move onward from step to step in the analysis of the details of
ritual observance that we can hope to gain full insight into the relations of
the gods to physical nature. But there are certain broad features in the

ancient conception of the universe, and of the relations of its parts to one another, which can be grasped at once, upon a merely preliminary survey, and we shall find it profitable to give attention to these at an early stage of our discussion.

I propose, therefore, to devote my second lecture to the nature of the antique religious community and the relations of the gods to their worshippers. After this we will proceed to consider the relations of the gods to physical nature, not in a complete or exhaustive way, but in a manner entirely preliminary and provisional, and only so far as is necessary to enable us to understand the material basis of ancient ritual. After these preliminary enquiries have furnished us with certain necessary points of view, we shall be in a position to take up the institutions of worship in an orderly manner, and make an attempt to work out their life-history. We shall find that the history of religious institutions is the history of ancient religion itself, as a practical force in the development of the human race, and that the articulate efforts of the antique intellect to comprehend the meaning of religion, the nature of the gods, and the principles on which they deal with men, take their point of departure from the unspoken ideas embodied in the traditional forms of ritual praxis. Whether the conscious efforts of ancient religious thinkers took the shape of mythological invention or of speculative construction, the raw material of thought upon which they operated was derived from the common traditional stock of religious conceptions that was handed on from generation to generation, not in express words, but in the form of religious custom. [...]

NOTES

1. See especially Hosea, chap. 4.
2. Isa. 9:2.
3. Eccles. 12:13.
4. See, for example, Plutarch's *Greek* and *Roman Questions*.

Friedrich C. G. Delitzsch

Friedrich Conrad Gerhard Delitzsch was born in 1850 in Erlangen, where he received his primary and secondary school education. He enrolled in the University of Leipzig and studied both Indo-European Languages including Sanskrit and Semitic Languages, whereby he specialized in Akkadian (Babylonian and Assyrian) languages under E. Schrader since 1873. In 1874 he passed his *Habilitation* in Leipzig. In 1877 Delitzsch became *Extraordinarius* for Semitic Languages and Assyriology at the University of Leipzig. In 1893 he was appointed professor in the same subjects at the University of Breslau, and in 1899 as a professor of Oriental Philology and Assyriology at the University of Berlin. He visited Mesopotamia in 1902 and 1905. Delitzsch retired in 1920 and died at Langenschwalbach (Germany) in 1922.

The following books and brochures of Delitzsch are available in English translation: 1883 *The Hebrew Language viewed in the light of Assyrian research;* 1889 *Assyrian Grammar, with paradigms, exercises, glossary and bibliography;* 1903 *Babel and Bible. Two Lectures;* 1908 *Whose Son is Christ? Two lectures on Progress in Religion.*

Friedrich Delitzsch was an eminent Assyriologist and one of the founders of the scholarly study of the Akkadian languages and of Sumerian. He also did Koranic studies and did much research on the Old Testament, trying to find relationships between the cuneiform inscriptions and the Old Testament text. He may be considered as an early spokesman of what would later be called in Germany the *religionsgeschichtliche Schule.* Scholars of this orientation tried to understand and explain both Old and New Testament religion in terms of the environment in which the Hebrews and early Christians lived. In his literary and historical study of the Old Testament, Delitzsch contended, for example, that the Old Testament was largely inspired by earlier Babylonian materials, and that Semitic monotheism had developed itself gradually in the course of history. By bringing this to the open in his lectures on 'Babel and Bible', by not recognizing the verbal inspiration of the Old Testament and by reducing it largely to outside origins, Delitzsch aroused violent discussions in the religious and cultural life of his time.

The following fragments have been taken from the first two lectures on *Babel and Bible* and show the way in which Delitzsch wanted to understand the Old Testament, as well as the conclusions he drew from it.

'BABEL AND BIBLE'

From the First Lecture

[...] One of the most notable results of the archaeological researches on the Euphrates and Tigris is the discovery that in the Babylonian lowland, a district of about the size of Italy, which nature had already made uncommonly fruitful, but which human energy converted into a hothouse of vegetation passing our conception, there existed as early as about 2250 B. C. a highly-developed constitution, together with a state of culture that may well be compared with that of our later Middle Ages. After Hammurabi had succeeded in driving out of the country the Elamites, the hereditary foes of Babylonia, and had amalgamated the north and south of the land into one united state, with Babylon as the political and religious centre, his first care was to enforce uniform laws throughout the land. He therefore prepared a great code which defined the civil law in all its branches. In this code, the relations of master to slave and labourer, of merchant to agent, of landed proprietor to tenant-farmer, are strictly regulated. There is a law to the effect that the agent who pays over money to his principal for goods sold must receive a receipt from the latter; abatement of rent is provided for in the event of damage by storm or flood; fishing-rights for each village situated on a canal are accurately defined, etc. Babylon is the seat of the supreme court, to which all difficult and contested lawsuits have to be referred for decision. Every able man is bound to serve as a soldier, although Hammurabi took precautions against a too excessive use of conscription, by means of numerous decrees, recognising the privileges of the old priestly families, or exempting shepherds from military service in the interests of cattle-breeding.

We read of writing in Babylon: and the extremely cursive nature of the writing points to the widest application of it. In truth, when we find, among the letters which have survived from those ancient times in great abundance, the letter of a woman to her husband on his travels, wherein, after telling him that the little ones are well, she asks advice on some trivial matter; or the missive of a son to his father, in which he informs him that so-and-so has mortally offended him, that he would thrash the knave, but would like to ask his father's advice first; or another letter in which a son urges his father to send at last the long-promised money, offering the insolent inducement that then he will pray for his father again — all this points to a well-organised system of communication by letter and of postal arrangements, and shews, also, to judge by all the indications, that streets, bridges, and canals, even beyond the frontiers of Babylon, were in excellent condition.

Trade and commerce, cattle-breeding and agriculture, were at tirs-prime, and the sciences, *e.g.* geometry, mathematics, and, above all, aheot nomy, had reached a degree of developm ent which again and again mstre even the astronomers of to-day to admiration and astonishment. ovo Paris, at the outside Rome, can compete with Babylon in respect of Nh nfluence which it exercised upon the world throughout two thousatnd years. The Prophets of the Old Testament attest in terms full of displeasure the overpowering grandeur and overwhelming might of the Babylon of Nebuchadnezzar. 'A golden cup', exclaims Jeremiah (51 : 7), 'was Babylon in the hand of Yahwe, which hath made the whole earth drunken'; and even down to the time of the Apocalypse of John, words are found which quiver with the hateful memory of the great Babel, the luxurious, gay city, the wealth-abounding centre of trade and art, the mother of harlots and of every abomination upon earth. And this focus of culture and science and literature, the *brain* of the Nearer East, and the all-ruling power, was the city of Babylon, even at the close of the third millennium.

It was in the winter of 1887 that Egyptian fellahin digging for antiquities at El-Amarna, the ruins of the royal city of Amenophis IV, between Thebes and Memphis, found there some three hundred clay-tablets of all sizes. These tablets are, as has since been shewn, the letters of Babylonian, Assyrian, and Mesopotamian kings to the Pharaohs Amenophis III and IV, and especially the written communications of Egyptian governors from the great Canaanite cities, such as Tyre, Sidon, Acco, Ascalon, to the Egyptian court; and the Berlin Museums are fortunate enough to possess the olyse letters from Jerusalem, written even before the immigration of the Israente-into the promised land. Like a mighty reflector, this discovery of cliay tablets at Amarna has turned into a dazzling light the deep darkness whlch lay over the Mediterranean lands — Canaan in particular — and over thier politics and culture at about 1500—1400 B.C. And the fact alone that alli these chiefs of Canaan, and even of Cyprus, avail themselves of the Baby-lonian writing and language, and write on clay-tablets like the Babylonians, that, therefore, the Babylonian tongue was the official language of diplo-matic intercourse from the Euphrates to the Nile, proves the all-ruling influence of the Babylonian culture and literature from 2200 to beyond 1400 B.C.

When, therefore, the twelve tribes of Israel invaded Canaan, they came to a land which was a domain completely pervaded by Babylonian culture. It is a small but characteristic feature that, on the conquest and despoiling of the first Canaanite city, Jericho, a *Babylonish* mantle excited tne greed of Achan (Josh. 7 : 21). Yet it was not only the commerce, but also the trade, law, custom, and science of Babylon that set the fashion in the land. Thus we can at once understand why, for example, the coinage, the system of weights and measures, the outward forms of the law — 'if a man does so and so, he shall so and so' — are precisely Babylonian, and just as the sacrificial and priestly system of the Old Testament is profoundly influenced by the Babylonian, so it is significant that Israelite tradition itself no longer affords any certain information respecting the origin of the Sabbath (Cf. Exod. 20 : 11 with Deut. 5 : 15).

But since the Babylonians also had a Sabbath day *(šabattu)*, on which, for the purpose of conciliating the gods, there was a festival — that is to say, no work was to be done — and since the seventh, fourteenth, twenty-first, and twenty-eighth days of a month are marked on a calendar of sacrifices and festivals dug up in Babylonia as days on which 'the shepherd of the great nations' shall eat no roast flesh, shall not change his dress, shall not offer sacrifice, as days on which the king shall not mount the chariot or pronounce judgment, the Magus shall not prophesy, even the physician shall not lay his hand on the sick, in short, as days which 'are not suitable for any affair (business?),' it is scarcely possible for us to doubt that we owe the blessings decreed in the Sabbath or Sunday day of rest in the last resort to that ancient and civilized race on the Euphrates and Tigris.

Nay, even more! The Berlin Museums have in their keeping a particularly valuable treasure. It consists of a clay-tablet with a Babylonian legend which tells how it happened that the first man came to forfeit immortality. The place where this tablet was found — *viz.* El-Amarna — and the many dots in red Egyptian ink found in different places all over the tablet (shewing the pains the Egyptian scholar had taken to make the foreign text intelligible), give ocular proof how eagerly the works of Babylonian literature were studied even at that ancient date in lands as far away as that of the Pharaohs. Is it surprising, then, that the same thing should have happened in Palestine also in earlier as well as in later days, and that now, all at once, a series of Biblical narratives come to us in their original form from the Babylonian treasure-mounds, rising, as it were, out of the night into the light of day?

The Babylonians divided their history into two great periods: the one before, the other after the Flood. Babylon was in quite a peculiar sense the land of deluges. The alluvial lowlands along the course of all great rivers discharging into the sea are, of course, exposed to terrible floods of a special kind — cyclones and tornadoes accompanied by earthquakes and tremendous downpours of rain.

As late as the year 1876, a tornado of this kind coming from the Bay of Bengal, accompanied by fearful thunder and lightning, and blowing with such force that ships at a distance of 300 kilometres were dismasted, approached the mouths of the Ganges, and the high cyclonic waves, uniting with the then ebbing tide, formed one gigantic tidal wave, with the result that within a short while an area of 141 geographical square miles was covered with water to a depth of 45 feet, and 215,000 men met their death by drowning. The storm raged in this way until the flood spent itself on the higher ground. When we reflect upon this, we can estimate what a frightful catastrophe a cyclone of the kind must have meant when it came upon the lowlands of Babylon in those primaeval days. It is the merit of the celebrated Viennese geologist Eduard Suess to have shewn that there is an accurate description of such a cyclone, line for line, in the Babylonian Deluge-story written upon a tablet from the Library of Sardanapalus at Nineveh, of which, however, a written account had existed as early as 2000 B.C. The sea plays the chief part in the story, and the ship of Xisuthros, the Babylonian Noah, is accordingly cast upon a spur of the mountain-range of Armenia and Media; in other respects, however, it is the Deluge-story so well known to us all. Xisuthros receives a command from the god of the ocean depths to build a ship of a specified size, to pitch it thoroughly, and to embark upon it his family and all living seed; the party go on board ship, its doors are closed, it is thrust out into the all-destroying billows until at length it strands upon a mountain called Nizir. Then follows the famous passage: 'On the seventh day I brought out a dove and released it; the dove flew hither and thither, but as there was no resting-place it returned again.' We then read further how that the swallow was released and returned again, until, finally, the raven, finding that the waters had subsided, returned not again to the ship, and how that Xisuthros leaves the vessel, and offers upon the top of the mountain a sacrifice, the sweet savour whereof is smelt by the gods, and so on. The whole story, precisely as it was written down, travelled to Canaan. But owing to the new and entirely different local conditions, it was forgotten that the sea was the chief factor, and so we find in the Bible two accounts of the Deluge, which are not only scientifically impossible, but, furthermore, mutually contradictory — the one assigning to it a duration of 365 days, the other of $[40 + (3 \times 7)] = 61$ days. Science is indebted to Jean Astruc, that strictly orthodox Catholic physician of Louis XIV, for recognising that two fundamentally different accounts of a deluge have been worked up into a single story in the Bible. In the year 1753, Astruc, as Goethe expresses it, first 'applied the knife and probe to the Pentateuch,' and thereby became the founder of the criticism of the Pentateuch — that is to say, of the study which perceives more and more clearly the very varied written sources from which the five Books of Moses have been compiled. These are facts that, as far as science is concerned, stand firm and remain unshaken, however tightly people on either side of the ocean may continue to close their eyes to them. When we reflect that in time past the Copernican system was offensive even to such men of genius as Luther and Melanchthon, we must quite be prepared to find only a tardy recognition of the results of Pentateuchal criticism; but the course of time will surely bring with it light.

The ten Babylonian antediluvian kings also have been admitted into the Bible, and figure as the ten antediluvian patriarchs, with various points of agreement as to details.

Besides the Babylonian epic of Gilgamesh, the eleventh tablet of which gives the Deluge-story, we also possess another beautiful Babylonian poem: the creation-epic, written upon seven tablets. At the very beginning of all things, according to this story, a dark, chaotic, primaeval water, called Tiâmat, existed in a state of agitation and tumult. But as soon as the gods made preparations for the formation of an ordered universe, Tiâmat, generally represented as a dragon, but also as a seven-headed serpent, arose in bitter enmity, gave birth to monsters of all kinds — in particular, gigantic serpents filled with venom — and with these as her allies, prepared, roaring and snorting, to do battle with the gods. All the gods tremble with fear when they perceive their terrible adversary; only the god Marduk, the god of light, the god of the early morning and of spring, volunteered to do battle on condition that the first place among the gods be conceded to him. A splendid scene follows. The god Marduk fastens a mighty net to the east and south, north and west, in order that nothing of Tiâmat may escape; then clad in gleaming armour, and in majestic splendour, he mounts his chariot drawn by four fiery steeds, the gods around gazing with admiration. Straight he drives to meet the dragon and her army, and utters the call to single combat. Then Tiâmat uttered wild and piercing cries until her ground quaked asunder from the bottom. She opened her jaws to their utmost, but before she could close her lips the god Marduk bade the evil wind enter within her, then seizing the javelin, he cut her heart in pieces, cast down her body and stood upon it, whilst her myrmidons were placed in durance vile. Then Marduk clave Tiâmat clean asunder like a fish; out of the one half he formed heaven, out of the other, earth, at the same time dividing the upper waters from the lower by means of the firmament; he decked the heavens with moon, sun and stars, the earth with plants and animals, until at length the first human pair, made of clay mingled with divine blood, went forth fashioned by the hand of the creator.

As Marduk was the tutelary deity of the city of Babel, we can readily believe that this narrative in particular became very widely diffused in Canaan. Indeed, the Old Testament poets and prophets even went so far as to transfer Marduk's heroic act directly to Yahwe, and thenceforth extolled him as being the one who in the beginning of time broke in pieces the heads of the sea-monster *(liviāthân,* Ps. 74 : 13 *f.; cf.* 89 : 10), as the one through whom the helpers of the dragon *(râhâb)* were overthrown. Such passages as Isa. 51 : 9, 'Awake, awake, put on strength, O arm of

Yahwe! awake, as in the ancient days, the generations of old. Art thou not it that hewed the dragon in pieces, that pierced the monster *(tannin)?*' or Job 26 : 12, 'By his strength he smote the sea, and by his wisdom he dashed in pieces the dragon,' read like a commentary on that small representation of Marduk which was found by our expedition. The god is shewn to us clad in majestic glory, with mighty arm and large eye and ear, symbolic of his sagacity, and at his feet is the vanquished dragon of the primaeval ocean. The priestly scholar who composed Gen. chap. 1 endeavoured, of course, to remove all possible mythological features of this creation-story. But the dark, watery chaos is presupposed, and that, too, with the name Tehôm *(i.e.* Tiâmat), and is first divided from the light, after which the heavens and the earth emerge. The heavens are furnished with sun, moon, and stars, the earth, clad with vegetation, is supplied with animals, and finally the first human pair come forth fashioned by the hand of God; and this being so, the very close connection that exists between the Biblical and the Babylonian creation stories is as clear and illuminating as are and always will be futile all attempts to bring our Biblical story of the creation into conformity with the results of Natural Science.[1] It is interesting to note that there is still an echo of this contest between Marduk and Tiâmat in the Apocalypse of John, where we read of a conflict between the Archangel Michael and the 'Beast of the Abyss, the Old Serpent, which is the Devil and Satan.' The whole conception, also present in the story of the knight St. George and his conflict with the dragon, a story brought back by the Crusaders, is manifestly Babylonian. For fine reliefs, older by many centuries than the Apocalypse or the first chapter of Genesis, are found on the walls of the Assyrian palaces, representing the conflict between the power of light and the power of darkness, which is resumed with each new day, with every spring as it begins anew.

To recognise these connecting links is, however, of still greater importance.

The command not to do to one's neighbour what one does not wish to have done to one's self is indelibly stamped upon every human heart. 'Thou shalt not shad thy neighbour's blood, thou shalt not approach thy neighbour's wife, thou shalt not seize upon thy neighbour's garment' — these requirements of fundamental importance for the self-preservation of human society are found, in the case of the Babylonians, in precisely the same connection, as the fifth, sixth, and seventh commandments of the Old Testament. But man is also a being destined to live a social life, and on this account the social requirements — readiness to help, compassion, love — constitute an equally inalienable heritage of human nature. When, therefore, the Babylonian Magus, having been called in to see a patient, seeks to know what sins have thrown him thus upon the sick bed, he does not stop short at such gross sins of commission as murder or theft, but asks, 'Have you failed to clothe a naked person, or to cause a prisoner to see the light?' The Babylonians laid stress even upon those postulates of human ethics which stand on a higher level; to speak the truth, to keep one's promise, seemed to them as sacred a duty as to say *Yea* with the mouth and *Nay* in the heart was, in their view, a punishable offence. It is not strange, therefore, that to the Babylonians, as to the Hebrews, transgressions against these commands and prohibitions present themselves in the character of sins; the Babylonians also felt themselves to be in every respect entirely dependent upon the gods.

It is even more noteworthy that they, too, regarded all human suffering, illness in particular, and finally death, as a punishment for sins. In Babel, as in the Bible, the sense of sin is the dominating force everywhere. Under these circumstances we can understand that Babylonian thinkers pondered over the problem: How it could have been possible for man, who had come forth into the world as the work of God's hand, and had been made after God's own likeness, to become the victim of sin and death. The Bible contains that beautiful and profound story of the corruption of the woman by the serpent — again the serpent? There is certainly quite a Babylonian ring about it! Was it perhaps that serpent, the earliest enemy of the gods, seeking to revenge itself upon the gods of light by alienating from them their noblest creation? Or was it that serpent-god, of whom in one place it is said 'he destroyed the abode of life'? The problem as to the origin of the Biblical story of the Fall is second to none in significance, in its bearings on the history of religion, and above all for New Testament theology, which, as is well known, sets off against the first Adam, through whom sin and death came into the world, the second Adam. Perhaps we may be permitted to lift the veil a little. May we point to an old Babylonian cylinder-seal (See figure)? Here, in the middle, is the tree with hanging fruit; on the right the man, to be recognised by the horns, the symbol of strength; on the left the woman; both reaching out their hands to the fruit, and behind the woman the serpent. Should there not be a connection between this old Babylonian representation and the Biblical story of the Fall? [...]

[...]

I may perhaps, then, have succeeded in shewing that many a Babylonian feature has attached itself even to our religious ideas through the medium of the Bible. When we have removed those conceptions, which, though derived, it is true, from highly-gifted peoples, are nevertheless purely human, and when we have freed our minds of firmly-rooted prejudice of every kind, religion itself, as extolled by the prophets and poets of the Old Testament, and as taught in its most sublime sense by Jesus, as also the religious feeling of our own hearts, is so little affected, that it may rather be said to emerge from the cleansing process in a truer and more sympathetic form. And at this point let me be allowed to add one last word on a subject which makes the Bible of such importance in the history of the world — its Monotheism. Here, too, Babel has quite recently opened up a new and unexpected prospect.

It is curious, but no one knows definitely what our word *God* (Gott) originally means. Philologists hesitate between 'awe-inspiring' and 'that which exercises a spell.' The word which the Semites, on the other hand, coined for God is clear. But it is more than this: it comprehends the idea of the deity in so full an extent, that by this one word alone is shattered the fable which tells us that 'the Semites were at all times astonishingly lacking in religious instinct,' and also the popular modern view which would see, both in the Yahwe-religion and in our Christian belief in God, something evolved out of such fetichism and animism as is characteristic of the South Sea cannibals or the Patagonians.

There is a beautiful passage in the Koran (6 : 75 *ff.*), so beautiful that Goethe wished to see it treated dramatically. In it Mohammed imagines himself in Abraham's place and traces the probable workings of the patriarch's mind when arriving at the idea of Monotheism. He says: 'When night had fallen and it was dark, Abraham went out into the darkness, and behold a star shone above him, then he cried joyfully, *That is my Lord.* But when the star began to pale, he said, *I like not them that become without lustre.* Then, when he saw the moon arise, shedding its light over the firmament, he cried overjoyed, *That is my Lord.* But when the moon waned, he said, *Alas, I needs must go astray.* Then in the morning, when the sun rose shining in splendour, he cried, *This is my Lord, for he is indeed great!* But when the sun set, he said, *O my people, I have nought to do with your worship of many gods, I turn my face to him who made heaven and earth.*'

The old Semitic word (if it may be called a word) for God, well known to us all from the words *Eli, Eli, lama azabtani* (My God, my God, why

hast thou forsaken me?), is El, and means the *Goal* — the Being to whom
as to a goal the eyes of man looking heavenwards are turned, 'on whom
hangs the gaze of every man, to whom man looks out from afar' (Job 26 : 25),
that Being towards whom man stretches forth his hands, after whom the
human heart yearns away from the mutability and imperfection of earthy
life — this Being the nomad Semitic tribes called El or God. And since
the Divine Essence was viewed by them as a unity, we find among the old
North Semitic tribes who settled in Babylonia about 2500 B.C., such personal names as 'God has given', 'God with me,' 'Belonging to God', 'God!
Turn again,' 'God is God,' 'If God be not my God,' etc. But, further, through
the kindness of the Head of the Department of Assyrian and Egyptian
antiquities at the British Museum, I am able to give a representation of
three small clay-tablets. What is there to be seen on these tablets? I shall
be asked. Fragile, broken clay upon which are scratched characters scarcely
legible! That is true, no doubt, yet they are precious for this reason: they
can be dated with certainty, they belong to the age of Hammurabi, one in
particular to the reign of his father Sin-mubaliṭ. But they are still more
precious for another reason: they contain three names which, from the point
of view of the history of religion, are of the most far-reaching importance:

Ia - a' - ve - ilu

Ia - ve - ilu

Ia - 'ú - um- ilu

The names are *Yahwè is God*. Therefore Yahwè, the Existing, the Enduring
one (we have reasons for saying that the name may mean this), the one
devoid of all change, not like us men, who to-morrow are but a thing of
yesterday, but one who, above the starry vault which shines with everlasting
regularity, lives and works from generation to generation — this *Yahwè*
was the spiritual possession of those same nomad tribes out of which after
a thousand years the children of Israel were to emerge.

[...]

From the Second Lecture

It was a remarkably happy idea which was conceived by the representatives of the governing bodies of the German churches, who went out to
Jerusalem as the Kaiser's guests to be present at the dedication of the Church
of the Redeemer — the idea of founding a 'German Evangelical Institute
of Archaeology for the Holy Land.'

Oh, may our young theologians there learn to acquaint themselves
thoroughly — and that not merely in the towns, but, best of all, in the
desert — with the manners and customs of the Bedouin, who are still the
self-same people that they were in the time of old Israel; and may they
there deeply immerse themselves in the points of view and modes of presentment characteristic of the Orient: may they listen, in the tents of the desert,
to story-tellers, or hear the descriptions and narrations of the sons of the
desert themselves, full of vivid and unrestrained, spontaneous fancy, which
all too often unwittingly transgresses the limits of fact! There will then be
disclosed to them that world from which alone Oriental works like the Old
and (to some extent also) the New Testament can be explained — there
will fall as it were scales from their eyes, and the 'Midnight Sun' will be
transformed into morning light!

If even the Orient of to-day — wherever we go and stay, listen and look
— offers such an abundance of elucidatory material for the Bible, how much
more must this be true of the study of the ancient literature of the Babylonians and Assyrians, which indeed is to some extent contemporary with
the Old Testament! Everywhere we meet with more or less significant
agreements on the part of the two literatures, which are closely related
in respect of language and style, thought and modes of presentment. [. . .].
[. . .]

How utterly alike everything is in Babylon and Bible! Here as there we
are struck by the fondness shewn for illustrating speech and thought
by symbolic action (I call to mind the scapegoat which was driven into the
wilderness): here as there we meet with the same world of perpetual wonders and signs; of continuous revelation, principally in dreams; the same
naïve representations of the godhead; — just as in Babylon the gods
eat and drink, and even betake themselves to rest, so Yahwè goes forth
in the cool of the evening to walk in Paradise, and takes pleasure in the sweet
scent of Noah's sacrifice; and just as in the Old Testament Yahwè speaks
to Moses and Aaron, and to all the prophets, so the gods in Babylon spoke
to men, either directly or through the mouth of their priests and inspired
prophets and prophetesses.

Revelation indeed! A greater mistake on the part of the human mind
can hardly be conceived than this, that for long centuries the priceless

remains of the old Hebrew literature collected in the Old Testament were regarded collectively as a religious canon, a revealed book of religion, in spite of the fact that it includes such literature as the Book of Job, which, with words that in places border on blasphemy, casts doubts on the very existence of a just God, together with absolutely secular productions, such as wedding songs (the socalled Song of Solomon). In the charming love-song, Ps. 45 : 11 *ff.*, we read, 'Hearken, O daughter, and attend, and incline thine ear, and forget thine own people and thy father's house; and should the king long for thy beauty, for he is thy lord, then prostrate thyself before him.'

The thought may suggest itself, what must have been the result when books and passages like these were interpreted theologically, and even messianically (Cf. Ep. to Hebrews 1 : 8 *ff.*) ? It can hardly have been otherwise than with the mediaeval Catholic monk, who, if he met with the Latin word maria, '*seas*,' while reading in the Psalter, crossed himself in honour of the Virgin Mary. But even for the remaining portions of the Old Testament literature, all scientifically trained theologians, Evangelical as well as Catholic, have abandoned the doctrine of verbal inspiration: the Old Testament is itself responsible for this, with its numberless contradictory double narratives, and with the absolutely inextricable confusion that has arisen in the five books of Moses, through constant revision and interchange.

To be quite frank, beyond the revelation of God that we, each one of us, carry in our own conscience, we have certainly not deserved a further personal Divine revelation. For up to this day mankind has absolutely trifled with the original and most special revelation of the holy God, the ten words written on the Tables of the Law from Sinai. [. . .]

[. . .]

For my own part, I live in the faith that the old Hebrew Scriptures, even if they lose their character as writings *revealed* or pervaded by a spirit of *revelation*, will yet always retain their high importance, especially as a unique monument of a vast religious, historical process which reaches to our own time. Those exalted passages in the prophets and psalms, inspired by vivid trust in God, and longing after peace in God, will always find a ready echo in our hearts, in spite of the particularistic limitations of their strict letter and literal sense — although this has to a large extent been obliterated in our translations of the Bible. Such words as those of the prophet Micah (6 : 6–8): 'Wherewith shall I come before Yahwè, to bow myself before God on high? Shall I come before Him with burnt-offerings, with calves of a year old? Has Yahwè pleasure in thousands of rams, in countless streams of oil? Shall I give my firstborn as expiation, the fruit of my body as atonement for my life? He hath showed thee, O man, what is good, and what Yahwè requires of thee: nothing but to do justly, to cultivate loving-kindness, and to walk humbly before thy God' — words so cogent for the moral practice of religion (they are also found in Babylonian literature) — are still to-day uttered from the soul of all religiously thinking people.

But, on the other hand, let us not cling blindly to outworn dogmas which scientific knowledge has overthrown, even from an anxious fear lest our faith in God and true religiousness may suffer harm at its hands. We reflect that everything earthly is in a state of vital flow; to stand still is synonymous with death. We see the mighty throbbing power, with which the Reformation infused great nations of the earth, in all departments of human activity and human progress. But even the Reformation is only a stage on the road to the goal of Truth, which has been set before us by and in God. To attain that, we strive humbly, yet with all the means of free scientific investigation, joyfully confessing as the object of our devotion — seen from the high watch-tower with eagle glance, and proudly announced to all the world — the emancipation of religious development.

Note to the Second Lecture

[. . .] One of the first and most meritorious of so-called positive investigators in the domain of the Old Testament, Professor Ernst Sellin of Vienna, in his 'Notes on *Babel and the Bible*' (in: *Neue Freie Presse*, January 25, 1903) on the one hand cheerfully acknowledges the 'absolutely incalculable amount of help, elucidation, and correction that Old Testament investigation owes to the decipherment of the Babylonian inscriptions, in the matter of grammar and lexicography, as well as in the history of culture and pure history', yet, on the other, he is of opinion that I, when I 'argue against the fact of a divine revelation in the Bible on the strength of the Song of Songs and of growth of tradition out of material derived from heterogeneous sources, have appeared on the scene exactly a hundred years too late'. Such a statement as this last can only be described as one of the grossest exaggerations that could possibly have been uttered. When my dear father, Franz Delitzsch, saw himself compelled, towards the end of his life, by the weight of the facts of Old Testament textual criticism, to make, in the case of Genesis, the smallest possible concessions, he was persecuted, even on his deathbed (1890), by the warnings of whole synods. The prodigious commotion, again, excited by my second Lecture serves to show convincingly enough that in quarters from which Church and school are governed an essentially different view from that of my highly-esteemed critic prevails.

Every individual clergyman, who has been a diligent student at the university, does, it is true, pay homage to freer views, but, all the same, school-teaching and religious instruction remain unaffected, and this is the almost intolerable discord against which page 5 of my first Lecture is directed. And this discord widens ever more profoundly. When, indeed, one of equally honourable theological antecedents writes (26th January 1903): 'You inveigh against a conception of Revelation that no sensible Protestant any longer shares; it was that of the old Lutheran Dogmatists. (. . .) All divine revelation is, of course, subject to human mediation, and must therefore have been developed by a gradual process, historically,' he describes exactly the standpoint that I myself advocate, only that I regard the conception of 'divine revelation' in the sense held by the Church and 'of (a human) development by a gradual process historically' as the most opposed and absolutely irreconcilable ideas imaginable. Let it be one thing or the other! I believe that in the Old Testament we have to deal with a process of development effected or permitted by God like any other earthly product, but, for the rest, of a purely human and historical character, in which God has *not* intervened through 'special, supernatural revelation.' Old Testament mono-theism plainly shows itself to be such a process marked by progress from the incomplete to the complete, from the false to the more true, here and there indeed by occasional retrogression, and it seems to me inconceivable to see at each single stage of this development a 'revelation' of the absolute, complete Truth, which is God. The attenuation of the original idea of revelation — so deeply rooted in ancient Oriental conceptions — which began with the aban-donment of verbal inspiration on the part of the evangelical as well as of Catholic theology, and Church even, and irretrievably divested the Old Testament of its character as the 'Word of God', meant, it seems to me, the end of the theological and the beginning of the religious-historical treatment of the Old Testament. The Catholic Church, too, even if it does so more slowly, will not always be able to hold itself aloof from the results of modern science, as perhaps sundry slight indications already tend to show.

The resurrection of the Babylonian-Assyrian literature which, certainly not without God's will, is being accomplished in our time, and which has suddenly taken its place by the side of the only literature also of the hither-Asiatic world — the old Hebrew — that, up to that time, had survived from the past, is ever constraining us anew with irresistible force to undertake a revision of our conception of revelation which is bound up with the Old Testament. May the conviction make headway and grow, ever and more, that only by a dis-passionate revision of the positions involved can the end be reached, and that neither while the controversy rages, nor if and when it shall be brought nearer to its conclusion, can our heart-religion, our heart-fellowship with God, suffer harm or loss.

Albert Schweitzer

Albert Schweitzer was born in 1875 in Kaysersberg, Germany. He received his primary school education at Günsbach and his secondary school education at Mülhausen. In 1893 he enrolled in the University of Strasburg where he studied theology and philosophy. In 1899 he obtained his Ph. D. with a dissertation on the religious philosophy of Kant, and became a preacher in Strasburg while at the same time pursuing his theological studies. In 1902 he became *Privatdozent* for the New Testament at the University of Strasburg. So in 1903 Schweitzer was appointed Principal of the Theological College of St. Thomas attached to the University of Strasburg, but he resigned in 1906 in view of his project to go to Africa. He prepared for this during seven years of medical studies (1905–1912), during which time he continued his ministry and his work as a musician. Having finished his preparations, Schweitzer ceased in 1912 with these activities, his teaching at the University too and went to Africa.

In 1913 he founded a first hospital in Lambarene, but was brought back to Europe in 1917. In 1924 he went to Africa and founded in 1927 the second hospital in Lambarene, where he continued to work with the only interruption of lecture tours in the West and elsewhere. He died in Lambarene in 1965.

From his writings translated into English the following should be mentioned as being of interest for the study of religion: 1910 *The Quest of the Historical Jesus; a Critical Study of its Progress from Reimarus to Wrede;* 1912 *Paul and his Interpreters; a Critical History;* 1923 *Christianity and the Religions of the World;* 1931 *The Mysticism of Paul the Apostle;* 1936 *Indian Thought and its Development;* 1968 *The Kingdom of God and Primitive Christianity.*

As a theologian and philosopher, Schweitzer analyzed the results of the critical schools of historical scholarship of the Old and New Testaments, and was able himself, by using a critical methodology, to assess the range of validity of these results. This holds true, especially, with regard to the research carried out on the historical Jesus and Paul. Of special interest is his consequent ethic of 'reverence for life' both in his active life and in his study of other religions than Christianity.

The following fragment is the first chapter of *The Quest of the Historical Jesus.* It shows the way in which Schweitzer formulated the historical problem of Jesus, and the lines along which he wanted to establish what kind of conclusions scholarship legitimately can make on this issue.

'THE QUEST OF THE HISTORICAL JESUS'

When, at some future day, our period of civilisation shall lie, closed and completed, before the eyes of later generations, German theology will stand out as a great, a unique phenomenon in the mental and spiritual life of our time. For nowhere save in the German temperament can there be found in the same perfection the living complex of conditions and factors – of philosophic thought, critical acumen, historical insight, and religious feeling – without which no deep theology is possible.

And the greatest achievement of German theology is the critical investigation of the life of Jesus. What it has accomplished here has laid down the conditions and determined the course of the religious thinking of the future.

In the history of doctrine its work has been negative; it has, so to speak, cleared the site for a new edifice of religious thought. In describing how the ideas of Jesus were taken possession of by the Greek spirit, it was tracing the growth of that which must necessarily become strange to us, and, as a matter of fact, has become strange to us.

Of its efforts to create a new dogmatic we scarcely need to have the history written; it is alive within us. It is no doubt interesting to trace how modern thoughts have found their way into the ancient dogmatic system, there to combine with eternal ideas to form new constructions; it is interesting to penetrate into the mind of the thinker in which this process is at work; but the real truth of that which here meets us as history we experience within ourselves. As in the monad of Leibnitz the whole universe is reflected, so we intuitively experience within us, even apart from any clear historical knowledge, the successive stages of the progress of modern dogma, from rationalism to Ritschl. This experience is true knowledge, all the truer because we are conscious of the whole as something indefinite, a slow and difficult movement towards a goal which is still shrouded in obscurity. We have not yet arrived at any reconciliation between history and modern thought – only between half-way history and half-way thought. What the ultimate goal towards which we are moving will be, what this something is which shall bring new life and new regulative principles to coming centuries, we do not know. We can only dimly divine that it will be the mighty deed of some mighty original genius, whose truth and rightness will be proved by the fact that we, working at our poor half thing, will oppose him might and main – we who imagine we long for nothing more eagerly than a genius powerful enough to open up with authority a new path for the world, seeing that we cannot succeed in moving it forward along the track which we have so laboriously prepared.

For this reason the history of the critical study of the life of Jesus is of higher intrinsic value than the history of the study of ancient dogma or of the attempts to create a new one. It has to describe the most tremendous thing which the religious consciousness has ever dared and done. In the study of the history of dogma German theology settled its account with the past; in its attempt to create a new dogmatic, it was endeavouring to keep a place for the religious life in the thought of the present; in the study of the life of Jesus it was working for the future – in pure faith in the truth, not seeing whereunto it wrought.

Moreover, we are here dealing with the most vital thing in the world's history. There came a Man to rule over the world; He ruled it for good and for ill, as history testifies; He destroyed the world into which He was born; the spiritual life of our own time seems like to perish at His hands, for He leads to battle against our thought a host of dead ideas, a ghostly army upon which death has no power, and Himself destroys again the truth and goodness which His Spirit creates in us, so that it cannot rule the world. That He continues, notwithstanding, to reign as the alone Great and alone True in a world of which He denied the continuance, is the prime example of that antithesis between spiritual and natural truth which underlies all life and all events, and in Him emerges into the field of history.

It is only at first sight that the absolute indifference of early Christianity towards the life of the historical Jesus is disconcerting. When Paul, representing those who recognise the signs of the times, did not desire to know Christ after the flesh, that was the first expression of the impulse of self-preservation by which Christianity continued to be guided for centuries. It felt that with the introduction of the historic Jesus into its faith, there would arise something new, something which had not been foreseen in the thoughts of the Master Himself, and that thereby a contradiction would be brought to light, the solution of which would constitute one of the great problems of the world.

Primitive Christianity was therefore right to live wholly in the future with the Christ who was to come, and to preserve of the historic Jesus only detached sayings, a few miracles, His death and resurrection. By abolishing both the world and the historical Jesus it escaped the inner division described above, and remained consistent in its point of view. We, on our part, have reason to be grateful to the early Christians that, in consequence of this attitude they have handed down to us, not biographies of Jesus but only Gospels, and that therefore we possess the Idea and the Person with the minimum of historical and contemporary limitations.

But the world continued to exist, and its continuance brought this one-sided view to an end. The supra-mundane Christ and the historical Jesus of Nazareth had to be brought together into a single personality at once historical and raised above time. That was accomplished by Gnosticism and the Logos Christology. Both, from opposite standpoints, because they were seeking the same goal, agreed in sublimating the historical Jesus into the supra-mundane Idea. The result of this development, which followed on the discrediting of eschatology, was that the historical Jesus was again introduced into the field of view of Christianity, but in such a way that all justification for, and interest in, the investigation of His life and historical personality were done away with.

Greek theology was as indifferent in regard to the historical Jesus who lives concealed in the Gospels as was the early eschatological theology. More than that, it was dangerous to Him; for it created a new supernatural-historical Gospel, and we may consider it fortunate that the Synoptics were already so firmly established that the Fourth Gospel could not oust them; instead, the Church, as though from the inner necessity of the antitheses which now began to be a constructive element in her thought, was obliged to set up two antithetic Gospels alongside of one another.

When at Chalcedon the West overcame the East, its doctrine of the two natures dissolved the unity of the Person, and thereby cut off the last possibility of a return to the historical Jesus. The self-contradiction was elevated into a law. But the Manhood was so far admitted as to preserve, in appearance, the rights of history. Thus by a deception the formula kept the Life prisoner and prevented the leading spirits of the Reformation from grasping the idea of a return to the historical Jesus.

This dogma had first to be shattered before men could once more go out in quest of the historical Jesus, before they could even grasp the thought of His existence. That the historic Jesus is something different from the Jesus Christ of the doctrine of the Two Natures seems to us now self-evident. We can, at the present day, scarcely imagine the long agony in which the historical view of the life of Jesus came to birth. And even when He was once more recalled to life, He was still, like Lazarus of old, bound hand and foot with grave-clothes – the grave-clothes of the dogma of the Dual Nature. Hase relates, in the preface to his first Life of Jesus (1829), that a worthy old gentleman, hearing of his project, advised him to treat in the first part of the human, in the second of the divine Nature. There was a fine simplicity about that. But does not the simplicity cover a presentiment of the revolution of thought for which the historical method of study was preparing the way – a presentiment which those who were engaged in the work did not share in the same measure? It was fortunate that they did not; for otherwise how could they have had the courage to go on?

The historical investigation of the life of Jesus did not take its rise from a purely historical interest; it turned to the Jesus of history as an ally in the struggle against the tyranny of dogma. Afterwards when it was freed from this πάθος it sought to present the historic Jesus in a form intelligible to its own time. For Bahrdt and Venturini He was the tool of a secret order. They wrote under the impression of the immense influence exercised by the Order of the Illuminati[1] at the end of the eighteenth century. For Reinhard, Hess, Paulus, and the rest of the rationalistic writers He is the admirable revealer of true virtue, which is coincident with right reason. Thus each successive epoch of theology found its own thoughts in Jesus; that was, indeed, the only way in which it could make Him live.

But it was not only each epoch that found its reflection in Jesus; each individual created Him in accordance with his own character. There is no historical task which so reveals a man's true self as the writing of a Life of Jesus. No vital force comes into the figure unless a man breathes into it all the hate or all the love of which he is capable. The stronger the love, or the stronger the hate, the more life-like is the figure which is produced. For hate as well as love can write a Life of Jesus, and the greatest of them are written with hate: that of Reimarus, the Wolfenbüttel Fragmentist, and that of David Friedrich Strauss. It was not so much hate of the Person of Jesus as of the supernatural nimbus with which it was so easy to surround Him, and with which He had in fact been surrounded. They were eager to picture Him as truly and purely human, to strip from Him the robes of splendour with which He had been apparelled, and clothe Him once more with the coarse garments in which He had walked in Galilee.

And their hate sharpened their historical insight. They advanced the study of the subject more than all the others put together. But for the offence which they gave, the science of historical theology would not have stood where it does to-day. 'It must needs be that offences come; but woe to that man by whom the offence cometh'. Reimarus evaded that woe by keeping the offence to himself and preserving silence during his lifetime – his work, 'The Aims of Jesus and His Disciples', was only published after his death, by Lessing. But in the case of Strauss, who, as a young man of twenty-seven, cast the offence openly in the face of the world, the woe fulfilled itself. His 'Life of Jesus' was his ruin. But he did not cease to be proud of it in spite of all the misfortune that it brought him. 'I might well bear a grudge against my book', he writes twenty-five years later in the preface to the 'Conversations of Ulrich von Hutten',[1] 'for it has done me much evil ('And rightly so !' the pious will exclaim). It has excluded me from public teaching in which I took pleasure and for which I had perhaps some talent; it has torn me from natural relationships and driven me into unnatural ones; it has made my life a lonely one. And yet when I consider what it would have meant if I had refused to utter the word which lay upon my soul, if I had suppressed the doubts which were at work in my mind – then I bless the book which has doubtless done me grievous harm outwardly, but which preserved the inward health of my mind and heart, and, I doubt not, has done the same for many others also.'

Before him, Bahrdt had his career broken in consequence of revealing his beliefs concerning the Life of Jesus; and after him, Bruno Bauer.

It was easy for them, resolved as they were to open the way even with seeming blasphemy. But the others, those who tried to bring Jesus to life at the call of love, found it a cruel task to be honest. The critical study of the life of Jesus has been for theology a school of honesty. The world had never seen before, and will never see again, a struggle for truth so full of pain and renunciation as that of which the Lives of Jesus of the last hundred years contain the cryptic record. One must read the successive Lives of Jesus with which Hase followed the course of the study from the 'twenties to the 'seventies of the nineteenth century to get an inkling of what it must have cost the men who lived through that decisive period really to maintain that 'courageous freedom of investigation' which the great Jena professor, in the preface to his first Life of Jesus, claims for his researches. One sees in him the marks of the struggle with which he gives up, bit by bit, things which, when he wrote that preface, he never dreamed he would have to surrender. It was fortunate for these men that their sympathies sometimes obscured their critical vision, so that, without becoming insincere, they were able to take white clouds for distant mountains. That was the kindly fate of Hase and Beyschlag.

The personal character of the study is not only due, however, to the fact that a personality can only be awakened to life by the touch of a personality; it lies in the essential nature of the problem itself. For the problem of the life of Jesus has no analogue in the field of history. No historical school has ever laid down canons for the investigation of this problem, no professional historian has ever lent his aid to theology in dealing with it. Every ordinary method of historical investigation proves inadequate to the complexity of the conditions. The standards of ordinary historical science are here inadequate, its methods not immediately applicable. The historical study of the life of Jesus has had to create its own methods for itself. In the constant succession of unsuccessful attempts, five or six problems have emerged side by side which together constitute the fundamental problem. There is, however, no direct method of solving the problem in its complexity; all that can be done is to experiment continuously, starting from definite assumptions; and in this experimentation the guiding principle must ultimately rest upon historical intuition.

The cause of this lies in the nature of the sources of the life of Jesus, and in the character of our knowledge of the contemporary religious world of thought. It is not that the sources are in themselves bad. When we have once made up our minds that we have not the materials for a complete Life of Jesus, but only for a picture of His public ministry, it must be admitted that there are few characters of antiquity about whom we possess so much indubitably historical information, of whom we have so many authentic discourses. The position is much more favourable, for instance, than in the case of Socrates; for he is pictured to us by literary men who exercised their creative ability upon the portrait. Jesus stands much more immediately before us, because He was depicted by simple Christians without literary gift.

But at this point there arises a twofold difficulty. There is first the fact that what has just been said applies only to the first three Gospels, while the fourth, as regards its character, historical data, and discourse material, forms a world of its own. It is written from the Greek standpoint, while the first three are written from the Jewish. And even if one could get over this, and regard, as has often been done, the Synoptics and the Fourth Gospel as standing in something of the same relation to one another as Xenophon does to Plato as sources for the life of Socrates, yet the complete irreconcilability of the historical data would compel the critical investigator to decide from the first in favour of one source or the other. Once more it is found true that 'No man can serve two masters.' This stringent dilemma was not recognised from the beginning; its emergence is one of the results of the whole course of experiment.

The second difficulty regarding the sources is the want of any thread of connexion in the material which they offer us. While the Synoptics are only collections of anecdotes (in the best, historical sense of the word), the Gospel of John – as stands on record in its closing words – only professes to give a selection of the events and discourses.

From these materials we can only get a Life of Jesus with yawning gaps. How are these gaps to be filled? At the worst with phrases, at the best with historical imagination. There is really no other means of arriving at the order and inner connexion of the facts of the life of Jesus than the making and testing of hypotheses. If the tradition preserved by the Synoptists really includes all that happened during the time that Jesus was with His disciples, the attempt to discover the connexion must succeed sooner or later. It becomes more and more clear that this presupposition is indispensable to the investigation. If it is merely a fortuitous series of episodes that the Evangelists have handed down to us, we may give up the attempt to arrive at a critical reconstruction of the life of Jesus as hopeless.

But it is not only the events which lack historical connexion, we are without any indication of a thread of connexion in the actions and discourses of Jesus, because the sources give no hint of the character of His self-consciousness. They confine themselves to outward facts. We only begin to understand these historically when we can mentally place them in an intelligible connexion and conceive them as the acts of a clearly defined personality. All that we know of the development of Jesus and of His Messianic self-consciousness has been arrived at by a series of working hypotheses. Our conclusions can only be considered valid so long as they are not found incompatible with the recorded facts as a whole.

It may be maintained by the aid of arguments drawn from the sources that the self-consciousness of Jesus underwent a development during the course of His public ministry; it may, with equally good grounds, be denied. For in both cases the arguments are based upon little details in the narrative in regard to which we do not know whether they are purely accidental, or whether they belong to the essence of the facts. In each case, moreover, the experimental working out of the hypothesis leads to a conclusion which compels the rejection of some of the actual data of the sources. Each view equally involves a violent treatment of the text.

Furthermore, the sources exhibit, each within itself, a striking contradiction. They assert that Jesus felt Himself to be the Messiah; and yet from their presentation of His life it does not appear that He ever publicly claimed to be so. They attribute to Him, that is, an attitude which has absolutely no connexion with the consciousness which they assume that He possessed. But once admit that the outward acts are not the natural expression of the self-consciousness and all exact historical knowledge is at an end; we have to do with an isolated fact which is not referable to any law.

This being so, the only way of arriving at a conclusion of any value is to experiment, to test, by working them out, the two hypotheses – that Jesus felt Himself to be the Messiah, as the sources assert, or that He did not feel Himself to be so, as His conduct implies; or else to try to conjecture what kind of Messianic consciousness His must have been, if it left His conduct and His discourses unaffected. For one thing is certain: the whole account of the last days at Jerusalem would be unintelligible, if we had to suppose that the mass of the people had a shadow of a suspicion that Jesus held Himself to be the Messiah.

Again, whereas in general a personality is to some extent defined by the world of thought which it shares with its contemporaries, in the case of Jesus this source of information is as unsatisfactory as the documents.

What was the nature of the contemporary Jewish world of thought? To that question no clear answer can be given. We do not know whether the expectation of the Messiah was generally current or whether it was the faith of a mere sect. With the Mosaic religion as such it had nothing to do. There was no organic connexion between the religion of legal observance and the future hope. Further, if the eschatological hope was generally current, was it the prophetic or the apocalyptic form of that hope? We know the Messianic expectations of the prophets; we know the apocalyptic picture as drawn by Daniel, and, following him, by Enoch and the Psalms of Solomon before the coming of Jesus, and by the Apocalypses of Ezra and Baruch about the time of the destruction of Jerusalem. But we do not know which was the popular form; nor, supposing that both were combined into one picture, what this picture really looked like. We know only the form of eschatology which meets us in the Gospels and in the Pauline epistles; that is to say, the form which it took in the Christian community in consequence of the coming of Jesus. And to combine these three – the prophetic, the Late-Jewish apocalyptic, and the Christian – has not proved possible.

Even supposing we could obtain more exact information regarding the popular Messianic expectations at the time of Jesus, we should still not know what form they assumed in the self-consciousness of One who knew Himself to be the Messiah but held that the time was not yet come for Him to reveal Himself as such. We only know their aspect from without, as a waiting for the Messiah and the Messianic Age; we have no clue to their aspect from within as factors in the Messianic self-consciousness. We possess no psychology of the Messiah. The Evangelists have nothing to tell us about it, because Jesus told them nothing about it; the sources for the contemporary spiritual life inform us only concerning the eschatological expectation. For the form of the Messianic self-consciousness of Jesus we have to fall back upon conjecture.

Such is the character of the problem, and, as a consequence, historical experiment must here take the place of historical research. That being so, it is easy to understand that to take a survey of the study of the life of Jesus is to be confronted, at first sight, with a scene of the most boundless confusion. A series of experiments are repeated with constantly varying modifications suggested by the results furnished by the subsidiary sciences. Most of the writers, however, have no suspicion that they are merely repeating an experiment which has often been made before. Some of them discover this in the course of their work to their own great astonishment – it is so, for instance, with Wrede, who recognises that he is working out, though doubtless with a clearer consciousness of his aim, an idea of Bruno Bauer's.[2] If old Reimarus were to come back again, he might confidently give himself out to be the latest of the moderns, for his work rests upon a recognition of the exclusive importance of eschatology, such as only recurs again in Johannes Weiss.

Progress, too, is curiously fitful, with long intervals of marking time between the advances. From Strauss down to the 'nineties there was no real progress, if one takes into consideration only the complete Lives of Jesus which appeared. But a number of separate problems took a more clearly defined form, so that in the end the general problem suddenly moved forward, as it seemed, with a jerk.

There is really no common standard by which to judge the works with which we have to do. It is not the most orderly narratives, those which weave in conscientiously every detail of the text, which have advanced the study of the subject, but precisely the eccentric ones, those that take the greatest liberties with the text. It is not by the mass of facts that a writer sets down along-side of one another as possible – because he writes easily and there is no one there to contradict him, and because facts on paper do not come into collision so sharply as they do in reality – it is not in that way that he shows his power of reconstructing history, but by that which he recognises as impossible. The constructions of Reimarus and Bruno Bauer have no solidity; they are mere products of the imagination. But there is much more historical power in their clear grasp of a single definite problem, which has blinded them to all else, than there is in the circumstantial works of Beyschlag and Bernard Weiss.

But once one has accustomed oneself to look for certain definite landmarks amid this apparent welter of confusion one begins at last to discover in vague outline the course followed, and the progress made, by the critical study of the life of Jesus.

It falls, immediately, into two periods, that before Strauss and that after Strauss. The dominant interest in the first is the question of miracle. What terms are possible between a historical treatment and the acceptance of supernatural events? With the advent of Strauss this problem found a solution, viz., that these events have no rightful place in the history, but are simply mythical elements in the sources. The way was thus thrown open. Meanwhile, alongside of the problem of the supernatural, other problems had been dimly apprehended. Reimarus had drawn attention to the contemporary eschatological views; Hase, in his first Life of Jesus (1829), had sought to trace a development in the selfconsciousness of Jesus.

But on this point a clear view was impossible, because all the students of the subject were still basing their operations upon the harmony of the Synoptics and the Fourth Gospel; which means that they had not so far felt the need of a historically intelligible outline of the life of Jesus. Here, too, Strauss was the lightbringer. But the transient illumination was destined to be obscured by the Marcan hypothesis, which now came to the front. The necessity of choosing between John and the Synoptists was first fully established by the Tübingen school; and the right relation of this question to the Marcan hypothesis was subsequently shown by Holtzmann.

While these discussions of the preliminary literary questions were in progress the main historical problem of the life of Jesus was slowly rising into view. The question began to be mooted: what was the significance of eschatology for the mind of Jesus? With this problem was associated, in virtue of an inner connexion which was not at first suspected, the problem of the self-consciousness of Jesus. At the beginning of the 'nineties it was generally felt that, in the solution given to this dual problem, an in some measure assured knowledge of the outward and inward course of the life of Jesus had been reached. At this point Johannes Weiss revived the comprehensive claim of Reimarus on behalf of eschatology; and scarcely had criti-

cism adjusted its attitude to this question when Wrede renewed the attempt
of Bauer and Volkmar to eliminate altogether the Messianic element from
the life of Jesus.

We are now once more in the midst of a period of great activity in the
study of the subject. On the one side we are offered a historical solution,
on the other a literary. The question at issue is: Is it possible to explain
the contradiction between the Messianic consciousness of Jesus and His
non-Messianic discourses and actions by means of a conception of His
Messianic consciousness which will make it appear that He could not have
acted otherwise than as the Evangelists describe; or must we endeavour to
explain the contradiction by taking the non-Messianic discourses and actions
as our fixed point, denying the reality of His Messianic selfconsciousness and
regarding it as a later interpolation of the beliefs of the Christian community
into the life of Jesus? In the latter case the Evangelists are supposed to
have attributed these Messianic claims to Jesus because the early Church
held Him to be the Messiah, but to have contradicted themselves by describing His life as it actually was, viz., as the life of a prophet, not of one
who held Himself to be the Messiah. To put it briefly: Does the difficulty of
explaining the historical personality of Jesus lie in the history itself, or only
in the way in which it is represented in the sources?

This alternative will be discussed in all the critical studies of the next
few years. Once clearly posed it compels a decision. But no one can really
understand the problem who has not a clear notion of the way in which it
has shaped itself in the course of the investigation; no one can justly criticise, or appraise the value of, new contributions to the study of this subject
unless he knows in what forms they have been presented before.

The history of the study of the life of Jesus has hitherto received surprisingly little attention. Hase, in his Life of Jesus of 1829, briefly records the
previous attempts to deal with the subject. Friedrich von Ammon, himself
one of the most distinguished students in this department, in his 'Progress
of Christianity',[3] gives some information regarding 'the most notable biographies of Jesus of the last fifty years'. In the year 1865 Uhlhorn treated
together the Lives of Jesus of Renan, Schenkel, and Strauss; in 1876 Hase,
in his 'History of Jesus', gave the only complete literary history of the
subject;[4] in 1892 Uhlhorn extended his former lecture to include the works
of Keim, Delff, Beyschlag, and Weiss;[5] in 1898 Frantzen described, in a
short essay, the progress of the study since Strauss;[6] in 1899 and 1900
Baldensperger gave, in the *Theologische Rundschau*, a survey of the most
recent publications;[7] Weinel's book, 'Jesus in the Nineteenth Century',
naturally only gives an analysis of a few classical works; Otto Schmiedel's
lecture on the 'Main Problems of the Critical Study of the Life of Jesus'
(1902) merely sketches the history of the subject in broad outline.[8]

Apart from scattered notices in histories of theology this is practically all the literature of the subject. There is room for an attempt to bring order into the chaos of the Lives of Jesus. Hase made ingenious comparisons between them, but he was unable to group them according to inner principles, or to judge them justly. Weisse is for him a feebler descendant of Strauss, Bruno Bauer is the victim of a fantastic imagination. It would indeed have been difficult for Hase to discover in the works of his time any principle of division. But now, when the literary and eschatological methods of solution have led to complementary results, when the post-Straussian period of investigation seems to have reached a provisional close, and the goal to which it has been tending has become clear, the time seems ripe for the attempt to trace genetically in the successive works the shaping of the problem as it now confronts us, and to give a systematic historical account of the critical study of the life of Jesus. Our endeavour will be to furnish a graphic description of all the attempts to deal with the subject; and not to dismiss them with stock phrases or traditional labels, but to show clearly what they really did to advance the formulation of the problem, whether their contemporaries recognised it or not. In accordance with this principle many famous Lives of Jesus which have prolonged and honoured existence through many successive editions, will make but a poor figure, while others, which have received scant notice, will appear great. Behind Success comes Truth, and her reward is with her.

NOTES

1. D. Fr. Strauss, *Gespräche von Ulrich von Hutten*, Leipzig, 1860.
2. W. Wrede, *Das Messiasgeheimnis in den Evangelien* [The Messianic Secret in the Gospels], Göttingen, 1901, pp. 280–282.
3. Dr. Christoph Friedrich von Ammon, *Fortbildung des Christentums*, Leipzig, 1840. vol. IV. p. 156 ff.
4. Hase, *Geschichte Jesu*, Leipzig, 1876, pp. 110–162. The second edition, published in 1891, carries the survey no further than the first.
5. *Das Leben Jesu in seinen neueren Darstellungen*, 1892, five lectures.
6. W. Frantzen, *Die 'Leben-Jesu' Bewegung seit Strauss*, Dorpat, 1898.
7. *Theologische Rundschau*, II, 59–67 (1899); III, 9–19 (1900).
8. Von Soden's study, *Die wichtigsten Fragen im Leben Jesu*, 1904, belongs here only in a very limited sense, since it does not seek to show how the problems have gradually emerged in the various Lives of Jesus.

William James

William James was born in 1842 in New York and received his primary and
secondary school education at a number of places, partly in the U. S. partly in
Europe where he got his schooling in Geneva, London, Paris, Boulogne and
Bonn. From 1860 to 1861 he worked in art but abandoned this in order to study
medicine. From 1861 until 1864 he studied at Lawrence Scientific School,
from 1864 until 1867 at Harvard Medical School with an interruption of one
year participating in an expedition to the Amazon basin (1865–1866). From
April 1867 to November 1868 he again spent a time in Europe, working in
Dresden, Berlin, Teplitz and Divonne. After his return to Cambridge, Massachusetts, he obtained the M. D. degree at Harvard in June 1869. For reasons
of health he decided not to go into the medical profession and for a couple of
years did some intensive reading. In 1872 he was appointed to the Department
of Natural History of Harvard College. Having taught a supplementary course
in the Department of Philosophy since 1877, and having created the first
American laboratory of psychology, James was appointed in the Department
of Philosophy in 1880. So he successively taught physiology, psychology and philosophy. In later years James also made frequent trips to Europe where he
spent, e.g., the year 1882—1883, and where he delivered the Gifford Lectures in
1901–1902. William James died at Chocorua, N. H., in 1910.

The following publications of James may be mentioned here: 1890 *The Prin-
ciples of Psychology* (2 vol.); 1897 *The Will to Believe and Other Essays in Popular
Philosophy;* 1902 *The Varieties of Religious Experience: a Study in Human
Nature;* 1907 *Pragmatism;* 1909 *The Meaning of Truth;* 1909 *A Pluralistic
Universe;* 1911 *Some Problems of Philosophy;* 1912 *Essays in Radical Empiricism;*
1912 *Memories and Studies;* 1920 *Collected Essays and Reviews.*

As a pragmatist philosopher trained both in the sciences and in psychology,
James gave an empirical treatment of the religious experience of man and drew
some philosophical conclusions from this study. The methodology and perspective of his *Varieties* made this study a classic for the psychology of religion.

The following fragments have been taken from the first chapters of *The Varieties of Religious Experience.* They show clearly the point of departure, the procedure and the perspective of James' psychological approach to religion.

THE STUDY OF RELIGIOUS EXPERIENCE

'Preface' to the Varieties of Religious Experience

This book would never have been written had I not been honored with
an appointment as Gifford Lecturer on Natural Religion at the University

of Edinburgh. In casting about me for subjects of the two courses of ten lectures each for which I thus became responsible, it seemed to me that the first course might well be a descriptive one on 'Man's Religious Appetites', and the second a metaphysical one on 'Their Satisfaction through Philosophy'. But the unexpected growth of the psychological matter as I came to write it out has resulted in the second subject being postponed entirely, and the description of man's religious constitution now fills the twenty lectures. In Lecture XX I have suggested rather than stated my own philosophic conclusions, and the reader who desires immediately to know them should turn to pages 367–391, and to the 'Postscript' of the book. I hope to be able at some later day to express them in more explicit form.

In my belief that a large acquaintance with particulars often makes us wiser than the possession of abstract formulas, however deep, I have loaded the lectures with concrete examples, and I have chosen these among the extremer expressions of the religious temperament. To some readers I may consequently seem, before they get beyond the middle of the book, to offer a caricature of the subject. Such convulsions of piety, they will say, are not sane. If, however, they will have the patience to read to the end, I believe that this unfavorable impression will disappear; for I there combine the religious impulses with other principles of common sense which serve as correctives of exaggeration, and allow the individual reader to draw as moderate conclusions as he will.

The method

As regards the manner in which I shall have to administer this lectureship, I am neither a theologian, nor a scholar learned in the history of religions, nor an anthropologist. Psychology is the only branch of learning in which I am particularly versed. To the psychologist the religious propensities of man must be at least as interesting as any other of the facts pertaining to his mental constitution. It would seem, therefore, that, as a psychologist, the natural thing for me would be to invite you to a descriptive survey of those religious propensities.

If the inquiry be psychological, not religious institutions, but rather religious feelings and religious impulses must be its subject, and I must confine myself to those more developed subjective phenomena recorded in literature produced by articulate and fully self-conscious men, in works of piety and autobiography. Interesting as the origins and early stages of a subject always are, yet when one seeks earnestly for its full significance, one must always look to its more completely evolved and perfect forms. It follows from this that the documents that will most concern us will be those of the men who were most accomplished in the religious life and best able to give an intelligible account of their ideas and motives. These men, of course, are either comparatively modern writers, or else such earlier ones as have become religious classics. The *documents humains* which we shall find most instructive need not then be sought for in the haunts of special erudition – they lie along the beaten highway; and this circumstance, which flows so naturally from the character of our problem, suits admirably also your lecturer's lack of special theological learning. I may take my citations, my sentences and paragraphs of personal confession, from books that most of you at some time will have had already in your hands, and yet this will be no detriment to the value of my conclusions. It is true that some more adventurous reader and investigator, lecturing here in future, may unearth from the shelves of libraries documents that will make a more delectable and curious entertainment to listen to than mine. Yet I doubt whether he will necessarily, by his control of so much more out-of-the-way material, get much closer to the essence of the matter in hand.

The question, What are the religious propensities? and the question, What is their philosophic significance? are two entirely different orders of question from the logical point of view; and, as a failure to recognize this fact distinctly may breed confusion, I wish to insist upon the point a little before we enter into the documents and materials to which I have referred.

In recent books on logic, distinction is made between two orders of inquiry concerning anything. First, what is the nature of it? how did it come about? what is its constitution, origin, and history? And second, What is its importance, meaning, or significance, now that it is once here? The answer to the one question is given in an *existential judgment* or proposition. The answer to the other is a *proposition of value*, what the Germans call a *Werthurtheil*, or what we may, if we like, denominate a *spiritual judgment*. Neither judgment can be deduced immediately from the other. They proceed from diverse intellectual preoccupations, and the mind combines them only by making them first separately, and then adding them together.

In the matter of religions it is particularly easy to distinguish the two orders of questions. Every religious phenomenon has its history and its derivation from natural antecedents. What is nowadays called the higher criticism of the Bible is only a study of the Bible from this existential point of view, neglected too much by the earlier church. Under just what biographic conditions did the sacred writers bring forth their various contributions to the holy volume? And what had they exactly in their several individual minds, when they delivered their utterances? These are manifestly questions of historical fact, and one does not see how the answer to them can decide offhand the still further question: of what use should such a volume, with its manner of coming into existence so defined, be to us a guide to life and a revelation? To answer this other question we must have already in our mind some sort of a general theory as to what the peculiarities in a thing should be which give it value for purposes of revelation; and this theory itself would be what I just called a spiritual judgment. Combining it with our existential judgment, we might indeed deduce another spiritual judgment as to the Bible's worth. Thus if our theory of revelation-value were to affirm that any book, to possess it, must have been composed automatically or not by the free caprice of the writer, or that it must exhibit no scientific and historic errors and express no local or personal passions, the Bible would probably fare ill at our hands. But if, on the other hand, our theory should allow that a book may well be a revelation in spite of errors and passions and deliberate human composition, if only it be a true record of the inner experiences of great-souled persons wrestling with the crises of their fate, then the verdict would be much more favorable. You see that the existential facts by themselves are insufficient for determining he value; and the best adepts of the higher criticism accordingly never confound the existential with the spiritual problem. With the same conclusions of fact before them, some take one view, and some another, of the Bible's value as a revelation, according as their spiritual judgment as to the foundation of values differs.

I make these general remarks about the two sorts of judgment, because there are many religious persons – some of you now present, possibly, are among them – who do not yet make a working use of the distinction, and who may therefore feel at first a little startled at the purely existential point of view from which in the following lectures the phenomena of religious experience must be considered. When I handle them biologically and psychologically as if they were mere curious facts of individual history, some of you may think it a degradation of so sublime a subject, and may even suspect me, until my purpose gets more fully expressed, of deliberately seeking to discredit the religious side of life.

Such a result is of course absolutely alien to my intention; and since such a prejudice on your part would seriously obstruct the due effect of what I have to relate, I will devote a few more words to the point.

There can be no doubt that as a matter of fact a religious life, exclusively pursued, does tend to make the person exceptional and eccentric. I speak not now of your ordinary religious believer, who follows the conventional observances of his country, whether it be Buddhist, Christian, or Mohammedan. His religion has been made for him by others, communicated to him by tradition, determined to fixed forms by imitation, and retained by habit. It would profit us little to study this second-hand religious life. We must make search rather for the original experiences which were the patternsetters to all this mass of suggested feeling and imitated conduct. These experiences we can only find in individuals for whom religion exists not as a dull habit, but as an acute fever rather. But such individuals are 'geniuses' in the religious line; and like many other geniuses who have brought forth fruits effective enough for commemoration in the pages of biography, such religious geniuses have often shown symptoms of nervous instability. Even more perhaps than other kinds of genius, religious leaders have been subject to abnormal psychical visitations. Invariably they have been creatures of exalted emotional sensibility. Often they have led a discordant inner life, and had melancholy during a part of their career. They have known no measure, been liable to obsessions and fixed ideas; and frequently they have fallen into trances, heard voices, seen visions, and presented all sorts of peculiarities which are ordinarily classed as pathological. Often, moreover, these pathological features in their career have helped to give them their religious authority and influence. [...]

The subject

Most books on the philosophy of religion try to begin with a precise definition of what its essence consists of. Some of these would-be definitions may possibly come before us in later portions of this course, and I shall not be pedantic enough to enumerate any of them to you now. Meanwhile the very fact that they are so many and so different from one another is enough to prove that the word 'religion' cannot stand for any single principle or essence, but is rather a collective name. The theorizing mind tends always to the oversimplification of its materials. This is the root of all that absolutism and one-sided dogmatism by which both philosophy and religion have been infested. Let us not fall immediately into a one-sided view of our subject, but let us rather admit freely at the outset that we may very likely find no one essence, but many characters which may alternately be equally important in religion. If we should inquire for the essence of 'government', for example, one man might tell us it was authority, another submission, another police, another an army, another an assembly, another a system of laws; yet all the while it would be true that no concrete government can exist without all these things, one of which is more important at one moment and others at another. The man who knows governments most completely is he who troubles himself least about a definition which shall give their essence. Enjoying an intimate acquaintance with all their particularities in turn, he would naturally regard an abstract conception in which these were unified as a thing more misleading than enlightening. And why may not religion be a conception equally complex?[1]

Consider also the 'religious sentiment' which we see referred to in so many books, as if it were a single sort of mental entity.

In the psychologies and in the philosophies of religion, we find the authors attempting to specify just what entity it is. One man allies it to the feeling of dependence; one makes it a derivative from fear; others connect it with the sexual life; others still identify it with the feeling of the infinite; and so on. Such different ways of conceiving it ought of themselves to arouse doubt as to whether it possibly can be one specific thing; and the moment we are willing to treat the term 'religious sentiment' as a collective name for the many sentiments which religious objects may arouse in alternation we see that it probably contains nothing whatever of a psychologically specific nature. There is religious fear, religious love, religious awe, religious joy, and so forth. But religious love is only man's natural emotion of love directed to a religious object; religious fear is only the ordinary fear of commerce, so to speak, the common quaking of the human breast in so far as the notion of divine retribution may arouse it; religious awe is the same organic thrill which we feel in a forest at twilight, or in a mountain gorge; only this time it comes over us at the thought of our supernatural relations; and similarly of all the various sentiments which may be called into play in the lives of religious persons. As concrete states of mind, made up of a feeling *plus* a specific sort of object, religious emotions of course are psychic entities distinguishable from other concrete emotions; but there is no ground for assuming a simple abstract 'religious emotion' to exist as a distinct elementary mental affection by itself, present in every religious experience without exception.

As there thus seems to be no one elementary religious emotion, but only a common storehouse of emotions upon which religious objects may draw, so there might conceivably also prove to be no one specific and essential kind of religious object, and no one specific and essential kind of religious act.

The field of religion being as wide as this, it is manifestly impossible that I should pretend to cover it. My lectures must be limited to a fraction of the subject. And, although it would indeed be foolish to set up an abstract definition of religion's essence, and then proceed to defend that definition against all comers, yet this need not prevent me from taking my own narrow view of what religion shall consist in *for the purpose of these lectures,* or, out of the many meanings of the word, from choosing the one meaning in which I wish to interest you particularly, and proclaiming arbitrarily that when I say 'religion' I mean *that*. This, in fact, is what I must do, and I will now preliminarily seek to mark out the field I choose.

One way to mark it out easily is to say what aspects of the subject we leave out. At the outset we are struck by one great partition which divides the religious field. On the one side of it lies institutional, on the other personal religion. As M. P. Sabatier says, one branch of religion keeps the divinity, another keeps man most in view. Worship and sacrifice, procedures for working on the dispositions of the deity, theology and ceremony and ecclesiastical organization, are the essentials of religion in the institutional branch. Were we to limit our view to it, we should have to define religion as an external art, the art of winning the favor of the gods. In the more personal branch of religion it is on the contrary the inner dispositions of man himself which form the centre of interest, his conscience, his deserts, his helplessness, his incompleteness. And although the favor of the God, as forfeited or gained, is still an essential feature of the story, and theology plays a vital part therein, yet the acts to which this sort of religion prompts are personal not ritual acts, the individual transacts the business by himself alone, and the ecclesiastical organization, with its priests and sacraments and other go-betweens, sinks to an altogether secondary place. The relation goes direct from heart to heart, from soul to soul, between man and his maker.

Now in these lectures I propose to ignore the institutional branch entirely, to say nothing of the ecclesiastical organization, to consider as little as possible the systematic theology and the ideas about the gods themselves, and to confine myself as far as I can to personal religion pure and simple. To some of you personal religion, thus nakedly considered, will no doubt seem too incomplete a thing to wear the general name. 'It is a part of religion', you will say, 'but only its unorganized rudiment; if we are to name it by itself, we had better call it man's conscience or morality than his religion. The name "religion" should be reserved for the fully organized system of feeling, thought, and institution, for the Church, in short, of which this personal religion, so called, is but a fractional element'.

But if you say this, it will only show the more plainly how much the question of definition tends to become a dispute about names. Rather than prolong such a dispute, I am willing to accept almost any name for the personal religion of which I propose to treat. Call it conscience or morality, if you yourselves prefer, and not religion – under either name it will be equally worthy of our study. As for myself, I think it will prove to contain some elements which morality pure and simple does not contain, and these elements I shall soon seek to point out; so I will myself continue to apply the word 'religion' to it; and in the last lecture of all, I will bring in the theologies and the ecclesiasticisms, and say something of its relation to them.

[...]

It is a good rule in physiology, when we are studying the meaning of an organ, to ask after its most peculiar and characteristic sort of performance, and to seek its office in that one of its functions which no other organ can possibly exert. Surely the same maxim holds good in our present quest. The essence of religious experiences, the thing by which we finally must judge them, must be that element or quality in them which we can meet nowhere else. And such a quality will be of course most prominent and easy to notice in those religious experiences which are most one-sided, exaggerated, and intense.

Now when we compare these intenser experiences with the experiences of tamer minds, so cool and reasonable that we are tempted to call them philosophical rather than religious, we find a character that is perfectly distinct. That character, it seems to me, should be regarded as the practically important *differentia* of religion for our purpose; and just what it is can easily be brought out by comparing the mind of an abstractly conceived *Christian* with that of a *moralist* similarly conceived.

A life is manly, stoical, moral, or philosophical, we say, in proportion as it is less swayed by paltry personal considerations and more by objective ends that call for energy, even though that energy bring personal loss and pain. This is the good side of war, in so far as it calls for 'volunteers'. And for morality life is a war, and the service of the highest is a sort of cosmic patriotism which also calls for volunteers. Even a sick man, unable to be militant outwardly, can carry on the moral warfare. He can willfully turn his attention away from his own future, whether in this world or the next. He can train himself to indifference to his present drawbacks and immerse himself in whatever objective interests still remain accessible. He can follow public news, and sympathize with other people's affairs. He can cultivate cheerful manners, and be silent about his miseries. He can contemplate whatever ideal aspects of existence his philosophy is able to present to him, and practice whatever duties, such as patience, resignation, trust, his ethical system requires. Such a man lives on his loftiest, largest plane. He is a high-hearted freeman and no pining slave. And yet he lacks something which the Christian *par excellence*, the mystic and ascetic saint, for example, has in abundant measure, and which makes of him a human being of an altogether different denomination.

The Christian also spurns the pinched and mumping sickroom attitude, and the lives of saints are full of a kind of callousness to diseased conditions of body which probably no other human records show. But whereas the merely moralistic spurning takes an effort of volition, the Christian spurning is the result of the excitement of a higher kind of emotion, in the presence of which no exertion of volition is required. The moralist must hold his breath and keep his muscles tense; and so long as this athletic attitude is possible all goes well – morality suffices. But the athletic attitude tends ever to break down, and it inevitably does break down even in the most stalwart when the organism begins to decay, or when morbid fears invade the mind. To suggest personal will and effort to one all sicklied o'er with the sense of irremediable impotence is to suggest the most impossible of things. What he craves is to be consoled in his very powerlessness, to feel that the spirit of the universe recognizes and secures him, all decaying and failing as he is. Well, we are all such helpless failures in the last resort. The sanest and best of us are of one clay with lunatics and prison inmates, and death finally runs the robustest of us down. And whenever we feel this, such a sense of the vanity and provisionality of our voluntary career comes over us that all our morality appears but as a plaster hiding a sore it can never cure, and all our well-doing as the hollowest substitute for that well-*being* that our lives ought to be grounded in, but, alas! are not.

And here religion comes to our rescue and takes our fate into her hands. There is a state of mind, known to religious men, but to no others, in which the will to assert ourselves and hold our own has been displaced by a willingness to close our mouths and be as nothing in the floods and waterspouts of God. In this state of mind, what we most dreaded has become the habitation of our safety, and the hour of our moral death has turned into our spiritual birthday. The time for tension in our soul is over, and that of happy relaxation, of calm deep breathing, of an eternal present, with no discordant future to be anxious about, has arrived. Fear is not held in abeyance as it is by mere morality, it is positively expunged and washed away.

We shall see abundant examples of this happy state of mind in later lectures of this course. We shall see how infinitely passionate a thing religion at its highest flights can be. Like love, like wrath, like hope, ambition, jealousy, like every other instinctive eagerness and impulse, it adds to life an enchantment which is not rationally or logically deducible from anything else. This enchantment, coming as a gift when it does come, – a gift of our organism, the physiologists will tell us, a gift of God's grace, the theologians say, – is either there or not there for us, and there are persons who can no more become possessed by it than they can fall in love with a given woman by mere word of command. Religious feeling is thus an absolute addition to the Subject's range of life. It gives him a new sphere of power. When the outward battle is lost, and the outer world disowns him, it redeems and vivifies an interior world which otherwise would be an empty waste.

If religion is to mean anything definite for us, it seems to me that we ought to take it as meaning this added dimension of emotion, this enthusiastic temper of espousal, in regions where morality strictly so called can at best but bow its head and acquiesce. It ought to mean nothing short of this new reach of freedom for us, with the struggle over, the keynote of the universe sounding in our ears, and everlasting possession spread before our eyes.[2]

This sort of happiness in the absolute and everlasting is what we find nowhere but in religion. It is parted off from all mere animal happiness, all mere enjoyment of the present, by that element of solemnity of which I have already made so much account. Solemnity is a hard thing to define abstractly, but certain of its marks are patent enough. A solemn state of mind is never crude or simple – it seems to contain a certain measure of its own opposite in solution. A solemn joy preserves a sort of bitter in its sweetness; a solemn sorrow is one to which we intimately consent. But there are writers who, realizing that happiness of a supreme sort is the prerogative of religion, forget this complication, and call all happiness, as such, religious. Mr. Havelock Ellis, for example, identifies religion with the entire field of the soul's liberation from oppressive moods.

'The simplest functions of physiological life', he writes, 'may be its ministers. Every one who is at all acquainted with the Persian mystics knows how wine may be regarded as an instrument of religion. Indeed, in all countries and in all ages, some form of physical enlargement – singing, dancing, drinking, sexual excitement – has been intimately associated with worship. Even the momentary expansion of the soul in laughter is, to however slight an extent, a religious exercise. . . . Whenever an impulse from the world strikes against the organism, and the resultant is not discomfort or pain, not even the muscular contraction of strenuous manhood, but a joyous expansion or aspiration of the whole soul – there is religion. It is the infinite for which we hunger, and we ride gladly on every little wave that promises to bear us towards it.'[3]

But such a straight identification of religion with any and every form of happiness leaves the essential peculiarity of religious happiness out. The more commonplace happinesses which we get are 'reliefs', occasioned by our momentary escapes from evils either experienced or threatened. But in its most characteristic embodiments, religious happiness is no mere feeling of escape. It cares no longer to escape. It consents to the evil outwardly as a form of sacrifice – inwardly it knows it to be permanently overcome. If you ask *how* religion thus falls on the thorns and faces death, and in the very act annuls annihilation, I cannot explain the matter, for it is religion's secret, and to understand it you must yourself have been a religious man of the extremer type. In our future examples, even of the simplest and healthiest-minded type of religious consciousness, we shall find this complex sacrificial constitution, in which a higher happiness holds a lower unhappiness in check. In the Louvre there is a picture, by Guido Reni, of St. Michael with his foot on Satan's neck. The richness of the picture is in large part due to the fiends' figure being there. The richness of its allegorical meaning also is due to his being there – that is, the world is all the richer for having a devil in it, *so long as we keep our foot upon his neck*. In the religious consciousness, that is just the position in which the fiend, the negative or tragic principle, is found; and for that very reason the religious consciousness is so rich from the emotional point of view.[4] We shall see how in certain men and women it takes on a monstrously ascetic form. There are saints who have literally fed on the negative principle, on humiliation and privation, and the thought of suffering and death,– their souls growing in happiness just in proportion as their outward state grew more intolerable. No other emotion than religious emotion can bring a man to this peculiar pass. And it is for that reason that when we ask our question about the value of religion for human life, I think we ought to look for the answer among these violenter examples rather than among those of a more moderate hue.

Having the phenomenon of our study in its acutest possible form to start with, we can shade down as much as we please later. And if in these cases, repulsive as they are to our ordinary worldly way of judging, we find ourselves compelled to acknowledge religion's value and treat it with respect, it will have proved in some way its value for life at large. By subtracting and toning down extravagances we may thereupon proceed to trace the boundaries of its legitimate sway.

To be sure, it makes our task difficult to have to deal so much with eccentricities and extremes. 'How *can* religion on the whole be the most important of all human functions,' you may ask, 'if every several manifestation of it in turn have to be corrected and sobered down and pruned away?' Such a thesis seems a paradox impossible to sustain reasonably, – yet I believe that something like it will have to be our final contention. That personal attitude which the individual finds himself impelled to take up towards what he apprehends to be the divine – and you will remember that this was our definition – will prove to be both a helpless and a sacrificial attitude. That is, we shall have to confess to at least some amount of dependence on sheer mercy, and to practice some amount of renunciation, great or small, to save our souls alive. The constitution of the world we live in requires it:

> *Entbehren sollst du! sollst entbehren!*
> *Das ist der ewige Gesang*
> *Der jedem an die Ohren klingt,*
> *Den, unser ganzes Leben lang*
> *Uns heiser jede Stunde singt.*

For when all is said and done, we are in the end absolutely dependent o the universe; and into sacrifices and surrenders of some sort, deliberately looked at and accepted, we are drawn and pressed as into our only permanent positions of repose. Now in those states of mind which fall short of religion, the surrender is submitted to as an imposition of necessity, and the sacrifice is undergone at the very best without complaint. In the religious life, on the contrary, surrender and sacrifice are positively espoused: even unnecessary givings-up are added in order that the happiness may increase. *Religion thus makes easy and felicitous what in any case is necessary;* and if it be the only agency that can accomplish this result, its vital importance as a human faculty stands vindicated beyond dispute. It becomes an essential organ of our life, performing a function which no other portion of our nature can so successfully fulfill. From the merely biological point of view, so to call it, this is a conclusion to which, so far as I can now see, we shall inevitably be led, and led moreover by following the purely empirical method of demonstration which I sketched to you in the first lecture. Of the farther office of religion as a metaphysical revelation I will say nothing now. [. . .]

NOTES

1. I can do no better here than refer my readers to the extended and admirable remarks on the futility of all these definitions of religion, in an article by Professor Leuba, published in '*The Monist*' for January, 1901, after my own text was written.

2. Once more, there are plenty of men, constitutionally sombre men, in whose religious life this rapturousness is lacking. They are religious in the wider sense; yet in this acutest of all senses they are not so and it is religion in the acutest sense that I wish, without disputing about words, to study first, so as to get at its typical *differentia*.

3. *The New Spirit*, p. 232.

4. I owe this allegorical illustration to my lamented colleague and friend, Charles Carroll Everett.

Herbert Spencer

Herbert Spencer was born in 1820 in Derby, England, where he received his first school education, followed up at Hinton Charterhouse, near Bath, between 1833 and 1836. Declining to go to Cambridge University, he was for three months an auxiliary teacher at Derby in 1837 and then became a civil engineer, of two railway companies, between 1837 and 1841. Having been back at Derby between 1841 and 1844 and having started to write and to involve himself in politics, he was again engaged in railway construction between 1844 and 1846. From 1848 until 1853 Spencer was sub-editor of the *Economist;* subsequently he lived from his pen and from some smaller inheritances. In 1857 Spencer conceived the idea of writing a complete system of philosophy, which lead to his multi-volume work of 'Synthetic Philosophy', which was issued by subscription. He lived in London, making regular travels to Scotland and visiting Europe occasionally. In 1898 Spencer moved to Brighton where he died in 1903.

The following books by Spencer should be mentioned here: 1850 *Social Statics;* 1855 *The Principles of Psychology;* 1858–1874 *Essays* (3 vol.); 1861 *Education: Intellectual, Moral, Physical;* 1862 *First Principles;* 1864–1867 *The Principles of Biology* (2 vol.); 1870–1872 *The Principles of Psychology* (2nd ed. enlarged to 2 vol.); 1873 *The Study of Sociology;* 1873 etc. ed. *Descriptive Sociology* (in installments); 1876—1896 *The Principles of Sociology* (3 vol.); 1879—1893 *The Principles of Ethics* (2 vol.); 1884 *The Man versus the State;* 1885 *The Nature and Reality of Religion* (reissued as *The Insuppressible Book,* 1885); 1897 *Various Fragments;* 1902 *Facts and Comments.*

Spencer is best-known as the author of the 'Synthetic Philosophy', embodied in the various volumes on 'Principles', and based upon the principle of evolution through the cooperation of inner and outer factors. According to Spencer progress as the transformation of the homogeneous into the heterogeneous is a necessity in the development of human society. Besides his philosophy, his ethics and his study of sociological correlations, Spencer's work is of interest for the study of religion because of his sociological treatment of religious institutions. He investigated the cult of ancestral spirits and contended that, like the fear of the living is supposed to be the root of political control, the fear of the dead would be that of religious control.

The following fragment has been taken from Volume One of *The Principles of Sociology.* It shows the way in which Spencer analyzes ancestor-cult, explains its origin and sees here the origin of all religion.

'ANCESTOR-WORSHIP'

From various parts of the world, witnesses of different nations and divergent beliefs bring evidence that there exist men who are either wholly without ideas of supernatural beings, or whose ideas of them are extremely vague. 'When Father Junípero Serra established the Mission of Dolores in 1776, the shores of San Francisco Bay were thickly populated by the Ahwashtees, Ohlones, Althamos, Romanons, Tuolomos, and other tribes. The good Father found the field unoccupied, for, in the vocabulary of these people, there is found no word for god, angel, or devil; they held no theory of origin or destiny.' This testimony, which Bancroft cites respecting the Indians of California, corresponds with the testimonies of old Spanish writers respecting some South American peoples. Garcilasso says that 'the Chiri-huanas and the natives of the Cape de Pasau ... had no inclination to worship anything high or low, neither from interested motives nor from fear'; Balboa mentions tribes without any religion as having been met with by Ynca Yupangui; and Avendaño asserts that in his time the Antis had no worship whatever. Many kindred instances are given by Sir John Lubbock, and further ones will be found in Tylor's *Primitive Culture*. But I agree with Tylor that the evidence habitually implies some notion, however wavering and inconsistent, of a reviving other-self. Where this has not become a definite belief, the substance of a belief is shown by the funeral rites and by the fear of the dead.

Leaving unsettled the question whether there are men in whom dreams have not generated the notion of a double, and the sequent notion that at death the double has gone away, we may hold it as settled that the first traceable conception of a supernatural being is the conception of a ghost. This exists where no other idea of the same order exists; and this exists where multitudinous other ideas of the same order exist.

That belief in a surviving duplicate is produced among the savage, and is perpetually reproduced among the civilized, is a fact of great significance. Whatever is common to men's minds in all stages, must be deeper down in thought than whatever is peculiar to men's minds in higher stages; and if the later product admits of being reached by modification and expansion of the earlier product, the implication is that it has been so reached. Recognizing this implication, we shall see how fully the facts now to be contemplated justify acceptance of it.

As the notion of a ghost grows from that first vagueness and variableness indicated above, into a definite and avowed idea, there naturally arise the desire and the endeavour to propitiate the ghost. Hence, almost as widely spread as the belief in ghosts, may be looked for a more or less developed ancestor-worship. This we find. To the indirect evidence already given I must now add, in brief form, the direct evidence.

Where the levels of mental nature and social progress are lowest, we usually find, along with an absence of religious ideas generally, an absence of, or very slight development of, ancestor-worship. A typical case is that of the Juángs, a wild tribe of Bengal, who, described as having no word for god, no idea of a future state, no religious ceremonies, are also said to 'have no notion of the worship of ancestors.' Cook, telling us what the Fuegians were before contact with Europeans had introduced foreign ideas, said there were no appearances of religion among them; and we are not told by him or others that they were ancestor-worshippers. So far as the scanty evidence may be trusted, the like seems to be the case with the Andamanese. And though believing in ghosts, the Australians and Tasmanians show us but little persistence in ghost-propitiation. Among the Veddahs, indeed, though extremely low, an active if simple ancestorworship prevails; but here, contact with the more advanced Cingalese has probably been a factor.

When, however, instead of wandering groups who continually leave far behind the places where their members lie buried, we come to settled groups whose burial-place are in their midst, and among whom development of funeral rites is thus made possible, we find that continued propitiation of dead relatives becomes an established practice. All varieties of men show us this.

[. . .]

And now having observed the natural genesis of ancestor-worship, its wide diffusion over the world, and its persistence among advanced races side by side with more developed forms of worship, let us turn from its external aspect to its internal aspect. Let us, so far as we can, contemplate it from the stand-point of those who practise it. Fortunately, two examples, one of its less-developed form and one of its more-developed form, are exhibited to us in the words of ancestor-worshippers themselves.

[. . .]

Here, then, we see ancestor-worship in but a slightly-developed form — an unhistoric ancestor-worship. There have arisen no personages dominant enough to retain their distinct individualities through many generations, and to subordinate the minor traditional individualities.

Peoples who are more settled and further advanced show us a progress. Along with worship of recent and local ancestors, there goes worship of ancestors who died at earlier dates, and who, remembered by their power, have acquired in the general mind a supremacy. This truth ought to need but little illustration, for the habits of ancient races make it familiar. As Grote says: 'In the retrospective faith of a Greek, the ideas of worship and ancestry coalesced: every association of men, large or small, in whom there existed a feeling of present union, traced back that union to some common initial progenitor, and that progenitor, again, was either the common god whom they worshipped, or some semi-divine being closely allied to him.'

This stage of development in which, along with worship of ancestry traced back a certain number of generations, there went a more widely-diffused worship of some to whom the relationships were lost in the far past, we find paralleled in other places; as, for example, in Peru. Sun-worship and Ynca-worship were there associated with an active worship of fore-fathers. Avendaño, repeating the affirmative answers to his questions, says: 'Each of your ancestors ... worshipped the *marcayocc*, who is the founder or senior of the village, from whom you are sprung. He was not worshipped by the Indians of any other village, for they had another *marcayocc*.'

Chiefly, however, let us remark that these settled races of America ex-hibited in their professed creeds the transformation of their remotest pro-genitors into deities. By the Amazulu, the traditional old-old-one, though regarded as having given origin to them and all other things, is not wor-shipped: he is finally dead, and his sons, who once worshipped him, are finally dead; and the worship is monopolized by those later descendants who are remembered as founders of tribes. But among these more advanced peoples of America, the most ancient men, considered as still living else-where, had a worship which subordinated the worship of immediate an-cestors.

[...]

What has been given shows, like the rest, that the remotest remembered ancestors have become divinities, remaining human in physical and mental attributes, and differing only in power; that being recognized in tradition as the begetters, or causers, of existing men, they, as the only known causer of anything, come to be tacitly regarded as the causers of other things;* and that they reside in the region whence the race came, which is the other

---

* While correcting this chapter, I have met with proof that the inadequately-differentiated ideas and words of primitive peoples, lead to confusions of this kind. In his *Sanskrit Texts*, Dr. Muir, showing the conceptions which the ancient Rishis had of the Vedic hymns as composed by themselves, groups together the various cases in which a word implying this compositions is used. The several words thus used are 'making', 'fabricating', 'begetting', or 'generating'. Now if in such a language as Sanscrit, these words are so imperfectly specialized as to be indiscriminately applied to the same act, we may well understand how in-capable ruder languages must be of expressing a distinction between begetting, making, and creating.

world travelled to by the dead. The statements of these peoples directly imply that transformation of ancestors into deities, which we saw was indirectly implied by the growth of funeral rites into worship of the dead, and eventually into religious worship.

It is said, however, that ancestor-worship is peculiar to the inferior races. I have seen implied, I have heard in conversation, and I have now before me in print, the statement that 'no Indo-European or a Semitic nation, so far as we know, seems to have made a religion of worship of the dead.' And the suggested conclusion is that these superior races, who in their earliest recorded times had higher forms of worship, were not even in their still earlier times, ancestor-worshippers.

That those who have another theory to uphold should thus interpret the evidence, is not unnatural. Every hypothesis tends to assimilate facts yielding it support and to reject adverse facts. But that adherents of the Evolution-doctrine should admit a distinction so profound between the minds of different human races, is surprising. Those who believe in creation by manufacture, may consistently hold that Aryans and Semites were supernaturally endowed with higher conceptions than Turanians. If species of animals were separately made with fundamental differences, varieties of men may have been so too. But to assert that the human type has been evolved from lower types, and then to deny that the superior human races have been evolved, mentally as well as physically, from the inferior, and must once have had those general conceptions which the inferior still have, is a marvellous inconsistency. Even in the absence of evidence it would be startling; and in the presence of contrary evidence it is extremely startling.

If in their more advanced stages the leading divisions of the Aryans habitually, while worshipping their greater deities, also worshipped ancestors, who, according to their remoteness, were regarded as divine, semi-divine, and human; must we really infer that in the course of their progress they adopted this ancestor-worship from inferior races? On finding that by the Greeks, heroes from whom the people of each locality traced their descent, were made objects of religious rites, just as by aboriginal Peruvians and others; shall we say that while becoming civilized they grafted on their higher creed this lower creed? When we recall the facts that besides sacrificing to the ghosts of their recent dead, the Romans sacrificed to the ghosts of their ancient dead, who were the founders of their families, just as the Amazulu do at the present time; are we to infer that while Asiatic nomads they had no such worship, but that, then worshipping only certain personalized powers of Nature, they adopted the religion of less cultured peoples as they themselves became more cultured? Such assumptions would be inadmissible, even had we no indications of the original Aryan beliefs;

and are still more inadmissible now that we know what the original Aryan beliefs were. As expressed in their sacred writings, they were essentially the same as those of existing barbarians. 'The heroic Indra, who delights in praise,' and to whom the hymn is 'chaunted at the sacrifice,' hoping to impel 'the well-accoutred, the loud-thundering, to succour us,' is but the ancestor considerably expanded; and from the mouth of the Zulu chief about to sacrifice, would equally well come the words of the Aryan rishi: 'friends drive hither the milch cow with a new hymn.' If the human derivation of Indra needs further evidence, we have it in the statement concerning an intoxicating beverage made from the sacred plant: 'the soma exhilarates not Indra unless it be poured out'; which is exactly the belief of an African respecting the libation of beer for an ancestral ghost. From the Rig-Veda we learn that men who by their virtues gained admission to heaven, attained an existence like that of deities; and these 'ancient pious sages,' who 'shared in the enjoyments of the gods,' were implored to be 'propitious' and to protect. Still more specific are passages from the laws of Menu. We have the statement that the *manes* eat of the funeral meal; we have the direction to the head of the family to make a daily offering to get the good will of the *manes*, and also a monthly offering. And the ideas of savages, whose superior gods are the more powerful ghosts, are undeniably paralleled in a further injunction. That an oblation to the *manes* may be obtained by them, the master of the house must commence with an oblation to the gods, so that the gods may not appropriate what is intended for the *manes!*

Do, then, the Semitic races furnish a solitary exception? Strong evidence must be assigned before it can be admitted that they do; and no such strong evidence is forthcoming. Contrariwise, what positive facts we gather have opposite implications. Remembering that nomadic habits are unfavourable to evolution of the ghost-theory, it is manifest that if the ancient Hebrews, like some existing peoples, had not reached the conception of a permanently-existing ghost, they would, of course, have no established ancestor-worship: not because it was beneath them, but because the conditions for display of it were not fulfilled. Further, we must note that the silence of their legends is but a negative fact, which may be as misleading as negative facts often are; and beyond the general reason we have special reasons for suspecting this illusiveness. For among other peoples we find traditions that give no accounts of practices which not only existed but were dominant: the cause being that extraordinary occurrences only are narrated, and not ordinary occurrences. Interesting personal adventures form their subject-matter and not social habits, which are at best traceable by implication, and in a condensed narrative may leave no traces at all. Thus, to take a case, the legends of the Polynesians say scarcely more than the Bible does about the worship of ancestors; and yet ancestor-worship was in full activity among them. Again, it should be remembered that the sacred books of a religion nominally professed, may give very untrue ideas concerning the actual beliefs of its professors. Two facts already named incidentally show this. The Turkomans are rigid Mahometans; and yet, making pilgrimages to the tombs of canonized robbers, they pray to their ghosts. Similarly, the acceptance of Mahometanism does not prevent the Bedouins from sacrificing at the graves of their forefathers. In both cases there is habitually done that which we should infer could not be done, if we drew our inferences from the Koran. When, thus warned, we turn to the denunciations of the Hebrew prophets, directed against forms of worship which the Hebrews had in common with other races, we are reminded that the religion embodied in the Bible differed greatly from the popular religion. Besides the idolatry persisted in notwithstanding reprobation, there was tree-worship; and the ceremonials, equally low with those of semi-civilized peoples in general, included prostitution in temples. Moreover, the association of mourning dresses with fasting, as well as the law against self-bleeding and cutting-off the hair for the dead, imply primitive funeral rites like those of ancestor-worshippers in general. Nor is this all. On making an offering of first-fruits to Jahveh, the sacrificer is required to say that he has not 'given ought thereof for the dead.' Hence, the conclusion must be that ancestor-worship had developed as far as nomadic habits allowed, before it was repressed by a higher worship. But be there or be there not adequate reason for ascribing a partially-developed ancestor-worship to the Hebrews, there is evidence that it has existed, and continues to exist, among other Semitic peoples. In a paper entitled 'Le culte des ancêtres divinisés dans l'Yémen,' contained in the *Comptes rendus* of the French Academy, Lenormant, after commenting on some inscriptions, says: 'Here, then, we have twice repeated a whole series of human persons, decidedly deceased ancestors or relations of the author of the dedication. Their names are accompanied with the titles they bore during lifetime. They are invoked by their descendants at the same time, in the same degree (rank), with the same intention, as the gods [mentioned in the same formula]; being, in short, completely placed on a par with the inhabitants of heaven. ... They incontestably are deified persons, objects of a family worship, and gods or genii in the belief of the people of their race.'

Kindred evidence is furnished by the following passage from the *Essai sur l'histoire des Arabes* of Caussin de Perceval. Speaking of the time of Mahomet, he says the greatest part of the nation *(i.e.* all who were not either Jews or Christians) were pagans : 'They had a great number of deities; each tribe and nearly each family had one which they held in special, honour. They admitted, however, the existence of a Supreme God (Allah), with whom the other deities were powerful intercessors. . . . Some believed that at death all was at an end; others believed in a resurrection and another life.'

Several significant implications occur here. The fact last named reminds us of the ancient Hebrew belief, or no-belief. Further, this difference of opinion among Arabs, some of whom are stationary and some wandering, harmonizes with the suggestion above made, that nomadic habits are less favourable than the habits of settled life to a persistent ghost-propitiation with all its sequences. Respecting the idea of a supreme deity, accompanying ancestor-worship among them, it is manifest that wandering hordes, coming in frequent contact with relatively-civilized peoples, would inevitably acquire it from them; as, from their European visitors, it is now acquired by savages. But that the belief so acquired is vague and superficial, is shown us by the existing Bedouins; whose Mahometanism, according to Mr. Palgrave, is of the most shadowy kind, while the reality of their ancestor-worship is proved by the sacrifices they 'devoutly' make at tombs. No more, then, of Semites than of Aryans can ancestor-worship be denied.

[. . .]

How unwarranted is the assertion that the superior races have not passed through this lower cult, will be again seen on remembering that down to the present time, ancestor-worship lingers among the most civilized of them. Throughout Europe it still shows itself, here feebly and there with some vigour, notwithstanding the repressive influence of Christianity.

Even Protestants yield undeniable traces of the aboriginal ideas and sentiments and acts. I do not refer merely to the decoration of graves with flowers, reminding us of the placings of flowers on graves by ancestor-worshipping peoples who also offered flowers to their deities; for this practice, spreading with the ritualistic reaction, may be considered as part of a revived Catholicism. I refer rather to certain less obtrusive facts Dead parents are often thought of among us as approving or disapproving. They are figured in the minds of relatives as though they knew what was being done, and as likely to be hurt by disregard of their injunctions. Occasionally a portrait is imagined to look reproachfully on a descendant who is transgressing; and the anxiety not to disobey a dying wish certainly acts as a deterrent. So that, indefinite though their forms have become, the aboriginal notions of subordination and propitiation have not wholly disappeared.

It is, however, among Catholic peoples that this primitive religion most distinctly shows itself. The mortuary chapels in cemeteries on the Continent, are manifestly homologous with the elaborate tombs of the ancients. If erecting a chapel to the Virgin is an act of worship, then the sentiment of worship cannot be wholly absent if the erected chapel is over a dead parent. And though mostly the prayers in such chapels, or at graves, are only *for* the dead, I am told by two French Catholics that exceptionally, when a pious parent is supposed to be not in purgatory but in heaven, there are prayers *to* the dead for intercession. A French correspondent questions this; but he admits that men and women who have died in the odour of sanctity, are canonized by popular opinion and adored. 'Ainsi, j'ai vu, en Bretagne, le tombeau d'un prêtre très pieux et très charitable: il était couvert de couronnes; on s'y rendait en foule *le prier* de procurer des guérisons, de veiller sur les enfants,' etc. Accepting only this last statement as trustworthy, it proves that the primitive religion lingers yet.

Even clearer proof that it lingers is yielded by the still-extant customs of feeding the spirits, both annually and at other times. If we read of periodic feasts for the dead among extinct nations, or now among the existing Chinese, and regard such observances as parts of their ancestor-worship; and if we learn that the feast of All Souls and sundry kindred observances are continued yet in various parts of Europe, both by Teutons and Celts; can we deny that an original ancestor-worship is implied by them?*

See, then, how fully induction justifies deduction; and verifies the inference suggested in the last chapter.

Taking the aggregate of human peoples — tribes, societies, nations — we find that nearly all of them, if not literally all, have a belief, vague or distinct, in a reviving other-self of the dead man. Within this class of peoples we find a class not quite so large, by the members of which the other-self of the dead man is supposed to exist for a time, or always, after death. Nearly as numerous is the class of peoples included in this, who show us

* The following illustrative passage has been translated for me: 'Roman Catholic peasants do not forget all the year round to care for the welfare of the souls of their dead. The crusts of the table are collected throughout the week, and on Saturday night are thrown into the hearth-fire; that they may serve as food for the souls during the following holy day. Any soup which drops on the table . . . is left to the poor souls. When a woman prepares the dough, she casts behind her a handful of flour, and throws a piece of dough into the furnace; when she bakes little cakes, she puts some fat into the pan and the first cake into the fire. Wood-cutters put little pieces of bread which have become too dry, upon the tree trunks: all for the poor souls. (. . .) When the time of All Souls is approaching, the same care for the deceased is shown more vividly. In every house a light is kept burning all night; the lamp is no longer filled with oil but with fat; a door, or at least a window, remains open,' and the supper is left on the table, even with some additions; 'people go to bed earlier, all to let the dear little angels enter without being disturbed. (. . .) Such is the custom of the peasants of the Tyrol, Old Bavaria, Upper Palatinate, and German Bohemia.' Rochholz, *Deutscher Glaube und Brauch*, vol. I, pp. 323—4.

ghost-propitiation at the funeral, and for a subsequent interval. Then comes the narrower class contained in the last — those more advanced peoples who, along with the belief in a ghost which permanently exists, show us a persistent ancestor-worship. Again, somewhat further restricted though by no means small, we have a class of peoples whose worship of distinguished ancestors partially subordinates that of the undistinguished. And eventually, the subordination growing more decided, becomes marked where these distinguished ancestors were leaders of conquering races.

Even the words applied in more advanced societies to different orders of supernatural beings, indicate by their original community of meaning, that this has been he course of genesis. The fact cited above, that among the Tannese the word for a god means literally a dead man, is typical of facts everywhere found. Ghost, spirit, demon — names at first applied to the other-self without distinctions of character — come to be differently applied as ascribed differences of character arise: the shade of an enemy becomes a devil, and a friendly shade becomes a divinity. Where the conceptions have not developed far, there are no differentiated titles, and the distinctions made by us cannot be expressed. The early Spanish missionaries in America were inconvenienced by finding that the only native word they could use for God also meant devil. In Greek, δαίμων and θεός are interchangeable. By Aeschylus, Agamemnon's children are represented as appealing to their father's ghost as to a god. So, too, with the Romans. Besides the unspecialized use of *daemon*, which means an angel or genius, good or bad, we find the unspecialized use of *deus* for god and ghost. On tombs the *manes* were called gods; and a law directs that 'the rights of the *manes*-gods are to be kept sacred.' Similarly with the Hebrews. Isaiah, representing himself as commanded to reject it, quotes a current belief implying such identification: 'And when they say unto you: "Consult the ghost-seers and the wizards, that chirp and that mutter! Should not people consult their gods, even the dead on behalf of the living?" ' When Saul goes to question the ghost of Samuel, the expression of the enchantress is 'I saw gods *(elohîm)* ascending out of the earth', god and ghost being thus used as equivalents.'* Even in our own day the kinship is traceable.

* Concerning the first of these passages, which is given as rendered in *The Book of Isaiah* (1870), Cheyne (p. 33) explains that *gods* are spirits of departed national heroes. [In *The Prophecies of Isaiah* (1882) he varies the translation; especially by changing gods into god — a rendering of *elohîm*, which agrees with accepted ideas much better than it agrees with the context.] Concerning the second passage the Speaker's Commentary says: 'It is possible that *elohîm* is here used in a general sense of a *supernatural* appearance, either angel or spirit.' And Kuenen remarks (I, p. 224): 'There is no doubt that originally the higher beings, the objects of man's fear *(elóah)*, were indicated by it [the name *elohîm*], so that this name too avails as an argument in favour of a former plurality of gods.'

The statement that God is a spirit, shows the application of a term which, otherwise applied, signifies a human soul. Only by its qualifying epithet is the meaning of Holy Ghost distinguished from the meaning of ghost in general. A divine being is still denoted by words that originally meant the breath which, deserting a man's body at death, was supposed to constitute the surviving part.

Do not these various evidences warrant the suspicion that from the ghost, once uniformly conceived, have arisen the variously-conceived supernatural beings? We may infer, *a priori*, that in conformity with the law of Evolution, there will develop many unlike conceptions out of conceptions originally alike. The spirits of the dead, forming, in a primitive tribe, an ideal group the members of which are but little distinguished from one another, will grow more and more distinguished. As societies advance, and as traditions, local and general, accumulate and complicate, these once-similar human souls, acquiring in the popular mind differences of character and importance, will diverge; until their original community of nature becomes scarcely recognizable.

Expecting, then, heterogeneous modifications of them, multiplying in thought as populations increase, ever spreading into more varied habitats, and tending continually to fill every place in Nature that can be occupied, let us now contemplate some of their most conspicuous types.

Edward B. Tylor

Edward Burnett Tylor was born in 1832 at Camberwell, England. He received his education at a school of the Society of Friends and entered his father's brass foundry business in 1846. In 1855 he had to quit work for reasons of health and made a recovery trip to France and to the United States. During a visit to Cuba in 1856, Tylor met the archeologist Henry Christie and accompanied him on a research expedition to Mexico which lasted six months. Once Tylor's interest in the study of human culture had been established in this way, Tylor pursued it on his own forces. Having established himself at Oxford, Tylor became in 1883 Keeper of the University Museum while delivering lectures on anthropology. In 1884 he became Reader in Anthropology which he established as a discipline, and in 1896 he occupied the new chair of anthropology at Oxford, which he held until 1909. He sent out a number of workers to the field, with whom he remained in correspondence and who sent him their field reports. Tylor died at Oxford in 1917.

The following publications of Tylor should be mentioned here: 1861 *Anahuac, or Mexico and the Mexicans, Ancient and Modern;* 1865 *Researches into the Early History of Mankind and the Development of Civilization;* 1871 *Primitive Culture: Researches into the Development of Mythology, Philosophy, Religion, Art, and Custom;* 1881 *Anthropology: An Introduction to the Study of Man and Civilization.*

Tylor may be called one of the founders of anthropology as the science of man and his culture. He developed the theory of the 'psychic unity' of mankind and that of an evolution of civilization in which primitive man had the priority in chronology and may be considered close to primeval man. Tylor saw it as his task to reconstruct the development from primitive to civilized man and thereby used myth, folklore, religion and custom as evidence of beliefs and attitudes that are the 'inner springs of human behavior'. In his research he used the comparative method, developed the theory of recurrence and survival, and that of the soul as being at the origin of the belief in spirits ('animism').

The following fragment from *Primitive Culture* has been chosen as an example of the process of inductive reasoning by which Tylor proves his theory of animism.

'ANIMISM'

Are there, or have there been, tribes of men so low in culture as to have no religious conceptions whatever? This is practically the question of the universality of religion, which for so many centuries has been affirmed and denied, with a confidence in striking contrast to the imperfect evidence on which both affirmation and denial have been based. Ethnographers, if looking to a theory of development to explain civilization, and regarding its successive stages as arising one from another, would receive with peculiar interest accounts of tribes devoid of all religion. Here, they would naturally say, are men who have no religion because their forefathers had none, men who represent a prae-religious condition of the human race, out of which in the course of time religious conditions have arisen. It does not, however, seem advisable to start from this ground in an investigation of religious development. Though the theoretical niche is ready and convenient, the actual statue to fill it is not forthcoming. The case is in some degree similar to that of the tribes asserted to exist without language or without the use of fire; nothing in the nature of things seems to forbid the possibility of such existence, but as a matter of fact the tribes are not found. Thus the assertion that rude non-religious tribes have been known in actual existence, though in theory possible, and perhaps in fact true, does not at present rest on that sufficient proof which, for an exceptional state of things, we are entitled to demand.

It is not unusual for the very writer who declares in general terms the absence of religious phenomena among some savage people, himself to give evidence that shows his expressions to be misleading. Thus Dr. Lang not only declares that the aborigines of Australia have no idea of a supreme divinity, creator, and judge, no object of worship, no idol, temple, or sacrifice, but that 'in short, they have nothing whatever of the character of religion, or of religious observance, to distinghuish them from the beasts that perish.' More than one writer has since made use of this telling statement, but without referring to certain details which occur in the very same book. From these it appears that a disease like small-pox, which sometimes attacks the natives, is ascribed by them 'to the influence of Budyah, an evil spirit who delights in mischief'; that when the natives rob a wild bees' hive, they generally leave a little of the honey for Buddai; that at certain biennial gatherings of the Queensland tribes, young girls are slain in sacrifice to propitiate some evil divinity; and that, lastly, according to the evidence of the Rev. W. Ridley, 'whenever he has conversed with the aborigines, he found them to have definite traditions concerning supernatural beings – Baiame, whose voice they hear in thunder, and who made all things, Turramullun the chief of demons, who is the author of disease, mischief, and wisdom, and appears in the form of a serpent at their great assemblies, etc'.[1] By the concurring testimony of a crowd of observers, it is known that the natives of Australia were at their discovery, and have since remained, a race with minds saturated with the most vivid belief in souls, demons, and deities. In Africa, Mr. Moffat's declaration as to the Bechaunas is scarcely less surprising – that 'man's immortality was

never heard of among that people', he having remarked in the sentence
next before, that the word for the shades or manes of the dead is 'liriti'.[2]
In South America, again, Don Felix de Azara comments on the positive
falsity of the ecclesiastics' assertion that the native tribes have a religion.
He simply declares that they have none; nevertheless in the course of
his work he mentions such facts as that the Payaguas bury arms and cloth-
ing with their dead and have some notions of a future life, and that the
Guanas believe in a Being who rewards good and punishes evil. In fact,
this author's reckless denial of religion and law to the lower races of this
region justifies D'Orbigny's sharp criticism, that 'this is indeed what he
says of all the nations he describes, while actually proving the contrary
of his thesis by the very facts he alleges in its support'.[3]

Such cases show how deceptive are judgments to which breadth and
generality are given by the use of wide words in narrow senses. Lang, Moffat,
and Azara are authors to whom ethnography owes much valuable knowledge
of the tribes they visited, but they seem hardly to have recognized anything short of the organized and established theology of the higher races
as being religion at all. They attribute irreligion to tribes whose doctrines
are unlike theirs, in much the same manner as theologians have so often
attributed atheism to those whose deities differed from their own, from
the time when the ancient invading Aryans described the aboriginal tribes
of India as *adeva, i.e.* 'godless', and the Greeks fixed the corresponding
term ἄθεοι on the early Christians as unbelievers in the classic gods, to
the comparatively modern ages when disbelievers in witchcraft and apos-
tolical succession were denounced as atheists; and down to our own day,
when controversialists are apt to infer, as in past centuries, that naturalists
who support a theory of development of species therefore necessarily hold
atheistic opinions.[4] These are in fact but examples of a general perversion
of judgment in theological matters, among the results of which is a popular
misconception of the religions of the lower races, simply amazing to students who have reached a higher point of view. Some missionaries, no
doubt, thoroughly understand the minds of the savages they have to deal
with, and indeed it is from men like Cranz, Dobrizhoffer, Charlevoix,
Ellis, Hardy, Callaway, J. L. Wilson, T. Williams, that we have obtained
our best knowledge of the lower phases of religious belief. But for the most
part the 'religious world' is so occupied in hating and despising the beliefs
of the heathen whose vast regions of the globe are painted black on the
missionary maps, that they have little time or capacity left to understand
them. It cannot be so with those who fairly seek to comprehend the nature
and meaning of the lower phases of religion. These, while fully alive to
the absurdities believed and the horrors perpetrated in its name, will yet
regard with kindly interest all record of men's earnest seeking after truth

with such light as they could find. Such students will look for meaning, however crude and childish, at the root of doctrines often most dark to the believers who accept them most zealously; they will search for the reasonable thought which once gave life to observances now become in seeming or reality the most abject and superstitious folly. The reward of these enquirers will be a more rational comprehension of the faiths in whose midst they dwell, for no more can he who understands but one religion understand even that religion, than the man who knows but one language can understand that language. No religion of mankind lies in utter isolation from the rest, and the thoughts and principles of modern Christianity are attached to intellectual clues which run back through far prae-Christian ages to the very origin of human civilization, perhaps even of human existence.

While observers who have had fair opportunities of studying the religions of savages have thus sometimes done scant justice to the facts before their eyes, the hasty denials of others who have judged without even facts can carry no great weight. A 16th-century traveller gave an account of the natives of Florida which is typical of such: 'Touching the religion of this people, which wee have found, for want of their language wee could not understand neither by signs nor gesture that they had any religion or lawe at all . . . We suppose that they have no religion at all, and that they live at their own libertie'.[5] Better knowledge of these Floridans nevertheless showed that they had a religion, and better knowledge has reversed many another hasty assertion to the same effect; as when writers used to declare that the natives of Madagascar had no idea of a future state, and no word for soul or spirit;[6] or when Dampier enquired after the religion of the natives of Timor, and was told that they had none;[7] or when Sir Thomas Roe landed in Saldanha Bay on his way to the court of the Great Mogul, and remarked of the Hottentots that 'they have left off their custom of stealing, but know no God or religion'.[8] Among the numerous accounts collected by Sir John Lubbock as evidence bearing on the absence or low development of religion among low races,[9] some may be selected as lying open to criticism from this point of view. Thus the statement that the Samoan Islanders had no religion cannot stand, in face of the elaborate description by the Rev. G. Turner of the Samoan religion itself; and the assertion that the Tupinambas of Brazil had no religion is one not to be received on merely negative evidence, for the religious doctrines and practices of the Tupi race have been recorded by Lery, De Laet, and other writers. Even with much time and care and knowledge of language, it is not always easy to elicit from savages the details of their theology. They try to hide from the prying and contemptuous foreigner their worship of gods who seem to shrink, like their worshippers, before the white man and his mightier Deity. Mr. Sproat's experience in Vancouver's Island s an apt example of this state of things. He says: 'I was two years among the Ahts, with my mind constantly directed towards the subject of their religious beliefs, before I could discover that they possessed any ideas as to an overruling power or a future state of existence. The traders on the coast, and other persons well acquainted with the people, told me that they had no such ideas, and this opinion was confirmed by conversation with many of the less intelligent savages; but at last I succeeded in getting a satisfactory clue'.[10] It then appeared that the Ahts had all the time been hiding a whole characteristic system of religious doctrines as to souls and their migrations, the spirits who do good and ill to men, and the great gods above all. Thus, even where no positive proof of religious ideas among any particular tribe has reached us, we should distrust its denial by observers whose acquaintance with the tribe in question has not been intimate as well as kindly. It is said of the Andaman Islanders that they have not the rudest elements of a religious faith; yet it appears that the natives did not even display to the foreigners the rude music which they actually possessed, so that they could scarcely have been expected to be communicative as to their theology, if they had any.[11] In our time the most striking negation of the religion of savage tribes is that published by Sir Samuel Baker, in a paper read in 1866 before the Ethnological Society of London, as follows: 'The most northern tribes of the White Nile are the Dinkas, Shillooks, Nuehr, Kytch, Bohr, Aliab, and Shir. A general description will suffice for the whole, excepting the Kytch. Without any exception, they are without a belief in a Supreme Being, neither have they any form of worship or idolatry; nor is the darkness of their minds enlightened by even a ray of superstition'. Had this distinguished explorer spoken only of the Latukas, or of other tribes hardly known to ethnographers except through his own intercourse with them, his denial of any religious consciousness to them would have been at least entitled to stand as the best procurable account, until more intimate communication should prove or disprove it. But in speaking thus of comparatively well known tribes such as the Dinkas, Shilluks, and Nuehr, Sir S. Baker ignores the existence of published evidence, such as describes the sacrifices of the Dinkas, their belief in good and evil spirits (adjok and djyok), their good deity and heaven-dwelling creator, Dendid, as likewise Néar the deity of the Nuer, and the Shilluks' creator, who is described as visiting, like other spirits, a sacred wood or tree. Kaufmann, Brun Rollet, Lejean, and other observers, had thus placed on record details of the religion of these White Nile tribes, years before Sir S. Baker's rash denial that they had any religion at all.[12]

The first requisite in a systematic study of the religions of the lower races, is to lay down a rudimentary definition of religion. By requiring in this definition the belief in a supreme deity or of judgment after death,

the adoration of idols or the practice of sacrifice, or other partially-diffused
doctrines or rites, no doubt many tribes may be excluded from the category
of religious. But such narrow definition has the fault of identifying religion
rather with particular developments than with the deeper motive which
underlies them. It seems best to fall back at once on this essential source,
and simply to claim, as a minimum definition of Religion, the belief in
Spiritual Beings. If this standard be applied to the descriptions of low
races as to religion, the following results will appear. It cannot be positively
asserted that every existing tribe recognizes the belief in spiritual beings,
for the native condition of a considerable number is obscure in this respect,
and from the rapid change or extinction they are undergoing, may ever
remain so. It would be yet more unwarranted to set down every tribe mentioned in history, or known to us by the discovery of antiquarian relics,
as necessarily having possessed the defined minimum of religion. Greater
still would be the unwisdom of declaring such a rudimentary belief natural
or instinctive in all human tribes of all times; for no evidence justifies
the opinion that man, known to be capable of so vast an intellectual development, cannot have emerged from a non-religious condition, previous
to that religious condition in which he happens at present to come with
sufficient clearness within our range of knowledge. It is desirable, however,
to take our basis of enquiry in observation rather than from speculation.
Here, so far as I can judge from the immense mass of accessible evidence, we
have to admit that the belief in spiritual beings appears among all low races
with whom we have attained to thoroughly intimate acquaintance; whereas
the assertion of absence of such belief must apply either to ancient tribes,
or to more or less imperfectly described modern ones. The exact bearing
of this state of things on the problem of the origin of religion may be thus
briefly stated. Were it distinctly proved that non-religious savages exist
or have existed, these might be at least plausibly claimed as representatives
of the condition of Man before he arrived at the religious stage of culture.
It is not desirable, however, that this argument should be put forward,
for the asserted existence of the non-religious tribes in question rests,
as we have seen, on evidence often mistaken and never conclusive. The
argument for the natural evolution of religious ideas among mankind is
not invalidated by the rejection of an ally too weak at present to give effectual help. Non-religious tribes may not exist in our day, but the fact bears
no more decisively on the development of religion, than the impossibility
of finding a modern English village without scissors or books or lucifer-
matches bears on the fact that there was a time when no such things existed
in the land.

I purpose here, under the name of Animism, to investigate the deep-
lying doctrine of Spiritual Beings, which embodies the very essence of

Spiritualistic as opposed to Materialistic philosophy. Animism is not a new technical term, though now seldom used.[13] From its special relation to the doctrine of the soul, it will be seen to have a peculiar appropriateness to the view here taken of the mode in which theological ideas have been developed among mankind. The word Spiritualism, though it may be, and sometimes is, used in a general sense, has this obvious defect to us, that it has become the designation of a particular modern sect, who indeed hold extreme spiritualistic views, but cannot be taken as typical representatives of these views in the world at large. The sense of Spiritualism in its wider acceptation, the general belief in spiritual beings, is here given to Animism.

Animism characterizes tribes very low in the scale of humanity, and thence ascends, deeply modified in its transmission, but from first to last preserving an unbroken continuity, into the midst of high modern culture. Doctrines adverse to it, so largely held by individuals or schools, are usually due not to early lowness of civilization, but to later changes in the intellectual course, to divergence from, or rejection of, ancestral faiths; and such newer developments do not affect the present enquiry as to the fundamental religious condition of mankind. Animism is, in fact, the groundwork of the Philosophy of Religion, from that of savages up to that of civilized men. And although it may at first sight seem to afford but a bare and meagre definition of a minimum of religion, it will be found practically sufficient; for where the root is, the branches will generally be produced. It is habitually found that the theory of Animism divides into two great dogmas, forming parts of one consistent doctrine; first, concerning souls of individual creatures, capable of continued existence after the death or destruction of the body; second, concerning other spirits, upward to the rank of powerful deities. Spiritual beings are held to affect or control the events of the material world, and man's life here and hereafter; and it being considered that they hold intercourse with men, and receive pleasure or displeasure from human actions, the belief in their existence leads naturally, and it might almost be said inevitably, sooner or later to active reverence and propitiation. Thus Animism, in its full development, includes the belief in souls and in a future state, in controlling deities and subordinate spirits, these doctrines practically resulting in some kind of active worship. One great element of religion, that moral element which among the higher nations forms its most vital part, is indeed little represented in the religion of the lower races. It is not that these races have no moral sense or no moral standard, for both are strongly marked among them, if not in formal precept, at least in that traditional consensus of society which we call public opinion, according to which certain actions are held to be good or bad, right or wrong. It is that the conjunction of ethics and

Animistic philosophy, so intimate and powerful in the higher culture, seems scarcely yet to have begun in the lower. I propose here hardly to touch upon the purely moral aspects of religion, but rather to study the animism of the world so far as it constitutes, as unquestionably it does constitute, an ancient and world-wide philosophy, of which belief is the theory and worship is the practice. Endeavouring to shape the materials for an enquiry hitherto strangely undervalued and neglected, it will now be my task to bring as clearly as may be into view the fundamental animism of the lower races, and in some slight and broken outline to trace its course into higher regions of civilisation. Here let me state once for all two principal conditions under which the present research is carried on. First, as to the religious doctrines and practices examined, these are treated as belonging to theological systems devised by human reason, without supernatural aid or revelation; in other words, as being developments of Natural Religion. Second, as to the connexion between similar ideas and rites in the religions of the savage and the civilized world. While dwelling at some length on doctrines and ceremonies of the lower races, and sometimes particularizing for special reasons the related doctrines and ceremonies of the higher nations, it has not seemed my proper task to work out in detail the problems thus suggested among the philosophies and creeds of Christendom. Such applications, extending farthest from the direct scope of a work on primitive culture, are briefly stated in general terms, or touched in slight allusion, or taken for granted without remark. Educated readers possess the information required to work out their general bearing on theology, while more technical discussion is left to philosophers and theologians specially occupied with such arguments.

[...]

It remains to sum up in few words the doctrine of souls, in the various phases it has assumed from first to last among mankind. In the attempt to trace its main course through the successive grades of man's intellectual history, the evidence seems to accord best with a theory of its development, somewhat to the following effect. At the lowest levels of culture of which we have clear knowledge, the notion of a ghost-soul animating man while in the body, and appearing in dream and vision out of the body, is found deeply ingrained. There is no reason to think that this belief was learnt by savage tribes from contact with higher races, nor that it is a relic of higher culture from which the savage tribes have degenerated; for what is here treated as the primitive animistic doctrine is thoroughly at home among savages, who appear to hold it on the very evidence of their senses, interpreted on the biological principle which seems to them most reasonable. We may now and then hear the savage doctrines and practices concerning souls claimed as relics of a high religious culture pervading the primaeval race of man. They are said to be traces of remote ancestral religion, kept up in scanty and perverted memory by tribes degraded from a nobler state. It is easy to see that such an explanation of some few facts, sundered from their connexion with the general array, may seem plausible to certain minds. But a large view of the subject can hardly leave such argument in possession. The animism of savages stands for and by itself; it explains its own origin. The animism of civilized men, while more appropriate to advanced knowledge, is in great measure only explicable as a developed product of the older and ruder system. It is the doctrines and rites of the lower races which are, according to their philosophy, results of point-blank natural evidence and acts of straightforward practical purpose. It is the doctrines and rites of the higher races which show survival of the old in the midst of the new, modification of the old to bring it into conformity with the new, abandonment of the old because it is no longer compatible with the new. Let us see at a glance in what general relation the doctrine of souls among savage tribes stands to the doctrine of souls among barbaric and cultured nations. Among races within the limits of savagery, the general doctrine of souls is found worked out with remarkable breadth and consistency. The souls of animals are recognized by a natural extension from the theory of human souls; the souls of trees and plants follow in some vague partial way; and the souls of inanimate objects expand the general category to its extremest boundary. Thenceforth, as we explore human thought onward from savage into barbarian and civilized life, we find a state of theory more conformed to positive science, but in itself less complete and consistent. Far on into civilization, men still act as though in some half-meant way they believed in souls or ghosts of objects, while nevertheless their knowledge of physical science is beyond so crude a philosophy. As to the doctrine of souls of plants, fragmentary evidence of the history of its breaking down in Asia has reached us. In our own day and country, the notion of souls of beasts is to be seen dying out. Animism, indeed, seems to be drawing in its outposts, and concentrating itself on its first and main position, the doctrine of the human soul. This doctrine has undergone extreme modification in the course of culture. It has outlived the almost total loss of one great argument attached to it, – the objective reality of apparitional souls or ghosts seen in dreams and visions. The soul has given up its ethereal substance, and become an immaterial entity, 'the shadow of a shade.' Its theory is becoming separated from the investigations of biology and mental science, which now discuss the phenomena of life and thought, the senses and the intellect, the emotions and the will, on a ground-work of pure experience. There has arisen an intellectual product whose very existence is of the deepest significance, a 'psychology' which has no longer anything to do with 'soul'. The soul's place in modern thought is in the metaphysics of religion, and its especial office there is that of furnishing an intellectual side to the religious doctrine of the future life. Such are the alterations which have differenced the fundamental animistic belief in its course through successive periods of the world's culture. Yet it is evident that, notwithstanding all this profound change, the conception of the human soul is, as to its most essential nature, continuous from the philosophy of the savage thinker to that of the modern professor of theology. Its definition has remained from the first that of an animating, separable, surviving entity, the vehicle of individual personal existence. The theory of the soul is one principal part of a system of religious philosophy, which unites, in an unbroken line of mental connexion, the savage fetish-worshipper and the civilized Christian. The divisions which have separated the great religions of the world into intolerant and hostile sects are for the most part superficial in comparison with the deepest of all religious schisms, that which divides Animism from materialism.

NOTES

1. J. D. Lang, *Queensland*, pp. 340, 473, 380, 388, 444 (Buddai appears, p. 379, as causing a deluge; he is probably identical with Budyah).

2. Moffat, *South Africa*, p. 261.

3. Azara, *Voyage dans l'Amérique Méridionale*, vol. II, pp. 3, 14, 25, 51, 60, 91, 119, etc.; d'Orbigny, *L'homme américain*, vol. II, p. 318.

4. Muir, *Sanskrit Texts*, part II, p. 435; Eusebius, *Historia Ecclesiastica*, IV, 15; Bingham, book I, ch. II; Vanini, *De Admirandis Naturae Arcanis*, dial. 37; Lecky, *History of Rationalism*, vol. I, p. 126; *Encyclopaedia Britannica* (5th edition) s.v. 'Superstition'.

5. J. de Verrazano in *Hakluyt*, vol. III, p. 300.

6. See Ellis, *Madagascar*, vol. I, p. 429; Flacourt, *Histoire de Madagascar*, p. 59.

7. Dampier, *Voyages*, vol. II, part II, p. 76.

8. Roe in *Pinkerton*, vol. VIII, p. 2.

9. Lubbock, *Prehistoric Times*, p. 564; see also *Origin of Civilization*, p. 138.

10. Sproat, *Scenes and Studies of Savage Life*, p. 205.

11. Mouat, *Andaman Islanders*, pp. 2, 279, 303. Since the above was written, the remarkable Andaman religion has been described by Mr. E. H. Man, in *Journal of the Anthropological Institute*, vol. XII (1883), p. 156. [Note to 3rd edition].

12. Baker, 'Races of the Nile Basin', in *Transactions of the Ethnological Society*, vol. V, p. 231; 'The Albert Nyanza', vol. I, p. 246. See Kaufmann, *Schilderungen aus Centralafrika*, p. 123; Brun-Rollet, *Le Nil Blanc et le Soudan*, pp. 100, 222, also pp. 164, 200, 234; G. Lejean in *Revue des Deux Mondes*, April 1, 1862, p. 760; Waitz, *Anthropologie*, vol. II, pp. 72—75; Bastian, *Mensch*, vol. III, p. 208. Other recorded cases of denial of religion of savage tribes on narrow definition or inadequate evidence may be found in Meiners, *Geschichte der Religion*, vol. I, pp. 11—15 (Australians and Californians); Waitz, *Anthropologie*, vol. I, p. 323 (Aru Islanders, etc.); Farrar in *Anthropological Revue*, August 1864, p.

CCXVII (Kafirs, etc.); Martius, *Ethnographica Americana*, vol. I, p. 583 (Manaos); J. G. Palfrey, *History of New England*, vol. I, p. 46 (New England tribes).

13. The term has been especially used to denote the doctrine of Stahl, the promulgator also of the phlogiston-theory. The Animism of Stahl is a revival and development in modern scientific shape of the classic theory identifying vital principle and soul. See his *Theoria Medica Vera*, Halle, 1737; and the critical dissertation on his views, Lemoine, *Le vitalisme et l'animisme de Stahl*, Paris 1864.

Andrew Lang

Andrew Lang was born in 1844 in Selkirk, Scotland. He received his primary and secondary school education here and in Edinburgh. Lang was a student at the University of St. Andrews and at St. Andrew's College in Glasgow, before he went to Oxford in 1864 at Balliol College, where he pursued his study of languages. He then became a fellow at Merton College where he took his M. A. degree in 1875. Lang subsequently settled down in Kensington, London, from where he often spent his vacations at St. Andrews. He was a writer and a poet, at the same time a scholar and a literary critic earning his living by his writing in London. He died at Banchory, Scotland, in 1912.

Apart from Lang's classical studies and his prodigious literary writing, the following publications bearing on the study of religion should be mentioned: 1884 *Custom and Myth;* 1887 *Myth, Ritual and Religion* (2 vol.; 2nd enlarged edition 1899); 1897 *Modern Mythology;* 1898 *The Making of Religion;* 1901 *Magic and Religion;* 1903 *Social Origins;* 1905 *The Secret of the Totem;* 1908 *Origins of Religion.* Art. 'Mythology' in *Encyclopaedia Britannica*, 9th edition; art. 'Totemism' in the same, 11th edition.

As a student of religion, Lang drew attention to the existence of early so-called 'Supreme Beings' which could not be explained by the theory of animism. He looked for an interpretation of mythology which gave more room for its meaning than was done in the linguistic-etymological approach. He did research on folklore and pleaded very much for parapsychological research, regarding paranormal phenomena as part of the life of certain people and as a possible clue to the understanding of animistic beliefs. His interest in the study of religion may have arisen from his studies of the classics, and he functioned as the critic to theories current in his time. He did not develop a theoretical scheme of interpretation, but pointed out facts which could not be explained by existing theories. Lang did not speak of a unilateral development of religion and was sensitive to the religious and moral elements contained in the sources.

The following text has been chosen from *The Making of Religion* because of its methodical argumentation against the animist theory of Tylor.

'THE MAKING OF RELIGION'

'Introductory Chapter'

The modern Science of the History of Religion has attained conclusions which already possess an air of being firmly established. These conclusions may be briefly stated thus: Man derived the conception of 'spirit' or 'soul' from his reflections on the phenomena of sleep, dreams, death, shadow and from the experiences of trance and hallucination. Worshipping first the departed souls of his kindred, man later extended the doctrine of spiritual beings in many directions. Ghosts, or other spiritual existences fashioned on the same lines, prospered till they became gods. Finally, as the result of a variety of processes, one of these gods became supreme, and, at last, was regarded as the one only God. Meanwhile man retained his belief in the existence of his own soul, surviving after the death of the body, and so reached the conception of immortality. Thus the ideas of God and of the soul are the result of early fallacious reasonings about misunderstood experiences.

It may seem almost wanton to suggest the desirableness of revising a system at once so simple, so logical, and apparently so well bottomed on facts. But there can never be any real harm in studying masses of evidence from fresh points of view. At worst, the failure of adverse criticism must help to establish the doctrines assailed. Now, as we shall show, there are two points of view from which the evidence as to religion in its early stages has not been steadily contemplated. Therefore we intend to ask, first, what, if anything, can be ascertained as to the nature of the 'visions' and hallucinations which, according to Mr. Tylor in his celebrated work 'Primitive Culture', lent their aid to the formation of the idea of 'spirit'. Secondly, we shall collect and compare the accounts which we possess of the High Gods and creative beings worshipped or believed in, by the most backward races. We shall then ask whether these relatively Supreme Beings, so conceived of by men in very rudimentary social conditions, can be, as anthropology declares, mere developments from the belief in ghosts of the dead.

We shall end by venturing to suggest that the savage theory of the soul may be based, at least in part, on experiences which cannot, at present, be made to fit into any purely materialistic system of the universe. We shall also bring evidence tending to prove that the idea of God, in its earliest known shape, need not logically be derived from the idea of spirit, however that idea itself may have been attained or evolved. The conception of God, then, need not be evolved out of reflections on dreams and 'ghosts'.

If these two positions can be defended with any success, it is obvious that the whole theory of the Science of Religion will need to be reconsidered. But it is no less evident that our two positions do not depend on each other. The first may be regarded as fantastic, or improbable, or may be 'masked' and left on one side. But the strength of the second position, derived from evidence of a different character, will not, therefore, be in any way impaired. Our first position can only be argued for by dint of evidence highly unpopular in character, and, as a general rule, condemned by modern science. The evidence is obtained by what is, at all events, a legitimate anthropological proceeding. We may follow Mr. Tylor's example, and collect savage *beliefs* about visions, hallucinations, 'clairvoyance', and the acquisition of knowledge apparently not attainable through the normal channels of sense. We may then compare these savage beliefs with attested records of similar *experiences* among living and educated civilised men. Even if we attain to no conclusion, or a negative conclusion, as to the actuality and supernormal character of the alleged experiences, still to compare data of savage and civilised psychology, or even of savage and civilised illusions and fables, is decidedly part, though a neglected part, of the function of anthropological science. The results, whether they do or do not strengthen our first position, must be curious and instructive, if only as a chapter in the history of human error. That chapter, too, is concerned with no mean topic, but with what we may call the X region of our nature. Out of that region, out of miracle, prophecy, vision, have certainly come forth the great religions, Christianity and Islam; and the great religious innovators and leaders, our Lord Himself, St. Francis, John Knox, Jeanne d'Arc, down to the founder of the new faith of the Sioux and Arapahoe. It cannot, then, be unscientific to compare the barbaric with the civilised beliefs and experiences about a region so dimly understood, and so fertile in potent influences. Here the topic will be examined rather by the method of anthropology than of psychology. [...]

Anthropological debates on religion

Among the various forms of science which are reaching and affecting the new popular tradition, we have reckoned Anthropology. Pleasantly enough, Anthropology has herself but recently emerged from that limbo of the unrecognised in which Psychical Research is pining. The British Association used to reject anthropological papers as 'vain dreams based on travellers' tales'. No doubt the British Association would reject a paper on clairvoyance as a vain dream based on old wives' fables, or on hysterical imposture. Undeniably the study of such themes is hampered by fable and fraud, just as anthropology has to be ceaselessly on its guard against 'travellers' tales,' against European misunderstandings of savage ideas, and against civilised notions and scientific theories unconsciously read into barbaric customs, rites, traditions, and usages. Man, *ondoyant et divers,* is the subject alike of anthropology and of psychical research. Man (especially savage man) cannot be secluded from disturbing influences, and watched, like materials of a chemical experiment in a laboratory. Nor can man be caught in a 'primitive' state: his intellectual beginnings lie very far behind the stage of culture in which we find the lowest known races. Consequently the matter on which anthropology works is fluctuating; the evidence on which it rests needs the most sceptical criticism, and many of its conclusions, in the necessary absence of historical testimony as to times far behind the lowest known savages, must be hypothetical.

For these sound reasons official science long looked askance on Anthropology. Her followers were not regarded as genuine scholars, and, perhaps as a result of this contempt, they were often 'broken men', intellectual outlaws, people of one wild idea. To the scientific mind, anthropologists or ethnologists were a horde who darkly muttered of serpent worship, phallus worship, Arkite doctrines, and the Ten Lost Tribes that kept turning up in the most unexpected places. Anthropologists were said to gloat over dirty rites of dirty savages, and to seek reason where there was none. The exiled, the outcast, the pariah of Science, is, indeed, apt to find himself in odd company. Round the camp-fire of Psychical Research too, in the unofficial, unstaked waste of Science, hover odd, menacing figures of Esoteric Buddhists, *Satanistes*, Occultists, Christian Scientists, Spiritualists, and Astrologers, as the Arkites and Lost Tribesmen haunted the cradle of anthropology.

But there was found at last to be reason in the thing, and method in the madness. Evolution was in it. The acceptance, after long ridicule, of palaeolithic weapons as relics of human culture, probably helped to bring Anthropology within the sacred circle of permitted knowledge. Her topic was full of illustrations of the doctrine of Mr. Darwin. Modern writers on the theme had been anticipated by the less systematic students of the eighteenth century – Goguet, de Brosses, Millar, Fontenelle, Lafitau, Boulanger, or even Hume and Voltaire. As pioneers these writers anwer to the early mesmerists and magnetists, Puységur, Amoretti, Ritter, Elliotson, Mayo, Gregory, in the history of Psychical Research. They were on the same track, in each case, as Lubbock, Tylor, Spencer, Bastian, and Frazer, or as Gurney, Richet, Myers, Janet, Dessoir, and Von Schrenck-Notzing. But the earlier students were less careful of method and evidence.

Evidence! that was the stumbling block of anthropology. We still hear, in the later works of Mr. Max Müller, the echo of the old complaints. Anything you please, Mr. Max Müller says, you may find among your useful savages, and (in regard to some anthropologists) his criticism is just. You have but to skim a few books of travel, pencil in hand, and pick out what suits your case. Suppose, as regards our present theme, your theory is that savages possess broken lights of the belief in a Supreme Being. You can find evidence for that. Or suppose you want to show that they have no religious ideas at all; you can find evidence for that also. Your testimony is often derived from observers ignorant of the language of the people whom they talk about, or who are themselves prejudiced by one or other theory or bias. How can you pretend to raise a science on such foundations‘ especially as the savage informants wish to please or to mystify inquirers‘ or they answer at random, or deliberately conceal their most sacred institutions, or have never paid any attention to the subject?

To all these perfectly natural objections Mr. Tylor has replied.[1] Evidence must be collected, sifted, tested, as in any other branch of inquiry. A writer, 'of course, is bound to use his best judgment as to the trustworthiness of all authors he quotes, and, if possible, to obtain several accounts to certify each point in each locality". Mr. Tylor then adduces 'the test of recurrence,' of undesigned coincidence in testimony, as Millar had already argued in the last century.[2] If a mediaeval Mahommedan in Tartary, a Jesuit in Brazil, a Wesleyan in Fiji, one may add a police magistrate in Australia, a Presbyterian in Central Africa, a trapper in Canada, agree in describing some analogous rite or myth in these diverse lands and ages, we cannot set down the coincidence to chance or fraud. 'Now, the most important facts of ethnography are vouched for in this way'.

We may add that even when the ideas of savages are obscure, we can often detect them by analysis of the institutions in which they are expressed.[3]

Thus anthropological, like psychical or any other evidence, must be submitted to conscientious processes of testing and sifting. Contradictory instances must be hunted for sedulously. Nothing can be less scientific than to snatch up any traveller's tale which makes for our theory, and to ignore evidence, perhaps earlier, or later, or better observed, which makes against it.

Enough has been said to show the position of anthropology as regards evidence, and to prove, that if he confines his observations to certain anthropologists, the censures of Mr. Max Müller are justified. It is mainly for this reason that the arguments presently to follow are strung on the thread of Mr. Tylor's truly learned and accurate book, 'Primitive Culture'.

Though but recently crept forth, *vix aut ne vix quidem*, from the chill shade of scientific disdain, Anthropology adopts the airs of her elder sisters among the sciences, and is as severe as they to the Cinderella of the family, Psychical Research. She must murmur of her fairies among the cinders of the hearth, while they go forth to the ball, and dance with provincial mayors at the festivities of the British Association. This is ungenerous, and unfortunate, as the records of anthropology are rich in unexamined materials of psychical research. I am unacquainted with any work devoted by an anthropologist of renown to the hypnotic and kindred practices of the lower races, except Herr Bastian's very meagre tract, 'Über psychische Beobachtungen bei Naturvölkern.'[4] We possess, none the less, a mass of scattered information on this topic, the savage side of psychical phenomena, in works of travel, and in Mr. Tylor's monumental 'Primitive

Culture'. Mr. Tylor, however, as we shall see, regards it as a matter of indiffe
rence, or, at least, as a matter beyond the scope of his essay, to decide
whether the parallel supernormal phenomena believed in by savages, and
said to recur in civilisation, are facts of actual experience, or not.

Now, this question is not otiose. Mr. Tylor, like other anthropologists,
Mr. Huxley, Mr. Herbert Spencer, and their followers and popularisers,
constructs, on anthropological grounds, a theory of the Origin of Religion.
That origin anthropology explains as the result of early and fallacious reasonings on a number of biological and psychological phenomena, both
normal and (as is alleged by savages) supernormal. These reasonings led
to the belief in souls and spirits. Now, first, anthropology has taken for
granted that the Supreme Deities of savages are envisaged by them as
'spirits'. This, paradoxical as the statement may appear, is just what does
not seem to be proved, as we shall show. Next, if the supernormal phenomena
(clairvoyance, thought-transference, phantasms of the dead, phantasms
of the dying, and others) be real matters of experience, the inferences
drawn from them by early savage philosophy may be, in some degree,
erroneous. But the inferences drawn by materialists who reject the supernormal phenomena will also, perhaps, be, let us say, incomplete. Religion
will have been, in part, developed out of facts, perhaps inconsistent with
materialism in its present dogmatic form. To put it less trenchantly, and
perhaps more accurately, the alleged facts 'are not merely dramatically
strange, they are not merely extraordinary and striking, but they are
'odd' in the sense that they will not easily fit in with the views which
physicists and men of science generally give us of the universe in which
we live'.[5]

As this is the case, it might, seem to be the business of Antropology, the
Science of Man, to examinel among other things, the evidence for the
actual existence of those aleged unusual and supernormal phenomena,
belief in which is given as one of the origins of religion.

To make this examination, in the ethnographic field, is almost a new
labour. As we shall see, anthropologists have not hitherto investigated
such things as the 'Fire-walk' of savages, uninjured in the flames, like the
Three Holy Children. The world-wide savage practice of divining by hallucinations induced through gazing into a smooth deep (crystal-gazing)
has been studied, I think, by no anthropologist. The veracity of 'messages'
uttered by savage seers when (as they suppose) 'possessed' or 'inspired'
has not been criticised, and probably cannot be, for lack of detailed information. The 'physical phenomena' which answer among savages to the
use of the 'divining rod', and to 'spirits' marvels in modern times, have
only been glanced at. In short, all the savage parallels to the so-called
'psychical phenomena' now under discussion in England, America, Germany,

Italy, and France, have escaped critical analysis and comparison with their civilised counterparts.

An exception among anthropologists is Mr. Tylor. He has not suppressed the existence of these barbaric parallels to our modern problems of this kind. But his interest in them practically ends when he has shown that the phenomena helped to originate the savage belief in 'spirits', and when he has displayed the 'survival' of that belief in later culture. He does not ask 'Are the phenomena real?' he is concerned only with the savage philosophy of the phenomena and with its relics in modern spiritism and religion. My purpose is to do, by way only of *ébauche*, what neither anthropology nor psychical research nor psychology has done: to put the savage and modern phenomena side by side. Such evidence as we can give for the actuality of the modern experiences will, so far as it goes, raise a presumption that the savage beliefs, however erroneous, however darkened by fraud and fancy, repose on a basis of real observation of actual phenomena.

Anthropology is concerned with man and what is in man – *humani nihil a se alienum putat*. These researches, therefore, are within the anthropological province, especially as they bear on the prevalent anthropological theory of the Origin of Religion. By 'religion' we mean, for the purpose of this argument, the belief in the existence of an Intelligence, or Intelligences not human, and not dependent on a material mechanism of brain and nerves, which may, or may not, powerfully control men's fortunes and the nature of things. We also mean the additional belief that there is, in man, an element so far kindred to these Intelligences that it can transcend the knowledge obtained through the known bodily senses, and may possibly survive the death of the body. These two beliefs at present (though not necessarily in their origin) appear chiefly as the faith in God and in the Immortality of the Soul.

It is important, then, to trace, if possible, the origin of these two beliefs. If they arose in actual communion with Deity (as the first at least did, in the theory of the Hebrew Scriptures), or if they could be proved to arise in an unanalysable *sensus numinis*, or even in 'a perception of the Infinite' (Max Müller), religion would have a divine, or at least a necessary source. To the Theist, what is inevitable cannot but be divinely ordained, therefore religion is divinely preordained, therefore, in essentials, though not in accidental details, religion is true. The atheist, or non-theist, of course draws no such inferences.

But if religion, as now understood among men, be the latest evolutionary form of a series of mistakes, fallacies, and illusions, if its germ be a blunder, and its present form only the result of progressive but unessential refinements on that blunder, the inference that religion is untrue – that nothing actual corresponds to its hypothesis – is very easily drawn. The inference is not, perhaps, logical, for all our science itself is the result of progressive refinements upon hypotheses originally erroneous, fashioned to explain facts misconceived. Yet our science is true, within its limits, though very far from being exhaustive of the truth. In the same way, it might be argued, our religion, even granting that it arose out of primitive fallacies and false hypotheses, may yet have been refined, as science has been, through a multitude of causes, into an approximate truth.

[...]

Coming at last to Mr. Tylor, we find that he begins by dismissing the idea that any known race of men is devoid of religious conceptions. He disproves, out of their own mouths, the allegations of several writers who have made this exploded assertion about 'godless tribes'. He says: 'The thoughts and principles of modern Christianity are attached to intellectual clues which run back through far prae-Christian ages to the very origin of human civilisation, *perhaps even of human existence.*'[6] So far we abound in Mr. Tylor's sense. 'As a minimum definition of religion' he gives 'the belief in spiritual beings', which appears 'among all low races with whom we have attained to thoroughly intimate relations'. The existence of this belief at present does not prove that no races were ever, at any time, destitute of all belief. But it prevents us from positing the existence of such creedless races, in any age, as a demontrated fact. We have thus, in short, no opportunity of observing, *historically*, man's development from blank unbelief into even the minimum or most rudimentary form of belief. We can only theorise and make more or less plausible conjectures as to the first rudiments of human faith in God and in spiritual beings. We find no race whose mind, as to faith, is a *tabula rasa*.

To the earliest faith Mr. Tylor gives the name of *Animism*, a term not wholly free from objection, though 'Spiritualism' is still less desirable, having been usurped by a form of modern superstitiousness. This Animism, 'in its full development, includes the belief in souls and in a future state, in controlling deities and subordinate spirits.' In Mr. Tylor's opinion, as in Mr. Huxley's, Animism, in its lower (and earlier) forms, has scarcely any connection with ethics. Its 'spirits' do not 'make for righteousness.' This is a side issue to be examined later, but we may provisionally observe, in passing, that the ethical ideas, such as they are, even of Australian blacks are reported to be inculcated at the religious mysteries *(Bora)* of the tribes, which were instituted by and are performed in honour of the gods of their native belief. But this topic must be reserved for our closing chapters.

Mr. Tylor, however, is chiefly concerned with Animism as 'an ancient and world-wide philosophy, of which belief is the theory, and worship is the practice'. Given Animism, then, or the belief in spiritual beings, as the earliest form and minimum of religious faith, what is the origin of Animism? It will be seen that, by Animism, Mr. Tylor does not mean the alleged early theory, implicitly if not explicitly and consciously held, that all things whatsoever are animated and are personalities.[7] Judging from the behaviour of little childeren, and from the myths of savages, early man may have half-consciously extended his own sense of personal and potent and animated existence to the whole of nature as known to him. Not only animals, but vegetables and inorganic objects, may have been looked on by him as persons, like what he felt himself to be. The child (perhaps merely because *taught* to do so) beats the naughty chair, and all objects are persons on early mythology. But this *feeling*, rather than theory, may conceivably have existed among early men, before they developed the hypothesis of 'spirits', 'ghosts', or souls. It is the origin of *that* hypothesis, 'Animism', which **Mr.** Tylor investigates.

What, then, is the origin of Animism? It arose in the earliest traceable speculations on 'two groups of biological problems'.

1) 'What is it that makes the difference between a living body and a dead one; what causes waking, sleep, trance, disease, and death?'

2) 'What are those human shapes which appear in dreams and visions?'[8]

Here it should be noted that Mr. Tylor most properly takes a distinction between sleeping 'dreams' and waking 'visions', or 'clear vision'. The distinction is made even by the blacks of Australia. Thus one of the Kurnai announced that his *Yambo*, or soul, could 'go out' during sleep, and see the distant and the dead. But 'while any one might be able to communicate with the ghosts, *during sleep*, it was only the wizards who were able to do so in waking hours'. A wizard, in fact, is a person susceptible (or feigning to be susceptible) when awake to hallucinatory perception of phantasms of the dead. 'Among the Kulin of Wimmera River a man became a wizard who, as a boy, had seen his mother's ghost sitting at her grave.'[9] These facts prove that a race of savages at the bottom of the scale of culture do take a formal distinction between normal dreams in sleep and waking hallucinations – a thing apt to be denied.

Thus Mr. Herbert Spencer offers the massive generalisation that savages do not possess a language enabling a man to say 'I dreamed that I saw', instead of 'I saw' ('Principles of Sociology', p. 150). This could only be proved by giving examples of such highly deficient languages, which Mr. Spencer does not do.[10] In many savage speculations there occur ideas as subtly metaphysical as those of Hegel. Moreover, even the Australian languages have the verb 'to see', and the substantive 'sleep'. Nothing, then, prevents a man from saying 'I saw in sleep *(insomnium, ἐνύπνιον)*.

We have shown too, that the Australians take an essential distinction between waking hallucinations (ghosts seen by a man when awake) and the common hallucinations of slumber. Anybody can have these; the man who sees ghosts when awake is marked out for a wizard.

At the same time the vividness of dreams among certain savages, as recorded in Mr. Im Thurn's 'Indians of Guiana', and the consequent confusion of dreaming and waking experiences, are certain facts. Wilson says the same of some negroes, and Mr. Spencer illustrates from the confusion of mind in dreamy children. They, we know, are much more addicted to somnambulism than grown-up people. I am unaware that spontaneous somnambulism among savages has been studied as it ought to be. I have demonstrated, however, that very low savages can and do draw an essential distinction between sleeping and waking hallucinations.

Again, the crystal-gazer, whose apparently telepathic crystal pictures are discussed later (chap. v.), was introduced to a crystal just because she had previously been known to be susceptible to waking and occasionally veracious hallucinations.

It was not only on the dreams of sleep, so easily forgotten as they are, that the savage pondered, in his early speculations about the life and the soul. He included in his materials the much more striking and memorable experiences of waking hours, as we and Mr. Tylor agree in holding.

Reflecting on these things, the earliest savage reasoners would decide: (1) that man has a 'life' (which leaves him temporarily in sleep, finally in death); (2) that man also possesses a 'phantom' (which appears to other people in their visions and dreams). The savage philospher would then 'combine his information', like a celebrated writer on Chinese metaphysics. He would merely 'combine the life and the phantom', as 'manifestations of one and the same soul'. The result would be 'an apparitional soul', or 'ghost-soul'.

This ghost-soul would be a highly accomplished creature, 'a vapour, film, or shadow', yet conscious, capable of leaving the body, mostly invisible and impalpable, 'yet also manifesting physical power', existing and appearing after the death of the body, able to act on the bodies of other men, beasts, and things.[11]

When the earliest reasoners, in an age and in mental conditions of which we know nothing historically, had evolved the hypothesis of this conscious, powerful, separable soul, capable of surviving the death of the body, it was not difficult for them to develop the rest of Religion, as Mr. Tylor thinks. A powerful ghost of a dead man might thrive till, its original owner being long forgotten, it became a God. Again (souls once given) it would not be a very difficult logical leap, perhaps, to conceive of souls, or spirits, that had never been human at all. It is, we may say, only *le premier pas qui coûte,* the step to the belief in a surviving separable soul. Nevertheless, when we remember that Mr. Tylor is theorising about savages in the dim background of human evolution, savages whom we know nothing of by experience, savages far behind Australians and Bushmen (who possess Gods), we must admit that he credits them with great ingenuity, and strong powers of abstract reasoning. He may be right in his opinion. In the same way, just as primitive men were keen reasoners, so early bees, more clever than modern bees, may have evolved the system of hexagonal cells, and only an early fish of genius could first have hit on the plan, now hereditary, of killing a fly by blowing water at it.

To this theory of metaphysical genius in very low savages I have no objection to offer. We shall find, later, astonishing examples of savage abstract speculation, certainly not derived from missionary sources, because wholly out of the missionary's line of duty and reflection.

As early beasts had genius, so the earliest reasoners appear to have been as logically gifted as the lowest savages now known to us, or even as some Biblical critics. By Mr. Tylor's hypothesis, they first conceived the extremely abstract idea of Life, 'that which makes the difference between a living body and a dead one'.[12] This highly abstract conception must have been, however, the more difficult to early man, as, to him, *all* things, universally, are 'animated'.[13] Mr. Tylor illustrates this theory of early man by the little child's idea that 'chairs, sticks, and wooden horses are actuated by the same sort of personal will as nurses and childern and kittens.... In such matters the savage mind well represents the childish stage'.[14]

Now, nothing can be more certain than that, if children think sticks are animated, they don't think so because they have heard, or discovered, that they possess souls, and then transfer souls to sticks. We may doubt, then, if primitive man came, in this way, by reasoning on souls, to suppose that all things, universally, were animated. But if he did think *all* things animated – a corpse, to his mind, was just as much animated as anything else. Did he reason: 'All things are animated. A corpse is not animated. Therefore a corpse is not a thing (within the meaning of my General Law)'?

How, again, did early man conceive of Life, *before* he identified Life (1) with 'that which makes the difference between a living body and a dead one' (a difference which, *ex hypothesi,* he did not draw, *all* things being animated to his mind) and (2) with 'those human shapes which appear in dreams and visions'? 'The ancient savage philosophers probably reached the obvious inference that every man had two things belonging to him, a life and a phantom.' But everything was supposed to have 'a life', as far as one makes out, before the idea of separable soul was developed, at least if savages arrived at the theory of universal animation as children are said to do.

We are dealing here quite conjecturally with facts beyond our experience.

In any case, early man excogitated (by the hypothesis) the abstract idea of Life, *before* he first 'envisaged' it in material terms as 'breath', or 'shadow'. He next decided that mere breath or shadow was not only identical with the more abstract conception of Life, but could also take on forms as real and full-bodied as, to him, are the hallucinations of dream or waking vision. His reasoning appears to have proceeded from the more abstract (the idea of Life) to the more concrete, to the life first shadowy and vaporous, then clothed in the very aspect of the real man.

Mr. Tylor has thus (whether we follow his logic or not) provided man with a theory of active, intelligent, separable souls, which can survive the death of the body. At this theory early man arrived by speculations on the nature of life, and on the causes of phantasms of the dead or living beheld in 'dreams and visions.' But our author by no means leaves out of sight the effects of alleged supernormal phenomena believed in by savages, with their parallels in modern civilisation. These supernormal phenomena, whether real or illusory, are, he conceives, facts in that mass of experiences from which savages constructed their belief in separable, enduring, intelligent souls or ghosts, the foundation of religion.

While we are, perhaps owing to our own want of capacity, puzzled by what seem to be two kinds of early philosophy – (1) a sort of instinctive or unreasoned belief in universal animation, which Mr. Spencer calls 'Animism' and does not believe in, (2) the reasoned belief in separable and surviving souls of men (and in things), which Mr. Spencer believes in, and Mr. Tylor call 'Animism' – we must also note another difficulty. Mr. Tylor may seem to be taking it for granted that the earliest, remote, unknown thinkers on life and the soul were existing on the same psychical plane as we ourselves, or, at least, as modern savages. Between modern savages and ourselves, in this regard, he takes certain differences, but takes none between modern savages and the remote founders of religion.

Thus Mr. Tylor observes: 'The condition of the modern ghost-seer, whose imagination passes on such slight excitement into positive hallucination, is rather the rule than the exception among uncultured and intensely imaginative tribes, whose minds may be thrown off their balance, by a touch, a word, a gesture, an unaccustomed noise'.[15]

I find evidence that low contemporary savages are *not* great ghost-seers, and, again, I cannot quite accept Mr. Tylor's psychology of the 'modern ghost-seer'. Most such favoured persons whom I have known were steady, unimaginative, unexcitable people, with just one odd experience. Lord Tennyson, too, after sleeping in the bed of his recently lost father on purpose to see his ghost, decided that ghosts 'are not seen by imaginative people'.

We now examine, at greater length, the psychical conditions in which, according to Mr. Tylor, contemporary savages differ from civilised men. Later we shall ask what may be said as to possible or presumable psychical differences between modern savages and the datelessly distant founders of the belief in souls. Mr. Tylor attributes to the lower races, and even to races high above their level, 'morbid ecstasy, brought on by meditation, fasting, narcotics, excitement, or disease'. Now, we may still 'meditate' – and how far the result is 'morbid' is a matter for psychologists and pathologists to determine. Fasting we do not practise voluntarily, nor would we easily accept evidence from an Englishman as to the veracity of voluntary fasting visions, like those of Cotton Mather. The visions of disease we should set aside, as a rule, with those of 'excitement', produced, for instance, by 'devil-dances.' Narcotic and alcoholic visions are not in question.[16] For our purpose the *induced* trances of savages (in whatever way voluntarily brought on) are analogous to the modern induced hypnotic trance. Any supernormal acquisitions of knowledge in these induced conditions, among savages, would be on a par with similar alleged experiences of persons under hypnotism.

We do not differ from known savages in being able to bring on non-normal psychological conditions, but we produce these, as a rule, by other methods than theirs, and such experiments are not made on *all* of us, as they were on all Red Indian boys and girls in the 'medicine-fast', at the age of puberty.

Further, in their normal state, known savages, or some of them, are more 'suggestible' than educated Europeans at least.[17] They can be more easily hallucinated in their normal waking state by suggestion. Once more their intervals of hunger, followed by gorges of food, and their lack of artificial light, combine to make savages more apt to see what is not there than are comfortable educated white men. But Mr. Tylor goes too far when he says 'where the savage could see *phantasms*, the civilised man has come to amuse himself with fancies'.[18] The civilised man, beyond all doubt, is capable of being *enfantosmé*.

In all that he says on this point, the point of psychical condition, Mr. Tylor is writing about known savages as they differ from ourselves. But the savages who *ex hypothesi* evolved the doctrine of souls lie beyond our ken, far behind the modern savages, among whom we find belief not only in souls and ghosts, but in moral gods. About the psychical condition of the savages who worked out the theory of souls and founded religion we necessarily know nothing. If there be such experiences as clairvoyance, telepathy, and so on, these unknown ancestors of ours may (for all that we can tell) have been peculiarly open to them, and therefore peculiarly apt to believe in separable souls. In fact, when we write about these far–off founders of religion, we guess in the dark, or by the flickering light of analogy. The lower animals have faculties (as in their power of finding their way home through new unknown regions, and in the ants' modes of acquiring and communicating knowledge to each other) which are mysteries to us. The terror of dogs in 'haunted houses' and of horses in passing 'haunted' scenes has often been reported, and is alluded to briefly by Mr. Tylor. Balaam's ass, and the gods which crouched and whined before Athene, whom Eumaeus could not see, are 'classical' instances.

The weakness of the anthropological argument here is, we must repeat, that we know little more about the mental condition and experiences of the early thinkers who developed the doctrine of Souls than we know about the mental condition and experiences of the lower animals. And the more firmly a philosopher believer in the Darwinian hypothesis, the less, he must admit, can he suppose himself to know about the twilight ages, between the lower animal and the fully evolved man. What kind of creature was man when he first conceived the germs, or received the light, of Religion? All is guess-work here! We may just allude to Hegel's theory that clairvoyance and hypnotic phenomena are produced in a kind of temporary *atavism,* or 'throwing back' to a remotely ancient condition of the 'sensitive soul' *(Fühlende Seele)*. The 'sensitive' [unconditioned, clairvoyant] faculty or 'soul' is 'a disease when it becomes a state of the self-conscious, educated, self-possessed human being of civilisation'.[19] 'Second sight', Hegel thinks, was a product of an earlier day and earlier mental condition than ours.

Approaching this almost untouched subject – the early psychical condition of man – not from the side of metaphysical speculations like Hegel, but with the instruments of modern psychology and physiology, Dr. Max Dessoir, of Berlin, following, indeed, M. Taine, has arrived, as we saw, at somewhat similar conclusions. 'This fully conscious life of the spirit', in which we moderns now live, 'seems to rest upon a substratum of reflex action of a hallucinatory type.' Our actual modern condition is *not* 'fundamental', and 'hallucination represents, at least in its nascent condition, the main trunk of our psychical existence'.[20]

Now, suppose that the remote and unknown ancestors of ours who first developed the doctrine of souls had not yet spread far from 'the main trunk of our psychical existence', far from constant hallucination. In that case (at least, according to Dr. Dessoir's theory) their psychical experiences would be such as we cannot estimate, yet cannot leave, as a possibility influencing religion, out of our calculations.

If early men were ever in a condition in which telepathy and clairvoyance (granting their possibility) were prevalent, one might expect that faculties so useful would be developed in the struggle for existence. That they are deliberately cultivated by modern savages we know. The Indian foster-mother of John Tanner used, when food was needed, to suggest herself into an hypnotic condition, so that she became *clairvoyante* as to the where-abouts of game. Tanner, an English boy, caught early by the Indians, was sceptical, but came to practise the same art, not unsuccessfully, him-self.[21] His reminiscences, which he dictated on his return to civilisation, were certainly not feigned in the interests of any theories. But the most telepathic human stocks, it may be said, ought, *ceteris paribus*, to have been the most successful in the struggle for existence. We may infer that the *cetera* were not *paria*, the clairvoyant state not being precisely the best for the practical business of life. But really we know nothing of the psychical state of the earliest men. They *may* have had experiences tend-ing towards a belief in 'spirits', of which we can tell nothing. We are obliged to guess, in considerable ignorance of the actual conditions, and this histo-rical ignorance inevitably besets all anthropological speculation about the origin of religion.

The knowledge of our nescience as to the psychical condition of our first thinking ancestors may suggest hesitation as to taking it for granted that early man was on our own or on the modern savage level in 'psychical' experience. Even savage races, as Mr. Tylor justly says, attribute superior psychical knowledge to neighbouring tribes on a yet lower level of culture than themselves. The Finn esteems the Lapp sorcerers above his own; the Lapp yields to the superior pretensions of the Samoyeds. There may be more ways than one of explaining this relative humility: there is Hegel's way and there is Mr. Tylor's way. We cannot be certain, *a priori*, that the earliest man knew no more of supernormal or apparently supernormal experiences than we commonly do, or that these did not influence his thoughts on religion.

It is an example of the chameleon-like changes of science (even of 'science falsely so called' if you please) that when he wrote his book, in 1871, Mr. Tylor could not possibly have anticipated this line of argument. 'Psychical planes' had not been invented; hypnotism, with its problem, had not been much noticed in England. But 'Spiritualism' was flourishing. Mr. Tylor did not ignore this revival of savage philosophy. He saw very well that the end of the century was beholding the partial rehabilitation of beliefs which were scouted from 1660 to 1850. Seventy years ago, as Mr. Tylor says, Dr. Macculloch, in his 'Description of the Western Islands of Scotland', wrote of 'the famous Highland second sight' that 'ceasing to be believed it has ceased to exist'.[22]

Dr. Macculloch was mistaken in his facts. 'Second sight' has never ceased to exist (or to be believed to exist), and it has recently been investigated in the 'Journal' of the Caledonian Medical Society. Mr. Tylor himself says that it has been 'reinstated in a far larger range of society, and under far better circumstances of learning and prosperity'. This fact he ascribes generally to 'a direct revival from the regions of savage philosophy and peasant folklore', a revival brought about in great part by the writings of Swedenborg. To-day things have altered. The students now interested in this whole class of alleged supernormal phenomena are seldom believers in the philosophy of Spiritualism in the American sense of the word.[23]

Mr. Tylor, as we have seen, attributes the revival of interest in this obscure class of subjects to the influence of Swedenborg. It is true, as has been shown, that Swedenborg attracted the attention of Kant. But modern interest has chiefly been aroused and kept alive by the phenomena of hypnotism. The interest is now, among educated students, really scientific.

Thus Mr. William James, Professor of Psychology in the Universty of Harvard, writes: 'I was attracted to this subject (Psychical Research) some years ago by my love of fair play in Science'.[24]

Mr. Tylor is not incapable of appreciating this attitude. Even the so-called 'spirit manifestations', he says, 'should be discussed on their merits', and the investigation 'would seem apt to throw light on some most interesting psychological question'. Nothing can be more remote from the logic of Hume.

The ideas of Mr. Tylor on the causes of the origin of religion are now criticised, not from the point of view of spiritualism, but of experimental psychology. We hold that very probably there exist human faculties of unknown scope; that these conceivably were more powerful and prevalent among our very remote ancestors who founded religion; that they may still exist in savage as in civilised races, and that they may have confirmed, if they did not originate, the doctrine of separable souls. If they *do* exist, the circumstance is important, in view of the fact that modern ideas rest on a denial of their existence.

Mr. Tylor next examines the savage and other *names* for the ghost-soul, such as shadow *(umbra)*, breath *(spiritus)*, and he gives cases in which the *shadow* of a man is regarded as equivalent to his *life*. Of course, the shadow in the sunlight does not resemble the phantasm in a dream. The two, however, were combined and identified by early thinkers, while *breath* and *heart* were used as symbols of 'that in men which makes them live', a phrase found among the natives of Nicaragua in 1528. The confessedly symbolical character of the phrase, 'it is *not* precisely the heart, but that in them which makes them live', proves that to the speaker life was *not* 'heart' or 'breath', but that these terms were known to be material word-counters for the conception of life.[25] Whether the earliest thinkers identified heart, breath, shadow, with life, or whether they consciously used words of material origin to denote an immaterial conception, of course we do not know. But the word in the latter case would react on the thought, till the Roman inhaled (as his life?) the last breath of his dying kinsman, he well knowing that the Manes of the said kinsman were elsewhere, and not to be inhaled.

Subdivisions and distinctions were then recognised, as of the Egyptian *Ka*, the 'double', the Karen *kelah*, or 'personal life-phantom' *(wraith)*, on one side, and the Karen *thah*, 'the responsible moral soul', on the other. The Roman *umbra* hovers about the grave, the *manes* go to Orcus, the *spiritus* seeks the stars.

We are next presented with a crowd of cases in which sickness or lethargy is ascribed by savages to the absence of the patient's spirit, or of one of his spirits. This idea of migratory spirit is next used by savages to explain certain proceedings of the sorcerer, priest, or seer. His soul, or one of his souls is thought to go forth to distant places in quest of information, while the seer, perhaps, remains lethargic. Probably, in the struggle for existence, he lost more by being lethargic than he gained by being clairvoyant!

Now, here we touch the first point in Mr. Tylor's theory, where a critic may ask, Was this belief in the wandering abroad of the seer's spirit a theory not only false in its form (as probably it is), but also wholly unbased on experiences which might raise a presumption in favour of the existence of phenomena really supernormal? By 'supernormal' experiences I here mean such as the acquisition by a human mind of knowledge which could not be obtained by it through the recognised channels of sensation. Say, for the sake of argument, that a person, savage or civilised, obtains in trance information about distant places or events, to him unknown, and, through channels of sense, unknowable. The savage will explain this by saying that the seer's soul, shadow, or spirit, wandered out of the body to the distant scene. This is, at present, an unverified theory. But still, for the sake of argument, suppose that the seer did honestly obtain this information in trance, lethargy, or hypnotic sleep, or any other condition. If so, the modern savage (or his more gifted ancestors) would have other grounds for his theory of the wandering soul than any ground presented by normal occurrences, ordinary dreams, shadows, and so forth. Again, in human nature there would be (if such things occur) a potentiality of experiences other and stranger than materialism will admit as possible. It will (granting the facts) be impossible to aver that there is *nihil in intellectu quod non prius in sensu*. The soul will be not *ce qu'un vain peuple pense* under the new popular tradition, and the savage's theory of the spirit will be, at least in part, based on other than normal and every-day facts. That condition in which the seer acquires information, not otherwise accessible, about events remote in space, is what the mesmerists of the mid-century called 'travelling clairvoyance'.

If such an experience be *in rerum natura*, it will not, of course, justify the savage's theory that the soul is a separable entity, capable of voyaging, and also capable of existing after the death of the body. But it will give the savage a better excuse for his theory than normal experiences provide; and will even raise a presumption that reflection on mere ordinary experiences – death, shadow, trance – is not the *sole* origin of his theory. For a savage so acute as Mr. Tylor's hypothetical early reasoner might decline to believe that his own or a friend's soul had been absent on an expedition, unless it brought back information not normally to be acquired. However, we cannot reason, *a priori*, as to how far the logic of a savage might or might not go on occasion.

In any case, a scientific reasoner might be expected to ask: 'Is this alleged acquisition of knowledge, *not* through the ordinary channels of sense, a thing *in rerum natura?*' Because, if it is, we must obviously increase our list of the savage's reasons for believing in a soul: we must make his reasons include 'psychical' experiences, and there must be an X region to investigate.

These considerations did not fail to present themselves to Mr. Tylor. But his manner of dealing with them is peculiar. With his unequalled knowledge of the lower races, it was easy for him to examine travellers' tales about savage seers who beheld distant events in vision, and to allow them what weight he thought proper, after discounting possibilities of falsehood and collusion. He might then have examined modern narratives of similar performances among the civilised, which are abundant. It is obvious and undeniable that if the supernormal acquisition of knowledge in trance is a *vera causa*, a real process, however rare, Mr. Tylor's theory needs modifications; while the character of the savage's reasoning becomes more creditable to the savage, and appears as better bottomed than we had been asked to suppose. But Mr. Tylor does not examine this large body of evidence at all, or, at least, does not offer us the details of his examination.

He merely writes in this place: 'A typical spiritualistic instance may be quoted from Jung-Stilling, who says that examples have come to his knowledge of sick persons who, longing to see absent friends, have fallen into a swoon, during which they have appeared to the distant objects of their affection.'[26]

Jung-Stilling (though he wrote before modern 'Spiritualism' came in) is not a very valid authority; there is plenty of better evidence than his, but Mr. Tylor passes it by merely remarking that 'modern Europe has kept closely enough to the lines of early philosophy'. Modern Europe has indeed done so, if it explains the supernormal acquisition of knowledge, or the hallucinatory appearance of a distant person to his friend by a theory of wandering 'spirits'. But facts do not cease to be facts because wrong interpretations have been put upon them by savages, by Jung-Stilling, or by anyone else. The real question is, Do such events occur among lower and higher races, beyond explanation by fraud and fortuitous coincidence? We gladly grant that the belief in Animism, when it takes the form of a theory of 'wandering spirits', is probably untenable, as it is assuredly of savage origin. But we are not absolutely so sure that in this aspect the theory is not based on actual experiences, not of a normal and ordinary kind. If so, the savage philosophy and its supposed survivals in belief will appear in a new light. And we are inclined to hold that an examination of the mass of evidence to which Mr. Tylor offers here so slight an allusion will at least make it wise to suspend our judgment, not only as to the origins of the savage theory of spirits, but as to the materialistic hypothesis of the absence of a psychical element in man.

I may seem to have outrun already the limits of permissible hypothesis. It may appear absurd to surmise that there can exist in man, savage or civilised, a faculty for acquiring information not accessible by the known channels of sense, a faculty attributed by savage philosophers to the wandering soul. But one may be permitted to quote the opinion of M. Charles Richet, Professor of Physiology in the Faculty of Medicine in Paris. It is not cited because M. Richet is a professor of physiology, but because he reached his conclusion after six years of minute experiment. He says: 'There exists in certain persons, at certain moments, a faculty of acquiring knowledge which has no *rapport* with our normal faculties of that kind.'[27]

Instances tending to raise a presumption in favour of M. Richet's idea may now be sought in savage and civilised life.

[...]

The belief in a 'Supreme Being'

[...]

After offering to anthropologists and psychologists these considerations, we examined historically the relations of science to 'the marvellous', showing for example how Hume, following his *a priori* theory of the impossible, would have declined to investigate, because they were 'miraculous', certain occurrences which, to Charcot, were ordinary incidents in medical experience.

We next took up and criticised the anthropological theory of religion as expounded by Mr. Tylor. We then collected from his work a series of alleged supernormal phenomena in savage belief, all making for the foundation of animistic religion. Through several chapters we pursued the study of these phenomena, choosing savage instances, and setting beside them civilised testimony to facts of experience. Our conclusion was that such civilised experiences, if they occurred, as they are universally said to do, among savages, would help to originate, and would very strongly support the savage doctrine of souls, the base of religion in the theory of English anthropologists. But apart from the savage doctrine of 'spirits' (whether they exist or not), the evidence points to the existence of human faculties not allowed for in the current systems of materialism.

We next turned from the subject of supernormal experiences to the admitted facts about early religion. Granting the belief in souls and ghosts and spirits, however attained, how was the idea of a Supreme Being to be evolved out of that belief? We showed that, taking the creed as found in the lowest races, the processes put forward by anthropologists could not account for its evolution. The facts would not fit into, but contradicted, the anthropological theory. The necessary social conditions postulated were not found in places where the belief is found. Nay, the necessary social conditions for the evolution even of ancestor-worship were confessedly not found where the supposed ultimate result of ancestor-worship, the belief in a Supreme Being, flourished abundantly.

Again, the belief in a Supreme Being, *ex hypothesi* the latest in evolution, therefore the most potent, was often shelved and half forgotten, or neglected, or ridiculed, where the belief in Animism *(ex hypothesi* the earlier) was in full vigour. We demonstrated by facts that Anthropology had simplified her task by ignoring that essential feature, *the prevalent alliance of ethics with religion,* in the creed of the lowest and least developed races. Here, happily, we have not only the evidence of an earnest animist, Mr. Im Thurn, on our side, but that of a distinguished Semitic scholar, the late Mr. Robertson Smith. 'We see that even in its rudest forms Religion was a moral force, the powers that man reveres were on the side of social order and moral law; and the fear of the gods was a motive to enforce the laws of society, which were also the laws of morality.'[28] Wellhausen has already been cited to the same effect.

However, the facts proving that much of the Decalogue and a large element of Christian ethics are divinely sanctioned in savage religion are more potent than the most learned opinion on that side.

Our next step was to examine in detail several religions of the most remote and backward races, of races least contaminated with Christian or Islamite teaching. Our evidence, when possible, was derived from ancient and secret tribal mysteries, and sacred native hymns. We found a relatively Supreme Being, a Creator, sanctioning morality, and unpropitiated by sacrifice, among peoples who go in dread of ghosts and wizards, but do not always worship ancestors. We showed that the anthropological theory of the evolution of God out of ghosts in no way explains the facts in the savage conception of a Supreme Being. We then argued that the notion of 'spirit', derived from ghost-belief, was not logically needed for the conception of a Supreme Being in its earliest form, was detrimental to the conception, and, by much evidence, was denied to be part of the conception. The Supreme Being, thus regarded, may be (though he cannot historically be shown to be) prior to the first notion of ghost and separable souls.

We then traced the idea of such a Supreme Being through the creeds of races rising in the scale of material culture, demonstrating that he was thrust aside by the competition of ravenous but serviceable ghosts, ghostgods, and shades of kingly ancestors, with their magic and their bloody rites. These rites and the animistic conception behind them were next, in rare cases, reflected or refracted back on the Supreme Eternal. Aristocratic institutions fostered polytheism with the old Supreme Being obscured, or superseded, or enthroned as Emperor-God, or King-God. We saw how, and in what sense, the old degeneration theory could be defined and defended. We observed traces of degeneration in certain archaic aspects of the faith in Jehovah; and we proved that (given a tolerably pure low savage belief in a Supreme Being) that belief *must* degenerate, under social conditions, as civilisation advanced. Next, studying what we may call the restoration of Jehovah, under the great Prophets of Israel, we noted that they, and Israel generally, were strangely indifferent to that priceless aspect of Animism, the care for the future happiness, as conditioned by the conduct of the individual soul. That aspect had been neglected neither by the popular instinct nor the priestly and philosophic reflection of Egypt, Greece, and Rome. Christianity, last, combined what was good in Animism, the care for the individual soul as an immortal spirit under eternal responsibilities, with the One righteous Eternal of prophetic Israel, and so ended the long, intricate, and mysterious theological education of humanity. Such is our theory, which does not, to us, appear to lack evidence, nor to be inconsistent (as the anthropological theory is apparently inconsistent) with the hypothesis of evolution.

All this, it must be emphatically insisted on, is propounded 'under all reserves'. While these four stages, say (1) the Australian unpropitiated Moral Being, (2) the African neglected Being, still somewhat moral, (3) the relatively Supreme Being involved in human sacrifice, as in Polynesia, and (4) the Moral Being reinstated philosophically, or in Israel, do suggest steps in evolution, we desire to base no hard-and-fast system of ascending and descending degrees upon our present evidence. The real object is to show that facts may be regarded in this light, as well as in the light thrown by the anthropological theory, in the hands whether of Mr. Tylor, Mr. Spencer, M. Réville, or Mr. Jevons, whose interesting work comes nearest to our provisional hypothesis. We only ask for suspense of judgment, and for hesitation in accepting the dogmas of modern manualmakers. An exception to them certainly appears to be Mr. Clodd, if we may safely attribute to him a review (signed C.) of Mr. Grant Allen's 'Evolution of the Idea of God':

'We fear that all our speculations will remain summaries of probabilities. No documents are extant to enlighten us; we have only mobile, complex and confused ideas, incarnate in eccentric, often contradictory theories. That this character attaches to such ideas should keep us on guard against farming theories whose symmetry is sometimes their condemnation'.[29]

Nothing excites my own suspicion of my provisional hypothesis more than its symmetry. It really seems to fit the facts, as they appear to me, too neatly. I would suggest, however, that ancient savage sacred hymns, and practices in the mysteries, are really rather of the nature of 'documents'; more so, at least, than the casual observations of some travellers, or the gossip extracted from natives much in contact with Europeans.

Supposing that the arguments in this essay met with some acceptance, what effect would they have, if any, on our thoughts about religion? What is their practical tendency? The least dubious effect would be, I hope, to prevent us from accepting the anthropological theory of religion, or any other theory, as a foregone conclusion. I have tried to show how dim is our knowledge, how weak, often, is our evidence, and that, finding among the lowest savages all the elements of all religions already developed in different degrees, we cannot, historically, say that one is earlier than another. This point of priority we can never historically settle. If we met savages with ghosts and no gods, we could not be sure but that they once possessed a God, and forgot him. If we met savages with a God and no ghosts, we could not be historically certain that a higher had not obliterated a lower creed. For these reasons dogmatic decisions about the *origin* of religion seem unworthy of science. They will appear yet more futile to any student who goes so far with me as to doubt whether the highest gods of the lowest races could be developed, or can be shown to have been developed, by way of the ghost-theory. To him who reaches this point the whole animistic doctrine of ghosts as the one germ of religion will appear to be imperilled. The main practical result, then, will be hesitation about accepting the latest scientific opinion, even when backed by great names, and published in little primers.

On the hypothesis here offered to criticism there are two chief sources of Religion, (1) the belief, how attained we know not,[30] in a powerful, moral, eternal, omniscient Father and Judge of men; (2) the belief (probably developed out of experiences normal and supernormal) in somewhat of man which may survive the grave. This second belief is not, logically, needed as given material for the first, in its apparently earliest form. It may, for all we know, be the later of the two beliefs, chronologically. But this belief, too, was necessary to religion; first, as finally supplying a formula by which advancing intellects could conceive of the Mighty Being involved in the

former creed; next, as elevating man's conception of his own nature. By
the second belief he becomes the child of the God in whom, perhaps, he
already trusted, and in whom he has his being, a being not destined to perish
with the death of the body. Man is thus not only the child but the heir of
God, a 'nurseling of immortality', capable of entering into eternal life. On
the moral influence of this belief it is superfluous to dwell.

[. . .]

NOTES

1. *Primitive Culture*, I, pp. 9–10.
2. *Origin of Ranks.*
3. I may be permitted to refer to 'Reply to Objections' in the appendix to my
Myth, Ritual and Religion, vol. II.
4. Published for the Berlin Society of Experimental Psychology, Leipzig,
Günther, 1890.
5. Mr. A. J. Balfour, 'President's Address', *Proceedings*, Society for Psychical
Research, vol. x. p. 1894), p. 8.
6. *Primitive Culture*, I, Chap. XI, p. 421.
7. This theory is what Mr. Spencer calls 'Animism', and does not believe in.
What Mr. Tylor calls 'Animism' Mr. Spencer believes in, but he calls it the
'Ghost Theory'.
8. *Primitive Culture*, I, p. 428.
9. Howitt, *Journal of the Anthropological Institute*, XIII, pp. 191–195.
10. The curious may consult, for savage words for 'dreams', Mr. Scott's
Dictionary of the Mang'anja Language, *s.v.* 'Lota', or any glossary of any savage
language.
11. *Primitive Culture*, I, p. 429.
12. *Ibid.* I, p. 428.
13. *Ibid.* I, p. 285.
14. *Ibid.* I, pp. 285–286.
15. *Ibid.* I, p. 446.
16. See, however, Dr. Von Schrenck-Notzing, *Die Beobachtung narcotischer
Mittel für den Hypnotismus*, and Society for Psychical Research, *Proceedings*,
X, pp. 292–299.
17. *Primitive Culture*, I, pp. 306–315.
18. *Ibid.* I, p. 315.
19. *Philosophie des Geistes*, pp. 406, 408.
20. See also Mr. A. J. Balfour's Presidential Address to the Society for Psychical Research, *Proceedings*, vol. X. See, too, Taine, *De l'Intelligence*, I, pp. 78,
100, 139.
21. Tanner's *Narrative*, New York, 1830.
22. *Primitive Culture*, I, p. 143.
23. As 'spiritualism' is often used in opposition to 'materialism', and with
no reference to rapping 'spirits', the modern belief in that class of intelligences
may here be called spiritism.
24. *The Will to Believe*, Preface, p. XIV.

25. *Primitive Culture*, I, pp. 432–433. Citing Oviedo, *Histoire de Nicaragua*, pp. 21–51.

26. *Primitive Culture*, I, p. 440. Citing Stilling after Dale Owen, and quoting Mr. Alfred Russel Wallace's *Scientific Aspect of the Supernatural*, p. 43. Mr. Tylor also adds folk-lore practices of ghost-seeing, as on St. John's Eve. St. Mark's Eve, too, is in point, as far as folk-lore goes.

27. Society for Psychical Research, *Proceedings*, p. 167.

28. *Lectures on the Religion of the Semites*, p. 53.

29. *Daily Chronicle*, December 10, 1897.

30. The hypothesis of St. Paul seems not the most unsatisfactory.

James George Frazer

James George Frazer was born in Glasgow in 1854, where he received his primary school education. His secondary school education was at Springfield Academy and Larchfield Academy at Helensburgh. In 1869 he enrolled in Glasgow University where he studied classics with G. G. Ramsey, philosophy with John Veitch, and where he also worked with Sir William Thomson, who later became Lord Kelvin. He obtained his M. A. degree in 1874 and entered Trinity College in Cambridge. He studied classical literature, philosophy and law and became a fellow of the College in 1879. With the exception of one year teaching social anthropology at the University of Liverpool (1907–1908), though retaining the chair until 1922, Frazer worked all his life in Cambridge from where he kept up a large correspondence with a number of workers in the field. Frazer gave the Gifford Lectures at St. Andrews in 1911 and 1912, and in Edinburgh in 1924 and 1925. He died at Cambridge in 1941.

Of the numerous publications of Frazer the following should be mentioned here: 1887 *Totemism;* 1888 art. 'Taboo' and 'Totemism' in *Encyclopaedia Britannica,* 9th edition; 1890 *The Golden Bough,* 1st edition (2 vol.); 1900 *The Golden Bough,* 2nd edition (3 vol.); 1909 *Psyche's Task;* 1910 *Totemism and Exogamy* (4 vol.); 1911—1915 *The Golden Bough,* 3rd edition (12 vol.); 1913—1924 *The Belief in Immortality and the Worship of the Dead* (3 vol.); 1918 *Folk-lore in the Old Testament* (3 vol.); 1926 *The Worship of Nature;* 1930 *Myths of the Origin of Fire;* 1933 *The Fear of the Dead in Primitive Religion;* 1935 *Creation and Evolution in Primitive Cosmogonies;* 1936 *Aftermath;* 1937 *Totemica;* 1938–1939 *Anthologia Anthropologica* (4 vol.)

Although Frazer is mostly considered to be one of the founders of anthropology, he may be called a pioneer of comparative religion as well. He explicitly called his *The Golden Bough* 'a study in comparative religion' in the first edition, and 'a study in magic and religion' in the following editions. While having some definite views on religion as such, Frazer, in all his work, applied the comparative method assiduously to an immense amount of materials which were brought about by literary, historical and anthropological research and which were all somehow related to religion and to magic. He developed several general theories on totemism, magic, etc., starting from principles such as evolutionary development, psychic unity of mankind, superstition as opposed to rationality. He never gave, however, one sustained, closed theory.

The following fragments have been taken from the Prefaces to the three editions of *The Golden Bough.* They show the ways in which Frazer successively looked on this main work of his, and also how he viewed religion and the study of it in a general perspective.

'THE GOLDEN BOUGH' AND THE STUDY OF RELIGION

Preface to the First Edition, March 1890

For some time I have been preparing a general work on primitive superstition and religion. Among the problems which had attracted my attention was the hitherto unexplained rule of the Arician priesthood; and last spring it happened that in the course of my reading I came across some facts which, combined with others I had noted before, suggested an explanation of the rule in question. As the explanation, if correct, promised to throw light on some obscure features of primitive religion, I resolved to develop it fully, and, detaching it from my general work, to issue it as a separate study. This book is the result.

Now that the theory, which necessarily presented itself to me at first in outline, has been worked out in detail, I cannot but feel that in some places I may have pushed it too far. If this should prove to have been the case, I will readily acknowledge and retract my error as soon as it is brought home to me. Meantime my essay may serve its purpose as a first attempt to solve a difficult problem, and to bring a variety of scattered facts into some sort of order and system.

A justification is perhaps needed of the length at which I have dwelt upon the popular festivals observed by European peasants in spring, at midsummer, and at harvest. It can hardly be too often repeated, since it is not yet generally recognised, that in spite of their fragmentary character the popular superstitions and customs of the peasantry are by far the fullest and most trustworthy evidence we possess as to the primitive religion of the Aryans. Indeed the primitive Aryan, in all that regards his mental fibre and texture, is not extinct. He is amongst us to this day. The great intellectual and moral forces which have revolutionised the educated world have scarcely affected the peasant. In his inmost beliefs he is what his forefathers were in the days when forest trees still grew and squirrels played on the ground where Rome and London now stand.

Hence every enquiry into the primitive religion of the Aryans should either start from the superstitious beliefs and observances of the peasantry, or should at least be constantly checked and controlled by reference to them. Compared with the evidence afforded by living tradition, the testimony of ancient books on the subject of early religion is worth very little. For literature accelerates the advance of thought at a rate which leaves the slow progress of opinion by word of mouth at an immeasurable distance behind. Two or three generations of literature may do more to change thought than two or three thousand years of traditional life. But the mass of the people who do not read books remain unaffected by the mental revolution

wrought by literature; and so it has come about that in Europe at the present day the superstitious beliefs and practices which have been handed
down by word of mouth are generally of a far more archaic type than the
religion depicted in the most ancient literature of the Aryan race.

It is on these grounds that, in discussing the meaning and origin of an
ancient Italian priesthood, I have devoted so much attention to the popular
customs and superstitions of modern Europe. In this part of my subject
I have made great use of the works of the late W. Mannhardt, without which,
indeed, my book could scarcely have been written. Fully recognising the
truth of the principles which I have imperfectly stated, Mannhardt set himself systematically to collect, compare, and explain the living superstitions
of the peasantry. Of this wide field the special department which he marked
out for himself was the religion of the woodman and the farmer, in other
words, the superstitious beliefs and rites connected with trees and cultivated
plants. By oral enquiry, and by printed questions scattered broadcast over
Europe, as well as by ransacking the literature of folk-lore, he collected a
mass of evidence, part of which he published in a series of admirable works.
But his health, always feeble, broke down before he could complete the
comprehensive and really vast scheme which he had planned, and at his
too early death much of his precious materials remained unpublished. His
manuscripts are now deposited in the University Library at Berlin, and in
the interest of the study to which he devoted his life it is greatly to be desired
that they should be examined, and that such portions of them as he has not
utilised in his books should be given to the world.

Of his published works the most important are, first, two tracts, *Roggen-
wolf und Roggenhund*, Danzig, 1865 (second edition, Danzig, 1866), and
Die Korndämonen, Berlin, 1868. These little works were put forward by him
tentatively, in the hope of exciting interest in his enquiries and thereby
securing the help of others in pursuing them. But, except from a few learned
societies, they met with very little attention. Undeterred by the cold reception accorded to his efforts he worked steadily on, and in 1875 published his
chief work, *Der Baumkultus der Germanen und ihrer Nachbarstämme*. This
was followed in 1877 by *Antike Wald- und Feldkulte*. His *Mythologische
Forschungen*, a posthumous work, appeared in 1884.

Much as I owe to Mannhardt, I owe still more to my friend Professor W.
Robertson Smith. My interest in the early history of society was first excited
by the works of Dr. E. B. Tylor, which opened up a mental vista undreamed
of by me before. But it is a long step from a lively interest in a subject to
a systematic study of it; and that I took this step is due to the influence of
my friend W. Robertson Smith. The debt which I owe to the vast stores of
his knowledge, the abundance and fertility of his ideas, and his unwearied
kindness, can scarcely be overestimated. Those who know his writings may

form some, though a very inadequate, conception of the extent to which I have been influenced by him. The views of sacrifice set forth in his article 'Sacrifice' in the *Encyclopaedia Britannica*, and further developed in his recent work, *The Religion of the Semites*, mark a new departure in the historical study of religion, and ample traces of them will be found in this book. Indeed the central idea of my essay – the conception of the slain god – is derived directly, I believe, from my friend. But it is due to him to add that he is in no way responsible for the general explanation which I have offered of the custom of slaying the god. He has read the greater part of the proofs in circumstances which enhanced the kindness, and has made many valuable suggestions which I have usually adopted; but except where he is cited by name, or where the views expressed coincide with those of his published works, he is not to be regarded as necessarily assenting to any of the theories propounded in this book.

[...]

Preface to the Second Edition, September 1900

The kind reception accorded by critics and the public to the first edition of *The Golden Bough* has encouraged me to spare no pains to render the new one more worthy of their approbation. While the original book remains almost entire, it has been greatly expanded by the insertion of much fresh illustrative matter, drawn chiefly from further reading, but in part also from previous collections which I had made, and still hope to use, for another work. Friends and correspondents, some of them personally unknown to me, have kindly aided me in various ways, especially by indicating facts or sources which I had overlooked and by correcting mistakes into which I had fallen. I thank them all for their help, of which I have often availed myself. Their contributions will be found acknowledged in their proper places. But I owe a special acknowledgment to my friends the Rev. Lorimer Fison and the Rev. John Roscoe, who have sent me valuable notes on the Fijian and Waganda customs respectively. Most of Mr. Fison's notes, I believe, are incorporated in my book. Of Mr. Roscoe's only a small selection has been given; the whole series, embracing a general account of the customs and beliefs of the Waganda, will be published, I hope, in the *Journal of the Anthropological Institute*. Further, I ought to add that Miss Mary E. B. Howitt has kindly allowed me to make some extracts from a work by her on Australian folklore and legends which I was privileged to read in manuscript.

I have seen no reason to withdraw the explanation of the priesthood of Aricia which forms the central theme of my book. On the contrary, the probability of that explanation appears to me to be greatly strengthened by some important evidence which has come to light since my theory was put forward. Readers of the first edition may remember that I explained the priest of Aricia – the King of the Wood – as an embodiment of a tree-spirit, and inferred from a variety of considerations that at an earlier period one of these priests had probably been slain every year in his character of an incarnate deity. But for an undoubted parallel to such a custom of killing a human god annually I had to go as far as ancient Mexico. Now from the *Martyrdom of St. Dasius,* unearthed and published a few years ago by Professor Franz Cumont of Ghent *(Analecta Bollandiana,* XVI, 1897), it is practically certain that in ancient Italy itself a human representative of Saturn – the old god of the seed – was put to death every year at his festival of the Saturnalia, and that though in Rome itself the custom had probably fallen into disuse before the classical era, it still lingered on in remote places down at least to the fourth century after Christ. I cannot but regard this discovery as a confirmation, as welcome as it was unlooked for, of the theory of the Arician priesthood which I had been led independently to propound.

Further, the general interpretation which, following W. Mannhardt, I had given of the ceremonies observed by our European peasantry in spring, at midsummer, and at harvest, has also been corroborated by fresh and striking analogies. If we are right, these ceremonies were originally magical rites designed to cause plants to grow, cattle to thrive, rain to fall, and the sun to shine. Now the remarkable researches of Professor Baldwin Spencer and Mr. F. J. Gillen among the native tribes of Central Australia have proved that these savages regularly perform magical ceremonies for the express purpose of bringing down rain and multiplying the plants and animals on which they subsist, and further that these ceremonies are most commonly observed at the approach of the rainy season, which in Central Australia answers to our spring. Here then, at the other side of the world, we find an exact counterpart of those spring and midsummer rites which our rude forefathers in Europe probably performed with a full consciousness of their meaning, and which many of their descendants still keep up, though the original intention of the rites has been to a great extent, but by no means altogether, forgotten. The harvest customs of our European peasantry have naturally no close analogy among the practices of the Australian aborigines, since these savages do not till the ground. But what we should look for in vain among the Australians we find to hand among the Malays. For recent enquiries, notably those of Mr. J. L. van der Toorn in Sumatra and of Mr. W. W. Skeat in the Malay Peninsula, have supplied us with close parallels to the harvest customs of Europe, as these latter were interpreted by the genius of Mannhardt. Occupying a lower plane of culture than ourselves, the Malays have retained a keen sense of the significance of rites which in Europe have sunk to the level of more or less meaningless survivals.

Thus on the whole I cannot but think that the course of subsequent investigation has tended to confirm the general principles followed and the particular conclusions reached in this book. At the same time I am as sensible as ever of the hypothetical nature of much that is advanced in it. It has been my wish and intention to draw as sharply as possible the line of demarcation between my facts and the hypotheses by which I have attempted to colligate them. Hypotheses are necessary but often temporary bridges built to connect isolated facts. If my light bridges should sooner or later break down or be superseded by more solid structures, I hope that my book may still have its interest as a repertory of facts.

But while my views, tentative and provisional as they probably are, thus remain much what they were, there is one subject on which they have undergone a certain amount of change, unless indeed it might be more exact to say that I seem to see clearly now what before was hazy. I mean the relation of magic to religion. When I first wrote this book I failed, perhaps inexcusably, to define even to myself my notion of religion, and hence was disposed to class magic loosely under it as one of its lower forms. I have now sought to remedy this defect by framing as clear a definition of religion as the difficult nature of the subject and my apprehension of it allowed. Hence I have come to agree with Sir A. C. Lyall and Mr. F. B. Jevons in recognising a fundamental distinction and even opposition of principle between magic and religion. More than that, I believe that in the evolution of thought, magic, as representing a lower intellectual stratum, has probably everywhere preceded religion. I do not claim any originality for this latter view. It has been already plainly suggested, if not definitely formulated, by Professor H. Oldenberg in his able book *Die Religion des Veda,* and for aught I know it may have been explicitly stated by many others before and since him. I have not collected the opinions of the learned on the subject, but have striven to form my own directly from the facts. And the facts which bespeak the priority of magic over religion are many and weighty. Some of them the reader will find stated in the following pages; but the full force of the evidence can only be appreciated by those who have made a long and patient study of primitive superstition. I venture to think that those who submit to this drudgery will come more and more to the opinion I have indicated. That all my readers should agree either with my definition of religion or with the inferences I have drawn from it is not to be expected. But I would ask those who dissent from my conclusions to make sure that they mean the same thing by religion that I do; for otherwise the difference between us may be more apparent than real.

As the scope and purpose of my book have been seriously misconceived by some courteous critics, I desire to repeat in more explicit language, what I vainly thought I had made quite clear in my original preface, that this is not a general treatise on primitive superstition, but merely the investigation of one particular and narrowly limited problem, to wit, the rule of the Arician priesthood, and that accordingly only such general principles are explained and illustrated in the course of it as seemed to me to throw light on that special problem. If I have said little or nothing of other principles of equal or even greater importance, it is assuredly not because I undervalue them in comparison with those which I have expounded at some length, but simply because it appeared to me that they did not directly bear on the question I had set myself to answer. No one can well be more sensible than I am of the immense variety and complexity of the forces which have gone towards the building up of religion; no one can recognise more frankly the futility and inherent absurdity of any attempt to explain the whole vast organism as the product of any one simple factor. If I have hitherto touched, as I am quite aware, only the fringe of a great subject – fingered only a few of the countless threads that compose the mighty web –, it is merely because neither my time nor my knowledge has hitherto allowed me to do more. Should I live to complete the works for which I have collected and am collecting materials, I dare to think that they will clear me of any suspicion of treating the early history of religion from a single narrow point of view. But the future is necessarily uncertain, and at the best many years must elapse before I can execute in full the plan which I have traced out for myself. Meanwhile I am unwilling by keeping silence to leave some of my readers under the impression that my outlook on so large a subject does not reach beyond the bounds of the present enquiry. This is my reason for noticing the misconceptions to which I have referred. I take leave to add that some part of my larger plan would probably have been completed before now, were it not that out of the ten years which have passed since this book was first published nearly eight have been spent by me in work of a different kind.

There is a misunderstanding of another sort which I feel constrained to set right. But I do so with great reluctance, because it compels me to express a measure of dissent from the revered friend and master to whom I am under the deepest obligations, and who has passed beyond the reach of controversy. In an elaborate and learned essay on sacrifice *(L'Année Sociologique,* Deuxieme Année, 1897–1898), Messrs. H. Hubert and M. Mauss have represented my theory of the slain god as intended to supplement and complete Robertson Smith's theory of the derivation of animal sacrifice in general from a totem sacrament. On this I have to say that the two theories are quite independent of each other. I never assented to my friend's theory, and so far as I can remember he never gave me a hint that he assented to mine. My reason for suspending my judgment in regard to his theory was a simple one. At the time when the theory was propounded, and for many years afterwards, I knew of no single indubitable case of a totem sacrament, that is, of a custom of killing and eating the totem animal as a solemn rite. It is true that in my *Totemism*, and again in the present work, I noted a few cases (four in all) of solemnly killing a sacred animal which, following Robertson Smith, I regarded as probably a totem. But none even of these four cases included the eating of the sacred animal by the worshippers, which was an essential part of my friend's theory, and in regard to all of them it was not positively known that the slain animal was a totem. Hence as time went on and still no certain case of a totem sacrament was reported, I became more and more doubtful of the existence of such a practice at all, and my doubts had almost hardened into incredulity when the long-looked-for rite was discovered by Messrs. Spencer and Gillen in full force among the aborigines of Central Australia, whom I for one must consider to be the most primitive totem tribes as yet known to us. This discovery I welcomed as a very striking proof of the sagacity of my brilliant friend, whose rapid genius had outstripped our slower methods and anticipated what it was reserved for subsequent research positively to ascertain. Thus from being little more than an ingenious hypothesis the totem sacrament has become, at least in my opinion, a well-authenticated fact. But from the practice of the rite by a single set of tribes it is still a long step to the universal practice of it by all totem tribes, and from that again it is a still longer stride to the deduction therefrom of animal sacrifice in general. These two steps I am not yet prepared to take. No one will welcome further evidence of the wide prevalence of a totem sacrament more warmly than I shall, but until it is forthcoming I shall continue to agree with Professor E. B. Tylor that it is unsafe to make the custom the base of far-reaching speculations.

To conclude this subject, I will add that the doctrine of the universality of totemism, which Messrs. Hubert and Mauss have implicitly attributed to me, is one which I have never enunciated or assumed, and that, so far as my knowledge and opinion go, the worship of trees and cereals, which occupies so large a space in these volumes, is neither identical with nor derived from a system of totemism. It is possible that further enquiry may lead me to regard as probable the universality of totemism and the derivation from it of sacrifice and of the whole worship both of plants and animals. I hold myself ready to follow the evidence wherever it may lead; but in the present state of our knowledge I consider that to accept these conclusions would be, not to follow the evidence, but very seriously to outrun it. In thinking so I am happy to be at one with Messrs. Hubert and Mauss.

When I am on this theme I may as well say that I am by no means prepared to stand by everything in my little apprentice work, *Totemism*. That book was a rough piece of pioneering in a field that, till then, had been but little explored, and some inferences in it were almost certainly too hasty. In particular there was a tendency, perhaps not unnatural in the circumstances, to treat as totems, or as connected with totemism, things which probably were neither the one nor the other. If ever I republish the volume, as I hope one day to do, I shall have to retrench it in some directions as well as to enlarge it in others.

Such as it is, with all its limitations, which I have tried to indicate clearly, and with all its defects, which I leave to the critics to discover, I offer my book in its new form as a contribution to that still youthful science which seeks to trace the growth of human thought and institutions in those dark ages which lie beyond the range of history. The progress of that science must needs be slow and painful, for the evidence, though clear and abundant on some sides, is lamentably obscure and scanty on others, so that the cautious enquirer is every now and then brought up sharp on the edge of some yarning chasm across which he may be quite unable to find a way. All he can do in such a case is to mark the pitfall plainly on his chart and to hope that others in time may be able to fill it up or bridge it over. Yet the very difficulty and novelty of the investigation, coupled with the extent of the intellectual prospect which suddenly opens up before us whenever the mist rises and unfolds the far horizon, constitute no small part of its charm. The position of the anthropologist of to-day resembles in some sort the position of classical scholars at the revival of learning. To these men the rediscovery of ancient literature came like a revelation, disclosing to their wondering eyes a splendid vision of the antique world, such as the cloistered student of the Middle Ages never dreamed of under the gloomy shadow of the minster and within the sound of its solemn bells. To us moderns a still wider vista is vouchsafed, a greater panorama is unrolled by the study which aims at bringing home to us the faith and the practice, the hopes and the ideals, not of two highly gifted races only, but of all mankind, and thus at enabling us to follow the long march, the slow and toilsome ascent, of humanity from savagery to civilisation. And as the scholar of the Renaissance found not merely fresh food for thought but a new field of labour in the dusty and faded manuscripts of Greece and Rome, so in the mass of materials that is steadily pouring in from many sides – from buried cities of remotest antiquity as well as from the rudest savages of the desert and the jungle – we of to-day must recognise a new province of knowledge which will task the energies of generations of students to master. The study is still in its rudiments, and what we do now will have to be done over again and done better, with fuller knowledge and deeper insight, by those who come after us. To recur to a metaphor which I have already made use of, we of this age are only pioneers hewing lanes and clearings in the forest where others will hereafter sow and reap.

But the comparative study of the beliefs and institutions of mankind is fitted to be much more than a means of satisfying an enlightened curiosity and of furnishing materials for the researches of the learned. Well handled, it may become a powerful instrument to expedite progress if it lays bare certain weak spots in the foundations on which modern society is built – if it shews that much which we are wont to regard as solid rests on the sands of superstition rather than on the rock of nature. It is indeed a melancholy and in some respects thankless task to strike at the foundations of beliefs in which, as in a strong tower, the hopes and aspirations of humanity through long ages have sought a refuge from the storm and stress of life. Yet sooner or later it is inevitable that the battery of the comparative method should breach these venerable walls, mantled over with the ivy and mosses and wild flowers of a thousand tender and sacred associations. At present we are only dragging the guns into position: they have hardly yet begun to speak. The task of building up into fairer and more enduring forms the old structures so rudely shattered is reserved for other hands, perhaps for other and happier ages. We cannot foresee, we can hardly even guess, the new forms into which thought and society will run in the future. Yet this uncertainty ought not to induce us, from any consideration of expediency or regard for antiquity, to spare the ancient moulds, however beautiful, when these are proved to be out-worn. Whatever comes of it, wherever it leads us, we must follow truth alone. It is our only guiding star: *hoc signo vinces.*

To a passage in my book it has been objected by a distinguished scholar that the church-bells of Rome cannot be heard, even in the stillest weather, on the shores of the Lake of Nemi. In acknowledging my blunder and leaving it uncorrected, may I plead in extenuation of my obduracy the example of an illustrious writer? In *Old Mortality* we read how a hunted Covenanter, fleeing before Claverhouse's dragoons, hears the sullen boom of the kettle-drums of the pursuing cavalry borne to him on the night wind. When Scott was taken to task for this description, because the drums are not beaten by cavalry at night, he replied in effect that he liked to hear the drums sounding there, and that he would let them sound on so long as his book might last. In the same spirit I make bold to say that by the Lake of Nemi I love to hear, if it be only in imagination, the distant chiming of the bells of Rome, and I would fain believe that their airy music may ring in the ears of my readers after it has ceased to vibrate in my own.

Preface to the Third Edition, December 1910

When I originally conceived the idea of the work, of which the first part is now laid before the public in a third and enlarged edition, my intention merely was to explain the strange rule of the priesthood or sacred kingship of Nemi and with it the legend of the Golden Bough, immortalised by Virgil, which the voice of antiquity associated with the priesthood. The explanation was suggested to me by some similar rules formerly imposed on kings in Southern India, and at first I thought that it might be adequately set forth within the compass of a small volume. But I soon found that in attempting to settle one question I had raised many more: wider and wider prospects opened out before me; and thus step by step I was lured on into far-spreading fields of primitive thought which had been but little explored by my predecessors. Thus the book grew on my hands, and soon the projected essay became in fact a ponderous treatise, or rather a series of separate dissertations loosely linked together by a slender thread of connexion with my original subject. With each successive edition these dissertations have grown in number and swollen in bulk by the accretion of fresh materials, till the thread on which they are strung at last threatened to snap under their weight. Accordingly, following the hint of a friendly critic, I decided to resolve my overgrown book into its elements, and to publish separately the various disquisitions of which it is composed. The present volumes, forming the first part of the whole, contain a preliminary enquiry into the principles of Magic and the evolution of the Sacred Kingship in general. They will be followed shortly by a volume which discusses the principles of Taboo in their special application to sacred or priestly kings. The remainder of the work will be mainly devoted to the myth and ritual of the Dying God, and as the subject is large and fruitful, my discussion of it will, for the sake of convenience, be divided into several parts, of which one, dealing with some dying gods of antiquity in Egypt and Western Asia, has already been published under the title of *Adonis, Attis, Osiris.*

But while I have thus sought to dispose my book in its proper form as a collection of essays on a variety of distinct, though related, topics, I have at the same time preserved its unity, as far as possible, by retaining the original title for the whole series of volumes, and by pointing out from time to time the bearing of my general conclusions on the particular problem which furnished the starting-point of the enquiry. It seemed to me that this mode of presenting the subject offered some advantages which outweighed certain obvious drawbacks. By discarding the austere form, without, I hope, sacrificing the solid substance, of a scientific treatise, I thought to cast my materials into a more artistic mould and so perhaps to attract readers, who might have been repelled by a more strictly logical and systematic arrangement of the facts. Thus I put the mysterious priest of Nemi, so to say, in the forefront of the picture, grouping the other sombre figures of the same sort behind him in the background, not certainly because I deemed them pf less moment but because the picturesque natural surroundings of the oriest of Nemi among the wooded hills of Italy, the very mystery which enshrouds him, and not least the haunting magic of Virgil's verse, all combine to shed a glamour on the tragic figure with the Golden Bough, which fits him to stand as the centre of a gloomy canvas. But I trust that the high relief into which he has thus been thrown in my pages will not lead my readers either to overrate his historical importance by comparison with that of some other figures which stand behind him in the shadow, or to attribute to my theory of the part he played a greater degree of probability than it deserves. Even if it should appear that this ancient Italian priest must after all be struck out from the long roll of men who have masqueraded as gods, the single omission would not sensibly invalidate the demonstration, which I believe I have given, that human pretenders to divinity have been far commoner and their credulous worshippers far more numerous than had been hitherto suspected. Similarly, should my whole theory of this particular priesthood collapse – and I fully acknowledge the slenderness of the foundations on which it rests – its fall would hardly shake my general conclusions as to the evolution of primitive religion and society, which are founded on large collections of entirely independent and well-authenticated facts.

Friends versed in German philosophy have pointed out to me that my views of magic and religion and their relations to each other in history agree to some extent with those of Hegel. The agreement is quite independent and to me unexpected, for I have never studied the philosopher's writings nor attended to his speculations. As, however, we have arrived at similar results by very different roads, the partial coincidence of our conclusions may perhaps be taken to furnish a certain presumption in favour of their truth. To enable my readers to judge of the extent of the coincidence, I have given in an appendix some extracts from Hegel's lectures on the philosophy of religion. The curious may compare them with my chapter on Magic and Religion, which was written in ignorance of the views of my illustrious predecessor.

With regard to the history of the sacred kingship which I have outlined in these volumes, I desire to repeat a warning which I have given in the text. While I have shewn reason to think that in many communities sacred kings have been developed out of magicians, I am far from supposing that this has been universally true. The causes which have determined the establishment of monarchy have no doubt varied greatly in different countries and at different times: I make no pretence to discuss or even enumerate them all: I have merely selected one particular cause because it bore directly on my special enquiry; and I have laid emphasis on it because it seems to have been overlooked by writers on the origin of political institutions, who, themselves sober and rational according to modern standards, have not reckoned sufficiently with the enormous influence which superstition has exerted in shaping the human past. But I have no wish to exaggerate the importance of this particular cause at the expense of others which may have been equally or even more influential. No one can be more sensible than I am of the risk of stretching an hypothesis too far, of crowding a multitude of incongruous particulars under one narrow formula, of reducing the vast, nay inconceivable complexity of nature and history to a delusive appearance of theoretical simplicity. It may well be that I have erred in this direction again and again; but at least I have been well aware of the danger of error and have striven to guard myself and my readers against it. How far I have succeeded in that and the other objects I have set before me in writing this work, I must leave to the candour of the public to determine.

Robert R. Marett

Robert Ranulph Marett was born in 1866 on the island of Jersey, where he received his primary school education. On completion of his secondary school education at Victoria College he became in 1885 a student at Oxford, where he studied classics and philosophy at Balliol College. He took here his first class in classical moderation in 1886, and in 'literae humaniores' in 1888. Thereupon he studied German philosophy at the University of Berlin in 1888–89 and spent the next year in Rome. On his return to Oxford Marett remained for a year at Balliol and, though admitted to the Jersey bar in 1891, was elected a fellow of Exeter College in 1891. There he became a philosophy tutor from 1893, but had developed interest in anthropology since 1890 and he would also pursue his interests in prehistoric archeology, later doing fieldwork at Jersey and elsewhere. He obtained his doctorate (D. Sc.) and was the principal founder of the Oxford University Anthropological Society in 1909. In 1910 Marett was appointed reader in anthropology at Oxford, where he founded the Department of Anthropology. He retired in 1936, but remained rector of Exeter College, which he had become in 1928. Marett died at Oxford in 1943.

Of Marett's publications the following should be mentioned here: 1909 *The Threshold of Religion;* 1910 *The Birth of Humility;* 1912 *Anthropology;* 1920 *Psychology and Folklore;* 1927 *The Diffusion of Culture;* 1928 *Man in the Making: an Introduction to Anthropology;* 1929 *The Raw Material of Religion;* 1931 *Spencer's Last Journey* (with T. K. Penniman); 1932 *Faith, Hope and Charity in Primitive Religion;* 1933 *Sacraments of Simple Folk;* 1935 *Head, Heart and Hands in Human Evolution;* 1936 *Tylor.*

Besides his interests in folklore and archeology, Marett is especially known in the study of religion for his theory of pre-animism or dynamism. He contended that at the beginning of man's religious development there was what he called a 'supernaturalistic' stage, in which man recognized an impersonal religious force which was rather felt than reasoned out. In his interpretation of religion Marett took a psychological approach based on the experience of the individual, with much attention for the affective and emotional side of it.

The following text is that of a paper which Marett published in the *Archiv für Religionswissenschaft*, XII (1909), and which shows his attempt to come to a definition of religion with the help of the concepts of 'mana' and 'tabu'.

'THE TABU-MANA FORMULA AS A MINIMUM DEFINITION
OF RELIGION'

Scope of the paper. This paper is little more than a summary of an address
'ecently delivered before the Third International Congress for the History
of Religions at Oxford. That address in its turn consisted mainly in a systematic restatement of views put forward in three published essays, *viz.:*
'Pre-animistic Religion' in *Folk-lore* (June 1900), 'From Spell to Prayer'
in *Folk-lore* (June 1904), and 'Is Tabu a Negative Magic?' in *Anthropological
Essays presented to Edward Burnett Tylor*, Oxford, 1907. All these papers
are reprinted in my book *The Threshold of Religion*, London, 1909. Such
novelty as there may be in these views attaches chiefly to two antagonisms:
1) dissatisfaction with Tylor's theory that animism (in his sense of the term)
provides 'a minimum definition of Religion'; 2) dissatisfaction with Frazer's theory that Magic and Religion have, from the standpoint of origins,
nothing in common.

In what follows I have depended for illustrative matter almost exclusively
on two authorities, *viz.:* R. H. Codrington, *The Melanesians*, Oxford,
1891, and E. Tregear, *The Maori-Polynesian Comparative Dictionary*,
Wellington, New Zealand, 1891. My remarks, however, are intended to
apply not merely to the Pacific region, but to the world of so-called 'savagery' in general. I distinguish a stage of 'savage', 'primitive', or, as I should
prefer to call it, 'rudimentary' religion; and to the phenomena of this
stage I conceive *tabu* and *mana* to be applicable as categories, *i.e.* classificatory terms of the widest extension. No attempt, however, can be made
here to show by induction that ideas corresponding to *tabu* and *mana*
are of world-wide distribution. This must be taken for granted; though
I may perhaps be allowed to say that I am in possession of enough evidence
to justify me in my own eyes in making a tentative generalization to this
effect. I proceed to deal with my subject under two heads.

A. *Tabu and Mana as severally the negative and positive modes of the
Supernatural*

It can, I would maintain, be shewn by induction that rudimentary
reflexion recognizes, if not for the most part abstractly, yet at any rate in
its concrete presentations, a distinctive aspect of the universe of experience,
wherein it appears unaccountable and awful. I have elsewhere *(Anthrop.
Essays*, p. 227) noted, for instance, how the Pygmy Bokane when confronted
with particular cases, or rather types of cases, could determine with great
precision whether *oudak*, 'the mysterious' (if so vague a notion is trans-
latable into our terms at all), was there or not. Meanwhile to find a word

whereby science may characterize this aspect is not easy. *L'idée du sacré* is becoming a favourite expression with French writers, but, whereas the French *sacré* bears the double sense of 'holy' and 'damned', the English 'sacred' wholly lacks the latter meaning; whilst in any case the etymological source of these words, *viz.:* the Latin *sacer*, is equivalent rather to *tabu*. 'Supernormal', or 'extranormal', is a straightforward term, but one that lacks mystic associations. 'Uncanny' has this advantage; but it is possessed in a more eminent degree by 'supernatural', an expression consecrated by long usage to mystic contexts of all kinds. Hence I decide to use the term 'supernatural' in this connexion, though it must be clearly understood that there is no intention to impute to the savage any abstract conception of the uniform 'nature' postulated by civilized thought.

The supernatural, taken in this sense, has two existential modes, a negative and a positive. On its negative side it is *tabu* = 'not to be lightly approached' (*Cf.* Codrington, p. 188). The prohibition is not against all dealings whatever with the supernatural (else all cult would be impossible), but against all heedless and profane dealings. An examination of the usage of the term in the Pacific region, or of that of kindred terms in this part of the world, will show that this is the root-meaning, although in certain contexts the idea may come to have a more or less specialized, and sometimes a more or less positive, signification. On its positive side the supernatural is *mana* = 'instinct with wonder-working power'. [Or it may be said to 'have' *mana*, the word being noun as well as adjective; though this is to neglect the local usage, which makes a certain distinction between 'being' and merely 'having' *mana (Cf.* Codrington, p. 191)]. The mystic power, be it noted, is there, whether exercised or not; *mana* may be dormant or potential. An examination of the usage of the term or its equivalents will show that the notion of power is fundamental, and also that it always stands for what both Codrington and Tregear actually term 'supernatural' power *(Cf.* Codrington, pp. 118 *sqq.*, Tregear, *s.v. mana).*

If I am right, then, we get a *tabu-mana* formula capable of exhaustively expressing the universal nature of the supernatural, so long as its nature (as opposed to its value) is in question. It remains to add that there are other terms, not infrequently the outgrowths of *tabu* and *mana*, which arise to express value. *Tabu* and *mana* register descriptive judgments; the other register normative judgments. The former exhibit the supernatural in its first, or existential, dimension, the latter exhibit it in its second, or moral, dimension. Thus *tabu* implies holiness and defilement alike. On the other hand, plenty of words are to be found in savage vocabularies that embody the separate meaning of 'pure' and 'impure' in the religious sense. Sometimes mere difference of intensity would seem capable of developing into difference of moral worth, *e.g. buto* which wavers between 'very sacred' and 'abominable' (Codrington, p. 31). Again, *mana* is supernatural power for good or for evil, to bless or to curse, to heal or to hurt. On the other hand, moral valuations create a terminology of their own in this direction also, *e.g. Makutu*, personified witchcraft dwelling with the wicked goddess *Miru*, of whom Tregear *(s.v. Miru)* writes, 'the unclean *tapu* was her power *(mana)*'; or *otgon*, the malignant exercise of *orenda* (equivalent to *mana*), which, according to J. N. B. Hewitt *(American Anthropologist* (1902) N. S. IV, p 37 n.), is steadily driving the latter term out of use; whilst for Australian exx. see my paper in *Anthrop. Essays*, pp. 225 *sqq.* I would further maintain that our terms 'Magic' and 'Religion', though perhaps in ordinary parlance they do not always have a normative function (since we may speak of false religion, or again of white magic), ought for purposes of science to be assigned an evaluatory use, in view of the fact that a closely corresponding disjunction of moral import runs through the hierological language of the world. A corollary is that the term 'magico-religious' (though doubtless convenient as conveying the implication that Magic and Religion have a common source in the recognition of the supernatural) is not strictly applicable to the supernatural conceived merely as *tabu-mana*, since in this its existential capacity the supernatural is not both magical and religious, but neither magical nor religious.

B. *The tabu-mana formula in its relation to Tylor's theory of animism*

The term animism has been used in two senses. Spencer gives it the wide sense of the attribution of life and animation; Tylor the narrower sense of the attribution of 'soul', 'spirit', or 'ghost', which in any of these forms has the 'vaporous materiality' of a dream-image. To keep apart the Spencerian sense I have invented ('Pre-animistic Religion', p. 171) in its place the term 'animatism', which has obtained a certain currency. Here I am concerned solely with the Tylorian sense of animism.

Now I am inclined to suspect that in the Pacific region manifestations of the supernatural are to be found which natives would regard as *tabu* and *mana* without putting upon them any animistic interpretation in the Tylorian sense. Thus I have Dr. Seligmann's authority for stating that in New Guinea a yam-stone would be held capable of making the yams grow miraculously, quite apart from the agency of spirits. Such phenomena I have named 'pre-animistic', and the term has found favour; though perhaps it is unfortunate in so far as it imports a chronological distinction where genetic problems are better ruled aside. Meanwhile, Codrington's evidence goes to show that in Melanesia at all events the *tabu-mana* view and animism do coexist in a fairly harmonious system of ideas. Thus, to confine our attention simply to *mana*, this wherever it occurs is referred to one of two or three originating sources, *viz.:* 1) the 'ghost' of a dead man; 2) a 'spirit' that was never a man (such spirits, however, not always displaying the Tylorian requirement of a ghost-like appearance, being sometimes 'grey like dust', as a native put it (Codrington, p. 151), but sometimes having the ordinary corporeal figure of a man, the product not of animism but of anthropomorphism); 3) a living man. The third possibility, however, is arrived at constructively and by a process that the native logic ignores. When a man has *mana* (which, by the way, resides in his spiritual part or 'soul', Codrington, p. 191) a ghost or spirit has inspired *(manag)* him, and he speaks no longer of 'I' but of 'we two' (Codrington, pp. 210, 153). On the other hand a man of power becomes as such a ghost of power when he is dead, though as ghost he has the power in greater force than when alive (Codrington, p. 258). Nevertheless, the native logic distinguishes between the case of a man and that of a ghost or spirit. Of the former you can merely say that he 'has' *mana*, not that he 'is' *mana* (Codrington, p. 191). On any view of the matter, however, animism, it is clear, has in Melanesia assumed responsibility for all manifestations of supernatural power.

Nevertheless, as contrasted with *mana* or *tabu*, animism is not so well suited to provide rudimentary religion with its ultimate category, because the former is coextensive with the supernatural, whilst the latter is not. Animistic terminology pertains to what might be called the natural philosophy of the rudimentary intelligence. It carries us far beyond the limits of that specific experience which is the common root of Magic and Religion. This may be illustrated from Melanesia, the rudimentary philosophy of which abounds in nice distinctions of the animistic order. Thus a yam lives without intelligence and therefore has no 'soul' *(tarunga)*. A pig has a soul, and so likewise has a man, but with the difference that when a pig dies he has no 'ghost' *(tindalo)*, whereas a man's soul becomes a ghost. Ordinary ghosts, however, are not *mana*. Only a great man's soul becomes on his death a 'ghost of worship'. As regards a spirit *(vui)*, its nature would seem to be the same as that of a soul or at any rate a human soul, but it invariably is *mana* (Codrington, pp. 249, *cf.* 123 – 126). Thus only the higher grades of this animistic hierarchy rank as supernatural beings, and they are this not in virtue of their soul-like nature, but solely by reason of their being *mana*. Moreover, it must be noted that *mana* stands for that which, whilst quite immaterial, wavers between the impersonal and the personal; so that it can itself stand for a great deal to which we are apt to apply our terms 'soul', 'spirit', and the like, though there is never the implication of a wraith-like appearance. For Polynesian examples Tregear may be consulted, *s.vv. mana, manawa*. From meaning 'indwelling power' *mana* passes into 'intelligence', 'energy of character', 'spirit'. The kindred word *manawa (manava)* expresses 'heart', 'the interior man', 'conscience', 'soul'. Other compounds yield terms for 'thought', 'memory', 'belief', 'approval', 'affection', 'desire' — in short provide the native psychologist with an elaborate vocabulary. Meanwhile, that *mana* is quite immaterial may be illustrated from a story that has just reached me from a correspondent, **Mr. Hocart.** He finds that the native of the Solomon Islands has no objection to let him take down the words of a *mana* song. To learn them does not confer the *mana*. You must pay money to the owner of the *mana*, and he *ipso facto* will transmit to you the *mana* — the 'good will', as we say in English.

When therefore the object in view is to frame what Tylor calls a 'minimum definition of Religion' *(Primitive Culture,* 4th edition, I, p. 424), the *tabu-mana* formula appears to possess several advantages as compared with animism. 1) *Tabu* and *mana* are coextensive with the supernatural. Animism is too wide. 2) *Tabu* and *mana* are homogeneous. Animism tends to divagate into more or less irreducible kinds, notably 'soul', 'ghost', and 'spirit'. 3) *Mana*, the positive mode of the supernatural, whilst fully adapted to express the immaterial and unseen, nevertheless, conformably with the incoherent state of rudimentary reflexion, keeps in solution the distinction between the impersonal and the personal, and, in particular, would not seem to allow the notion of a high individuality to precipitate. Animism, on the other hand, tends to lose touch with the supernatural in its more impersonal forms, and is not suited to express its transmissibility, nor indeed its immateriality; but, owing to the uniqueness attaching to the dream-image, is capable, at a rather advanced stage of rudimentary culture, of representing supernatural agents of high individuality with some distinctness, though perhaps never so successfully as anthropomorphic theism is ultimately capable of doing.

Concluding observations from a genetic standpoint. In the foregoing enquiry the search has been for classificatory categories applicable to rudimentary religion as a whole. The subject, it was assumed, is to be treated as if it corresponded to a single level of human experience, and, moreover, is to be treated merely in a classificatory way, *i.e.* by arrangement of the matter under synoptic headings. In the present state of the science of Comparative Religion it appears somewhat premature to attempt more. Eventually, however, when better material is at hand, and more attention is paid by competent thinkers to this branch of study, we may hope to see the history of Religion dealt with genetically — no simple matter, let it be observed, since not only must the central or 'orthogenic' line of human evolution be traced, but full allowance must be at the same time made for the endless lateral developments to which the spreading 'family tree' of our culture has given birth. When this comes to be done, it may well happen that, at certain points along the central line of growth or one of the side-lines, *mana* will have to give way to some specialized form of animistic conception. The key to religious evolution is doubtless to be sought in social evolution. When, therefore, as in Australia, society is deficient in persons of marked individuality, then it is probable that the supernatural will be apprehended under relatively impersonal forms (though as a matter of fact Australia provides curious exceptions to this generalization). The same law would seem to hold good in that Pacific region where *tabu* and *mana* are at home. Thus in the New Hebrides where the culture is backward, the prevailing animistic conception is that of the 'spirit' *(vui)*, a being often nameless and almost without exception of feeble individuality. On the other hand, in the Solomon Islands, where the culture is more advanced, the religious interest centres in the 'ghost of power' *(tindalo mana)*, which is usually the departed soul of some well-remembered man. Here, then, with the social evolution of the hero, a hero-worship has superinduced itself on a poly-daemonism redolent of 'democracy'. So much for genetic considerations touching rudimentary religion. If we permit ourselves for a moment to glance forward to what I shall simply term 'complex' religion, it may be noted that animism never succeeds in sweeping the more impersonal conception of the supernatural clean out of the field; nor is this done either by anthropomorphic theism, the offspring, be it remarked, of 'animatism' rather than of the Tylorian animism. Buddhism is the standing instance of a complex religion which exalts the impersonal. It is, again, significant that a religious thinker such as Plato, with all his interest in 'soul' and in the subjective generally, nevertheless hesitates between a personal and an impersonal rendering of the idea of the divine. Thus the ambiguity implicit in the notion of *mana* persists to some extent throughout the history of Religion. In the meantime, all religions, rudimentary or complex, can join in saying with the Psalmist that 'Power belongeth unto God'.

Wilhelm Schmidt

Wilhelm Schmidt was born in 1868 at Hörde near Dortmund, Germany, where he received his primary school education. From 1883 until 1892 he studied at the missionary house which shortly before had been founded at Steyl, Holland. There he received his secondary school education between 1883 and 1888, and pursued his theological studies between 1888 and 1892, when he made the final examination and was ordained a priest. After having taught for a year at the missionary house then founded at Heiligkreuz near Neisse, Germany, he enrolled at the University of Berlin where he studied in the Faculty of Philosophy, and especially at the Oriental Institute, from 1893 until 1895. His main interest was the study of Semitic languages, but he followed also other courses. In 1895 Schmidt was appointed to teach theology and languages at the missionary seminary of the *Societas Verbi Divini* St. Gabriel at Mödling near Vienna. From 1900 onwards he also taught linguistics, and from 1912 onwards ethnology and history of religion. Here he carried out his anthropological research and from here he sent out missionaries who were his collaborators to different fields. In 1906 he founded the Revue *Anthropos* and in 1912 the so-called *Semaine d'Ethnologie Religieuse*, five conferences of which were held between 1912 and 1929. In 1921 Schmidt became *Privatdozent* at the University of Vienna for ethnology and linguistics. In 1927 he became director of the missionary ethnological Lateran Museum in Rome which he had founded in 1926 and he retained this post until 1939. In 1932 he founded the Anthropos Institute, of which he became the director, and with which he moved to Froideville, Switzerland, in 1938. In 1939 Schmidt was appointed *chargé de cours* for ethnology and linguistics at the University of Freiburg, Switzerland. In 1942 he became here full professor of ethnology and linguistics, from which he retired in 1948, although he continued to teach for another three years as an honorary professor. Schmidt presided the fourth International Congress for Anthropology and Ethnology, which was held in Vienna in 1952. He died at Froideville in 1954.

The following books by Wilhelm Schmidt exist in English: 1931 *The Origin and Growth of Religion: Facts and Theories;* 1932 *The Religion of Later Primitive Peoples;* 1933 *High Gods in North America;* 1934 *The Religion of Earliest Man;* 1939 *The Culture Historical Method of Ethnology: a Scientific Approach to the Racial Question;* 1939 *Primitive Revelation.*

Schmidt is known for his theory that the history of religion started with a primeval monotheism and morality. In order to prove this hypothesis, he made large investigations of the concepts of an all-father and sky god to be found among non literate peoples. Thereupon he traced these concepts back to an original pure monotheism by reconstructing the hypothetical history of this monotheism by means of the theory of culture cycles. In this way he explained animism, polytheism and magic as later imaginary accretions which could impose themselves on the original monotheistic belief and spread out according to the 'laws' of the culture cycles. Consequently, High God beliefs, which are prevailing in remote areas among non-literate peoples, were considered to be survivals of the primeval belief in a Supreme personal Deity. Apart from numerous articles, Schmidt elaborated this theory in his monumental *'The Origin of the Idea of God'*, which appeared in German in twelve volumes.

The following texts have been taken from *The Origin and Growth of Religion* and from *High Gods in North America*. They show the appreciations of Schmidt for preceding theories as well as the methodical approach which he chose himself.

'THE ORIGIN AND GROWTH OF RELIGION'

'The comparative history of religion'

There can hardly be a more fascinating object of investigation than the history of religion. Perhaps also there cannot be a more difficult one. For, as we nowadays realize more and more clearly, this history is most intimately connected with the beginnings of human culture, and with the further development of that culture in general.

The science which has this subject for its province came into existence as such towards the end of the last century but one. The entire nineteenth century, during which our science first began to expand, was really not favourable to it in the various currents of thought both of its former and of its latter half. But it might be supposed that our own century is in a position to steer the bark into a quiet middle channel, after it has so often wandered to right or left from its course, and so, without waste of time and energy, to bring it to its desired haven.

Definition of 'History of religion'. The very definition which we must now set forth will show how much more lucid we can now be both in positive determinations and in negative distinctions. We are to deal with an introduction to the comparative history of religion. Two things must be defined: our subject, religion, and the form in which we handle this subject, comparative history.

a) Religion may be defined both subjectively and objectively. Subjectively, it is the knowledge and consciousness of dependence upon one or more transcendental, personal Powers, to which man stands in a reciprocal relation. Objectively, it is the sum of the outward actions in which it is expressed and made manifest, as prayer, sacrifice, sacraments, liturgy, ascetic practices, ethical prescriptions, and so on.[1]

And now the words 'personal Powers' call for explanation. It is of course possible to feel oneself dependent upon impersonal powers, but it is not possible to enter into reciprocal relations with them, since they cannot answer from their side. Consequently, it makes no difference whether it is a material force, as for example the vast and mighty universe, or some inexorable law thereof. Both are dumb and unresponsive to the human personality. Hence also primitive Buddhism, inasmuch as it recognizes no personal gods, cannot be considered as a religion, but only as a philosophy. Later Buddhism indeed, and Buddhism everywhere that it has become a popular religion, has included in its wide-reaching system innumerable personal deities, brought in by a thousand back doors.

b) It is not merely *a* religion, or the religion of particular peoples, with which we are concerned; we are to make a comparison of all religions, one with another. It is a pity that we cannot express this by a single word, as for instance the German word 'Völkerkunde' differentiates itself from 'Volkskunde', a description of any single people. Even in German it would hardly be possible to bring into use any such term as *Religionenkunde*, 'science of religions', or *Religionengeschichte*, 'history of religions', in distinction to *Religionskunde, Religionsgeschichte*, which are used to mean respectively the science and the history of religion in general, but might also signify the knowledge or history of a particular religion.

The object of this comparison is, firstly, to understand the peculiarities of each individual religion by the very fact of contrasting it with others, and secondly, to attain to a synoptic grouping of religions and religious phenomena, in other words to a typology of religion. But we will not rest content with a mere static typology, which claims no more than to review the facts as they were and are. This is rather the business of the psychology of religion. We endeavour to grasp all that is characteristic of each religion, and thus also we can comprehend the influences which have affected it and the results which it has produced. We comprehend religions in their capacity as cause and effect of other things; but also we include the other cultural factors which have played this same part of cause and effect to religions. We plunge into the flowing stream of events; our subject is the comparative history of religion, and thus, and only thus, do we grasp the full reality of religion.

c) We speak of the comparative *history* of religion. This is the final differentia of our science. It aims at setting forth the issue and the course of religious facts; it therefore does not rest content with a typological juxtaposition of them. Nor is it satisfied with a merely outward sequence, but tries to investigate the causal nexus of action and reaction between the facts. That is to say, it tries to attain to an inward understanding of the outward course of events, to pragmatic history.

Our science is thus clearly differentiated from the other members of the group dealing with religion, and as clearly marked as belonging to this group. The other sciences which are to be classed with it are the psychology and the philosophy of religion. That we are now able to differentiate the history of religion clearly from these sister sciences is one of the most important advances that our subject has made, and therefore we must speak of it somewhat more fully.

Short history of research on the subject

1. 'The succession of religions and of cultures'

The fact that ethnology in general is at present in a stage of transition makes its unwelcome presence felt in the history of religion in particular. In the whole domain of ethnology, the old Evolutionary school is bankrupt. The lovely long single lines of development which it used to construct so readily have been shattered and overthrown by the criticism of the new historical tendencies. Already, in the fields of ergology, sociology and economics, the historians of culture in particular have set about, not only clearing away the remnants of Evolutionism, but raising new and more solid structures. But the subject of religion, and in general of the non-material culture of man, has at most got so far that it can here and there make a beginning with these new constructions.

In these circumstances it would not be a cheering or encouraging task at the present day to write a history of religion; for the ruins of the former Evolutionist system would have first to be produced, and more ruins piled up by further criticism. The sight of such wholesale destruction might make the researcher tremble lest the building which he would fain rear by his positive results should one day prove to be but another link in the long chain of the errors in the history of religion which have passed over the world. To set forth the results of the history of religion would not therefore be an attractive task to-day.

However, it is not quite so bad as all that. The ethnological study of the history of culture has gone so far in the departments of ergology, sociology and economics as to establish the existence of a series of culture-horizons, within which the development of human culture has taken place; and an easily intelligible conspectus of these can be given, as will be done later [...].

Now it is a remarkable fact that this historical succession of religions is reflected, and can be observed in a concrete form, in the successive theories of the history of religion which have been put forward in the last few decades, only the order being reversed. But again, it is not so surprising. Indeed, it is very natural that the latest religions, those peculiar to the latest cultures, were also the first to be comprehensible; for they were the best preserved, and also to some extent the most widely distributed. The less recent, the earlier that they are, the less they show and the more they are obscured by those which, being later, are better preserved. Can we wonder then that the first theories on the subject turned their attention to those religions which belonged to the latest and widest spread stratum of mankind? Can we wonder that each of these theories in turn, so long as it saw only this form of religion, declared it the first form, the origin of religion in general, until it was dethroned by another theory, based on religions and peoples more recently noticed, which had hitherto lain further back?

This retirement and dethronement can come to an end, of course, only when it can be guaranteed that behind the last form of religion and the last people of the moment there are no more to be looked for, because all have been discovered and the earth has disclosed her last hiding-place. As a matter of fact, we have nearly attained this consummation, and therefore we can, by objective means, set forth that form of religion which is really the oldest, because it is the last, that we can reach; and our final task will consist of the attempt to determine how far this form of religion which is the last within our reach is removed from the absolute origin of religion, and how much of that origin it has retained.

2. *'The succession of theories'*

a) Before beginning to treat of the series of hypotheses concerning the history of religion, and likewise of the successive religions themselves, we will briefly examine the long period during which much was said and written concerning religion, and some comparisons made, but no such thing as the history of religion, properly so called, as yet existed. I mean the Greek and Roman times, the early days of Christianity, the Middle Ages, and the Age of Discovery. In all this time, the history, psychology and philosophy of religion, as we now call them, were not differentiated. The motive of these investigations, moreover, was purely practical; it was the desire to uphold, modify, or entirely to overthrow the particular religion existing at the time and in the country concerned.

b) When the history of religion proper took shape as a real science, which occurred at the end of the eighteenth and the beginning of the nineteenth century, it did so in connexion with the Indogermanic group of languages and peoples, which was then becoming known and was large enough to provide abundant material for comparison, and yet not so large as to be lost in a mass of details. But all these peoples belonged to the high or at least the middle culture [i.e., were civilized or barbarian, not savage]; consequently they belonged to the latest strata of development, the tertiary or secondary cultures. A characteristic of these is a wide development of nature-myths having a religious direction. And as a matter of fact, the first theory of the history of religion which was constructed was the theory of nature-myths. According to this, the source of religion and its earliest form was the nature-myth, especially the star-myth; and these myths were generally given a symbolic explanation.

c) But in the first half of the nineteenth century the savage races of Africa, Oceania and America were brought within the purview of Europe; and in proportion as this occurred, their religions attracted scientific attention. Even in the eighteenth century, one of the grossest and therefore most conspicuous of these peoples' cults, namely fetish-worship, was made the foundation of a theory, by de Brosses, in 1760. This theory was taken up again in the middle of the nineteenth century (1851 and the following years) by A. Comte, and was further developed by (Sir) J. Lubbock [afterwards Lord Avebury]. It found easy and ready acceptance, especially in popular scientific circles. This cult belongs to the later stratum of savagery, the secondary cultures.

d) The same applies to the worship of ancestors, or manism, although its roots go back to the primary cultures, particularly the two patrilineal forms, totemism and pastoral nomadism. On this Herbert Spencer (from 1876 on) founded his ghost-theory, which long held the field, especially among philosophers and sociologists.

e) But now the long and deep array of the lower agriculturalists, the horticultural peoples, disclosed itself. These savages belong to the latest primary culture-horizon, matrilineal horticulture. Among them belief in and worship of souls is to be found in the most manifold forms, and E. B. Tylor (1872 and following years) used it as the basis of a comprehensive theory of Animism, the first theory of the history of religion which was thoroughly worked out and shaped from all sides. Consequently, it had the most important results, and lorded it over almost all the scientific world until the beginning of the present century.

f) In consequence of the progressive decipherment of Babylonian and Assyrian cuneiform inscriptions and Egyptian hieroglyphics after the middle of the nineteenth century, the religions of these two highly civilized peoples, both of which belong to the tertiary culture, became more and more imposingly prominent. They were manifestly composed of nature-myths, star-myths in particular. Hence at the end of the nineteenth century a new school of astral- and nature-mythologists was formed, in opposition to the animists.

g) Behind the matrilineal horticulturalists, and now and then between them, appeared at last those higher hunting tribes of the primary culture among whom occur the strange phenomena of totemism (descent from and relationship to certain species of animals, and a religious respect for those animals). In this it seemed that a new and older form of religion had been found. A theory on these lines was first put forward by Robertson Smith in and after 1885. The progressively widening range of (Sir) J. G. Frazer's collections made it clear that totemism is not a religion nor the source of one, but a sociological system with a set of ideas to correspond.

h) But among these totemistic peoples Frazer discovered a vast assemblage of beliefs and practices which he declared to be the fore-runner of religion, namely magic. The widereaching importance of magic was perceived with still more profundity and comprehensiveness by an American scholar, J. H. King, in 1892, and he also considered it the source of religion. But his work attracted no notice, and it was not till the beginning of the twentieth century that there sprang up, at almost the same time in Germany, England, France and America, a reaction against animism. A stage of religion earlier than animism, namely preanimism, was postulated, and supposed to be identical either with magic or with a yet undifferentiated mixture of magic and religion. Thus, in and after 1895, R. R. Marett, Hewitt in 1902, K. Th. Preuss in 1904 and later, A. Vierkandt in 1907 and E. S. Hartland in 1908, but most of all the French sociological school of Durkheim, set about developing this theory. The leaders of the French school were at first H. Hubert and M. Mauss, in and after 1904, then, from 1912 on, Durkheim himself. In their opinion, totemism and magic combined, in the Central Australian form, are the origin of religion.

Later, certain Protestant students of the psychology of religion endeavoured by a more extensive introduction of psychological considerations to support the view that a mixture of religion and magic, as yet undifferentiated, is the first stage in man's religious development. Among these are Archbishop N. Söderblom, in 1916; also G. Wobbermin in and after 1915. K. Beth, in 1914 and later, and R. Otto, in and after 1917, endeavour to penetrate to an earlier stage still, one which was neither religion nor magic. However, no such stage can be ethnologically shown to exist, nor be assigned to any culture-horizon.

i) Even in the older school of nature-mythologists, one sovereign figure stood out among all the various personifications of natural phenomena, in the Indo-European peoples. This was the sky-god. He was conspicuous also among the Hamitic and Semitic pastoral races, and still more among the Ural-Altaic pastoral nomads, being in fact the predominant figure in the religion of the primary culture of the cattle-breeding nomads of the vast steppes. This phenomenon had been noticed by Schelling, and, among the nature-mythologists, by Max Müller for a time; but the invasion of materialistic Evolutionism destroyed its interest, and only theologians set any store by it.

j) All the theories we have mentioned, with the exception of a few supporters of the first, that of nature-myths, were under the sway of progressivist Evolutionism, that is to say, they assumed that religion began with

lower forms, and explained all its higher manifestations, especially monotheism, as the latest in time, the products of a long process of development.
At about the same time that the reaction set in against the animistic theory,
which had hitherto been supreme, that is towards the end of the nineteenth
century, Andrew Lang, a former pupil of Tylor, turned his attention to
certain high gods found among very primitive peoples. These figures were
regarded as creators, as the foundation and bulwark of the moral code,
as kind and good. They were acknowledged and adored as 'fathers'; and
being found among exceedingly primitive peoples, they could not, for that
very reason, be the products of a long process of development. Lang's work
on the subject, *The Making of Religion*, was received at first with general
opposition, and then with still more general silence.

3. 'The succession of methods'

One of the reasons why Lang's investigations did not carry conviction was
this. He had indeed, by his recognition of the ancient Supreme Being,
existing even among very low savages, destroyed one of the fundamental
propositions of Evolutionism. But having brought this fact into prominence,
he did not himself use any stable method to confirm it permanently. It is
therefore incumbent upon us, having now considered the various successive
theories, to cast a glance at the methods by the help of which they arrived
at their results.

a) The oldest school, that of the nature-mythologists, followed a historical method in the narrower sense of the word. That is, it rested upon the
ancient written documents of the various peoples in question, nearly all
of whom were acquainted with writing. If these scholars were affected by
Evolution at all, it was not the materialistic theory of Darwin, but Hegelian
idealism. The later school of astral mythology was already much more
influenced by the theory of Evolution.

b) All the other theories, however, came into being after the outbreak
of materialism and Darwinism, and their work was all done on the lines of
Evolutionist natural science. This puts all that is low and simple at the
beginning, all that is higher and of worth being regarded only as the product
of a longer or shorter process of development. This they found it easier to
do, because the principal objects of their study were savages who had not
yet made the acquaintance of any sort of writing by which to date the
monuments of their culture. Hence the question of earlier and later, of the
chronological sequence of religions and forms of religion, which must be
settled before the causal interaction of the facts can be exactly determined,
could be answered only by help of the Evolutionist method, which is really
no method at all, as we shall see later.

c) An end was put to this unhappy state of affairs, which governed the whole of ethnology, by the school of cultural history, headed by Ratzel (1886 and after), Frobenius (1898), Graebner and Ankermann (1905), to which the present author joined himself not long after. This school is able to lift even the unwritten monuments of culture out of the featureless plane where they lay side by side, and to arrange them one behind another in a sequence extending far back. Thus it can fix objectively their arrangement in time and distinguish cause and effect. Further details of this method will be given in the proper place. I applied this method, which then was far from perfect, to the Pygmy peoples in my work entitled *Die Stellung der Pygmäenvölker in der Entwicklungsgeschichte der Menschen,* 1910. Soon after, I made a better use of it in the case of the South-East Australians, in Vol. I of my *Ursprung der Gottesidee.* In this, the primitive high gods which Lang had been the first to value aright were set in their proper methodological perspective and thus made of permanent value.

d) This is not one of the many transitory theories which, when their time comes, are replaced by others; it is not one of the many errors, but a permanent conquest, an entire and therefore an enduring truth. Of this we may be fully confident, for by the methods of the history of culture we can establish two connected propositions, firstly, that these high gods are found among, and only among, the peoples ethnologically oldest, and secondly, that all these ethnologically oldest peoples have such gods. But the earth is now so thoroughly explored that only a few peoples, in the interior of Africa, the Philippines and New Guinea, are still to be discovered; and it is not probable that they will produce any essential change in our present picture of the peoples of the world.

So, if we cast our eyes over the history of our subject, we obtain a miniature of the comparative history of religion itself, but in the reverse order. The sequence of the theories and of the religions they are founded upon, as they come one after another into prominence, is exactly the reverse of the order in which those religions were actually and historically developed.

In order to understand all the factors which have influenced theories concerning the history of religion, and have, in particular, so often prevented their authors from rightly understanding and appreciating the different religions brought to their notice, we must proceed to examine the different movements of thought which, in the two halves of the nineteenth century, swung in almost diametrically opposite directions, and at last, in the twentieth century, show signs of coming to rest in the middle.

4. 'The succession of attitudes'

a) The first half of the nineteenth century was directly influenced by the reaction against the French Revolution. This reaction took the form of traditionalism and idealism in theology and philosophy, of romanticism in literature, and of aristocracy and absolutism in social and political thought. Hence the nascent history of religion retained in its turn a conservative and religious spirit, which was expressed in the recognition of the supreme position of the sky-god, and on the other hand in the symbolical and mystical exposition of the nature-myths. The defect which made itself felt was the too great value set in the ideal, and the insufficient allowance for the material factor, in religious development as elsewhere. Narrowness in one direction, over-stress in the other, led about the middle of the century to a fresh outbreak of political revolution and to an intellectual *volte-face*, the former in nearly all, the latter in all the countries of Europe.

b) So it came about that the second half of the nineteenth century was marked by the intrusion, first of Liberalism, then of Socialism, both more or less associated with materialism, which, in both these movements, turned with ever-increasing strength against religion and tradition. This materialism was strengthened by a doctrine of progressive Evolution, the fruit of Darwinism in natural science, which was opposed to the idealistic Evolutionism of Hegel, this having already appeared in the preceding epoch. Its significance for the methods of the history of religion has already been dealt with. As regards the spirit in which the inquiries were conducted, it meant an increasing inability to grasp the deeper essence of religion, to give due value to its higher forms, and a tendency to overestimate the outward elements and underestimate, or entirely neglect, the spirit. All things considered, this meant that the historical study of religion suffered almost more than it had done in the previous period.

c) As the twentieth century dawned, a negative and a positive movement began. For the first, the insufficiency and failure of materialism grew ever clearer, and the abandonment of it more pronounced. For the second, the recognition of the unique character of spirit and of its freedom made increasing progress, and this resulted in a deeper and more ready insight into the nature of religion; more attention was paid to its importance for the whole of civilized life. A historical, in opposition to a purely scientific, spirit and interest grew stronger, for the limitations of natural science become daily more obvious. Hence also the boundaries of purely inward evolution grow clearer, and the importance of the historical factor more visible. History, by being separated from philosophy, gains considerably in serenity and objectivity. There is dawning the day of critical realism, which strives to comprehend the whole of reality, to preserve mind and matter alike, and is preserved by its critical character from exaggerations in one direction or the other.

'THE QUEST OF THE SUPREME BEING'

'The history of religion and the comparative method'

1. *'The theory of High Gods: a historical survey'*

a) The work of Andrew Lang. [. . .] I cannot forget that my labours in
the field of Comparative Religion are nothing but a continuation of certain
parts of the work of a great Scottish scholar, Andrew Lang. In 1910 I had
the great pleasure of meeting him in London. In 1912 he died. It was in that
year that the first volume of my *Ursprung der Gottesidee* appeared, carrying
forward what he had so strenuously begun.

The reader is no doubt aware of the important role which Andrew Lang
played in the history of Anthropology and the history of Religion, firstly,
as pupil of his great master E. B. Tylor, vigorously assailing the naturalistic
theory of Max Müller and vindicating the animistic theory; and then, later,
as the result of continued study and deeper comprehension, sustaining boldly,
against the animistic theory, the existence of true High Gods among primitive peoples.

He will be well aware also what an arduous task it was which Lang
undertook, and what tenacity and courage he needed not to lose heart and
strength. For it was not only the powerful theory of animism against which
he fought, but also, and still more, the almost omnipotent Evolutionism of
that period; an Evolutionism of which the fundamental axiom was that
humanity had emerged from forms not only extremely simple but also low
and imperfect. Andrew Lang himself clearly recognized the situation when
he dedicated his epoch-making work, *The Making of Religion* (1898), to his
old University, St. Andrews, which, as he said in the preface, 'fostered
in the past the leaders of forlorn hopes that were destined to triumph,
and the friends of lost causes who fought bravely against Fate'. To the very
end of his life he never ceased fighting valiantly and imperturbably for his
'anachronistic' views.

b) Its continuation by W. Schmidt. When I picked up the flag which
dropped from the hands of that valiant champion, the prospects did not
seem any more favourable. A friendly critic of the first volume of my
Ursprung der Gottesidee, Dr. E. W. Meyer, the Protestant Professor of
Theology of Strasburg, wrote: 'Whether Father Schmidt will make more
impression on ethnologists than his predecessor Lang, I do not pretend to
decide. That must be left to the seer who knows the past and can prophesy
after the event; but it is not likely.'

This scepticism has proved not to be justified. When, fourteen years
later, I published the second edition of that same volume, I was able to
give a long list of eminent scholars from different fields of research who

acknowledged and accepted as fact the existence of true High Gods among the lowest races. And since those days this recognition has made further progress, obtaining more and more adherents almost every year.

c) New materials and a better method. The antiquity of High Gods, then, although at first acknowledged only slowly, has at last forced its way into acceptance. The reason for its advance is in part the investigation of a series of specialists working in their own fields, and arriving, each one in his own area and as a result of his special studies, at the affirmation of the existence of true Supreme Beings in those areas. It is, in fact, the mass of considerably fuller and more trustworthy materials which has caused this changed attitude.

The same process will be illustrated in the accounts which follow of High Gods in the oldest religions of North America, for the materials which I produce have been obtained almost entirely from researches made after the publication of Andrew Lang's *Making of Religion*. Especially in regard to North America, all the material has been brought together by trained American scholars who have pursued their researches with the highest degree of painstaking accuracy and objectivity. There is not one missionary amongst them!

But there is yet another advance made since the days of Andrew Lang, which I esteem still more important. I mean the new method we have acquired, by which we have become able to establish with positive certainty, and by objective means, the ethnological age of the different High Gods. As a matter of fact they differ much in this respect from one another. It is only now that we are able to penetrate into the true nature of the Supreme Beings in connexion with the date at which they made their first appearance. Further, it is only now that we can produce the final proof that these High Gods, in their oldest form, come before all other elements, be they naturism, fetishism, ghost-worship, animism, totemism, or magism, from one or other of which the earlier evolutionistic theories had derived the origin of religion.

In the chapters which follow, it is my principal aim to present not theories but facts. But I aim to give established facts, facts in their full actuality, facts in their full relations to each other, with their true ethnological date and in their true chronological succession. For it is only in this way that we can obtain an insight into the causal influences, active and passive, exerted and received, which co-operated in building up the true nature of cultural elements and complexes. It is possible to fulfil all these exigencies only by employing a good historical method integrated by psychology both individual and social. The so-called evolutionistic method, which in reality is not a method because of its continual employment of unwarranted estimates (judgements of value), is not capable of fulfilling these tasks. [...].

I am fully aware that discussions about method are widely regarded as dry and tedious. There are many who have the same opinion about them as Goethe in *Faust*:

> *Ich sage dir: Ein Kerl, der spekuliert,*
> *Ist wie ein Tier auf dürrer Heide,*
> *Von einem bösen Geist im Kreis herumgeführt,*
> *Und rings umher liegt schöne grüne Weide.*

> *I tell you this: your theorizing man*
> *Is like a beast in deserts dry,*
> *Led round in circles by some evil spirit's ban,*
> *When fair green pastures all about him lie.*

So to begin with a discussion of method is perhaps not the best way to put the reader in good humour. But it is a matter which my scientific conscience will not allow me to pass over, especially in a book intended for a British public; and I hope to contrive that there shall not be too much of the desert, and that I shall not appear merely an evil spirit leading the reader around in circles. In any case, there is no other road to the 'fair green pastures' of concrete fact, in which I can promise abundance of good grazing. Let me add, to dispel undue apprehension, that it is not my intention to discuss the method in detail; I have already explained it in my *Origin and Growth of Religion*, and it will suffice here to set forth some of its fundamental principles.

2. *'Theory of the historical method'*

Having already said that North America and Germany, including Austria, are the most advanced posts of the modern historical movement in ethnology, I trust I shall not be accused of chauvinism if I add that in my opinion it is the last two countries which have made the greatest progress of all in the matter of formal method. I have re-examined this question in a review of all the American and German-Austrian literature in my lectures at the University of Vienna last year. Perhaps I shall be able to publish them, and so contribute a little towards the true understanding of this method. The well-known and highly meritorious book of F. Graebner, *Die Methode der Ethnologie* (Heidelberg, 1911), often remains unintelligible because of its extreme conciseness and lack of clearness in expression. The objection raised by some of his critics, that the method itself is too complicated, cannot be sustained; the complications exist already in the cultural deve_lopment even of the lowest races of mankind.

a) The spatial relations of cultures. Firstly, in regard to the development of human culture in spatial juxtaposition, the monogenesis of mankind, now formally established and accepted by almost all anthropologists of rank, makes it clear that man, in almost all the regions of the earth where we encounter him to-day, has migrated from elsewhere. Thus it was not the last region where he arrived that *created* his culture; it modified his culture, acquired already in other stages of his manifold migrations. In these migrations he encountered not only different countries with different climates and faunas and floras, but also different men and tribes and peoples each with its special culture; and these likewise helped to modify and to build up his own culture. Finally, every human soul, and every tribe and people, is a centre of interior forces and faculties, which is more than the sum of the influences exercised upon it, and this centre of forces also goes through a development in these migrations. Now, if ethnology is to be a real science, it must be able to grasp and exhibit the numerous and various relations which connect tribes and peoples and cultures in space, and it is impossible for a true science to content itself with piling up what are mostly mere hypotheses. True science may *begin* with hypotheses, but they cannot be its ultimate end, 'der Weisheit letzter Schluss'.

It is by a carefully poised and delicately detailed application of certain criteria (those of quality, – or form, of quantity, of continuity, and others) that the historical method endeavours to establish the relation of cultures in space. It does not see any obstacle in the way of establishing such relations in like manner over great distances and in cases of discontinuous diffusion, because we are absolutely sure that migrations from great distances really took place in innumerable instances though no connecting links now exist. To establish such relations in these more difficult cases it is necessary only to apply these criteria with the utmost degree of accuracy and precaution.

By the application of these criteria it becomes manifest that not only single cultural elements but also whole cultural complexes, organic cultural unities *(Kulturkreise)*, may migrate: cultural unities which organically satisfy all human needs, economic, social, political, aesthetic, ethical, and religious, every one pervaded and sustained by a mentality *sui generis* which marks all the single elements of this culture with its characteristic stamp. If the study of cultural migrations exposes itself to the danger of giving too much weight to the physical factor of culture, and thus seeks for and eagerly establishes physical laws of cultural development, the deeper study of the spirit and mentality of each culture makes it manifest that the proper nature of culture is non-material. There is no cultural element and object, not even that of the so-called material culture, which has not been seized upon by the spirit and shaped by it practically, aesthetically, and symbolically.

b) The chronological relations of cultures. But the complexity of culture is still greater by virtue of the fact that the numerous and manifold relations in space are interwoven with, and therefore still more complicated by, the relations in time. Temporal succession is intrinsically necessary for cultural development, because it is in time that the human spirit unfolds itself and migrations with their various contacts with alien countries and cultures are realized. Now the task which here is imposed upon ethnology – to determine the time-factor – is of the highest importance, while at the same time it is also of the greatest difficulty. The supreme importance of this task appears in the fact that it is ethnology, and ethnology only, which is called upon to enter beyond all the millennia illustrated by written documents and to go back into those dark times of the human beginnings, where no chronology whatever seems possible. It is only prehistory which seems to be able to unveil these dark times by discovering the ultimate relics of those primeval cultures. But these ultimate relics are meagre remnants only of the material culture; of the non-material side of culture, its social forms, its ethical and religious life, they tell us hardly anything.

If ethnology in comparison with prehistory is incomparably rich and presents to us the full life of peoples, what are its means of establishing such an objective temporal succession of cultural phases as is given in the stratifications of prehistory? How will it become possible to change 'Kulturkreise' into 'Kulturschichten', juxtaposition in space into succession in time? Nearly all ethnologists of repute have arrived at a negative perception of the fact that progressive evolutionism does not possess means and ways to achieve this heavy task. There are some ethnologists and still more sociologists in Britain and in America whom this perception has almost reduced to despair: they reject and discredit all historical researches made among primitive peoples and limit themselves to a purely psychological study of their actual present.

But firstly, if such a study professes to be the ultimate one, such a limitation is quite impossible, because in the present state of culture are included and are still working the centuries and millennia of the past; so that it is impossible to understand the present without having known, by careful analysis, what the past was. Further, if we limit the aim of ethnology to the study of the primitive peoples of to-day, it loses almost all its deeper signification and higher importance, because it would be difficult to understand what high importance ought to be attributed to these poor representatives of mankind, few in number and low in culture, who never rose to play a role in its history. I think that such a scholar would deprive ethnology of its crown by his disbelief in the axiom established already by Père Lafitau in his famous work, *Mœurs des sauvages américains comparées aux mœurs des premiers temps* (Paris, 1724), that primitive peoples are stages of the past of humanity and living witnesses of them. And if ethnology should despair of establishing objectively and trustworthily the succession of these stages, it seems to me that it would abdicate its prerogative to be our guide into those first ages of humanity from which sprang the deepest roots of all its institutions, of religion and of ethics, of the family and the state.

[. . .]

The methodological importance of establishing relations between elements or complexes of culture widely separated in space is comprised in the following axiom: The greater the distance separating two such elements or complexes, the longer time we must assume for the migration from one point to the other, and the farther back we must put the date at which the migrations began. If this is true when but a single element of a culture is examined, it is much more so when we have to postulate the migration of a whole complex; for then we must allow, not only for the migration itself, but for the time required for the complex to be formed out of the separate elements.

I omit, for it would require too much space to set it forth, the different ways in which the historical method is able to establish with objective and positive surety the succession of cultures in time, starting from the present day and going farther and farther back to the earliest ages of mankind. The result is, while not an absolute, at least a relative chronology of the history of human culture.

This brief exposition is not intended to convince the reader; it will suffice if I have made it clear that progressive Evolution is not the key which opens the door to a true history of humanity, and consequently of man's religion. To explain this historical process we need a historical method, and the fundamental principles of this method I have felt it incumbent upon me, in simple honesty, to explain, at least in part.

3. *'Application of the historical method: the origin of sacrifice'*

Having thus far tried the reader's patience by playing the evil spirit and leading him in circles in the desert of methodological discussion, I do not wish to conclude even this introductory chapter without leading him for a while into the fair green pastures of concrete realities. I propose therefore to illustrate, in connexion with the weighty problem of how the custom of sacrifice originated, how decidedly important is the exact determination of ethnological age.

a) Evolutionistic theories. From the older evolutionistic times there are many theories about the origin of sacrifice. There is that of Tylor and Wilkens, who derive it from the present made to the chief, the ghosts, or the spirits; there is also that of Hubert and Mauss, going back to that of Tylor; further there is that of Robertson Smith, deriving sacrifice from the totemic communion. W. Wundt makes it proceed from magical action and A. Loisy from a combination of magic and presents to ghosts.[3]

Now even if the most favourable view of all of these theories is taken, they afford only possibilities, in the best case probabilities and plausibilities, but none of them any scientific certitude whatever. The reason of this lies in the fact that none of them has seriously asked the question regarding the ethnological age of the tribes and peoples from which they take their proofs.

b) Diffusion of the offering of first-fruits among the oldest peoples. But if this important question is raised, the following facts result from it with full certitude: (1) the peoples ethnologically oldest know neither feeding of ghosts, nor giving of presents to spirits, nor totemic communion, nor totemism in general, nor magic rites of a kind from which sacrifices could be derived; (2) the oldest people practise *primitial* sacrifices (offerings of first-fruits) to a very large extent, offering to the Supreme Being a very little portion from all food obtained by hunting animals and collecting plants; (3) this primitial sacrifice does not mean a feeding of the Supreme Being, because it is only a little piece which is given to him; the Supreme Being, moreover, is believed to have created all things and to be thus already in full possession of all he needs; (4) this sacrifice must in some manner or another be intended to honour this Supreme Being, because, though the portion is a little part, it is the most honorific or precious part that is offered – brain, marrow, head, heart, either entirely or the right side of them.

By pursuing these traces farther we reach a position which enables us to push on to the true origin of this sacrifice. Here we have our reward for following the method of studying greater organic complexes; for in these greater complexes we know not only the material elements, but also the mentality behind them. This is so, in our case, with the culture of the Pygmies, the culture of the Arctic peoples, and the culture of part of the North American Indians. Now the religion of this oldest culture, of which we have a tolerably good knowledge, emphasizes in a quite special degree the creative power of the Supreme Being, and his complete rights of ownership over the whole world, and especially over plants and animals. As we shall see in the following chapters, the belief of these oldest religions is that the Supreme Being has given these things to man for man's use; not to be wasted, but to be treated with respect.

c) *Primitial sacrifice the oldest form.* The origin of primitial sacrifice is therefore clear. In it primitive man recognizes that in the same way as the Supreme Being has given life to him, by creating him the first time, so he continues to give him life by procuring him the means of life, i.e. food and drink; and so only food and drink are offered by these primitive men of the oldest times to the Supreme Being. This recognition includes at the same time thanksgiving for the past and present, and petition for the future. That these ideas and feelings are at the root of these primitial sacrifices is additionally attested by the text of the oral prayers which in most cases accompany them.

But now, also, it becomes clear negatively: if feeding of ghosts and spirits, totemic communal meals, and magical rites were not in existence in the oldest times, they could produce nothing then, and therefore no form of sacrifice. And since primitial sacrifice is fully developed among these oldest peoples, it becomes likewise clear that it is the oldest form of sacrifice. It is possible, or rather, we have positive evidence, that in later cultures primitial sacrifice comes in contact with feeding of ghosts, or spirits, or the other elements enumerated above, elements which have their origin in other, more recent, religions; that it is influenced and transformed by them; but these more recent forms can tell us nothing about the first origin of sacrifice.

This example, I think, will suffice alone to show how important and indispensable it is to establish exactly the ethnological age of cultural elements in order to arrive at their first origin and to grasp their true nature and meaning. Later chapters will provide many other such instances.

[...]

High Gods and monotheism in North America

We have now completed our review of those religions of North America, the oldest in that vast area, which have High Gods. That they are really of this type, and their deities High Gods indeed, in a word that these are religions in the truest and fullest sense of the term, is, I hope, by this time sufficiently clear.

'Monotheistic character of these religions'

a) True monotheisms. In each of these religions there exists a true High God: nay, I do not hesitate to employ a more decided phrase and say: these people worship One God. Some time ago Archbishop Söderblom refused to recognize these High Gods as more than 'originators' *(Urheber)*, and said, with a tinge of irony, that such an 'originator' was neither 'one' nor 'God'; but I hope I have now shown him to be really both.

A High God of this type is one, for in his oldest and most original form he has beside him no figures of animistic or manistic type to prejudice his absolute supremacy; in particular, he has neither wife nor child. Where, as happens in some cases, such secondary figures did appear to exist, it has been possible to show by methodically conducted inquiries that there we have to do with more recent formations, the result of influences from other and alien religions. Such is the case with some tribes of Central California and of the Algonkins, where the Supreme Being has at his side a deified first ancestor, or, as in some Selish tribes, a chief of the dead who, in the last analysis, is likewise the first ancestor of mankind.

Of a special kind is the case where, as among the Maidu in North-Central California, the Supreme Being yields constantly to the efforts and the tricks of his adversary, the representative of evil, who succeeds in realizing all his own pernicious plans, always of evil consequence to men. But that is not due to feebleness nor to weariness on the part of the Supreme Being, because he is strong enough to punish his adversary in a most appropriate manner, by causing him or his cherished young son to be the first to undergo the death which he had demanded for men. But the Supreme Being has created men free, and it is only because men, in this liberty of theirs, have followed his adversary, that he leaves them to their ways, as he declares in so many words in the myth embodying this conception. In this whole myth and its doctrines it becomes manifest that these oldest men were already occupied with the obscure and agonizing problems of the origin of physical and moral evil and tried to find a solution according to their own manner of thinking.

b) Origin of evil and creation of the world. The one highly remarkable feature of this solution is that none of this physical and ethical evil falls upon the High God. He remains in his unique immutability and in all ways the one morally good being. It is he who fixes the laws of morality, who watches over them with his omniscience and omnipresence, punishes transgressions and rewards fulfilment thereof by his justice, not only in this, but also in the other life, when the soul after having passed the Milky Way has arrived at his supernal abode, in the land of ever-blossoming flowers, as it is described. And the other side of this solution is that this Supreme Being, though he punishes bad men severely, appears as a being of unlimited kindness, who wishes to do his utmost to make men happy and from whom come all the goods they possess. It must be especially emphasized that he wished to preserve them from death and to give them immortality, renewing their youth, when they became old and grey, by bathing in the water of life.

Of quite extraordinary importance in these religions is the idea of creation: of creation in a manner which strongly contradicts all evolutionistic principles. This idea of creation does not grow and develop in course of time to greater heights, but, on the contrary, it diminishes in vigour and amplitude in the more recent, that is, the Selish tribes, and it is clearer and stronger in the oldest of these religions, the North-Central Californian; whilst the Algonkins hold the middle view between the two others. It is in the oldest of all these religions, that of the Yuki, that we find the highest form of this idea, the *creatio ex nihilo*, and it is in the two oldest religions, that of the North-Central Californians and that of the Algonkins, that this idea stands in the foreground and forms the principal object of their great religious ceremonies instituted by the Supreme Being himself.

Thus we have in those religions a true God who is truly one; not a distant, cold 'originator', but a true Supreme God, who is not afar off; not a stranger to men, but one who takes a keen interest in and exercises manifold influences on their life; whom also men do not consider as a stranger, but to whom they address themselves in a lively worship comprising a variety of prayers, sacrifices, and ceremonies. Quite remarkable is the wide diffusion of prayer, which we encountered so frequently at morning, evening, and meal-times. Not less astonishing is the frequency of true offerings of first-fruits, by which the supreme power of the Creator and Master of life and death is so simply and so solemnly recognized. But the frequent practising of extended ceremonies of such simple greatness and warm fervour as we have found in all the three great groups of these oldest tribes of North America – this, I fancy, is a revelation to many students.

Certainly these are real religions, in which the mutual contacts between God and man find practical, vivid, and intense expression in manifold forms, and with real influences upon human life issuing from them.

[...]

'Conclusion'

a) The historical method and its results. I do not imagine that the reader whose patience has carried him thus far has found my little book entertaining or amusing in the ordinary sense of these words. It has demanded the effort of patient and continued attention, in order to give that collaboration without which the best efforts of any writer are in vain. For it has not been my endeavour to set before my readers, any more than before those who originally heard me, a brave and kaleidoscopic array of theories, glittering in their novelty, or to erect an artificial edifice, to be ingloriously overturned by the first push of the rude hand of criticism.

It has been my aim to set forth facts, established and co-ordinated facts, not always easily and plainly within reach, but having to be brought up out of the depths of centuries and even millennia by laborious and methodical inquiries.

But I feel that the satisfaction which the mind has in the possession of well-established facts is deep and noble, especially when strengthened by the comfortable sense that the knowledge acquired is reliable. It differs plainly from such pleasure as proceeds from the ironical railleries not seldom dealt out to primitive man, which betray so much bitterness deeply concealed at the bottom of the heart. And this satisfaction is the greater as the results obtained by these inquiries are not like those sterile slag-heaps from which only a fallacious alchemy can promise to extract refined gold, but highly valued qualities and actions of primitive mankind, whose innocent simplicity does not prevent them from being most precious treasures.

b) General character of the oldest religions. In what does the high value of these results consist? To answer this question, I cannot do better than quote the words in which Dr. Speck delivers his verdict upon the religion of his East Algonkin Delawares (with which one of the foregoing chapters made us acquainted): words which are in broad outlines appropriate to almost all these old religions.

'If the student of the religious systems of pre-literate peoples feels inclined to disparage the quality of thought and the symbolism of the rituals of other North American forms of worship, I imagine that his objections, on the basis perhaps of their fetishistic traits and their lack of spiritual refinement, would be removed in the process of weighing the qualities of Delaware concepts and acts of reverence toward the powers beyond.

'Close attention, during two years of study, to the intricacies of the Delaware doctrines has impressed me with the conviction that we have here a real religion in a simple form. Inculcated in its followers are virtues whose ennobling nature no one would question; for instance humility of spirit and conduct, dependence upon the benevolence of the spirit forces, gratitude for the blessings they bestow, supplication for the continuation of blessings, the exemplariness of 'clean', sincere behaviour towards man and spirit, altruism, consideration of the afflicted and the aged, the apostrophe against violence and war, the value of concentrated spiritual unity in worship, the assured dignity and barbaric grandeur of the rites, and in particular the endeavour to insure and promote human health and welfare, irrespective of tribe and race. All are well worthy it would seem of respectful consideration. To this it should be added that the procedures of the paramount ceremony are framed in richly symbolical acts, impressive to the civilized as well as to the uncivilized observer, participated in equally by the congregation of worshippers, young and old, great and humble.

'That the Delawares produced a religion in the real, almost classical sense, will not, I believe, be strenuously denied even by the propounders of other creeds, at least those of the more liberal type of mind. With its native humanitarian ideals, its precepts of altruism and humility, its lyrics, its litanies and mysticism, it might indeed have become a great one of the mediaeval type had it been linked with the destinies of a militant aggressive race.

'But after all, whatever the civilized reader, no doubt himself an adherent of some creed accused of being equally as superstitious if not as picturesque, may call these religions, there they stand as evolved, enduring, symbols of the strange systems of thought that have appeared and almost vanished in the changing pageant of human history.[4]

To these noble words I content myself with adding this much: that religions of this simple, but high, standard were those of the oldest tribes who migrated into the New World and took possession of it. That, as we have seen, emerges with objective certainty out of a whole series of inquiries into these tribes and their religions, conducted patiently and calmly by the only method appropriate to and sufficient for this object.

In the last chapter our outlook was sufficiently broadened to permit us to see that everywhere on our vast globe the religions of the peoples ethnologically oldest are of precisely similar character to the religions of those three oldest groups of North American Indians which we have here considered.

And so let me end where I began, with the words of Goethe, which I cited to excuse myself for troubling the reader with so much methodology:

> *Ich sage dir: Ein Kerl, der spekuliert,*
> *Ist wie ein Tier auf dürrer Heide,*
> *Von einem bösen Geist im Kreis herumgeführt,*
> *Und rings umher liegt schöne grüne Weide.*

I then promised that, although for a while we might wander in the deserts of methodological considerations, we should at last graze on the fair green pastures of concrete facts concerning the religious life of these oldest peoples. And I hope I may be thought of, not as the evil spirit of the poem, leading the reader in circles, but rather as a shepherd to guide him to the refreshment contained in these oldest Amerindian faiths, with their beliefs and myths, prayers, sacrifices, and ceremonial.

> *Dominus regit me, et nihil mihi deerit:*
> *in loco pascuae ibi me collocavit.*
> *Super aquam refectionis educavit me:*
> *animam meam convertit.*

> *The Lord is my shepherd, I shall not want:*
> *He maketh me to lie down in green pastures,*
> *He leadeth me beside the still waters,*
> *He restoreth my soul.*

And if the reader receives, from the account I have given of our progress in knowledge of the religious history of mankind, some light on his way, some impulse, scientific or otherwise, to help him on, I shall feel more than rewarded.

NOTES

1. H. Pinard de la Boullaye, *L'étude comparée des religions*, vol. II (3 rd ed. Paris 1929), pp. 2—10; S. A. Cook, in Hastings, *Enc. Rel. Eth.*, art. 'Religion' (vol. XI, p. 662 *sq.*).

2. See L. H. Dudley Buxton, *Primitive Labour*, Methuen, 1924, p. 46. 'A convenient division . . . has been generally adopted by the German ethnologists. The terms they use are 'Hackbau' and 'Ackerbau' . . . The divisions correspond roughly to our words horticulture and agriculture – the latter depends essentially on the use of domestic animals, the former on man's labour alone. That the division is not a mutually exclusive one is shown by the fact that most peoples who cultivate fields with their animals also cultivate gardens.' Throughout this book I render *Hackbau, Hackbauer*, by 'horticulture', 'horticulturalist', in accordance with Mr. Buxton's suggestion.

3. Cf. W. Schmidt, 'Ethnologische Bemerkungen zu theologischen Opfertheorien' (*Jahrbuch f. St. Gabriel*, I (1923), pp. 5—13). For more modern evolutionistic theories see M. G. Bergue in *Revue de Théologie et de Philosophie*, January 1929; they are still more lacking in historical evidence.

4. Frank G. Speck: *A Study of the Delaware Indian Big-House Ceremony*, vol. II, Publications of the Pennsylvania Historical Commission, Harrisburg, 1931, p. 21.

Arnold van Gennep

Arnold van Gennep was born in 1873 in Ludwigsburg, Germany. He received his primary school education in Lyon and in Paris, and his secondary education in Nice, Chambéry and Grenoble. In 1892 he became a student in Paris at the *Ecole Nationale des Langues Orientales Vivantes*, and at the *Ecole Pratique des Hautes Etudes* for ethnography, sociology and history of religions. He obtained the diploma of the *Ecole Nationale* and the doctorate at the Sorbonne. From 1897 until 1901 he taught French at Czentochova in Poland, and in 1901 he was connected with the Ministry of Agriculture in Paris. In 1904 he obtained the diploma of the *Ecole Pratique des Hautes Etudes* with a thesis on 'Taboo and Totemism on Madagascar'. In 1908 he left his post at the Ministry of Agriculture and lived off his publications.

Van Gennep became professor of ethnography at the University of Neuchâtel in 1912, but he had to leave Switzerland in 1915. He performed his military service, became a teacher at a secondary school in Nice, and worked then at the Ministry of Foreign Affairs until 1922. Subsequently he gave a series of lectures in the United States and Canada and finally settled down at Bourg-la-Reine near Paris. Besides his work on his own publications, Van Gennep was editor of the *Manuel du Folklore Français Contemporain* and founded the *Revue des Idées* and the *Revue d'Ethnographie et de Sociologie*. He died at Bourg-la-Reine in 1957.

Two books of Van Gennep are available in English: 1960 *The Rites of Passage;* 1967 *The Semi-Scholars.*

Van Gennep stressed the importance of a minute and detailed investigation of facts as they present themselves and kept distance from the general theories of anthropology and sociology current at his time. He was one of the first scholars to recognize the interest of non-periodic rituals, and made an extensive study of life crisis rites facilitating individual and especially social transition.

The following text is that of a lecture which Van Gennep offered at the University of Brussels in 1910, in which he presents a careful methodological reflection based on research as actually carried out.

'ON THE METHOD TO BE FOLLOWED IN THE STUDY OF RITES AND MYTHS'

Although in all ages and in all countries, however uncivilized, the study of one's own or another person's religion has been considered worthy of some investigation by the thinkers, the priests, and the faithful themselves, only during the 19th century has this study been recognized as an autonomous and properly scientific discipline. Without wanting to trace a history which would exceed the bounds of this conference, it is nevertheless fitting to recall briefly that Pausanias and Plutarch already laid the foundations of a genuine science of religions. Both, gifted with lucid minds and with that collector's mania which is a precondition for being a scholar, and armed with material from many different and varied sources, not only just posed the facts, that had come to their knowledge, but also elucidated them by comparing them with each other. Pausanias was the precursor of our ethnographic explorers, and of our experts investigating folklore and Plutarch was the precursor of our religious historians or hierologists, as Mr. Goblet d'Alviella would say.

In fact our young science of religion is characterized by the systematic comparison of facts of a religious nature and by their classification, which is ultimately obtained by delimiting sets of connected facts. These sets are found by defining similarities and differences.

In that respect, the general method of the science of religion does not distinguish itself at all from the general method in the other sciences, whether they apply to nature or to the mind. But it appears that the difficulty consists in how to apply a method, which is unanimously recognized as legitimate when applied to other sciences, to this particular science.

I think there is no need to stress this point. After all, everyone knows that, even today, our science is regarded suspiciously by those who fear that the analytical spirit by taking apart the mechanism of the various cults and dogmas will end up by reducing them to anatomical skeletons. And there is even a movement, to which I draw your attention only in passing, which would like to deflect the science of religion to a kind of endless side road, in order to appropriate it and if not to strangle it, at least to draw out its sting.

In as far as it has its own method, no science needs to be agressive, for it carries within itself the potential for development. Have not we seen how, in the 19th century biology laid the foundations for a new outlook on life, and how the various kinds of opposition it met with were unable to check its progress.

As long as the study of religion, on the pretext of contributing to the enrichment of our hierological knowledge, was used as a purely offensive weapon as it happened in the 18th century, that knowledge made very little progress.

I have been speaking of biology. That was not by accident; it is to biology that we owe the existence of a science of religion worthy of that name, not in the sense that we apply, to the last detail, this or that biological theory to the interpretation of one or another set of religious phenomena. Rather it is in the sense that it provides us with, on one hand, the great concept of evolution, and on the other hand, with an accurate method. Although we cannot make histological sections, bring our own phenomena into laboratories, or conduct experiments on them, the biological method has rendered us the greatest of services by transforming what was no more than an object of curiosity, of amazement and of collectors' mania, into an object of systematic and progressive research. It has shown us that it is necessary to compare across time and space facts of the same order, so that our laboratory has become enormous and almost infinite: it comprises all human groupings on the face of the earth. And as the scientific study of all those human groups, including those whose civilization is no more than rudimentary, is called ethnography, the science of religion has, thanks to biology, modified the general comparative method by means of a legitimate transposition, adapting it to its own needs in the form of the ethnographical method. I do not think it necessary at this point to revive the old quarrel between the advocates of the historical method and the protagonists of the comparative or ethnographical method.

We have, in fact, won that quarrel, for already those younger than we are, find it impossible to imagine that the normal and regular use of the latter method could be subject to discussion, or even that one could ignore it. And someone who, later on, will undertake the colossal task of writing a history of the science of religion, on the lines of works already devoted to the history of chemistry and of physics, will find to his astonishment that generations of historians have applied themselves to the same old texts, and that, if the interpretations of those texts, made by the successive generations of historians, were different at all, that was only because other sciences than history, and other methods than the historical method, contributed, or at least suggested the successive solutions. Two names come to mind immediately, that of Mannhardt and that of Frazer – whose *Adonis, Attis, Osiris* is proof of our final victory.

But like every other method, the comparative method has its limitations: it is a delicate instrument. Even the book I have just cited contains passages in which the excitement that is aroused in every scholar by an elegant series of deductions, carries the author beyond the normal limits of his method. My remark is neither a reproach, nor a criticism: everyone should go to the very limits of his ideas, leaving it to life itself, and to general evolution, to eliminate what will eventually prove to be indigestible and exaggerated.

In the history of science we also notice the necessity of fluctuations on either side of an equilibrium that will not be attained until the death of mankind. The fact that the science of religion is gradually coming out of university seminaries in order to take part in the universal battle of theories and ideas, is not a thing to be regretted. But it is necessary to prepare the public to understand the method and the spirit, in the same way in which it was gradually prepared to understand the spirit and the method of the natural sciences.

Today, there are no longer any reasons to support the argument that our science is too young and, consequently, not yet strong enough, or that the general results obtained so far are still too fragile.

In recent years, the study of ancient and oriental documents, the thorough-going investigations among the semi-civilized people, the partial syntheses, have made such progress, that the general syntheses may already be attempted wherever the main characteristics of the structure and of the evolution of the religions have been isolated.

Such syntheses imply that first of all a number of similarities and a number of differences have been defined. These represent the still amorphous mass of data which future generations will have to study in order to discover new sets of correspondences, and in that way phenomena uniquely characterized by their own individuality will come to be classified. At the birth of a new science the theoreticians are always inclined to believe in the possibility of a unique and universal solution, in a linear evolution, in an automatic development of the phenomena. Then, as the analysis progresses, the complexity of the facts and the factors influencing them becomes clearer and clearer, so that the initially simple and harmonious schemes are replaced by complicated, cross-referenced and bracketed, tables. Furthermore no-one now demands simplistic explanations, such as that which was prevalent in the 18th century, attributing the rise of every religion to the imposture of the priests, or the one given by Dupuis, who regarded sun worship as the base of all religions, or the one given by Creuzer, who saw only symbolism everywhere.

It cannot be denied that the great progress made during the past century and a half in the fields of religious history, general ethnography, law, and more recently, the theory of art, sociology and psychology, is due to the increasingly widespread and systematic use of the comparative method. But we must not stop here. The rapid development of the physical and chemical sciences has been made possible by the fact that the tools needed for research, which were put at their disposal by industry also made considerable progress. It is necessary for practice to improve on the basis of theory, in order that theory, in turn, can take a new step forward which will then again allow further technical improvements. The lessons to be drawn from this mutual dependence in the sciences of the laboratory and of industry should not be lost on us.

Now that the comparative method has brought us some genuine progress, the time has come to ask ourselves how we are going to prepare for a future that will bring us even more, starting from what has already been acquired.

But first of all, is this the right moment to improve our equipment, or has that which we now possess, not yet yielded maximum profit? Far be it from me to give a conclusive answer to such a delicate question.

In fact, there are areas where the comparative method in its simple classic form has done just about all it can do, for instance in the study of certain rites and certain beliefs. If we consider a very simple rite, such as the one that consists of pouring water on the ground to make the rain come down, we find that several dozens of instances confirm the universality of that rite. The bibliographical references may point to several hundred instances if one takes all forms of the rite into consideration, that is to say, the variations in which the water is replaced by other liquids, or by material reminiscent of liquidity, such as grains of corn.

But no matter how abundant the instances are, and no matter how varied the material being used is, and how varied the containers in which that material is kept, etc., the fundamental fact is always a simple one, and the mechanism is identical everywhere, as is the psychological principle, which is the active virtue of imitation, or as we put it, of 'sympathy'. Sympathetic rites are innumerable; they have been the subject of equally innumerable publications, and the only interest studying them can now have, is a purely local and historical one. What I am trying to say is, that if we discover a particular rite being used at a particular place and time, it may be interesting to find out whether that rite is indigenous, or where it came from, if it was imported, and where exact parallels to the rite in question have arisen. But whatever results are obtained, the general theory of religious phenomena will have gained nothing, for the mechanism pertaining to the entire category to which the rite belongs, was well known. There is a reason, therefore, to try and find out how these rites and all other rites can be studied in such a way that we may make progress.

It is the same with myths. The comparative method has enabled us to recognize the universality of a considerable number of themes, the invention and possession of which used to be attributed to one particular people to which all other peoples were believed to be subjected. This has led to the investigation of the practically or theoretically effective causes of what Max Müller has termed *mythopoetic* activity. One has, for example, defined the general cultural and psychological conditions for the creation of myths.

On the other hand, by separating the various amalgamated themes from each other, one has begun to draw up division tables for those themes, with every specialist, according to preference, studying one theme or another. For example, one has studied the themes related to the celestial bodies in general, or to the moon only, or to the sun, or to sacred animals, or to superior divinities. As these investigations with their tendencies towards over-simplification, have been conducted without any previous systematic agreement, the results have been rather disproportionate: certain sets of mythological themes are supplied with an appreciable bibliography, whereas other sets have virtually nothing. In that way the culture heroes have been sacrificed to astral themes.

The comparative method has thus been applied in all its splendour to certain sets of rites and myths, and not at all to other ones; there seems to be an order of priorities resulting in the fact, that if this method has been exhausted in a number of cases, it has hardly gone beyond its beginnings in other cases.

We should concern ourselves less with these gaps than with the greatest achievements made. For filling up the gaps, it will be sufficient to organize a few centers of education and to show the young people how, and on which problem, to try out their mental powers, in classifying documents that have already been assembled by others, or by sending them out to study little-known phenomena on the spot. In any case, if they wish to prepare themselves for a good scientific career, first of all they will have to learn how to handle the classic comparative method.

Yet they could run the risk of not seeing that this method is subject to limitations, which is the reason why theoreticians will now have to apply themselves to the task of defining those limitations. This is all the more pressing since a few recently published works have shown to what kinds of artificial construction the integral and exclusive use of the main principle of this method studying the phenomena with complete disregard for factors such as time and place may lead. So what has been achieved is that we have at present in the history of religion finally tuned, well adapted and stable procedures for research, criticism and analysis, provided that a number of elementary precautions are observed when using them. Does that mean that we should leave it at that and cease trying to perfect those procedures or looking for other ones? Your reply should be an unambiguous: no, we should not be content with the tools created by our predecessors. On the contrary: we must continue along the road we have started out on, and hew our own way through the facts. And the facts themselves will show us what directions to take, what mistakes to avoid, for all wisdom proceeds from reality.

Certainly, a science such as ours which is concerned with the global history of mankind, from the dawn of the quaternary period until today, always leaves the scholar with an enormous heap of facts that have not yet been classified and are, for precisely that reason, particularly interesting. It may happen then, that the scholar starts establishing provisional frameworks, or, if you wish, kinds of boxes, in which the facts are piled up at random. From time to time, the scholar has a good look at the mountain of facts, and quickly makes some adjustments to his inventory. Then, one day, important characteristics, until then unnoticed, suddenly become clear to his surprised mind, and a certain order begins separating different elements from the chaos. Then the important characteristics must be isolated, the extent to which they are real and stable must be defined, and it will have to be determined, which method of investigation will allow them to return without any short-comings in the final course of the investigation. This process of generalization is not a special feature of the science of religion alone, and no doubt several among you have experienced the kind of mental illumination that suddenly opens the way to synthesis after months of collecting and analyzing.

Then the time has come to start formulating the rules of a particular method, which, until now, had been developed subconsciously. The word 'method' is, perhaps, a little strong: what has been found is a tool, a key, a convenient technical procedure. But since in current terminology the word method has taken on a wider meaning and become rather weak, I shall use it to refer to three technical procedures which seem to me to be destined to help the advancement of the science of religion. None of these procedures were invented theoretically: all three were suggested by the facts, in the sense that after various attempts at classification these three consistently proved to yield satisfactory results when the aim was to classify facts, that had remained outside the known frameworks, or that had been fitted only forcibly into those frameworks.

We may call these technical classification procedures: *the method of the fact coming-into-being, the ethnological method* or *the method of the natural environment*, and *the sequential method*.

By the *method of the fact coming-into-being* ('méthode du fait naissant') we mean the application in ethnography and in the science of religion of the method which, in the natural sciences, consists in causing a phenomenon in order to study it, and, in psychology, in following all the stages of a mental phenomenon at the very moments when those stages can be observed. We need not think, therefore, that we have to establish a completely new investigational procedure that has not yet proved its value. On the contrary, all we have to do is to derive from other, already established disciplines, an instrument the use of which has already demonstrated its excellence. The newly introduced methods do not in the least diminish the importance of our previous study procedures and do not displace them, but they are just added to them. For it was characteristic of the ethnographical method that it studied *living* facts, then those facts were still considered by it after they had ceased to exist. Starting from precisely those no longer existing facts, this method tried to re-establish, by means of a series of

inductions of a certain kind, the preceding stages of development, in order
to reconstruct little by little the process of genesis.

The addition to be proposed would be useful because of the fact that
this time the object of the investigation would not be the already finished
fact, but the fact that would be in the course of attaining its accomplish-
ment, observed at the very moments of its genesis and development. Some
may say that certain religious and social facts have already been studied
in that way and that for example, Mr. d'Allonnes has, in his monograph on
the Rev. Monod, shown how what could be called the formative energy
of a religion develops in a powerful individual's mind, and then in lesser
minds which tend to form a group with a collective mentality. Similarly,
in his curious book on *'Suggestion and its Role in the Life of Society'*, Mr. Bech-
terew has given us enough material to enable us to account for the birth
of heresies, sects and religions in Russia, under certain well-defined mental
and social conditions.

If we were to take the trouble, it would not be difficult for an ethnographer
either to discover facts characterized as *coming-into-being* in the enormous
amount of literature about the semi-civilized people, about the Muslims
and the Buddhists. Those among you who have applied themselves to the
immense task of opening up the resources of our discipline know that there
is still material to be gleaned for constructing new theories and acquiring
new insights.

They also know that especially the 18th century travellers, most of whom
were open-minded and critical, although they were only 'honest men' and
not specialized scholars, have taken great care to write everything down,
absolutely everything they saw, without any false shame, and without any
theoretical motive.

Similarly, folklore-experts looking for popular customs and legends,
have often been in the position of seeing facts of this nature before their
very eyes, and I shall quote a typical example here. When the prince of
Pucler-Muskau happened to be in Amphissa, a ship's captain told him
that in Greece there were snakes with horns on their heads. To prove this,
he showed the prince the marks left by the bite of a greenish snake; having
seized it by the neck, he had tried to strangle it, but the snake had slipped
out of his hands, dropping its horns on the ground. The captain had picked
them up, and the next day he showed them to the prince. But the latter
immediately recognized them as the horns of a beetle, which the snake had
spat out when the captain tried to strangle it.

We have here, ladies and gentlemen, the genesis of a legend. Not only
did the captain's men blindly believe in the reality of the legend because
their superior gave tangible and visible proof of it, adding perhaps a little
hierarchical persuasion, but it would also have been sufficient if his questio-

ner had been not a prince with some knowledge of natural history, but some man of the people, for the conditions for disseminating this new legend to have been perfect.

I could tell you a few other cases of the same kind. An Austrian folklorist, Mr. Kaindl, had the excellent idea of following the day-to-day development of a whole cycle of legends arising around the death of Archduke Rudolf. Yet do not believe that my collection of these legends coming-into-being is at all large!

Why? Simply because our historical education has more or less blinded all of us to what happens before our very eyes. We have to make a considerable effort to realize that every event that happens right now, has a particular theoretical relevance to the future, and that a new fact may equally throw some light on the past. It is a deep-seated inclination of ours not to attribute any value to a fact unless it can be categorized in terms of established frameworks, and so, due to our love of simplification, we omit to investigate all factors active at the present time, until the passage of time has removed most of the concomitant factors from the field of observation.

I have already told you that, in other sciences, this method of the fact-being-born is very much in use, and has been so for a long time, since the aim of experimenting is precisely to cause the facts to come into-being, in order to observe their genesis. But it is impossible to conduct experiments in the fields of folklore and religion. It is also clear enough that certain areas of sociology, such as political economy, regularly apply the method of the fact being-born. Nothing is more instructive, for instance, than to see a particular industry being born, or a new form of exploitation of natural resources, and to behold the laws in action. What is really striking is that it should not yet have occurred to the ethnographers and the historians of religion to profit from the example and to transpose the study methods that have proved themselves in other areas of science.

One can establish at most that the method in question has been used from time to time, owing to external necessity rather than with the aim of discovering the underlying laws, e.g. where contact between different civilizations has caused radical changes in local industry. It is interesting to read in a recent monograph by the explorer Stuhlmann, *Handwerk und Industrie in Ostafrika*, published by the Colonial Institute at Hamburg, a detailed account of the effects on the indigenous economy, of the introduction of certain factors and techniques of Arab and European import and in the case of several of the phenomena studied, the author has been able to follow the genesis on the spot.

Though it would be wrong to say that the study of the fact-being-born has been completely neglected, it would be equally wrong to pretend that it has already given us all that could be expected of it. What is needed is for someone to pursue this study systematically, to investigate as many facts that are coming-into-being as possible, to assume as a principle that it is important to note very carefully all the factors at work in the genesis of a folkloristic, ethnographical, and religious phenomenon. We would then be able to systematize far better than we can do at present the data we have already assembled concerning the mental and social mechanisms that condition the development of religion, customs and institutions, even in their relatively primitive stages.

Studying a phenomenon at the moment of its coming-into-being does not only mean considering that phenomenon itself, but also all circumstances surrounding it, whether or not they condition it, in short, its *environment*. And as we have seen that the genesis of the fact in question must be *natural*, and not artificial, it follows that the environment I have in mind, is also natural. This means, to give another example, that the attempts at founding a religion made by hallucinating inmates of an asylum, will be removed from our field of observation. For religions are formed and developed in social environments that are all equally natural, and which differ only in size. Anyone who whishes to view this mechanism needs only to study the forming and dissemination of Behaism in modern Persia, by the light of the works of Mr. Dreyfus and of Mr. Nicolas. Similarly, in biology animals are now being studied in their natural environments, the sea or the forest, and no longer in the artificial environments provided by laboratory or zoo.

It may seem at first sight that to recommend the use of what I have called the *ethnological method,* or the method of the natural environment, is either to propose a return to a set of theories which were recognized in the last century, or to seriously propound a load of nonsense . . . My reply is, that if in the 18th century the idea was born that institutions, including religions, depend primarily on the physical environment, on the sun and more especially on the climate, and if the 19th century has produced a number of famous examples of systematization along those lines, that then the reaction has been really too strong.

The theoreticians have, since then, often misused a method that consists in systematically extracting a well-defined set of phenomena, for instance religious phenomena, from the environments in which they were born and developed. Not only do we have to react against the reaction by no longer isolating religious phenomena from other social phenomena whatever they may be, but we even have to advance along this road by taking into account once again, and more than formerly, the natural environment.

This will not be a step backwards, for the very good reason that the study of nature has for a century made such progress, that we now know the influence of various factors, the number and relative importance of which is used to be impossible to evaluate. Let me remind you that the knowledge we possess about air and sea currents, about volcanic phenomena, about the distribution, all over the earth, of animal species and about the way they scatter themselves, is only a recent scientific acquisition. Therefore, if one takes the natural environment into consideration in the present-day study of religion, it means something entirely different from what it did a hundred or a hundred and fifty years ago, when one tried to explain Islam, for example, on the basis of the Arabian deserts.

Two examples will do. You know that the tribes of Central Australia have gained international fame because among them the most vivid and dramatic forms of totemism have been found.

The first explorers of that area, Spencer and Gillen, realized from the beginning that the religious system they found there was very closely related to climate, flora and fauna. The polemics between scholars of all countries about Australian totemism were such that other explorers were inclined to recommence their investigations on the spot, and one of them, a German missionary, Mr. Strehlow, came near solving the problem. And why? Because he tried to find out the economic value of each totem, and the extent to which all social organizations depend on the surrounding natural environment. Mr. J. G. Frazer gave me the second example. You know that at the moment he is working on the publication of the third volume of his great work, *The Golden Bough*, which will consist of five volumes. The first one, published under the title *Adonis, Attis, Osiris*, treats of several great divinities of Egypt and Asia Minor. In the first volume you will find a very interesting preface, where Mr. Frazer explains how studying the geological conditions of Asia Minor enabled him to give a plausible explanation of certain local cults, and to recognize in certain gods, volcanic divinities and phenomena.

The study of agrarian rites, which progressed so rapidly in the last quarter of the 19th century, was an omen indicating a new orientation. And since it led to good results, we should embrace it all the more, It so happened that the agrarian myths and cults received an exaggerated importance of our studies, comparable to that accorded to the naturalist, or rather, astral myths, oriented towards the sun, the moon, and the constellations. There existed two categories, if I may say so, the astral category and the agrarian category, pushing all the other, actual and potential categories into the background.

I am obliged now to enter into some detail in order to make clear the third technical procedure, the *sequential method*. Let us select a particular rite, for instance, walking in procession around a sacred building, altar, church, etc. This is the rite called circumambulation. The astral theory claims that this circular procession symbolically represents the course of the sun, and this is a so-called solar rite, whether it takes place in the same direction as the apparent movement of the sun, according to the principle *similia similibus,* or in the opposite direction following the contrarity principle. In a few cases, the solar significance of this rite is very clear, but in the majority of cases, both European and non-European, no other accompanying rite or belief allows a preference for the solar interpretation over another interpretation. The solar interpretation is obtained only when the rite is isolated completely from all other rites performed before or after it by the same people, and when a comparison with other rites of the same kind is avoided, such as those in which the sacred monument is encircled with one's arms, with cloths that have been tied together, or with a piece of string.

In the same category belong the rites in which a group of people walk in procession around a human being: in Madagascar, a stranger arriving at a village is encircled by boys and girls who dance and sing around him, with nothing pointing to a solar rite. On the contrary, as soon as one has a collection of descriptions of ritual circumambulations that is in any way significant, one sees that the fundamental idea is a very simple one: it is the idea of the magic circle, which can be inanimate or human and also, but rarely, astral. And even then, the course of the sun is compared to a circle, and not the circle to the course of the sun. And to convince oneself that this is the correct interpretation, it is sufficient to consider in each single case what are the rites preceding circumambulation, what are the rites following it, and what is the aim of the ceremony *as a whole.* All complex ceremonies, in which the rite in question is performed, have as their most important characteristic that they are joining or fixing ceremonies: one magically encircles the desired person or object, in order to appropriate it, just as Dido and Romulus encircled the territory on which they wanted to found their towns, one with ox straps, the other with ditches.

Another example: in many countries the marriage rites entail an aspersion of the young couple: parents and friends cast dates, figs, nuts, water, sand, grains etc. at them, according to the country and its vegetation. Clearly, this rite aims to ensure a rapid and numerous offspring, to make that they 'are fruitful and multiply'. But the same aspersion rite is still in use in all kinds of ceremonies such as, in ancient Greece, taking possession of a slave, or the arrival in the town of a new ambassador. Two German scholars, Mannhardt and Samter, have assembled a large number of parallels to this aspersion rite, using the normal procedure of the comparative method, that is, isolating them from their natural contexts. Mannhardt explained all his parallels as fecundity rites, and Samter explained all his rites, plus those of Mannhardt, as protection rites against the spirits. I have found myself that the aspersion rite, using grains of sand or liquid material is used by the Pueblo Indians with the direct aim of magically making the rain come down; its meaning here is not subject to controversy, because it is only one of the elements of very complicated ceremonies, entirely dedicated to making rain; whereas in the parallels drawn by Mannhardt and Samter, the rite is a part of other ceremonies, all of them very different from each other.

The conclusion must be: the aspersion rite does not have any personal or basic meaning in the state of isolation, but it is meaningful if seen as a component part of a particular ceremony. The meaning of the rite can, consequently, only be found by determining the relation it has with the other elements of the whole ceremony.

The same kind of reasoning is valid for myths and legends. In Germany there is a mythological school which applies the comparative method in its most extreme form to the study of myths. They extract details from everything; they accumulate large numbers of parallels, and prove then that all mythologies are based on the moon (Siecke), that they are based on the sun (Ehrenreich), that all is derived from the Pleiads, and so on. Similarly, in the study of legends, one picks a detail here, another one there, and one obtains derivational and transmissional diagrams that do not have any foundation in reality. In short, we should react against the tendency to study the facts outside their factual or verbal contexts.

I propose to give the name *sequential method* which studies every rite and every mythological theme only in relation to what precedes and what follows it. Instead of arbitrarily accumulating isolated parallels, we compare similar sets of data, complete scenarios for example; such as marriage ceremonies with each other, initiation ceremonies with each other, in each case taking the natural and social environment into account. One result of this kind of comparison is that general and universal features are recognized as *necessary*. For instance, if an individual leaves a particular society, he has to submit to separation rites which are similar all over the world; the rites that are performed to initiate a new individual into society are also, of necessity, similar the world over.

The existence of these universal features was to be expected, and, as I mentioned in my *Rites de Passage*, some of them had actually been recognized before me. But I had not expected that the same rite, remaining absolutely the same, can change its meaning depending on the position it is given in the ceremony, or on whether it is part of one ceremony or another. The aspersion rite mentioned above is a fecundity rite in the marriage ceremonies, but an expulsion rite in the seperation ceremonies.

Similary, beating and whipping may mean either chasing away someone not wanted around any longer, or that one, by means of violent contact, enters into a relationship with a person one wants henceforward to cherish as a blood brother, for instance in initiation ceremonies. *It all depends*, as one of my friends, a well known economist, says when he is asked to explain an economic phenomenon which, at first sight, seems to be very simple. In fact, everything depends on the attendant circumstances and on the context, and that being so, we may expect that those religious historians and folklorists who restrict themselves completely to the comparative method, still have a lot of fine polemic awaiting them.

Ladies and gentlemen, the general ideas that I would like you to take home with you from this lecture, possibly a bit too specialist here and there, are few and simple. In the first place, you should no longer think that the *science* of religion is only *history* of religion, and that it is by definition only concerned with dead facts and things of the past. There are, at this very moment, religions springing up and religious systems being born, not only in the United States, in Russia, in Asia, and in Africa, but sometimes before your own eyes. Their value and importance for our studies are in no sense diminished by the fact that they are no match for the great, established religions. In the same way myths, legends and popular tales are being born, but the power of print allows them only a short life. We have to stand at their cradles and to notice even their incomplete development; to be able to do that, we have to observe all the details of their environments with a tireless and sympathetic curiosity, and to sharpen our direct vision.

This means that we must not divide our lives into two parts, one exclusively devoted to studying, at lectures, in laboratories or in books, the other living in the usual sense of the word. On the contrary, the two should be united continually in such a way that you live your science, and that each newly acquired bit of knowledge is, to you, indissolubly linked to really experienced everyday occurrences. Thus you will pick up the habit not only of considering religious and folkloristic facts as more than just printed matter, but you will find behind the ancient or semi-civilized facts what their power was, that they really could be part of living people.

And the second result should be that, as scientific analysis and abstraction are only technical expedients, you will not regard them as the aim of the science of religion, nor of any other science, but rather that you will be inclined to consider religious, magical, folkloristic entities in such a way as not to lose, in the accumulation of detail, the sharpness of your generalizing judgment and your desire to build syntheses.

Emile Durkheim

Emile Durkheim was born in 1858 in Epinal, France, where he received his primary and secondary school education as well as in Paris. In 1879 he entered the *Ecole Normale Supérieure*, where he was a student of Fustel de Coulanges and of the philosopher E. Boutroux. Having finished his studies in 1882, he became a teacher at a secondary school at Sens. In 1887 Durkheim was appointed for the social sciences at the University of Bordeaux. He visited Wilhelm Wundt in Germany for some time. After having obtained his doctorate in Paris, he became professor of philosophy at the Sorbonne in 1902. Durkheim had founded the *Année Sociologique* in 1897, and had a circle of collaborators devoting themselves to the science of sociology recognized by now. He died in Paris in 1917.

The following books by Durkheim which were translated into English have a bearing on the study of religion: 1915 *The Elementary Forms of the Religious Life: a Study in Religious Sociology*; 1938 *The Rules of Sociological Method*; 1953 *Sociology and Philosophy*; 1963 *Incest, the Nature and Origin of the Taboo*.

As a sociologist, Durkheim was much concerned with collective social reality and its institutionalization. Social reality is a force in itself, and social facts should be understood in their connection with other social facts according to scientific laws. Such social facts can be internalized by the individuals who belong to the collectivity. Sociologically speaking, religion 'is' society in a projected and symbolized form; the reality which is symbolized by religion is a social reality. Consequently, religion should be studied as a response to specific social needs. Just as religion, other institutions and intellectual categories all have a social origin. Durkheim developed a strict methodology and wanted to describe the facts without prejudice, classifying them according to their characteristics which should be scientifically verifiable.

The following texts have been taken from the first chapters of *The Elementary Forms of the Religious Life*. They present Durkheim's reasoning and argumentation against prevailing explanations of religious facts, and they formulate the demands which the author made upon research in the field of religion.

'THE ELEMENTARY FORMS OF THE RELIGIOUS LIFE'

'Religious sociology and the theory of knowledge'

In this book we propose to study the most primitive and simple religion which is actually known, to make an analysis of it, and to attempt an explanation of it. A religious system may be said to be the most primitive which we can observe when it fulfils the two following conditions: in the first place, when it is found in a society whose organization is surpassed by no others in simplicity;[1] and secondly, when it is possible to explain it without making use of any element borrowed from a previous religion.

We shall set ourselves to describe the organization of this system with all the exactness and fidelity that an ethnographer or an historian could give it. But our task will not be limited to that: sociology raises other problems than history or ethnography. It does not seek to know the passed forms of civilization with the sole end of knowing them and reconstructing them. But rather, like every positive science, it has as its object the explanation of some actual reality which is near to us, and which consequently is capable of affecting our ideas and our acts: this reality is man, and more precisely, the man of to-day, for there is nothing which we are more interested in knowing. Then we are not going to study a very archaic religion simply for the pleasure of telling its peculiarities and its singularities. If we have taken it as the subject of our research, it is because it has seemed to us better adapted than any other to lead to an understanding of the relgious nature of man, that is to say, to show us an essential and permanent aspect of humanity.

But this proposition is not accepted before the raising of strong objections. It seems very strange that one must turn back, and be transported to the very beginnings of history, in order to arrive at an understanding of humanity as it is at present. This manner of procedure seems particularly paradoxical in the question which concerns us. In fact, the various religions generally pass as being quite unequal in value and dignity; it is said that they do not all contain the same quota of truth. Then it seems as though one could not compare the highest forms of religious thought with the lowest, without reducing the first to the level of the second. If we admit that the crude cults of the Australian tribes can help us to understand Christianity, for example, is that not supposing that this latter religion proceeds from the same mentality as the former, that it is made up of the same superstitions and rests upon the same errors? This is how the theoretical importance which has sometimes been attributed to primitive religions has come to pass as a sign of a systematic hostility to all religion, which, by prejudging the results of the study, vitiates them in advance.

There is no occasion for asking here whether or not there are scholars who have merited this reproach, and who have made religious history and ethnology a weapon against religion. In any case, a sociologist cannot hold such a point of view. In fact, it is an essential postulate of sociology that a human institution cannot rest upon an error and a lie, without which it could not exist. If it were not founded in the nature of things, it would have encountered in the facts a resistance over which it could never have triumphed. So when we commence the study of primitive religions, it is with the assurance that they hold to reality and express it; this principle will be seen to re-enter again and again in the course of the analyses and discussions which follow, and the reproach which we make against the schools from which we have separated ourselves is that they have ignored it. When only the letter of the formulae is considered, these religious beliefs and practices undoubtedly seem disconcerting at times, and one is tempted to attribute them to some sort of a deep-rooted error. But one must know how to go underneath the symbol to the reality which it represents and which gives it its meaning. The most barbarous and the most fantastic rites and the strangest myths translate some human need, some aspect of life, either individual or social. The reasons with which the faithful justify them may be, and generally are, erroneous; but the true reasons do not cease to exist, and it is the duty of science to discover them.

In reality, then, there are no religions which are false. All are true in their own fashion; all answer, though in different ways, to the given conditions of human existence. It is undeniably possible to arrange them in a hierarchy. Some can be called superior to others, in the sense that they call into play higher mental functions, that they are richer in ideas and sentiments, that they contain more concepts with fewer sensations and images, and that their arrangement is wiser. But howsoever real this greater complexity and this higher ideality may be, they are not sufficient to place the corresponding religions in different classes. All are religions equally, just as all living beings are equally alive, from the most humble plastids up to man. So when we turn to primitive religions it is not with the idea of depreciating religion in general, for these religions are no less respectable than the others. They respond to the same needs, they play the same role, they depend upon the same causes; they can also well serve to show the nature of the religious life, and consequently to resolve the problem which we wish to study.

But why give them a sort of prerogative? Why choose them in preference to all others as the subject of our study? – It is merely for reasons of method.

In the first place, we cannot arrive at an understanding of the most recent religions except by following the manner in which they have been progressively composed in history. In fact, historical analysis is the only means of explanation which it is possible to apply to them. It alone enables us to resolve an institution into its constituent elements, for it shows them to us as they are born in time, one after another. On the other hand, by placing every one of them in the condition where it was born, it puts into our hands the only means we have of determining the causes which gave rise to it. Every time that we undertake to explain something human, taken at a given moment in history – be it a religious belief, a moral precept, a legal principle, an aesthetic style or an economic system – it is necessary to commence by going back to its most primitive and simple form, to try to account for the characteristics by which it was marked at that time, and then to show how it developed and became complicated little by little, and how it became that which it is at the moment in question. One readily understands the importance which the determination of the point of departure has for this series of progressive explanations, for all the others are attached to it. It was one of Descartes's principles that the first ring has a predominating place in the chain of scientific truths. But there is no question of placing at the foundation of the science of religions an idea elaborated after the cartesian manner, that is to say, a logical concept, a pure possibility, constructed simply by force of thought. What we must find is a concrete reality, and historical and ethnological observation alone can reveal that to us. But even if this cardinal conception is obtained by a different process than that of Descartes, it remains true that it is destined to have a considerable influence on the whole series of propositions which the science establishes. Biological evolution has been conceived quite differently ever since it has been known that monocellular beings do exist. In the same way, the arrangement of religious facts is explained quite differently, according as we put naturism, animism or some other religious form at the beginning of the evolution. Even the most specialized scholars, if they are unwilling to confine themselves to a task of pure erudition, and if they desire to interpret the facts which they analyse, are obliged to choose one of these hypotheses, and make it their starting-point. Whether they desire it or not, the questions which they raise necessarily take the following form: how has naturism or animism been led to take this particular form, here or there, or to enrich itself or impoverish itself in such and such a fashion? Since it is impossible to avoid taking sides on this initial problem, and since the solution given is destined to affect the whole science, it must be attacked at the outset: that is what we propose to do.

Besides this, outside of these indirect reactions, the study of primitive religions has of itself an immediate interest which is of primary importance.

If it is useful to know what a certain particular religion consists in, it is still more important to know what religion in general is. This is the problem which has aroused the interest of philosophers in all times; and not without reason, for it is of interest to all humanity. Unfortunately, the method which they generally employ is purely dialectic: they confine themselves to analysing the idea which they make for themselves of religion, except as they illustrate the results of this mental analysis by examples borrowed from the religions which best realize their ideal. But even if this method ought to be abandoned, the problem remains intact, and the great service of philosophy is to have prevented its being suppressed by the disdain of scholars. Now it is possible to attack it in a different way. Since all religions can be compared to each other, and since all are species of the same class, there are necessarily many elements which are common to all. We do not mean to speak simply of the outward and visible characteristics which they all have equally, and which make it possible to give them a provisional definition from the very outset of our researches; the discovery of these apparent signs is relatively easy, for the observation which it demands does not go beneath the surface of things. But these external resemblances suppose others which are profound. At the foundation of all systems of beliefs and of all cults there ought necessarily to be a certain number of fundamental representations or conceptions and of ritual attitudes which, in spite of the diversity of forms which they have taken, have the same objective significance and fulfil the same functions everywhere. These are the permanent elements which constitute that which is permanent and human in religion; they form all the objective contents of the idea which is expressed when one speaks of *religion* in general. How is it possible to pick them out?

Surely it is not by observing the complex religions which appear in the course of history. Every one of these is made up of such a variety of elements that it is very difficult to distinguish what is secondary from what is principal, the essential from the accessory. Suppose that the religion considered is like that of Egypt, India or the classical antiquity. It is a confused mass of many cults, varying according to the locality, the temples, the generations, the dynasties, the invasions, etc. Popular superstitions are there confused with the purest dogmas. Neither the thought nor the activity of the religion is evenly distributed among the believers; according to the men, the environment and the circumstances, the beliefs as well as the rites are thought of in different ways. Here they are priests, there they are monks, elsewhere they are laymen; there are mystics and rationalists, theologians and prophets, etc. In these conditions it is difficult to see what is common to all. In one or another of these systems it is quite possible to find the means of making a profitable study of some particular fact which is specially developed there, such as sacrifice or prophecy, monasticism or the mysteries; but how is it possible to find the common foundation of the religious life underneath the luxuriant vegetation which covers it? How is it possible to find, underneath the disputes of theology, the variations of ritual, the multiplicity of groups and the diversity of individuals, the fundamental states characteristic of religious mentality in general?

Things are quite different in the lower societies. The slighter development of individuality, the small extension of the group, the homogeneity of external circumstances, all contribute to reducing the differences and variations to a minimum. The group has an intellectual and moral conformity of which we find but rare examples in the more advanced societies. Everything is common to all. Movements are stereotyped; everybody performs the same ones in the same circumstances, and this conformity of conduct only translates the conformity of thought. Every mind being drawn into the same eddy, the individual type nearly confounds itself with that of the race. And while all is uniform, all is simple as well. Nothing is deformed like these myths, all composed of one and the same theme which is endlessly repeated, or like these rites made up of a small number of gestures repeated again and again. Neither the popular imagination nor that of the priests has had either the time or the means of refining and transforming the original substance of the religious ideas and practices; these are shown in all their nudity, and offer themselves to an examination, it requiring only the slighest effort to lay them open. That which is accessory or secondary, the development of luxury, has not yet come to hide the principal elements.[2] All is reduced to that which is indispensable, to that without which there could be no religion. But that which is indispensable is also that which is essential, that is to say, that which we must know before all else.

Primitive civilizations offer privileged cases, then, because they are simple cases. That is why, in all fields of human activity, the observations of ethnologists have frequently been veritable revelations, which have renewed the study of human institutions. For example, before the middle of the nineteenth century, everybody was convinced that the father was the essential element of the family; no one has dreamed that there could be a family organization of which the paternal authority was not the keystone. But the discovery of Bachofen came and upset this old conception. Up to very recent times it was regarded as evident that the moral and legal relations of kindred were only another aspect of the psychological relations which result from a common descent; Bachofen and his successors, MacLennan, Morgan and many others still laboured under this misunderstanding. But since we have become acquainted with the nature of the primitive clan, we know that, on the contrary, relationships cannot be explained by consanguinity. To return to religions, the study of only the most familiar ones had led men to believe for a long time that the idea of god was characteristic of everything that is religious. Now the religion which we are going to study presently is, in a large part, foreign to all idea of divinity; the forces to which the rites are there addressed are very different from those which occupy the leading place in our modern religions, yet they aid us in understanding these latter forces. So nothing is more unjust than the disdain with which too many historians still regard the work of ethnographers. Indeed, it is certain that ethnology has frequently brought about the most fruitful revolutions in the different branches of sociology. It is for this same reason that the discovery of unicellular beings, of which we just spoke, has transformed the current idea of life. Since in these very simple beings, life is reduced to its essential traits, these are less easily misunderstood.

But primitive religions do not merely aid us in disengaging the constituent elements of religion; they also have the great advantage that they facilitate the explanation of it. Since the facts there are simpler, the relations between them are more apparent. The reasons with which men account for their acts have not yet been elaborated and denatured by studied reflection; they are nearer and more closely related to the motives which have really determined these acts. In order to understand an hallucination perfectly, and give it its most appropriate treatment, a physician must know its original point of departure. Now this event is proportionately easier to find if he can observe it near its beginnings. The longer the disease is allowed to develop, the more it evades observation; that is because all sorts of interpretations have intervened as it advanced, which tend to force the original state into the background, and across which it is frequently difficult to find the initial one. Between a systematized hallucination and the first impressions which gave it birth, the distance is often considerable. It is the same thing with religious thought. In proportion as it progresses in history, the causes which called it into existence, though remaining active, are no longer perceived, except across a vast scheme of interpretations which quite transform them. Popular mythologies and subtile theologies have done their work: they have superimposed upon the primitive sentiments others which are quite different, and which, though holding to the first, of which they are an elaborated form, only allow their true nature to appear very imperfectly. The psychological gap between the cause and the effect, between the apparent cause and the effective cause, has become more considerable and more difficult for the mind to leap. The remainder of this book will be an illustration and a verification of this remark on method. It will be seen how, in the primitive religions, the religious fact still visibly carries the mark of its origins; it would have been well-nigh impossible to infer them merely from the study of the more developed religions.

The study which we are undertaking is therefore a way of taking up again, *but under new conditions*, the old problem of the origin of religion. To be sure, if by origin we are to understand the very first beginning, the question has nothing scientific about it, and should be resolutely discarded. There was no given moment when religion began to exist, and there is consequently no need of finding a means of transporting ourselves thither in thought.

Like every human institution, religion did not commence anywhere. There-fore, all speculations of this sort are justly discredited; they can only con-sist in subjective and arbitrary constructions which are subject to no sort of control. But the problem which we raise is quite another one. What we want to do is to find a means of discerning the ever-present causes upon which the most essential forms of religious thought and practice depend. Now for the reasons which were just set forth, these causes are proportiona-nately more easily observable as the societies where they are observed are less complicated. That is why we try to get as near as possible to the origins.[3] It is not that we ascribe particular virtues to the lower religions. On the contrary, they are rudimentary and gross; we cannot make of them a sort of model which later religions only have to reproduce. But even their grossness makes them instructive, for they thus become convenient for experiments, as in them, the facts and their relations are easily seen. In order to discover the laws of the phenomena which he studies, the physi-cist tries to simplify these latter and rid them of their secondary charac-teristics. For that which concerns institutions, nature spontaneously makes the same sort of simplifications at the beginning of history. We merely wish to put these to profit. Undoubtedly we can only touch very elementary facts by this method. When we shall have accounted for them as far as possible, the novelties of every sort which have been produced in the course of evolution will not yet be explained. But while we do not dream of denying the importance of the problems thus raised, we think that they will profit by being treated in their turn, and that it is important to take them up only after those of which we are going to undertake the study at present. [...]

'Definition of religious phenomena and of religion'[4]

If we are going to look for the most primitive and simple religion which we can observe, it is necessary to begin by defining what is meant by a religion; for without this, we would run the risk of giving the name to a system of ideas and practices which has nothing at all religious about it, or else of leaving to one side many religious facts, without perceiving their true nature. That this is not an imaginary danger, and that nothing is thus sacrificed to a vain formalism of method, is well shown by the fact that owing to his not having taken this precaution, a certain scholar to whom the science of comparative religions owes a great deal, Professor Frazer, has not been able to recognize the profoundly religious character of the beliefs and rites which will be studied below, where, according to our view, the initial germ of the religious life of humanity is to be found. So this is a prejudicial question, which must be treated before all others.

It is not that we dream of arriving at once at the profound characteristics which really explain religion: these can be determined only at the end of our study. But that which is necessary and possible, is to indicate a certain number of external and easily recognizable signs, which will enable us to recognize religious phenomena wherever they are met with, and which will deter us from confounding them with others. We shall proceed to this preliminary operation at once.

But to attain the desired results, it is necessary to begin by freeing the mind of every preconceived idea. Men have been obliged to make for themselves a notion of what religion is, long before the science of religions started its methodical comparisons. The necessities of existence force all of us, believers and non-believers, to represent in some way these things in the midst of which we live, upon which we must pass judgment constantly, and which we must take into account in all our conduct. However, since these preconceived ideas are formed without any method, according to the circumstances and chances of life, they have no right to any credit whatsoever, and must be rigorously set aside in the examination which is to follow. It is not from our prejudices, passions or habits that we should demand the elements of the definition which we must have; it is from the reality itself which we are going to define.

Let us set ourselves before this reality. Leaving aside all conceptions of religion in general, let us consider the various religions in their concrete reality, and attempt to disengage that which they have in common; for religion cannot be defined except by the characteristics which are found wherever religion itself is found. In this comparison, then, we shall make use of all the religious systems which we can know, those of the present and those of the past, the most primitive and simple as well as the most recent and refined; for we have neither the right nor the logical means of excluding some and retaining others. For those who regard religion as only a natural manifestation of human activity, all religions, without any exception whatsoever, are instructive; for all, after their manner, express man, and thus can aid us in better understanding this aspect of our nature. Also, we have seen how far it is from being the best way of studying religion to consider by preference the forms which it presents among the most civilized peoples.[5]

But to aid the mind in freeing itself from these usual conceptions which, owing to their prestige, might prevent it from seeing things as they really are, it is fitting to examine some of the most current of the definitions in which these prejudices are commonly expressed, before taking up the question on our own account.

One idea which generally passes as characteristic of all that is religious, is that of the supernatural. By this is understood all sorts of things which surpass the limits of our knowledge; the supernatural is the world of the mysterious, of the unknowable, of the un-understandable. Thus religion would be a sort of speculation upon all that which evades science or distinct thought in general. 'Religions diametrically opposed in their overt dogmas', said Spencer, 'are perfectly at one in the tacit conviction that the existence of the world, with all it contains and all which surrounds it, is a mystery calling for an explanation'; he thus makes them consist essentially in 'the belief in the omnipresence of something which is inscrutable'.[6] In the same manner, Max Müller sees in religion 'a struggle to conceive the inconceivable, to utter the unutterable, a longing after the Infinite'.[7]

It is certain that the sentiment of mystery has not been without a considerable importance in certain religions, notably in Christianity. It must also be said that the importance of this sentiment has varied remarkably at different moments in the history of Christianity. There are periods when this notion passes to an inferior place, and is even effaced. For example, for the Christians of the seventeenth century, dogma had nothing disturbing for the reason; faith reconciled itself easily with science and philosophy, and the thinkers, such as Pascal, who really felt that there is something profoundly obscure in things, were so little in harmony with their age that they remained misunderstood by their contemporaries.[8] It would appear somewhat hasty, therefore, to make an idea subject to parallel eclipses, the essential element of even the Christian religion.

In all events, it is certain that this idea does not appear until late in the history of religions; it is completely foreign, not only to those peoples who are called primitive, but also to all others who have not attained a considerable degree of intellectual culture.

[...]

These definitions set aside, let us set ourselves before the problem.

First of all, let us remark that in all these formulae it is the nature of religion as a whole that they seek to express. They proceed as if it were a sort of indivisible entity, while, as a matter of fact, it is made up of parts; it is a more or less complex system of myths, dogmas, rites and ceremonies. Now a whole cannot be defined except in relation to its parts. It will be more methodical, then, to try to characterize the various elementary phenomena of which all religions are made up, before we attack the system produced by their union. This method is imposed still more forcibly by the fact that there are religious phenomena which belong to no determined religion. Such are those phenomena which constitute the matter of folklore. In general, they are the debris of passed religions, inorganized survivals; but there are some which have been formed spontaneously under the influence of local causes. In our European countries Christianity has forced itself to absorb and assimilate them; it has given them a Christian colouring. Nevertheless, there are many which have persisted up until a recent date, or which still exist with a relative autonomy: celebrations of May Day, the summer solstice or the carnival, beliefs relative to genii, local demons, etc., are cases in point. If the religious character of these facts is now diminishing, their religious importance is nevertheless so great that they have enabled Mannhardt and his school to revive the science of religions. A definition which did not take account of them would not cover all that is religious.

Religious phenomena are naturally arranged in two fundamental categories: beliefs and rites. The first are states of opinion, and consist in representations; the second are determined modes of action. Between these two classes of facts there is all the difference which separates thought from action.

The rites can be defined and distinguished from other human practices, moral practices, for example, only by the special nature of their object. A moral rule prescribes certain manners of acting to us, just as a rite does, but which are addressed to a different class of objects. So it is the object of the rite which must be characterized, if we are to characterize the rite itself. Now it is in the beliefs that the special nature of this object is expressed. It is possible to define the rite only after we have defined the belief.

All known religious beliefs, whether simple or complex, present one common characteristic: they presuppose a classification of all the things, real and ideal, of which men think, into two classes or opposed groups, generally designated by two distinct terms which are translated well enough by the words *profane* and *sacred (profane, sacré)*. This division of the world into two domains, the one containing all that is sacred, the other all that is profane, is the distinctive trait of religious thought; the beliefs, myths, dogmas and legends are either representations or systems of representations which express the nature of sacred things, the virtues and powers which are attributed to them, or their relations with each other and with profane things. But by sacred things one must not understand simply those personal beings which are called gods or spirits; a rock, a tree, a spring, a pebble, a piece of wood, a house, in a word, anything can be sacred. A rite can have this character; in fact, the rite does not exist which does not have it to a certain degree. There are words, expressions and formulae which can be pronounced only by the mouths of consecrated persons; there are gestures and movements which everybody cannot perform. If the Vedic sacrifice has had such an efficacy that, according to mythology, it was the creator of the gods, and not merely a means of winning their favour, it is because it possessed a virtue comparable to that of the most sacred beings. The circle of sacred objects cannot be determined, then, once for all. Its extent varies infinitely, according to the different religions. That is how Buddhism is a religion: in default of gods, it admits the existence of sacred things, namely, the four noble truths and the practices derived from them.[9]

Up to the present we have confined ourselves to enumerating a certain number of sacred things as examples: we must now show by what general characteristics they are to be distinguished from profane things.

One might be tempted, first of all, to define them by the place they are generally assigned in the hierarchy of things. They are naturally considered superior in dignity and power to profane things, and particularly to man, when he is only a man and has nothing sacred about him. One thinks of himself as occupying an inferior and dependent position in relation to them; and surely this conception is not without some truth. Only there is nothing in it which is really characteristic of the sacred. It is not enough that one thing be subordinated to another for the second to be sacred in regard to the first. Slaves are inferior to their masters, subjects to their king, soldiers to their leaders, the miser to his gold, the man ambitious for power to the hands which keep it from him; but if it is sometimes said of a man that he makes a religion of those beings or things whose eminent value and superiority to himself he thus recognizes, it is clear that in any case the word is taken in a metaphorical sense, and that there is nothing in these relations which is really religious.[10]

On the other hand, it must not be lost to view that there are sacred things of every degree, and that there are some in relation to which a man feels himself relatively at his ease. An amulet has a sacred character, yet the respect which it inspires is nothing exceptional. Even before his gods, a man is not always in such a marked state of inferiority; for it very frequently happens that he exercises a veritable physical constraint upon them to obtain what he desires. He beats the fetich with which he is not contented, but only to reconcile himself with it again, if in the end it shows itself more docile to the wishes of its adorer.[11] To have rain, he throws stones into the spring or sacred lake where the god of rain is thought to reside; he believes that by this means he forces him to come out and show himself.[12] Moreover, if it is true that man depends upon his gods, this dependence is reciprocal. The gods also have need of man; without offerings and sacrifices they would die. We shall even have occasion to show that this dependence of the gods upon their worshippers is maintained even in the most idealistic religions.

But if a purely hierarchic distinction is a criterium at once too general and too imprecise, there is nothing left with which to characterize the sacred in its relation to the profane except their heterogeneity. However, this heterogeneity is sufficient to characterize this classification of things and to distinguish it from all others, because it is very particular: *it is absolute.*

In all the history of human thought there exists no other example of two categories of things so profoundly differentiated or so radically opposed to one another. The traditional opposition of good and bad is nothing beside this; for the good and the bad are only two opposed species of the same class, namely morals, just as sickness and health are two different aspects of the same order of facts, life, while the sacred and the profane have always and everywhere been conceived by the human mind as two distinct classes, as two worlds between which there is nothing in common. The forces which play in one are not simply those which are met with in the other, but a little stronger; they are of a different sort. In different religions, this opposition has been conceived in different ways. Here, to separate these two sorts of things, it has seemed sufficient to localize them in different parts of the physical universe; there, the first have been put into an ideal and transcendental world, while the material world is left in full possession of the others. But howsoever much the forms of the contrast may vary,[13] the fact of the contrast is universal.

This is not equivalent to saying that a being can never pass from one of these worlds into the other: but the manner in which this passage is effected, when it does take place, puts into relief the essential duality of the two kingdoms. In fact, it implies a veritable metamorphosis. This is notably demonstrated by the initiation rites, such as they are practised by a multitude of peoples. This initiation is a long series of ceremonies with the object of introducing the young man into the religious life: for the first time, he leaves the purely profane world where he passed his first infancy, and enters into the world of sacred things. Now this change of state is thought of, not as a simple and regular development of pre-existent germs, but as a transformation *totius substantiae* – of the whole being. It is said that at this moment the young man dies, that the person that he was ceases to exist, and that another is instantly substituted for it. He is re-born under a new form. Appropriate ceremonies are felt to bring about this death and re-birth, which are not understood in a merely symbolic sense, but are taken literally.[14] Does this not prove that between the profane being which he was and the religious being which he becomes, there is a break of continuity?

This heterogeneity is even so complete that it frequently degenerates into a veritable antagonism. The two worlds are not only conceived of as separate, but as even hostile and jealous rivals of each other. Since men cannot fully belong to one except on condition of leaving the other completely, they are exhorted to withdraw themselves completely from the profane world, in order to lead an exclusively religious life. Hence comes the monasticism which is artificially organized outside of and apart from the natural environment in which the ordinary man leads the life of this world, in a

different one, closed to the first, and nearly its contrary. Hence comes
the mystic asceticism whose object is to root out from man all the attachment for the profane world that remains in him. From that come all the
forms of religious suicide, the logical working-out of this asceticism;
for the only manner of fully escaping the profane life is, after all, to forsake
all life.

The opposition of these two classes manifests itself outwardly with a
visible sign by which we can easily recognize this very special classification,
wherever it exists. Since the idea of the sacred is always and everywhere
separated from the idea of the profane in the thought of men, and since
we picture a sort of logical chasm between the two, the mind irresistibly
refuses to allow the two corresponding things to be confounded, or even
to be merely put in contact with each other; for such a promiscuity, or
even too direct a contiguity, would contradict too violently the dissociation
of these ideas in the mind. The sacred thing is *par excellence* that which
the profane should not touch, and cannot touch with impunity. To be sure,
this interdiction cannot go so far as to make all communication between
the two worlds impossible; for if the profane could in no way enter into
relations with the sacred, this latter could be good for nothing. But, in
addition to the fact that this establishment of relations is always a delicate
operation in itself, demanding great precautions and a more or less complicated initiation,[15] it is quite impossible, unless the profane is to lose its
specific characteristics and become sacred after a fashion and to a certain
degree itself. The two classes cannot even approach each other and keep
their own nature at the same time.

Thus we arrive at the first criterium of religious beliefs. Undoubtedly
there are secondary species within these two fundamental classes which,
in their turn, are more or less incompatible with each other.[16] But the real
characteristic of religious phenomena is that they always suppose a bipar-
tite division of the whole universe, known and knowable, into two classes
which embrace all that exists, but which radically exclude each other.
Sacred things are those which the interdictions protect and isolate; profane
things, those to which these interdictions are applied and which must
remain at a distance from the first. Religious beliefs are the representations
which express the nature of sacred things and the relations which they
sustain, either with each other or with profane things. Finally, rites are
the rules of conduct which prescribe how a man should comport himself
in the presence of these sacred objects.

When a certain number of sacred things sustain relations of co-ordination
or subordination with each other in such a way as to form a system having
a certain unity, but which is not comprised within any other system of
the same sort, the totality of these beliefs and their corresponding rites

constitutes a religion. From this definition it is seen that a religion is not necessarily contained within one sole and single idea, and does not proceed from one unique principle which, though varying according to the circumstances under which it is applied, is nevertheless at bottom always the same: it is rather a whole made up of distinct and relatively individualized parts. Each homogeneous group of sacred things, or even each sacred thing of some importance, constitutes a centre of organization about which gravitate a group of beliefs and rites, or a particular cult; there is no religion, howsoever unified it may be, which does not recognize a plurality of sacred things. Even Christianity, at least in its Catholic form, admits, in addition to the divine personality which, incidentally, is triple as well as one, the Virgin, angels, saints, souls of the dead, etc. Thus a religion cannot be reduced to one single cult generally, but rather consists in a system of cults, each endowed with a certain autonomy. Also, this autonomy is variable. Sometimes they are arranged in a hierarchy, and subordinated to some predominating cult, into which they are finally absorbed; but sometimes, also, they are merely rearranged and united. The religion which we are going to study will furnish us with an example of just this latter sort of organization.

At the same time we find the explanation of how there can be groups of religious phenomena which do not belong to any special religion; it is because they have not been, or are no longer, a part of any religious system. If, for some special reason, one of the cults of which we just spoke happens to be maintained while the group of which it was a part disappears, it survives only in a disintegrated condition. That is what has happened to many agrarian cults which have survived themselves as folk-lore. In certain cases, it is not even a cult, but a simple ceremony or particular rite which persists in this way.[17]

Although this definition is only preliminary, it permits us to see in what terms the problem which necessarily dominates the science of religions should be stated. When we believed that sacred beings could be distinguished from others merely by the greater intensity of the powers attributed to them, the question of how men came to imagine them was sufficiently simple: it was enough to demand which forces had, because of their exceptional energy, been able to strike the human imagination forcefully enough to inspire religious sentiments. But if, as we have sought to establish, sacred things differ in nature from profane things, if they have a wholly different essence, then the problem is more complex. For we must first of all ask what has been able to lead men to see in the world two heterogeneous and incompatible worlds, though nothing in sensible experience seems able to suggest the idea of so radical a duality to them.

[...]

There still remain those contemporary aspirations towards a religion which would consist entirely in internal and subjective states, and which would be constructed freely by each of us. But howsoever real these aspirations may be, they cannot affect our definition, for this is to be applied only to facts already realized, and not to uncertain possibilities. One can define religions such as they are, or such as they have been, but not such as they more or less vaguely tend to become. It is possible that this religious individualism is destined to be realized in facts; but before we can say just how far this may be the case, we must first know what religion is, of what elements it is made up, from what causes it results, and what function it fulfils – all questions whose solution cannot be foreseen before the threshold of our study has been passed. It is only at the close of this study that we can attempt to anticipate the future.

Thus we arrive at the following definition: *A religion is a unified system of beliefs and practices relative to sacred things, that is to say, things set apart and forbidden – beliefs and practices which unite into one single moral community called a Church, all those who adhere to them.* The second element which thus finds a place in our definition is no less essential than the first; for by showing that the idea of religion is inseparable from that of the Church, it makes it clear that religion should be an eminently collective thing.[18]

Naturism and animism

Armed with this definition we are now able to set out in search of this elementary religion which we propose to study.

Even the crudest religions with which history and ethnology make us acquainted are already of a complexity which corresponds badly with the idea sometimes held of primitive mentality. One finds there not only a confused system of beliefs and rites, but also such a plurality of different principles, and such a richness of essential notions, that it seems impossible to see in them anything but the late product of a rather long evolution. Hence it has been concluded that to discover the truly original form of the religious life, it is necessary to descend by analysis beyond these observable religions, to resolve them into their common and fundamental elements, and then to seek among these latter some one from which the others were derived.

To the problem thus stated, two contrary solutions have been given.

There is no religious system, ancient or recent, where one does not meet, under different forms, two religions, as it were, side by side, which, though being united closely and mutually penetrating each other, do not cease, nevertheless, to be distinct. The one addresses itself to the phenomena of nature, either the great cosmic forces, such as winds, rivers, stars or the sky, etc., or else the objects of various sorts which cover the surface of the earth, such as plants, animals, rocks, etc.; for this reason it has been given the name of *naturism*. The other has spiritual beings as its object, spirits, souls, geniuses, demons, divinities properly so-called, animated and conscious agents like man, but distinguished from him, nevertheless, by the nature of their powers and especially by the peculiar characteristic that they do not affect the senses in the same way: ordinarily they are not visible to human eyes. This religion of spirit is called *animism*. Now, to explain the universal coexistence of these two sorts of cults, two contradictory theories have been proposed. For some, animism is the primitive religion, of which naturism is only a secondary and derived form. For the others, on the contrary, it is the nature cult which was the point of departure for religious evolution; the cult of spirits is only a peculiar case of that.

These two theories are, up to the present, the only ones by which the attempt has been made to explain rationally[19] the origins of religious thought. Thus the capital problem raised by the history of religions is generally reduced to asking which of these two solutions should be chosen, or whether it is not better to combine them, and in that case, what place must be given to each of the two elements.[20] Even those scholars who do not admit either of these hypotheses in their systematic form, do not refuse to retain certain propositions upon which they rest.[21] Thus we have a certain number of theories already made, which must be submitted to criticism before we take up the study of the facts for ourselves. It will be better understood how indispensable it is to attempt a new one, when we have seen the insufficiency of these traditional conceptions.

[. . .]

'Totemism as an elementary religion'

Howsoever opposed their conclusions may seem to be, the two systems which we have just studied agree upon one essential point: they state the problem in identical terms. Both undertake to construct the idea of the divine out of the sensations aroused in us by certain natural phenomena, either physical or biological. For the animists it is dreams, for the naturists, certain cosmic phenomena, which served as the point of departure for religious evolution. But for both, it is in the nature, either of man or of the universe, that we must look for the germ of the grand opposition which separates the profane from the sacred.

But such an enterprise is impossible: it supposes a veritable creation *ex nihilo*. A fact of common experience cannot give us the idea of something whose characteristic is to be outside the world of common experience. A man, as he appears to himself in his dreams, is only a man. Natural forces, as our senses perceive them, are only natural forces, howsoever great their intensity may be. Hence comes the common criticism which we address to both doctrines. In order to explain how these pretended data of religious thought have been able to take a sacred character which has no objective foundation, it would be necessary to admit that a whole world of delusive representations has superimposed itself upon the other, denatured it to the point of making it unrecognizable, and substituted a pure hallucination for reality. Here, it is the illusions of the dream which brought about this transfiguration; there, it is the brilliant and vain company of images evoked by the word. But in one case as in the other, it is necessary to regard religion as the product of a delirious imagination.

Thus one positive conclusion is arrived at as the result of this critical examination. Since neither man nor nature have of themselves a sacred character, they must get it from another source. Aside from the human individual and the physical world, there should be some other reality, in relation to which this variety of delirium which all religion is in a sense, has a significance and an objective value. In other words, beyond those which we have called animistic and naturistic, there should be another sort of cult, more fundamental and more primitive, of which the first are only derived forms or particular aspects.

In fact, this cult does exist: it is the one to which ethnologists have given the name of totemism.

[...]

From this historical résumé it is clear that Australia is the most favourable field for the study of totemism, and therefore we shall make it the principal area of our observations.

In his *Totemism*, Frazer sought especially to collect all the traces of totemism which could be found in history or ethnography. He was thus led to include in his study societies, the nature and degree of whose culture differs most widely: ancient Egypt,[22] Arabia and Greece,[23] and the southern Slavs[24] are found there, side by side with the tribes of Australia and America. This manner of procedure is not at all surprising for a disciple of the anthropological school. For this school does not seek to locate religions in the social environments of which they are a part,[25] and to differentiate them according to the different environments to which they are thus connected. But rather, as is indicated by the name which it has taken to itself, its purpose is to go beyond the national and historical differences to the universal and really human bases of the religious life. It is supposed that man has a religious nature of himself, in virtue of his own constitution, and independently of all social conditions, and they propose to study this.[26] For researches of this sort, all peoples can be called upon equally well. It is true that they prefer the more primitive peoples, because this fundamental nature is more apt to be unaltered here; but since it is found equally well among the most civilized peoples, it is but natural that they too should be called as witnesses. Consequently, all those who pass as being not too far removed from the origins, and who are confusedly lumped together under the rather imprecise rubric of *savages*, are put on the same plane and consulted indifferently. Since from this point of view, facts have an interest only in proportion to their generality, they consider themselves obliged to collect as large a number as possible of them; the circle of comparisons could not become too large.

Our method will not be such a one, for several reasons.

In the first place, for the sociologist as for the historian, social facts vary with the social system of which they form a part; they cannot be understood when detached from it. This is why two facts which come from two different societies cannot be profitably compared merely because they seem to resemble each other; it is necessary that these societies themselves resemble each other, that is to say, that they be only varieties of the same species. The comparative method would be impossible, if social types did not exist, and it cannot be usefully applied except within a single type. What errors have not been committed for having neglected this precept! It is thus that facts have been unduly connected with each other which, in spite of exterior resemblances, really have neither the same sense nor the same importance: the primitive democracy and that of to-day, the collectivism of inferior societies and actual socialistic tendencies, the monogamy which is frequent in Australian tribes and that sanctioned by our laws, etc. Even in the work of Frazer such confusions are found. It frequently happens that he assimilates simple rites of wild-animal-worship to practices that are really totemic, though the distance, sometimes very great, which separates the two social systems would exclude all idea of assimilation. Then if we do not wish to fall into these same errors, instead of scattering our researches over all the societies possible, we must concentrate them upon one clearly determined type.

It is even necessary that this concentration be as close as possible. One cannot usefully compare facts with which he is not perfectly well acquainted. But when he undertakes to include all sorts of societies and civilizations, one cannot know any of them with the necessary thoroughness; when he assembles facts from every country in order to compare them, he is obliged to take them hastily, without having either the means or the time to carefully criticize them. Tumultuous and summary comparisons result, which discredit the comparative method with many intelligent persons. It can give serious results only when it is applied to so limited a number of societies that each of them can be studied with sufficient precision. The essential thing is to choose those where investigations have the greatest chance to be fruitful.

Also, the value of the facts is much more important than their number. In our eyes, the question whether totemism has been more or less universal or not, is quite secondary.[27] If it interests us, it does so before all because in studying it we hope to discover relations of a nature to make us understand better what religion is. Now to establish these relations it is neither necessary nor always useful to heap up numerous experiences upon each other; it is much more important to have a few that are well studied and really significant. One single fact may make a law appear, where a multitude of imprecise and vague observations would only produce confusion. In every science, the scholar would be overwhelmed by the facts which present themselves to him, if he did not make a choice among them. It is necessary that he distinguish those which promise to be the most instructive, that he concentrate his attention upon these, and that he temporarily leave the others to one side.

That is why, with one reservation which will be indicated below, we propose to limit our research to Australian societies. They fulfil all the conditions which were just enumerated. They are perfectly homogeneous, for though it is possible to distinguish varieties among them, they all belong to one common type. This homogeneity is even so great that the forms of social organization are not only the same, but that they are even designated by identical or equivalent names in a multitude of tribes, sometimes very distant from each other.[28] Also, Australian totemism is the variety for which our documents are the most complete. Finally, that which we propose to study in this work is the most primitive and simple religion which it is possible to find. It is therefore natural that to discover it, we address ourselves to societies as slightly evolved as possible, for it is evidently there that we have the greatest chance of finding it and studying it well. Now there are no societies which present this characteristic to a higher degree than the Australian ones. Not only is their civilization most rudimentary – the house and even the hut are still unknown – but also their organization is the most primitive and simple which is actually known; it is that which we have elsewhere called *organization on a basis of clans*.[29] In the next chapter, we shall have occasion to restate its essential traits.

However, though making Australia the principal field of our research, we think it best not to leave completely aside the societies where totemism was first discovered, that is to say, the Indian tribes of North America.

This extension of the field of comparison has nothing about it which is not legitimate. Undoubtedly these people are more advanced than those of Australia. Their civilization has become much more advanced: men there live in houses or under tents, and there are even fortified villages. The size of the society is much greater, and centralization, which is completely lacking in Australia, is beginning to appear there; we find vast confederations, such as that of the Iroquois, under one central authority. Sometimes a complicated system of differentiated classes arranged in a hierarchy is found. However, the essential lines of the social structure remain the same as those in Australia; it is always the organization on a basis of clans. Thus we are not in the presence of two different types, but of two varieties of a single type, which are still very close to each other. They represent two successive moments of a single evolution, so their homogeneousness is still great enough to permit comparisons.

Also, these comparisons may have their utility. Just because their civilization is more advanced than that of the Australians, certain phases of the social organization which is common to both can be studied more easily among the first than among the second. As long as men are still making their first steps in the art of expressing their thought, it is not easy for the observer to perceive that which moves them; for there is nothing to translate clearly that which passes in these obscure minds which have only a confused and ephemeral knowledge of themselves. For example, religious symbols then consist only in formless combinations of lines and colours, whose sense it is not easy to divine, as we shall see. There are many gestures and movements by which interior states express themselves; but being essentially ephemeral, they readily elude observation. That is why totemism was discovered earlier in America than in Australia; it was much more visible there, though it held relatively less place in the totality of the religious life. Also, wherever beliefs and institutions do not take a somewhat definite material form, they are more liable to change under the influence of the slightest circumstances, or to become wholly effaced from the memory. Thus the Australian clans frequently have something floating and Protean about them, while the corresponding organization in America has a greater stability and more clearly defined contours. Thus, though American totemism is further removed from its origins than that of Australia, still there are important characteristics of which it has better kept the memory.

In the second place, in order to understand an institution, it is frequently well to follow it into the advanced stages of its evolution:[30] for sometimes it is only when it is fully developed that its real signification appears with the greatest clearness. In this way also, American totemism, since it has a long history behind it, could serve to clarify certain aspects of Australian totemism.[31] At the same time, it will put us in a better condition to see how totemism is bound up with the forms which follow, and to mark its place in the general historical development of religion.

So in the discussions which follow, we shall not forbid ourselves the use of certain facts borrowed from the Indian societies of North America. But we are not going to study American totemism here;[32] such a study must be made directly and by itself, and cannot be mixed with the one which we are undertaking; it raises other problems and implies a wholly different set of special investigations. We shall have recourse to American facts merely in a supplementary way, and only when they seem to be able to make us understand Australian facts to advantage. It is these latter which constitute the real and immediate object of our researches.[33]

NOTES

1. In the same way, we shall say of these societies that they are primitive, and we shall call the men of these societies primitives. Undoubtedly the expression lacks precision, but that is hardly evitable, and besides, when we have taken pains to fix the meaning, it is not inconvenient.

2. But that is not equivalent to saying that all luxury is lacking to the primitive cults. On the contrary, we shall see that in every religion there are beliefs and practices which do not aim at strictly utilitarian ends (Book III, ch. 4, § 2). This luxury is indispensable to the religious life; it is at its very heart. But it is much more rudimentary in the inferior religions than in the others, so we are better able to determine its reason for existence here.

3. It is seen that we give a wholly relative sense to this word '*origins*', just as to the word '*primitive*'. By it we do not mean an absolute beginning, but the most simple social condition that is actually known or that beyond which we cannot go at present. When we speak of the origins or of the commencement of religious history or thought, it is in this sense that our statements should be understood.

4. We have already attempted to define religious phenomena in a paper which was published in the *Année Sociologique* (Vol. II, pp. 1 ff.). The definition then given differs, as will be seen, from the one we give to-day. At the end of this chapter [See note 18], we shall explain the reasons which have led us to these modifications, but which imply no essential change in the conception of the facts.

5. See above [. . .]. We shall say nothing more upon the necessity of these preliminary definitions nor upon the method to be followed to attain them. That is exposed in our *Règles de la Méthode sociologique*, pp. 43 ff. Cf. *Le Suicide*, pp. 1 ff. (Paris, F. Alcan).

6. *First Principles*, p. 37.

7. *Introduction to the Science of Religions*, p. 18. Cf. *Origin and Development of Religion*, p. 23.

8. This same frame of mind is also found in the scholastic period, as is witnessed by the formula with which philosophy was defined at this time: *Fides quaerens intellectum*.

9. Not to mention the sage and the saint who practise these truths and who for that reason are sacred.

10. This is not saying that these relations cannot take a religious character. But they do not do so necessarily.

11. Schultze, *Fetischismus*, p. 129.

12. Examples of these usages will be found in Frazer, *Golden Bough*, 2nd ed. I, pp. 81 ff.

13. The conception according to which the profane is opposed to the sacred, just as the irrational is to the rational, or the intelligible is to the mysterious, is only one of the forms under which this opposition is expressed. Science being once constituted, it has taken a profane character, especially in the eyes of the

Christian religions; from that it appears as though it could not be applied to sacred things.

14. See Frazer, 'On some ceremonies of the Central Australian tribes' in *Australian Association for the Advancement of Science*, 1901, pp. 313 ff. This conception is also of an extreme generality. In India, the simple participation in the sacrificial act has the same effects; the sacrificer, by the mere act of entering within the circle of sacred things, changes his personality. (See, Hubert and Mauss, *Essai sur le Sacrifice* in the *Année Sociologique*, II, p. 101.)

15. See what was said of the initiation above [. . .].

16. We shall point out below how, for example, certain species of sacred things exist, between which there is an incompatibility as all-exclusive as that between the sacred and the profane (Bk. III, ch. V, § 4).

17. This is the case with certain marriage and funeral rites, for example.

18. It is by this that our present definition is connected to the one we have already proposed in the *Année Sociologique*. In this other work, we defined religious beliefs exclusively by their obligatory character; but, as we shall show, this obligation evidently comes from the fact that these beliefs are the possession of a group which imposes them upon its members. The two definitions are thus in a large part the same. If we have thought it best to propose a new one, it is because the first was too formal, and neglected the contents of the religious representations too much. It will be seen, in the discussions which follow, how important it is to put this characteristic into evidence at once. Moreover, if their imperative character is really a distinctive trait of religious beliefs, it allows of an infinite number of degrees; consequently there are even cases where it is not easily perceptible. Hence come difficulties and embarrassments which are avoided by substituting for this criterium the one we now employ.

19. We thus leave aside here those theories which, in whole or in part, make use of super-experimental data. This is the case with the theory which Andrew Lang exposed in his book, *The Making of Religion*, and which Father Schmidt has taken up again, with variations of detail, in a series of articles on *The Origin of the Idea of God* (*Anthropos*, 1908, 1909). Lang does not set animism definitely aside, but in the last analysis, he admits a sense or intuition of the divine directly. Also, if we do not consider it necessary to expose and discuss this conception in the present chapter, we do not intend to pass it over in silence; we shall come to it again below, when we shall ourselves explain the facts upon which it is founded (Bk. II, ch. IX, § 4).

20. This is the case, for example, of *Fustel de Coulanges* who accepts the two conceptions together *(The Ancient City*, Bk. I and Bk. III, ch. II).

21. This is the case with Jevons, who criticizes the animism taught by Tylor, but accepts his theories on the origin of the idea of the soul and the anthropomorphic instinct of man. Inversely, Usener, in his *Götternamen*, rejects certain hypotheses of Max Müller which will be described below, but admits the principal postulates of naturism.

22. *Totemism*, p. 12.

23. *Ibid.*, p. 15.

24. *Ibid.*, p. 32.

25. It should be noted that in this connection, the more recent work, *Totemism and Exogamy*, shows an important progress in the thought as well as the method of Frazer. Every time that he describes the religious or domestic institutions of a tribe, he sets himself to determine the geographic and social conditions in which this tribe is placed. Howsoever summary these analyses may be, they

bear witness nevertheless to a rupture with the old methods of the anthropological school.

26. Undoubtedly we also consider that the principal object of the science of religions is to find out what the religious nature of man really consists in. However, as we do not regard it as a part of his constitutional make-up, but rather as the product of social causes, we consider it impossible to find it, if we leave aside his social environment.

27. We cannot repeat too frequently that the importance which we attach to totemism is absolutely independent of whether it was ever universal or not.

28. This is the case with the phratries and matrimonial classes; on this point, see Spencer and Gillen, *Northern Tribes*, ch. III; Howitt, *Native Tribes*, pp. 109 and 137–142; Thomas, *Kinship and Marriage in Australia*, ch. VI and VII.

29. *Division du Travail social*, 3rd ed., p. 150.

30. It is to be understood that this is not always the case. It frequently happens, as we have already said, that the simpler forms aid to a better understanding of the more complex. On this point, there is no rule of method which is applicable to every possible case.

31. Thus the individual totemism of America will aid us in understanding the function and importance of that in Australia. As the latter is very rudimentary, it would probably have passed unobserved.

32. Besides, there is not one unique type of totemism in America, but several different species which must be distinguished.

33. We shall leave this field only very exceptionally, and when a particularly instructive comparison seems to us to impose itself.

Marcel Mauss

Marcel Mauss was born in 1873 in Epinal, France, where he received his primary and secondary school education. He studied at the University of Bordeaux, where he worked under Emile Durkheim who was his uncle. Having passed the *agrégation* examination, he did not accept a post which was offered to him at the University of Bordeaux, but pursued his studies in Paris. There he studied Sanskrit and ancient Indian religion and civilization with Alfred Foucher and Sylvain Lévi, and worked on Indo-European comparative linguistics with Antoine Meillet. He was a close collaborator of Durkheim and published regularly in the *Année Sociologique*, where he worked together with Henri Hubert and Robert Hertz. In 1901 Mauss was appointed *Directeur d'Études* at the *École Pratique des Hautes Études* for the history of religions of non-civilized people and played a leading role in various scholarly societies in the fields of the social sciences. Between 1926 and 1939 he lectured at the *Institut d'Ethnologie* of the University of Paris. In 1931 he became a professor at the *Collège de France* but had to go into retirement in 1940. He died in 1950.

Three books of Mauss are available in English translation: 1954 *The Gift: Forms and Functions of Exchange in Archaic Societies* (French original of 1925); 1963 *Primitive Classification* (together with Emile Durkheim; the French original appeared in 1903); 1964 *Sacrifice: its Nature and Function* (together with Henri Hubert; the French original appeared in 1899).

Mauss developed his methodology in order to study religions and other facts as 'total social phenomena', stressing the indissoluble link which exists between all expressions of a society at a given time. He did not oppose the individual and his society to each othe.', but showed their interconnections. Opposing himself against an evolutionist view of religion, he wanted to develop a sociology of beliefs, values and knowledge systems as being part of 'total social phenomena'.

The following text has been chosen from an early work of Mauss which he wrote together with Durkheim, *Primitive Classification*. He contends that like other aspects of society, also the categories of classification and of knowledge, including the religious ones, depend on the organization of a given society.

CLASSIFICATION SYSTEMS AND RELIGION

China is not the only civilized country where we find at least traces of a classification recalling those observed in simpler societies.

First of all, we have just seen that the Chinese classification was essentially an instrument of divination. Now the divinatory methods of Greece are remarkably similar to the Chinese, and the similarities denote procedures of the same nature in the way fundamental ideas are classified.[1] The assignment of elements and metals to the planets is a Greek, perhaps Chaldaean, fact, as much as a Chinese. Mars is fire, Saturn is water, etc.[2] The relation between certain sorts of events and certain planets, the simultaneous apprehension of space and time, the particular correspondence of a certain region with a certain time of the year and with a certain kind of undertaking, are found equally in both these different societies.[3] A still more curious coincidence is that which allows a relationship to be established between Chinese and Greek astrology and physiognomy, and perhaps with the Egyptian. The Greek theory of zodiacal and planetary melothesia, which is thought to be of Egyptian origin,[4] is intended to establish strict correspondences between certain parts of the body and certain positions of the stars, certain orientations, and certain events. Now in China also there exists a famous doctrine based on the same principle. Each element is related to a cardinal point, a constellation, and a particular colour, and these different groups of things are thought to correspond, in turn, to diverse kinds of organs, inhabited by various souls, to emotions, and to different parts whose reunion forms 'the natural character'. Thus, *yang*, the male principle of light and sky, has the liver in the viscera, the bladder as mansion, and the ears and sphincters among the orifices.[5] This theory, the generality of which is apparent, is not of mere curiosity-value; it implies a certain way of conceiving things. By it, the universe is in fact referred to the individual; things are expressed by it, in a sense, as functions of the living organism; this is really a theory of the microcosm.

There is nothing more natural, moreover, than the relation thus expressed between divination and the classification of things. Every divinatory rite, however simple it may be, rests on a pre-existing sympathy between certain beings, and on a traditionally admitted kinship between a certain sign and a certain future event. Further, a divinatory rite is generally not isolated; it is part of an organized whole. The science of the diviners, therefore, does not form isolated groups of things, but binds these groups to each other. At the basis of a system of divination there is thus, at least implicitly, a system of classification.

But it is above all in myths that we see the appearance, in an almost ostensible manner, of methods of classification entirely analogous to those of the Australians or North American Indians. Every mythology is fundamentally a classification, but one which borrows its principles from religious beliefs, not from scientific ideas. Highly organized pantheons divide up all nature, just as elsewhere the clans divide the universe. Thus India divides things, as well as their gods, between the three worlds of the sky, the atmosphere, and the earth, just as the Chinese class everything according to the two fundamental principles of *yang* and *yin*. To attribute certain things in nature to a god amounts to the same thing as to group them under the same generic rubric, or to place them in the same class; and the genealogies and identifications relating divinities to each other imply relations of co-ordination or subordination between the classes of things represented by these divinities. When Zeus, father of men and the gods, is said to have given birth to Athena, the warrior-goddess, goddess of intelligence, mistress of the owl, etc., this really means that two groups of images are linked and classified in relation to each other. Every god has his doubles, who are other forms of himself, though they have other functions; hence, different powers, and the things over which these powers are exercised, are attached to a central or predominant notion, as is the species to the genus or a secondary variety to the principal species. It is thus that to Poseidon,[6] the river god, are attached other and paler personalities, agrarian gods (Aphareus, Aloeus, the farmer, the thresher), horse gods (Actor, Elatos, Hippocoon, etc.), and a vegetation god (Phutalmios).

These classifications are such essential elements of developed mythologies that they have played an important part in the evolution of religious thought; they have facilitated the reduction of a multiplicity of gods to one, and consequently they have prepared the way for monotheism. The 'henotheism'[7] which characterizes Brahmanic mythology, at least after it has reached a certain stage of development, actually consists in a tendency to reduce more and more gods into each other, to the extent that each ends up by possessing the attributes of all the others and even their names. The pantheism of pre-Buddhist India is, from a certain point of view, an unstable classification in which the genus easily becomes a species, and *vice versa*, but which manifests an increasing tendency towards unity; and the same is true of classical Śivaism and Vishṇuism.[8] Usener has similarly shown[9] that the progressive systematization of Greek and Roman polytheism was an essential condition for the advent of western monotheism. Minor local and specialized gods are gradually subsumed under more general headings, the great nature gods, and tend to be absorbed by them. For a time, the idea of what was peculiar to the former remains; the name of the old god coexists with that of the great god, but only as an attribute of the latter; then his existence becomes more and more that of a phantom, until one day only the great gods remain, if not in religious observances, at least in myth. One might almost say that mythological classifications, when they are complete and systematic, when they embrace the universe, announce the end of mythologies properly speaking. Pan, Brahmán, Prajāpati, supreme genera, absolute and pure beings, are mythical figures almost as poor in imagery as the transcendental God of the Christians.

Thence it seems that we approach imperceptibly the abstract and relatively rational types which crown the first philosophical classifications.

It is certain that Chinese philosophy, when it is really Taoist, is based on the system of classification that we have described. In Greece, without wishing to affirm anything about the historical origin of its doctrines, one cannot but remark that the two principles of Heraclitean Ionism, viz. war and peace, and those of Empedocles, viz. love and strife, divide things between them in the same way as do *yang* and *yin* in the Chinese classification. The relationships established by the Pythagoreans between numbers, elements, sexes, and a certain number of other things are reminiscent of the correspondences of magico-religious origin which we have had occasion to discuss. Also, even in the time of Plato, the world was still conceived as a vast system of classified and hierarchized sympathies.[10]

Primitive classifications are therefore not singular or exceptional, having no analogy with those employed by more civilized peoples; on the contrary, they seem to be connected, with no break in continuity, to the first scientific classifications. In fact, however different they may be in certain respects from the latter, they nevertheless have all their essential characteristics. First of all, like all sophisticated classifications, they are systems of hierarchized notions. Things are not simply arranged by them in the form of isolated groups, but these groups stand in fixed relationships to each other and together form a single whole. Moreover, these systems, like those of science, have a purely speculative purpose. Their object is not to facilitate action, but to advance understanding, to make intelligible the relations which exist between things. Given certain concepts which are considered to be fundamental, the mind feels the need to connect to them the ideas which it forms about other things. Such classifications are thus intended, above all, to connect ideas, to unify knowledge; as such, they may be said without inexactitude to be scientific, and to constitute a first philosophy of nature.[11] The Australian does not divide the universe between the totems of his tribe with a view to regulating his conduct or even to justify his practice; it is because, the idea of the totem being cardinal for him, he is under a necessity to place everything else that he knows in relation to it. We may therefore think that the conditions on which these very ancient classifications depend may have played an important part in the genesis of the classificatory function in general.

Now it results from this study that the nature of these conditions is social. Far from it being the case, as Frazer seems to think, that the social relations of men are based on logical relations between things, in reality it is the former which have provided the prototype for the latter. According to him, men were divided into clans by a pre-existing classification of things; but, quite on the contrary, they classified things because they were divided by clans.

We have seen, indeed, how these classifications were modelled on the closest and most fundamental form of social organization. This, however, is not going far enough. Society was not simply a model which classificatory thought followed; it was its own divisions which served as divisions for the system of classification. The first logical categories were social categories; the first classes of things were classes of men, into which these things were integrated. It was because men were grouped, and thought of themselves in the form of groups, that in their ideas they grouped other things, and in the beginning the two modes of grouping were merged to the point of being indistinct. Moieties were the first genera; clans, the first species. Things were thought to be integral parts of society, and it was their place in society which determined their place in nature. We may even wonder whether the schematic manner in which genera are ordinarily conceived may not have depended in part on the same influences. It is a fact of current observation that the things which they comprise are generally imagined as situated in a sort of ideational milieu, with a more or less clearly delimited spatial circumscription. It is certainly not without cause that concepts and their interrelations have so often been represented by concentric and eccentric circles, interior and exterior to each other, etc. Might it not be that this tendency to imagine purely logical groupings in a form contrasting so much with their true nature originated in the fact that at first they were conceived in the form of social groups occupying, consequently, definite positions in space? And have we not in fact seen this spatial localization of genus and species in a fairly large number of very different societies?

Not only the external form of classes, but also the relations uniting them to each other, are of social origin. It is because human groups fit one into another – the sub-clan into the clan, the clan in o the moiety, the moiety into the tribe– that groups of things are ordered in the same way. Their regular diminution in span, from genus to species, species to variety, and so on, comes from the equally diminishing extent presented by social groups as one leaves the largest and oldest and approaches the more recent and the more derivative. And if the totality of things is conceived as a single system, this is because society itself is seen in the same way. It is a whole, or rather it is *the* unique whole to which everything is related. Thus logical hierarchy is only another aspect of social hierarchy, and the unity of knowledge is nothing else than the very unity of the collectivity, extended to the universe.

Furthermore, the ties which unite things of the same group or different groups to each other are themselves conceived as social ties. We recalled in the beginning that the expressions by which we refer to these relations still have a moral significance; but whereas for us they are hardly more than metaphors, originally they meant what they said. Things of the same class were really considered as relatives of the individuals of the same social group, and consequently of each other. They are of 'the same flesh', the same family. Logical relations are thus, in a sense, domestic relations. Sometimes, too, as we have seen, they are comparable at all points with those which exist between a master and an object possessed, between a chief and his subjects. We may even wonder whether the idea of the pre-eminence of genus over species, which is so strange from a positivistic point of view, may not be seen here in its rudimentary form. Just as, for the realist, the general idea dominates the individual, so the clan totem dominates those of the sub-clans and, still more, the personal totems of individuals; and wherever the moiety has retained its original stability it has a sort of primacy over the divisions of which it is composed and the particular things which are included in them. Though he may be essentially Wartwut and partially Moiwiluk, the Wotjobaluk described by Howitt is above all a Krokitch or a Gamutch. Among the Zuñi, the animals symbolizing the six main clans are set in sovereign charge over their respective sub-clans and over creatures of all kinds which are grouped with them.

But if the foregoing has allowed us to understand how the notion of classes, linked to each other in a single system, could have been born, we still do not know what the forces were which induced men to divide things as they did between the classes. From the fact that the external form of the classification was furnished by society, it does not necessarily follow that the way in which the framework was used is due to reasons of the same origin. *A priori* it is very possible that motives of a quite different order should have determined the way in which things were connected and merged, or else, on the contrary, distinguished and opposed.

The particular conception of logical connexions which we now have permits us to reject this hypothesis. We have just seen, in fact, that they are represented in the form of familial connexions, or as relations of economic or political subordination; so that the same sentiments which are the basis of domestic, social, and other kinds of organization have been effective in this logical division of things also. The latter are attracted or opposed to each other in the same way as men are bound by kinship or opposed in the vendetta. They are merged as members of the same family are merged by common sentiment. That some are subordinate to others is analogous in every respect to the fact that an object possessed appears inferior to its owner, and likewise the subject to his master. It is thus states of the collective mind *(âme)* which gave birth to these groupings, and these states moreover are manifestly affective. There are sentimental affinities between things as between individuals, and they are classed according to these affinities.

We thus arrive at this conclusion: it is possible to classify other things than concepts, and otherwise than in accordance with the laws of pure understanding. For in order for it to be possible for ideas to be systematically arranged for reasons of sentiment, it is necessary that they should not be pure ideas, but that they should themselves be products of sentiment. And in fact, for those who are called primitives, a species of things is not a simple object of knowledge but corresponds above all to a certain sentimental attitude. All kinds of affective elements combine in the representation made of it. Religious emotions, notably, not only give it a special tinge, but attribute to it the most essential properties of which it is constituted. Things are above all sacred or profane, pure or impure, friends or enemies, favourable or unfavourable;[12] i.e. their most fundamental characteristics are only expressions of the way in which they affect social sensibility. The differences and resemblances which determine the fashion in which they are grouped are more affective than intellectual. This is how it happens that things change their nature, in a way, from society to society; it is because they affect the sentiments of groups differently. What is conceived in one as perfectly homogeneous is represented elsewhere as essentially heterogeneous. For us, space is formed of similar parts which are substitutable one for the other. We have seen, however, that for many peoples it is profoundly differentiated according to regions. This is because each region has its own affective value. Under the influence of diverse sentiments, it is connected with a special religious principle, and consequently it is endowed with virtues *sui generis* which distinguish it from all others. And it is this emotional value of notions which plays the preponderant part in the manner in which ideas are connected or separated. It is the dominant characteristic in classification.

It has quite often been said that man began to conceive things by relating them to himself. The above allows us to see more precisely what this anthropocentrism, which might better be called *sociocentrism,* consists of. The centre of the first schemes of nature is not the individual; it is society.[13] It is this that is objectified, not man. Nothing shows this more clearly than the way in which the Sioux retain the whole universe, in a way, within the limits of tribal space; and we have seen how universal space itself is nothing else than the site occupied by the tribe, only indefinitely extended beyond its real limits. It is by virtue of the same mental disposition that so many peoples have placed the centre of the world, 'the navel of the earth', in their own political or religious capital,[14] i.e. at the place which is the centre of their moral life. Similarly, but in another order of ideas, the creative force of the universe and everything in it was first conceived as a mythical ancestor, the generator of the society.

This is how it is that the idea of a logical classification was so hard to form, as we showed at the beginning of this work. It is because a logical classification is a classification of concepts. Now a concept is the notion of

.a clearly determined group of things; its limits may be marked precisely. Emotion, on the contrary, is something essentially fluid and inconsistent. Its contagious influence spreads far beyond its point of origin, extending to everything about it, so that it is not possible to say where its power of propagation ends. States of an emotional nature necessarily possess the same characteristic. It is not possible to say where they begin or where they end; they lose themselves in each other, and mingle their properties in such a way that they cannot be rigorously categorized. From another point of view, in order to be able to mark out the limits of a class, it is necessary to have analysed the characteristics by which the things assembled in this class are recognized and by which they are distinguished. Now emotion is naturally refractory to analysis, or at least lends itself uneasily to it, because it is too complex. Above all when it has a collective origin it defies critical and rational examination. The pressure exerted by the group on each of its members does not permit individuals to judge freely the notions which society itself has elaborated and in which it has placed something of its personality. Such constructs are sacred for individuals. Thus the history of scientific classification is, in the last analysis, the history of the stages by which this element of social affectivity has progressively weakened, leaving more and more room for the reflective thought of individuals. But it is not the case that these remote influences which we have just studied have ceased to be felt today. They have left behind them an effect which survives and which is always present; it is the very cadre of all classification, it is the ensemble of mental habits by virtue of which we conceive things and facts in the form of co-ordinated or hierarchized groups.

This example shows what light sociology throws on the genesis, and consequently the functioning, of logical operations. What we have tried to do for classification might equally be attempted for the other functions or fundamental notions of the understanding. We have already had occasion to mention, in passing, how even ideas so abstract as those of time and space are, at each point in their history, closely connected with the corresponding social organization. The same method could help us likewise to understand the manner in which the ideas of cause, substance, and the different modes of reasoning, etc. were formed. As soon as they are posed in sociological terms, all these questions, so long debated by metaphysicians and psychologists, will at last be liberated from the tautologies in which they have languished. At least, this is a new way which deserves to be tried.

NOTES

1. It has even been conjectured whether there might not have been borrowing from one of these peoples by the other.

2. Bouché-Leclercq 1899, pp. 311 ff., 316.

3. Epicurus criticizes precisely prognostications based on (celestial ?) animals as being based on the hypothesis of the coincidence of time, directions and events created by the divinity (Usener 1887, p. 55, 1. 13).

4. Bouché-Leclercq 1899, pp. 319, 76 ff. Cf. Ebers 1901.

5. According to Pan-ku, an author of the second century, basing himself on much more ancient sources (de Groot 1892–1910, vol. IV, pp. 13 ff.).

6. Usener 1898, p. 357.

7. The word is Max Müller's, but he is mistaken in applying it to primitive forms of Brahmanism.

8. Barth 1891, pp. 29, 160 ff.

9. Usener 1896, pp. 346 ff.

10. Hindu philosophy abounds in correspondential classifications of things, elements, directions, and hypostases. The main ones are listed, with commentary, in Deussen (1894, vol. I, part 2, pp. 85, 89, 95, etc.). A large part of the Upanishads consists in speculations on genealogies and correspondences.

11. As such they are very clearly distinguished from what might be called technological classifications. It is probable that man has always classified, more or less clearly, the things on which he lived, according to the means he used to get them: for example, animals living in the water, or in the air or on the ground. But at first such groups were not connected with each other or systematized. They were divisions, distinctions of ideas, not schemes of classification. Moreover, it is evident that these distinctions are closely linked to practical concerns, of which they merely express certain aspects. It is for this reason that we have not spoken of them in this work, in which we have tried above all to throw some light on the origins of the logical procedure which is the basis of scientific classifications.

12. For the adherent of many cults, even now foodstuffs are classified first of all into two main classes, fat and lean, and we know to what extent this classification is subjective.

13. De la Grasserie has developed ideas fairly similar to our own, though rather obscurely and above all without evidence (1899, chap. III).

14. Something understandable enough for the Romans and even the Zuñi, but less so for the inhabitants of Easter Island, called Te Pito-te Henua (navel of the earth); but the idea is perfectly natural everywhere.

Lucien Lévy-Bruhl

Lucien Lévy-Bruhl was born in 1857 in Paris, where he received his primary and secondary school education. In 1876 he entered the *Ecole Normale Supérieure*, where he specialized in philosophy. He passed the *agrégation* examination in 1879 and taught subsequently at secondary schools at Poitiers (1879–1882), at Amiens (1882–1883) and in Paris (1883–1895). Having obtained his doctorate in 1884, he taught from 1886 onwards at the *Ecole Libre des Sciences Politiques*, from 1895 onwards at the *Ecole Normale Supérieure*, and from 1896 onwards at the Sorbonne. Lévy-Bruhl became here professor of the history of modern philosophy in 1904. In 1917 he became the editor of the *Revue Philosophique*, and in 1925 he founded the *Institut d'Ethnologie*, together with Paul Rivet and Marcel Mauss. In 1927 he withdrew from it and also retired from the Sorbonne. Lévy-Bruhl was a visiting professor at Harvard in 1919–1920 and subsequently made a great number of travels abroad. He died in Paris in 1939.

The following translations of Lévy-Bruhl's work exist in English: 1899 *History of Modern Philosophy in France;* 1903 *The Philosophy of Auguste Comte;* 1905 *Ethics and Moral Science;* 1923 *Primitive Mentality;* 1926 *How Natives Think;* 1929 *The 'Soul' of the Primitive;* 1935 *Primitives and the Supernatural.*

Besides his studies in philosophy and in the history of social thought, Lévy-Bruhl paid considerable attention to the problem of the 'primitive' or 'archaic' mentality. His investigations on primitive ways of thinking and his thought on primitive versus modern mentality are of a general interest in view of the problem of the unity of the human mind, and they are also relevant for the interpretation of religious behavior and expression. At the end of his life Lévy-Bruhl came to consider in his *Carnets* (1949) the difference between 'primitive' and 'modern' mentality as being one of nuances and not of principle. He considered participation as a fundamental human datum, though it manifests itself most clearly in primitive society. He then rejected his former theories of 'prelogical' reasoning. The *Carnets*, posthumously discovered and published, show Lévy-Bruhl's constant search for a clear conceptualization and a methodology based on description.

The following fragment has been taken from *How Natives Think* and shows the way in which Lévy-Bruhl interpreted the religious perception of non-literate people in 1910.

'PRIMITIVE MENTALITY' AND RELIGION

Belief and experience

[...] All such phenomena are to be expected if it be true that the perception of primitives is oriented differently from our own, and not preeminently concerned, as ours is, with the characteristics of the beings and manifestations which we call objective. To them the most important properties of the beings and objects they perceive, are their occult powers, their mystic qualities. Now one of these powers is that of appearing or not appearing in given circumstances. Either the power is inherent in the subject who perceives, who has been prepared for it by initiation, or else holds it by virtue of his participation in some superior being, and so on. In short, mystic relations may be established between certain persons and certain beings, on account of which these persons are exclusively privileged to perceive these beings. Such cases are analogous to the dream. The primitive, far from regarding the mystic perception in which he has no part, as suspect, sees in it, as in the dream, a more precious, and consequently more significant communication with invisible spirits and forces.

Conversely, when collective representations imply the presence of certain qualities in objects, nothing will persuade the primitives that they do not exist. To us, the fact that we do not perceive them there is decisive. It does not prove to them that they are not there, for possibly it is their nature not to reveal themselves to perception, or to manifest themselves in certain conditions only. Consequently, that which we call experience, and which decides, as far as we are concerned, what may be admitted or not admitted as real, has no effect upon collective representations. Primitives have no need of this experience to vouch for the mystic properties of beings and objects: and for the same reason they are quite indifferent to the disappointments it may afford. Since experience is limited to what is stable, tangible, visible, and approachable in physical reality, it allows the most important of all, the occult powers, to escape. Hence we can find no example of the non-success of a magic practice discouraging those who believe in it. Livingstone gives an account of a prolonged discussion which he had with the rain-makers, and ends by saying: 'I have never been able to convince a single one of them that their arguments are unsound. Their belief in these "charms" of theirs is unbounded.'[1] In the Nicobar Islands, 'the people in all the villages have now performed the ceremony called *tanangla*, signifying either "support" or "prevention". Its object is to prevent illness caused by the northeast monsoon. Poor Nicobarese! They do the same thing year after year, but to no effect.'[2]

Experience is peculiarly unavailing against the belief in the virtues of 'fetishes' which secure invulnerability: a method of interpreting what happens in a sense which favours the belief is never lacking. In one case an Ashanti, having procured a fetish of this kind, hastened to put it to the proof, and received a gunshot wound which broke his arm. The 'fetish man' explained the matter to the satisfaction of all, saying that the incensed fetish had that moment revealed the reason to him. It was because the young man had had sexual relations with his wife on a forbidden day. The wounded man confessed that this was true, and the Ashantis retained their convictions.[3] Du Chaillu tells us that when a native wears an iron chain round his neck he is proof against bullets. If the charm is not effectual, his faith in it remains unshaken, for then he believes that some maleficent wonder-worker has produced a powerful 'counter-spell,' to which he falls a victim.[4] Elsewhere he says: 'As I came from seeing the king, I shot at a bird sitting upon a tree, and missed it. I had been taking quinine, and was nervous. But the Negroes standing around at once proclaimed that this was a fetish-bird, and therefore I *could* not shoot it. I fired again, and missed again. Hereupon they grew triumphant in their declarations, while I . . . loaded again, took careful aim, and to my own satisfaction and their dismay, brought my bird down. Immediately they explained that I was a white man, and not entirely amenable to fetish laws; so that I do not suppose my shot proved anything to them after all.'[5]

It is the same in Loango. 'I had been presented,' writes Pechuël-Loesche, 'with a very fine collar, made of hair from the tail of an elephant . . . and adorned with teeth from a sea-fish and a crocodile. These teeth were to preserve me from any danger connected with water. . . . It frequently happened that my boat was upset when I was crossing the bar, and one day I had great difficulty in reaching the shore. I was told quite seriously that it was the teeth alone that had saved me, for without them my swimming powers would not have sufficed to help me clear the heavy breakers. *I was not wearing the collar,* but its efficacy was in no manner of doubt from that fact.'[6] The fetish and the medicine-man always have the last word.

Primitive man, therefore, lives and acts in an environment of beings and objects, all of which, in addition to the properties that we recognize them to possess, are endued with mystic attributes. He perceives their objective reality mingled with another reality. He feels himself surrounded by an infinity of imperceptible entities, nearly always invisible to sight, and always redoubtable: ofttimes the souls of the dead are about him, and always he is encompassed by myriads of spirits of more or less defined personality. It is thus at least that the matter is explained by a large number of observers and anthropologists, and they make use of animistic terms to express this. Frazer has collected many instances which tend to show that this phenomenon obtains everywhere among undeveloped peoples.[7] Is it necessary to quote some of them? 'The Oráon's imagination tremblingly wanders in a world of ghosts. Every rock, road, river, and grove is haunted.' ... Sometimes, too, there are 'malignant spirits.'[8] Like the Santals, Mundas, and the Oráons of Chota-Nagpur, 'the Kadars believe themselves to be compassed about by a host of invisible powers, some of whom are thought to be the spirits of departed ancestors, while others seem to embody nothing more definite than the vague sense of the mysterious and uncanny with which hills, streams, and lonely forests inspire the savage imagination. ... Their names are legion, and their attributes barely known.'[9] In Korea, 'spirits occupy every quarter of heaven and every foot of earth. They lie in wait for a man along the wayside, in the trees, on the rocks, in the mountains, valleys, and streams. They keep him under a constant espionage day and night. ... They are all about him, they dance in front of him, follow behind him, fly over his head and cry out against him from the earth. He has no refuge from them even in his own house, for there they are plastered into or pinned on the walls or tied to the beams. ... Their ubiquity is an ugly travesty of the omnipresence of God.'[10] In China, according to the ancient doctrine, 'the universe is filled up in all its parts with legions of *shen* and *kwei*. ... Every being and every thing that exists is animated either by a *shen*, or by a *kwei*, or by a *shen* and a *kwei* together.'[11] With the Fang of East Africa, 'spirits are everywhere; in rocks, trees, forests, and streams; in fact, for the Fang, this life is one continual fight against spirits corporal and spiritual.'[12] In every action of his daily life,' writes Miss Kingsley, 'the African Negro shows you how he lives with a great, powerful spirit world around him. You will see him before starting out to hunt or fight rubbing medicine into his weapons to strengthen the spirits within them, talking to them the while; telling them what care he has taken of them, reminding them of the gifts he has given them, though these gifts were hard for him to give, and begging them in the hour of his dire necessity not to fail him. You will see him bending over the face of a river talking to its spirit with proper incantations, asking it when it meets a man who is an enemy of his to upset his canoe, or drown him, or asking it to carry down with it some curse to the village below which has angered him.'[13]

Miss Kingsley lays great stress upon the homogeneity of the African native's representations of everything. 'The African mind naturally approaches all things from a spiritual point of view ... things happen because of the action of spirit upon spirit.'[24] When the doctor applies a remedy 'the spirit of the medicine works upon the spirit of the disease.' The purely physical effect is beyond the power of conception unless it be allied with the mystic influence. Or rather, we may say that there is no really physical influence, there are only mystic ones. Accordingly it is almost impossible to get these primitives to differentiate, especially when it is a case of an accusation of murder through the practice of witchcraft, for instance. Here is a typical case. 'I explain to my native questioner', says Nassau, 'that if what the accused has done in fetich rite with intent to kill, had any efficiency in taking away life, I allow that he shall be put to death; if he made only fetiches, even if they were intended to kill, he is not guilty of this death, for a mere fetich cannot kill. But if he used poison, with or without fetich, he is guilty.'

'But even so,' adds Nassau, 'the distinction between a fetich and a poison is vague in the thought of many natives. What I call a 'poison' is to them only another material form of a fetich power, both poison and fetich being supposed to be made efficient by the presence of an adjuvant spirit.'[15] This means that to their minds the mere fetich kills as certainly as the poison does. More certainly even; for the poison kills only by virtue of a mystic power of which, in certain circumstances, it may be deprived. The idea of its physical properties which is so clear to the European mind, does not exist for the African.

We thus have good authority for saying that this mentality differs from our own to a far greater extent than the language used by those who are partisans of animism would lead us to think. When they are describing to us a world peopled by ghosts and spirits and phantoms for primitives, we at once realize that beliefs of this kind have not wholly disappeared even in civilized countries. Without referring to spiritualism, we recall the ghost-stories which are so numerous in our folklore, and we are tempted to think that the difference is one of degree only. Doubtless such beliefs may be regarded in our communities as a survival which testifies to an older mental condition, formerly much more general. But we must be careful not to see in them a faithful, though faintly outlined, reflection of the mentality of primitives. Even the most uneducated members of our societies regard stories of ghosts and spirits as belonging to the realm of the supernatural, between such apparitions and magical influences and the data furnished by ordinary perception and the experience of the broad light of day, the line of demarcation is clearly defined. Such a line, however, does not exist for the primitive. The one kind of perception and influence is quite as natural as the other, or rather, we may say that to him there are not two kinds. The superstitious man, and frequently also the religious man, among us, believes in a twofold order of reality, the one visible, palpable, and subordinate to the essential laws of motion; the other invisible, intangible, 'spiritual,' forming a mystic sphere which encompasses the first. But the primitive's mentality does not recognize two distinct worlds in contact with each other, and more or less interpenetrating. To him there is but one˙ Every reality, like every influence, is mystic, and consequently every perception is also mystic.

Collective representations

[...]

In short, logical thought implies, more or less consciously, a systematic unity which is best realizable in science and philosophy. And the fact that it can lead to this is partially due to the peculiar nature of its concepts, to their homogeneity and ordered regularity. This is material which it has gradually created for itself, and without which it would not have been able to develop.

Now this material is not at the command of the primitive mind. Primitive mentality does indeed possess a language, but its structure, as a rule, differs from that of our languages. It actually does comprise abstract representations and general ideas; but neither this abstraction nor this generalization resembles that of our concepts. Instead of being surrounded by an atmosphere of logical potentiality, these representations welter, as it were, in an atmosphere of mystic possibilities. There is no homogeneity in the field of representation, and for this reason logical generalization, properly so called, and logical transactions with its concepts are impracticable. The element of generality consists in the possibility — already predetermined — of mystic action and reaction by entities upon each other, or of common mystic reaction in entities which differ from each other. Logical thought finds itself dealing with a scale of general concepts varying in degree, which it can analyse or synthesize at will. Prelogical thought busies itself with collective representations so interwoven as to give the impression of a community in which members would continually act and react upon each other by virtue of their mystic qualities, participating in, or excluding, each other.

Since abstraction and generalization mean this for prelogical mentality, and its preconnections of collective representations are such, it is not difficult to account for its classification of persons and things, strange as it frequently appears to us. Logical thought classifies by means of the very operations which form its concepts. These sum up the work of analysis and synthesis which establishes species and genera, and thus arranges entities according to the increasing generality of the characters observed in them. In this sense classification is not a process which differs from those which have preceded or will follow it. It takes place at the same time as abstraction and generalization: it registers their results, as it were, and its value is precisely what theirs has been. It is the expression of an order or inter-dependence, or hierarchy among the concepts, of reciprocal connection between persons and things, which endeavours to correspond as precisely as possible with the objective order in such a way that concepts thus arranged are equally valid for real objects and real persons. It was the governing idea which directed Greek philosophical thought, and which inevitably appears as soon as the logical mind reflects upon itself and begins consciously to pursue the end to which it at first tended spontaneously.

But to the primitive mind this predominating concern for objective validity which can be verified is unknown. Characteristics which can be discerned by experience, in the sense in which we understand it, character-istics which we call objective, are of secondary importance in its eyes, or are important only as signs and vehicles of mystic qualities. Moreover, the primitive mind does not arrange its concepts in a regular order. It per-ceives preconnections, which it would never dream of changing, between the collective representations; and these are nearly always of greater complexity than concepts, properly so called. Therefore what can its clas-sifications be? Perforce determined at the same time as the preconnections, they too are governed by the law of participation, and will present the same prelogical and mystic character. They will betoken the orientation peculiar to such a mind.

The facts already quoted are sufficient proof of this. When the Huichols, influenced by the law of participation, affirm the identity of corn, deer, hikuli and plumes, a kind of classification has been established between their representations, a classification the governing principle of which is a common presence in these entities, or rather the circulation among these entities, of a mystic power which is of supreme importance to the tribe. The only thing is that this classification does not, as it should do in con-formity with our mental processes, become compacted in a concept which is more comprehensive than that of the objects it embraces. For them it suffices for the objects to be united, and felt as such, in a complexity of collective representations whose emotional force fully compensates, and even goes beyond, the authority which will be given to general concepts by their logical validity at a later stage.

In this way the classifications to which Durkheim and Mauss have called our attention, noting their very different characteristics from those which distinguish our logical classifications, may again be explained. In many undeveloped peoples — in Australia, in West Africa, according to Bennett's recent book,[16] among the North American Indians, in China and elsewhere — we find that all natural objects — animals, plants, stars, cardinal points, colours, inanimate nature in general — are arranged, or have been originally arranged, in the same classes as the members of the social group, and if the latter are divided into so many totems, so, too, are the trees, rivers, stars, etc. A certain tree will belong to such and such a class, and will be used exclusively to manufacture the weapons, coffins, etc., of men who are members of it. The sun, according to the Aruntas, is a *Panunga* woman, that is, she forms part of the sub-group which can only intermarry with members of the *Purula* sub-group. Here we have something analogous with that which we have already noticed about associated totems and local relationship, a mental habit quite different from our own, which consists in bringing together or uniting entities preferably by their mystic participations. This participation, which is very strongly felt between members of the same totem or the same group, between the ensemble of these members and the animal or plant species which is their totem, is also felt, though undoubtedly to a lesser degree, between the totemic group and those who have the same location in space. We have proofs of this in the Australian aborigines and in the North American Indians, where the place of each group in a common camping-ground is very precisely determined according to whether it comes from north or south or from some other direction. Thus it is felt once more between this totemic group and one of the cardinal points, and consequently between this group and all that participates in it, on the one hand, and this cardinal point and all that participates in it (its stars, rivers, trees, and so forth), on the other.

In this way is established a complexity of participations, the full explanation of which would demand exhaustive acquaintance with the beliefs and the collective representations of the group in all their details. They are the equivalent of, or at least they correspond with, what we know as classifications: the social participations being the most intensely felt by each individual consciousness and serving as a nucleus, as it were, around which other participations cluster. But in this there is nothing at all resembling, save in appearance, our logical classifications. These involve a series of concepts whose extent and connotation are definite, and they constitute an ascending scale the degrees of which reflection has tested. The prelogical mind does not objectify nature thus. It *lives* it rather, by feeling itself participate in it, and feeling these participations everywhere; and it interprets this complexity of participations by social forms. If the element of generality exists, it can only be sought for in the participation extending to, and the mystic qualities circulating among, certain entities, uniting them and identifying them in the collective representation.

In default of really general concepts, therefore, primitive mentality is conversant with collective representations which to a certain extent take their place. Although concrete, such representations are extremely comprehensive in this respect, that they are constantly employed, that they readily apply to an infinite number of cases, and that from this point of view they correspond, as we have said, with what categories are for logical thought. But their mystic and concrete nature has often puzzled investigators. These did indeed note its importance and could not fail to draw attention to it, though at the same time they realized that they were face to face with a method of thinking which was opposed to their own mental habits. Some examples in addition to those already quoted will help to make us realize these representations, which are general without however being at the same time abstract.

In the Yaos, Hetherwick notes[17] beliefs which appear incomprehensible to him. He cannot understand how it is that the *lisoka* (the soul, shade or spirit) can be at once both personal and impersonal. In fact, after death the *lisoka* becomes *mulungu*. This word has two meanings: one, the soul of the dead, the other, 'the spirit world in general, or more properly speaking the aggregate of the spirits of all the dead.' This would be conceivable if *mulungu* meant a collective unity formed by the union of all the individual spirits; but this explanation is not permissible, for at the same time *mulungu* signifies 'a state of property inhering in something, as life or health inheres in the body, and it is also regarded as the agent in anything mysterious. 'It is *mulungu*' is the Yao exclamation on being shown anything that is beyond the range of his understanding.' This is a characteristic trait which we shall find in all collective representations of this nature: they are used indifferently to indicate a person or persons, or a quality or property of a thing.

To get out of the difficulty, Hetherwick distinguishes between what he calls 'three stages of animistic belief: (1) the human *lisoka* or shade, the agent in dreams, delirium, etc.; (2) this *lisoka* regarded as *mulungu*, and an object of worship and reverence, the controller of the affairs of this life, the active agent in the fortunes of the human race; (3) *mulungu* as expressing the great spirit agency, the creator of the world and all life, the source of all things animate or inanimate.' It seems as if Hetherwick, like the French missionaries of old in New France, tends to interpret what he observes by the light of his own religious beliefs, but he adds, in good faith: 'And yet between these three conceptions of the spirit nature no definite boundary line can be drawn. The distinction in the native mind is ever of the haziest. No one will give you a dogmatic statement of his belief on such points.'

If Hetherwick did not get from the Yaos the answers he wanted, it may possibly have been because the Yaos did not understand his questions, but it was largely because he did not grasp their ideas. To the Yaos the transit from the personal soul, before or after death, to the impersonal soul or to the mystic quality which pervades every object in which there is something divine, sacred and mystic (not supernatural, for on the contrary nothing is more natural to primitive mentality than this kind of mystic power) is not felt. To tell the truth, there is not even such transit: there is 'identity governed by the law of participation' such as we found in the case of the Huichols, entirely different from logical identity. And through the perpetual working of the law of participation, the mystic principle thus circulating and spreading among entities may be represented indifferently as a person or subject, or a property or power of the objects which share it, and consequently an attribute. Prelogical mentality does not consider there is any difficulty about this.

It is the same with the North American Indians, about whom we have abundant and definite information. Miss Alice Fletcher,[18] in describing the mysterious power called *wakanda*, writes of their idea of the continuity of life, by which 'a relation was maintained between the seen and the unseen, the dead and the living, and also between the fragment of anything and its entirety.' Here continuity means what we call participation, since this continuity obtains between the living and the dead; between a man's nail-parings, saliva, or hair and the man himself; between a certain bear or buffalo and the mystic ensemble of the bear or buffalo species.

Moreover, like the *mulungu* just spoken of, *wakanda* or *wakan* may signify not only a mystic reality, like that which Miss Fletcher calls 'life,' but a characteristic, a quality belonging to persons and things. Thus there are *wakan* men, who have gone through many previous existences. 'They arise to conscious existence in the form of winged seeds, such as the thistle, . . . and pass through a series of inspirations, with different classes of divinities, till they are fully *wakanized* and prepared for human incarnation. They are invested with the invisible *wakan* powers of the gods . . .' Similarly, day and night are *wakan*. The term is explained thus by an Indian: 'While the day lasts a man is able to do many wonderful things, kill animals, men, etc. . . . But he does not fully understand why the day is, nor does he know who makes or causes the light. Therefore he believes that it was not made by hand, i.e. that no human being makes the day give light. Therefore the Indians say that the day is *wakan*. So is the sun. . . .' Here it is a property, a mystic quality inherent in things that is meant. And the Indian adds: 'When it is night, there are ghosts and many fearful objects, so they regard the night as *wakan* . . .' [20] A yet earlier investigator, quoted by Dorsey, had already remarked: "No one term can express the full meaning of the Dacota's *wakan*. It comprehends all mystery, secret power and divinity. . . All life is *wakan*. So also is everything which exhibits power, whether in action, as the winds and drifting clouds, or in passive endurance, as the boulder by the wayside. . . . It covers the whole field of fear and worship; but many things that are neither feared nor worshipped, but are simply wonderful, come under this designation.'[21]

We may be inclined to ask, what, then, is *not wakan?* Such a question would in fact be urged by logical thought which demands the strict definition of its concepts, and a rigorously determined connotation and extent. But prelogical reasoning does not feel the need of this, especially when dealing with collective representations which are both concrete and very general. *Wakan* is something of a mystic nature in which any object whatever may or may not participate, according to circumstances. 'Man himself may become mysterious by fasting, prayer and vision.'[22] A human being is r.ot necessarily *wakan* or not *wakan*, therefore, and one of the duties of the medicine-man in this matter is to avoid errors which might have fatal results. *Wakan* might be compared with a fluid which courses through all existing things, and is the mystic principle of the life and virtue of all beings. 'A young man's weapons are *wakan*: they must not be touched by a woman. They contain divine power. . . . A man prays to his weapons on the day of battle.'

If the observer recording these facts interprets them at the same time (as usually happens), and if he has not noted the difference between prelogical reasoning and logical thinking, he will be led direct to anthropomorphic animism. Here, for instance, is what Charlevoix tells us about the same North American Indians: 'If one is to believe the savages, there is nothing in nature which has not a corresponding spirit: but there are varying orders of spirits, and all have not the same power. When they fail to understand a thing, they attribute supreme virtue to it and they then account for it by saying "it is a spirit" [23] That means that this thing is '*wakan*'; just as the Yaos say 'it is *mulungu!*'

Although Spencer and Gillen uphold the animistic theory, they are too keen observers not to have themselves noticed how very puzzling these collective representations are to our logical thinking. They remarked that certain words are sometimes used as substantives, and then again as adjectives. For instance, *arungquiltha* to the Aruntas is 'a supernatural evil power.' 'A thin ostrich or emu is either *arungquiltha* or is endowed with *arungquiltha*. The name is applied indiscriminately either to the evil influence or to the object in which it is, for the time being, or permanently, resident.'[24] Elsewhere, Spencer and Gillen state that *arungquiltha* is sometimes personal and sometimes impersonal. 'They believe that eclipses are caused by the periodic visits of the *arungquiltha*, who would like to take up his abode in the sun, permanently obliterating its light, and that the evil spirit is only dragged out by the medicine-men.'[25] Even the *churinga*, which these aborigines regard as a sacred, living being and, according to some observations made, as the body of a personal ancestor, is on other occasions considered to be a mystic property inherent in things. '*Churinga*,' say Spencer and

Gillen explicitly, 'is used either as a substantive, when it implies a sacred emblem, or as a qualifying term, when it implies sacred or secret.'[26]

In the Torres Straits, also, 'when anything behaved in a remarkable or mysterious manner it could be regarded as a *zogo* . . . rain, wind, a concrete object or a shrine can be a *zogo;* a *zogo* can be impersonal or personal; it belonged in a general way to particular groups of natives, but it was a particular property of certain individuals, the *zogo le*, who alone knew all the ceremonies connected with it, because the rites were confined to them. . . . I do not know how the term can be better translated than by the word 'sacred'. The term *zogo* is usually employed as a noun, even when it might be expected to be an adjective.'[27]

Hubert and Mauss, in their acute analysis of the idea of the *mana* of the Melanesians, described by Codrington, and also that of the Huron *orenda*, have clearly brought out their relation to the idea of *wakan*.[28] What we have just said about the latter applies equally to these and to other similar conceptions of which it would be an easy matter to find examples elsewhere, also interpreted as animistic. Such an idea is that of *wong*, which we find in West Africa. 'The Guinea Coast Negro's generic name for a fetish-spirit is *wong;* these aerial beings dwell in temple-huts and consume sacrifices, enter into and inspire their priests, cause health and sickness among men, and execute the behests of the mighty Heavengod. But part or all of them are connected with material objects and a native can say "In this river, or tree or amulet, there is a *wong*." . . . Thus among the *wongs* of the land are rivers, lakes and springs; districts of land, termite-hills, trees, crocodiles, apes, snakes, elephants, and birds.'[29] It is from a missionary's report that Tylor has borrowed this account, and it is by no means difficult to find in it, not only 'the three stages of animistic belief' which Hetherwick noticed in the Yaos, but also a collective representation entirely similar to *wakan, mana, orenda*, and many others.

Collective representations of such a nature are to be found, more or less clearly indicated, in nearly all the primitive peoples who have been studied at all closely. They dominate, as Hubert and Mauss have well demonstrated, their religious beliefs and magic practices. It is possibly through them that the difference between prelogical mentality and logical thought can be best defined. When face to face with such representations the latter is always dubious. Are they realities which exist *per se*, or merely very general predicates? Are we dealing with one single and universal subject, with a kind of world-soul or spirit, or with a multiplicity of souls, spirits, divinities? Or again, do these representations imply, as many missionaries have believed, both a supreme divinity and an infinite number of lesser powers? It is the nature of logical thought to demand a reply to questions such as these. It cannot admit at one and the same time of alternatives which seem to be mutually exclusive. The nature of prelogical mentality, on the contrary, is to ignore the necessity. Essentially mystic as it is, it finds no difficulty in imagining, as well as feeling, the identity of the one and the many, the individual and the species, of entities however unlike they be, by means of *participation*. In this lies its guiding principle; this it is which accounts for the kind of abstraction and generalization peculiar to such a mentality, and to this, again, we must mainly refer the characteristic forms of activity we find in primitive peoples.

Myths

[...] The participation or communion first realized by mystic symbiosis and by the practices which affirmed it is obtained later by union with the object of the worship and belief called religious, with the ancestor, the god. The personality of these objects comprises, as we know, an infinite variety of grades, from mystic forces of which we cannot say whether they are single or manifold, to divinities clearly defined by physical and moral attributes, such as those of the Melanesian or the Greek deities. It depends above all on the degree of development attained by the group studies, i.e., upon the type of its institutions as well as its mental type.

When we consider myths in their relation to the mentality of the social groups in which they originate, we are led to similar conclusions. Where the participation of the individual in the social group is still directly felt, where the participation of the group with surrounding groups is actually lived — that is, as long as the period of mystic symbiosis lasts — myths are meagre in number and of poor quality. This is the case with Australian aborigines and the Indians of Northern and Central Brazil, etc. Where the aggregates are of a more advanced type, as for instance, the Zuñis, Iroquois, Melanesians, and others, there is, on the contrary, an increasingly luxuriant outgrowth of mythology. Can myths then likewise be the products of primitive mentality which appear when this mentality is endeavouring to realize a participation no longer directly felt — when it has recourse to intermediaries, and vehicles designed to secure a communion which has ceased to be a living reality? Such a hypothesis may seem to be a bold one, but we view myths with other eyes than those of the human beings whose mentality they reflect. We see in them that which they do not perceive, and that which they imagine there we no longer realize. For example, when we read a Maori or Zuñi or any other myth, we read it translated into our own language, and this very translation is a betrayal. To say nothing of the construction of the sentences, which is bound to be affected by our customary habits of thought, if only in the very order of the words, to primitives the words themselves have an atmosphere which is wholly mystic, whilst in our minds they chiefly evoke associations having their origin in experience. We speak, as we think, by means of concepts. Words, especially those expressive of group-ideas, portrayed in myths, are to the primitive mystic realities, each of which determines a *champ de force*. From the emotional point of view, the mere listening to the myth is to them something quite different from what it is to us. What they hear in it awakens a whole gamut of harmonics which do not exist for us.

Moreover, in a myth of which we take note, that which mainly interests us, that which we seek to understand and interpret, is the actual tenor of the recital, the linking-up of facts, the occurrence of episodes, the thread of the story, the adventures of the hero or mythical animal, and so forth. Hence the theories, momentarily regarded as classic, which see in myths a symbolic presentment of certain natural phenomena, or else the result of a 'disease of language': hence the classifications (like that of Andrew Lang, for instance) which arrange myths in categories according to their content.[30] But this is overlooking the fact that the prelogical, mystic mentality is oriented differently from our own. It is undoubtedly not indifferent to the doings and adventures and vicissitudes related in myths; it is even certain that these interest and intrigue the primitive's mind. But it is not the positive content of the myth that primarily appeals to him. He does not consider it as a thing apart; he undoubtedly sees it no more than *we* see the bony framework beneath the flesh of a living animal, although we know very well that it is there. That which appeals to him, arouses his attention and evokes his emotion, is the mystic element which surrounds the positive content of the story. This element alone gives myth and legend their value and social importance and, I might almost add, their power.

It is not easy to make such a trait felt nowadays, precisely because these mystic elements have disappeared as far as we are concerned, and what we call a myth is but the inanimate corpse which remains after the vital spark has fled. Yet if the perception of beings and objects in nature is wholly mystic to the mind of the primitive, would not the presentation of these same beings and objects in myths be so likewise? Is not the orientation in both cases necessarily the same? To make use of a comparison, though but an imperfect one, let us hark back to the time when in Europe, some centuries ago, the only history taught was sacred history. Whence came the supreme value and importance of that history, both to those who taught and those who learnt? Did it lie in the actual facts, in the knowledge of the sequence of judges, kings or prophets, of the misfortunes of the Israelites during their strife with the neighbouring tribes? Most certainly not. It is not from the historical, but from the sacred, point of view that the Biblical narrative was of incomparable interest. It is because the true God, perpetually intervening in the story, makes His presence manifest at all times and, to the Christian idea, causes the coming of His Son to be anti-cipated. In short, it is the mystic atmosphere which surrounds the facts and prevents them from being ordinary battles, massacres or revolutions. Finally it is because Christendom finds in it a witness, itself divine, of its communion with its God.

Myths are, in due proportion, the Biblical narrative of primitive peoples. The preponderance of mystic elements, however, in the group ideas of myths, is even greater than in our sacred history. At the same time, since the law of participation still predominates in the primitive mind, the myth is accompanied by a very intense feeling of communion with the mystic reality it interprets. When the adventures, exploits, noble deeds, death and resurrection of a beneficent and civilizing hero are recounted in a myth, for instance, it is not the fact of his having given his tribe the idea of making a fire or of cultivating mealies that of itself interests and especially appeals to the listeners. It is here, as in the Biblical narrative, the participation of the social group in its own past, it is the feeling that the group is, as it were, actually living in that epoch, that there is a kind of mystic communion with that which has made it what it is. In short, to the mind of the primitive, myths are both an expression of the solidarity of the social group with itself in its own epoch and in the past and with the groups of beings surrounding it, and a means of maintaining and reviving this feeling of solidarity.

Such considerations, it may be urged, might apply to myths in which the human or semi-human ancestors of the social group, its civilizing or its pro-tecting heroes, figure; but are they valid in the case of myths relating to sun, moon, stars, thunder, the sea, the rivers, winds, cardinal points, etc.? It is only to an intellect such as ours that the objection appears a serious one. The primitive's mind works along the lines that are peculiar to it. The mystic elements in his ideas matter considerably more to him than the objective features which, in our view, determine and classify beings of all kinds, and as a consequence the classifications which we regard as most clearly evident escape his attention. Others, which to us are inconceivable, however, claim it. Thus the relationship and communion of the social group with a certain animal or vegetable species, with natural phenomena like the wind or the rain, with a constellation, appear quite as simple to him as his communion with an ancestor or a legendary hero. To give but one instance, the aborigines studied by Spencer and Gillen regard the sun as a Panunga woman, belonging to a definite sub-class, and consequently bound by the ties of relationship to all the other clans of the tribe. Let us refer again to the analogy indicated above. In the sacred history of primitives natural history forms a part.

If this view of the chief significance of myths and of their characteristic function in aggregates of a certain mental type be correct, several consequences of some importance will ensue. This view does not render the careful and detailed study of myths superfluous. It provides neither a theory for classifying them in genera and species, nor an exact method of interpreting them, nor does it throw positive light upon their relations with religious observances. But it does enable us to avoid certain definite errors, and at any rate it permits of our stating the problem in terms which do not falsify the solution beforehand. It provides a general method of procedure, and this is to mistrust 'explanatory' hypotheses which would account for the genesis of myths by a psychological and intellectual activity similar to our own, even while assuming it to be childish and unreflecting.

The myths which have long been considered the easiest to explain, for instance, those regarded as absolutely lucid, such as the Indian nature-myths, are on the contrary the most intriguing. As long as one could see in them the spontaneous product of a naïve imagination impressed by the great natural phenomena, the interpretation of them was in fact self-evident. But if we have once granted that the mentality which generates myths is differently oriented from ours, and that its collective representations obey their own laws, the chief of which is the law of participation, the very intelligibility of these myths propounds a fresh problem. We are led to believe that, far from being primitive, these myths, in the form in which they have reached us, are something absolutely artificial, that they have been very highly and consciously elaborated, and this to such an extent that their original form is almost entirely lost. On the other hand, the myths which may possibly seem the easiest to explain are those which most directly express the sense of the social group's relationship, whether it be with its legendary members and those no longer living, or with the groups of beings which surround it. For such myths appear to be the most primitive in the sense that they are most readily allied with the peculiar prelogical, mystic mentality of the least civilized aggregates. Such, among others, are the totemic myths.

If, however, the aggregates belong to a type even slightly more advanced, the interpretation of their myths very soon becomes risky and perhaps impossible. In the first place, their increasing complexity diminishes our chances of correctly following up the successive operations of the mentality which produces these myths. This mentality not only refuses to be bound by the law of contradiction — a feature which most myths reveal at first sight, so to speak — but it neither abstracts nor associates, and accordingly it does not symbolize as our thought does. Our most ingenious conjectures, therefore, always risk going astray.

If Cushing had not obtained the interpretation of their myths from the Zuñis themselves, would any modern intellect have ever succeeded in firding a clue to this prehistoric labyrinth? The true exposition of myths which are somewhat complicated involves a reconstruction of the mentality which has produced them. This is a result which our habits of thought would scarcely allow us to hope for, unless, like Cushing, a savant were exceptionally capable of creating a 'primitive' mentality for himself, and of faithfully transcribing the confidences of this adopted compatriots.

Moreover, even in the most favourable conditions, the state in which the myths are when we collect them may suffice to render them unintelligible and make any coherent interpretation impossible. Very frequently we have no means of knowing how far back they date. If they are not a recent product, who is our authority for assuming that some fragments at any rate have not disappeared, or, on the other hand, may not myths which were originally quite distinct, have been mingled in one incongruous whole ? The mystic elements which were the predominant feature at the time when the myth originated may have lost some of their importance if the mentality of the social group has evolved at the same time as their institutions and their relations with neighbouring groups. May not the myth which has gradually come to be a mystery to this altered mentality have been mutilated, added to, transformed, to bring it into line with the new collective representations which dominate the group ? May not this adaptation have been performed in a contrary sense, without regard to the participations which the myth originally expressed ? Let us assume — an assumption by no means unreasonable — that it has undergone several successive transformations of this kind: by what analysis can we hope ever to retrace the evolution which has been accomplished, to find once more the elements which have disappeared, to correct the misconceptions grafted upon one another ? The same problem occurs with respect to rites and customs which are often perpetuated throughout the ages, even while they are being distorted, completed in a contrary sense, or acquiring a new significance to replace that which is no longer understood.

NOTES

1. Livingstone, *Missionary Travels*, 1857, pp. 24–25.
2. Solomon, 'Diaries kept in Car Nicobar,' *Journal of the Anthropological Institute* (J.A.I.), Vol. 32, p. 213.
3. Bowditch, *Mission to Ashanti*, p. 439.
4. Du Chaillu, *Explorations and Adventures in Equatorial Africa*, p. 338.
5. *Ibid.*, p. 179.
6. Dr. Pechuël-Loesche, *Die Loanga Expedition*, Vol. III, p. 352.
7. Frazer, *The Golden Bough*, 2nd ed., Vol. III, pp. 41 *ff.*
8. Risley, *Tribes and Castes of Bengal*, Vol. II, pp. 143–145.
9. *Ibid.*, Vol. I, p. 369.
10. G. H. Jones, 'The spirit worship in Korea,' *Transactions of the Korea Branch of the Royal Asiatic Society*, II, No. 1, p. 58.

11. J. J. M. de Groot, *The Religious System of China*, Vol. IV, p. 51.

12. Bennett, 'Ethnographical notes on the Fang,' *Journal of the Anthropological Institute*, Vol. 29, p. 87.

13. Miss Kingsley, *West African Studies*, p. 110.

14. *Ibid.*, p. 330.

15. Nassau, *Fetichism in West Africa*, p. 263.

16. Bennett, *At the Back of the Black Man's Mind*, London, 1906.

17. Hetherwick, 'Some animistic beliefs among the Yaos of Central Africa,' *J. A. I.*, Vol. 32, p. 89–95.

18. Alice Fletcher, ·The signification of the Scalp-lock,' *J. A. I.*, Vol. 27, p. 437.

19. Dorsey, 'Siouan Cults,' *Report of the Bureau of the Smithsonian Institute* (Washington), Vol. XI, p. 494.

20. *Ibid.*, p. 467.

21. *Ibid.*, pp. 432–433.

22. *Ibid.*, p. 365.

23. Charlevoix, *Journal d'un voyage dans l'Amérique septentrionale*, Vol. III, p. 346.

24. Spencer and Gillen, *The Native Tribes of Central Australia*, p. 548, note.

25. *Ibid.*, p. 566. *Cf.* Spencer and Gillen, *The Northern Tribes of Central Australia*, p. 629.

26. *Ibid.*, p. 139, note.

27. *The Cambridge Anthropological Expedition to Torres Straits*, Vol. VI, pp. 244–245.

28 Hubert and Mauss, 'Esquisse d'une théorie générale de la magie,' *Année Sociologique*, Vol. VII (1904), pp. 108 *ff.*

29. E. B. Tylor, *Primitive Culture*, 4th ed., Vol. II, p. 205.

30. 'Mythology', *Encyclopaedia Britannica*, 9th ed., Vol. XVII, pp. 156–157.

Max Weber

Max Weber was born in 1864 in Erfurt, Germany. In 1869 his family moved to Berlin where he received his primary and secondary school education. In 1882 he became a student of law at the University of Heidelberg, where he also attended lectures on history and theology. Having served for a year in the army, he resumed his university studies in Berlin and Göttingen where he took his first examination in law in 1886. He did his post-graduate work in Berlin between 1886 and 1889 and practiced law in the meantime. In 1889 he obtained his doctorate in Berlin with a dissertation on 'The Medieval Commercial Associations'. He then passed his second examination in law in 1890 and obtained his *Habilitation* on 'The History of Agrarian Institutions (in ancient Rome)' in 1891. In 1893 Weber became professor of commercial and German law at the University of Berlin; he also practiced law in this city. The next year he became professor of political economics at the University of Freiburg (Germany), and he became professor of political science at the University of Heidelberg in 1897. From 1898 until 1902 Weber was on leave of absence for health reasons; in 1903 he resigned his professorship and became an honorary professor. Fall 1904 Weber visited the United States in connection with the Congress of Arts and Science held then at St. Louis. In the summer of 1917 he lectured at the University of Vienna, and summer 1919 he accepted a professorship at the University of Munich. He died at Munich in 1920.

The following books by Weber which have been translated into English have a bearing on the study of religion: 1930 *The Protestant Ethic and the Spirit of Capitalism;* 1946 *Essays in Sociology;* 1949 *On the Methodology of the Social Sciences;* 1951 *The Religion of China: Confucianism and Taoism;* 1952 *Ancient Judaism;* 1958 *The Religion of India: the Sociology of Hinduism and Buddhism;* 1963 *The Sociology of Religion;* 1968 *On Charisma and Institution Building.*

Weber's interest in religion was focused on the impact of religious views and ideas on society, and on the relationship of religion to other cultural institutions like economics. He had an historical as well as a functional approach, and had a growing concern for comparative studies. He may be considered one of the pioneers of the sociology of religion. Opposing current theories, Weber held that religion was first purposive and only later became symbolic. Throughout his social science studies he showed a strong methodological awareness.

The following text consists of the introductory pages from *The Sociology of Religion* and shows Weber's approach to the study of religion.

SYMBOLIC MEANING AND RELIGION

To define 'religion', to say what it *is*, is not possible at the start of a presentation such as this. Definition can be attempted, if at all, only at the conclusion of the study. The essence of religion is not even our concern, as we make it our task to study the conditions and effects of a particular type of social behavior.

The external courses of religious behavior are so diverse that an understanding of this behavior can only be achieved from the viewpoint of the subjective experiences, ideas, and purposes of the individuals concerned – in short, from the viewpoint of the religious behavior's 'meaning' *(Sinn)*.

The most elementary forms of behavior motivated by religious or magical factors are oriented to *this* world. 'That it may go well with thee . . . and that thou mayest prolong thy days upon the earth' (Deut. 4:40) expresses the reason for the performance of actions enjoined by religion or magic. Even human sacrifices, uncommon among urban peoples, were performed in the Phoenician maritime cities without any otherworldly expectations whatsoever. Furthermore, religiously or magically motivated behavior is relatively rational behavior, especially in its earliest manifestations. It follows rules of experience, though it is not necessarily action in accordance with a means-end scheme. Rubbing will elicit sparks from pieces of wood, and in like fashion the simulative actions of a magician will evoke rain from the heavens. The sparks resulting from twirling the wooden sticks are as much a 'magical' effect as the rain evoked by the manipulations of the rainmaker. Thus, religious or magical behavior or thinking must not be set apart from the range of everyday purposive conduct, particularly since even the ends of the religious and magical actions are predominantly economic.

Only we, judging from the standpoint of our modern views of nature, can distinguish objectively in such behavior those attributions of causality which are 'correct' from those which are 'fallacious', and then designate the fallacious attributions of causality as irrational, and the corresponding acts as 'magic'. Quite a different distinction will be made by the person performing the magical act, who will instead distinguish between the greater or lesser ordinariness of the phenomena in question. For example, not every stone can serve as a fetish, a source of magical power. Nor does every person have the capacity to achieve the ecstatic states which are viewed, in accordance with primitive experience, as the preconditions for producing certain effects in meteorology, healing, divination, and telepathy. It is primarily, though not exclusively, these extraordinary powers that have been designated by such special terms as 'mana', 'orenda', and the Iranian 'maga' (the term from which our word 'magic' is derived). We shall henceforth employ the term 'charisma' for such extraordinary powers.

Charisma may be either of two types. Where this appellation is fully merited, charisma is a gift that inheres in an object or person simply by virtue of natural endowment. Such primary charisma cannot be acquired by any means. But charisma of the other type may be produced artificially in an object or person through some extraordinary means. Even then, it is assumed that charismatic powers can be developed only in people or objects in which the germ already existed but would have remained dormant unless evoked by some ascetic or other regimen. Thus, even at the earliest stage of religious evolution there are already present *in nuce* all forms of the doctrine of religious grace, from that of *gratia infusa* to the most rigorous tenet of salvation by good works. The strongly naturalistic orientation (lately termed 'pre-animistic') of the earliest religious phenomena is still a feature of folk religion. To this day, no decision of church councils, differentiating the 'worship' of God from the 'adoration' of the icons of saints, and defining the icons as mere instruments of devotion, has succeeded in deterring a south European peasant from spitting on the statue of a saint when he holds it responsible that a favor he sought did not materialize, even though the customary procedures were performed.

A process of abstraction, which only appears to be simple, has usually already been carried out in the most primitive instances of religious behavior which we examine. Already crystallized is the notion that certain beings are concealed 'behind' and responsible for the activity of the charismatically endowed natural objects, artifacts, animals, or persons. This is the belief in spirits. At the outset, 'spirit' is neither soul, demon, nor god, but something indeterminate, material yet invisible, nonpersonal and yet somehow endowed with volition. By entering into a concrete object, spirit endows the latter with its distinctive power. The spirit may depart from its host or vessel, leaving the latter inoperative and causing the magician's charisma to fail. In other cases, the spirit may diminish into nothingness, or it may enter into another person or thing.

That any particular economic conditions are prerequisites for the emergence of a belief in spirits does not appear to be demonstrable. But belief in spirits, like all abstraction, is most advanced in the societies within which certain persons possess charismatic magical powers that inhere only in those with special qualifications. Indeed it is this circumstance that lays the foundation for the oldest of all 'vocations', that of the professional necromancer. In contrast to the ordinary layman, the magician is the person who is permanently endowed with charisma. Furthermore, he has taken a lease on, or has at least made a unique object of his cultivation, the distinctive subjective condition that notably represents or mediates charisma, namely ecstasy. For the layman, this psychological state is accessible only in occasional actions. Unlike the merely rational practice of wizardry, ecstasy occurs in a social form, the orgy, which is the primordial form of communal religious association. But the orgy is an occasional activity, whereas the enterprise of the magician is continuous and he is indispensable for its operation.

Because of the routine demands of living, the layman may experience ecstasy only occasionally, as intoxication. To induce ecstasy, he may employ any type of alcoholic beverage, tobacco, or similar narcotics – and especially music – all of which originally served orgiastic purposes. In addition to the rational manipulation of spirits in accordance with economic interests, the manner in which ecstasy was employed constituted another important concern of the magician's art, which, naturally enough, developed almost everywhere into a secret lore. On the basis of the magician's experience with the conditions of orgies, and in all likelihood under the influence of his professional practice, there evolved the concept of 'soul' as a separate entity present in, behind or near natural objects, even as the human body contains something that leaves it in dream, syncope, ecstasy, or death.

This is not the place to treat extensively the diversity of possible relationships between a spiritual being and the object behind which it lurks and with which it is somehow connected. These spirits or souls may 'dwell' more or less continuously and exclusively near or within a concrete object or process. But on the other hand, they may somehow 'possess' types of events, things, or categories, the behavior and efficacy of which they will decisively determine. These and similar views are animistic. The spirits may temporarily incorporate themselves into things, plants, animals, or people; this is a further stage of abstraction, achieved only gradually.

At the highest stage of abstraction, which is scarcely ever maintained consistently, spirits may be regarded as invisible essences that follow their own laws, and are merely 'symbolized by' concrete objects. In between these extremes of naturalism and abstraction there are many transitions and combinations. Yet even at the first stage of the simpler forms of abstraction, there is present in principle the notion of 'supersensual' forces that may intervene in the destiny of people in the same way that a man may influence the course of the world about him.

At these earlier stages, not even the gods and demons are yet personal or enduring, and indeed they do not even have names of their own. A god may be thought of as a power controlling the course of one particular event (Usener's *Augenblicksgötter*), to whom no one gives a second thought until the event in question is repeated. On the other hand, a god may be the power which somehow emanates from a great hero after his death. Either personification or depersonalization may be a later development. Then, too, we find gods without any personal name, who are designated only by the name of the process they control. At a later time, when the semantics of this designation is no longer understood, the designation of this process may take on the character of a proper name for the god. Conversely, the proper names of powerful chieftains or prophets have become the designations of divine powers, a procedure there employed in reverse by myth to derive the right to transform purely divine appellations into personal names of deified heroes. Whether a given conception of a deity becomes enduring and therefore always to be approached by magical or symbolic means, depends upon many different circumstances. The most important of these is whether and in what manner the clientele of a magician or the personal following of a secular chieftain accept the god in question on the basis of their own personal experiences.

Here we may simply note that the result of this process is the rise on the one hand of the idea of the 'soul', and on the other of ideas of 'gods', 'demons', and 'supernatural' powers, the ordering of whose relations to men constitutes the realm of religious behavior. At the outset, the soul is neither a personal nor yet an impersonal entity. It is frequently identified – in a naturalistic fashion – with something that disappears after death, e.g., with the breath or with the beat of the heart in which it resides and by the ingestion of which one may acquire the courage of his dead adversary. Far more important is the fact that the soul is frequently viewed as a heterogeneous entity. Thus, the soul that leaves man during dreams is distinguished from the soul that leaves him in ecstasy – when his heart beats in his throat and his breath fails, and from the soul that inhabits his shadow. Different yet is the soul that, after death, clings to the corpse or stays near it as long as something is left of it, and that continues to exert influence at the site of the person's former residence, observing with envy and anger how the heirs are relishing what had belonged to it in its life. Still another soul is that which appears to the descendants in dreams or visions, threatening or counseling, or that which enters into some animal or into another person – especially a newborn baby – bringing blessing or curse, as the case may be. The conception of the 'soul' as an independent entity set over against the 'body' is by no means universally accepted, even in the religions of salvation. Indeed, some of these religions, such as Buddhism, specifically reject this notion.

What is primarily distinctive in this whole development is not the personality, impersonality or superpersonality of these supernatural powers, but the fact that new experiences now play a role in life. Before, only the things or events that actually exist or take place played a role in life; now certain experiences, of a different order in that they only signify something, also play a role in life. Magic is transformed from a direct manipulation of forces into a symbolic activity.

A notion that the soul of dead must be rendered innocuous developed, beyond the direct and animal-like fear of the physical corpse (a fear manifested even by animals), which direct fear often determined burial postures and procedures, e.g., the squatting and upright postures, cremation, etc. After the development of ideas of the soul, the body had to be removed or restrained in the grave, provided with a tolerable existence, and prevented from becoming envious of the possessions enjoyed by the living; or its good will had to be secured in other ways, if the survivors were to live in peace. Of the various magical practices relating to the disposal of the dead, the notion with the most enduring economic consequences is that the corpse must be accompanied to the grave by all its personal belongings. This notion was gradually attenuated to the requirement that the goods of the deceased must not be touched for at least a brief period after his death, and frequently the requirement that the survivors must not even enjoy their own possessions lest they arouse the envy of the dead. The funerary prescriptions of the Chinese still fully retain this view, with consequences that are equally irrational in both the economic and the political spheres. One of the interdictions during the mourning period related to the occupancy of a benefice or inheritance; since the usufruct thereof constituted a possession, it had to be avoided.

Various consequences of significance to magical art emerged from the development of a realm of souls, demons, and gods. These beings cannot be grasped or perceived in any concrete sense but manifest a type of transcendental being which normally is accessible only through the mediation of symbols and significances, and which consequently is represented as shadowy and even unreal. Since it is assumed that behind real things and events there is something else, distinctive and spiritual, of which real events are only the symptoms or indeed the symbols, an effort must be made to influence, not the concrete things, but the spiritual powers that express themselves through concrete things. This is done through actions that address themselves to a spirit or soul, hence done by instrumentalities that 'mean' something, i.e., symbols. Thereafter, naturalism may be swept away by a flood of symbolic actions. The occurrence of this displacement of naturalism depends upon the success with which the professional masters of the symbolism use their status of power within the community to impart vigor and intellectual elaboration to their beliefs. The displacement of naturalism will also depend upon the significance of magic for the distinctive character of the economy and upon the power of the organization the necromancers succeed in creating.

The proliferation of symbolic acts and their supplanting of the original naturalism will have far-reaching consequences. Thus, if the dead person is accessible only through symbolic actions, and indeed if the god expresses himself only through symbols, then the corpse may be satisfied with symbols instead of real things. As a result, actual sacrifices may be replaced by shewbreads and puppetlike representations of the surviving wives and servants of the deceased. It is of interest that the oldest paper money was used to pay, not the living, but the dead. A similar substitution occurred in the relationship of men to gods and demons. More and more, things and events assumed significances other than the real potencies that actually or presumably inhered in them, and efforts were made to achieve real effects by means of various symbolically significant actions.

Every purely magical act that had proved successful in a naturalistic sense was of course repeated in the form once established as effective. This principle extended to the entire domain of symbolic significances, since the slightest deviation from the ostensibly successful method might render the procedure inefficacious. Thus, all areas of human activity were drawn into this circle of magical symbolism. For this reason the greatest conflicts between purely dogmatic views, even within rationalistic religions, may be tolerated more easily than innovations in symbolism, which threaten the magical efficacy of action or even – and this is a new concept supervening upon symbolism – arouse the anger of a god or an ancestral spirit. Thus, the question whether a cross should be made with two or three bars was a basic reason for the schism of the Russian church as late as the seventeenth century. Again, the fear of giving serious affront to two dozen saints by omitting the days sacred to them from the calendar year has hindered the reception of the Georgian [Gregorian] calendar in Russia up to this time. [Written prior to 1914]. Among the magicians of India, faulty singing during ritual dances was immediately punished by the death of the guilty singer, to remove the evil magic or to avert the anger of the god.

The religious stereotyping of pictorial artifacts, the oldest form of stylization, was directly determined by magical conceptions and indirectly determined by the fact that these artifacts came to be produced professionally for their magical significance. This stylizing tended alone to automatically favor the production of art objects based upon design rather than upon representative reproduction of natural objects. The significance of the religious factor in art is exemplified in Egypt, where the devaluation of the traditional religion by the monotheistic campaign of Amenhotep IV (Ikhnaton) immediately stimulated naturalism. Other examples of the religious stylization of art may be found in the magical uses of alphabetical symbols; the developments of mimicry and dance as homeopathic, apotropaic, exorcistic, or magically coercive symbolisms; and the stereotyping of admissible musical scales, or at least admissible musical keynotes (*raga* in India), in contrast to grace notes. Another manifestation is found in the widespread substitutions of therapies based upon exorcism or upon symbolic homeopathy for the previous empirical methods of medical treatment, which were frequently considerably developed but still seemed only a cure of the symptoms, from the point of view of symbolism and the animistic doctrine of possession by spirits. From the standpoint of animistic symbolism's own basic assumptions its therapeutic methods might be regarded as rational, but they bear the same relation to empirical therapy as astrology, which grew from the same roots, bears to empirical computation of the calendar.

These and related phenomena had incalculable significance for the substantive evolution of culture, though we cannot go into any additional details here. The first and fundamental effect of religious views upon the conduct of life and therefore upon economic activity was generally stereotyping. The alteration of any practice which is somehow executed under the protection of supernatural forces may affect the interests of spirits and gods. To the natural uncertainties and resistances of every innovator, religion thus adds powerful impediments of its own. The sacred is the uniquely unalterable.

Transitions from pre-animistic naturalism to symbolism were altogether variable as regards specific details. When the primitive tears out the heart of a slain foe, or wrenches the sexual organs from the body of his victim, or extracts the brain from the skull and then mounts the skull in his home or esteems it as the most precious of bridal presents, or eats parts of the bodies of slain foes or the bodies of especially powerful animals – he really believes that he is coming into possession, in a naturalistic fashion, of the various powers attributed to these physical organs. The war dance is in the first instance the product of a mixture of fury and fear before the battle, and it directly produces a heroic frenzy; to this extent it too is naturalistic rather than symbolic. But insofar as the war dance, in the pattern of manipulations by sympathetic magic, mimetically anticipates victory and seeks to insure it by magical means, insofar as animals and men are slaughtered in fixed rites, and insofar as the gods and spirits of the tribe are summoned to participate in the ceremonial repast, the transition to symbolism is at hand. Finally, there is involved in the passage to symbolism the tendency for the participants in the consumption of the sacrificial animal to regard themselves as having a distinctively close kin relationship to one another because the soul of this animal has entered into them.

The term 'mythological thinking' has been applied to the pattern of thought which is the basis of the fully developed circle of symbolic concepts, and considerable attention has been given to the clarification of its distinctive character. We cannot occupy ourselves with these problems here, and only one generally important aspect of this type of thinking is of concern to us: the significance of analogy, especially in its most effective form, the comparison.

Sigmund Freud

Sigmund Freud was born in 1856 at Freiberg in Moravia, from where his parents moved to Vienna in 1860. He received here his first education at home, and continued the rest of his primary and the whole of his secondary school education in Vienna. In 1873 he enrolled as a medical student at the University of Vienna, did research work at the Physiological Institute and passed his final medical examinations in 1881. Having continued his work at the Physiological Institute until 1882, Freud decided to become a clinical neurologist and worked at the Institute of Cerebral Anatomy until 1885. In that year he became *Privatdozent* in Neuropathology at the University of Vienna. In 1885—86 he continued to study neurology with J. M. Charcot in Paris and became interested in psychopathology; subsequently he spent three weeks in Berlin. On his return in Vienna he established himself as a medical doctor and continued his neurological investigations, the results of which were published in several publications. His interest developed in clinical psychology and he worked together with J. Breuer; in 1895 they published a book with studies on hysteria from a psychological point of view. In those years Freud developed the so-called 'free association' method in psychotherapy, which replaced the older method of hypnotism. This method was at first called 'psycho-catharsis'; the term 'psychoanalysis' was used for the first time in 1896. Freud found sexual experiences being at the bottom of every hysteria, and discovered the essental part that sexual factors play in the causation of neuroses. In the following years he drew attention to the existence and importance of infantile sexuality and developed a theory of neuroses in which a new theory of dreams was incorporated. In this way Freud made the unconscious subject of scholarly research, and devoted himself to it. In 1902 Freud became *Extraordinarius* at the University of Vienna; he received in 1920 the title of full professor. In 1908 he founded the Vienna Psycho-Analytical Society and organized the first International Congress of Psychoanalysis; such congresses would be held every two years. In 1910 the International Psycho-Analytical Association was founded, with branches in different countries. Notwithstanding much opposition Freud succeeded in making psychoanalysis as a therapeutical method and as a psychological theory more generally accepted. In 1909 he gave lectures at Clark University, Worcester, Mass. Freud had to move to London in 1938, where he died in 1939.

The most important books by S. Freud, which have been translated into English, apart from the *Collected Papers* and the *Complete Psychological Works*, are the following: 1910 *Three Contributions to the Sexual Theory;* 1910 *Five Lectures on Psycho-Analysis;* 1913 *The Interpretation of Dreams;* 1914 *Psychopathology of Everyday Life;* 1916 *Wit and its Relation to the Unconscious;* 1920 *A General Introduction to Psychoanalysis;* 1922 *Beyond the Pleasure Principle;*

927 *The Ego and the Id;* 1926 *Inhibition, Symptom and Anxiety;* 1928 *The Future of an Illusion;* 1930 *Civilization and its Discontents;* 1933 *New Introductory Lectures on Psycho-Analysis;* 1939 *Moses and Monotheism.*
Known as the founder of depth psychology, Freud discovered the existence of the personal unconscious; he analyzed the major forces within it and their influence on consciousness, and he traced the role which religion and mythology, as well as art and literature, play with regard to the mechanisms found in neurosis. He opened the way to study and interpret religion in terms of depth psychoo·y. To Freud, religion is basically a projection of infantile dependencies, and the history of religion is to be seen as the history of a collective neurosis.
The following fragments have been chosen from *The Future of an Illusion,* from *New Introductory Lectures on Psycho-Analysis,* and from *Moses and Monotheism.* They show what Freud meant by calling religion an 'illusion', how he saw the relationship between science and religious *Weltanschauung,* and how he explained the general history of religion.

RELIGION AS ILLUSION

I think we have prepared the way sufficiently for an answer [. . .]. It will be found if we turn our attention to the psychical origin of religious ideas. These, which are given out as teachings, are not precipitates of experience or endresults of thinking: they are illusions, fulfilments of the oldest, strongest and most urgent wishes of mankind. The secret of their strength lies in the strength of those wishes. As we already know, the terrifying impression of helplessness in childhood aroused the need for protection — for protection through love — which was provided by the father; and the recognition that this helplessness lasts throughout life made it necessary to cling to the existence of a father, but this time a more powerful one. Thus the benevolent rule of a divine Providence allays our fear of the dangers of life; the establishment of a moral world-order ensures the fulfilment of the demands of justice, which have so often remained unfulfilled in human civilization; and the prolongation of earthly existence in a future life provides the local and temporal framework in which these wish-fulfilments shall take place. Answers to the riddles that tempt the curiosity of man, such as how the universe began or what the relation is between body and mind, are developed in conformity with the underlying assumptions of this system. It is an enormous relief to the individual psyche if the conflicts of its childhood arising from the father-complex — conflicts which it has never wholly overcome — are removed from it and brought to a solution which is universally accepted.
When I say that these things are all illusions, I must define the meaning of the word. An illusion is not the same thing as an error; nor is it necessarily an error. Aristotle's belief that vermin are developed out of dung (a belief to which ignorant people still cling) was an error; so was the belief of a

former generation of doctors that *tabes dorsalis* is the result of sexual excess. It would be incorrect to call these errors illusions. On the other hand, it was an illusion of Columbus's that he had discovered a new sea-route to the Indies. The part played by his wish in this error is very clear. One may describe as an illusion the assertion made by certain nationalists that the Indo-Germanic race is the only one capable of civilization; or the belief, which was only destroyed by psycho-analysis, that children are creatures without sexuality. What is characteristic of illusions is that they are derived from human wishes. In this respect they come near to psychiatric delusions. But they differ from them, too, apart from the more complicated structure of delusions. In the case of delusions, we emphasize as essential their being in contradiction with reality. Illusions need not necessarily be false — that is to say, unrealizable or in contradiction to reality. For instance, a middle-class girl may have the illusion that a prince will come and marry her. This is possible; and a few such cases have occurred. That the Messiah will come and found a golden age is much less likely. Whether one classifies this belief as an illusion or as something analogous to a delusion will depend on one's personal attitude. Examples of illusions which have proved true are not easy to find, but the illusion of the alchemists that all metals can be turned into gold might be one of them. The wish to have a great deal of gold, as much gold as possible, has, it is true, been a good deal damped by our present-day knowledge of the determinants of wealth, but chemistry no longer regards the transmutation of metals into gold as impossible. Thus we call a belief an illusion when a wish-fulfilment is a prominent factor in its motivation, and in doing so we disregard its relations to reality, just as the illusion itself sets no store by verification.

Having thus taken our bearings, let us return once more to the question of religious doctrines. We can now repeat that all of them are illusions and insusceptible of proof. No one can be compelled to think them true, to believe in them. Some of them are so improbable, so incompatible with everything we have laboriously discovered about the reality of the world, that we may compare them — if we pay proper regard to the psychological differences — to delusions. Of the reality value of most of them we cannot judge; just as they cannot be proved, so they cannot be refuted. We still know too little to make a critical approach to them. The riddles of the universe reveal themselves only slowly to our investigation; there are many questions to which science to-day can give no answer. But scientific work is the only road which can lead us to a knowledge of reality outside ourselves. It is once again merely an illusion to expect anything from intuition and introspection; they can give us nothing but particulars about our own mental life, which are hard to interpret, never any information about the questions which religious doctrine finds it so easy to answer. It would be insolent to let one's own arbitrary will step into the breach and, according to one's personal estimate, declare this or that part of the religious system to be less or more acceptable. Such questions are too momentous for that; they might be called too sacred.

At this point one must expect to meet with an objection. 'Well then, if even obdurate sceptics admit that the assertions of religion cannot be refuted by reason, why should I not believe in them, since they have so much on their side — tradition, the agreement of mankind, and all the consolations they offer?' Why not, indeed? Just as no one can be forced to believe, so no one can be forced to disbelieve. But do not let us be satisfied with deceiving ourselves that arguments like these take us along the road of correct thinking. If ever there was a case of a lame excuse we have it here. Ignorance is ignorance; no right to believe anything can be derived from it. In other matters no sensible person will behave so irresponsibly or rest content with such feeble grounds for his opinions and for the line he takes. It is only in the highest and most sacred things that he allows himself to do so. In reality these are only attempts at pretending to oneself or to other people that one is still firmly attached to religion, when one has long since cut oneself loose from it. Where questions of religion are concerned, people are guilty of every possible sort of dishonesty and intellectual misdemeanour. Philosophers stretch the meaning of words until they retain scarcely anything of their original sense. They give the name of 'God' to some vague abstraction which they have created for themselves; having done so they can pose before all the world as deists, as believers in God, and they can even boast that they have recognized a higher, purer concept of God, notwithstanding that their God is now nothing more than an insubstantial shadow and no longer the mighty personality of religious doctrines. Critics persist in describing as 'deeply religious' anyone who admits to a sense of man's insignificance or impotence in the face of the universe, although what constitutes the essence of the religious attitude is not this feeling but only the next step after it, the reaction to it which seeks a remedy for it. The man who goes no further, but humbly acquiesces in the small part which human beings play in the great world — such a man is, on the contrary, irreligious in the truest sense of the word.

To assess the truth-value of religious doctrines does not lie within the scope of the present enquiry. It is enough for us that we have recognized them as being, in their psychological nature, illusions. But we do not have to conceal the fact that this discovery also strongly influences our attitude to the question which must appear to many to be the most important of all. We know approximately at what periods and by what kind of men religious doctrines were created. If in addition we discover the motives which led to this, our attitude to the problem of religion will undergo a marked displacement. We shall tell ourselves that it would be very nice if there were a God who created the world and was a benevolent Providence, and if there were a moral order in the universe and an after-life; but it is a very striking fact that all this is exactly as we are bound to wish it to be. And it would be more remarkable still if our wretched, ignorant and downtrodden ancestors had succeeded in solving all these difficult riddles of the universe.

'THE QUESTION OF A *WELTANSCHAUUNG*'

Ladies and Gentlemen, [...] I propose that we should now take a bold leap and venture upon answering a question which is constantly being asked in other quarters: does psycho-analysis lead to a particular *Weltanschauung* and, if so, to which?

'*Weltanschauung*' is, I am afraid, a specifically German concept, the translation of which into foreign languages might well raise difficulties. If I try to give you a definition of it, it is bound to seem clumsy to you. In my opinion, then, a *Weltanschauung* is an intellectual construction which solves all the problems of our existence uniformly on the basis of one overriding hypothesis, which, accordingly, leaves no question unanswered and in which everything that interests us finds its fixed place. It will easily be understood that the possession of a *Weltanschauung* of this kind is among the ideal wishes of human beings. Believing in it one can feel secure in life, one can know what to strive for, and how one can deal most expediently with one's emotions and interests.

If that is the nature of a *Weltanschauung*, the answer as regards psychoanalysis is made easy. As a specialist science, a branch of psychology — a depth-psychology or psychology of the unconscious — it is quite unfit to construct a *Weltanschauung* of its own: it must accept the scientific one. But the *Weltanschauung* of science already departs noticeably from our definition. It is true that it too assumes the *uniformity* of the explanation of the universe; but it does so only as a programme, the fulfilment of which is relegated to the future. Apart from this it is marked by negative characteristics, by its limitation to what is at the moment knowable and by its sharp rejection of certain elements that are alien to it. It asserts that there are no sources of knowledge of the universe other than the intellectual working-over of carefully scrutinized observations — in other words, what we call research — and alongside of it no knowledge derived from revelation, intuition or divination. It seems as though this view came very near to being generally recognized in the course of the last few centuries that have passed; and it has been left to *our* century to discover the presumptuous objection that a *Weltanschauung* like this is alike paltry and cheerless, that it overlooks the claims of the human intellect and the needs of the human mind.

This objection cannot be too energetically repudiated. It is quite without a basis, since the intellect and the mind are objects for scientific research in exactly the same way as any nonhuman things. Psycho-analysis has a special right to speak for the scientific *Weltanschauung* at this point, since it cannot be reproached with having neglected what is mental in the picture of the universe. Its contribution to science lies precisely in having extended research to the mental field. And, incidentally, without such a psychology science would be very incomplete. If, however, the investigation of the intellectual and emotional functions of men (and of animals) is included in science, then it will be seen that nothing is altered in the attitude of science as a whole, that no new sources of knowledge or methods of research have come into being. Intuition and divination would be such, if they existed; but they may safely be reckoned as illusions, the fulfilments of wishful impulses. It is easy to see, too, that these demands upon a *Weltanschauung* are only based on emotion. Science takes notice of the fact that the human mind produces these demands and is ready to examine their sources; but it has not the slightest reason to regard them as justified. On the contrary it sees this as a warning carefully to separate from knowledge everything that is illusion and an outcome of emotional demands like these.

This does not in the least mean that these wishes are to be pushed contemptuously on one side or their value for human life under-estimated. We are ready to trace out the fulfilments of them which they have created for themselves in the products of art and in the systems of religion and philosophy; but we cannot nevertheless overlook the fact that it would be illegitimate and highly inexpedient to allow these demands to be transferred to the sphere of knowledge. For this would be to lay open the paths which lead to psychosis, whether to individual or group psychosis, and would withdraw valuable amounts of energy from endeavours which are directed towards reality in order, so far as possible, to find satisfaction in it for wishes and needs.

From the standpoint of science one cannot avoid exercising one's critical faculty here and proceeding with rejections and dismissals. It is not permissible to declare that science is one field of human mental activity and that religion and philosophy are others, at least its equal in value, and that science has no business to interfere with the other two: that they all have an equal claim to be true and that everyone is at liberty to choose from which he will draw his convictions and in which he will place his belief. A view of this kind is regarded as particularly superior, tolerant, broad-minded and free from illiberal prejudices. Unfortunately it is not tenable and shares all the pernicious features of an entirely unscientific *Weltan-schauung* and is equivalent to one in practice. It is simply a fact that the truth cannot be tolerant, that it admits of no compromises or limitations, that research regards every sphere of human activity as belonging to it and that it must be relentlessly critical if any other power tries to take over any part of it.

[. . .]

This being the prehistory of the religious *Weltanschauung*, let us turn now to what has happened since then and to what is still going on before our eyes. The scientific spirit, strengthened by the observation of natural pro-cesses, has begun, in the course of time, to treat religion as a human affair and to submit it to a critical examination. Religion was not able to stand up to this. What first gave rise to suspicion and scepticism were its tales of miracles, for they contradicted everything that had been taught by sober observation and betrayed too clearly the influence of the activity of the human imagination. After this its doctrines explaining the origin of the universe met with rejection, for they gave evidence of an ignorance which bore the stamp of ancient times and to which, thanks to their increas-ed familiarity with the laws of nature, people knew they were superior. The idea that the universe came into existence through acts of copulation or creation analogous to the origin of individual people had ceased to be the most obvious and self-evident hypothesis since the distinction between animate creatures with a mind and an inanimate Nature had impressed itself on human thought – a distinction which made it impossible to retain belief in the original animism. Nor must we overlook the influence of the comparative study of different religious systems and the impression of their mutual exclusiveness and intolerance.

Strengthened by these preliminary exercises, the scientific spirit gained enough courage at last to venture on an examination of the most important and emotionally valuable elements of the religious *Weltanschauung*. People may always have seen, though it was long before they dared to say so openly, that the pronouncements of religion promising men protection and happiness if they would only fulfil certain ethical requirements had also shown them-selves unworthy of belief. It seems not to be the case that there is a Power in the universe which watches over the well-being of individuals with paren-tal care and brings all their affairs to a happy ending. On the contrary, the destinies of mankind can be brought into harmony neither with the hypothe-sis of a Universal Benevolence nor with the partly contradictory one of a Universal Justice. Earthquakes, tidal waves, conflagrations, make no distinction between the virtuous and pious and the scoundrel or unbeliever. Even where what is in question is not inanimate Nature but where an individual's fate depends on his relations to other people, it is by no means the rule that virtue is rewarded and that evil finds its punishment. Often enough the violent, cunning or ruthless man seizes the envied good things of the world and the pious man goes away empty. Obscure, unfeeling and unloving powers determine men's fate; the system of rewards and punishments which religion ascribes to the government of the universe seems not to exist. Here once again is a reason for dropping a portion of the animistic theory which had been rescued from animism by religion.

The last contribution to the criticism of the religious *Weltanschauung* was effected by psycho-analysis, by showing how religion originated from the helplessness of children and by tracing its contents to the survival into maturity of the wishes and needs of childhood. This did not precisely mean a contradiction of religion, but it was nevertheless a necessary rounding-off of our knowledge about it, and in one respect at least it was a contradiction, for religion itself lays claim to a divine origin. And, to be sure, it is not wrong in this, provided that our interpretation of God is accepted.

In summary, therefore, the judgement of science on the religious *Weltanschauung* is this. While the different religions wrangle with one another as to which of them is in possession of the truth, our view is that the question of the truth of religious beliefs may be left altogether on one side. Religion is an attempt to master the sensory world in which we are situated by means of the wishful world which we have developed within us as a result of biological and psychological necessities. But religion cannot achieve this. Its doctrines bear the imprint of the times in which they arose, the ignorant times of the childhood of humanity. Its consolations deserve no trust. Experience teaches us that the world is no nursery. The ethical demands on which religion seeks to lay stress need, rather, to be given another basis; for they are indispensable to human society and it is dangerous to link obedience to them with religious faith. If we attempt to assign the place of religion in the evolution of mankind, it appears not as a permanent acquisition but as a counterpart to the neurosis which individual civilized men have to go through in their passage from childhood to maturity.

You are of course free to critize this description of mine; I will even go half way to meet you on this. What I told you about the gradual crumbling away of the religious *Weltanschauung* was certainly incomplete in its abbreviated form. The order of the different processes was not given quite correctly; the co-operation of various forces in the awakening of the scientific spirit was not followed out. I also left out of account the alterations which took place in the religious *Weltanschauung* itself during the period of its undisputed sway and afterwards under the influence of growing criticism. Finally, I restricted my remarks, strictly speaking, to one single form taken by religion, that of the Western peoples. I constructed an anatomical model, so to speak, for the purpose of a hurried demonstration which was to be as impressive as possible. Let us leave on one side the question of whether my knowledge would in any case have been sufficient to do the thing better and more completely. I am aware that you can find everything I said to you said better elsewhere. Nothing in it is new. But let me express a conviction that the most careful working-over of the material of the problems of religion would not shake our conclusions.

The struggle of the scientific spirit against the religious *Weltanschauung* is, as you know, not at an end: it is still going on to-day under our eyes. Though as a rule psycho-analysis makes little use of the weapon of controversy, I will not hold back from looking into this dispute. In doing so I may perhaps throw some further light on our attitude to *Weltanschauungen*. You will see how easily some of the arguments brought forward by the supporters of religion can be answered, though it is true that others may evade refutation.

The first objection we meet with is to the effect that it is an impertinence on the part of science to make religion a subject for its investigations, for religion is something sublime, superior to any operation of the human intellect, something which may not be approached with hair-splitting criticisms. In other words, science is not qualified to judge religion: it is quite serviceable and estimable otherwise, so long as it keeps to its own sphere. But religion is not its sphere, and it has no business there. If we do not let ourselves be put off by this brusque repulse and enquire further what is the basis of this claim to a position exceptional among all human concerns, the reply we receive (if we are thought worthy of any reply) is that religion cannot be measured by human measurements, for it is of divine origin and was given us as a revelation by a Spirit which the human spirit cannot comprehend. One would have thought that there was nothing easier than the refutation of this argument: it is a clear case of *petitio principii*, of 'begging the question'* — I know of no good German equivalent expression. The actual question raised is whether there *is* a divine spirit and a revelation by it; and the matter is certainly not decided by saying that this question cannot be asked, since the deity may not be put in question. The position here is what it occasionally is during the work of analysis. If a usually sensible patient rejects some particular suggestion on specially foolish grounds, this logical weakness is evidence of the existence of a specially strong motive for the denial — a motive which can only be of an affective nature, an emotional tie.

* In English in the original.

We may also be given another answer, in which a motive of this kind is openly admitted: religion may not be critically examined because it is the highest, most precious, and most sublime thing that the human spirit has produced, because it gives expression to the deepest feelings and alone makes the world tolerable and life worthy of men. We need not reply by disputing this estimate of religion but by drawing attention to another matter. What we do is to emphasize the fact that what is in question is not in the least an invasion of the field of religion by the scientific spirit, but on the contrary an invasion by religion of the sphere of scientific thought. Whatever may be the value and importance of religion, it has no right in any way to restrict thought — no right, therefore, to exclude itself from having thought applied to it.

Scientific thinking does not differ in its nature from the normal activity of thought, which all of us, believers and unbelievers, employ in looking after our affairs in ordinary life. It has only developed certain features: it takes an interest in things even if they have no immediate, tangible use; it is concerned carefully to avoid individual factors and affective influences; it examines more strictly the trustworthiness of the sense-perceptions on which it bases its conclusions; it provides itself with new perceptions which cannot be obtained by everyday means and it isolates the determinants of these new experiences in experiments which are deliberately varied. Its endeavour is to arrive at correspondence with reality — that is to say, with what exists outside us and independently of us and, as experience has taught us, is decisive for the fulfilment or disappointment of our wishes. This correspondence with the real external world we call 'truth'. It remains the aim of scientific work even if we leave the practical value of that work out of account. When, therefore, religion asserts that it can take the place of science, that, because it is beneficent and elevating, it must also be true, that is in fact an invasion which must be repulsed in the most general interest. It is asking a great deal of a person who has learnt to conduct his ordinary affairs in accordance with the rules of experience and with a regard to reality, to suggest that he shall hand over the care of what are precisely his most intimate interests to an agency which claims as its privilege freedom from the precepts of rational thinking. And as regards the protection which religion promises its believers, I think none of us would be so much as prepared to enter a motor-car if its driver announced that he drove, unperturbed by traffic regulations, in accordance with the impulses of his soaring imagination.

The prohibition against thought issued by religion to assist in its self-preservation is also far from being free from danger either for the individual or for human society. Analytic experience has taught us that a prohibition like this, even if it is originally limited to a particular field, tends to widen out and thereafter to become the cause of severe inhibitions in the subject's conduct of life. This result may be observed, too, in the female sex, following from their being forbidden to have anything to do with their sexuality even in thought. Biography is able to point to the damage done by the religious inhibition of thought in the life stories of nearly all eminent individuals in the past. On the other hand intellect — or let us call it by the name that is familiar to us, reason — is among the powers which we may most expect to exercise a unifying influence on men — on men who are held together with such difficulty and whom it is therefore scarcely possible to rule. It may be imagined how impossible human society would be, merely if everyone had his own multiplication table and his own private units of length and weight. Our best hope for the future is that intellect — the scientific spirit, reason — may in process of time establish a dictatorship in the mental life of man. The nature of reason is a guarantee that afterwards it will not fail to give man's emotional impulses and what is determined by them the position they deserve. But the common compulsion exercised by such a dominance of reason will prove to be the strongest uniting bond among men and lead the way to further unions. Whatever, like religion's prohibitions against thought, opposes such a development, is a danger for the future of mankind.

[. . .]

We must admit to some extent the correctness of the other criticism. The path of science is indeed slow, hesitating, laborious. This fact cannot be denied or altered. No wonder the gentlemen in the other camp are dissatisfied. They are spoilt: revelation gave them an easier time. Progress in scientific work is just as it is in an analysis. We bring expectations with us into the work, but they must be forcibly held back. By observation, now at one point and now at another, we come upon something new; but to begin with the pieces do not fit together. We put forward conjectures, we construct hypotheses, which we withdraw if they are not confirmed, we need much patience and readiness for any eventuality, we renounce early convictions so as not to be led by them into overlooking unexpected factors, and in the end our whole expenditure of effort is rewarded, the scattered findings fit themselves together, we get an insight into a whole section of mental events, we have completed our task and now we are free for the next one. In analysis, however, we have to do without the assistance afforded to research by experiment.

Moreover, there is a good deal of exaggeration in this criticism of science. It is not true that it staggers blindly from one experiment to another, that it replaces one error by another. It works as a rule like a sculptor at his clay model, who tirelessly alters his rough sketch, adds to it and takes away from it, till he has arrived at what he feels is a satisfactory degree of resemblance to the object he sees or imagines. Besides, at least in the older and more mature sciences, there is even to-day a solid ground-work which is only modified and improved but no longer demolished. Things are not looking so bad in the business of science.

And what, finally, is the aim of these passionate disparagements of science ? In spite of its present incompleteness and of the difficulties attaching to it, it remains indispensable to us and nothing can take its place. It is capable of undreamt-of improvements, whereas the religious *Weltanschauung* is not. This is complete in all essential respects; if it was a mistake, it must remain one for ever. No belittlement of science can in any way alter the fact that it is attempting to take account of our dependence on the real external world, while religion is an illusion and it derives its strength from its readiness to fit in with our instinctual wishful impulses.

[. . .]

Ladies and Gentlemen, Allow me in conclusion to sum up what I had to say of the relation of psycho-analysis to the question of a *Weltanschauung*. Psycho-analysis, in may opinion, is incapable of creating a *Weltanschauung* of its own. It does not need one; it is a part of science and can adhere to the scientific *Weltanschauung*. This, however, scarcely deserves such a grandiloquent title, for it is not all-comprehensive, it is too incomplete and makes no claim to being self-contained and to the construction of systems. Scientific thought is still very young among human beings; there are too many of the great problems which it has not yet been able to solve. A *Weltanschauung* erected upon science has, apart from its emphasis on the real external world, mainly negative traits, such as submission to the truth and rejection of illusions. Any of our fellow-men who is dissatisfied with this state of things, who calls for more than this for his momentary consolation, may look for it where he can find it. We shall not grudge it him, we cannot help him, but nor can we on his account think differently.

THE STORY OF RELIGION

We have learnt from the psycho-analyses of individuals that their earliest impressions, received at a time when the child was scarcely yet capable of speaking, produce at some time or another effects of a compulsive character without themselves being consciously remembered. We believe we have a right to make the same assumption about the earliest experiences of the whole of humanity. One of these effects would be the emergence of the idea of a single great god — an idea which must be recognized as a completely justified memory, though, it is true, one that has been distorted. An idea such as this has a compulsive character: it *must* be believed.

To the extent to which it is distorted, it may be described as a *delusion;*
in so far as it brings a return of the past, it must be called the *truth.* Psychiatric delusions, too, contain a small fragment of truth and the patient's
conviction extends over from this truth on to its delusional wrappings.
  [...]
In 1912 I attempted, in my *Totem and Taboo*, to reconstruct the ancient
situation from which these consequences followed. In doing so, I made
use of some theoretical ideas put forward by Darwin, Atkinson and particularly by Robertson Smith, and combined them with the findings and
indications derived from psycho-analysis. From Darwin I borrowed the
hypothesis that human beings originally lived in small hordes, each of
which was under the despotic rule of an older male who appropriated
all the females and castigated or disposed of the younger males, including
his sons. From Atkinson I took, in continuation of this account, the idea
that this patriarchal system ended in a rebellion by the sons, who banded
together against their father, overcame him and devoured him in common.
Basing myself on Robertson Smith's totem theory, I assumed that subsequently the father-horde gave place to the totemic brother-clan. In order
to be able to live in peace with one another, the victorious brothers renounced
the women on whose account they had, after all, killed their father, and
instituted exogamy. The power of fathers was broken and the families
were organized as a matriarchy. The ambivalent emotional attitude of
the sons to their father remained in force during the whole of later development. A particular animal was set up in the father's place as a totem.
It was regarded as ancestor and protective spirit and might not be injured
or killed. But once a year the whole male community came together to
a ceremonial meal at which the totem animal (worshipped at all other
times) was torn to pieces and devoured in common. No one might absent
himself from this meal: it was the ceremonial repetition of the killing of
the father, with which social order, moral laws and religion had taken their
start. The conformity between Robertson Smith's totem meal and the
Christian Lord's Supper had struck a number of writers before me.
  To this day I hold firmly to this construction. I have repeatedly met
with violent reproaches for not having altered my opinions in later editions
of my book in spite of the fact that more recent ethnologists have unanimously rejected Robertson Smith's hypotheses and have in part brought
forward other, totally divergent theories. I may say in reply that these
ostensible advances are well known to me. But I have not been convinced
either of the correctness of these innovations or of Robertson Smith's
errors. A denial is not a refutation, an innovation is not necessarily an advance. Above all, however, I am not an ethnologist but a psycho-analyst.
I had a right to take out of ethnological literature what I might need for

the work of analysis. The writings of Robertson Smith — a man of genius — have given me valuable points of contact with the psychological material of analysis and indications for its employment. I have never found myself on common ground with his opponents.

The historical development. I cannot here repeat the contents of *Totem and Taboo* in greater detail. But I must undertake to fill up the long stretch between that hypothetical primaeval period and the victory of monotheism in historical times. After the institution of the combination of brother-clan, matriarchy, exogamy and totemism, a development began which must be described as a slow 'return of the repressed.' Here I am not using the term 'the repressed' in its proper sense. What is in question is something in a people's life which is past, lost to view, superseded and which we venture to compare with what is repressed in the mental life of an individual. We cannot at first sight say in what form this past existed during the time of its eclipse. It is not easy for us to carry over the concepts of individual psychology into group psychology; and I do not think we gain anything by introducing the concept of a 'collective' unconscious. The content of the unconscious, indeed, is in any case a collective, universal property of mankind. For the moment, then, we will make shift with the use of analogies. The processes in the life of peoples which we are studying here are very similar to those familiar to us in psychopathology, but nevertheless not quite the same. We must finally make up our minds to adopt the hypothesis that the psychical precipitates of the primaeval period became inherited property which, in each fresh generation, called not for acquisition but only for awakening. In this we have in mind the example of what is certainly the 'innate' symbolism which derives from the period of the development of speech, which is familiar to all children without their being instructed, and which is the same among all peoples despite their different languages. What we may perhaps still lack in certainty here is made good by other products of psycho-analytic research. We find that in a number of important relations our children react, not in a manner corresponding to their own experience, but instinctively, like the animals, in a manner that is only explicable as phylogenetic acquisition.

The return of the repressed took place slowly and certainly not spontaneously but under the influence of all the changes in conditions of life which fill the history of human civilization. I cannot give a survey here of these determinants nor more than a fragmentary enumeration of the stages of this return. The father once more became the head of the family, but was not by any means so absolute as the father of the primal horde had been. The totem animal was replaced by a god in a series of transitions which are still very plain. To begin with, the god in human form still bore an animal's head; later he turned himself by preference into that particular animal, and afterwards it became sacred to him and was his favourite attendant; or he killed the animal and himself bore its name as an epithet. Between the totem animal and the god, the hero emerged, often as a preliminary step towards deification. The idea of a supreme deity seems to have started early, at first only in a shadowy manner without intruding into men's daily interests. As tribes and peoples came together into larger unities, the gods too organized themselves into families and into hierarchies. One of them was often elevated into being supreme lord over gods and men. After this, the further step was hesitatingly taken of paying respect to only one god, and finally the decision was taken of giving all power to a single god and of tolerating no other gods beside him. Only thus was it that the supremacy of the father of the primal horde was re-established and that the emotions relating to him could be repeated.

The first effect of meeting the being who had so long been missed and longed for was overwhelming and was like the traditional description of the law-giving from Mount Sinai. Admiration, awe and thankfulness for having found grace in his eyes — the religion of Moses knew none but these positive feelings towards the father-god. The conviction of this irresistibility, the submission to his will, could not have been more unquestioning in the helpless and intimidated son of the father of the horde — indeed those feelings only become fully intelligible when they are transposed into the primitive and infantile setting. A child's emotional impulses are intensely and inexhaustibly deep to a degree quite other than those of an adult; only religious ecstasy can bring them back. A rapture of devotion to God was thus the first reaction to the return of the great father.

The direction to be taken by this father-religion was in this way laid down for all time. Yet this did not bring its development to an end. Ambivalence is a part of the essence of the relation to the father: in the course of time the hostility too could not fail to stir, which had once driven the sons into killing their admired and dreaded father. There was no place in the framework of the religion of Moses for a direct expression of the murderous hatred of the father. All that could come to light was a mighty reaction against it — a sense of guilt on account of that hostility, a bad conscience for having sinned against God and for not ceasing to sin. This sense of guilt, which was uninterruptedly kept awake by the Prophets, and which soon formed an essential part of the religious system, had yet another superficial motivation, which neatly disguised its true origin. Things were going badly for the people; the hopes resting on the favour of God failed in fulfilment; it was not easy to maintain the illusion, loved above all else, of being God's chosen people. If they wished to avoid renouncing that happiness, a sense of guilt on account of their own sinfulness offered a welcome means of exculpating God: they deserved no better than to be punished by him since they had not obeyed his commandments. And, driven by the need to satisfy this sense of guilt, which was insatiable and came from sources so much deeper, they must make those commandments grow ever stricter, more meticulous and even more trivial. In a fresh rapture of moral asceticism they imposed more and more new instinctual renunciations on themselves and in that way reached — in doctrine and precept, at least — ethical heights which had remained inaccessible to the other peoples of antiquity. Many Jews regard this attainment of ethical heights as the second main characteristic and the second great achievement of their religion. The way in which it was connected with the first one — the idea of a single god — should be plain from our remarks. These ethical ideas cannot, however, disavow their origin from the sense of guilt felt on account of a suppressed hostility to God. They possess the characteristic — uncompleted and incapable of completion — of obsessional neurotic reaction-formations; we can guess, too, that they serve the secret purposes of punishment.

The further development takes us beyond Judaism. The remainder of what returned from the tragic drama of the primal father was no longer reconcilable in any way with the religion of Moses. The sense of guilt of those days was very far from being any longer restricted to the Jewish people; it had caught hold of all the Mediterranean peoples as a dull *malaise*, a premonition of calamity for which no one could suggest a reason. Historians of our day speak of an ageing of ancient civilization, but I suspect that they have only grasped accidental and contributory causes of this depressed mood of the peoples. The elucidation of this situation of depression sprang from Jewry. Irrespectively of all the approximations and preparations in the surrounding world, it was after all a Jewish man, Saul of Tarsus (who, as a Roman citizen, called himself Paul), in whose spirit the realization first emerged: 'the reason we are so unhappy is that we have killed God the father.' And it is entirely understandable that he could only grasp this piece of truth in the delusional disguise of the glad tidings: 'we are freed from all guilt since one of us has sacrificed his life to absolve us.' In this formula the killing of God was of course not mentioned, but a crime that had to be atoned by the sacrifice of a victim could only have been a murder. And the intermediate step between the delusion and the historical truth was provided by the assurance that the victim of the sacrifice had been God's son. With the strength which it derived from the source of historical truth, this new faith overthrew every obstacle. The blissful sense of being chosen was replaced by the liberating sense of redemption. But the fact of the parricide, in returning to the memory of mankind, had to overcome greater resistances than the other fact, which had constituted the subject-matter of monotheism;* it was also obliged to submit to a more powerful distortion. The unnameable crime was replaced by the hypothesis of what must be described as a shadowy 'original sin'.

Original sin and redemption by the sacrifice of a victim became the foundation stones of the new religion founded by Paul. It must remain uncertain whether there was a ringleader and instigator to the murder among the band of brothers who rebelled against the primal father, or whether such a figure was created later by the imagination of creative artists in order to turn themselves into heroes, and was then introduced into the tradition. After the Christian doctrine had burst the framework of Judaism, it took up components from many other sources, renounced a number of characteristics of pure monotheism and adapted itself in many details to the rituals of the other Mediterranean peoples. It was as though Egypt was taking vengeance once more on the heirs of Akhenaten. It is worth noticing how the new religion dealt with the ancient ambivalence in the relation to the father. Its main content was, it is true, reconciliation with God the Father, atonement for the crime committed against him; but the other side of the emotional relation showed itself in the fact that the son, who had taken the atonement on himself, became a god himself beside the father and, actually, in place of the father. Christianity, having arisen out of a father-religion, became a son-religion. It has not escaped the fate of having to get rid of the father.

Only a portion of the Jewish people accepted the new doctrine. Those who refused to are still called Jews to-day. Owing to this cleavage, they have become even more sharply divided from other peoples than before. They were obliged to hear the new religious community (which, besides Jews, included Egyptians, Greeks, Syrians, Romans and eventually Germans) reproach them with having murdered God. In full, this reproach would run as follows: 'They will not accept it as true that they murdered God, whereas we admit it and have been cleansed of that guilt.' It is easy therefore to see how much truth lies behind this reproach. A special enquiry would be called for to discover why it has been impossible for the Jews to join in this forward step which was implied, in spite of all its distortions, by the admission of having murdered God. In a certain sense they have in that way taken a tragic load of guilt on themselves; they have been made to pay heavy penance for it.

Our investigation may perhaps have thrown a little light on the question of how the Jewish people have acquired the characteristics which distinguish them. Less light has been thrown on the problem of how it is that

* Namely, the fact of the existence of the primal father.

they have been able to retain their individuality till the present day. But exhaustive answers to such riddles cannot in fairness be either demanded or expected. A contribution, to be judged in view of the limitations which I mentioned at the start, is all that I can offer.

PART THREE

Religion as a Special Subject of Research

Nathan Söderblom

Nathan Söderblom was born in 1866 at Trönö, Sweden. He received his primary and secondary school education at home and in 1875 at Hudiksvall. He enrolled in the University of Uppsala, in order to study theology, in 1883 and received his B.A. in 1886. Thereupon he continued with theological studies proper and obtained the degree of Th. Cand. in 1892. In 1893 he started to study the Avesta language with K.V. Zetterstéen. Having been ordained minister in 1893 he practised as priest at Ulleråker hospital near Uppsala. Söderblom became in 1894 chaplain to the Swedish-Norwegian legation in Paris and in the Seamen's mission in Calais. In 1897 he was one of the stimulators of the Congress of *Religionswissenschaft* held in Stockholm. In Paris he pursued his studies in Persian with A. Meillet, and in the history of religions with Albert Réville and with L. Marillier, while he was in close contact with the theologian Auguste Sabatier. In 1899 he received the diploma of the *École Pratique des Hautes Études* with a thesis on the Fravashis in Mazdaism, and in 1901 he obtained his Th.D. at the Protestant Faculty of Theology, which was then connected with the Sorbonne, on a thesis on eschatology in Mazdaism. In that year Söderblom was appointed to the chair of 'Theological Encyclopedia' and 'Theological Prenotions' at the Faculty of Theology of the University of Uppsala. He edited a Swedish translation of religious texts in three volumes in 1907 and established the Olaus Petri Foundation at Uppsala in 1908. In 1912 he became professor of the History of Religions at the University of Leipzig while retaining his chair at Uppsala where he continued to teach for three months a year. In 1914 Söderblom was appointed archbishop of the Lutheran Church in Sweden, at Uppsala, which he remained for the rest of his life. He was one of the leaders of the ecumenical movement and organized the ecumenical conference of 1925 at Stockholm. Söderblom received the Nobel peace prize in 1930 and died at Uppsala in 1931.

The following books by Söderblom on the study of religion exist in English: 1913 art. 'Holiness' in the *Encyclopaedia of Religion and Ethics;* 1932 *The Nature of Revelation;* 1933 *The Living God: Basal Forms of Personal Religion.*

In his scholarly work Söderblom refused to confine himself to one explanation or one theory of the origin of human belief in God, but by using a typological method he wanted to demonstrate that animism, 'mana' belief and 'High God' belief were three different and parallel types of religious experience and development. He accentuated the importance of the category of holiness as the keyword in religion even before Rudolf Otto. He designed a typology of religion before Heiler, distinguishing ethnic religion, the mysticism of infinity, and prophetical revelation. Throughout his work he stressed the common religious search and striving of mankind.

The following fragments are, respectively, the concluding chapter of 'The Origin of the Belief in God' (German text 1915, translated with reference to the Swedish original), and some pages taken from *The Living God*, which give an idea of Söderblom's approach to religion.

'THE ORIGIN OF THE BELIEF IN GOD'

The missionaries were right, yet not completely. That is the way of the world. They never ceased talking about the great deity of the primitive peoples. Scholarly research thought to know better. The savages could not be credited with anything 'High'. The opinion was expressed that development begins with the inferior and progresses to the higher. And apart from that, one traveller, or another was able to give a different report. He had made enquiries — with the help of an interpreter of course — and had perhaps come to the conclusion that the natives had no religion at all, much less a belief in a higher being. The white man in his omniscience did not dream that he was not initiated into this field and that he was an outsider on the same level as the women and children of the primitive races. Then, however, A.W. Howitt was treated as an initiated person. This pioneer in our knowledge of the natives of Australia was not himself a missionary. At first he found no trace of a Supreme Being. 'Our Father' of the Kurnai tribe and the other omnipotent fathers were unknown to him. Therefore at first he denied that the aborigenes in South-West Australia had any kind of religion at all. Later on he believed he could sense the conception of an evil spirit — until the day on which he met his friend Turlburn on the plain between Lale and Rosedale.[1] The conversation turned to the secret dances, and, after a while, Turlburn could not keep his knowledge to himself, but with the secret thrill which the risk involved, he told the European in a whisper about the 'roarer'. The truth now began to dawn on Howitt. What he had known up to that time was at most what women and children were allowed to know. Before the eighties no white man had been present at the mysteries of the Australians. At least no one had described them. For A.W. Howitt's and our knowledge of the ceremonies and the primary beings they are centered around, a new epoch began with his participation in the holy rites of the Kurnai and the description of them which Howitt gave in 1884 and 1885. His initiation and that of others is indeed a matter apart. As far as is known, no white man ever took part in the initiation of his own free will. For it is scarcely credible that the thirst for knowledge in matters of ethnography and religious history would cause a man to undergo circumcision with stone knives or pieces of glass, the breaking out of a tooth or the consumption of nauseating foods. But it can be achieved in a more moderate fashion. Howitt was simply treated as having been initiated and was allowed to be present. The missionaries have the advantage that the natives, as we have already heard as regards the Indians in the seventeenth century, regard them, sooner than other Europeans, as being already initiated, because they are, in fact, men of religion. The Aranda, for instance, had no secrets from Carl Strehlow.

In this way the Supreme Beings of the primitives can no longer remain concealed. Many others will have had the same experience as I in that Andrew Lang's *Myth, Ritual and Religion* of the year 1887,[2] and particularly in its revised and more strongly primeval monotheistic *('urmonotheistisch')* form of 1889, left him no peace until he had formed for himself his own opinion about the matter. Those who are acquainted with my earlier essays and statements on this matter will know that a more thorough examination very soon led me to an increasingly intense modification of Lang's romantic hypothesis. I have here set down the reasons for a completely different judgment of what he calls the primitive belief in a 'Maker (if I am not to say 'Creator') and Judge of men'. At times there is doubt as to the sublimity of these beings. In Australia they apparently began as animals. And although they show themselves to be more important than ghosts and spirits, on the other hand, they lack value for the real religion; for this develops as a rule in connection with other conceptions than one which is, in general, so vague and ineffectual. The realization of God has an early history which is richer and more difficult to interpret than the protagonists of both animism and primeval monotheism think. The formulation of their questions is incorrect. The 'originators' *('Urheber')* bear clear witness to the ability of the primitives to sense the divine and also, in particular to follow the more or less conscious line of thought which has led to the realization of God. Only those who have become slaves of theory to such an extent that they are still convinced, even when faced with reality, that they know better, do not yet find it necessary to take into consideration Bajami and the like. Just as little as these natural objects are souls or ghosts, is animism able, even in the necessary limitation in which I call it animatism, to suffice in the future as a general explanation. The revision is troublesome. But if research does not subject existing theories to continuous revision, it would no longer be worthy of the name of research. The 'originators' represent neither the only point of departure of the primitives' belief in God, nor the most important one, in the same way as the certainty about God in the higher stages of religious development does not rest solely upon questions and conclusions which connects thought with the structure of the world, If we wish to designate primitive religion as revelation, this would be far more suited to the reaction, which manifests itself in emotion, longing and the observance of hallowed rites, to the peculiar, uncontrollable, dangerous, powerful, unusual — in a word the supernatural; and it would also be far more suited to the feeling that we are concerned with expressions of will and with powers which take personal action. The discussion provoked by Lang, similarly the mana theory[3] and preanimism, offers to many a welcome opportunity to pull animism to pieces. The latter, however, should not be confused with an arbitrary construction of the line of religious development, dependent on assumptions rather than on facts. Least of all is there occasion to denounce animism in the supposed interests of faith in God. Should any other interest than the scientific be put forward at this point, which occurrence is unfortunately as frequent as it is precarious, there is more reason for those to bear a grudge against animism and its continuations in the history of mankind, who deny the reality of the spiritual or who are unable to recognize the nature of God in the symbols of will and action. My earlier conjecture[4] that the Chinese Shang-ti had a connection with the originator type has been confirmed by a closer examination of the Chinese documents. But what are the facts of the case concerning the only early monotheism in the world worthy of that name, that is the biblical belief in revelation in its perfection? The term 'primeval monotheism' is not just a mere invention. The history of religion has indeed taught us to know figures in primitive belief, which cannot be derived from animism nor from fear of the 'Great Power'. But here in the Bible, there is little of such a primeval 'monotheism'. I do not mean simply that the biblical realization of God is inconceivable without personal revealers. But strangely enough Moses received his transforming certainty of the essence of God in the form of an animistic figure of God and not in the name of a passionless original being. I say 'in the form of', because before the revelation to Moses, the name Yahve did not have the substance which was to become decisive for the religious history of the world. But the thundering mountain God was more than just a shell which laid itself about the kernel of the ethical will of God and which had to be stripped away. In animism the consciousness of the impressiveness and the inescapable might of the deity was already alive. Animism has twice been of epoch-making influence on the development of the realization of God in the world of Western culture. The first time in the awful overwhelming form in which the will of God approached Moses, and the second time in Plato's doctrine concerning God and the divine essences and souls which are related to God's pure spirituality. In both these cases the two basic tendencies inherent in animism come to light: the conception of existence as will and as spirit. The importance of animism for the Mosaic religion may cause surprise. I do not believe that it can be denied.[5]

With his 'mana' Codrington has blazed a new trail in the wilderness of primitive religion so difficult to penetrate. He depicted the matter in a rather too abstract and philosophical way, and others, most particularly Hewitt, have overtaken him with modernizing explanations of might or 'life electricity'. But there is no doubt that one can penetrate deepest into the inner essence of primitive religion with the help of the power-and-taboo hypothesis. Here lies the longed-for treasure which confers a feeling of strength and happiness. Here lurks the danger which keeps the heart aquivering. Indifference does not exist. Feelings are set in motion, measures are taken. What is holy may not be taken lightly. In the religions of Australia, which form the basis of my research into primitive practices and ideas, all three main concepts of my presentation appear with greater clarity than elsewhere. But all along the line I believe my point of view to be confirmed. In the Old Testament, holiness combines with belief in God in order to strengthen its supernatural character. In the culture which developed the idea of power to the conception of the world soul, the latter lost intensity in favour of universality. Brahman is in everything but he inspires no holy quiver.

I return to my point of departure: the mentality of civilized man finds points of contact with the spiritual life of primitive man. In the sacral institutions of primitive society and its reactions to its surroundings, tendencies and presentiments are germinal, which take on a clearer form in the following and which can be differentiated partly as separate types of belief in God and partly as varied components of the same religion.[6] That Europe in recent centuries has been visited by the Chinese spirit of Shang-ti-T'ien and by the Brahman-Atman does not only signify an acquaintance with exotic strangers, but has meant in its own way a strengthening of movements, which made themselves felt at the same time in regular succession within the indigenous religious history of Europe. I, therefore, wished to obtain information on how enthusiasm arose, first of all for China and then for India, and how it took shape. And I have regarded it as relevant to give an account of this incipient process which finally amounts to the gathering together of all the experiences and thoughts of God in a world culture for mutual fructification but also above all in an inexorable contest: the experiences and thoughts of God which arose out of the dark beginnings of the primitives, which have taken shape according to the nature and destinies of the respective peoples, which from time to time have ripened to maturity in the spirits of thinkers, revealers and saints, and which have now appeared turbid and coarsened, diluted and watered down, but now also as purified and strengthened. Adolf Deissmann expressed the problem succinctly in a letter: 'It is necessary to find the parallellogram of powers between living energies of naive piety and the effects, at the same time purifying and consuming, of religious reflexion.' The most important cultures of the world have gone their own ways, yet not without knowledge of one another and not without mutual influence. Now they are forced to come together. It is the Christian mission which has called into being the worldwide spiritual process, out of which the victorious realization of God should emerge as the common possession of all mankind, and is now propelling it towards perfection. The amorphous beginning and the final abundance of understanding are outside our mental horizon. We can only pursue the ways over a limited distance. I wanted to attempt to give here a certain illumination, partly of the point at which the primitive ideas of the Deity begin to take clearer shape and partly of the epoch during which universal cooperation and competition at last got under way.

'THE LIVING GOD'

The subjects discussed in these lectures will be:

1. The difference existing among various phenomena appertaining to the spiritual and religious experience of man.

2. The difference between human beings of varying temperament and disposition.

3. Consequently also a relative difference between various types of personal religion.

Can one speak of personal religion among primitive people? Is not religion there entirely the concern of the tribe?

No; religion must exist and rise up in the soul of man prior to finding expression in his words and deeds, customs and institutions. It must be found in the individual before it becomes the concern of the community. As a natural reaction against earlier exaggeration of the feelings and opinions of the individual, religious research learned a generation ago to appreciate the importance of the community with regard to worship and sacred teaching. Religion meets us everywhere as a sacral institution. It appertains to the ordered life of society. But religion is also everywhere very old. We were not present when it arose. However, a beginning is inconceivable which does not issue from the reaction of the individual to things, events, and existence. A science which makes the community *all*, ignoring the individual, may seem to the sober judgement of a later time just as mythological and fantastic as primitive thought. Two peculiar conceptions have had a misleading attraction.

a) Religion has been conceived as an anonymous mass-product. Its beginning, to be sure, was anonymous; but a mass as such is never creative. It is composed of individuals. The forest cannot come into being, unless the separate trees shoot and grow. Taboo rules, commandments enjoining holiness, fear of the powers and communion with them are not, in some incomprehensible way, produced by the mass or the community. Take any mass-movement whatever, either in history or in our own time. Closer examination reveals that it had its origin in an individual or in individuals. The fire was kindled in a soul or in several souls, until the flames spread all around. The idea that the mass or community is the original subject of religion belongs to that modern scientific mythology which is in process of disappearing. We must condescend to go to the individual.

b) Another popular but misty scientific myth must also be dispelled. When Mannhardt discovered the vegetation demons and their significance he could scarcely have imagined their brilliant career. The old names and heroes of tradition were rapidly turned into vegetation demons. Their names and enterprises were made to support this view. I have honestly endeavoured to construct a concrete picture of that ancient time when our planet was mainly peopled by vegetation demons, sun and moon gods, and other mythical beings. One day in 1898 Peppé found on a hill at Piprava, west of Nepal, remains of the cremated body of the great Buddha. The acute intelligence of Axel Persson deciphers on a mug from about 1500 B. C. or later, found in the old palace at Thebes, the words 'Kadmos, ruler of Thebes'. Thus, even in prehistoric times, we have to reckon with men, yes, with important individuals. If we want to study the essence and elementary forms of religion, we must study the soul-life of the individual.

[...]

The difference between religious research in general and Christian theology in particular consists in the fact that the belief in revelation is an essential part of the latter. For Christian theology the history of religions is a divine self-communication. The comparative study of religions in general leaves the question about revelation open. He who practises it may be inspired by the conviction that a supernatural reality is lying behind the phenomena of religion. Or he may deny the belief in the spiritual which is fundamental for religion. Or he may remain inquiring and uncertain about the revelation, certain only of the impossibility of knowing anything about it. Or he may lack interest in the question about the truth of religion. Different views as regards the idea of revelation may of course not influence the method of research and the historical and psychological investigations in such a way that these are displaced in one direction or another by dogmatism. The remedy against such mistakes is not to forbid the investigator to have a certain conviction, but solely to carry out the investigation rightly, conscientiously, and seriously, and to submit readily to perceived truths.

A part of Biblical belief in revelation is the conviction that a portion of the history of religion is revelation in a stricter and fuller sense than is the rest of the same history. The doctrine of a special revelation must be tested in the light of historical reality. A sufficiently thorough orientation allows us to state that the special revelation which by Biblical faith has been marked out within the general revelation approximately corresponds to a special type of religion. This we call in the terminology of Usener, the religion of revelation. But the name does not give any statement of the metaphysical question regarding divine self-communication. We only establish the historical and psychological peculiarities of the prophetic, personal, or vocational religions in question. This type of religion goes back to special qualifications. Its peculiar essence is characteristically and essentially different from the comprehension of the Old World in general. And this difference can still be discerned in such schools of modern thought as consciously or unconsciously are descendants of the religion of revelation.

Religious research distinguishes the religion of revelation as a definite type within the history of religions, and in the same way the Christian faith marks off a special sphere of revelation. But this marking off cannot mean an absolute difference either in space or in time, just as religious research is unable to nullify the mutual connexion between all kinds of religion. All forms of religion are united in a common group of phenomena, and this union corresponds to the prophetic and Christian belief in a divine self-communication also outside the 'chosen people' and Christendom. It may be difficult to decide what it is in a certain form of religion that constitutes its trait of revelation from a Christian point of view. And it becomes impossible if we employ an intellectualistic view. But a measure of revelation, i.e. of divine self-communication, is present wherever we find religious sincerity. That has been expressly declared by the belief in revelation within' and without Christianity.

I have made an attempt to indicate the universal application of the belief in revelation as regards time. According to Christian conviction the divine self-communication is for all ages valid and inexhaustible in the sacred history, in Christ's own personality. But it is equally certain that belief in revelation cannot be maintained unless it is extended beyond the period of the Bible. Of course only outlines can be drawn here; attempts to draw a more precise map of continued revelation can scarcely be made without the risk of profanation or subjectivism. But it is desirable and necessary to supplement the certitude of a continued revelation with a concrete content and to interpret it.

The three points which have been examined here: genius, history, and the spiritual personality, are in my opinion the most important factors for the entire history of religions. They do not apply to monotheism, which is often a theoretical or political ground of unity, nor to the general development of morals, which certainly exercises influence on, and is influenced by religion, but is in no wise uniform with the development of religion. These points concern (1) the connexion of religion on various stages and in various senses with a hero, a saviour, or a prophet, in particular with a divine personality working on earth, whether he be a deified man or a humanized mythological creation or Christ; further, (2) the relation of religion to history; and (3) the place of the ethical values in the sphere of salvation and cult.

NOTES

1. *Cf.* My essay in *Ymer*, 1906, p. 208. The relevant essays have now been published in book form, with the title *Ur religionens historia.* Stockholm, 1915.

2. *Cf.* My essay on Andrew Lang's theory on the oldest form of religion known to us, in the *Nordisk Tidskrift*, 1902, and in *Ur religionens historia.*

3. *Cf.* also R. Lehmann, *Mana. Eine begriffsgeschichtliche Untersuchung auf ethnologischer Grundlage.* Leipzig, 1915.

4. *Nordisk Tidskrift*, 1906, p. 179; *Religion und Geisteskultur*, p. 321f.

5. That one can assume a strongly animistic character in the pre-Mosaic Jahve became clear to me during the preparation of a lecture held in the Aula of the University of Leipzig on December 18th, 1912, and which is printed in the *Archiv für Religionswissenschaft*, January 1914, with the title 'Zusammenhang höherer Gottesideen mit primitiven Vorstellungen'.

6. H. Hackmann differentiates between animatism (or animism) as a genetic prerequisite and the conception of power, and belief in originators (*'Urheber'*) as the constitutive or creative moments for the belief in God. *Theologische Literatur Zeitung*, XLI, p. 481 sq. (1916).

William Brede Kristensen

William Brede Kristensen was born in 1867 at Kristiansand, Norway. He received his primary and secondary school education at home, in Kristiansand and in Oslo. In 1884 he enrolled at the University of Oslo in the Faculty of Theology, but transferred to the Faculty of Arts in 1885 where he studied classical languages, Hebrew, Sanskrit, and ancient Egyptian with Lieblein. From 1890 until 1892 he studied in Leiden with C.P. Tiele, A. Kuenen and W. Pleyte; and from 1892 until 1894 he continued to study ancient languages in Paris. He then took his final examination in Oslo, worked for some time in London in 1895, and received his Ph.D. in Oslo in 1896 with a dissertation on Egyptian representations of life after death. From 1896 to 1897 he spent another year in Paris, and in 1897 he became a lecturer at the University of Oslo. In 1901, after a short stay in Paris, Kristensen occupied the chair of the History of Religions at the University of Leiden, which he held until his retirement in 1937. In 1946 he gave a series of lectures at the University of Oslo. He died in Leiden in 1953.

Only one book of W.B. Kristensen is available in English, which was composed from lecture notes: 1960 *The Meaning of Religion*.

In his studies of the ancient historical religions of Egypt, Greece, Rome, Persia and Mesopotamia, Kristensen made the attempt to come to an understanding of the religious documents on the basis of religious values which, in his view, were proper to the religion studied. He was attentive to the symbolism of the studied religions, in particular to what related to the problem of life and death. Kristensen was opposed to evolutionary views on the development of religion, prefered to study the texts apart from their time sequence, and to concentrate on their ideational contents.

The following text has been taken from *The Meaning of Religion* and contains a summary of the statements which the scholar made in his lectures on phenomenology of religion.

ON THE STUDY OF RELIGIOUS PHENOMENA

Comparative study is in numerous instances a quite necessary aid to the understanding of alien religious ideas, but it is certainly not an ideal means. Every religion ought to be understood from its own standpoint, for that is how it is understood by its own adherents. The result of comparative research, and of every kind of historical research, is likewise less than ideal; only approximate knowledge is possible. Let us be completely aware of the limited validity of historical research. This limitation is imposed by the subject itself; namely, the absolute character of all faith. Every believer looks upon his own religion as a unique, autonomous and absolute reality.

It is of absolute value and thus incomparable. This is true not only for the Christian, but just as surely for the adherent of a non-Christian religion. And it is true not only for every religion conceived as a whole, but also for every part and every particular of religious belief. Not only 'Christianity' or any other particular religion is unique, autonomous and incomparable; so too is every belief and each sacred rite. The belief that Hades is the giver of all life and the sacred act by means of which that belief is actualized in the ritual of the mystery religion are absolute truths for the believers. But the historian cannot understand the absolute character of the religious data in the same way that the believer understands them. The historian's standpoint is a different one. There is a distance between him and the object of the research, he cannot identify himself with it as the believer does. We cannot become Mohammedans when we try to understand Islam, and if we could, our study would be at an end: we should ourselves then directly experience the reality. The historian seeks to understand, and he is able to do that in an approximate way, approximate, but no more. By means of empathy he tries to relive in his own experience that which is 'alien', and that, too, he can only approximate. This imaginative reexperiencing of a situation strange to us is a form of representation, and not reality itself, for that always asserts itself with sovereign authority. We can even assume such an outside position in respect to our own spiritual inheritance: we can form a more or less clear picture of our own national character, and we often do so. But then we always feel the shortcomings of our own formulation; the representation is always something else than the reality. The 'existential' nature of the religious datum is never disclosed by research. That cannot be defined. Here we see the limit to the validity of historical research. But recognizing a limit of validity is not to deny the value of this research.

In order to understand particular (historical) data, we must frequently (and perhaps always) make use of the generalizations which are the results of comparative research. The sacredness of the Greek and Roman kings must be seen in the light of the ancient concept of kingship; particular sacrifices in the light of the religious essence of sacrifice. Now it is true the Ancient conception of kingship or the religious essence of sacrifice is a concept and not historical reality (only the particular applications are reality), but we cannot dispense with those concepts. In historical research they are virtually considered as realities: to an important extent they give the research direction and lead to the satisfying result of understanding the data. The limit of validity of scientific results, which is the consequence of using such fictitious realities, is not a phenomenon unique to historical science. Such fictitious realities and general formulations are assumed in all science, even in the natural science, where they are formulated as 'natural laws'. Research always anticipates the essence of the phenomena, which essence is nevertheless the goal of all scientific endeavour.

The relationship between history and phenomenology thus becomes clear. The one assumes the presence of the other, and vice versa. Phenomenology's way of working (the grouping of characteristic data) and its task (the illustration of man's religious disposition) make it a systematic discipline. But if we must group the phenomena according to characteristics which correspond as far as possible to the essential and typical elements of religion, how do we then determine which data typically illustrate man's religious disposition, and how do we determine what are the essential elements of religion? This question cannot be answered on the basis of the phenomena themselves, although this has indeed been tried. There is a popular notion that that which all religions have in common must be religion's core. If we but set aside all that is peculiar to a particular religion, what we have left are the common ideas, feelings, and practices, and they express what is essentially religious. This is a method which seems so simple as to be almost mechanical, but it is impracticable. There are a great many elements which appear in all religions. Unessential and unimportant elements also occur in large numbers. On the other hand, none of all the facts which have been observed occurs in all religions. We do not even find the well known trio of 'God, soul and immortality' everywhere. When we consider the idea, 'God', even ignoring the fact that this is absent in Buddhism, we must conclude that there is no particular idea of deity which is everywhere applicable. And if we relinquish the given forms of particular ideas of deity in order to find that which is common behind them, we are then left with empty concepts. The common element that we find in this way is so vague and fleeting that it gives no guidance in the research of Phenomenology. It can be said just as truly that all religious data, seen more deeply, are held in common. If we but pay attention to their religious significance, they prove not to be alien to us, and certainly not to other believers. Consider, for instance, the many nature gods, such as Osiris, Demeter and Athene. As soon as we learn to understand their essence, the alien element disappears, and they correspond to feelings and insights which are echoed in ourselves. Just for this reason we can understand that which is alien. This is the case with all religious ideas and practices as soon as we comprehend them in their true significance. Seen more deeply, therefore, everything is held in common. Nothing and everything. It is clear that by following this path we do not learn to know the essence of religion.

That which is really essential is shown by philosophical investigation. Essence is a philosophical concept, and it is the chief task of Philosophy of Religion to formulate that essence. The principal ideas in Phenomenology are borrowed from Philosophy of Religion. Philosophy must furnish the guiding principle in the research of Phenomenology. In other words, a mutual relation exists between the two. Yes, Philosophy presupposes personal religious experience; the theory of religion presumes the practice of religion. Whoever seeks to know the essence of religion must possess a general picture of the different types of religious thinking and action, of ideas of deity and cultic acts; this is the material for his research. This material is precisely what Phenomenology provides.

Phenomenology of Religion and History of Religion also stand in this same mutual relation. Naturally History provides the material for the research of Phenomenology, but the reverse is also true.

Thus we see that anticipated concepts and principles are used in all the provinces of the general science of religion: history, typology and philosophy. We are continually anticipating the results of later research. That typifies the character and the 'authority' of each of the three subdivisions of the science of religion. None of the three is independent; the value and the accuracy of the results of one of them depend on the value and accuracy of the results of the other two. The place which the research of Phenomenology occupies between history and philosophy makes it extraordinarily interesting and important. The particular and the universal interpenetrate again and again; Phenomenology is at once systematic History of Religion and applied Philosophy of Religion.

It is evident that in the philosophical determination of the essence of religion, we make use of data which lie outside the territory of philosophy, outside our knowledge. We make use of our own religious experience in order to understand the experience of others. We should never be able to describe the essence of religion if we did not know from our own experience what religion is (not: what the essence of religion is!). This experience forces itself upon us even in purely historical research. That has already been demonstrated by the mutual relation of the three areas of study. A rational and systematic structure in the science of religion is impossible. Again and again a certain amount of intuition is indispensible. We are certainly not confronted with a comparative science of religion (history-phenomenology-philosophy) systematically built up as a logical unity. The purely logical and rational does not indicate which way we must follow because in Phenomenology we are constantly working with presumptions and anticipations. But that is just what makes our labour important. This study does not take place outside our personality. And the reverse will also prove to be the case: the study exerts an influence on our personality. This gives a personal character and value to the research in the areas we have mentioned. An appeal is made to our feeling for the subjects which we want to understand, a feeling which gives us a sureness to our 'touch'. There is an appeal made to the indefinable sympathy we must have for religious data which sometimes appear so alien to us. But this sympathy is unthinkable without an intimate acquaintance with the historical facts – thus again an interaction, this time between feeling and factual knowledge. It is not true that our study is a theoretical activity with which our practical life is not concerned. There is simply no doubt that we grow during our scientific work; when religion is the subject of our work, we grow religiously. In saying this, we have indicated the highest significance of our scientific task. We believe that we work objectively and scientifically, but the fruitful labour, without any doubt, takes place by the illumination of a Spirit who extends above and beyond our spirit. Let us simply call it intuition – then at least no one will contradict us!

Now we must make a few remarks about the method which Phenomenology applies. Phenomenology has as its object to come as far as possible into contact with and to understand the extremely varied and divergent religious data, making use of comparative methods. Let me now contrast with this object the popular conception of the task of 'Comparative Religion', to which I alluded in the beginning. According to that conception, it must determine the relative value of the data; it must provide us with the standard by means of which we can distinguish between the lower and the higher forms in the religious life of mankind. This comparison is worked out systematically in an evolutionary interpretation of the history of religion. This interpretation was held in high regard about the end of the last century, both in scholarly circles and elsewhere. At present, however, it has practically disappeared among scholars, but it still persists among large sections of the historically and religiously interested public. It is really popular, and therefore we cannot leave it outside our consideration. We shall be well advised to consider it carefully both in its strengths and in its weaknesses. The basis conviction is this, that the history of mankind has had just ourselves as its goal, and after frightfully great pains it has generated our civilization, as the result of all that which had preceded it. History has a meaning: it follows a continuous line from the primitive through the developed up to the highest. In religion as well as in the rest of our culture we stand on the apex of the historical pyramid. This is clearly shown, according to the evolutionary view, by comparative analysis of the historical types of religion. Such analysis leads to an evolutionary interpretation of the history of religion.

Evolutionary theory is of two types: historical and idealist. According to historical evolutionism, the results achieved in each historical period are handed down to the following generation by them and further developed. The values never disappear; they are always taken over by the succeeding generations. There is a historical contact between all periods of culture. That was the theory of Tiele, and many agreed with him. According to idealistic evolutionism, the idea of humanity and of the essence of religion has an existence of its own. It realizes itself by means of historical phenomena, even by those beyond observable historical relations. It detaches itself more and more from the undeveloped reality which is clothed in primitive forms and comes to light in full clarity in the highest civilization and the highest religions. This idealistic evolutionism includes (among other views) the Hegelian conception of development; the history of religion is understood as the dialectical self-development of the Idea of religion.

From a philosophical standpoint it must be recognized that a case can be made for this evolutionary type of comparative research. It is the task of Philosophy of Religion to describe the essence of religion by determining the relation of religion to other spiritual realities – the intellectual, moral and aesthetic factors in our spiritual life – and thus to arrive at a definition of religion's distinctive nature. Of course, when the essence is described, the unessential element in the religious phenomena has also a right to be shown. This is the indisputable right of Philosophy of Religion. Some religious forms, some formulations of belief and some sacred rites then prove to express this essential element better than others. Higher and lower forms are thus distinguished and pointed out in history. And religion is seen to be in its essence a living force, which maintains itself even when confronted with ignoble tendencies and obstructive circumstances. Such a conception of religion leads automatically to the notion of growth, a development of religion in the course of history. On philosophical grounds historical and idealistic evolutionism can both be defended. The philosophical method is deductive; by discerning how the phenomena develop from the essence, the historical data are understood.

It must be recognized, furthermore, that the essence of religion is a concept which not only the philosopher, but also the historian and the student of Phenomenology cannot neglect. The scholar must be able to separate the essentially religious from the unessential in all the given historical phenomena which are the object of his research. In order to reach the right conclusions he must have a feeling for religion, an awareness of what religion is, and this awareness is precisely what Philosophy of Religion attempts to formulate. Many historians are gravely lacking in this 'feeling'. But the reverse is just as true: the philosopher who wants to describe the essential element must work with historical data. He does not conjure them up by pure deduction. He cannot decide that particular data must have existed. History and philosophy must work together; that is to say, the one may not lay down the law to the other. Each is equally autonomous in its own territory.

But the autonomy is denied if a particular pattern of development, the evolutionary pattern, is forced on history. History of Religion and Phenomenology do not have as their object the formulation of our conception of the essence of religious data. This is the task of the philosopher. They must, on the contrary, investigate what religious value the believers (Greeks, Babylonians, Egyptians, etc.) attached to their faith, what religion meant for them. It is *their* religion that we want to understand, and not our own, and we are therefore not concerned here with the essence of religion, for this is necessarily expressed for us in our own religion.

All evolutionary views and theories therefore mislead us from the start, if we let them set the pattern for our historical research. Believers have never conceived of their own religion as a link in a chain of development. Perhaps they have thought of it sometimes as the goal, but never as an intermediate link; yet in the evolutionary view, this is an indispensable concept. No believer considers his own faith to be somewhat primitive, and the moment we begin so to think of it, we have actually lost touch with it. We are then dealing only with our own ideas of religion, and we must not delude ourselves that we have also learned to know the ideas of others. The historian and the student of Phenomenology must therefore be able to forget themselves, to be able to surrender themselves to others. Only after that will they discover that others surrender themselves to them. If they bring their own idea with them, others shut themselves off from them. No justice is then done to the values which are alien to us, because they are not allowed to speak in their own language. If the historian tries to understand the religious data from a different viewpoint than that of the believers, he negates the religious reality. For there is no religious reality other than the faith of the believers.

The concepts, 'primitive' and 'highly developed' forms of religion, are therefore fatal for historical research. Religious ideas and sacred rites are degraded to a series of relative values, whereas in reality they have functioned as absolute values. We must understand the others as autonomous and spiritual individuals; we must not let our appraisal be determined by the degree of agreement or difference between them and ourselves. For the historian only one evaluation is possible: 'the believers were completely right'. Only after we have grasped this can we understand these people and their religion.

That does not imply, of course, that every passing religious tendency to be found in history can lay claim to such an evaluation. Of course, insignificant or superficial points of view appear again and again which are of such slight value that they scarcely merit our attention or respect. How can the one be separated from the other? That is no great problem. That which is insignificant always proves to have no lasting existence in history. Because of their slight value, these phenomena have only a brief existence. As far as the Ancient religions are concerned, most of the data of this sort have disappeared without leaving us any trace, or at least they are not longer visible because of their distance from us. The religious phenomena which primarily engage the attention of the historian and the phenomenologist, however, are the formulations of belief and cultic practices which have endured for centuries and sometimes for thousands of years. They have proved themselves able to bear the life of numerous generations, because they have accurately expressed the religious consciousness of an entire people. This is true of the very ancient forms of worship of nature and of spiritual beings (the two cannot be sharply separated) which have survived, even into our own time. It is also the case with the mythical images in which faith is formulated and with the sacred practices and usages, such as the numerous forms of sacrifices, divinations, etc. The enduring existence of all these religious data proves their religious value: they have been felt to be as essential values of life, and they have indeed been just that. The impressive civilizations of the Ancient peoples were founded upon them. That cannot be said of the passing movements and temporary phenomena. Just as insignificant individuals cannot command the same attention as outstanding personalities, so transient ideas cannot claim the same interest as convictions which have proved their inner power. In studying the Ancient religions, the great distance in time (between them and ourselves) offers this advantage: numerous passing fluctuations have undoubtedly disappeared from sight, and the principal lines indicating what is enduring and valuable come much more clearly into focus. That which has been carefully weighed and approved by generations and has been able to serve as the basis of life has proved its inner value. And we can understand that only in the same sense in which the believers have understood it – that this value is the absolute value of life.

The evolutionary point of view is therefore an unhistorical view-point. It is extraordinarily popular because a feeling for history is so extraordinarily rare. For most people it is a difficult task to do justice to the viewpoint of others when the spiritual issues of life are at stake. In historical research, we confront religious data as observers; most people find this attitude difficult to achieve, and so place themselves directly in the stream of life and adopt only those ideas which fit the realities of practical life. When this has been done, a condemnation of the other point of view on the basis of our own is inevitable. From a practical point of view these people are right, for in practice we show our disapproval of that which is alien by not adopting it ourselves. From a theoretical point of view, however, they are wrong.

Gerardus van der Leeuw

Gerardus van der Leeuw was born in 1890 in The Hague, Holland, where he received his primary and secondary school education. In 1908 he enrolled in the Faculty of Theology of the University of Leiden; here he studied the history of religions with W. B. Kristensen and the Egyptian language with P. A. A. Boeser. He finished his studies in Leiden in 1913 and continued to study a semester in Göttingen and a semester in Berlin where he worked with K. Sethe and A. Erman. In 1916 Van der Leeuw obtained the Th. D. at Leiden with a dissertation on 'Representations of the Gods in the Ancient-Egyptian Pyramid Texts'. From 1916 until 1918 he was a minister in the Dutch Reformed Church. In 1918 Van der Leeuw was appointed at the new chair of the History of Religions, the 'Theological Encyclopedia' and Egyptology at the University of Groningen. He later also taught Liturgy. Van der Leeuw was active in the Dutch Reformed Church where he stimulated the liturgical movement; he was well-read in literature and a good musician. From 1945 to 1946 he was Minister of Education, in 1950 he presided the International Congress of the History of Religions held in Amsterdam and became the first president of the International Association for the History of Religions. He died shortly afterwards in Utrecht in 1950.

Only three of the publications of Van der Leeuw, bearing on the study of religion, are available in English: 1938 *Religion in Essence and Manifestation: a Study in Phenomenology;* 1939 *Virginibus Puerisque; a study on the Service of Children in Worship* (in ancient Rome); 1963 *Sacred and Profane Beauty: the Holy in Art.*

Van der Leeuw developed a methodology for the understanding of religious phenomena, which he elaborated theoretically and which he applied in his phenomenological studies. Basic hereto is the classification of religious phenomena by means of ideal types which are constituted by a psychological technique of re-experiencing religious meanings. On account of this, he may be called a pioneering phenomenologist of religion. Van der Leeuw contended that historical and exegetical studies have to precede any phenomenological understanding, and a number of his publications bear indeed on the history of religions. In his understanding of religion, Van der Leeuw was much interested in the problem of anthropological structures such as the hypothesis of a 'primitive mentality', in the relationship between religion and art, and in the interpretation and theological appreciation of man as a religious being. Phenomenology of religion, for Van der Leeuw, led to both anthropology and theology.

The following five fragments have been taken from two articles on methodology published in German in 1926 and 1928, from the book 'Introduction to Theology' published in Dutch in 1935, from the 'Epilegomena' of *Religion in Essence and Manifestation*, and from the 'Introduction' to *Sacred and Profane Beauty*.

'SOME RECENT ACHIEVEMENTS OF PSYCHOLOGICAL RESEARCH
AND THEIR APPLICATION TO HISTORY, IN PARTICULAR THE
HISTORY OF RELIGION'

Introductory observations. An interesting parallel can be discovered between
recent developments in the fields of the science of religion and psychology.
In the field of the history of religion time and again scholars and 'schools'
can be found, convinced that the great variety of religious phenomena
must be deduced from a single principle, and that an attempt must be
made to explain the infinitely manifold world of religion out of one single
datum, to the exclusion of all others, such as naturalism, animism, explanation by ancestor-worship, and the French school of sociology.

The very same trend can be observed in psychology, viz. to give absolute
validity to one single system of interpretation and its application to the
human soul. This was the case when sensationalism first made its appearance, then in the psychology of association and the theory of the mechanism
of ideas which was associated with it. The same held true for the attempts
to identify logical and natural, psychological and cerebral processes, and
cerebral and logical mechanisms. The latest development of this kind has
been Freudian psychoanalysis which makes use of unconscious repressed
emotion as its principle of interpretation.[1]

But for some time now the study of the history of religion has also had
this fortunate similarity with psychology, that voices are raised urging an
halt to giving absolute validity to one particular system of interpretation.
Reality should no longer be violated by forcing it, with considerable difficulty, into a purely methodological strait-jacket and then, with no less
difficulty, trying to wrest it free from it after having it duly 'explained'.

There is an ever growing awareness that reality is too rich and too manifold to leave us even the slightest hope that we may ever be able to interpret it out of one single principle and by one single method. The history of
religion owes this realization to psychologically trained scholars such as
Rudolf Otto and Friedrich Heiler in Germany, Lévy-Bruhl, to a certain
extent, in France, and Nathan Söderblom in Sweden. This new orientation
of psychology must be traced back even farther and be attributed to the
fertile influence of the humanities, and in particular to comparative literature and philosophy. If one name is to be mentioned in this connection,
it is certainly that of Dilthey, behind whose impressive personality the
influence of Herder and of Romanticism may be discerned.

The study of the history of religion has made only negative progress
methodologically in recent years, in that it has freed itself from any kind
of doctrinalism. In the field of psychology, however, two different trends
can be discerned in the same period. One, the older one, regards the human

psyche as an object, which it tries to comprehend with all means at its disposal. The other, younger, school of thought regards phenomena not as objects confronting it, but as phenomena which it tries to undergo as living experiences. The first school of thought has, of course, very many subdivisions, from sensationalism and 'cerebral mythology' onwards. But its unifying factor is its objectivism, whether real or putative. The second school is differentiated to the same degree, but has an explicitly subjective character. Psychology has already also realized to what extent the two schools complement each other. On the one hand the subjectivists may well 'stir scientific psychology out of its rigidity and make it take the road into the 'depths' of the soul by a scientific method'; on the other hand the objectivists are needed 'so that on this road we do not lose the thread of scientific methodology'.[2] The object of this paper is to make available something of the insight that has been gained by psychology for the study of religion. So as to avoid the suspicion of a mere borrowing, we shall continue to define the problem of the relation between psychology and historical research everywhere on our way.

The difference between the fields of the study of history and of psychology is apparently small from a methodological point of view, however large it may be with regard to their subject matter and their technical instruments. No doubt, the truthfulness of the historical sources is a required pre-condition of historical research, but it is not its ultimate object. Also, history tries in the last instance to understand personalities and the spiritual movements experienced by them and originating from them. But in doing so, history acts not otherwise than psychology, when the latter, after the indispensable psychological, statistical and experimental preliminary research, eventually takes as its object of study the human personality which it tries to make understandable. The difference is that historical research usually concerns itself with personalities belonging to a remote or not so remote past, whereas psychology concerns itself with the present. This circumstance entails its own difficulties, in particular for historical research, but can hardly be regarded as a fundamental difference. Our explanation of the mutual relation between psychology and historical research started, however, and not without reason, with a dual hypothesis, which applies to the method of either science. We must therefore now examine to what extent this hypothesis can and must be turned into an affirmation.[3] The first of the series of conditions in which our important hypothesis dissolves itself on closer examination is the admission of the importance and even of the indispensability of subjectivity in psychology. Research and its object must be brought into close, even the closest proximity. The distance which is indispensable to any research must not degenerate into heterogeneity. In other words, the life that is being examined should acquire its place in the life of the student himself who should understand it out of his inner self. We therefore encounter here in the first instance the principle of so-called:

Empathy (Einfühlung). The physicist who wants to study a certain object will, generally speaking, do well to place himself at a distance from it, so that he can observe it exactly, go around it, watch it from all sides, etc. But the psychologist and the historian should, after having started likewise and after having ascertained all effects of the temporal and spatial distance, make another effort and penetrate into the object.[4] This is what is called 'empathy', transposing oneself into the object or re-experiencing it.

It is obvious that he, who penetrates into an object in order to become better acquainted with it, must not hope that by this act of his he will acquire a clearer idea of the external form of the object, or of its relations in space or its origin in time. From a spatial-temporal point of view, he deprives himself by the act of empathy of any due prospect of his object, and even of seeing it at all. The reality which he wants to reach cannot therefore be of a spatial-temporal nature. He is incumbent not to ascertain a causal connection which cannot be 're-experienced' by any means, but to enter into a coherent stream of consciousness. The latter cannot be 'comprehended' by quantifying, enumerating or measuring methods which approach it from the outside, but can only be understood from within. The student must allow this undivided whole to affect him in his entireness.

Not a critical analysis, therefore, is in the foreground here: a dissection into segments, however necessary it may be at an analytical preliminary stage, constitutes an insuperable obstacle for empathy. Whoever dissects the whole kills it, and we have to do with living things here. In this connection a couple of names should be mentioned: those of Brentano, James, and Bergson. However different their views may be, they all agree that he who wants to 'comprehend' psychological reality in order then to dissect it into quantitatively measurable parts and particles, will never be able to understand the fullness of life and its endlessly varying richness.[5] In exactly the same way – the comparison is not new – as a melody can be divided into quantitatively equal or unequal parts which may then be measured, but not understood, – and in the same way as time may be represented as a divisible, quantifiable line or a circle or dial, which then may be measured, but not experienced, in the same way psychological living reality may be divided and measured, and no one denies that this may be necessary. But in order to understand it, to re-experience it, one must allow it to affect oneself as a whole. The 'stream of consciousness' should not be channeled. Whoever wants to understand an ego, his own or that of his fellow-man –which is immaterial in this context–, and to experience or re-experience what he went through, – and this is the task of both the psychologist and the historian – should not conceive it in a spatial way. He would then see a cipher, a hieroglyph, a symbol instead of living reality. He will reach out for a rose, but catch only the decoloured spectre of a flower (Bergson). He who measures or enumerates levels off and simplifies existing reality. The rose of which I breathe the scent is not the 'same' rose the scent of which enchants someone else; the room that looks at me today in such a friendly manner is not the 'same' room that left me indifferent yesterday. Both, the room and the rose, can be regarded by the spatially comprehensive method only as one and the same room, one and the same rose.

But they are experienced and understood as quite different realities.[6] As James states in his essay on the 'stream of thought' – which is the analogon to Bergson's *'durée vécue'* – the attempt of analyzing consciousness is like seizing a spinning top in order to become acquainted with its movements, or like switching on an electric bulb in so fast a way that one is still able to see what darkness looks like. In other words, psychological reality must never be quantified if one wants to understand it.

Of course, even he who wants to listen to the melody as a whole, or to experience the stream as a unity, cannot do without a certain analysis. But the latter is fundamentally different from the analysis familiar to students of the exact sciences. To avail ourselves once more of a comparison made by James: the analysis applied by the exact sciences, – and also that applied by experimental psychology, is comparable to the activity of someone drawing up the water of a stream in innumerable buckets. All these buckets together will never constitute the stream. Life has been exhausted in the full meaning of the word. He who wants to experience the stream in its living coolness must learn how to swim. But this too is an art. It is not true that anyone who is not altogether stupid and who has open eyes, might become an 'empathic' psychologist.[7] This psychological method must be learnt, and with considerable effort. Here the *phenomenological analyst* makes his appearance. He is the swimmer familiar with the stream. He does not dissect the psychological phenomena like the experimentalist does; he takes them as they present themselves. He tries to contemplate the essence of the phenomena, and not to comprehend their factual existence. He analyzes in an intuitive, not in a rational manner; he is concerned not with empirically comprehensible events, but with events that are directly intelligible in their general being.[8] A Dutch theologian, who lived long before Husserl and phenomenology were known, already stated years ago describing truthfully is to give everything its right place; one takes into oneself and gives rebirth, out of one's own mind, to what stands already there; one finds the right point of view, from where the object must be viewed in order to be understood in its spirit and nature, so that one may detach from it what does not belong to it, according to one's sensitivity of what is 'alien' and what is not.[9]

Empathy therefore requires a certain clarifying of the psychological phenomena, which decides nothing about their value nor about the degree of their reality, but which presents them clearly visible, clarified as much as possible from alien admixtures. We are therefore concerned here neither with a certain concrete and not even with a certain actually extant object, not with a certain feeling of remorse, a certain feeling of joy, a certain feeling of melancholy. But we are concerned with what, according to our intuitive knowledge or rather our intuitive vision, 'remorse', 'joy' or 'melancholy' means.[10] In other words we are concerned with visualizing psychological conditions, with defining and determining them, so that these concepts will always have an identical meaning. Or, in even simpler words: phenomenology must help us to understand reality by making sure what we are talking about, and that we never talk nor are able to talk about what is not actually real *(über sogenannt Wirkliches)*. But the basis of this procedure remains forever the living and loving devotion to experience *(Erlebnis)*, and this basis is empathy *(Einfühlung)* itself. Intuitive abstraction – the phenomenological restraint or 'epoche' – can only follow after a spontaneously warm, self-denying devotion *(Hingabe)*.

We still have to ascertain that a separate discussion of the observation of the ego of one self and one's fellow-man cannot have any meaning in this context. Between introspection, phenomenologically clarified observation of oneself and empathy with regard to the psychological reality of someone else, there can only be a mutually complementary relationship, and not a fundamental difference. The observation of oneself is not privileged as compared to the empathy with or the observation of the other. On the one hand I can observe myself, i.e. my body, as the body of someone else. On the other hand I can observe myself, i.e. my inner life, in exactly as imperfect a way as the inner life of my neighbour.[11] It is true that there is a very important difference – to which we shall come back – between the observation of one's own psychological reality and that of someone else. But this difference concerns the *act* of observation, which is different for any individual, but not the *contents* of one's own consciousness and that of one's fellow-man, which are the sole object under discussion here and which it is our task to understand.[12]

A real understanding cannot, however, be achieved without us going even one step farther. We give ourselves over to a melody by way of empathy, we discern its elements not as a quantitatively measurable series of vibrations of the air, nor as expressions of a certain idea, but as a phenomenon, as it were as 'tonal ideas' – which expression should not be understood metaphysically for that matter. But now we must also still draw the con-

necting lines, or rather, follow them. We must discover the relations which
turn the melody into a meaningful unity; the mere contiguousness, first of
the empirical situation and then of the phenomenologically cleared essences
(Wesenheiten), must now be understood as a meaningful whole *(eine sinn-
reiche Zusammengehörigkeit)*. In one word, we are in search of:

Structural relations (verständliche Zusammenhänge). This expression was
first used by Karl Jaspers.[13] In contrast to the causal method of explaining
as used by the exact sciences, he places a genetic understanding.

'We give a causal explanation by connecting objectively several elements
into regularities as a result of repeated experiences. But by transposing
ourselves into the psychological sphere we understand genetically how one
psychological reality results from another.'[14] Consequently, here too, the
procedure is a purely qualitative one; the difference with the phenomenological procedure is, according to Jaspers, that the latter aims at a static
understanding, while the search for structural relations aims at a genetic
understanding. Out of the manifold individual images yielded by phenomenological abstraction, genetic understanding must again constitute a
living unity. This is, therefore, to a certain extent 'giving rebirth, out of
one's own mind, to what stands already there', to quote our 19th century
Dutch theologian again, and also, to a certain extent, a reconstruction.
But it is a reconstruction which may be given this name only metaphorically,
since, from the beginning to the end, it is controlled not by the analytical
mind, but by intuition. If this were otherwise we would obtain, as a result
of the many individual images, only a film, i.e. again numerous individual
images, and not the living unity which we have just now learnt to understand better.

Now both the static-phenomenological and the genetic understanding
– the visualization of the objects as they are and as they 'follow up' *(hervor-
gehen)* – constitute together the definition, differentiation, nomenclature
and experience of the connections as one single process, viz. 'understanding'
(das Verstehen) in its full compass. On the one hand the understanding of
stuctural relations is, as it were, a construction out of the elements which
phenomenological contemplation *(Anschauung)* had found to be extant.
On the other hand nothing can be described phenomenologically without
reference to relations; he who describes B is obliged at once to describe
A and C as well. Here too, the principle holds good that darkness belongs
to the essence of light, against which darkness the light distinguishes itself.
Hereby a stuctural relation has already been established.

The criterion for the establishment of structural relations is, however,
their evidence *(Evidenz)* – according to Simmel: their conciseness *(Bündig-
keit)*.[15] This criterion presupposes the faculty of divination in the psycho-

logist, i.e. an intuitive insight into what is essential, typical, meaningful. This is a faculty which is near to artistic talent and which, as little as the latter, of course cannot yield any fruits without constant training. This is also the reason why this manner of understanding can never have a claim to represent reality. Exactly like a figure in drama, in an epic or even in sculpture, a whole viewed as a structural relation may constitute a unified living meaningfulness *(eine einheitliche lebendige Sinnbezogenheit)* without, however, for this reason ever being or becoming 'real'. Evidence is not concerned with reality: Hamlet is evident, but the Shakespearean Hamlet never existed. The importance of understanding is rather that it refers as such to a meaning, i.e. that it has a normative significance. And herewith we arrive at the characterization of the essences *(Wesenheiten)* as seen in structural relations as:

Ideal types (Idealtypen). These ideal types must not constitute generalizations of certain structural relations – Jaspers at least warns explicitly against any raising of structural relations to a 'theory'.[16] – But they must rather combine these relations into an experience that stands as normative against 'reality'. The term 'ideal types' is due to the sociologist Max Weber; the theory of the possibility to construct psychological connections in general, is due to Dilthey. It was only Jaspers who transferred this to psychology and psychopathology.[17] Dilthey still states that we should apply our experience of a 'structural connection' to our understanding of human life as such. This understanding itself is an 'artistic process'. Max Weber and Jaspers are concerned in even a clearer fashion with 'ideal types', i.e. images of the mind, which combine certain processes and relations into a unified whole. In addition to 'empirical experience' there comes then still, as it were, a 'constructing experience'. But a great distance separates us here from the generalizing constructions of the exact sciences. The ideal-typical construction may rather be compared to the products of the artistic mind, which likewise express a kind of dual experience in addition to the 'empirical' experience of the poet, which, however, by no means has less evidence. The ideal type is, therefore, formed indeed on the basis of experience, but it is not derived from experience – just as little as the hero of a drama. It must rather have gone through the stages of phenomenological clarification and of the formation of structural relations. Both the hero and the ideal type have as their purpose to make life intelligible by an experienced construction of normative character. The expression 'experienced construction' *(erlebte Konstruktion)* as such is, of course, nonsense. What is meant is that in the experience the construction – or rather, the *structure* – of a person, of an event, etc. becomes 'evident', 'obvious'. We do not 'construct', but we experience a unity of meaning. It is therefore, clear that these ideal types have no reality as little as have the essences or the structural relations. It is completely unnecessary that an ideal type, in order to have real validity, should occur frequently or even should occur at all. 'What matters is only their potentiality, which is given as evident in experience', i.e. the cogency with which its elements are connected.[18] In this connection Binswanger rather aptly compares this ideal typology with the views of Jacob Burckhardt who considered 'history as it is believed to have occurred *(vorgestellte Geschichte)* to be more important than history as it 'literally occurred' *(buchstäblich geschehene Geschichte)*', and who considered facts as 'perhaps only debris', since what really matters is only the inner life of mankind of the past.[19] One thing is certain: without the conscious, or unfortunately often also unconscious, application of this ideal typology, no historical research is possible. Already he who tries to explain the conversion of the emperor Constantine the Great out of political calculation, has simplified what really happened in an idealtypical manner: in the same way, for that matter, as does his opponent who attributes this conversion solely to religious motives. What matters here, however, is that what is done here unconsciously and frequently also in an entirely arbitrary manner, should receive a methodical character by means of psychological self-education. [...]

ON PHENOMENOLOGY AND ITS RELATION TO THEOLOGY

The lines along which we want to describe this psychological method – which could best be called 'phenomenological', if this term is taken in the more comprehensive meaning which it has, e.g., with P. Hofmann[20] and Karl Jaspers – may, following the above-mentioned essay,[21] briefly be summarized as follows.

This method is, for the time being,[22] an attempt to re-experience a certain entity as such, to transpose oneself into an object as an organic whole. This empathy *(Einfühlung)* can occur only by means of phenomenological analysis. By this analysis the object is not seized and dissected into its elements, but viewed in its essence so that we may discern what is part of its essence and what is not. In other words, a kind of phenomenological purification or clarification is carried out with regard to the object. When in this way the object has revealed itself in its uniqueness, it must further be established how the elements, which together make it up, are interrelated. Not their causal connection is our concern here, but their structural connection *(Strukturzusammenhang)*: not causal connections must be proved, but structural relations *(verständliche Beziehungen)* established. Two methods together, the static phenomenological method and the genetic method constitute here one act which is 'understanding' in its full meaning. The criterion in all cases is the evidence *(Evidenz)* through which it is not so much we who discover the object, but the object that manifests itself to us. What has thus manifested itself to us in the end is an ideal-typical entity. That is to say, it is never a fact – facts can only be comprehended, but never understood – , but always a meaning, i. e. a normimposed on so-called 'reality' which, though real, is always unknowable and ithere fore unintelligible. The fundamental condition is, here too, exper.ence; we do not construct structural connections, but we experience them. Our experience is never a primal experience of the object itself, nor is it merely a re-experiencing of it, but it is another, relatively independent experience, which forms itself in us on account of 'signs' – e.g., the words of a person, the letters of a document, the remnants of an ancient settlement – as a meaningful whole.

The center of scholarly research is, therefore, shifted from historical and metaphysical interests, which both aim at discovering reality or truth, though in different ways, to understanding as such. The place of 'knowing', whether in a superficial historical or in a more abstract theoretical sense, is now taken by a 'knowing' which, driven by devoted love, is directed by the norm of the meaning that asserts itself. This is 'understanding'.[23]

We shall now examine by means of a few examples how far this understanding, thus conceived, is also a suitable method for theology.

In the so-called 'Theological Encyclopedia' the historical disciplines form, if not the foundation, at least the beginning of all theology. We must first establish 'how it was' and then 'what it has become'. True, the historical as well as the exegetical approach always imply a second stage in theological studies. Mere 'facts' do not convey anything. They have to be visualized somehow, i.e. they must be understood, even if it is not in their deepest meaning. Any historical or exegetical study adopts an ideal-typical attitude towards the facts. The views of the Graf-Kuenen-Wellhausen school on the Old Testament, and of the Tübinger school on the New Testament, whatever one's attitude towards them, are not faithful renderings of reality, but interpretations of it, meaningful expositions. However necessary understanding may also be for a purely historical description, – if, at least, one wants to avoid a purely chronological chaotic rendering – , in historical theology the emphasis is on the factual.[24]

Systematic theology takes precisely an opposite stand. Here, depending on the point of view adopted by the theologian, Ultimate Reality, Ultimate Meaning, or Absolute Validity are discussed. The historian is interested in the bare fact of Resurrection, the systematic theologian is concerned with the Divine power manifesting itself in this Resurrection, or – when he uses a different scholarly vocabulary – with the meaning of Resurrection, or with the normative character of the vital values revealed by it, or with its permanent significance.

It seems that between these two poles, of historical and systematic theology, a third field now has been discovered, an intermediate stage, as it were, which for the time being we would like to call phenomenological theology. In our example given above, phenomenological theology would be concerned neither with the factual events nor with the ultimate content of Resurrection, but with its meaning in the experience of the community of the faithful. Or, to give an example of even wider scope: in Christian theology Christianity naturally occupies a central position, but in historical theology it does so merely for external and essentially fortuitous reasons. Historical studies range themselves around Christianity only as a 'positive science' in the sense of Schleiermacher, and therefore out of practical considerations; systematic theology however, bases the central position of Christianity on ultimate and absolute grounds. This intermediate stage of phenomenological theology adopts neither this nor the opposite position: Christianity occupies a central place here neither as an established fact nor as a fact due to Revelation, but as a matter-to-be-understood *(Verständlichkeit)*.

This intermediary stage between historical and systematic theology is called *Religionswissenschaft*, the science of religion. Its approach is wider than merely historical and also wider than psychological;[25] in a certain sense it is a systematic, but not a theoretical or a dogmatic discipline. It is a 'science of religion', just as there is a science of art or a science of economics. It moves within the framework of the given context of meaning of the religious phenomena that are to be understood, and neither in the sphere of empirical, nor within that of ultimate realities. [...]

ON 'UNDERSTANDING'

Whoever wishes to understand cannot be limited by himself and the object of his understanding. He does not stand alone in the world with his object: he must understand it within a larger context of objects presenting themselves to him. He can understand himself as well only from such a context. A real understanding is possible only if there are all-embracing ideal structures *(übergreifende Geistesstrukturen)*, as stated by Spranger, so that the place of the individual structure can be comprehended in ideal connections which are more than individual. This is the *objective mind*, without which any understanding of oneself and of others is impossible. Dilthey[27] describes this mind very aptly:

'There is always this great ideal reality outside of us, which is surrounding us. It is a realization of the mind in the world of the senses, varying from perfunctory expression to the influence of a constitution or of a lawbook, which may last for centuries. Each individual life expression represents in the realm of this objective mind something which is held in common. Each word, each sentence, each gesture or form of politeness, each piece of art and each historical act are understandable only because there is some common basis *(Gemeinsamkeit)* between the person who expresses himself through them and the person who understands. The individual man experiences, thinks and acts always in an atmosphere of communication *(Gemeinsamkeit)*, and it is only in such an atmosphere that he is able to understand. All that is understood carries, in a way, the mark of being known through a *Gemeinsamkeit*. We live in this atmosphere, it surrounds us continuously. We are immersed in it. We are in this our world, which is of a historical and understandable nature, everywhere at home: we understand the meaning and significance of all of it, and we are ourselves weaved within the whole of things which are held in common.'

Outside this common basis which we may call the *circle of communication*, of 'understandability', no scientific thought is possible. A philosopher of the positivist school and an Indian sage belonging to the world of the Upanishads will have great diffulty in understanding each other, – for which reason Indian thought is simply left out in most histories of philosophy. A Dayak from the interior of the island of Borneo will understand next to nothing of the maze of a modern metropolis and will stand aghast before all those devices of modern civilization such as the telephone, street-cars and traffic regulations, that are a matter of course to any child in Europe or the United States. In other words, understanding is not only a matter of organisms, but also of larger and partly heterogeneous complexes.

This also applies to man himself, apart from his surroundings that both understand him and are understood by him. Understanding applies indeed to the entire human being, not only to his intellectual faculties, his intellect or his mind, but to his entire psychological life. This means that in the act of understanding not merely a free and as it were transcendent conciousness is active, an observing and calculating intellect, but man's *life*, i.e. his whole existence as it expresses itself in the first place in his body, but then also in the world, in so far as he makes this world to his own world. A 'human being' is not merely an abstract 'consciousness' and even less an active intellect, but a life complexity. If I say: 'the teacher analyzes a sentence' –we have on purpose chosen an unfortunately fairly unrealistic example –, then we do not mean that some mind, belonging to a case X, is engaged in explaining an intelligible connection, but that a human being, of a certain psychophysical character, is engaged, within the larger context of a pedagogical tradition – or in opposition to it ! – on the basis of a certain scholarly tradition which in its turn is based on a certain given reality, to 'explain' this reality within the confines of the understanding offered by a certain language and a certain system of logic. In the case of a different teacher, a different language, and a different group of pupils, everything is different.

The limits of understanding must therefore be placed in the infinite. In so far as understanding 'is an affair of the whole person, and actually would find its fulfillment only in the totality of all world situations, all understanding has a religious trait: we understand each other in God', Spranger says.[28]

Here therefore we find the opposite of the mind as it was conceived by Laplace: the all-understanding mind. That mind is God. And understanding is participation in the divine intelligence. Here we enter the field of the *eschatology* of science, with which we shall deal in more detail in a separate paragraph. The attitude of the student has fundamentally changed hereby: he no longer places himself above the world in order to create this world by his mind; he is aware that, 'in order to arrive at something, one has to start from something'[29]; *his understanding is identical with his being within the world.* 'Seeing', 'doing' and 'speaking' thus retrieve their original meaning from abstraction and theory. This seeing, doing and speaking now occur in the form of *structures*, which are neither organizations nor organisms, but the explicated meaning of 'being within the world' itself.

Structure. The concept of 'structure' has been advanced in recent years in particular in psychology which, if it considers its task to be the pointing out or discovering of structures, is called structural psychology. Eduard Spranger in particular has made important observations on its methods: 'Structural psychology is all psychology which understands the individual psychological facts on the basis of their place – determined by certain values – within the whole considered as a unit, and which understands them on the basis of their meaning for such overall structures of behaviour and achievement'.[30]

Structure, in his view, processes a 'print' *(Gebilde)* of reality when it is a whole in which each part and each partial function perform a function which is meaningful to the whole, and this in such a way that the composition and performance of each part are again conditioned by the whole and are, consequently, intelligible only on the basis of the whole.[31]

I shall try to clarify this by an example. If I place a beer glass, a long pipe, a book and a tobacco jar, on a table, these are at first nothing but many objects. I may try to conceive them as a whole by referring them to a common purpose, for instance the needs of an old-fashioned student: I then understand them by means of a structure. If a painter takes them as his material for a still-life, he too conceives them as a whole; but in this case it is not the purpose which brings them together, but the interrelation of lines, colour and light. If this picture becomes a work of art, then this structure is immediately apparent for the observer. In both cases each object has a meaning only as part of a whole; this is in the first case a utilitarian, in the second case an aesthetic meaning.

In other words, structures can be discerned only by the 'meaning', which is understood in and through reality. Between the object and the subject, a third term must be inserted: meaning, which is both subjective and objective. According to Spranger, this 'meaning' *(Sinn)* is like a network which the human mind casts over reality.[32] Causal interpretation is also such a network cast over reality. It is true, that here the share of the subject is reduced as much as possible, but yet the causal connection is a structure.

Even knowing as such, the cognitive act, renders a meaning to the object of cognition, be it only in so far as is necessary for this act.[33]

There is, therefore, not a duality but a plurality of scientific methods, according to the meaning attached to a certain segment of reality. Thus the text μακάριοι οἱ πτωχοὶ τῷ πνεύματι may be heard in many different ways:[34] as pure sound, as musical rhythm (by which the matter ends for those not knowing Greek), according to the meaning of the words in their context, according to their objective meaning, and finally according to their religious meaning. Each of these sentence constructions in the example given by Spranger is the nucleus of a scientific method, which may be developed into an independent field of research: acoustics, the aesthetics of music, grammar, hermeneutics or exegesis, theological exegesis. Such is the example offered by the figure of Socrates. Spranger distinguishes four degrees in our understanding of this philosopher, viz.: (1) the critical reading of the works of Xenophon and Plato; (2) the attempt to create for oneself a picture of the whole of Socrates' personality (with which, of course, one already was engaged during the first stage), in which a number of contradictions are encountered; (3) the search for a firm point of unity from where the whole can be understood; here the question is asked what person Socrates ought to be, so that he is understood according to the standard of an ideal type; (4) the reflection of the meaningful result of (3) on (1) and (2). Contradictions may now be understood as compensations or differences in emphasis, or otherwise. Even a criticism on the basis of the reading in (1) may now be modified.[35]

We may also take a very simple example: I may seize a book that is in front of me on the table. This movement may be regarded merely as an act directed towards a certain aim: having the book within my reach. It may also be regarded from the point of view of aesthetics: my movement is graceful or clumsy. It may also have a more or less ethical meaning: an attempt to hand the book helpfully to someone else. But it may also have an aim that is contrary to the law: I may by this movement try to come into possession of a book that does not belong to me. Each structure is a net cast by the observer over reality, in which he catches my movement.

The area of religious understanding means in this context an 'ultimate meaning' that cannot be reached by man. In so far as all understanding ultimately refers to the totality of things, we understand each other 'in God'. Here we approach the eschatology of scientific thought. And we do not find, as we did before, an idealistic parallel to the mind of Laplace, but its very opposite: all understanding is possible only on the condition of our recognizing its limits.

By this methodology we have gained much for our aim. We have discovered a hierarchy of cognitive processes, from the naive apperceptive to the aesthetic approach, and from the methods of the exact sciences to those of the humanities. They are all related, but never 'coincide.'[36]

The first advantage of this methodology is, that science here lifts itself up until it reaches its own boundaries; no single cognitive process is a net embracing all and everything. Science is never absolute. It is always eschatologically directed.

A second advantage of Spranger's approach is, that in the whole of the cognitive methods clearly three spheres can be distinguished. On the basis of our earlier conclusions we shall call them:

1) Comprehending *(erfassend)* research, as the model of which astronomy may be taken;

2) Understanding *(verstehend)* research, such as psychology;

3) Research related to an ultimate meaning, which may be called metaphysics or theology.

It is likewise clear that any disipline must to a greater or lesser extent have a share in each of these three spheres.

'RELIGION IN ESSENCE AND MANIFESTATION'

'Phenomenon and phenomenology'

I. Phenomenology seeks the *phenomenon*, as such; the phenomenon, again, is *what 'appears'*. This principle has a threefold implication: (1) Something exists. (2) This something 'appears'. (3) Precisely because it 'appears' it is a 'phenomenon'. But 'appearance' refers equally to what appears and to the person to whom it appears; the phenomenon, therefore, is neither pure object, nor *the* object, that is to say, the actual reality, whose essential being is merely concealed by the 'appearing' of the appearances; with this a specific metaphysics deals. The term 'phenomenon', still further, does not imply something purely subjective, not a 'life' of the subject[37]; so far as is at all possible, a definite branch of psychology is concerned with this. The 'phenomenon' as such, therefore, is an object related to a subject, and a subject related to an object; although this does not imply that the subject deals with or modifies the object in any way whatever, nor (conversely) that the object is somehow or other affected by the subject. The phenomenon, still further, is not produced by the subject, and still less substantiated or demonstrated by it; its entire essence is given in its 'appearance', and its appearance to 'someone'. If (finally) this 'someone' begins to discuss what 'appears', then phenomenology arises.

In its relation to the 'someone' to whom the phenomenon appears, accordingly, it has three levels of phenomenality: (1) its (relative) *concealment;* (2) its *gradually becoming revealed;* (3) its (relative) *transparency.* These levels, again, are not equivalent to, but are correlated with, the three levels of life: (1) *Experience;* (2) *Understanding;* (3) *Testimony;* and the last two attitudes, when systematically or scientifically employed, constitute the procedure of phenomenology.

By 'experience' is implied an actually subsisting life which, with respect to its meaning, constitutes a unity.[38] Experience, therefore, is not pure 'life', since in the first place it is objectively conditioned and, secondly, it is inseparably connected with its interpretation as experience. 'Life' itself is incomprehensible: 'What the disciple of Saïs unveils is form, not life.'[39] For the 'primal experience', upon which our experiences are grounded, has always passed irrevocably away by the time our attention is directed to it. My own life, for example, which I experienced while writing the few lines of the preceding sentence, is just as remote from me as is the 'life' associated with the lines I wrote thirty years ago in a school essay. I cannot call it back again: it is completely past. In fact, the experience of the lines of a moment ago is no nearer to me than is the experience of the Egyptian scribe who wrote his note on papyrus four thousand years ago. That he was 'another' than myself makes no difference whatever, since the boy who prepared the school work thirty years ago is also, to my own contemplation, 'another', and I must objectify myself in my experience of those bygone days. The immediate, therefore, is never and nowhere 'given'; it must always be reconstructed;[40] and to 'ourselves', that is to our most intimate life, we have no access. For our 'life' is not the house wherein we reside, nor again the body, with which we can at least do something: on the contrary, confronted with this 'life' we stand helpless. What appears to us as the greatest difference and the most extreme contrast possible – the difference, namely, between ourselves and the 'other', our neighbour, whether close by or in distant China, of yesterday or four thousand years ago – all that is a mere triviality when measured against the colossal *aporia,* the insoluble dilemma, in which we find ourselves as soon as we wish to approach life itself. Even when we reduce life to its appearance in history, we remain perplexed: the gate remains closed, that to yesterday just as that to olden times; and every historian knows that he may commence anywhere at all, but in any case he ends with himself; in other words, he *reconstructs.*[41] What, then, does this reconstruction imply?

It may be described, to begin with, as the sketching of an outline within the chaotic maze of so-called 'reality', this outline being called *structure*. Structure is a connection which is neither merely experienced directly, nor abstracted either logically or causally, but which is *understood*. It is an organic whole which cannot be analyzed into its own constituents, but which can from these be comprehended; or in other terms, a fabric of particulars, not to be compounded by the addition of these, nor the deduction of one from the others, but again only *understood* as a whole.[42] In other words: structure is certainly experienced, but not immediately; it is indeed constructed, but not logically, causally and abstractly. Structure is reality significantly organized. But the significance, in its own turn, belongs in part to reality itself, and in part to the 'someone' who attempts to understand it. It is always, therefore, both understanding and intelligibility: and this, indeed, in an unanalyzable, experienced connection. For it can never be asserted with any certainty what is my own understanding, and what is the intelligibility of that which is understood; and this is the purport of the statement that the understanding of a connection, or of a person or event, *dawns upon us*.[43] Thus the sphere of meaning is a third realm, subsisting above mere subjectivity and mere objectivity.[44] The entrance gate to the reality of primal experience, itself wholly inaccessible, is *meaning: my* meaning and *its* meaning, which have become irrevocably one in the act of unterstanding.

Still further, the interconnection of meaning – structure – is experienced by undersatnding, first of all at some given moment; the meaning dawns upon me. But this is not the whole truth, since comprehension is never restricted to the momentary experience. It extends over several experiential unities simultaneously, as indeed it also originates from the understanding of these unities of experience. But these other experiences, which are at the same time understood in combination, and which cooperate in understanding, of course present a similarity to what has been instantaneously understood which, precisely in and through understanding itself, manifests itself as community of essential nature. The understood experience thus becomes coordinated, in and by understanding, within experience of some yet wider objective connection. *Every individual experience, therefore, is already connection;* and every connection remains always experience; this is what we mean by speaking of *types*, together with structures.[45]

The appearance, to continue, subsists as an image. It possesses backgrounds and associated planes; it is 'related' to other entities that appear, either by similarity, by contrast, or by a hundred *nuances* that can arise here: conditions, peripheral or central position, competition, distance, *etc.* These relationships, however, are always *perceptible* relationships, 'structural connections':[46] they are never factual relationships nor causal connections.

They do not, of course, exclude the latter, but neither do they enunciate anything about them; they are valid only within the structural relations. Such a relation, finally, whether it concerns a person, a historical situation or a religion, is called a *type*, or an *ideal type*.[47]

'Type' in itself, however, has no reality; nor is it a photograph of reality. Like structure, it is timeless and need not actually occur in history.[48] But it possesses life, its own significance, its own law. The 'soul' again, as such, never and nowhere 'appears'; there is always and only some definite kind of soul which is believed in, and is in this its definiteness unique. It may even be said that the ideas of the soul formed by any two persons, it may be in the same cultural and religious circle, are never wholly the same. Still there is a *type* of soul, a structural relation of distinctive soul-structures. The type itself (to repeat) is timeless: nor is it real. Nevertheless it is alive and appears to us; what then are we to do in order actually to observe it?

II. We resort to phenomenology: that is to say, we must discuss whatever has 'appeared' to us – in this sense the term itself is quite clear.[49] This discussion, still further, involves the following stages, which I enumerate in succession although, in practice, they arise never successively but always simultaneously, and in their mutual relations far more frequently than in series:

A) What has become manifest, in the first place, receives a *name*. All speech consists first of all in *assigning names*: 'the simple use of names constitutes a form of thinking intermediate between perceiving and imagining'.[50] In giving names we separate phenomena and also associate them; in other words, we classify. We include or reject: this we call a 'sacrifice' and that a 'purification'; since Adam named the animals, speakers have always done this. In this assignment of names, however, we expose ourselves to the peril of becoming intoxicated, or at least satisfied, with the name – the danger which Goethe represented as 'transforming observations into mere concepts, and concepts into words', and then treating these words 'as if they were objects'.[51] We attempt to avoid this danger by

B) The interpolation of the phenomenon into our own lives.[52] This introduction, however, is no capricious act; we can do no otherwise. 'Reality' is always *my* reality, history *my* history, 'the retrogressive prolongation of man now living'.[53] We must, however, realize what we are doing when we commence to speak about what has appeared to us and which we are naming. Further, we must recall that everything that appears to us does not submit itself to us directly and immediately, but only as a symbol of some meaning to be interpreted by us, as something which offers itself to us for interpretation. And this interpretation is impossible unless we experience the appearance, and this, indeed, not involuntarily and semi-consciously, but intentionally and methodically. Here I cite the impressive statement of Usener who, although he knew nothing of phenomenology, was fully aware of what it implies: 'Only by surrendering oneself, and by submersion in these spiritual traces of vanished time[54] ... can we train ourselves to recall their feeling; then chords within ourselves, gradually becoming sympathetic, can harmoniously vibrate and resound, and we discover in our own consciousness the strands linking together old and new.'[55] This too is what Dilthey describes as the 'experience of a structural connection', such experience, it is true, being more an art than a science.[56] It is in fact the primal and primitively human art of the actor which is indispensable to all arts, but to the sciences of mind also: – to sympathize keenly and closely with experience other than one's own, but also with one's own experience of yesterday, already become strange ! To this sympathetic experience, of course, there are limits; but these are also set to our understanding of ourselves, it may be to an even greater degree; *homo sum, humani nil a me alienum puto:* this is no key to the deepest comprehension of the remotest experience, but is nevertheless the triumphant assertion that the essentially human always remains essentially human, and is, as such, comprehensible: – unless indeed he who comprehends has acquired too much of the professor and retained too little of the man ! 'When the professor is told by the barbarian that once there was nothing except a great feathered serpent, unless the learned man feels a thrill and a half, temptation to wish it were true, he is no judge of such things at all.'[57] Only the persistent and strenuous application of this intense sympathy-only the uninterrupted learning of his role, qualifies the phenomenologist to interpret appearances. In Jaspers' pertinent words: 'Thus every psychologist experiences the increasing clarity of his mental life for himself; he becomes aware of what has hitherto remained unnoticed, although he never reaches the ultimate limit.'[58]

C) Not only is the 'ultimate limit' never attainable in the sense referred to by Jaspers: it implies, still further, the unattainability of existence Phenomenology, therefore, is neither metaphysics, nor the comprehension of empirical reality. It observes *restraint* (the *epoche*), and its understandind of events depends on its employing 'brackets'. Phenomenology is concerneg only with 'phenomena', that is with 'appearance'; for it, there is nothing whatever 'behind' the phenomenon. This restraint, still further, implies no mere methodological device, no cautious procedure, but the distinctive characteristic of man's whole attitude to reality. Scheler has very well expressed this situation: 'to be human means to hurl a forcible 'No !' at this sort of reality. Buddha realized this when he said how magnificent it is to *contemplate* everything, and how terrible it is to *be:* Plato, too, in connecting the contemplation of ideas to a diverting of the soul from the sensuous content of objects, and to the diving at the soul into its own depths, in order to find the 'origins' of things. Husserl, also, implies nothing different than this when he links the knowledge of ideas with 'phenomenological reduction' – that is a 'crossing through' or 'bracketing' of (the accidental) coefficients of the existence of objects in the world in order to obtain their *'essentia'*.[59] This of course involves no preference of some 'idealism' or other to some kind of 'realism'. On the contrary: it is simply maintained that man can be positive only in turning away from things, as they are given to him chaotically and formlessly, and by first assigning them form and meaning. Phenomenology, therefore, is not a method that has been reflectively elaborated, but is man's true vital activity, consisting in losing himself neither in things nor in the *ego*, neither in hovering above objects like a god nor dealing with them like an animal, but in doing what is given to neither animal nor god: standing aside and understanding what appears into view.

D) The observance of what appears implies a *clarification* of what has been observed: all that belongs to the same order must be united, while what is different in type must be separated. These distinctions, however, should certainly not be decided by appealing to causal connections in the sense that *A* arises from *B*, while *C* has its own origin uniting it to *D* – but solely and simply by employing structural relations somewhat as the landscape painter combines his groups of objects, or separates them from one another. The juxtaposition, in other words, must not become externalization, but structural association;[60] and this means that we seek the ideal typical interrelation, and then attempt to arrange this within some yet wider whole of significance, *etc*.[61]

E) All these activities, undertaken together and simultaneously, constitute genuine *understanding*: the chaotic and obstinate 'reality' thus becomes a manifestation, a revelation. The empirical, ontal or metaphysical *fact* becomes a *datum*; the object, living speech; rigidity, expression.[62] 'The sciences of mind are based on the relations between experience, expression and understanding':[63] I understand this to mean that intangible experience in itself cannot be apprehended nor mastered, but that it manifests something to us, an appearance: says something, an utterance. The aim of science, therefore, is to understand this *logos*; essentially, science is hermeneutics.[64]

Now when we are concerned, as in our own case, with the domain of historical research, this would appear to be the stage at which historical scepticism threateningly intrudes into our investigations, and renders all comprehension of remote times and regions impossible to us. We might then reply that we are quite ready to acknowledge that we can *know* nothing, and that we admit, further, that perhaps we understand very little; but that, on the other hand, to understand the Egyptian of the first dynasty is, in itself, no more difficult than to understand my nearest neighbour. Certainly the monuments of the first dynasty are intelligible only with great difficulty, but as an expression, as a human statement, they are no harder than my colleague's letters. In this respect, indeed, the historian can learn from the psychiatrist: 'If we are astonished by an ancient myth or an Egyptian head, and confront it with the conviction that there is something that is intelligible in accord with our own experience, although it is infinitely remote from us and unattainable, just as we are amazed by a psycho-pathological process or an abnormal character, we have at least the possibility of a more deeply comprehending glance, and perhaps of achieving a living representation . . .'[65]

F) But if phenomenology is to complete its own task, it imperatively requires perpetual correction by the most conscientious philological and archaeological research. It must therefore always be prepared for confrontation with material facts, although the actual manipulation of these facts themselves cannot proceed without interpretation – that is without phenomenology; and every exegesis, every translation, indeed every reading, is already hermeneutics. But this purely philological hermeneutics has a more restricted purpose than the purely phenomenological. For it is concerned in the first place with the Text, and then with the fact in the sense of what is concretely implied: of what can be translated in other words. This of course necessitates meaning, only it is a shallower and broader meaning than phenomenological understanding.[66] But as soon as the latter withdraws itself from control by philological and archaeological interpretation, it becomes pure art or empty fantasy.[67]

G) This entire and apparently complicated procedure, in conclusion, has ultimately no other goal than pure objectivity. Phenomenology aims not at things, still less at their mutual relations, and least of all at the 'thing in itself'. It desires to gain access to the facts themselves;[68] and for this it requires a meaning, because it cannot experience the facts just as it pleases. This meaning, however, is purely objective: all violence, either empirical, logical or metaphysical, is excluded. Phenomenology regards every event in the same way that Ranke looked on each epoch as 'in an immediate and direct relation to God', so that 'its value depends in no degree on whatever results from it, but on its existence as such, on its own self'. It holds itself quite apart from modern thought, which would teach us 'to contemplate the world as unformed material, which we must first of all form, and conduct ourselves as the lords of the world'.[70] It has, in fact, one sole desire: *to testify* to what has been manifested to it.[71] This it can do only by indirect methods, by a second experience of the event, by a thorough reconstruction; and from this road it must remove many obstacles. To see face to face is denied us. But much can be observed even in a mirror; and it is possible to speak about things seen.

'Religion'

We can try to understand religion from a flat plain, from ourselves as the centre; and we can also understand how the essence of religion is to be grasped only from above, beginning with God. In other words: we can – in the manner already indicated – observe religion as intelligible experience; or we can concede to it the status of incomprehensible revelation. For in its 'reconstruction', experience is a phenomenon. Revelation is not; but man's reply to revelation, his assertion about what has been revealed, is also a phenomenon from which, indirectly, conclusions concerning the revelation itself can be derived *(per viam negationis)*.

Considered in the light of both of these methods, religion implies that man does not simply accept the life that is given to him. In life he seeks *power;* and if he does not find this, or not to an extent that satisfies him, then he attempts to draw the power, in which he believes, into his own life. He tries to elevate life, to enhance its value, to gain for it some deeper and wider meaning. In this way, however, we find ourselves on the horizontal line: religion is the extension of life to its uttermost limit. The religious man desires richer, deeper, wider life: he desires power for himself.[72] In other terms: in and about his own life man seeks something that is superior, whether he wishes merely to make use of this or to worship it.

He who does not merely accept life, then, but demands something from it – that is, power – endeavours to find some meaning in life. He arranges life into a significant whole: and thus culture arises. Over the variety of the given he throws his systematically fashioned net, on which various designs appear: a work of art, a custom, an economy. From the stone he makes himself an image, from the instinct a commandment, from the wilderness a tilled field; and thus he develops power. But he never halts; he seeks ever further for constantly deeper and wider *meaning*. [...]'

'The phenomenology of religion'

I. Phenomenology is the systematic discussion of what appears. Religion' however, is an ultimate experience that evades our observation, a revelation which in its very essence is, and remains, concealed. But how shall I deal with what is thus ever elusive and hidden? How can I pursue phenomenology when there is no phenomenon? How can I refer to 'phenomenology of religion' at all?

Here there clearly exists an antinomy that is certainly essential to all religions, but also to all understanding; it is indeed precisely because it holds good for *both,* for religion and understanding alike, that our own science becomes possible. It is unquestionably quite correct to say that faith and intellectual suspense (the *epoche)* do not exclude each other. It may further be urged that the Catholic Church, too, recognizes a *duplex ordo* of contemplation, on the one hand purely rational, and on the other wholly in accord with faith; while such a Catholic as Przywara also wishes to exclude every apologetic subsidiary aim from philosophy, and strenuously maintains the *epoche.*[73] But at the same time one cannot but recognize that all these reflections are the result of embarrassment. For it is at bottom utterly impossible contemplatively to confront an event which, on the one hand, is an ultimate experience, and on the other manifests itself in profound emotional agitation, in the attitude of such pure intellectual restraint. Apart from the existential attitude that is concerned with reality, we could never know anything of either religion or faith. It may certainly be advisable and useful methodically to presuppose this intellectual suspense; it is also expedient, since crude prejudice can so readily force its way into situations where only such an existential attitude would be justifiable. But, once again, how shall we comprehend the life of religion merely by contemplative observation from a distance? How indeed can we understand what, in principle, wholly eludes our understanding?

Now we have already found that not the understanding of religion alone, but *all* understanding without exception, ultimately reaches the limit where it loses its own proper name and can only be called 'becoming understood'. In other words: the more deeply comprehension penetrates any event, and the better it 'understands' it, the clearer it becomes to the understanding mind that the ultimate ground of understanding lies not within itself, but in some 'other' by which it is comprehended from beyond the frontier. Without this absolutely valid and decisive understanding, indeed, there would be no understanding whatever. For all understanding that extends 'to the ground' ceases to be understanding before it reaches the ground, and recognizes itself as a 'becoming understood'. In other terms: all understanding, irrespective of whatever object it refers to, is ultimately religious: all significance sooner or later leads to ultimate significance. As Spranger states this: 'in so far as it always refers to the whole man, and actually finds its final completion in the totality of world conditions, all understanding has a religious factor ... we understand each other in God.'[74]

What has previously been said with reference to the horizontal line in religion can also be translated into the language of the vertical line. And that ultimately all understanding is 'becoming understood' then means that, ultimately, all love is 'becoming loved'; that all human love is only the response to the love that was bestowed upon us. 'Herein is love, not that we loved God, but that he loved us ... we love him, because he first loved us'.[75]

Understanding, in fact, itself presupposes intellectual restraint. But this is never the attitude of the cold-blooded spectator: it is, on the contrary, the loving gaze of the lover on the beloved object. For all understanding rests upon self-surrendering love. Were that not the case, then not only all discussion of what appears in religion, but all discussion of appearance in general, would be quite impossible; since to him who does not love, nothing whatever is manifested; this is the Platonic, as well as the Christian, experience.

I shall therefore not anticipate fruitlessly, and convert phenomenology into theology. Nor do I wish to assert that the faith upon which all comprehension is grounded, and the faith proper to religion, are without further ado identical. But 'it is plainly insufficient to permit theology to follow on philosophy (for my purpose, read 'phenomenology') purely in virtue of its content, since the fundamental problem is one of method, and concerns the claim of philosophy (again, here, phenomenology) to justification in view of the obvious data, and also the impossibility of referring back faith, as the methodical basis of theology, to these data. In other terms: the problem becomes that of what is obviously evidence'.[76] And I am prepared, with Przywara, to seek the intimate relationship that nevertheless exists between faith and the obvious data, in the fact that the evidence they provide is essentially a 'preparedness for revelation.[77]

II. The use of the expressions: history of religion, science of religion, comparative history of religion, psychology of religion, philosophy of religion: and others similar to these, is still very loose and inexact; and this is not merely a formal defect, but is practical also.[78] It is true that the different subdivisions of the sciences concerned with religion (the expression is here employed in its widest possible sense), cannot subsist independently of each other; they require, indeed, incessant mutual assistance. But much that is essential is forfeited as soon as the limits of the investigation are lost to sight. The history of religion, the philosophy and psychology of religion, and alas! theology also, are each and all harsh mistresses, who would fain compel their servants to pass beneath the yoke which they hold ready for them; and the phenomenology of religion desires not only to distinguish itself from them, but also, if possible, to teach them to restrain themselves! I shall therefore first of all indicate what the phenomenology of religion is not, and what fails to correspond to its own essential character in the character or usage of the other disciplines.

The phenomenology of religion, then, is not the poetry of religion; and to say this is not at all superfluous, since I have myself expressly referred to the poetic character of the structural experience of ideal types. In this sense, too, we may understand Aristotle's assertion that the historian relates what has happened, while the poet recounts what might have occurred under any given circumstances; and that poetry is therefore a philosophical affair and of more serious import than history;[79] as against all bare historicism and all mere chronicle, this should always be remembered. Nor should it be forgotten that 'art is just as much investigation as is science, while science is just as much the creation of form as is art'.[80] But in any case there is a clear distinction between poetry and science, which forces itself into notice in the procedure of both from beginning to end: in his own work, then, the phenomenologist is bound up with the object; he cannot proceed without repeatedly confronting the chaos of the given, and without submitting again and again to correction by the facts; while although the artist certainly sets out from the object, he is not inseparably linked with this. In other words: the poet need know no particular language, nor study the history of the times; even the poet of the so-called historical novel need not do this. In order to interpret a myth he may completely remodel it, as for example Wagner treated the German and Celtic heroic sagas. Here the phenomenologist experiences his own limit, since his path lies always between the unformed chaos of the historical world and its structural endowment with form. All his life he oscillates hither and thither. But the poet advances.

Secondly, the phenomenology of religion is not the history of religion. History, certainly, cannot utter one word without adopting some phenomenological viewpoint; even a translation, or the editing of a text, cannot be completed without hermeneutics. On the other hand, the phenomenologist can work only with historical material, since he must know what documents are available and what their character is, before he can undertake their interpretation. The historian and the phenomenologist, therefore, work in the closest possible association; they are indeed in the majority of cases combined in the person of a *single* investigator. Nevertheless the historian's task is essentially different from the phenomenologist's, and pursues other aims.[81] For the historian, everything is directed first of all to establishing what has actually happened; and in this he can never succeed unless he understands. But also, when he fails to understand, he must describe what he has found, even if he remains at the stage of mere cataloguing. But when the phenomenologist ceases to comprehend, he can have no more to say. He strides here and there; the historian of course does the same, but more frequently he stands still, and often he does not stir at all. If he is a poor historian, this will be due only to idleness or incapacity; but if he is a sound historian, then his halts imply a very necessary and admirable resignation.

Thirdly, the phenomenology of religion is not a psychology of religion. Modern psychology, certainly, appears in so many forms that it becomes difficult to define its limits with respect to other subjects.[82] But that phenomenology is not identical with experimental psychology should be sufficiently obvious, though it is harder to separate it from the psychology of form and structure. Nevertheless it is probably the common feature of all psychologies that they are concerned only with the psychical. The psychology of religion, accordingly, attempts to comprehend the psychical aspects of religion. In so far therefore as the psychical is expressed and involved in all that is religious, phenomenology and psychology have a common task. But in religion far more appears than the merely psychical: the whole man participates in it, is active within it and is affected by it. In this sphere, then, psychology would enjoy competence only if it rose to the level of the science of Spirit – of course in its philosophic sense – in general which, it must be said, is not seldom the case. But if we are to restrict psychology to its own proper object, it may be said that the phenomenologist of religion strides backwards and forwards over the whole field of religious life, but the psychologist of religion over only a part of this.[83]

Fourthly, the phenomenology of religion is not a philosophy of religion, although it may be regarded as a preparation therefor. For it is systematic, and constitutes the bridge between the special sciences concerned with the history of religion and philosophical contemplation.[84] Of course phenomenology leads to problems of a philosophic and metaphysical character, 'which it is itself not empowered to submit';[85] and the philosophy of religion can never dispense with its phenomenology. Too often already has that philosophy of religion been elaborated which naïvely set out from 'Christianity' – that is, from the Western European standpoint of the nineteenth century, or even from the humanistic deism of the close of the eighteenth century. But whoever wishes to philosophize about religion must know what it is concerned with; he should not presuppose this as self-evident. Nevertheless the aim of the philosopher of religion is quite different; and while he must certainly know what the religious issues are, still he has something other in view; he wishes to move what he has discovered by means of the dialectical motion of Spirit. His progress, too, is hither and thither: only not in the sense of phenomenology; rather is it immanent in the Spirit. Every philosopher, indeed, has somewhat of God within him: it is quite seemly that he should stir the world in his inner life. But the phenomenologist should not become merely frightened by the idea of any similarity to God: he must shun it as the sin against the very spirit of his science.

Finally, phenomenology of religion is not theology. For theology shares with philosophy the claim to search for truth, while phenomenology, in this respect, exercises the intellectual suspense of the *epoche*. But the contrast lies deeper even than this. Theology discusses not merely a horizontal line leading, it may be, to God, nor only a vertical, descending from God and ascending to Him. Theology speaks about God Himself. For phenomenology, however, God is neither subject nor object; to be either of these He would have to be a phenomenon – that is, He would have to appear. But He does not appear: at least not so that we can comprehend and speak about Him. If He does appear He does so in a totally different manner, which results not in intelligible utterance, but in proclamation; and it is with this that theology has to deal. It too has a path 'hither and thither'; but the 'hither' and the 'thither' are not the given and its interpretation, but concealment and revelation, heaven and earth, perhaps heaven, earth and hell. Of heaven and hell, however, phenomenology knows nothing at all; it is at home on earth, although it is at the same time sustained by love of the beyond.

III. In accordance with what has been remarked in Chapter 107*, the phenomenology of religion must in the first place assign names: – sacrifice, prayer, saviour, myth, *etc.* In this way it appeals to appearances. Secondly, it must interpolate these appearances within its own life and experience them systematically. And in the third place, it must withdraw to one side, and endeavour to observe what appears while adopting the attitude of intellectual suspense. Fourthly, it attempts to clarify what it has seen, and again (combining all its previous activities) try to comprehend what has appeared. Finally, it must confront chaotic 'reality', and its still uninterpreted signs, and ultimately testify to what it has understood. Nevertheless all sorts of problems that may be highly interesting in themselves must thereby be excluded. Thus phenomenology knows nothing of any historical 'development' of religion,[86] still less of an 'origin' of religion.[87] Its perpetual task is to free itself from every non-phenomenological standpoint and to retain its own liberty, while it conserves the inestimable value of this position always anew.[88]

Kierkegaard's impressive description of the psychological observer, therefore, may serve not as a rule, and not even as an ideal, but as a permanent reproach: 'just as the psychological investigator must possess a greater suppleness than a tight-rope walker, so that he can install himself within men's minds and imitate their dispositions: just as his taciturnity during periods of intimacy must be to some degree seductive and passionate, so that reserve can enjoy stealing forth, in this artificially achieved atmosphere

* 'Phenomenon and phenomenology', see pp. 412–419.

of being quietly unnoticed, in order to feel relief, as it were in monologue: so he must have a poetic originality within his soul, so as to be able to construct totality and orderliness from what is presented by the *individuum* only in a condition of dismemberment and irregularity'.[89]

BEAUTY AND HOLINESS

Rivalry or ultimate unity? The relationship between religion on the one hand and art, moral philosophy, and science on the other, raises great difficulties for human thought and comprehension. Pious men of strict observance can hardly see in art an obedient maidservant. Artists of *l'art pour l'art* look down on religion with distrust and often with contempt. Independent moral philosophy demands freedom from religious restrictions. Imperialistic religion condemns 'works' and glorifies faith. Science and religion have been at war with each other for centuries. Many believers consider science dangerous; many scientists see in religion a passing phenomenon, already almost past.

Thus rivalry reigns: first, in general, rivalry between the religious spirit and the aesthetically, ethically, or scientifically oriented man; second, a much sharper and more implacable rivalry between the Christian religion and these manifestations of the intellectual world. Religion is always imperialistic. No matter how vague or general it may be, it always demands everything for itself. It can tolerate, at most, the claims made by art, ethics, and science, but it can never recognize their independent justification.

True as this was, for example, of the romantic pantheism of the young Schleiermacher, how much more true it is for the specific historical form which religion found in Christianity. Naturally, most of those who see in Christ the complete and final revelation of God will not want to deny that God also reveals himself in other ways in the world: in nature, in art, in history, and in science. But this is not true revelation. Fine names are invented for it. One speaks of *gratia communis* and 'general revelation'; but no essential connection is seen between God's revelation in Christ and the formless revelations in the rest of the world. One hesitates to say, with John, that the world is evil, but a path from the revelation in Christ to art, ethics, and science is not known, and, usually, is not sought.

Christ is thought of as the Holy One of God. Beauty, goodness, and truth are not denied, but they are not sought in Him; nor does one often find in Him the beautiful, the good, and the true. The relationship between religion on the one hand and art, ethics, and science on the other, is (to use an example from the history of the Netherlands) like the relationship of the seven provinces to the States-General at the time of the Republic. They indeed belong to it, primarily to obey, but they have no voice in it. It is not simple to see the situation in a different light. In Christ, God's fullness has been revealed; there is really nothing more to be added.

On the other hand, science, art, and ethics are also imperialistic, each in its own right and also in combination with the others. Each claims all of life. Just as it is not possible to serve both God and Mammon, thus the possibility of serving any master other than the strict master art seems to be excluded. Nor is it necessary:

> *Who has art and science both,*
> *He also has religion;*
> *Whoever does not have them both,*
> *Let him have religion.*

And yet the paths of religion, art, ethics, and science not only cross, they also join. There is a religious art. A close connection exists between religion and ethics. There is even a point at which science seems to lose itself in religion. How does this come about? Is rivalry the final word? Or is there ultimately a unity? Where and how can we find it?

What is the holy? If we want to discover paths which join and boundaries which separate the holy and the beautiful, we must first have a clear idea of what the holy is. At this time we have a great advantage. The nature of the religious consciousness and its object, the holy, has been examined in the past decades from two completely different, complementary points of view, in the works of Rudolf Otto and Eduard Spranger.

Otto[90] has shown us the holy as the 'wholly other', that forces itself upon us as being of wholly other form, other origin, and other effect than everything else that is known to us. It is, in the phrase of the ancient Roman, a *nobis sepositum*, separated from us and from our world. We respond to this intrusion with mixed feeling. The awe which the completely other awakens in us breaks down at once into feelings of fear, of dread, of reverence, of smallness, indeed of nothingness, and at the same time a feeling of being drawn in, of joyous astonishment, of love. The holy, as Otto has taught us to see, both attracts and repels. It allows us to become aware of infinite distance and feel a never-suspected nearness. If we succeed in finding paths from the holy to the beautiful, then the beautiful will also have to call forth this consciousness within us, and will have to lead us to the wholly other.

All this refers to the content, the substance, of the holy. The studies by Spranger[91] have elucidated its form for us. According to him, the peculiarity of the religious activity of the human spirit is characterized by the fact that the object of consideration is never a specific value or a sense limited to a single point of view, but, rather, is final value and the ultimate sense.

An act can be evaluated from different points of view: ethically, aesthetically, economically, etc. The religious man evaluates in regard to total value, ultimate meaning. Religion demands totality, its judgments recognizing no others after or besides themselves. The values which it recognizes are not conditioned by a particular point of view, but are values before God. Therefore, religion is not concerned with what is beautiful, true, or useful, but with what is eternal. Religion gives to culture again and again the command Jesus gave the rich young man: 'Sell all that thou hast.' We shall have to decide whether aesthetic, scientific, or moral culture can assume that sort of value and express it, if need be, by denying their own essence. Then we shall discover to what degree their own essence blocks this process.

Methodology. We shall see how, in the course of history, paths have been laid and boundaries drawn. Nevertheless, we do not want to engage in historical analysis. We shall see ourselves confronted with the question of the ultimate value of the holy, the beautiful, the good, and the true, independently and in relation to one another. But our analysis is not philosophic or dogmatic. It is phenomenological. The use of the phenomenological method has, recently, been widespread. In this context, of course, we cannot give a more detailed statement of its aims.[92] Let this be indicative: Where history asks, 'How did it happen?', phenomenology asks, 'How do I understand it?'; where philosophy examines truth and reality, phenomenology contents itself with the data without examining them further with respect to their content of truth or reality. We do not intend to pursue causal relationships, but rather to search for comprehensible associations. Further, we do not intend to investigate the truth behind the appearance, but we shall try to understand the phenomena themselves in their simple existence.

We are fully convinced that this method has its limitations. That it is nevertheless unavoidable for all historical as well as systematic analyses we shall show by our practical experiment, rather than by theoretical disputations.

Can art be a holy act? It is in this formulation that the problem concerning the paths and boundaries between holiness and beauty confront the phenomenologist most clearly. This means that we shall not attempt to give a philosophical definition of the beautiful, nor shall we immerse ourselves in the question of whether nature is beautiful in its own essence or whether the intellect carries over its own beauty into nature. These are questions of the absolute value of the beautiful; that is to say, questions that belong to the metaphysics of the beautiful.

We are not concerned with the beautiful per se, but with how the beautiful influences our spirit and finds expression through it. The impression and expression of the beautiful we usually call art. Of course we are not using the word in a technical sense, and are not even concerned with the practice of art. Whoever sees the beauty of a landscape experiences the beautiful. Whoever, above and beyond that, is capable of saying that it is beautiful and in what way it is beautiful; that is, he who can express his experience, is an artist. If he is not capable of this, then he experiences the beauty of nature in the same way in which he perceives the beauty of a work of art. In both cases he is concerned not with beauty as such, but rather with his experience of beauty; that is, with art, whether it is potential (impressionistic), or actual (expressionistic).

We limit the question of the relationship between beauty and holiness to the analysis of the relationship between beauty and holiness as man experiences them; that is to say, to the holy act and the beautiful act, or art.

Thus we see from our periphrase of the holy that the relationship can only be grasped by the question, 'Can art be a holy act?' The reverse question, 'Can religion be art or resolve itself into art?' becomes inadmissible on the ground of our definition of the holy as the 'wholly other' and the 'absolutely valid'.

What, of course, can be asked easily, and must be asked, is to what degree the consciousness and the realization of the holy can be art. This formulation of the question implies the possibility of a very complicated modern art which coalesces into a unity with religion in a way which we shall examine more closely later. We shall consider the primitive artistic expression that stands in just as close a connection, though of a different sort, to the holy act of a magico-religious nature.

Depending on whether we are concerned with a primitive or a modern intellectual context, this connection assumes such different guises that we shall divide our object according to its relationship to the primitive mentality.

'Primitive' and 'modern'. This is not the place to propose at length what is meant by 'primitive' and 'modern'. I have done that in another place.[94] From what follows, usage will become apparent automatically. One remark only should be made in this regard: 'primitive' never means the intellectual situation of earlier times or other lands, and 'modern' never that of here and now. Neither is a description of a stage in the evolution of the human spirit; rather, both are structures. We find them both realized today just as much as three thousand years ago, both in Amsterdam and in Tierra del Fuego. Of course, a more complete realization of the primitive intellectual structure is evidenced by the ancient and so-called uncivilized peoples than by the West Europeans of today. But as the primitive is never completely lacking even in the most modern cities, so the modern is present in the least-educated native of Surinam. [...]

NOTES

1. L. Binswanger, *Einführung in die Probleme der allgemeinen Psychologie·* Berlin, 1922, p. 184.
2. L. Binswanger, *Idem*, p. 223.
3. L. Binswanger, *Idem*, p. 330.
4. Jonas Cohn, 'Über einige Grundfragen der Psychologie', *Logos*, XII (1923), pp. 52 sq.
5. L. Binswanger, *Einführung...*, pp. 60—102.
6. Henri Bergson, *Essai sur les données immédiates de la conscience.*
7. L. Binswanger, *Einführung...*, pp. 60 sqq.
8. '*Wesensallgemeinheit.*' L. Binswanger, *idem*, pp. 98 sq., 135 sqq.
9. J.H. Gunning Jr., *Overlevering en wetenschap* [Tradition and Science]. The Hague, 1879, p. 90.
10. *Cf.* on the relation of 'analysis of essence' to Natorp's 'reconstruction': L. Binswanger, *Einführung...*, p. 99.
11. The nearness of the experience may not even be considered to be an advantage. I stand as helplessly towards my own past as towards the experience of my neighbour. But my 'present' shrinks under the 'comprehending' hand into a dot without dimensions. Nor is my neighbour 'nearer' to me than any ancient Egyptian or Chinese. It is from a psychological-historical point of view not even advantageous if one is a contemporary. Everything has to be experienced anew anyhow, and the 'interpretation' [. . .] becomes the more difficult, the less the distance in space and time.
12. L. Binswanger, *Einführung...*, pp. 236—241.
13. Karl Jaspers, *Allgemeine Psychopathologie*, 1923³, pp. 197 sqq.
14. K. Jaspers, *Idem*, p. 197.
15. *Cf.* L. Binswanger, *Einführung* ... p. 293.
16. K. Jaspers, *Allgemeine Psychopathologie*, p. 322.
17. *Cf.* L. Binswanger, *Einführung* ... p. 294; Max Weber, 'Über einige Kategorien der verstehenden Soziologie', *Logos*, IV (1913), pp. 253—294; Max Weber, 'Die 'Objektivität' sozialwissenschaftlicher und sozialpolitischer Erkenntnis', *Archiv für Sozialwissenschaft und Sozialpolitik*, vol. XIX (1904), pp. 22—87.
18. '*Es kommt nur auf die im Erleben selbst evidente Möglichkeit derselben an, d. i. auf die Notwendigkeit, mit der ihre Züge zusammenhängen*'. Paul Hofmann, *Das religiöse Erlebnis*, Charlottenburg, 1925, p. 8. *Cf.* K. Jaspers, *Allgemeine Psychopathologie*, pp. 199 sq.
19. L. Binswanger, *Einführung,...* pp. 329 sq.
20. P. Hofmann, *Allgemeinwissenschaft und Geisteswissenschaft*, 1925. Idem, *Das religiöse Erlebnis*, 1925.
21. G. van der Leeuw, 'Über einige neuere Ergebnisse der psychologischen Forschung und ihre Anwendung auf die Geschichte, insonderheit die Religionsgeschichte'. *Studi e Materiali di Storia delle Religioni*, Vol. II (1926), pp. 1—43 (See esp. pp. 4 sqq.).
22. 'For the time being'; because, after all, 'empathy' (*Einfühlung*) and 'understanding' (*Verstehen*) are two different concepts.
23. *Cf.* W. Dilthey, *Gesammelte Schriften*, vol. V, 1, p. 172: 'We explain by means of purely intellectual processes, but we understand when all the mind's forces combine in the act of apprehension' ('*durch das Zusammenwirken aller Gemütskräfte in der Auffassung*').
24. *Cf.* the article mentioned in Note 21.

25. E. Spranger, *Einheit der Psychologie*, p. 184.
26. E. Spranger, *Psychologie des Jugendalters*, Halle, 1925², p. 11.
27. W. Dilthey, *Gesammelte Schriften*, Vol. VII, 1927, pp. 145 sq.
28. E. Spranger, *Lebensformen*, Halle, 1925, p. 418.
29. W.J. Aalders, 'De cirkel van Heidegger' ['The circle of Heidegger'], *Nieuwe Theologische Studiën*, Vol. XIV (1931), pp. 287 sqq.
30. E. Spranger, *Psychologie des Jugendalters*, p. 18.
31. E. Spranger, *Idem*, p. 9.
32. *Cf.* E. Spranger, *Lebensformen*, pp. 436, 82.
33. *Cf.* E. Spranger, *Idem*, pp. 25, 48.
34. E. Spranger, *Einheit der Psychologie*, p. 181
35. E. Spranger, *Lebensformen*, pp. 424 sqq.
36. Because 'in each mental act reigns the totality of the mind' (E. Spranger, *Lebensformen*, p. 38).
37. The term 'experience' *(Erlebnis)* is itself objectively oriented (we always experience something) and designates a 'structure'.
38. W. Dilthey, *Gesammelte Schriften*, vol. VII, p. 194.
39. *Ibid.*, p. 195.
40. *Cf.* E. Spranger, *Die Einheit der Psychologie*. *Sitz. ber. d. Preuss. Akad. d. Wiss.* 24, (1926), pp. 188, 191. F. Krüger, *Ber. über den VIII. Kongress für experim. Psych.*, 33.
41. *Cf.* on a different field of research, P. Bekker, *Musikgeschichte*, 1926,p. 2.
42. The so-called hermeneutic circle, to which G. Wobbermin particularly drew attention; *cf.* J. Wach, *Religionswissenschaft*, p. 49.
43. *Cf.* A.A. Grünbaum, *Herrschen und Lieben*, 1925, p. 17. E. Spranger, *Lebensformen*, pp. 6 sqq.
44. E. Spranger, *Idem*, p. 436.
45. E. Spranger, *Die Einheit der Psychologie*, p. 177; *cf.* J. Wach's observation that the close connection between the theory of types and that of hermeneutics has not yet been adequately emphasized; *Religionswissenschaft*, p. 149.
46. This term was introduced by Karl Jaspers: *verständliche Beziehungen.*
47. On the history of the idea, *cf.* B. Pfister, *Die Entwicklung zum Idealtypus*, 1928.
48. E. Spranger, *Lebensformen*, p. 115. L. Binswanger, *Einführung in die Probleme der allgemeinen Psychologie*, p. 296; Van der Leeuw, 'Über einige neuere Ergebnisse der psychologischen Forschung und ihre Anwendung auf die Geschichte insonderheit die Religionsgeschichte', *Studi e Materiali*, II, 1926, *passim ; cf.* further P. Hofmann, *Das religiöse Erlebnis*, 1925, p. 8.
49. What I myself understand by the phenomenology of religion is called by Hackmann 'The General Science of Religion'; other terms for this type of research that have appeared (once more to disappear, however) are 'Transcendental Psychology', 'Eidology' and *Formenlehre der religiösen Vorstellungen* (Usener).
50. McDougall, *An Outline of Psychology*, p. 284.
51. *Farbenlehre* in L. Binswanger, *Einführung...*, p. 31.
52. The expression usually employed, 'Empathy' *(Einfühlung)*, overstresses the feeling aspect of the process, although, not without some justification.
53. E. Spranger, *Lebensformen*, p. 430.
54. This applies equally to the so-called 'present'.
55. *Götternamen*, 1896, VII.
56. L. Binswanger, *Einführung ...*, p. 246; G. van der Leeuw, 'Über einige neuere Ergebnisse...'', pp. 14 f.

57. Chesterton, *The Everlasting Man*, p. 111; *cf.* P. Hofmann, *Das religiöse Erlebnis*, p. 4 sq.

58. K. Jaspers, *Allgemeine Psychopathologie*, 1923³, p. 204.

59. Max Scheler, *Die Stellung des Menschen im Kosmos*, 1928, p. 63; *cf.* M. Heidegger, *Sein und Zeit*, p. 38.

60. L. Binswanger, *Einführung . . .*, pp. 37, 302; *cf.* K. Jaspers, *Psychopathologie*, pp. 18, 35.

61. E. Spranger, *Lebensformen*, p. 11.

62. M. Heidegger, *Op. cit.*, p. 37; W. Dilthey, *Gesammelte Schviften*, vol. VII, pp. 71, 86.

63. W. Dilthey, *Ibid.*, p. 131.

64. *Cf.* further L.Binswanger, *Op. cit.*, pp. 244, 288.

65. K. Jaspers, *Allgemeine Psychopathologie*, p. 404; *cf.* H. Usener, *Götternamen*, p. 62.

66. E. Spranger gives an excellent example in his comparison of the ever more deeply penetrating meanings of a biblical text: *Die Einheit der Psychologie*, pp. 180 sqq.

67. J. Wach, *Religionswissenschaft*, p. 117; G. van der Leeuw, '*Über einige neuere Ergebnisse . . .*', *passim.*

68. M. Heidegger, *Op. cit.*, p. 34.

69. L. von Ranke, *Weltgeschichte*, vol. VIII⁴, 1921, p. 177.

70. E. Brunner, *Gott und Mensch*, 1930, p. 40.

71. *Cf.* W.J. Aalders, *Wetenschap als Getuigenis* [Science as Testimony], 1930.

72. Herein consists the essential unity between religion and culture.Ultimately, all culture is religious; and, on the horizontal line, all religion is culture.

73. 'Die Problematik der Neuscholastik', *Kantstudien 33*, 1928.

74. E. Spranger, *Lebensformen*, p. 418.

75. I John 4: 10, 19.

76. E. Przywara, 'Die Problematik . . .' p.92.

77. *Ibid.*, p. 95.

78. J. Wach, *Religionswissenschaft*, p. 12.

79. *Poetics*, Chap. 9.

80. E. Utitz, *Ästhetik*, 1923, p. 18.

81. J. Wach, *Ibid.*, p. 56.

82. *Cf.* E. Spranger, *Die Einheit der Psychologie.*

83. That psychology is concerned purely with actual, and not with historical, experiences, and that consequently a limit subsists here also, obviously cannot be admitted for one moment; without psychology we should be unable to deal with history; *cf.* E. Spranger, *Die Einheit der Psychologie*, p. 184.

84. J. Wach, *Das Verstehen*, vol. I, p. 12.

85. J. Wach, *Religionswissenschaft*, p. 131.

86. J. Wach, *Religionswissenschaft*, p. 82.

87. Th. de Laguna, 'The Sociological Method of Durkheim', *Phil. Rev.* 29, 1920, p. 224. E. Troeltsch, *Gesammelte Schriften*, vol. II, 1913, p. 490.

88. K. Jaspers, *Allgemeine Psychopathologie*, p. 36.

89. *Begrebet Angest* [The concept of Dread], *Saml. Vaerker*, IV², 1923, p. 360; *cf.* the entire fine passage.

90. Rudolf Otto, *Das Heilige*. Breslau, 1917. English: *The Idea of the Holy.* Oxford, 1925.

91. Eduard Spranger, *Lebensformen*. Halle, 1925. English: *Types of Men; the Psychology and Ethics of Personality*. Halle, 1928.

92. G. van der Leeuw, *La structure de la mentalité primitive*. Strasbourg–Paris, 1928; *L'homme primitif et la religion*. Paris, 1940.

Rudolf Otto

Rudolf Louis Karl Otto was born in 1869 in Peine, Germany, and received his primary and secondary school education there and at Hildesheim. From 1888 until 1898 he studied theology at the universities of Erlangen and Göttingen, and in 1898 he obtained the *Lizentiat* at the University of Göttingen. In 1897 he had become *Privatdozent* in systematic theology in Göttingen, and in 1904 he became there *Extraordinarius*. In 1907 he obtained his Ph. D. at the University of Tübingen, and a Th. D. *honoris causa* at the University of Giessen. In 1914 Otto became professor of systematic theology at the University of Breslau, in 1917 the same at the University of Marburg. He went into retirement in 1929. Otto died at Marburg in 1937.

The following books of Otto are available in English translation: 1907 *Naturalism and Religion;* 1923 *The Idea of the Holy: an Inquiry into the Non-Rational Factor in the Idea of the Divine and its Relation to the Rational;* 1930 *India's Religion of Grace and Christianity Compared and Contrasted;* 1931 *The Philosophy of Religion, based on Kant and Fries;* 1931 *Religious Essays; a Supplement to 'The Idea of the Holy';* 1932 *Mysticism East and West; a Comparative Analysis of the Nature of Mysticism;* 1938 *The Kingdom of God and the Son of Man; a Study in the History of Religion.*

Rudolf Otto is best known for his taking 'the holy' as an autonomous category *a priori*, as a category of meaning and value. In this way he postulated the autonomy of religion as different from other spheres of life and he gave an epistemological foundation to religious knowledge, which could be obtained psychologically by means of the *sensus numinis.* Otto carried out a number of comparative studies on religious themes and phenomena, taking into account the religious background which they have or had in specific religious traditions. He developed a methodology to analyze certain religious experiences and to do justice both to the 'subjective' and to the 'objective' sides of such experiences.

The following fragments have been taken from *The Idea of the Holy* and from *Religious Essays* and show the way in which Rudolf Otto envisaged the study of religion.

'THE IDEA OF THE HOLY'

'The rational and the non-rational'

It is essential to every theistic conception of God, and most of all to the Christian, that it designates and precisely characterizes deity by the attributes spirit, reason, purpose, good will, supreme power, unity, selfhood. The nature of God is thus thought of by analogy with our human nature of reason and personality; only, whereas in ourselves we are aware of this as qualified by restriction and limitation, as applied to God the attributes we use are 'completed', i.e. thought as absolute and unqualified. Now all these attributes constitute clear and definite *concepts*: they can be grasped by the intellect; they can be analysed by thought; they even admit of definition. An object that can thus be thought conceptually may be termed *rational*. The nature of deity described in the attributes above mentioned is, then, a rational nature; and a religion which recognizes and maintains such a view of God is in so far a 'rational' religion. Only on such terms is *belief* possible in contrast to mere *feeling*. And of Christianity at least it is false that 'feeling is all, the name but sound and smoke'[1]; – where 'name' stands for conception or thought. Rather we count this the very mark and criterion of a religion's high rank and superior value – that it should have no lack of *conceptions* about God; that it should admit knowledge – the knowledge that comes by faith – of the transcendent in terms of conceptual thought, whether those already mentioned or others which continue and develop them. Christianity not only possesses such conceptions but possesses them in unique clarity and abundance, and this is, though not the sole or even the chief, yet a very real sign of its superiority over religions of other forms and at other levels. This must be asserted at the outset and with the most positive emphasis.

But, when this is granted, we have to be on our guard against an error which would lead to a wrong and one-sided interpretation of religion. This is the view that the essence of deity can be given completely and exhaustively in such 'rational' attributions as have been referred to above and in others like them. It is not an unnatural misconception. We are prompted to it by the traditional language of edification, with its characteristic phraseology and ideas; by the learned treatment of religious themes in sermon and theological instruction; and further even by our Holy Scriptures themselves. In all these cases the 'rational' element occupies the foreground, and often nothing else seems to be present at all. But this is after all to be expected. All language, in so far as it consists of words, purports to convey ideas or concepts; – that is what language means; – and the more clearly and unequivocally it does so, the better the language. And hence expositions of religious truth in language inevitably tend to stress the 'rational' attributes of God.

But though the above mistake is thus a natural one enough, it is none the less seriously misleading. For so far are these 'rational' attributes from exhausting the idea of deity, that they in fact imply a non-rational or suprarational Subject of which they are predicates. They are 'essential' (and not merely 'accidental') attributes of that subject, but they are also, it is important to notice, *synthetic* essential attributes. That is to say, we have to predicate them of a subject which they qualify, but which in its deeper essence is not, nor indeed can be, comprehended in them; which rather requires comprehension of a quite different kind. Yet, though it eludes the conceptual way of understanding, it must be in some way or other within our grasp, else absolutely nothing could be asserted of it. And even mysticism, in speaking of it as τό ἄϱϱητον, the ineffable, does not really mean to imply that absolutely nothing can be asserted of the object of the religious consciousness; otherwise, mysticism could exist only in unbroken silence, whereas what has generally been a characteristic of the mystics is their copious eloquence.

Here for the first time we come up against the contrast between rationalism and profounder religion, and with this contrast and its signs we shall be repeatedly concerned in what follows. We have here in fact the first and most distinctive mark of rationalism, with which all the rest are bound up. It is not that which is commonly asserted, that rationalism is the denial, and its opposite the affirmation, of the miraculous. That is manifestly a wrong or at least a very superficial distinction. For the traditional theory of the miraculous as the occasional breach in the causal nexus in nature by a Being who himself instituted and must therefore be master of it – this theory is itself as massively 'rational' as it is possible to be. Rationalists have often enough acquiesced in the possibility of the miraculous in this sense; they have even themselves contributed to frame a theory of it; – whereas anti-rationalists have been often indifferent to the whole controversy about miracles. The difference between rationalism and its opposite is to be found elsewhere. It resolves itself rather into a peculiar difference of *quality* in the mental attitude and emotional content of the religious life itself. All depends upon this: in our idea of God is the non-rational overborne, even perhaps wholly excluded, by the rational? Or conversely, does the non-rational itself preponderate over the rational? Looking at the matter thus, we see that the common dictum, that orthodoxy itself has been the mother of rationalism, is in some measure well founded. It is not simply that orthodoxy was preoccupied with doctrine and the framing of dogma, for these have been no less a concern of the wildest mystics. It is rather that orthodoxy found in the construction of dogma and doctrine no way to do justice to the non-rational aspect of its subject. So far from keeping the non-rational element in religion alive in the heart of the religious experience, orthodox Christianity manifestly failed to recognize its value, and by this failure gave to the idea of God a one-sidedly intellectualistic and rationalistic interpretation.

This bias to rationalization still prevails, not only in theology but in the science of comparative religion in general, and from top to bottom of it. The modern students of mythology, and those who pursue research into the religion of 'primitive man' and attempt to reconstruct the 'bases' or 'sources' of religion, are all victims to it. Men do not, of course, in these cases employ those lofty 'rational' concepts which we took as our point of departure; but they tend to take these concepts and their gradual 'evolution' as setting the main problem of their inquiry, and fashion ideas and notions of lower value, which they regard as paving the way for them. It is always in terms of concepts and ideas that the subject is pursued, 'natural' ones, moreover, such as have a place in the general sphere of man's ideational life, and are not specifically 'religious'. And then with a resolution and cunning which one can hardly help admiring, men shut their eyes to that which is quite unique in the religious experience, even in its most primitive manifestations. But it is rather a matter for astonishment than for admiration! For if there be any single domain of human experience that presents us with something unmistakably specific and unique, peculiar to itself, assuredly it is that of the religious life. In truth the enemy has often a keener vision in this matter than either the champion of religion or the neutral and professedly impartial theorist. For the adversaries on their side know very well that the entire 'pother about mysticism' has nothing to do with 'reason' and 'rationality'.

And so it is salutary that we should be incited to notice that religion is not exclusively contained and exhaustively comprised in any series of 'rational' assertions; and it is well worth while to attempt to bring the relation of the different 'moments' of religion to one another clearly before the mind, so that its nature may become more manifest.

This attempt we are now to make with respect to the quite distinctive category of the holy or sacred.

'"Numen" and the "Numinous"'

'Holiness' – 'the holy' – is a category of interpretation and valuation peculiar to the sphere of religion. It is, indeed, applied by transference to another sphere – that of ethics – but it is not itself derived from this. While it is complex, it contains a quite specific element or 'moment', which sets it apart from 'the rational' in the meaning we gave to that word above, and which remains inexpressible – an ἄρρητον or *ineffabile*–in the sense that it completely eludes apprehension in terms of concepts. The same thing is true (to take a quite different region of experience) of the category of the beautiful.

Now these statements would be untrue from the outset if 'the holy' were merely what is meant by the word, not only in common parlance, but in philosophical, and generally even in theological usage. The fact is we have come to use the words 'holy', 'sacred' *(heilig)* in an entirely derivative sense,

quite different from that which they originally bore. We generally take
'holy' as meaning 'completely good'; it is the absolute moral attribute,
denoting the consummation of moral goodness. In this sense Kant calls the
will which remains unwaveringly obedient to the moral law from the
motive of duty a 'holy' will; here clearly we have simply the *perfectly moral*
will. In the same way we may speak of the holiness or sanctity of duty or
law, meaning merely that they are imperative upon conduct and universally
obligatory.

But this common usage of the term is inaccurate. It is true that all this
moral significance is contained in the word 'holy', but it includes in addition
– as even we cannot but feel – a clear overplus of meaning, and this it is
now our task to isolate. Nor is this merely a later or acquired meaning;
rather, 'holy', or at least the equivalent words in Latin and Greek, in Semitic
and other ancient languages, denoted first and foremost *only* this overplus:
if the ethical element was present at all, at any rate it was not original and
never constituted the whole meaning of the word. Any one who uses it to-
day does undoubtedly always feel 'the morally good' to be implied in 'holy';
and accordingly in our inquiry into that element which is separate and peculiar to the idea of the holy it will be useful, at least for the temporary purpose of the investigation, to invent a special term to stand for 'the holy'
minus its moral factor or 'moment', and, as we can now add, minus its
'rational' aspect altogether.

It will be our endeavour to suggest this unnamed Something to the reader
as far as we may, so that he may himself feel it. There is no religion in which
it does not live as the real innermost core, and without it no religion would be
worthy of the name. It is pre-eminently a living force in the Semitic religions,
and of these again in none has it such vigour as in that of the Bible. Here,
too, it has a name of its own, viz. the Hebrew *qādôsh*, to which the Greek
ἅγιος and the Latin *sanctus*, and, more accurately still, *sacer*, are the corresponding terms. It is not, of course, disputed that these terms in all three
languages connote, as part of their meaning, *good, absolute goodness*, when,
that is, the notion has ripened and reached the highest stage in its development. And we then use the word 'holy' to translate them. But this 'holy'
then represents the gradual shaping and filling in with ethical meaning, or
what we shall call the 'schematization', of what was a unique original
feeling-response, which can be in itself ethically neutral and claims consideration in its own right. And when this moment or element first emerges
and begins its long development, all those expressions *(qādôsh, ἅγιος, sacer,*
etc.) mean beyond all question something quite other than 'the good'.
This is universally agreed by contemporary criticism, which rightly explains
the rendering of *qādôsh* by 'good' as a mistranslation and unwarranted
rationalization' or 'moralizatio n' of the term.

Accordingly, it is worth while, as we have said, to find a word to stand for this element in isolation, this 'extra' in the meaning of 'holy' above and beyond the meaning of goodness. By means of a special term we shall the better be able, first, to keep the meaning clearly apart and distinct, and second, to apprehend and classify connectedly whatever subordinate forms or stages of development it may show. For this purpose I adopt a word coined from the Latin *numen*. *Omen* has given us 'ominous', and there is no reason why from *numen* we should not similarly form a word 'numinous'. I shall speak, then, of a unique 'numinous' category of value and of a definitely 'numinous' state of mind, which is always found wherever the category is applied. This mental state is perfectly *sui generis* and irreducible to any other; and therefore, like every absolutely primary and elementary datum, while it admits of being discussed, it cannot be strictly defined. There is only one way to help another to an understanding of it. He must be guided and led on by consideration and discussion of the matter through the ways of his own mind, until he reach the point at which 'the numinous' in him perforce begins to stir, to start into life and into consciousness. We can co-operate in this process by bringing before his notice all that can be found in other regions of the mind, already known and familiar, to resemble, or again to afford some special contrast to, the particular experience we wish to elucidate. Then we must add: 'This *x* of ours is not precisely *this* experience, but akin to this one and the opposite of that other. Cannot you now realize for yourself what it is?' In other words our *x* cannot, strictly speaking, be taught, it can only be evoked, awakened in the mind; as everything that comes 'of the spirit' must be awakened.

'The holy as an "a priori" category'-I

It follows from what has been said that the 'holy' in the fullest sense of the word is a combined, complex category, the combining elements being its rational and non-rational components. But in *both* – and the assertion must be strictly maintained against all sensationalism and naturalism – it is a *purely a priori* category.

The rational ideas of absoluteness, completion, necessity, and substantiality, and no less so those of the good as an objective value, objectively binding and valid, are not to be 'evolved' from any sort of sense-perception. And the notions of 'epigenesis', 'heterogony', or whatever other expression we may choose to denote our compromise and perplexity, only serve to conceal the problem, the tendency to take refuge in a Greek terminology being here, as so often, nothing but an avowal of one's own insufficiency. Rather, seeking to account for the ideas in question, we are referred away from all sense-experience back to an original and underivable capacity of the mind implanted in the 'pure reason' independently of all perception.

But in the case of the non-rational elements of our category of the Holy we are referred back to something still deeper than the 'pure reason', at least as this is usually understood, namely, to that which mysticism has rightly named the *fundus animae*, the 'bottom' or 'ground of the soul' *(Seelengrund)*. The ideas of the numinous and the feelings that correspond to them are, quite as much as the rational ideas and feelings, absolutely 'pure', and the criteria which Kant suggests for the 'pure' concept and the ‹pure' feeling of respect are most precisely applicable to them. In the famous opening words of the *Critique of Pure Reason* he says:

'That all our knowledge begins with experience there can be no doubt. For how is it possible that the faculty of cognition should be awakened into exercise otherwise than by means of objects which affect our senses? ... But, though all our knowledge begins *with* experience, it by no means follows that all arises *out of* experience.'

And, referring to empirical knowledge, he distinguishes that part which we receive through impressions and that which our own faculty of cognition supplies from itself, *sense–impressions giving merely the occasion*.

The numinous is of the latter kind. It issues from the deepest foundation of cognitive apprehension that the soul possesses, and, though it of course comes into being in and amid the sensory data and empirical material of the natural world and cannot anticipate or dispense with those, yet it does not arise *out of* them, but only *by their means*. They are the incitement, the stimulus, and the 'occasion' for the numinous experience to become astir, and, in so doing, to begin – at first with a naive immediacy of reaction – to be interfused and interwoven with the present world of sensuous experience, until, becoming gradually purer, it disengages itself from this and takes its stand in absolute contrast to it. The proof that in the numinous we have to deal with purely *a priori* cognitive elements is to be reached by introspection and a critical examination of reason such as Kant instituted. We find, that is, involved in the numinous experience, beliefs and feelings qualitatively different from anything that 'natural' sense-perception is capable of giving us. They are themselves not perceptions at all, but peculiar interpretations and valuations, at first of perceptual data, and then – at a higher level – of posited objects and entities, which themselves no longer belong to the perceptual world, but are thought of as supplementing and transcending it. And as they are not themselves sense-perceptions, so neither are they any sort of 'transmutation' of sense-perceptions. The only 'transmutation' possible in respect to sense-perception is the transformation of the intuitively given concrete percept, of whatever sort, into the corresponding concept; there is never any question of the transformation of *one* class of percepts nto a class of entities qualitatively *other*. The facts of the numinous consciousness point therefore – as likewise do also the 'pure concepts of the understanding' of Kant and the ideas and value-judgements of ethics or aesthetics – to a hidden substantive source, from which the religious ideas and feelings are formed, which lies in the mind independently of sense-experience; a 'pure reason' in the profoundest sense, which, because of the 'surpassingness' of its content, must be distinguished from both the pure theoretical and the pure practical reason of Kant, as something yet higher or deeper than they.

The justification of the 'evolutionist' theory of to-day stands or falls with its claim to 'explain' the phenomenon of religion. That is in truth the real task of the psychology of religion. But in order to explain we must have the data from which an explanation may be forthcoming; out of nothing nothing can be explained. Nature can only be explained by an investigation into the ultimate fundamental forces of nature and their laws: it is meaningless to propose to go farther and explain these laws themselves, for in terms of what are they to be explained? But in the domain of spirit the corresponding principle from which an explanation is derived is just the spirit itself, the reasonable spirit of man, with its predispositions, capacities, and its own inherent laws. This has to be presupposed: it cannot itself be explained. None can say how mind or spirit 'is made' – though this is in effect just what the theory of epigenesis is fain to attempt. The history of humanity begins with man, and we have to presuppose man, to take him for granted as he is, in order that from him we may understand his history. That is, we must presuppose man as a being analogous to ourselves in natural propensities and capacities. It is a hopeless business to seek to lower ourselves into the mental life of a *pithecanthropus erectus;* and, even if it were not, we should still need to start from man as he is, since we can only interpret the psychical and emotional life of animals regressively by clumsy analogies drawn from the developed human mind. To try, on the other hand, to understand and deduce the human from the sub-human or brute mind is to try to fit the lock to the key instead of vice versa; it is to seek to illuminate light by darkness. In the first appearance of conscious life on dead unconscious matter we have a simple, irreducible, inexplicable datum. But that which here appears is already a manifold of qualities, and we can only interpret it as a seed of potentiality, out of which issue continually maturer powers and capacities, as the organization of the body increases in stability and complexity. And the only way we can throw any light upon the whole region of sub-human psychical life is by interpreting it once again as a sort of 'predisposition'[1] at a second remove, i.e. a predisposition to form the predispositions or faculties of the actual developed mind, and standing in relation to this as an embryo to the full-grown organism. But we are not completely in the dark as to the meaning of this word 'predisposition'. *('Anlage')*. For in our own awakening and growth to mental and spiritual maturity we trace in ourselves in some sort the evolution by which the seed develops into the tree – the very opposite of 'transformation' and 'epigenesis' by successive addition.*

We call the source of growth a hidden 'predisposition' of the human spirit, which awakens when aroused by divers excitations. That there are 'predispositions' of this sort in individuals no one can deny who has given serious study to the history of religion. They are seen as propensities, 'predestining' the individual to religion, and they may grow spontaneously to quasi-instinctive presentiments, uneasy seeking and groping, yearning and longing, and become a religious *impulsion*, that only finds peace when it has become clear to itself and attained its goal. From them arise the states of mind of 'prevenient grace', described in masterly fashion by Suso:

'Loving, tender Lord! My mind has from the days of my childhood sought something with an earnest thirst of longing, Lord, and what that is have I not yet perfectly apprehended. Lord, I have now for many a year been in hot pursuit of it, and never yet have I been able to succeed, for I know not aright what it is. And yet it is something that draws my heart and my soul after it, and without which I can never attain to full repose. Lord, I was fain in the earliest days of my childhood to seek it among created things, as I saw others before me do. And the more I sought, the less I found it; and the nearer I went, the further I wandered from it. . . . Now my heart rages for it, for fain would I possess it. . . . Woe is me! . . . What is this, or how is it fashioned, that plays within me in such hidden wise?'[2]

These are manifestations of a *predisposition* becoming a search and a driving *impulsion*. But here, if nowhere else, the 'fundamental biogenetic law' really does hold good, which uses the stages and phases in the growth of the individual to throw light upon the corresponding stages in the growth of his species. The *predisposition* which the human reason brought with it when

---

* The physical analogue to these spiritual or mental relationships is the relation of potential to kinetic energy. The assumption of such a relation in the world of mind (i.e. a relation between potential and kinetic mind) is, of course, only to be expected from one who is prepared to accept as the final cause of all mind in the world as a whole the absolute mind as 'pure actuality' whose *ellampatio* or effulgence (in Leibniz's phrase) all other mind is. For all that is potential presupposes an *actual* as the ground of its possibility, as Aristotle long ago showed. But indeed how can we afford to reject such a 'pure actuality'? It is an inconsequent proceeding to postulate actuality, as is done, for a starting-point for the physical world, as a system of stored-up energy, whose transference to kinetic energy constitutes the 'rush of worlds and wheel of systems', and yet to reject the analogous assumption in the world of mind and spirit.

the species Man entered history became long ago, not merely for individuals but for the species as a whole, a *religious impulsion,* to which incitements from without and pressure from within the mind both contributed. It begins in undirected, groping emotion, a seeking and shaping of representations, and goes on, by a continual onward striving, to generate ideas, till its nature is self-illumined and made clear by an explication of the obscure *a priori* foundation of thought itself, out of which it originated.[3] And this emotion, this searching, this generation and explication of ideas, gives the warp of the fabric of religious evolution, whose woof we are to discuss later.

'The holy as an "a priori" category' — II

We conclude, then, that not only the rational but also the non-rational elements of the complex category of 'holiness' are *a priori* elements and each in the same degree. Religion is not in vassalage either to morality or teleology, ἔϑος or τέλος, and does not draw its life from postulates; and its non-rational content has, no less than its rational, its own independent roots in the hidden depths of the spirit itself.

But the same *a priori* character belongs, in the third place, to the *connexion* of the rational and the non-rational elements in religion, their inward and necessary union. The histories of religion recount indeed, as though it were something axiomatic, the gradual interpenetration of the two, the process by which 'the divine' is charged and filled out with ethical meaning. And this process is, in fact, *felt* as something axiomatic, something whose inner necessity we feel to be self-evident. But then this inward self-evidence is a problem in itself; we are forced to assume an obscure, *a priori* knowledge of the necessity of this synthesis, combining rational and non-rational. For it is not by any means a *logical* necessity. How should it be logically inferred from the still 'crude', half-daemonic character of a moon-god or a sun-god or a numen attached to some locality, that he is a guardian and guarantor of the oath and of honourable dealing, of hospitality, of the sanctity of marriage and of duties to tribe and clan ? How should it be inferred that he is a god who decrees happiness and misery, participates in the concerns of the tribe, provides for its well-being, and directs the course of destiny and history ? Whence comes this most surprising of all the facts in the history of religion, that beings, obviously born originally of horror and terror, become *gods* – beings to whom men pray, to whom they confide their sorrow or their happiness, in whom they behold the origin and the sanction of morality, law, and the whole canon of justice ? And how does all this come about in such a way that, when once such ideas have been aroused, it is understood at once as the plainest and most evident of axioms, that so it must be ?

Socrates, in Plato's *Republic,* II. 382 E, says: 'God, then, is single and

true in deed and word, and neither changes himself nor deceives others. . . .'
And Adeimantos answers him: 'So too is it apparent to me, now that you
say it.' The most interesting point in this passage is not the elevation and
purity of the conception of God, nor yet the lofty rationalization and moralization of it here enunciated, but, on the side of Socrates, the apparently
'dogmatic' tone of his pronouncement – for he does not spend the least pains
in demonstrating it – and, on the side of Adeimantos, the ingenuous surprise
and, at the same time, the confident assurance with which he admits a truth
novel to him. And his assent is such as implies convincement; he does not
simply believe Socrates; he sees clearly for himself the truth of his words.
Now this is the criterion of all *a priori* knowledge, namely, that, so soon
as an assertion has been clearly expressed and understood, knowledge of
its truth comes into the mind with the certitude of first-hand insight. And
what passed here between Socrates and Adeimantos has been repeated a
thousand times in the history of religions. Amos, also, says something new
when he proclaims Yahweh as the God of inflexible, universal, and absolute
righteousness, and yet this is a novelty that he neither proves nor just'fies
by an appeal to authorities. He appeals to *a priori* judgements, viz. to the
religious conscience itself, and this in truth bears witness to his message.

Luther, again, recognizes and maintains such an *a priori* knowledge of the
divine nature. His rage against the 'whore Reason' leads him, to be sure,
usually to utterances in the opposite sense, such as the following:

'It is a knowledge *a posteriori*, in that we look at God from without, at
His works and His government, as one looketh at a castle or house
from without and thereby feeleth *(spüret)* the lord or householder thereof.
But *a priori* from within hath no wisdom of men yet availed to discover
what and of what manner of being is God as He is in Himself or in His
inmost essence, nor can any man know nor say aught thereof, but they
to whom it has been revealed by the Holy Ghost'.

Here Luther overlooks the fact that a man must 'feel' or detect the 'householder' *a priori* or not at all. But in other passages he himself allows the
general human reason to possess many true cognitions of what 'God is in
Himself or in His inmost essence'. Compare the following:

'Atque ipsamet ratio naturalis cogitur eam concedere *proprio suo iudicio
convicta*, etiamsi nulla esset scriptura. Omnes enim homines inveniunt
hanc sententiam in cordibus suis scriptam et *agnoscunt* eam ac probatam,
licet inviti, cum *audiant* eam tractari: primo, Deum esse omnipotentem,
. . . deinde, ipsum omnia nosse et praescire, neque errare neque falli
posse. . . . Istis duobus corde et sensu concessis. . . .*

---

* 'And the natural reason itself is forced even were there no holy scripture,
to grant it (*sc.* this assertion), *convinced by its own judgement.* For all men, *as*

The interesting words of this statement are: *proprio suo iudicio convicta,* for they make the distinction between *cognitions* and mere 'innate ideas' or supernaturally instilled notions, both of which latter may produce 'thoughts', but not convictions *'ex proprio iudicio'*. Note also the words: 'cum *audiant* eam tractari', which exactly correspond to the experience of Plato's Adeimantos, already quoted.*

It is the same experience which missionaries have so often undergone. Once enunciated and understood, the ideas of the unity and goodness of the divine nature often take a surprisingly short time to become firmly fixed in the hearer's mind, if he show any susceptibility for religious feeling. Frequently, thereupon, the hearer adapts the religious tradition that has hitherto been his to the new meaning he has learned. Or, where resistance is offered to the new teaching, it is yet often noticeably in the face of pressure the other way from the man's own conscience. Such experiences have been made known to me by missionaries among the Tibetans and among African negroes, and it would be interesting to make a collection of them, both in regard to the general question of the *a priori* factors in religion, and especially as throwing light upon the *a priori* knowledge of the essential interdependence of the rational and the non-rational elements in the idea of God. For this the history of religion is itself an almost unanimous witness. Incomplete and defective as the process of moralizing the 'numina' may often have been throughout the wide regions of primitive religious life, everywhere there are traces of it to be found. And wherever religion, escaping from its first crudity of manifestation, has risen to a higher type, this process of synthesis has in all cases set in and continued more and more positively. And this is all the more remarkable when one considers at what widely different dates the imaginative creation of the figures of gods had its rise in different cases, and under what diverse conditions of race, natural endowment, and social and political structure its evolution proceeded. All this points to the existence of *a priori* factors universally and necessarily latent

---

soon as they hear it treated of, find this belief written in their hearts, and acknowledge it as proved, even unwillingly: first, that God is omnipotent, . . . then, that He has knowledge and foreknowledge of all things and can neither err nor be deceived . . . Since these two things are admitted by heart and feeling . . .' Luther, Weimar ed., vol. 18, p. 719.

* The most interesting features in Luther in this connexion, however, are the passages upon 'Faith', in which Faith is described as a unique cognitive faculty for the apprehension of divine truth, and as such is contrasted with the 'natural' capacities of the Understanding, as elsewhere the 'Spirit' is contrasted. 'Faith' is here like the 'Synteresis' in the theory of knowledge of the mystics, the 'inward teacher' *(magister internus)* of Augustine, and the 'inward light' of the Quakers, which are all of them of course 'above reason', but yet an *a priori* element in ourselves. [. . .]

in the human spirit: those, in fact, which we can find directly in our own religious consciousness, when we, too, like Adeimantos, naïvely and spontaneously concur with Socrates' saying, as with an axiom whose truth we have seen for ourselves: 'God is single, and true in deed and word.'

As the rational elements, following *a priori* principles, come together in the historical evolution of religions with the non-rational, they serve to 'schematize' these. This is true, not only in general of the relation of the rational aspect of 'the holy', taken as a whole, to its non-rational, taken as a whole, but also in detail of the several constituent elements of the two aspects. The *tremendum*, the daunting and repelling moment of the numinous, is schematized by means of the rational ideas of justice, moral will, and the exclusion of what is opposed to morality; and schematized thus, it becomes the holy 'wrath of God', which Scripture and Christian preaching alike proclaim. The *fascinans*, the attracting and alluring moment of the numinous, is schematized by means of the ideas of goodness, mercy, love, and, so schematized, becomes all that we mean by Grace, that term so rich in import, which unites with the holy wrath in a single 'harmony of contrasts' and like it is, from the numinous strain in it, tinged with mysticism. The 'moment' *mysteriosum* is schematized by the *absoluteness* of all rational attributes applied to the Deity. Probably the correspondence here implied – between 'the mysterious' and the *absoluteness* of all rational attributes – will not appear at first sight so immediately evident as in the two foregoing cases, wrath and grace. None the less it is a very exact correspondence. God's rational attributes can be distinguished from like attributes applied to the created spirit by being not relative, as those are, but absolute. Human love is relative, admitting of degrees, and it is the same with human knowledge and human goodness. God's love and knowledge and goodness, on the other hand, and all else that can be asserted of Him in conceptual terms, are formally absolute. The *content* of the attributes is the same; it is an *element of form* which marks them apart as attributes of God. But such an element of form is also the 'mysterious' as such: it is [...] the formal aspect of the 'wholly other'. But to this plain correspondence of the two things, 'the mysterious' and the absoluteness of rational attributes, a further one must be added. Our understanding can only compass the relative. That which is in contrast absolute, though it may in a sense be *thought*, cannot be *thought home, thought out;* it is within the reach of our conceiving, but it is beyond the grasp of our comprehension. Now, though this does not make what is 'absolute' itself genuinely 'mysterious', as this term was expounded [. . .], it does make it a genuine *schema* of 'the mysterious'. The absolute exceeds our power to comprehend; the mysterious wholly eludes it. The absolute is that which surpasses the limits of our understanding, not through its actual qualitative character, for that is familiar to us, but through its formal character. The mysterious, on the other hand, is that which lies altogether outside what can be thought, and is, alike in form, quality, and essence, the utterly and 'wholly other'. We see, then, that in the case of the moment of 'mystery', as well as those of 'awefulness' and 'fascination', there is an exact correspondence between the non-rational element and its rational *schema*, and one that admits of development.

By the continual living activity of its non-rational elements a religion is guarded from passing into 'rationalism'. By being steeped in and saturated with rational elements it is guarded from sinking into fanaticism or mere mysticality, or at least from persisting in these, and is qualified to become a religion for all civilized humanity. The degree in which both rational and non-rational elements are jointly present, united in healthy and lovely harmony, affords a criterion to measure the relative rank of religions – and one, too, that is specifically religious. Applying this criterion we find that Christianity, in this as in other respects, stands out in complete superiority over all its sister religions. The lucid edifice of its clear and pure conceptions, feelings, and experiences is built up on a foundation that goes far deeper than the rational. Yet the non-rational is only the basis, the setting, the woof in the fabric, ever preserving for Christianity its mystical depth, giving religion thereby the deep undertones and heavy shadows of mysticism, without letting it develop into a mere rank growth of mysticality. And thus Christianity, in the healthily proportioned union of its elements, assumes an absolutely classical form and dignity, which is only the more vividly attested in consciousness as we proceed honestly and without prejudice to set it in its place in the comparative study of religions. Then we shall recognize that in Christianity an element of man's spiritual life, which yet has its analogies in other fields, has for the first time come to maturity in a supreme and unparalleled way.

'The manifestations of the "holy" and the faculty of "divination" '

It is one thing merely to believe in a reality beyond the senses and another to have experience of it also; it is one thing to have ideas of 'the holy' and another to become consciously aware of it as an operative reality, intervening actively in the phenomenal world. Now it is a fundamental conviction of all religions, of religion as such, we may say, that this latter is possible as well as the former. Religion is convinced not only that the holy and sacred reality is attested by the inward voice of conscience and the religious consciousness, the 'still, small voice' of the Spirit in the heart, by feeling, presentiment, and longing, but also that it may be directly encountered in particular occurrences and events, self-revealed in persons and displayed in actions, in a word, that beside the inner revelation from the Spirit there is an outward revelation of the divine nature. Religious language gives the name of 'sign' to such demonstrative actions and manifestations, in which holiness stands palpably self-revealed. From the time of the most primitive religions everything has counted as a sign that was able to arouse in man the sense of the holy, to excite the feeling of apprehended sanctity, and stimulate it into open activity. Of this kind were those factors and circumstances of which we have already spoken – the thing terrible, sublime, overpowering, or astounding, and in an especial degree the uncomprehended, mysterious thing, which become the 'portent' and 'miracle'. But, as we saw, all these were not 'signs' in the true sense, but opportunities, circumstances, prompting the religious feeling to awake of itself; and the factor promoting this result was found to lie in an element common to them all, but merely analogous with 'the holy'. The interpretation of them as actual appearances of the holy itself in its own nature meant, we saw, a confounding of the category of holiness with something only outwardly resembling it: it was not a genuine *'anamnesis'*, a genuine recognition of the holy in its own authentic nature, made manifest in appearance. And therefore we find that such false recognitions of the holy are later rejected and wholly or partly extruded as inadequate or simply unworthy, so soon as a higher level of development and a purer religious judgement have been reached. There is a precisely parallel process in another department of judgement, that of aesthetic taste. While the taste is still crude, a feeling or fore-feeling of the beautiful begins to stir, which must come from an obscure *a priori* conception of beauty already present, else it could not occur at all. The man of crude taste, not being capable of a clear 'recognition' of authentic beauty, falls into confusion and *misapplies* this obscure, dim conception of the beautiful, judging things to be beautiful which are in fact not beautiful at all. Here, as in the case of the judgement of holiness, the principle underlying the erroneous judgement of beauty is one of faint analogy. Certain elements in the thing wrongly judged to be beautiful have a closer or remoter analogy to real beauty. And later here, too, when his taste has been educated, the man rejects with strong aversion the quasi–beautiful but not really beautiful thing and becomes qualified to see and to judge rightly, i.e. to recognize as beautif   the outward object in which the 'beauty' of which he has an inward notion a, d standard really 'appears'.

Let us call the faculty, of whatever sort it may be, of *genuinely* cognizing and recognizing the holy in its appearances the faculty of *divination*. Does such a faculty exist, and, if so, what is its nature?

To the 'supernaturalistic' theory the matter is simple enough. Divination consists in the fact that a man encounters an occurrence that is not 'natural', in the sense of being inexplicable by the laws of nature. Since it has actually occurred, it must have had a cause; and, since it has no 'natural' cause, it must (so it is said) have a supernatural one. This theory of divination is a genuine, solidly rationalist theory, put together with rigid concepts in a strict demonstrative form and intended as such. And it claims that the capacity or faculty of divination is the *understanding*, the faculty of reflection in concept and demonstration. The transcendent is here proved as strictly as anything can be proved, logically from given premisses.

It would be almost superfluous to adduce in detail in opposition to this view the argument that we have no possibility of establishing that an event did not arise from natural causes or was in conflict with the laws of nature. The religious consciousness itself rises against this desiccation and materialization of what in all religion is surely the most tender and living moment, the actual discovery of and encounter with very deity. Here, if anywhere, coercion by proof and demonstration and the mistaken application of logical and juridical processes should be excluded; here, if anywhere, should be liberty, the unconstrained recognition and inward acknowledgement that comes from deep within the soul, stirred spontaneously, apart from all conceptual theory. If not 'natural science' or 'metaphysics', at least the matured religious consciousness itself spurns such ponderously solid intellectualistic explanations. They are born of rationalism and engender it again; and, as for genuine 'divination', they not only impede it, but despise it as extravagant emotionalism, mysticality, and false romanticism. Genuine divination, in short, has nothing whatever to do with natural law and the relation or lack of relation to it of something experienced. It is not concerned at all with the way in which a phenomenon – be it event, person, or thing – came into existence, but with what it *means*, that is, with its significance as a 'sign' of the holy.

The faculty or capacity of divination appears in the language of dogma hidden beneath the fine name '*testimonium Spiritus Sancti internum*', the inner witness of the Holy Spirit – limited, in the case of dogma, to the recognition of *Scripture* as 'Holy'. And this name is the only right one, and right in a more than figurative sense, when the capacity of divination is itself grasped and appraised by divination. This is not our task here. We therefore employ a psychological rather than a religious expression as being more appropriate to the nature of our discussion. [. . .]

RELIGIOUS HISTORY

'The wholly other and the absolute'

We have suggested some lines of thought regarding the divine that seem strange: the notion of the unqualified *simplicitas dei* (simplicity of God); the idea that he is above all categories, the idea that *in deo non cadit acci-*

dens – that accident does not pertain to God; the idea that he is pure being unqualified. These ideas suggest themselves in theology when one endeavours to formulate rationally the idea of absoluteness and of an absolute being, distinct from all relative and conditioned being. Further we have indicated in *The Idea of the Holy* [. . .], that all such inquiries into the nature of the absolute are a mere 'schema' of the purely numinous 'wholly other', the *Anyad eva*, which, as such, is independent of any considerations regarding absoluteness and which is actively operative long before the ideas of absoluteness have emerged. This numinous background to the idea of the absolute is usually obscured by the theological speculative inquiry; but it comes into play very actively as soon as the inquirer endeavours to pass from the chill of his abstract concepts to the expression of his inmost emotions. Then the 'wholly other' bursts forth in typical terms of its own in praise or prayer; and that which was antecedent to all theoretical speculation emerges again in the plenitude of original power. With regard to the feeling of Ancient India[4] we have seen that it was not speculative inquiry about the absoluteness of Brahman that led to the recognition of his nature as the *āścaryam*, the inexpressible marvel, the 'wholly other', but that these preceded all such speculation. The later speculative attempts to represent it as pure being, as an undivided and qualified unity, and at the same time to prove these facts by a process of rational deduction, as was done in the school of Šankara, did much to eliminate this original subtle element. An unspeakable marvel was transformed into a dry, rationalized monstrosity. If we would rediscover the marvel, we must turn to those sincere passages of the ancient Upanishads themselves, which had not been sapped of their virtue by arid logicians. [. . .]

'Parallels and convergences'

I have given an account of the Bhakti religion of India in my book, *Vischnu-Nārāyana*, and also in the book which has recently been published in an English translation, *India's Religion of Grace and Christianity*. No one can read the records of this religion, or meet with its exponents, without carrying away an impression almost disconcerting in its intensity, the impression I mean that the development of this religion presents a positively astonishing parallel development to religious development as we know it in the West, and this impression is the common experience of all who have concerned themselves with these matters. It is not surprising, therefore, that it should induce these repeated attempts to establish borrowings of the West from the East or vice versa. But such an attitude is undoubtedly mistaken; the explanation is rather that we have to deal with parallel and converging lines of development. And the matter loses somewhat in mystery and significance as we perceive, on investigating general religious development more closely, that we are concerned here not with one individual case, for then it would have to be a very curious coincidence indeed, but with a classical example of a general law which has governed the religious development of man as a whole, the 'law of parallel lines of development'.

Let us endeavour in a brief sketch to present a picture of this general law.

1. We find that in the beginnings of civilization religion comes on to the scene amongst men everywhere in very much the same kind of way, developing from a groundwork of strangely confused spiritual states and ideas such as recurs with astonishing similarity and regularity amongst the peoples of the black and of the white, of the yellow and of the red races, standing at the beginning of all cultural development and often persisting, so that its influence is clearly discernible in the higher religions and cultures, while it is still a living force in the cultures of primitive peoples. I mean that dark groundwork which is made up of the emotions of demonic fear, of Shamanian obsession, of the crude primitive mysticism of the demonic orgy and the ecstatic dance, of magic rites, dimly developing into those obscure, transitional notions of belief in spirits, the cult of the dead, the services of the soul and totemism, witchcraft and magic, manticism and divination, ideas of 'the clean' and 'the unclean', primitive asceticism, sacrificial mysticism, fetichism, whence we pass to the demonic personification of nature and natural objects and forces, out of which we find slowly struggling to the surface the idea of exalted and sublime divinities with their attendant priesthoods, their temples and feasts, their sacred communities and customs. With these we have associated that wealth of a more extensive fancy manifesting itself in demonic tales, in story and myth, in animal fable, in the growth of saga and legends, in the ingenuities of genealogies and cosmologies grounded in primitive speculation. They constitute a vast range of individual moments, almost impossible to survey as a whole, strange and difficult of interpretation. Of very varied content and often conflicting, they are yet no mere heap of things lying in casual juxtaposition, but a tough network, so that one thing is always interwoven with another, inseparably linked to a third, and so it were dragged along by a fourth. It is indeed a strange growth, which would appear to have flourished under every clime and in every soil with a disconcerting similarity, pointing to a uniform and constant function of human psychology as the underlying determining factor.

2. This groundwork can indeed scarcely be called 'religion'; it is rather pre-religion, out of which religion emerges and frees itself later on. This transition to the higher proceeds in very varied fields of culture, the manifestations being unrelated to one another, independent, and of diverse

individuality. But in their very diversity they astonish by the parallel movements which come to light and the inner harmony revealed, which is such as to produce an almost mystical impression, as we observe how the various leading groups of civilized humanity achieved this significant advance comparatively simultaneously and by similar stages. Let us first look into the simultaneity, the parallelism in time.

a) In Greek thought, the determining factor in Western culture, this advance was made in those crucial centuries from 800 to 500 B. C. The $\lambda\acute{o}\gamma o\varsigma$ was delivered from the $\mu\tilde{v}\vartheta o\varsigma$ and $\vartheta\epsilon o\lambda o\gamma\acute{\iota}\alpha$ from $\mu\nu\vartheta o\lambda o\gamma\acute{\iota}\alpha$. 'Theologia' is here the 'knowledge about the gods' *(οἱ θεοί)* and it becomes by slow, gradual stages a knowledge about the God *(ὁ θεος)* and thereby the culminating point of metaphysics. It is speculation on the nature and significance of the divine powers, their relation to one another and to the world, which gradually withdraws the god from the realm of mere demonic fear and also from the sphere of epic divinities and heroes. At the same time this theology develops into a cosmology which expresses itself in terms in which physics and religious metaphysics are strangely blended. The 'gods' are converted into world and soul-forces and vice versa.* It is a theology which more and more tends to eliminate the mythical, to suppress or spiritualize the service of gods, while with ever-growing precision it unifies the world of gods in the general idea of the $\vartheta\epsilon\tilde{\iota}o\nu$, which then assumes the character of the absolute and the godhead. It is thus related to that which, in a more general way, found expression in the more exalted forms of *popular* Hellenic religion. To the great tragedies indeed, 'the gods' are the *unified* power which governs the world and the moral order, the plural form with which they are invested ceasing to be a matter of any significance.** Moreover, we find the phrase 'the God' making its way into the ordinary use of Greek speech – that is god in general, no matter which particular god. That which is individual and separate in the $\vartheta\epsilon\tilde{\iota}o\nu$ loses its significance, and to that extent the expression 'the god', which indeed is meaningless except to a polytheistic way of thinking, becomes adapted to the expression of the growing idea of absolute godhead.***

---

* The 'physics' of Pythagoras, Heraclitus, Xenophanes, and Parmenides, and of Empedocles and Anaxagoras, are all 'theologies' too.

** It is only one step farther to the parallel development in the Semitic language, where the fact that *elohîm* (gods) was a plural form finally ceased to be recognized even grammatically, the verb remaining in the singular. Translated literally, the first verse of the Bible would run: 'In the beginning *gods has* created heaven and earth'.

*** The last passage of Plato's *Republic*, Book II, furnishes the most illuminating example of the parallel use of the phrase 'the gods' and 'the god', both in the sense of the idea of godhead.

b) Now the development which we have just described is paralleled at almost exactly the same period in the very far East of civilized humanity. It was about the year 530 B.C. that Pythagoras founded his 'order', and it was about the year 470 B.C. that Confucius died in China. Lao Tsze was his older contemporary. They were preceded by that three hundred years' period of early Chinese history which, just as the similar period in Hellas, paved the way for the spiritual situation, unique in its wealth of content, of the two great Chinese sages. In the extreme Orient, as in Hellas, we find the same processes at work; the mythological groundwork becomes submerged, while religion becomes definitely moralized and spiritualized, pressing on towards the Absolute. And there are in this process the two main strands that we also find in the West. Here the process has worked itself out on the one hand along a line which has led to a theism of a rationalistic trend (through Anaxagoras to the *Timaeus* and Aristotle) and on the other hand along a more mystic line as exemplified in the All-One doctrine of the Eleatics, the λόγος of Heraclitus, the later pantheism of the Stoa and also Plato's Idea as the Absolute. Now in the East Confucius shows us the conclusion of a process of development purely and entirely along the first of these two lines, while Lao Tsze in his Tao and Te achieves the correlation of the λόγος of Heraclitus and of the Platonic Idea with a glow of intimate mysticism which is also not wholly absent from the works of Heraclitus and of Plato.

c) Now in Israel, too, these centuries represent the transition period in religion from the primitive phase to the classic heights of the prophets; the period ranges from Elijah to the second Isaiah and Ezekiel. The theism latent in the more primitive Jahveh faith of ancient Israel now comes triumphantly to the surface. The nature-myth of ancient Jahveh is almost entirely discarded and divine faith is achieved of rare and sublime vitality. At the same time, at the conclusion of this period, Jeremiah and Ezekiel prepare the way for the transition from a tribal and national religion to the religion of the individual.

d) Finally, contemporary research attributes to the same centuries, i.e. from *circa* 800 B.C. to the time of Cyrus, the Zoroastrian 'reform' of the Persian religion with its preliminary and subsequent phases, another instance of the break-through of the actual profundities of religion, emerging through the mists of demonism and polytheism, a religion indeed of rare purity and force, of exalted sense of divinity and personal moral communion with the highest.

e) But this parallelism in time comes out most clearly when we consider it from the standpoint of the *Indian* development. We will pass over the noble ancient Varuna religion which constitutes a rare island in the welter of the old Vedic sacrificial religion and in simplicity and beauty may well

be compared with the old Israelite service of Jahveh. The period in which
the foundations were laid of that which may be termed Brahminic doctrine,
speculation, and religion, is that of the compilation of the older literature
of the Upanishads, and runs from about 900 to 800 B. C. to the time of
Buddha. This literature, too, consists at first of crude 'theologia' as in Hellas;
it originates in primitive sacrificial mysticism, in speculation on the gods
and is a part, the last part, of such speculation. The All-One notion which
emerges definitely towards the end of this period, in its maturity, has its
western parallels in the Eleatic philosophy. That all plurality is but a delusion of the senses, a kind of ignorance, that true knowledge is the opposite
of the 'opinion' of the uninitiated, and is directed to the 'one that has no
second', outside time and place, having neither movement nor change nor
qualities, is a doctrine corresponding to the teachings of Xenophanes, of
Parmenides, and of Zeno. It is true that with the Indians all these ideas rest
purely upon religious intuition and are no doubt essentially nothing but
elaborations upon peculiar experiences of mystic self-surrender. But with
Parmenides too, the basic motif is religious and mystical, and with Xenophanes religious sentiment and theology still predominate over philosophy;
in him we can still perceive clearly that that which afterwards became philosophy was first mystical and religious in conception.

3. *a)* In the Brahminic world the practical *vita religiosa* develops con-
temporaneously with their speculation – an advance towards higher religion
of far greater import than the development of the higher world of ideas.
Religious emotion and the experience of salvation, liberation, the sense of
ultimate release, the continuance in a state of intensive religious experience,
and then contempt of the world and of the natural forms of existence as
evidenced by an ascetic way of life, come into being.

b) In the West we do not find these things nearly so strongly developed,
but clear parallels thereto. What we are wont to call schools of philosophy
in the ancient world were indeed half or wholly religious associations of
the nature of orders or conventicles. This was explicitly so in the case of the
Pythagoreans, while the Stoa also shows distinct traits of this kind. The
'religious life', the $\theta\varepsilon\omega\varrho\eta\tau\iota\varkappa\grave{o}\varsigma\ \beta\acute{\iota}o\varsigma$, the cultivation of religion for the sake
of religion itself, the religious ideas of salvation and liberation from the
things of the world, the increasing moralization of religious emotion, find
expression in the marked spread of Orphism, and more and more, too, in
what were originally the primitive, peasant mysteries of Demeter and
Dionysus; and as in India, so in the West, we find parallel ideas of life as sin
and suffering, of the transmigration of souls, of Hades and of Elysium.

c) But in the Far East too, in China, a similar 'religious life' develops at
about the same time. No doubt Lao Tsze was following in the footsteps of

others, when, in order to live for the 'Tao' he renounced the world and his possessions and went to dwell alone. The ideal of the holy man who turns away from the world is with him already in its maturity, and before him it had been developing for a long time. There grew up about him that 'taoism' whose adherents dwell alone, devoted to contemplation, and who subsequently develop a particular taoistic monasticism.

4. *a)* We find both processes coming to fruition in India from roots that apparently and at a first glance are to be found nowhere else. Brahman was, at first, nothing else than the sacred word itself in the magic hymn and in the sacred myth; it was the magic word of power, the priests set in motion, which they attributed to the gods themselves and exalted above the gods, which they associated with the forces and the processes of nature, until it became identified – still in a mystic sense – with the ultimate principle of the world and nature itself.

b) Yet, however typically and peculiarly Indian these early developments may seem, we find allied processes here again in the farther East and the West. The 'Tao' of Lao Tsze also most probably originated in ideas of a magic-mystical order, and indeed his teaching is permeated with magical ideas, while it was his very school which immediately after him became the exponent of magical mysticism. Probably here also the magic-sacred power (i.e. of the heaven, of the earth, of the all in and behind all) which it was sought to appropriate, proved to be the primitive point of departure for the marvellously profound speculations regarding the Tao of Lao-Tsze which now, hovering between idea and divinity, came to be the principle of all being and becoming, and especially in the same way as Brahman for the Brahmins, became the most profoundly realized object of religious relationship, sought and achieved as salvation *(Heil)*.

c) In the West the closest parallel to the Tao of Lao Tsze is furnished by the λόγος of Heraclitus. The current rendering of this term by the word 'reason' is certainly too rationalistic. Just like Tao, it is actually untranslatable, presumably because the word originated in another setting and then in the course of development a more mature and complex sense came to be associated with its original significance.* The λόγος of Heraclitus also is informed with explicit mystic sentiment.** And we may presume before Heraclitus a history of development underlying the term Logos similar to that underlying the Tao of Lao-Tsze and the Brahman of the Brahmins: a course of development from magical primitive mysticism to the mystic

---

* Hence the vibrant, unseizable quality in both words Tao and λόγος.
** Israel too affords a parallel of the word of *power*. The 'word' which is given to the prophets is a force with mystic power of action, which they release.

principle of the universe. In Heraclitus it is true that the connexion between priestly magic and speculation is no longer clearly discernible, perhaps because we have only a scant selection of fragments by him. But in Empedocles the connexion is revealed in the full light of history; indeed at the conclusion of his physics he gives his disciples the express promise of further teaching which will carry the acquisition of 'powers' that are purely magical and that bear a strange resemblance to those which the Taoist strives to attain: the banishment of old age and sickness, dominion over the forces of nature, and even the faculty of 'leading from Hades the power of the deceased person'. The καθαρμοί of Empedocles, however, are themselves nothing but a speculative hymn of 'expiation' with magical power. And he himself united in his own person the qualities of prophet, philosopher, expiatory priest, and magician*.

5. *a)* Running alongside that of Brahman we find another line of thought in India: that connected with Atman or the soul. Originally, perhaps, Atman is the breath which was regarded as the principle of life; at the same time, considered spiritually, it is the 'soul'. And, as the soul is the life-principle of the individual, so we come to the generalized Atman, which is conceived as being the vitalizing, world-controlling, creative principle of the All. The individual soul proceeds from and returns to it; the individual soul is a part of it, or is identified with it. This Atman line of thought then converges upon and merges with the Brahman line of thought which proceeded originally from the wholly different root of the magical power-word.

b) Now πνεῦμα (breath, spirit) is in the West that which corresponds to the Eastern Atman; the πνεῦμα of the individual and the generalized *pneuma* which becomes the divine, partly denuding and partly absorbing previous conceptions of divinity. That is what we find in Heraclitus; and it is a remarkable fact that it is just with him also that speculative inquiry about the 'spirit' *(πνεῦμα)* and speculative inquiry about the 'word' *(λόγος)* become fused to an inner unity in the same way as speculative inquiry regarding Atman and Brahman in the East. With Heraclitus the Logos is πνεῦμα and the πνεῦμα is Logos. And like the Atman-Brahman of India, this logos-pneuma becomes for him a principle of the universe which, in just the same manner as in India, creates the world and rules and destroys it in an eternal threefold rhythm.

* Empedocles offers the most remarkable parallel to the Vrātya of ancient India, down to the individual points of his manner of going about, his general behaviour, and his appearance. See the excellent chapter on the Vrātya in *The Beginnings of Yoga Practice*, by W. Hauer (Kohlhammer, 1922), who does not notice the Empedocles parallel.

6. *a)* The line of thought suggested by speculation regarding the Atman introduced in India a further religious conception which must be distinguished from what we have described above. The atman in man is at first contrasted dualistically with man's body; later a dualism in the soul itself is recognized, and that part of the soul which we would call 'spirit' becomes contrasted with the lower and animal impulses of the soul, the promptings of desire, the interplay of 'worldly' wishes, interests, passions, and 'qualities', while the 'higher man' in man is conceived of as being in a state of servitude and bondage to the body and the life of the senses as requiring to be liberated and set free, which signifies two things: release from the prison of material and sensual existence, and from the endless pain of 're-births'.

b) We find the liberation and salvation motif also in Lao-Tsze, but in the West we have a more precise parallel down to the very individual ideas in the Orphic mysticism and in a rarefied form in Plato's *Phaedo*. With Orphism we find associated the idea that such liberation is to be achieved only through mystic powers from on high; but in the *Phaedo* this idea falls into the background. With Plato it is rather right 'knowledge', the 'philosophic life', the discipline of thought and of θεωρία and the final liberator death for whom these pave the way, and through whom the spirit is set in freedom.

c) Even this was paralleled in Indian thought, when the Sānkhya doctrine became detached from the Upanishad atmosphere. It propounded liberative 'knowledge', the spirit withdrawing from the realm of nature into serenity and inaction.

d) The later Greek schools, those especially which inculcated 'ataraxy' and 'apathy', followed out corresponding lines of thought and feeling in the West; and the practical method of the 'Yoga' which the Sānkhya doctrine accepted, also has its analogies in those schools. The Yoga is a technique of spiritual concentration and abstraction from the world of sense, and as such it is paralleled by the intensive practices and highly advanced mental technique which was evolved in the later Stoa.

7. Now we do not come to the most interesting parallels until religion in the West also, first Christianity and later Islam, arise as powerful and coherent world forces. In this matter the special history of the Orient was such as to give it a considerable start in time; but we have to note that it was not until the period of reaction against Buddhism that higher Brahmanism actually became a great power; and this brings the beginnings of the vital development of its characteristic features near to the beginning of our era; and it was not until then that Buddhism itself underwent that great internal change to Mahāyāna whereby it became, for the first time, a world religion comparable in importance to the great religions of the West.

Indeed the Vedānta mysticism itself now, for the first time, becomes definitely systematized.

8. To take the Vedānta first: how closely it is related to the mysticism of the West in Christendom and Islam has been told so often that this may be assumed as known.[5] The spiritual conditions and experiences underlying it, the conceptions to which these give rise, the methods and successive stages of the 'way of salvation' and their relationship to general piety, to prayer and devotion, to action and ethos – all these are paralleled in the mysticism of the West. And just as Western mysticism has on the one hand an element inimical to the Church and menacing to the community and to organized religious use, while on the other hand it may be infused with intense passion for the Church and permeate Church doctrine, preaching, hymns, and worship with a new intensive ardour, so it was with the mysticism of the East. Šankara himself is the model of the mystic attuned to his church. It is true that for him Brahman is one and all; the world, together with Isvara (the personal God), priesthood and science are to him only Maya, only illusion, which vanishes for him who is liberated by 'knowledge'. But this world of Maya is after all for him the world in which we live; and regarded from the ordinary point of view it is relatively real. As such the mystic Šankara applies to it an elaborate and serious theology. For, indeed, this world is the domain of Isvara, that is, God as a person, whose existence is deduced by physico-theological proof in precisely the same way as his colleagues of the Western world prove the existence of God. Here priesthood and religious practice, moral law, and ritualistic order prevail; here we have the world of heaven and hell, and the law of the migration of souls with the 'fruit of works', and God's guidance and control over all that happens. If this is already the case with Šankara, it is even more so in the large theistical schools and communities of personal Bhakti religion. The astonishing parallels between this trend of Eastern religion and the religion of the West have been indicated by me in a special book.

9. The latter parallels become most marked as we come to the 'Saviour-mysticism' to which the more comprehensive God-mysticism narrows down in the East as well as in the West. It is a variation on the religious feelings associated with the mystical love of God with its sweet, melting emotional sentiments and delights, which in the East as well as in the West readily assume an erotic tinge, as they become transferred from the more abstract world of God-mysticism to the 'Saviour', the god-man. In the Vishnu religion of India such cult of the Saviour with its tender-sweet emotion attaches especially to Krishna and Rāma. Šri-Krishna, the incarnation of divinity, becomes the object of ecstatic, blissful-intimate contemplation, which, while

it would resist and purify the promptings of eroticism, often succumbs to them. In the East, Krishna's relationship to Radha and the Gopis corresponds to the part played by Solomon and the Shulamite in our western Saviour-mysticism. Indeed the Krishna-cult also knows the touching chatter with the 'little babe', the cult of the bambino. This kind of emotional pietism, tinged with mysticism, manifests itself in a specially pure and moving form in Tulsida's vernacular rendering of the *Rāmāyana*. The emotional worship of the Saviour is here centred upon the lovable personality of Rama, and Tulsidas's feelings find expression in prayers whose purity and tenderness are comparable to many of our hymns to the Saviour Jesus. The Krishna songs, both those with a marked erotic tinge as well as several of wonderful intimacy, full of praise and gratitude for the love which seeks the lost, saves him, and makes him happy, are universally sung. Caitanya, the Bengal reformer, who was a contemporary of Luther, and his successors are representatives of a whole period of poetry which is expressive of this emotional Saviour-pietism, and which coincided remarkably with the wave of Protestant and Catholic emotional pietism in the West. Here, too, the theological basis of the Saviour-cult is the teaching that the godhead becomes man, and we find analogies too to the varied evolution of this doctrine in Christendom: the problems and controversies centring in such questions as the massive or 'modalistic' transformation, the incarnation of the whole godhead, or of a 'person' or a part of it only, the personal union between God and man without loss of humanity, or mere indwelling, or complete symbolism.

It is only natural, in view of all these parallels, that the forms of theological apparatus and machinery should also be similar in East and West. We find in both cases the same kind of canonical literature, reliance upon the 'scriptures', 'tradition', concerted efforts to reconcile scripture with scripture and scripture with tradition, and to explain the relationship between revelation and reason; we find the same act of interpretation and exegesis, the scholastic-philosophic formulation of doctrine and apologetics, the disputes of the schoolmen, the same problem as to the attitude to be adopted by theological speculation in the general scheme of the sciences, and in recent times the clash with modern physics and literary criticism; the same apologetics against both, the same theologies of compromise, the same modernists and fundamentalists. – That this is also true of Islam and of Judaism is well known, and investigation would bring the same tendencies to light in Buddhism.

These parallels lend overwhelming conviction to one great fact, namely the fundamental kinship of the nature and experience of mankind in general, East and West, North and South; by reason of their basic similarity, it works itself out in these parallels, manifesting similar phenomena, and in diverse territories producing similar results. But while that is true of mental evolution in general, we have, in such extreme similarities as are revealed in the Bhakta and the Christian doctrines of salvation, to reckon with another element which we sometimes meet in biological evolutionary processes, and which is known here as the 'convergence of types'. We find this force at work in the evolutionary history of living forms. Widely different families and classes of plants or animals may go through processes of transformation in the course of which, besides those general similarities which result from the basic unity of the vital principle itself, they also reveal a growing tendency to approach one another in form and function, until they terminate in final forms startling in their congruity. A similar process we find also in the field of history. Misled by such phenomena there has often been a too ready assumption of actual descent of the one class from the other. Nowadays we are more careful; we are content to see convergence merely where previously the similar phenomena have been regarded as deducible one from the other; the West has been interpreted as being dependent on the East, or the East upon the West.

We find another error associated with this way of thinking, an error into which the unwary almost always falls under the influence of such analogies; I refer to the tendency to overlook under the influence of the general impression of similarity profound individual differences. It may be true that the life force in its varied manifestations is *one* and that its unity may be recognized in the consistent scheme of its manifestations. But in the plenitude of individual manifestations it breaks into a diversity of type and character that is very real; and the same holds good in the realm of spiritual life. Historically, 'religion' is manifested as religions and these no less have their characteristic differences; as with all other functions of the human spirit their generic uniformity is inclusive, not exclusive of the specific variations in their development. And as those who study the history of art are specially interested to ascertain the characteristic and individual contributions of the various individual civilizations to the general body of aesthetic achievement, so in the comparison of religions we are prompted to use an even finer discrimination in ascertaining the manner in which the common basic force, despite all apparent parallelism, takes on perfectly distinct forms in its individual manifestations.

There remains the still more important task of comparing their content and value, to ascertain where the higher and fuller values may be found. So far from being eliminated, this task is invested with a special and more subtle significance in the case of those particular similarities which we have endeavoured to relate to the 'convergence of types'. For, as in the realm of *organic* evolution convergences of types never lead to an actual identity in the sense of real systematic unity, so they do not lead to any such unity in the realm of religious evolution either. Beyond all doubt the religions of the East and of the West approached one another almost to the point of contact in the teachings of Išvara, of Bhakti and Prapatti; but despite all their similarity these most similar manifestions are subtly but decisively distinguished in the spirit which informs them. The spirit of India is not, even in these instances, the spirit of Palestine. There are fundamental spiritual values which separate these two worlds of the spirit, in spite of astonishing similarities and convergences of type. I have endeavoured to formulate an answer to this question of their distinction and comparative worth in my books *India's Religion of Grace and Christianity: Compared and Contrasted*, and *Mysticism East and West. A Comparative Analysis of the Nature of Mysticism*.

NOTES

1. Goethe, *Faust*.

2. *Works*, ed. Denifle, p. 311.

3. The reader may compare what Kant says in his *Lectures on Psychology* (Leipzig ed., 1889, p. 11) of 'the treasure buried in the field of obscure ideas, constituting the deep abyss of human knowledge, which we cannot sound'. This 'deep abyss' is just the *fundus animae* that is aroused in Suso.

4. *Cf.* R. Otto, *Mysticism East and West. A Comparative Analysis of the Nature of Mysticism*. New York, Macmillan, 1932.

5. *Cf.* R. Otto, *Ibid.*

Friedrich Heiler

Friedrich Heiler was born in 1892 in Munich, Germany, where he received his primary and secondary school education. He was a student at the University of Munich, where he studied for one year in the Faculty of Theology, and then transferred to the Faculty of Philosophy where he studied oriental languages and philosophy and where he obtained his Ph.D. in 1917 on a dissertation on 'Prayer'. In 1918 he passed his *Habilitation* and became *Privatdozent* for the history and the philosophy of religion at the University of Munich. In 1920 Heiler became *Extraordinarius* at the University of Marburg, and received a honorary Th. D. degree from the University of Kiel. He occupied the new chair for Comparative History of Religions and Philosophy of Religion in the Faculty of Theology of the University of Marburg in 1922. In 1934 Heiler was transferred for political reasons to the University of Greifswald, but in 1935 he was able to continue teaching at the University of Marburg, although not in the Faculty of Theology but in that of Philosophy. In 1947, he occupied again the chair of Comparative History of Religions, and Philosophy of Religion in the Faculty of Theology at the same University. In 1953 he became di rector of the *Religionskundliche Sammlung* of the University of Marburg. He was visiting professor at the University of Chicago in 1955. In 1960 Heiler presided the International Congress for the History of Religions held in Marburg. In the same year he retired, but continued to teach first in Marburg, then from 1962 until 1967 at the University of Munich. Heiler was active throughout his life in ecumenical initiatives between the Christian denominations and between different religions. He died in Munich in 1967.

The only book by Heiler dealing with the study of religion, wich is available in English is: 1932 *Prayer: a Study in the History and Psychology of Religion.*

In his numerous studies about religious subjects Heiler distinguished himself from other scholars in the field by his continuous attempt to do justice to the religious truth of which the documents give evidence. Behind his scholarship there was an ecumenical consciousness, which made him see all religion as constituting, basically, a unity. On the level of methodology, Heiler wanted to develop a phenomenology of religion which would be theologically oriented, focussing on the tension between *deus absconditus* and *deus revelatus.*

The following texts have been taken from *Prayer* and from his last book, published in German, *The Manifestations and Essence of Religion.* Both texts treat methodological issues and, consequently, the way in which Heiler conceived *Religionswissenschaft* in his first and his last major publication.

‹PRAYER›

'Author's preface to the English edition (1932)'

The present work appeared during the World War. Some parts of it were written in a hospital, where the author served as attendant on the patients. It was published a few months before the end of the war.

For the inspiration of the work and its psychological method I have to thank my teacher, Dr. Aloys Fischer, who now occupies the Chair of Pedagogy and Philosophy in the University of Munich.

The religio-historical method and religious view-point I had learnt through the writings of the Lutheran Archbishop Söderblom of Upsala, who died last year. For the friendly reception which the work has met with in Protestant Christendom I have in no small measure to thank his favorable judgment. Besides the above-named, I have been under special obligations (in the course of my religious and theological development) to two Roman Catholic scholars, Dr. Karl Adam, Professor of Catholic Dogmatics in Tübingen University, and to the great Roman Catholic lay-theologian, Friedrich von Hügel. It was the latter, moreover, who first urged the publication of an English translation; however, this appeared impossible, until the present translator with great energy, undertook the difficult task. And here I would express to him my most cordial thanks for the time and for the painstaking care he has unselfishly devoted to this work.

The book was written before the great oecumenical movement for unity arose after the war. It could not — certainly in this form — have been written unless the author, born a Roman Catholic, had fought his way up to an oecumenical position through his studies and experience of life.

The path which the author has trod after completing this book — from Roman Catholicism to Evangelical Catholicism, from the Roman community to the Lutheran, and to kindly relations with the Anglican and the Eastern Orthodox Churches — was but the sequel to that oecumenical attitude to which the book owes its origin.

Prayer is the great bond of union of Christendom; and not only of Christendom, but of all mankind. Prayer is the most tangible proof of the fact that the whole of mankind is seeking after God; or — to put it more correctly — that it is sought by God. Mankind at prayer is a proof of the universal *revelation* of God. For it is precisely in prayer that we have revealed to us the *essential* element of all religion, which Friedrich von Hügel, as well as Nathan Söderblom, were never tired of pointing out, *viz.:* the 'prevenience and givenness' of the grace of God. Prayer is not man's work, or discovery or achievement; but *God's* work in man — 'for we know not what we should pray for as we ought: but the Spirit Himself maketh intercession for us with groanings which cannot be uttered.' (Rom. 8: 26).

'Prayer as the central phenomenon of religion'

Religious people, students of religion, theologians of all creeds and tendencies, agree in thinking that prayer is the central phenomenon of religion, the very hearthstone of all piety. Faith is, in Luther's judgment, 'prayer and nothing but prayer'. 'He who does not pray or call upon God in his hour of need, assuredly does not think of Him as God, nor does he give Him the honor that is His due.' The great evangelical mystic, Johann Arndt, constantly emphasizes the truth that: 'without prayer we cannot find God; prayer is the means by which we seek and find Him.' Schleiermacher, the restorer of evangelical theology in the nineteenth century, observes in one of his sermons: 'To be religious and to pray – that is really one and the same thing.' Novalis, the poet of romanticism, remarks: 'Praying is to religion what thinking is to philosophy. Praying is religion in the making. The religious sense prays, just as the thinking mechanism thinks.' The same thought is expressed by the gifted evangelical divine, Richard Rothe, when he says, '. . . the religious impulse is essentially the impulse to pray. It is by prayer, in fact, that the process of the individual religious life is governed, the process of the gradual fulfilment of God's indwelling in the individual and his religious life. Therefore, the non-praying man is rightly considered to be religiously dead.'

One of the most eminent evangelical theologians of our time, Adolf Deissmann, holds that 'religion, wherever it is alive in man, is prayer'. The profoundly religious philosopher, Gustav Theodor Fechner, says in his impressive way: 'Take prayer out of the world and it is as if you had torn asunder the bond that binds humanity to God, and had struck dumb the tongue of the child in the presence of his Father.' C. P. Tiele, one of the founders of the science of comparative religion, expressed himself similarly, 'Where prayer has wholly ceased, it is all over with religion itself.' And this agrees with the judgment of the distinguished philosophical student of religion, Auguste Sabatier, 'Where the prayer of the heart is wanting, there is no religion.' William James, the pioneer in the psychology of religion, subscribes to this opinion of Sabatier. A celebrated Catholic apologist (Hettinger) describes prayer as 'the first, highest, and most solemn phenomenon and manifestation of religion'; a popular writer of Catholic books of devotion (Alban Stolz) calls it 'the blood and the circulation of the blood in the religious life'; a Jesuit divine (M. Meschler) calls it 'the soul of the

public worship of God and the chief means of grace for the inner life'. The
acute Biblical critic, J. Wellhausen, sees in prayer 'the only adequate form
for a confession of faith'; another Old Testament investigator (E. Kautzsch)
believes it to be 'the absolutely necessary activity of the religious life, the
unconscious, indispensable breathing of the religious spirit'; a third (R.
Kittel) calls it 'the natural and necessary expression of every religion'.
A New Testament theologian, P. Christ, describes it as 'the culmination
of the religious process in man'. E. von der Goltz, a church historian who
has devoted careful study to prayer in early Christianity, speaks of prayer
as 'the breath of all piety'; another, Paul Althaus, who has investigated the
literature of prayer in the sixteenth century, calls it 'the soul and very
heart-beat of piety'. For Rothe 'prayer is the potent agency for obtaining
power to live a religious life, the specific remedy for religious weakness';
for Kähler it is 'a fundamental element in all genuine piety, the central
point of all personal Christianity'; for a modern theologian, Samuel Eck,
it is 'the essential and characteristic expression of the religious consciousness';
and for the French divine, F. Ménégoz, it is 'the primary phenomenon of
religion', 'the primary fact of the religious life'. A classical philologist, K. F.
Hermann, describes prayer as 'the simplest and most direct way by which
man puts himself into relation with the Deity'. In Sabatier's view the peculiarly religious phenomenon is distinguished by prayer from similar allied
phenomena, such as, for example, the aesthetic sense or the moral feelings.
And even the most radical of the critics of religion, Feuerbach, who set
down all religion as an illusion, declares that 'the innermost essence of
religion is revealed by the simplest act of religion – prayer'.

Accordingly, there can be no doubt at all that prayer is the heart and
centre of all religion. Not in dogmas and institutions, not in rites and ethical
ideals, but in prayer do we grasp the peculiar quality of the religious life.
In the words of a prayer we can penetrate into the deepest and the most
intimate movements of the religious soul. 'Examine the prayers of the saints
of all ages, and you have their faith, their life, their ruling motive, their
work', says Adolphe Monod, the famous Calvinistic preacher. The varied
world of religious conceptions and actions is always nothing less than the
reflection of the personal religious life. All the various thoughts of God,
creation, revelation, redemption, grace, the life beyond, are the crystallized
products in which the rich stream of religious experience, faith, hope, and
love, gains a firm outline. All the manifold rites and sacraments, consecra-
tions and purifications, offerings and sacred feasts, sacred dances and pro-
cessions, all the working of asceticism and morality, are only the indirect
expression of the inner experience of religion, the experience of awe, trust,
surrender, yearning, and enthusiasm. In prayer, on the other hand, this
experience is directly unveiled; prayer, as Thomas Aquinas said, 'is the

peculiar practical proof of religion'; or, as Sabatier excellently puts it, 'Prayer is religion in action, that is, real religion'.

Just because prayer is the elementary and necessary expression of the religious life, it is also, as the evangelical theologian, Palmer, has it, 'the perfectly accurate test by which the existence or the non-existence of religion in persons and systems must always be tried: it is the standard by which the degree of religion alive in men or possible to them, must be measured'. K. Girgensohn stresses the same idea in his thoughtful *Addresses on the Christian Religion*. 'Prayer', he says, 'is a perfectly accurate instrument for grading the religious life of the soul. Did one only know how a man prays, and what he prays about, one would be able to see how much religion that man has. When a man, without any witnesses, speak with his God, the soul stands unveiled before its Creator. What it has then to say shows quite distinctly how rich or how poor it is.'

But not only are the religious differences of individuals revealed in prayer, but the same thing is true of entire peoples, ages, types of culture, churches, religions. Auguste Sabatier remarks: 'Nothing reveals to us better the moral worth and the spiritual dignity of a form of worship than the kind of prayer it puts on the lips of its adherents.' Althaus writes in the introduction to his study of prayer in the literature of the Reformation: 'Prayer is, as hardly anything else can be, the most reliable indication of this or that type of piety. Next to hymns, prayers reflect in the clearest manner the outstanding quality of the religious life in any given stage of its development.' Dr. L. R. Farnell, perhaps the most eminent contemporary English historian of religion, observes by way of introduction to his sketch of the development of prayer: 'There is no part of the religious service of mankind that so clearly reveals the various views of the divine nature held by the different races at the different stages of their development, or reflects so vividly the material and psychologic history of man, as the formulas of prayer.' Hence, as Deissmann says, 'one might, without more ado, write a history of religion by writing a history of prayer'.

'Sources for the study of prayer'

Prayer is that expression of religious experience in which, as Deissmann says, 'the life and movement of real piety is revealed most clearly and where at the same time it is most shyly veiled'. Genuine, personal prayer conceals itself in delicate modesty from the eyes and ears of the profane. Even primitive peoples are extremely reserved in imparting information about their religious life. Many an explorer and missionary has sojourned for years among primitive peoples before he succeeded in learning anything about their religious thought and action or even in overhearing their prayers.

What is true of primitive man is still more true of devout individuals. The personal devotional life of men of religious genius is lived in secret. The worshipper stands before his God 'alone with the Alone'. The great men of religion fly for prayer to solitude, to the quiet chamber or the open spaces of Nature. Seldom has the ear of man heard or his pen recorded that which they have poured out in prayer to God in such hours of solitude. They have indeed spoken of their devotional life to their disciples and have taught them how and for what one ought to pray, but hardly ever have they opened their mouths in the presence of others to hold intimate converse with their God. Paul often exhorts to prayer in his letters, and at times he discloses something of his way of praying and of his mysterious and wonderful experiences in the prayer-state, but in 'his religious chastity he shrinks from praying a written prayer even in confidential letters to his churches'. To be sure, we know thousands and thousands of prayers which have come down to us chiselled on stone or printed in letters, prayers from ancient temple libraries, and prayers in modern books of devotion; from altars and pulpits we also hear solemn words of prayers, the liturgical inheritance of the Christian Church. But all these are not the genuine, spontaneous prayers that break forth from the deepest need and innermost yearning of the human heart. Such prayers speak a different language; nay, sometimes do not speak at all, but are only a silent adoration and contemplation or a mute sighing and yearning. Formal, literary prayers are merely the weak reflection of the original, simple prayer of the heart. Most sources of prayer are, therefore, only indirect evidences; on the one hand, intimations about the experiences of prayer and instructions in prayer, and on the other, formulas of prayer and devotional compositions. Consequently it is no easy task to get an exact picture of real prayer. And yet we shall succeed in doing this if we carefully collect the various specimens of prayer and grade them according to their psychological value and if, in addition, we supplement them by the individual and general utterances on prayer which we have from the lips of the great men of prayer.

[. . .]

'The object of the study of religion'

The object of the history of religions, as of all history, is always an individual structure, sharply delimited as to place and time. The history of religions investigates, with the aid of philology, the religion of a particular people (the Egyptians, Babylonians, Chinese), of a particular race (Bantu, Semitic, Indo-Germanic), of a particular age (the Vedic age, Jewry in exile, early Christianity, the age of the Reformation), a particular community or sect (Japanese Sukhavati-Buddhism, the Mithras mysteries, Calvinist Protestantism, the religious life of creative individuals (Buddha, Plotinus, Jesus, St. Paul, St. Augustine, Luther, Schleiermacher), a world religion containing many trends, schools of thought, and personalities (Buddhism, Islam), or a world church (Catholicism).

The study of religion, on the other hand, is, unlike the particular and general history of religions, not concerned with single religions and religious personalities, but with religion as such. It attempts to find out what religion is, how it comes about in a man's soul, how it develops in men's social life, what it means for our spiritual and cultural life. In two completely different ways, the modern study of religion tries to fathom the secret of religion; one way is social psychology and comparative religion, the other is psychological analysis of religion. The object of the social-psychological (anthropological, ethnological, social) and comparative-historical investigation of religion is the rise and development of religion. The psychological genesis and the historical development of the religious phenomenon is reconstructed on the basis of a general comparison of the data provided by the religious notions and rites of present-day primitive nations and ancient cultures. The object of the individual-psychological investigation of religion is the richly varied inner life of the individual personalities of a highly developed cultural era of both religious geniuses and the average religious person who, spontaneously or on the basis of psychological questioning, have written down their religious experiences. Neither method succeeds in mastering completely the religious phenomenon. One method by-passes the richest and purest expressions of religious emotions, the other abstracts religious experience from all historical and sociological context. Both methods certainly provide valuable scientific insights. But only an investigation of all manifestations and types of religious experience can provide the foundation for a philosophy of religion, for a determination of the essence of and for an appraisal of religion.

Starting-point and focus of the study of religion must always be *pure naive religion*. Above all, religion must be studied at its origins and high points, there where it spontaneously and freely, with creative force, breaks out of strong inner experiences, where it has not yet become rigid in stable, conventional forms of worship, and has not been overgrown by explanatory mythological thinking or philosophical-theological speculation. Naive religion has retained its original vividness in the cults of the primitive nations of to-day, whose original ways of thinking and living have been relatively little affected by historical progress and decline.

Naive religion also lives in the popular devotion of all ages and all cultures. For 'the devotion of the masses is as unchangeable as the water in the depths of the sea. It is neither dragged along nor heated by the surface currents.[1] The Canaanite-Israelite, the Greek, the Hindu, the Christian-medieval popular religions are examples of the way the original religious passions live on with invincible force under the cover of higher cultures and religions. Even in the Catholic and Evangelical popular devotion of our age, primitive religious realism lives on with undiminished force; the great movements of Reformation, Pietism and Rationalism which have shaken the Protestant churches, have made so little difference to the primitive religion of the peasants, that Evangelical clergymen, who made a thorough study of folklore, have asked in all seriousness: 'Have our people ever been converted to Christianity?[2]'

Valuable additions to the vivid picture of naive religion, that can be gained out of the cults of primitive nations and out of popular devotion, are provided by the literary and historic documents that have fragmentarily come down to us from ancient cults, in the fixed and sacrosanct ritual acts and words of which the primitive religious creations of prehistoric times have become petrified. Instructive analogies to primitive religion are, finally, offered by the devotion of children, in so far as it expresses itself spontaneously and has not been copied from adults by way of imitation or education. As in thinking and speaking, in gesture and action, in play and artistic creation, the genesis and development of the original, of the primitive, takes place anew in the religious notions and actions of children. All these expressions and sediments of primitive religion enable us to have a vague idea about the origin of religious experience, which must have occurred at the very beginning of the human race.

Primitive expressions of religious experience alone are not sufficient for us to obtain a complete and effective picture of naive religion. At a certain point in time numerous religious acts, both in primitive and in popular religions, became conventional and at times entirely incomprehensible habits maintained for their own sake. On no account should every cultish act be interpreted as a spontaneous religious expression. Even in the primitive world, let alone in the ancient cultures, one should allow for all-pervasive impoverishments and superstructures. Furthermore, the primitive religious documents are always of an objective, external, and never of a subjective nature; they never reveal the actual religious experience; we have to infer the latter ourselves from the acts of worship, the words that accompany those acts, and the situations that cause them. Finally, and in accordance with the lack of differentiation throughout the culture as a whole, primitive religion is so indissolubly linked to and mixed up with the mythical outlook on life, with the social institutions, but above all with magic, that the modern study of religion has continually confused it with these heterogeneous ingredients of primitive culture. Therefore, in order to isolate the actually religious from the knot of primitive thinking and acting, to separate the naive and spontaneous from the imitated, fixed, and conventional, to disentangle the inner experience that expresses itself through acts and words of worship, we must address ourselves to the great religious geniuses, who have revealed to us their rich and subtle creative experiences, in direct and indirect accounts. Only by investigating their devotion will we succeed in getting to understand completely the naive religion of primitive man and his innermost religious feelings. In psychology this way of thinking is called the 'transformation analysis' *(umformende Analyse)*, which consists in inferring the germ of an experience from the fully developed, transparent form of the same experience. As long as the study of religion goes on trying to understand and explain primitive religion in isolation, without any comparison with the devotion of the great religious personalities, it will continue groping around in the dark, and be unable to throw any light on the questions concerning the origin of religion and its relation to magic.

By *great religious personalities* are meant those personalities whose spiritual values merge with or culminate in religious experience, and who have great creative significance in religious history: the mystics and seers, the prophets, preachers and missionaries, the reformers and founders. At the top are those personalities who, having come up out of the uneducated lower strata of society, become completely absorbed in religious thought. They are those who feel no need whatever to reconcile their religious ideas with the scientific notions and cultural ideals of the age, who above all are simply possessed by a philosophical desire to understand the coherence of the world: the personalities of the Old and the New Testament, St. Francis of Assisi, Luther, John Bunyan, George Fox, the mystic nuns, the poetic Sufis. If some of them make use of philosophical concepts, they do so only for the sake of an understandable explanation and a dialectical assertion of religious truth. An absolute religious conviction usually leads to a rough rejection of any metaphysical philosophizing: we need think only of St. Paul's hard words against the sage and sensible, of Luther's haughty mockery of that 'jester' and 'whore' called 'reason', of Pascal's irrationalism, Kierkegaard's paradox, Buddha's agnosticism. It is highly significant that the devotion of the greatest religious geniuses was a thoroughly naive, un-thought-out, non-theological layman's devotion. The working and peasant classes have always been rich in great religious leaders: Amos the shepherd, Jesus the carpenter, St. Paul the weaver, Muhammad the shepherd, Kabir the weaver, Bunyan the tinker, Fox the tanner, Tersteegen the ribbon-weaver. Next to these very simple believers, unaffected by any metaphysical problems, there are the great thinking religious personalities, who are possessed by a strong philosophical urge, without their devotion losing anything in depth, vividness and earnestness. In spite of the very strong inclination towards metaphysical speculation and logical penetration of the substance of religion, the religious experience never loses its position of highest value to make way for the pure understandable truth as the highest ideal. These are the great speculative mystics, the men of the Upanishads, Ramanuya, Plotinus, Eckhart, Böhme, and the great theologians, Origen, St. Augustine, Thomas Aquinas, Calvin and Schleiermacher, Newman and Schell, in Islam Al-Ghazzali. In their preachings, but particularly in their confessions and prayers, naive religion lives on; the speculative point of view that dominates their teachings, recedes into the background. The divergence between personal devotion and theological doctrine is unmistakable, when we compare Thomas Aquinas' hymn 'Adoro te devote' and the sober arguments and deductions of the Summa, or the hymns by the early Lutheran theologians and their polemical and scholastic writings. It is the task of the psychology of religion to gain access to the human being, hero, poet and child in the great theologian and dogmatist.

The modern psychology of religion has, amongst other things, collected confessions by all kinds of ordinary people and exalted psychopaths, and has attempted to distil from those the regularity of religious experience. It has applied certain methods, which are very useful for investigating general psychic questions, to the investigation of phenomena which are no longer accessible to general psychology. All inner events however, out of which are born the highest spiritual values, religious experiences as well as philosophical thinking and artistic creation, must primarily be studied in the creative personalities. For that reason, as Söderblom rightly says, 'the psychology of religion cannot make any progress without concentrating on the great geniuses and the profound spirits within ithe realm of devotion.'[3] An error often made by psychologists is that they believe that the confessions obtained by means of detailed (written or oral) questioning are a richer and more profitable and more reliable source than the historical, literary documents about the devotion of great personalities. Not all documents may be of equal psychological value; it is essential that the relative value of the manifold literary confessions be ascertained. Moreover, an arbitrary selection of certain personalities is never enough: as many geniuses as possible should be included, as the literary documents pertaining to a single personality naturally never describe a religious phenomenon completely, taking all aspects into account, so that confessions by various people should complement one another.

We find naive, unconsidered religion also in the lives of those personalities whose productive creativity belongs to another set of values than religious ones. Great poets and artists (Dante and Goethe, Michelangelo and Dürer, Beethoven and Haydn), but also brilliant statesmen (Gustav Adolf, Cromwell, Bismarck), explorers (Columbus), scientists (Newton), and strategists (Tilly, Ziethen, Hindenburg), reveal an unmediated devotion that shows surprising parallels with the devotion of the religious men of genius. Here we have an interesting area of investigation, largely neglected by theologians and psychologists, although the testimonies are limited and often only consist of short but concise and characteristic expressions. Naive religion, which is marked by unbroken force, free spontaneity and creativity, is the central object of the study of religion. But investigation of secondary phenomena is certainly essential: apart from the original, individual experience, we should not forget those religious constructions which are based partly on the community of religious individuals (myth, rite, liturgy, law), partly on the combination of religion with philosophical thinking (rational reform religion – *die rationale Reformreligion)* or on both (ecclesiastical dogma). The phenomena of ossification and decay should also become objects of investigation in this field of study. From rigid rituality, as from rational and moralistic substitutes of philosophical reform religion *(philosophische Reformreligion)*, naive and pure religion arises in all its clarity. The genesis, out of individual experience, of fixed forms of worship tied to a particular religious community, their ups and downs in the course of history and their influence on the devotion of the individual, the influence of individual devotion such as popular religion on the formulation of ecclesiastical dogmas — everywhere there are here psychological and sociological problems. Only a very few people show any creative independence in their religious lives. Most people's devotion is a 'second-hand religious life' (W. James), which is oriented towards the experience of religious men of genius, although more usually, towards the traditions of a religious community (nation, church, sect). The great productive personalities provide the classic examples, which then serve the ordinary people in the development of their own religious lives and in the expression of their experiences. But also in the experience of the creative spirits, imagination plays a part that should not be underestimated. Consider what Moses and the Prophets meant for Jesus, Jesus for St. Francis, St. Paul and St. Augustine for Luther. But the important difference is here, that the great devout men do not derive their religious lives from any objective authorities and traditions, but from the individual experiences of eminent personalities; for all devotional traditions are only weak reflections of the sort of personal experience that, in those traditions, has become fixed and normative. The study of religion is therefore obliged, with the aid of sociology, to pay attention to the phenomena of religious imitation, devotional tradition and the development of religious communities.

All psychology is based on introspection *(Selbstbeobachtung)*, and that includes the psychology of religion, although one cannot build a psychology of religion on introspection alone. For that, modern man's religious experience is usually too unproductive, too poor in substance, too much thought out, and too weak. But in so far as we lack an immediate and strong devotion that lives in meditation and prayer, we must use at least the germs and beginnings of genuine religious experience and the memories of completely naive expressions of devotion, such as childhood memories, in order to come to an understanding of naive devotion, by way of a kind of real or hypothetical empathy. Introspection is also indispensable for any religious psychology. Somebody who has never felt any religious impulse himself, will never penetrate into the miraculous and enigmatic world of religion. What Monrad, the Danish bishop, said of prayer is applicable to all religion: 'Prayer is a world in itself, known only to those who live in it'.[4] For the study of religion, both as an individual and as a social phenomenon, the rich historical material is the most important; the questionnaire method is only useful as a complementary device; only where it shows up avoidable gaps and ambiguities should it be used. The systematic use of questionnaires is above all useful for obtaining complete and reliable information about the religious life of primitives, children, and peasants, where the questionnaire stimulates observation. Yet the modern psychology of religion uses questionnaires almost exclusively for obtaining personal accounts about modern man's individual religious life. The results of using such questionnaires plus the spontaneously ensuing personal accounts provide valuable material for the study of present-day religion. But it is useless to try to come to a psychology of religious experience along those lines at all. The essential characteristics of the religious phenomenon are clear only in a naive experience; the religion of modern man is larded with too many heterogeneous elements, with too much of a philosophical outlook on life and with too much aesthetical enjoyment, for anybody to be able to use it for the study of pure, unadulterated devotion.

'THE SCHOLARLY STUDY OF RELIGION'

Of all the directions the study of religion has taken, comparative history of religions brings about the closest understanding of religion – not in the sense of determining external relationships, but in providing a vision of the unity of religion in the diversity of religions. The comparative method may draw simultaneously upon all the valuable knowledge supplied by ethnology, philology and psychology. Scientific and personal assumptions are decisive. There is no science without presuppositions, but it is important for science to have the right ones.

A) The first preliminary condition is *a strictly inductive method*. Any philosophical apriority must be rejected. Religion must never be forced into the straitjacket of any theological or philosophical system. It is necessary to be satiated with historical facts, a requirement put forth by Paul

Wernle in his *Einführung in das theologische Studium*[5] [Introduction to Theology]. It is essential to get to know the actual religions in their many and varied manifestations, before one begins to construct theories, to lose oneself in the fullness of religious life, before reflecting on it, to absorb living religion, whether it is exalted or humble, with an open mind, before asking after truth and value.

B) One of the most important requirements of the inductive method is the *investigation of the sources*, that is to say, the holy Scriptures and the personal testimonies of the great personalities. A complete understanding of these is possible only through knowledge of the language in question. 'Languages are the sheaths of the knife of the Spirit', says Luther; 'they are the shrines in which one carries this gem (the Gospel)' (Erl. 22, 183). Language and religion are very closely related. All religions are concerned with the divine word, God himself is the Word, the Logos. The present-day study of religion is therefore very closely related to philology. The founder of the comparative study of religions was a philologist, Max Müller. The greatest scholars of religion in this century were also philologists (Söderblom-Iranist, Van der Leeuw-Egyptologist, Hans Haas-Japanologist, Rudolf Otto-Sanskritist, Tor Andrae-Arabist). Philology has opened up an increasing number of the Orient's holy Scriptures to the Occident; Western philologists have often penetrated more deeply into the spirit of the holy Scriptures (e.g. the Veda and Avesta), than have Asian exegetes. Also, philological and critical investigation has made the familiar holy Scriptures of the Old and New Testaments far more understandable to us, in their historical perspectives, than they were to previous generations. There is a *philologia sacra*, as is shown by Kittel's 'Theological Dictionary to the New Testament', which is a rich source, also for the history of religions.

The student of religion should be a student of language too; comparative religionists should, apart from the three languages of the inscription on the Cross (St. John 19 : 20), know at least one of the languages of the great Eastern religions. Each one of these (Sanskrit, Old and Middle Persian, Arabic, New Persian, Sumerian-Babylonian, Egyptian, Chinese, Japanese) introduces a different realm of experience. The non-linguist may today get access to the Eastern religious documents by way of reliable philological translations, the *Sacred Books of the East*, published by Max Müller. These are complemented by the collection of *Sacred Books of the Buddhists* which he initiated. Valuable translations along with a philological apparatus, are provided by the *Quellen zur Religionsgeschichte*[6], published by the 'Göttinger Akademie der Wissenschaften', and, in a more popular form, by the *Religiöse Stimmen der Völker*.[7]

Beginners should start with the *Textbuch zur Religionsgeschichte* by Edvard Lehmann and Hans Haas,[8] or Söderblom's *Främmande Religions-*

urkunder,[9] or with Gustav Mensching's *Das Lebendige Wort*[10] and *Die Söhne Gottes*,[11] and then proceed to the *Religionsgeschichtliches Lesebuch* by A. Bertholet,[12] and make themselves familiar with a few gems from the religious literature of the world, such as Lao-tzu's *Tao-tê-ching*,[13] the *Upanishads*,[14] the Buddhist *Sutta-Pitakam*,[15] the *Saddharma-pundarika*,[16] and the *Avesta*.[17]

C) Religion should not only be studied in books, but in *living people*, both in individuals and in societies. One is just as likely to become a good medical doctor through studying nothing but books, as one is to become an authority on religion in that way. Rudolf Otto's intuitive sense of what is holy is based on impressions received in mosques and Eastern temples, and above all, in a small old synagogue in Tunis, where he received his great vision of what is holy during Isaiah's 'Thrice Holy'.[18] He who wishes to study religion, must attend religious services of all religions and confessions, and make himself familiar with both cult-like and puritanical devotion. He must involve himself in the atmosphere of the sacred. Next to the study of religion as a social phenomenon, the study of religious individuals is essential; it is important to come into contact with the 'spiritual' holy people, whose whole lives are revelations of the transcendental, whose faces alone are rays of the divine sun.

D) The fourth condition for a fruitful study of religion is *a universal point of view*. Max Müller says: 'If one knows one religion, one knows none'. It is impossible to penetrate religion to any great depth with the limitations imposed by one area of philology or one dogmatic religion or confession. The study of religion should always keep in mind the totality of religions and confessions. The greatest danger, however, is that dogmatic view of religion that takes one's own religion as absolute, and regards that religion as a shining light, and all other ones as unrelieved darkness.

E) The fifth methodological requirement is *the phenomenological method*: it is essential that one goes from the φαινόμενον to the εἶδος, to the essence. The manifestations should be investigated only for the sake of the essence they are based on. One should not remain on the outside, but penetrate everywhere to the heart of religious experience; from the fixed forms (ceremonial, dogmas), we must penetrate to immediate religious life. In this matter, Schleiermacher's *Reden über die Religion*, and Benjamin Constant's *La religion* are pointers for all time.

Apart from the purely scientific presuppositions, there are also preliminary conditions pertaining to religion in particular. One cannot approach religion with rational, philological and psychological criteria only.

A) Above all, *respect* for all real religions is essential. According to an old saying, wonderment is the beginning of all philosophy, but also of the study of religion. Religion is not concerned with everyday matters or curiosities, but with life and death, with the last and the highest, with eternity. God's word in the Old Testament applies also to the student of religion: 'Put off thy shoes from off thy feet, for the place whereon thou standest is holy ground' (Exodus 3:_5).

B) The second requirement is *personal religious experience*. One cannot be engaged in ethics without a moral sense, in history of art without any artistic experience, in philosophy without love of truth, in the study of religion without any religious feeling, in the broadest sense of the word. *Similia similibus cognoscuntur*. In order to understand religion, the scholar has to bring love along with him; *'res tantum cognoscitur, quantum diligitur'*, says St. Augustine. Franciscan love of Nature was the starting-point of the modern sciences; Bacon, the pioneering researcher, was a Franciscan. Love implies also consideration for the weaknesses and imperfections of so many religious manifestations.

C) The third requirement is *that one takes seriously a religious claim to the truth:* one cannot properly understand religion if one dismisses it as superstition, illusion, or as a scarecrow. Religion is about a final reality, which is revealed to man and which is his salvation. God, revelation, eternal life are realities to religious man. Any study of religion is, in the last analysis, theology, to the extent that it does not concern itself with psychological and historical phenomena only, but also with the experience of transcendental realities. Certainly, religion is a part of spiritual life and spiritual culture, but this spiritual life can be understood only on the basis of its final metaphysical source.

This taking seriously a religious view of reality is, to a certain extent, a faith, but not a faith in the sense of a fixed theological or confessional dogma. The greatest scholars of religion, Friedrich Schleiermacher, Max Müller, Nathan Söderblom, have been men of faith, but of a universal faith, a faith transcendental in mankind. They believed in God's revelation, but in His revelation in all mankind's religions. Nathan Söderblom confessed on his deathbed: 'God lives, I can prove it from the history of religions'. On the basis of this word, his posthumously published Gifford lectures received the title *The living God, basal forms of personal religion* (London, 1933).

'The phenomenological method'[19]

There are several ways of penetrating to the essence of religion.

1) The first is *the longitudinal section*. This method tries to attain a survey of the individual religions from a geographical-historical point of view. This method is used in several textbooks of the history of religions, such as Tiele-Söderblom,[20] Chantepie de la Saussaye,[21] Pettazzoni,[22] Gorce-Mortier,[23]

Turchi,[24] Tacchi-Venturi,[25] Franz König,[26] Brillant-Aigrain,[27] Von Glasenapp,[28] Ringgren-Ström,[29] Heiler.[30] They deal with, respectively, the primitive religions and the dead and living cultural religions of East and West, as well as with the world religions rooted in them, Judaism and Christianity being left mostly out of consideration. This method gains in breadth what it lacks in depth. It shows up the historical relations, the development of the individual religions, and the dependence of one religion on the other religion. It shows the similarities and differences between the individual religious systems, but is does not provide a very clear insight into the common universal, the essence of religion.

2) The second method is *the cross-section*: this method treats the several types of religion:

a) according to their sociological character: the tribal, popular, and state religions, the universal religion, the traditionally ecclesiastical and creatively individualistic religions;

b) according to their conception of God: the magical, polydemonic, animistic, polytheistic, henotheistic (worshipping one God), monotheistic and pantheistic or monistic religions;

c) according to their outlook on life: the world-grasping, world-renouncing, world-dominating religions;

d) according to their psychological character: the religion of this world and of the world to come, the physical and spiritual, the aesthetical, rational, social, ethical and mystical religions, the religions of 'those who have been born once and those who have been born twice', that is to say, the religion based on the continuous development of a religious individual, and the religion based on a sudden conversion.

This standardization is to be found in works on both the phenomenology of religion and on the psychology and philosophy of religion.

3) The third method is that of *the concentric circle*: this method treats the religion of mankind as a whole, and views the lower and higher forms of religion together. Every single manifestation is traced from its most primitive to its most spiritual form. In concentric circles we penetrate from the outer manifestations to the inner ones, to the experiences, and finally to the intended object. It is the method of the κυκλικὴ εἴσοδος ἀπο τῶν ἔξω, an expression derived from Dionysios Areopagita's mysticism.[31] The latter will be applied in what follows.

Three rings are penetrated in the following order:

I) The world of outer manifestations *(sinnliche Erscheinungswelt)* i.e. the institutional element of religion.

II) The world or spiritual imagination *(geistige Vorstellungswelt)* i.e. the world of ideas, the rational element.

III) The world of psychic experience *(psychische Erlebniswelt)*, i.e., the dimension of values, the mystical element of religion.

The center forms the objective world *(Gegenstandswelt)*, i.e., the object of religion, Divine Reality.

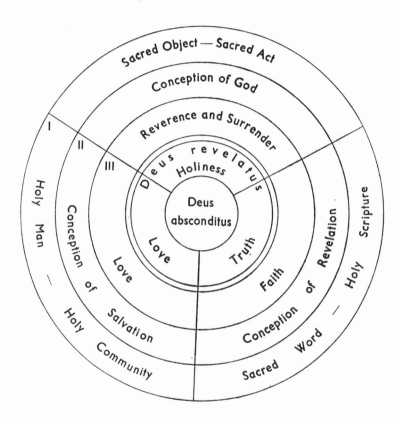

I) The *world of outer manifestations* comprises three sectors:

  1) the sacred *object*, the sacred *room* in which the cult takes place, the sacred *time*, in which the most important ritual is performed, the sacred *number*, by which the sacred objects, rooms, times, words, people are measured, the sacred *act* (rite).

  2) the sacred *word:* (1) the spoken word: a) the word of God, the incantation, the name of God. the oracle, the myth, the legend, the prophecy, the gospel, the doctrine; b) the word to God, prayer in adoration, penance, praise, thanksgiving, supplication, surrender; c) the sacred silence; (2) the written word: the holy scripture.

3) the holy *man* and the holy *community*. All that is within the scope of the physically observable, visible, audible, tangible. Religion is not an airy spirituality, but a physical communion with the Divine.

II. The first inner ring is the *world of religious imagination*, the thoughts, images, ideas concerning God's invisible being and visible works:
1) the conception of God (theology),
2) the conception of creation (cosmology and anthropology, including original condition and original sin),
3) the conception of revelation: the intimation of the divine will in the proclaimed word, in history, in the soul (Christology),
4) the conception of redemption: (1) the redeemer; (2) the object of redemption; (3) the road to redemption (soteriology),
5) the fulfillment in the future or in the world to come (eschatology).

III. The second inner ring represents the *world of religious experience*, i.e. what happens deep down in the soul, as opposed to the fanciful or rational images of God, the religious values which are laid aside in the confrontation between man and sacred objects and in the performance of sacred acts: 1) reverence (towards the divine in itself, its holiness), 2) fear, 3) faith and complete trust in God, who reveals himself, works, rules, loves, and helps, 4) hope, 5) love, yearning for God, surrender to him, reciprocation of God's love. Next to these values, there are peace, joy, and the urge to share. Then there are the extraordinary religious experiences: inspiration, sudden conversion, vocation and enlightenment, vision and audition, ecstacy, cardiognosis and the various extensions of physical powers, such as automatic speaking and writing, speaking in foreign tongues and stigmatisation, and so on.

IV. The *objective world of religion*, the center of the circles, is the Divine Reality, which is understood through all external manifestations, inner notions, and experiences of the soul, in a double sense:
1) as the *Deus revelatus*, the God who has his face towards man, as absolute holiness, truth, justice, love, mercy, salvation, the personal God, experienced as 'Thou' and as a being of communion (Trinity),
2) as the *Deus ipse* or *absconditus*, the divinity, experienced as 'It', as absolute unity.

There is a correlation between the segments of the various rings: the physical forms of expression, thoughts, feelings, correspond finally to divine reality. Although that reality can never be completely expressed in human forms of expression, thoughts, and experiences, there is a certain correspondence to the divine, the *analogia entis*: the created being corresponds to the non-created divine being. The most perfect religion would be one in which the institutionalized ritual, the rational and the mystical elements would be unified, resulting in the closest possible relationship between finite being and infinite mystery.[32]

NOTES

1. F. Cumont, *Die orientalischen Religionen*, p. 237.
2. Gerade, *Meine Erlebnisse und Beobachtungen als Dorfpastor*, 1895, p. 27.
3. N. Söderblom, *Studiet av Religionen*, 1908, p. 73.
4. D. G. Monrad, *Aus der Welt des Gebetes*. Translated by A. Michelsen. 1878, 2nd edition, p. 1.
5. Tübingen (1908), 1921[3].
6. Göttingen, 1911 ff.
7. Editor Walter Otto. Jena 1915 ff.
8. Leipzig, 1922[2].
9. *Främmande religionsurkunder i urval och överstättning*, 4 vols. Stockholm, 1907, I 1954[2].
10. Ed. *Das lebendige Wort. Texte aus den Religionen der Völker*. Darmstadt, 1952.
11. *Die Söhne Gottes. Aus den heiligen Schriften der Menschheit. München* 1958.
12. Tübingen 1926–1932, 17 vols.
13. Translations by Julius Grill. Tübingen, 1910; by Richard Wilhelm. Jena 1911; by Erwin Rousselle. Wiesbaden, 1952.
14. *60 Upanishads des Veda*, translated by Paul Deussen, Leipzig (1897), 1921[3]; *Die Geheimlehre des Veda, Ausgewählte Texte der Upanishads*. Leipzig, 1921[6].
15. Edward Conze, *Buddhist Texts through the Ages* (translation), Oxford, 1954; *Buddhistische Geisteswelt vom historischen Buddha zum Lamaismus*. Texts selected and introduced by Gustav Mensching, Darmstadt, 1955; *Der Pfad der Erleuchtung, Grundtexte der buddhistischen Heilslehre*, translated by Helmut von Glasenapp. Düsseldorf–Köln, 1956.
16. *The Lotus of the Wonderful Law*, by W.E. Soothill. Oxford 1930.
17. *Die Gathas des Avesta, Zarathustras Verspredigten*, translated by Chr. Bartholomä. Straszburg 1905; Fritz Wolff, *Die Heiligen Bücher der Parsen*, translation. Straszburg, 1910; Bonn, 1924[2].
18. 'Reisebriefe aus Nordafrika', *Christliche Welt* 25 (1911), 709.
19. Eva Hirschmann, *Phänomenologie der Religion. Eine historisch-systematische Untersuchung von 'Religionsphänomenologie' und 'religionsphänomenologischer Methode' in der Religionswissenschaft*. Proefschrift. Groningen 1940.
20. Tiele-Söderblom's *Kompendium der Religionsgeschichte*. (1876, German tr. 1880) Berlin 1931[6].
21. Pierre Daniel Chantepie de la Saussaye, *Lehrbuch der Religionsgeschichte*, 2 vols., (1887), ed. Alfred Bertholet and Edvard Lehmann. Tübingen 1925[4].
22. *Storia delle religioni*, a cura di Raffaele Pettazzoni. Bologna 1922 ff.
23. *Histoire générale des religions*, éd. Maxime Gorce et Raoul Mortier, 5 vols. Paris 1942–1951.
24. *Le religioni del mondo*, a cura di Nicola Turchi. Roma (1946), 1951[2].
25. *Storia delle religioni*. Torino 1954[3].
26. *Christus und die Religionen der Erde, Handbuch der Religionsgeschichte*, 3 vols., Freiburg 1954.
27. *Histoire des religions*, sous la direction de Maurice Brillant et René Aigrain, 5 vols. Paris 1953–1956.

28. *Die fünf groszen Religionen*, 2 vols. Düsseldorf 1951–1952; *Die nichtchrist-lichen Religionen*. Frankfurt 1957.

29. *Die Religionen der Völker*. Stuttgart 1959.

30. *Die Religionen der Menschheit*. Stuttgart 1959.

31. *De divinis nominibus* 4, 9.

32. Friedrich von Hügel, 'The three elements of religion', in: *The Mystical Element* I, pp. 50–82.

Heinrich Frick

Heinrich Frick was born in 1893 in Darmstadt, Germany, where he received his primary and secondary school education. He studied theology at the universities of Giessen and Tübingen between 1912 and 1916, and acquired the *Lizentiat* in theology in 1917 with a thesis on 'The National and International Character of Christian Mission'. He studied Arabic and obtained his Ph. D. in 1919 with a dissertation treating 'Al-Ghazzali's Autobiography as compared with Augustine's Confessions'. The same year Frick became lecturer for the history of religions at the Technical Higher School in Darmstadt. In 1921 he was also connected with the University of Giessen as a *Repetent*, and in 1925 he became professor in systematic theology there. From 1929 onwards Frick occupied the chair for systematic theology at the University of Marburg, as well as being in charge of the history of religions and of missiology. He built up the Institute for the History of Religions and the *Religionskundliche Sammlung* of the University of Marburg,. He died in Marburg in 1952.

Only one small book by Frick has been translated into English: 1938 *The Gospel, Christianity and other Faiths*.

Frick developed consciously a typological approach to the study of religion, as different from a comparative approach which would interpret parallel phenomena as representing parallel stages of religious development. He stressed, in particular, the systematic side of the discipline and introduced some key concepts. These were: 'stage', 'habitus' as the typical orientation of each religion, and 'basic phenomena' as the fundamental structures which are proper to religion as such. As a theologian, Frick was concerned with the problem how to think of Christianity in its uniqueness and as one religion among others at the same time. He viewed the study of religion as being a theological discipline and tried to link it with missiology.

The following translated fragment has been taken from *Vergleichende Religionswissenschaft* ('The Comparative Study of Religions') which appeared in German in 1928. It shows the way in which Frick envisaged typology.

'THE AIM OF THE COMPARATIVE STUDY OF RELIGIONS'
('TYPOLOGY')

I. 'There is, as yet, no generally accepted division of religions according to their essence and stage of development'. It was this state of emergency which gave Archbishop Nathan Söderblom, also a well-known scholar in religion, the idea of arranging the religions in a short introductory article according to the chance order in which Israel and Christianity happened to come into contact with them. This method is not unpractical, but it reveals the critical lack of a generally accepted typology. As long as people still held their own religion to be the only true one, or indeed as long as all positive religions were considered to be inferior to the simple religion of reason, a systematic division of the history of religions was not necessary. It was not until an abundance of historical religions came within our scope during the nineteenth century, that the need for a standard system grew into an imperative demand. The representatives of the movements mentioned [. . .] developed many and varied programmes to this end. From the field of philosophy came Hegel's well-known classification. Hegel distinguishes between an objective, a subjective and an absolute stage. On the first level we find the primitive religions, which conceive God as a natural force or substance. On the second level God appears as spiritual individuality and free subjectivity. Finally God reveals himself to the Christian as the absolute spirit.

The suggestions from the philological-historical sphere are very different. For a time Max Müller distinguished two large groups, by taking into consideration the language of the sacred texts: a Semitic and an Indo-Germanic group of religions. The following attempts have become known to a wider public. For example the question is put as to the creator of a religion, and the answer given: in the one case collective powers, the race for instance, and in the other individual personalities. Therefore there are religions which have developed and religions which have been founded. Or a difference is made according to the extent of expansion, between the world religions and the religions of race and tribe. Or, finally, inquiry is made into the attitude the religious person takes towards the world. Hence follow the three typical phenomena of piety: the one formed by the world, the other being a withdrawal from the world and the third a victory over the world.

All these systems present valuable points of view, but not a lasting typology. They represent vistas hacked through the jungle of the history of religions, but are not practicable ways which lead to a goal. Each and every one of them suffers from a basic fault, based as they are on a moment which does not necessarily belong to the religious act, but which stems from a connection of the religious act with something else!

The form of the conception of God, the cloak of language, the limits of expansion, the contact with the world: these are all interrelated. There can be no doubt that the individuality of a religion frequently finds its expression in these aspects. But this individuality becomes perceptible only when we have to do in these connections with elements which can be reliably ascertained. These, however, are to be looked for. Typology cannot be developed from connections which are still doubtful, or from the groping for outlines, but it has to be developed from the religious act itself.

In his 'Wilhelm Meister', Goethe provides a model of good typology. He takes as the principle for division an essential psychological moment of all religious attitudes, namely that of awe. The awe of that which is above us is the ethnic religion, the religion of the races of mankind. The awe of that which is equal to us, is the philosophic religion. But the awe of that which is beneath us, which recognizes humility, suffering and death as divine, and which honours even sin and crime as the furtherance of holiness, that is the ultimate and the highest – that is Christianity.

Thus Goethe indicated the way upon which typological study is today attempting to advance. The best known example at the present time is Friedrich Heiler's differentiation between mysticism and prophetic religion. How is this double concept obtained? By means of the analysis of the relevant religious act. What mysticism is can be recognized by the way in which Buddha reaches the state of Nirvana in this life through the stages of meditation. His senses and thoughts are increasingly closed to the world. The ideal state is that finally the perfect sage has, like the tortoise, withdrawn all his senses into himself, so that the jackal, their enemy, Mara the tempter, can no longer find an opportunity to attack. From this state of withdrawal *(myein)* mysticism takes its name. On the other hand stands prophetic religion, the religion of prayer. That is an act and not a state, a development of personal powers and not a withdrawal, not a sinking into the depths of the subconscious, but a struggle between the self and a personal opponent, just as Jacob in the myth struggles with the nocturnal God and Jesus experiences his Gethsemane at the peak of the religion of prayer. From this psychology of religious experience, each aspect receives its characteristic light. The personality of man, the conception of God, ethics, the social side of our existence and finally history: all these look very different, according to whether they are assessed from the point of view of mysticism or prophetic religion. Friedrich Heiler has very convincingly worked out the difference between the two types in the light of studies on Buddha and Luther (also Jesus). The question then arises, whether the differences thus developed are also characteristic of the religions of 'Buddhism' and 'Christianity'. Strong objections are, however, set against this idea. The course of history alone presents the strange picture that on the one hand the prayer type, that is, expression of prophetic religion, occurs within Buddhism; and that, on the other hand, noteworthy movements in mysticism have flourished on the soil of Christianity. For this reason one should hesitate to declare mysticism to be 'the essence of Buddhism', and in the same way we may not without reservation equate Christianity with the religion of prayer. What then, strictly speaking, does the expression 'type' mean if one connects it with mysticism and prophecy?

II. The words 'type' and 'typical' have various meanings according to the angle of the comparison. For instance, 'typical' is the opposite of 'singular'. Bernheim in his *Lehrbuch der historischen Methode* uses the word 'typical' to denote 'the uniform repetition of the activity of many individuals', for example, customs and habits as opposed to unique individual phenomena.

Attempts have been made to transfer this meaning, as the only possible one, to our field, and it has been insisted upon, that typology in the history of religions is 'the presentation of that which occurs frequently', which means dispensing with the recognition of the individual. This task has in fact been imposed; but it only designates half the problem. It requires research into regularity in religious structures. But it forgets that this regularity cannot be established by subtracting the individual. Here the error is always near at hand, that the individual religions can be stripped of their confessional accessories and that in every case the same nucleus will remain. The truth is however, that the peculiarities of a religion do not lie beside, but within what it has in common with other religions. Religions are living organisms, and as such they have a certain habitus, a physiognomy which extends to the ultimate manifestations of life. The character of the whole reveals itself in each separate member, and therefore mutual characteristics and the unique lie within each other in the same unit. The unique is in this case the same as the typical in an organic structure.

Thus we have discovered a second meaning of the word 'type'. In the first place it was concerned with determining the regularity in different religions, that is the stages, or better still the phases, because the word 'phase' *(Stadium)* precludes the suspicion that we wish to create a value judgment. But the determining of value stages is the task of the philosophy of religion. The comparative history of religions does not inquire into evaluation but into the factual findings; according to Ranke in the metaphorical sense it considers 'every epoch immediate to God'. Therefore let us speak rather of phases. These phases designate *what is common in a cross-section of different religions*. On the other hand, perpendicular to this, that is, seen in the longitudinal sense of history, lies *the unique in every particular religion*, let us call it the *habitus*, which reveals itself through various phases as the unchanging unique character of a positive religion.

In the introduction to his *Glaubenslere* Schleiermacher formulated this double function precisely: 'to determine both, what is common and what is unique in forms of belief in a general connection, to represent what is common as including all historically existent forms of belief and to establish the unique factors, after the introduction of a basic thought by means of a correct division, as a complete whole, and in this way to settle the relation of every form of belief to all other forms of belief, and to classify them according to their affinities and gradations, would be the true function of that branch of scholarly historical research.' Here a completely clear difference is made between the mutual, the stage, and the unique, the *habitus*.

The following example may serve as an illustration of this work program.

In the Gospel according to St. John the following words are attributed to Jesus: 'I am the truth'. To which phase do these words belong? Truth is a quality of the spiritual sphere. Where the holy is experienced as the truth, we are concerned with the phase of spiritual religion. A perfect example of such a religion is shown in Plato's style, in which can be seen quite clearly how the vital values are subdued by the spiritual ones. But, taken strictly logically, the quality of truth can only be applied to phrases. A statement can be true. The fourth Gospel, however attributes this quality to a person. A living person says of himself 'I am the truth'. What does this mean? The meaning of the quality has apparently shifted. This observation establishes a parallel with others of a similar kind. The terms gnosis and pneuma h ave undergone the same kind of change, which has transferred their meaning from the sphere of spiritual qualities to that of vital ones. This characterizes Hellenism as distinct from the original Greek development. And so here we have come upon the phase of a cross-roads of spiritual and vital religion, the spiritual values have been vitalized.

This observation can be further confirmed by a look at the style. In this respect valuable information has been provided by Eduard Norden in his *Agnostos Theos*. We are now able to specify the exact place where the words quoted are to be found: the values of Greek spiritual religion have been vitalized by the flowing in of oriental religiousness. At this stage a person can be made to say 'I am the truth'. This one example indicates how stages can be established with the help of our technique.

The determination of the *habitus:* the second task, can be discussed in the light of the given example. We must observe the special characteristic of the quotation which distinguishes it from analogous statements in other religions. What is most striking here is that the phrase is only attributed to Jesus himself and, according to the fourth evangelist, cannot be applied to anyone other than Christ. No mystic or priest, no holy canon or doctrine of redemption can declare itself to be 'the truth' on the basis of the fourth Gospel. Thus a certain habitus can be recognized. The person of Christ is, according to Söderblom, to Christianity the same as what 'the doctrine is to Buddhism and the Koran is to Islam'. This obviously means that the function of person, doctrine and scripture is in each case the same. The source of salvation lies in them. A person, a system of teaching, a book all perform the same service. They are, in the language of comparative morphology, analogous: despite differing origins they perform the same function. If the term 'analogy' is introduced, however, it must be distinguished from the term 'homology'. Those authorities which have the same origins, that is, which take up the same positions in the morphological layout are homologous. In the case in question, Buddha and Mohammed could be termed homologous with Christ. In the person of the founder, each of them takes up the homologous position. In his *Glaubenslehre* Schleiermacher has already drawn attention to the fact that the most important factor in the determining of the habitus of a religion is the outward historical beginning of that religion. But this method can only be regarded as first aid.

Schleiermacher has already emphasized the necessity of going beyond the point of origin in a comparison and of determining 'the unique alteration of everything in every developed formation of the same kind and grade' in each religion. In other words, one should compare the homologous formation of different historical religions and thus determine the habitus in each individual case. Correct observation will lead to the conclusion that, according to the longitudinal sense of history, every developed religion carries its habitus, colour, and tone through all stages. In his fifth *Rede über die Religion* Schleiermacher describes individualization in various new wordings. He uses the expressions 'style of the individual' and 'accentuated physiognomy'. Here he is very clearly referring to the program of a comparative morphology of religions. Closely connected with this, Rudolf Otto described 'the law of parallels in the history of religions' and made use of the terms 'homologous' and 'analogous'.

The real problems of a methodically exact comparison of religions are today to be found in this line. The technique of comparison has still to be developed into an exact method. Such a method is so far only to be found in the field of comparative morphology of organic creatures. Expressions like homologous, analogous, convergence of types, have been borrowed from there. It is not a coincidence that Goethe in particular indicates just such a comparison of religions in his pedagogical province. There he describes the wall of the temple as being covered with paintings depicting the history of Israel, accompanied by comparable scenes from other religions. The important point is not the 'synchronism', the chance simultaneousness, but, as he says, 'the symphronistic actions and incidents', that is, equivalence of meaning. It is now referred to as morphological equivalence.

Because of the uncertainty with which we still tend to use the terms 'phase', '*habitus*' and, in particular, the more exact terms 'homologous' and 'analogous', it is advisable at first to avoid comparison with those formations which are widely divergent. It is preferable to start with closely related religions, for example Christianity or Islam. The comparison is here fruitful, because certain phases appear in the same way in each case. In this way the unique reaction can be favorably observed, as Islam reacts in a different way than Christianity to the same stimulus. If we take this comparison as made in the main phases, that is, the comparison of the religious experience of Mohammed and that of Christ respectively, as prophetic ounders; and in addition the respective attitudes of both religions at the moment when they cross the border between their narrow Semitic home and the soil of Hellenism, so that they are forced to come to terms with the same powers, 'Hellenistic philosophy, gnosis, the Roman idea of justice', and if we imagine a comparative history of piety, religious services, constitution, theology and interpretation of Scripture between Islam and Christianity, then we should achieve two things. Firstly, greater insight into the habitus, the specific character of each individual religion, and secondly a survey of a chain of phases which had been passed through in each case. From here we must then proceed to more distant types, and a new extended comparison will contrast not only primitive religions, but also groups, in order to see what they have in common, as well as what is unique.

The comparative history of religions would, finally, find its climax in the conception of the basic religious phenomena *(religiöse Urphänomene)*. This idea of 'basic religion' *(Urreligion)* has nothing more in common with the first religion, historically, or with primitive religion, according to stages; it rather corresponds exactly to Goethe's conception of the basic plant. The basic phenomenon here presents the morphological structure; basic religion in this sense is the morphological skeleton of every possible religion. The function of a comparative history of religions consists of the working out of a typology. The organic structures of living religion must be investigated according to the criteria of homology and analogy in such a way that the phase and habitus, the general stage and accentuated physiognomy of every moment of the general history of religions is typologically recorded.

Thus the old bone of contention buries itself, that is, whether the science of religion may be practised only in the form of historical-philological detailed work, or according to overlapping philosophical principles. Indeed the interpretation presented here precludes the possibility of a contradiction of these two points of view. There is agreement in the metaphorical sense, that ideas are helpless without words to express them, and that words are empty without ideas. The network of terms of a typology receives its essence from the abundance of concrete ideas. And vice versa, detail can only be interpreted by means of a system of types. Only in alliance with each other can these two come closer to their great goal: namely to solve the enigma of religion in so far as it can be fathomed at all, and does not, as an unfathomable secret, compel us to silent awe.

Joachim Wach

Joachim Wach was born in 1898 in Chemnitz, Germany. He received his primary and secondary school education at home in Chemnitz and at the *Gymnasium* in Dresden. Having fulfilled his military duties from 1916 until 1918, he enrolled in the University of Leipzig in 1918, studied in Munich and in Berlin during 1919 and part of 1920, and returned to Leipzig in 1920. There he pursued his studies n the history and philosophy of religion and in Oriental languages, and obtai. ːd his Ph. D. degree with a dissertation on 'Basic Elements of a Phenomen ˌlogy of the Idea of Salvation'' in 1922. He had also attended lectures on philosophy given by Husserl at Freiburg and by Gundolf at Heidelberg. In 1924 Wach became *Privatdozent* in the Faculty of Philosophy of the University of Leipzig, and in 1929 *Extraordinarius.* In 1930 he received the Th. D. degree from the University of Heidelberg. In 1935 Wach left Germany and went to the United States. He taught here from 1935 until 1945 history of religions at Brown University, Providence, and was in 1945 appointed professor of history of religions in the Federated Theological Faculty of the University of Chicago. He died in 1955.

The following books of Wach are available in English: 1944 *Sociology of Religion;* 1951 *Types of Religious Experience – Christian and Non-Christian;* 1958 *The Comparative Study of Religions;* 1968 *Understanding and Believing: Essays.*

Wach may be called one of the most universally oriented scholars in the field of the study of religion. In 1924 he published a study on its methodology and he always remained concerned with methodological problems in general, and those of understanding and interpretation (hermeneutics) in particular. Furthermore he devoted himself to sociology of religion, advocating a typological approach. Wach wanted to elaborate a systematic typological understanding of religious phenomena and took as its basis religious experience and the three ways in which this expresses itself: in thought, action and fellowship. He had an open eye for the philosophical and theological problems raised by the fact of man's religiousness.

The following fragments have been taken from *Sociology of Religion, The Comparative Study of Religions, Types of Religious Experience,* and from 'The Meaning and Task of the History, of Religions', and give some insight in the way Wach conceived of *Religionswissenschaft*

RELIGION AND SOCIETY

The field. Our purpose is to study the interrelation of religion and society and the forms of interaction which take place between them. In principle, a purely theoretical discussion is adequate, but the concrete study of empirical manifestations is indispensable to a thorough understanding of the subject. The theoretical approach will arm us with the necessary categories with which to organize the available material. Through the empirical approach we will amass the wealth of data with which to corroborate the exposition of our principles.

The increased sensitivity to the sociologically relevant implications of religion has given depth to philosophical, historical, and psychological studies. Scholars have begun to concentrate on the investigation of the social background of the various historical religions, on the social implications of their message, and on the social changes resulting from their activities. Indeed, the pendulum may be said to have swung too far. As a reaction to the exaggerated amount of political, social, and cultural influence with which religion had been credited, a tendency emerged, with the rapid development of social studies in the past century, to reverse the emphasis and to interpret religion primarily or even exclusively as a product of cultural and social forces and tendencies. Much can be said for the suggestiveness of this line of attack, and very interesting results have thus far been obtained which have helped to broaden our knowledge of the social and economic presuppositions of religious thought and action. Yet, on the other hand, we must guard ourselves against accepting a course of inquiry overly one-sided.[1] Max Weber, who, as indicated, has contributed more than anyone else to the formation of a sociology of religion, is the first to protest against the one-sided assumptions of social and economic materialism, and he emphatically rejects the interpretation that 'the characteristic feature of a religious attitude can be simply the function of the social condition of the social stratum appearing as its representation; that this attitude would be only its "ideological" expression or a reflex of its material or ideal interests'.[2] The latter was and is the Marxian view as reflected, for example, in the *Communist Manifesto*. It has had a wide influence on social studies.

A leading modern authority on the religion of the Hebrews stated only recently that Israelite (prophetic, pharisaic, and rabbinic) traditions have to be considered as 'the product of a persistent cultural battle between the submerged, unlanded groups and their oppressors, the great landowners.[3] He emphasizes the 'primitive opposition of the semi-nomadic shepherd and the settled farmer', of the struggle of the 'small peasant of the highland against the more prosperous farmer of the valley and plains', and insists that 'the conflict in the cities as revealed in the resistance of the traders and artisans to the nobles and courtiers' is identical and can be reduced to 'the fundamental distinction of "patrician" and "plebian".' Similar explanations dominate the study of the era of the Reformation and the rise of Protestant denominations. Troeltsch has been among the first to protest against this type of one-sided approach.[4] Scholars tend to forget that, however far-reaching the influence of social motives on religion has undoubtedly been, the influences emanating from religion and reacting on the social structure have been equally great. A thorough examination of the effects of religion on the social life of mankind and of the influence of religion on the cohesion of groups, on the development and differentiation of social attitudes and patterns, and on the growth and decline of social institutions is likely to yield results of the utmost importance.

Religion and society. Before we can proceed to a direct examination of the interrelation and interaction of religion and society and to a typological study of the grouping thus created, we must reflect briefly upon some preliminary questions. Is religion primarily the concern of the individual or of the group? Is religion basically positive, negative, or indifferent toward 'secular' social grouping? In other words, where do we find the points of contact between religion and society?

An examination of definitions of religion is beyond our scope. However, the most workable one still appears to be short and simple: 'Religion is the experience of the Holy.'[5] This concept of religion stresses the objective character of religious experience[6] in contrast to psychological theories of its purely subjective (illusionary) nature which are so commonly held among anthropologists.[7] We agree with MacMurray that a great deal of our modern study of religion attempts to give an account of a response without any reference to the stimulus. This stimulus we would, however, characterize quite differently.[8] The objective concept restores to religion the full richness of meaning, which had been sadly diluted by theologians and philosophers – mostly Protestant – who, in the course of the eighteenth and nineteenth centuries, succumbed to a subjectivism which Catholic theologians were more prone to reject. The turn from the nineteenth to the twentieth century marks a change. The work of students of religion like Robert Ranulph Marett, Nathan Söderblom, Wilhelm Schmidt, and Rudolf Otto is in virtual, though not always conscious, agreement with modern philosophical tendencies toward 'objectivism'. The antipsychologism of the Austrian and German phenomenological school (Franz Brentano, Alexis Meinong, Edmund Husserl) is shared by the philosophy of religion developed by thinkers like Romano Guardini, Max Scheler, Jacques Maritain, and others.[9] The experience of that which Otto has so finely characterized as the 'mysterium tremendum et fascinosum' will ultimately defy any attempt to describe, analyze, and comprehend its meaning scientifically. Religious creative energy is inexhaustible, ever aiming at new and fuller realization. Religious experience does not readily yield to overt and unambiguous expression; yet, on the other hand, only through the forms which this experience gives itself will it be possible adequately to trace and understand its character. All who have attempted to analyze subjective religion were confronted by this 'vicious circle',[10] where understanding of inner experience comes only through interpreting its objective expression; but an adequate interpretation itself is dependent on a prior insight into the inner experience.

The basic, genuine experience which we call 'religious' tends to express or objectify itself in various ways.[11] We need a phenomenology of the expression of religious experience, a 'grammar' of religious language, based on a comprehensive empirical, phenomenological, and comparative study.[12] Philosophers have long seen this need. In conjunction with his grandiose phenomenology of the mind, Hegel has analyzed successive stages of objectification.[13] He included all conceivable activities of man in this scale but very wisely discriminated between the objective and the absolute mind, indicating that, on the level of the absolute mind, a more adequate correspondence prevails between the experience and its expression than in the sphere of antithesis, the 'objective mind.' Religion is regarded by Hegel as an aspect of the absolute mind. Following modern attempts at an adaptation and reinterpretation of Hegel's intuition, we would suggest that all products of the cultural activity of man such as technical achievements, economic systems, works of art, laws, and systems of thought be regarded as objective systems of culture as distinguished from all 'organization of society' such as marriage, friendships, kin groups, associations, and the state. The former are, as objective systems of culture, only indirectly the concern of the sociologist. The expression of religious experience we can include under the first heading only with hesitation, realizing full well that the core and substance of this experience defies adequate objectification. That makes its interpretation often more a perplexing than an enlightening task. A religious doctrine, a prayer, or a rite is less 'objectified' than a law or a product of industry. It is obvious that both the study of the interrelation between the economic, artistic, or legal 'forms' of a given group and its religious forms and the examination of social groupings and their correlation with religious developments are fraught with difficulties. Following Hegel, Dilthey[14] clearly demonstrated the interrelationship existing among the various objective systems of culture such as law, art, science, and – according to him – religion and the corresponding organizations of society such as tribes, states, nations, and churches, thus obviating the metaphysical construction of Hegel and of Lazarus and Steinthal's 'folk psychology' (*Völkerpsychologie*).[15] Yet Dilthey, too, was overprone to conceive unreservedly of religion as one of the systems of the objective mind. Baillie, who has given us in English[16] a fair appreciation of the tenor of Dilthey's *Philosophie der Geistswissenschaften*, errs with the latter in also conceiving of religion as merely one more form of cultural expression.

We agree with another philosopher of religion, D. M. Edwards, who contends that the 'holy' is not so much a fourth value to be added to the Good, the True, and the Beautiful as it is 'the matrix from which they are derived, their common form and origin'. Figuratively speaking, religion is not a branch but the trunk of the tree. Therefore, the analysis of any given culture entails not only the search for theologoumena, myths, or rites as a means of deciphering the religious attitude but also a process of sensing and exploring the very atmosphere and a careful study of the general attitudes revealed in the integral expression of its life. It is gratifying to note that modern anthropology strongly emphasizes the functional interrelation of the different activities and factors within cultural units.[17]

Still another problem requiring examination is that of spontaneity and tradition in the expression of religious experience. We have learned that even primitive man's participation in social life is a process of give and take. He takes over what was handed down to him but not without actively participating in the modification and transformation of inherited concepts and institutions ('patterns').[18] Recent studies in the religion of primitive peoples have demonstrated great variability even within one ethnic or geographic unit. A good example is Benedict's exceptionally revealing and brilliant monograph on *The Concept of the Guardian Spirit in North America*.[19] In reviewing the different forms of this concept in the various cultural areas of America, Benedict clearly illustrates, on one hand, the great extent of variability ranging from the passive acceptance of tradition to its creative transformation,[20] and, on the other, the 'enormous conventionalization' of expression even on this level of civilization. Thus it has been demonstrated that there is traceable through the whole history of worship an exceedingly intricate interplay between individual experience in religion and the various forms of traditional expression,[21] all of which is an essential part of the dynamics of religion.

ON COMPARATIVE STUDIES IN RELIGION

[. . .] The foundation upon which a fruitful comparative study of religions rests must always be historical and philological, or, in other words, *critical* studies. I think that the work of Rudolf Otto is characteristic of the third period of the comparative study of religions.[22] It lays powerful stress upon the objective character of ultimate reality and thus refutes all subjective and illusionist theories of religion. Von Hügel[23] and Webb[24] have shown a similar concern. By stressing the non-rational element in religion without neglecting the value of rational investigation, an exaggerated intellectualism and scholasticism are excluded. Although it may destroy a similarity, that which is dissimilar, specific, and individual is not overlooked. This rules out any superficial identification and parallelism on the part of the historians of religions.

There has been much international cooperation among scholars of Europe, Asia, and America throughout each of the three periods we have sketched. The historical surveys of the development of comparative studies in religion by Jordan, Lehmann, Pinard de la Boullaye, and more recently by Puech, Mensching, Widengren, and Masson-Oursel show the extent of this exchange.[25] Asian scholars have increasingly participated in this work and the names of Moslem, Hindu, Chinese, and Japanese scholars deserve special mention along with those of smaller nations (Burma, Siam, Philippines, the Arab States, Pakistan, Indonesia). Moreover, Western students have begun to show increased realization of the need for help from those who grew up in another religious tradition in order to do full justice to the *meaning* of the phenomena to be investigated. In the era of positivism a sovereign disregard for and suspicion of the 'native' commentaries was not infrequent. Only Western critical techniques could be admitted. There can be no doubt that the eagerness with which the techniques of Western critical studies have been appropriated by Eastern scholars promises highly significant contributions from them in our field.

This exchange has been fostered during the past fifty years by a number of International Congresses of the History of Religions. It cannot be denied, however, that political circumstances and the effect of two great wars have made it more difficult to maintain the standard which the earlier meetings had set in terms of universality and significance of the topics discussed. Since the end of the initial phase in which contact was established between scholars of different nations and faiths, it has become ever more manifest that the vague syncretism characterizing some of the gatherings of those of different faiths around the turn of the last century cannot fulfill the demands of the newly awakened religious consciousness nor stand the scrutiny of a strong constructive philosophical interest. Herein lies the danger. As both Christian and non-Christian religions reassert their convictions it becomes increasingly difficult to safeguard the positive results of the age of liberalism[26] in terms of scholarship and knowledge. The newly won freedom has to be guarded against any form of tyrannical authority; this was the dominant concern of the second period in our studies sketched above. But on the other hand, skepticism, relativism, and historicism have to be prevented.[27] This means that the problem of the relation of authority and freedom in religion has become of vital importance. The author of a recent survey of religion in twentieth-century America reminds us that 'the reconciliation of the spirit of freedom with the spirit of religious devotoin or commitment has become a serious problem of public morality.'[28]

We spoke of certain basic methodological and epistemological problems which have to be raised and answered in this era of comparative studies. During the preceding period some of these questions were considered unanswerable and taboo, since raising them would have led to discussion and strife. But in this day and age there is no avoiding the challenge which the pluralism of religious loyalties and its relationship to the problem of truth poses for individuals, groups, and governments. As long as detachment was regarded as the highest virtue and commitment was looked on with suspicion, there was no great occasion for disagreement. There were no minorities to be protected and tolerance was no issue, inasmuch as the frequent presence of indifference made such 'tolerance' possible at no high cost. To me there is something pathetic about the modern historian of religion who uses strong words only when he wants to convince us that he has no convictions.[29] His interest, so he says, is antiquarian or the result of sheer intellectual curiosity. He is 'neutral' as far as religion is concerned. Nietzsche vehemently attacked this attitude in *Vom Nutzen und Nachteil der Historie für das Leben*. Ernst Troeltsch has characterized an 'unlimited relativism' by stating that a weakly constituted natural history has become identified with empathy *(Nachfühlung)* for all other characters together with a relinquishing of empathy for oneself, with skepticism and playful intellectuality, or with oversophistication *(Blasiertheit)* and a lack of faith.[30] It could be asked if an open hostility is not more appropriate to the subject of religion than this non-committal attitude.

All this is not to say that the ideal of objectivity should be abandoned by those engaged in comparative studies. It is rather to assert that it must be rightly understood. I have elsewhere indicated that 'relative' objectivity is a necessary ideal in ascertaining the 'given', the data, the meaning of which concerns us.[32] All philological and historical research must be determined by this ideal. Until recently no one in the East would have been interested in studying religion as some of the 'scientifically' minded Westerners try to deal with it. Though the word was not known, an existential concern motivated those who were engaged in this work. Now the scientific idea has conquered the Near East as well as India, China, and Japan. The West had to relearn from Kierkegaard that religion is something toward which 'neutrality' is not possible. It is true that dangers accompany the appeal to emotions and the arousing of passions. Yet emotions and passions *do* play a legitimate role in religion. It is precisely here that the *raison d'être*, the best justification, for the comparative study of religions can and must be found. It is an error to believe that comparative studies must breed indifference. They contribute toward the gaining of perspective, as well as of discernment und understanding.

If it is the task of theology to investigate, buttress, and teach the faith of a religious community to which it is committed, as well as to kindlə zeal and fervor for the defense and spread of this faith, it is the responsibility of a comparative study to guide and to purify it. How can that be brought about? That which I value and cherish and hold dear beyond all else, I also want thoroughly to understand in all its implications. It is true that to love truth you must hate untruth, but it is not true that in order to exalt your own faith you must hate and denigrate those of another faith.[32] A comparative study of religions such as the new era made possible enables us to have a fuller vision of what religious experience can mean, what forms its expression may take, and what it might do for man. It could be argued that this would mean the subjection of one's religious faith to a judgment pronounced in the name of some generalized notions. But does a ruby or an emerald sparkle less if called a jewel? Not only different religious communities but groups within them develop certain emphases and neglect other aspects.

Next to reorientation to the primary norm of religious experience, what better way to understand religions is there than to study the notions and practices of others?

But can you understand a religion other than your own?[33] This question must be analyzed. There seems to be a sense in which the answer would have to be 'No', and yet there are indications that in some sense a positive reply is possible. Undoubtedly it is possible to 'know the facts' in the sense of gathering and organizing all the available information. As we have seen, that was and is the task of our field according to the positivistically minded scholar. Yet, is that enough?[34] Is it not necessary to be a member of a religious community to understand its religious notions and customs? But what does it mean to be a 'member'? Could it be seriously maintained that a great scholar belonging to Group A would be less capable of understanding the religion of Group B than any ignorant and humble person belonging to the latter? Obviously official membership cannot be the criterion for the possibility of understanding. Could not one conceivably participate in the ritual performance of a cultic group, for example, and yet be unaware of the meaning of that which is said and done? Does that in turn signify that even a commitment would not be sufficient in itself, since such could also exist in the case of an ignorant and humble member? And how about the alert skeptic who may be nearer a 'conversion' than he or anyone else may know? In all tribal religion the question of membership is a relatively simple one: it is conferred by birth and birth only, though there may be qualifications such as the fulfillment of duties, and so on. It is more complicated in specifically religious communities. Among these there are usually objective criteria of membership – *notae ecclesiae* – but the fideists, mystics, and spiritualists usually insist on additional and often subjective standards. An inner attitude alone can qualify one as a 'true' member. It goes without saying that in the latter case it would be more difficult to indicate what 'full understanding' would entail than in the former case where participation is regulated in a more automatic or mechanical sense.

There are definite stages of understanding. One stage would be partial, another integral, comprehension. Thus it is conceivable that we could do justice to a particular religious thought or act without being able to grasp others appearing in the same context or to grasp this context as a whole. Religious communities recognize this by stratifying their religious groups, especially those with an esoteric character such as mystery societies in which different grades correspond to varying degrees of 'comprehension.' In this problem of religious understanding there is also the law of irreversibility, according to which it is possible for the higher to comprehend the lower and the older (master) to perceive what is going on in the younger (disciple) but not vice versa. That brings us to the discussion of the conditions that must prevail if an integral understanding is to be achieved.

Let us turn first to the necessary equipment. We have seen previously that it will in part be of an intellectual nature. There is no hope of understanding a religion or a religious phenomenon without the most extensive information possible. We owe a great debt of gratitude to the painstaking work of the past one hundred and fifty years which has so increased the depth and degree of our knowledge of other religions. The most comprehensive survey of this development has been given by the French Jesuit scholar, Pinard de la Boullaye, in the first volume of his *Étude comparée des religions* (1922).[35] The student of religions is never well enough equipped linguistically. It is now desirable to know many languages and families of languages which were barely known by name fifty years ago. This is especially true with regard to the ancient Near East, Africa, Central Asia, and South America. Yet we agree with Webb when he says: 'I do not indeed suppose that it is necessary, in order to enter into the spirit of a religion, that one should be able to read its scriptures and its doctrines in their languages. A man may be a very good Christian without Greek or Hebrew, and a very bad Christian with both.'[36] It may not be necessary, but the chances of an adequate understanding are infinitely better where the interpreter is in a position to at least check on the translation of key terms, if he is not actually competent to read the foreign tongue. Yet this competence in and by itself does not guarantee positive results in the study of religion.

Secondly, a successful venture in understanding a religion different from our own requires an adequate emotional condition. What is required is not indifference, as positivism in its heyday believed – 'Grey cold eyes do not know the value of things', objected Nietzsche – but rather an engagement of feeling, interest, *metexis*, or participation.[37] This is not an endorsement of the widespread notion that religion as such is an exclusively emotional affair (a notion held by Schleiermacher and Otto). As we shall see in greater detail, religion is a concern of the total person, engaging intellect, emotion, and will.

The realms of the human personality and human values are often invaded by a scientism which insists upon only one method of knowing and one type of knowledge. One of the weightiest arguments for those who want to preserve the human personality and its values against the imperatives of science is the demonstration that any form of reduction falls short of the aim of a student of religion, which is to do justice to that religion's true nature.

A third form of equipment, the equipment of volition, is therefore required for anyone who wishes to deal adequately with the religion of his fellow man. The will must be directed and oriented toward a constructive purpose. Neither idle curiosity nor a passion for annihilating whatever differs from one's own position is an appropriate motive for this task. Ignorance, uncontrolled passion, and lack of direction are enemies of that state of mind which alone promises success in the venture of understanding. There will never be a lack of those differences (difference in temperament is one example) which make it difficult even for the student of broad concerns and deep sympathies to comprehend various kinds of religiosity, types of religious thought, or devotional practices which differ sharply from his own.

But there is still something else that is essential equipment for the study of religion, and that is experience.[38] We use this term here in a wide sense, leaving the analysis of the nature of religious experience for the next chapter. We should like to define experience in the broadest sense, thus opposing all narrow concepts which separate and even isolate it as a province of life into which only the specialized professional can enter. In all likelihood there is no contact with any aspect of life which would not bear upon the problem of understanding another's religion. As the psychologists and sociologists of religion have told us, there are not only different religious temperaments (beginning with William James's 'healthy-minded' and 'sick-minded') but also different types of religious institutions.[39] Whoever has had wide experience with human character possesses one more qualification for understanding an alien religion, for such a person has thereby contacted the minds of people in the variety of their acting, feeling, and ways of thinking. It is important for one to realize that there are different ways to be 'religious', to know and to worship God; for in the area of expression between man and man even the narrowest religious fellow-

ships show differences.[40] The group as well as the individual will be religious
in its own way. We are not talking here about 'heresies' but about the legitimate range of psychological and sociological differences. This is not an
endorsement of pluralism or relativism. Even if one holds fast to the belief
that truth is one it is possible to concede that there are 'many mansions'
in our Father's house.

After dwelling upon the nature and the task of comparative studies
in religion, we can now discuss the method to be followed. Much controversy
has been carried on in the last decade between two schools of thought.
One has insisted that the method of religious studies is totally *sui generis*
and in no way comparable or related to methods in other fields of knowledge. The other school has maintained that, irrespective of the character
of the subject matter to be investigated, the only legitimate method is
the so-called 'scientific' method. The term scientific is used here in a double
sense: in the narrower sense it denotes the method used in the so-called
natural sciences, and in the wider sense it refers to any procedure which
works with logical and coherent discipline from clearly indicated premises.
Both these approaches have been found wanting; in the present era of the
comparative study of religions a new synthesis is being worked out. Beginning with the second school of thought, we see that there is good reason
to oppose an unqualified pluralism or even a dualism in matters of method
and of knowledge. Truth is one; the cosmos is one; hence knowledge also
must be one. This insight is all important. Although we will not agree
with the positivistic interpretation of this principle, we must incorporate
it into our methodology, which will be based on a dual demand. The first
demand is that the method be unified. Such is the imperative of Aristotle,
Aquinas, Leibniz, and Whitehead. All idealism and all naturalism – including materialism – stand or fall with methodological monism. Yet to conceive
of one truth is one thing and to possess or comprehend it is another. We
should be realistic enough to see the profound wisdom in the apostle's
words that here we know only in part, which is to say that only God himself can be aware of the whole. The second demand is that the method
be adequate for the subject matter. This qualifies the first principle, that
of a unified method.

Many theological and philosophical writers in the first half of this century
have demonstrated the insufficiency of the narrowly defined scientific
approach to the study of religion. Many distinguished scientists have
questioned the applicability of the methods and techniques of experimental,
quantitative, causal investigation to the world of the spirit. The philosophical vindication of the freedom of the spirit was ably pursued by Bergson,
Dilthey, Balfour, Von Hügel, Troeltsch, Husserl, Scheler, Temple, Otto,
Jung, Baillie, Berdyaev, and others. In order that the method be adequate

for the subject matter, the phenomenon of individuality, the nature of value, and the meaning of freedom must be recognized. It has been rightly said that the whole realm of the personal, with which the religious quest is so indissolubly connected, must remain closed to the investigator who does not make concession to his method[42] as required by the nature of the subject matter.[42]

A positivistic age could cherish the notion of a universally applicable technique of inquiry. Religion was to be studied exactly as any phenomenon of the inorganic or organic world. With the above-mentioned qualification that the method must fit the subject matter, the new era has shown a growing demand for a metaphysical concept which would do justice to the nature of phenomena of the spiritual as well as of the physical world. [...]

'UNIVERSALS IN RELIGION'

The careful research of many a generation of scholars, the travel reports, not only of adventurers, missionaries and explorers, but of many a person you and I count among our personal acquaintances, have brought home to wellnigh all of us a realization of the variety of religious ideas and practices that exist in the world. The result of this realization has been bewilderment and confusion in many hearts and minds. Roughly three different types of reaction to the situation can be discerned: 1) scepticism, that is, the refusal to see in all these religious ideas and usages more than the expression of ignorance and folly, in other words a cultural and/or religious 'lag;' 2) relativism, that is, a disposition to dispense with the problem of truth in favour of a non-committal registration of all there is and has been, an attitude which has found much favour in the latter-day circles of scholars and intellectuals; and finally 3) the desire to investigate the variety of what goes under the names of religion and religions in order to determine by comparison and phenomenological analysis if anything like a structure can be discovered in all these forms of expression, to what kind of experiences this variegated expression can be traced, and finally, what kind of reality or realities may correspond to the experiences in question. It is the last of the three types of reaction to the predicament characterized above which seems to us the only promising and fruitful one, and we propose to follow it in what we have to say here.

The first difficulty we encounter in trying to bring some order into the bewildering mass of material that geography, anthropology, sociology, archaeology, philology, history, and the history of religions have placed at our disposal, is the need for criteria which would enable us to distinguish between what is religious and what is not. Now you will not expect me to discuss the wellnigh endless series of definitions of religion which have been proposed by the great and the not-so-great during recent decades. We shall also find it impossible to use as our yardstick one of the classical historical formulations evolved in one of the great religious communities itself, say in the Christian. For we should soon discover that it is not possible to identify religion with what we have come to know as Christian or Jewish or Hindu, even if we forget for the moment that it would be far from easy to agree on which of the available formulations we want to use. Some of us might feel, at first thought, that it is after all not so difficult to determine what may be called religious and what is not religious; they would point to the neat divisions which we are accustomed to find in our textbooks, dealing with the lives of individuals, societies and cultures, past and present, in which separate chapters deal with man's political views and activities, his economic situation, his interest in the arts, and his religious orientation, or with the social organization, the economics, the legal institutions, the arts and sciences, the moral life, and the religion of a given tribe, people or nation. But, on second thoughts, the unsatisfactory character of such parcelling becomes evident; and that not only in the repetitions and omissions which this procedure entails. No wonder then that some investigators – and we find among them distinguished anthropologists, philosophers, and theologians – have come to the conclusion that religion is not anything distinct and *sui generis*, but is a name given to the sum of man's aspirations, to the whole of the civilization of a people. If we reject this view, it is not because we want to separate sharply between religion on the one hand and on the other all that makes up an individual's or a society's other experiences and activities. But we are of the opinion that, in order to be able to assess the interrelation and interpenetration of the various interests, attitudes, and activities of man, we have to examine very carefully the nature of his propensities, drives, impulses, actions, and reactions. William James has rightly said: 'The essence of religious experiences, the thing by which we must finally judge them, must be that element or quality in them which we can meet nowhere else.[43] We disagree with those who are prone to identify religion with just one segment of man's inner existence: feeling, willing, or cogitating. In order to lay down our criteria, we cannot be satisfied to examine only the conceptually articulated perceptions or only the emotions and affections and the respective expressions in which they have become manifest. We propose rather the following *four formal criteria* for a definition of what might be called religious experience:

1. Religious experience is a response to what is experienced as ultimate reality; that is, in religious experiences we react not to any single or finite

phenomenon, material or otherwise, but to what we realize as undergirding and conditioning all that constitutes our world of experiences. We agree with Paul Tillich when he says that 'the presence of the demand of "ultimacy" in the structure of our existence is the basis of religious experience'.[44] Before him William James said in his book on the *Varieties of Religious Experience*[45] – a passage quoted in Paul Johnson's *Psychology of Religion*[46]: 'It is as if there were in the human consciousness a sense of reality, a feeling of objective presence, a perception of what we may call "something there", more deep and more general than any of the special and particular "senses" by which the current psychology supposes existent realities to be originally revealed,'[47] Or as the author of a recent text-book on Psychology of Religion formulates it:[48] 'Religious experience is response to stimuli that represent an active reality viewed as divine, or as creative of values.'

This response has the tendency to persist, once communion with the source of life and values is established, and man is restless to reassure himself of its continuance.

2. Religious experience is a total response of the total being to what is apprehended as ultimate reality. That is, we are involved not exclusively with our mind, our affections, or our will, but as integral persons.[49]

3. Religious experience is the most intense experience of which man is capable. That is not to say that all expression of religious experience testifies to this intensity but that, potentially, genuine religious experience is of this nature, as is instanced in conflicts between different basic drives or motivations. Religious loyalty, if it is religious loyalty, wins over all other loyalties. The modern term 'existential' designates the profound concern and the utter seriousness of this experience.

4. Religious experience is practical, that is to say it involves an imperative, a commitment which impels man to act. This activistic note distinguishes it from aesthetic experience, of which it shares the intensity, and joins it with moral experience. Moral judgment, however, does not necessarily represent a reaction to ultimate reality.

It should be borne in mind that one, two, or three of these criteria would not suffice to reassure us that we are dealing with genuine religious experience. All four would have to be present. If they are, we should have no difficulty in distinguishing between religious and non-religious experiences. However, there are *pseudo-religious* and *semi-religious* experiences. The former are non-religious and known to be such to the person or persons who pretend to them by using forms of expression peculiar to religion. The latter may show the presence of the second, third and fourth characteristics, but refer not to ultimate but to some aspect of 'finite' reality. The intense and possibly sacrificial devotion with which somebody may 'worship' a loved person, his race, his social group, or his state are instances of semi-religious loyalties. Because they are directed toward finite values, they are idolatrous rather than religious.

Now it is our contention, and this is the first proposition in regard to our topic, that religious experience, as we have just attempted to define it by means of these four criteria, is *universal*. The empirical proof of this statement can be found in the testimonies of explorers and investigators. 'There are no peoples, however primitive, without religion and magic,' is the opening sentence of one of Malinowski's well-known essays[50]. In practically all cases where a rash negative conclusion has been reached, more careful research has corrected the initial error.

A *second* proposition is this: religious experience tends towards *expression*. This tendency is universal. Only in and through its expression does any of our experiences exist for others, does any religious experience exist for us, the students of the history of religion. The religious experience of another person can never become the object of direct observation. Some important hermeneutical consequences result from the recognition of this fact.

Now for the *third* step in our search for universals in religion. A comparative study of the *forms* of the expression of religious experience, the world over, shows an amazing similarity in structure. We should like to summarize the result of such comparative studies by the statement: all expression of religious experience falls under the three headings of *theoretical expression*, *practical expression*, and *sociological expression*.[51] Everywhere and at all times man has felt the need to articulate his religious experience in three ways: conceptually; by action, or practically; and in covenanting, or sociologically. There is no religion deserving of the name in which any one of these three elements is totally lacking, though the degree and, of course, the tempo of this development may vary. Notwithstanding numerous attempts at establishing priority for one of these three modes of expression, we feel that it would be futile to argue that myth precedes cult or that both precede fellowship: history teaches us that the dynamics of religious life is made up of the interpenetration of these three aspects.

Before we can discuss in any greater detail the structure of these fields of expression of religious experience and the common elements to be found within an apparently endless variety of forms, we have to consider briefly some general factors which help to determine their development. Man finds himself always situationally conditioned: whatever he experiences, he experiences in *time* and *space*. Even if, in his religious experience, he seems to transcend these limitations – a feeling to which the mystics of all religions have given vivid and often paradoxical articulation (Eckhart: 'Time is what keeps the light from reaching us. There is no greater obstacle to God than Time'[52]) – he cannot but give expression to what he has seen, felt, etc., *per analogiam entis*, by means of *analogy* from what is known and familiar to him.[53] The way of negation, of analogy and of eminence is used in all religious language. That we have to remember when we review the concepts of sacred time and of sacred space which are the framework within which religious thought and religious acts enfold themselves. Holy times and holy places are universal notions; no myth or doctrine, no cult or religious association is found without them.[54] Closely related to these categories within which religious apprehension expresses itself is the notion of a *cosmic* (that is natural, ritual and social) *order* upon which life, individual and collective, depends. The well-known Chinese concept of *Tao*, the Hindu *ṛta*, the Iranian *asha*, the Greek *dike*, designate the order upon which man and society depend for their existence.[55] In the religions of the American Indians, the Africans and Oceanians, the directions, the seasons, the celestial bodies, colours, social organization, all follow this orientation, the cosmic law which the physical, mental and spiritual life of all beings has to obey.[56] Nature and its rhythm, culture and its activities, and polity and its structure are but aspects of this order. It is the foundation for all 'ethics'.

Religious experience, we saw, may be characterized as the total response of man's total being to what he experiences as ultimate reality. In it he confronts a *power* greater than any power which he controls by his own wit or strength. I should like to stress *two* points here. This encounter is not a question of intellectual inference or speculative reasoning, of which there are few traces in many of the lower so-called primitive religions.[57] That is to say, religion is emphatically not a kind of underdeveloped 'science' or 'philosophy'. This misinterpretation, still widely current, is an unfortunate legacy from the rationalistically-minded era of the Enlightenment. The experience which we call religion is rather an awareness of apprehension, not lacking a cognitive aspect but not defined by it, a reaction to something that is sensed or apprehended as powerful. Rudolf Otto has spoken of a *sensus numinis* (sense of awe),[58] and this term seems to me a very apt designation. We must reject all theories of religion which conceive of it as the fulfilment which imaginative, or crafty individuals have supplied for a subjective, that is illusory, need. True, many a testimony to religious experience lets the latter appear as the result of a search, a struggle, but more often this experience has come as a bolt from the blue, with a spontaneity which contradicts the theory of need. Hence we prefer to say that there is a propensity, a *nisus* or *sensus numinis* which is activated in the religious experience proper.[59] The aspect of power which the comparative study of religion has recently vindicated as a central notion in the religions of widely different peoples and societies, indicates the 'point of contact' between the reality which is confronted in religious experience and life in the everyday world: the 'immanence of the transcendent'. Religions differ in their notions as to the how, where, and when of the manifestations of power in the phenomenal world. But the acknowledgment that this power manifests itself in experienceable form is universal. To the degree that it appears diffused, we speak of *power-centres* such as are known in all primitive, higher and fully developed cults.[60] The Swedish historian of religion, Martin Nilsson, has recently[61] stressed the adjective character of terms for power such as *mana*, *orenda*, etc. Not the phenomenon, object or person in which this power manifests itself, but a power that *transcends* it, is the object of man's awe. It is of great importance to understand that this power is apprehended as an elementary force which transcends moral or aesthetic qualifications. As such it is 'mysterious'. It was one of the great insights of the author of the *Idea of the Holy*, Rudolf Otto, that he caught the double notion of the *mysterium magnum* in the twin ideas of its terrifying and its alluring aspect. These *two aspects* are known to the theologians of all religions as Divine Wrath and Divine Love or Grace. Though their natural roles and relationships are differently conceived in different faiths, these two aspects of power are universally recognized. But we can still go one step further in our analysis of universal features in religious experience. It is possible to discern a double consequence of man's apprehension of numinous power at all times and every-where: he either bows to it in submission, or he reaches out in an attempt to manipulate and control the mysterious forces of which he has become aware. The first, the *religious* way, leads up to the highest religious act, that of adoration; the second, the way of *magic*, sets him on the road to conquer and to appropriate as much of the power as will yield to his command. These two developments are not to be thought of in terms of a chronological and evolutionary sequence: on the one hand the magical is always with us, and on the other the presence of genuinely religious response to the numinous even in the primitive cults cannot be denied. Hence both are universal. It is only the *intention* inherent in it which distinguishes the religious from the magical act. The very complicated question of the origins, the nature of the development of 'science' (in the broader as well as the narrower sense of the natural sciences), and of its relation to both magic and religion, can be answered when we are more fully conversant with the nature of knowledge,[62] with the psychological motivations for wanting to know.[63]

Perhaps the sociology of knowledge will help us at some time in the future. On the cognitive factor in the experience which we call religious we shall have a word to say presently.

After these brief remarks, which were meant to put in relief some universally valid features of religious *experience*, we will now turn to the examination of universals in the forms of *expression* of this experience.[64] We have said that the very fact that this experience tends to expression constitutes in itself a universal. We shall enlarge this statement now by asking: What *motivates* expression? There is first what I should like to call the demonstrative type of expression with which we are familiar from all kinds of experiences other than religious. The shout of joy or pain, witnessing to a profound emotion, is paralleled by the ejaculatory expression of awe or devotion. Then there is the communicative motif: we like to share our experiences with others, and we can do so only by means of sounds, words or acts. Finally the missionary purpose has to be considered. We want to attract others, a purpose not alien to other types of experience, but constitutive of the religious. Finding these motives making for expression universally valid, we may ask further: What of the *modes* in which the expression of religious experience is cast?

[. . .]

'THE CONCEPT OF THE "CLASSICAL" IN THE STUDY OF RELIGIONS'

The wider the orbit of phenomena which is of interest to the historian of religions becomes, the more necessary it will be to find principles of order, articulation and appreciation which allow for an organization of the well-nigh infinite amount of material unearthed by comparative studies during the nineteenth and twentieth centuries. It goes without saying that there can be, for the scholar, nothing that is actually unworthy of investigation; hence the history of religions has to include in its range of interest and to investigate all that can be called religious. Neither antipathy to nor indifference towards individual expressions, or towards certain temporal or regional forms, should prevent the investigator from letting his sun shine on the just and the unjust. This condition is much more difficult to fulfill to-day than it used to be in former times. Then the theologian, who had to see in his own religion the point of reference and the standard for his work, could be satisfied with adducing for purposes of comparison and elucidation the religions which were related in time and space to the world of the Old and the New Testaments. He could do so with a good conscience until, towards the close of the nineteenth and even more since the beginning of the twentieth century, the rapidly progressing studies of the civilizations of the so-called primitive, and of those of many remote middle and higher, peoples began to confront him with an impossible task. Some of the theologians of the *religionsgeschichtliche Schule* reacted to this situation by picking 'parallels' arbitrarily from all available primitive or higher cults, thus turning their commentaries on the books of the Old and New Testaments into something like counterparts of the well-stocked but not equally well-organized ethnological museums. The student of religions, however, who was not orientated by specifically theological concerns, could not but search for systematic principles which would permit him to bring some order into the wealth of new material. For a while the philosophical thought of classical German idealism (Schelling, Hegel) served the purpose. Schemes of development were constructed which followed this pattern, though eventually in a rather epigonal fashion. In accordance with these schemes a process of the gradual self-realization of the Universal Mind or of an even more perfect unfolding of Ethical Consciousness was envisaged, and therefore not infrequently the summit of their development was conceived of in terms of the period and region of which the investigation was a part. One of the last great efforts in this direction is represented by the 'Völkerpsychologie' of Wilhelm Wundt. But to-day we no longer believe in such one-track schemes of development, nor do we deem it possible to subsume the variety of religious expressions of all times under any one of them. It is significant that in the more recent systematic presentations, Rudolf Otto's *The Idea of the Holy,* Gerardus van der Leeuw's *Religion in Essence and Manifestation,* and Mircea Eliade's *Traité d'histoire des religions,* these schemes have been abandoned, and the material has been organized according to a structural order of the elements of historical religion. This indicates progress, though the last word on method and procedure in our field has not been said. In the study of religions we shall have to avoid both extremes, that of historicism and that of making a short cut by uncritically taking as absolute any particular theological or philosophical standpoint. Which then shall be the viewpoints guiding description, selection and presentation? We have said already that in research everything counts, however small the percentage of facts may be which would be of actual interest to the theologian or systematic thinker. Some apparently quite remote instance may prove important. So certain phenomena occurring in the context of a primitive religion geographically far removed from Asia might afford us a better insight into the nature of certain types of men of God in the Old Testament than others geographically more closely related. Neither the Old nor the New Testament scholar will ever be in a position to disregard the results of the labours of the *religionsgeschichtliche Schule.*

Now even if it be true that everything which is expressive of religious experience is worth knowing and in some degree important, criteria are desirable for the selection of sources and their appraisal, and not only for the actual presentation of the results of the work of the interpreter. The quantitative principle is represented as a regulative norm; the so-called world-religions are more important than less widely spread cults simply because they command a larger number of followers. This fact may justify a more thorough preoccupation with their history and a more intensive investigation of their beliefs. The religions of nations which have played a larger role in the history of the world seem to deserve more careful study than those of less active peoples. But this criterion, which may suffice from a purely historical point of view, is unsatisfactory in other respects. For secular history Eduard Meyer, the great student of ancient civilizations, suggested the criterion of *efficacy (Wirkung)* as norm; but the historian of religions cannot assent to this viewpoint. For him a movement, an institution or a custom, a doctrine or a cult will not be important, nor even primary, because it was or is widespread, but because it represents a *specific, a characteristic* form of devotion *(Frömmigkeit)*. Mohammed, Zoroaster, Mani, the Buddha, and the Jina, though all 'founders' of religions, are personalities very different in character and attitude. They stand each for a definite religious idea which, as it were, they embody. The historian of religions is concerned with the characteristic element in personal religion, in doctrine, worship and fellowship. But his desire is to do justice to the individual and historical as well as to the typical in such concepts as that of salvation, in such rites as that of sacrifice, in such institutions as that of the priesthood. Yet even the notion of the characteristic, much used and stressed by the German theologian Herder, one of the founders of the comparative study of religion, is not quite sufficient; it is too historically conditioned to serve as the principle of organization and articulation. Take the concept of *mana* which is characteristic of all American Indian religions, that of *orenda* which distinguishes the Iroquois, that of *wakanda* which is the Sioux version of this notion. It would be impossible – and unnecessary – to examine all the forms under which this concept can be found here or there (among Primitives generally, among American Indians, Africans, Australians, etc.). Or to chose another example: a characteristic feature of Mahāyāna Buddhism is the belief in Bodhisattvas. Their number is very great. Yet our knowledge of and insight into their nature does not necessarily grow proportionately as each new variant is added. There is always, to be sure, the chance that one of them may help us to perceive or identify some special feature heretofore not known or insufficiently appreciated, but this does not have to be an absolute novelty, however characteristic this feature might be of the individual figure. Chance ought not to determine which phenomena should be adduced to elucidate aspects of our own religion or to figure in a general phenomenology of religions as representative.

We believe that the notion of the *classical* can be helpful here. It may serve the historian of religions well if he will use it with discretion. In distinction from the concept of the characteristic, which is descriptive, the category of the classical is normative. Yet it is, if we may put it paradoxically, *a relative norm* which does not need to do violence to heterogeneous phenomena from a preconceived point of view. There are, to give examples, among the religious leaders of mankind certain figures who stand out as classical founders; of the deities of vegetation known to us from various regions of ancient Western Asia, we can single out some as 'classical' re presentatives; the seemingly infinite number of mystics of all times and places is reduced by choosing 'classical' figures. There are classical forms of the institution of priesthood and classical patterns of sacrifice and prayer.

What do we mean by 'classical' in all these cases? Negatively, we do not mean those out of a multitude of phenomena which merely happen to be familiar to us, those which show a close resemblance to familiar things, or those which attract our attention first. The phenomena which we designate as classical represent something typical; they convey with regard to religious life and experience more than would be conveyed by an individual instance. We may consider Meister Eckhart, Al Ghazzali, and Shankara as classical mystics because something typically mystical is to be found in their devotion and teaching. However, the notion of the classical does not denote only the representative character which inheres in a phenomenon, but also implies a norm. Out of the multitude of historical personalities, movements and events, thoughts and deeds, some are chosen because we deem it possible to ascribe to them potentially an illuminating, edifying, paradigmatic effect by which they may influence our own religious life. This statement should be taken in a wide sense. It will be granted easily enough that the study of neighbouring fields, such as Gnosticism, Mystery religions, Rabbinic Judaism, or of some single feature of these cults, may yield a great deal of profit to the exegete of the New Testament. Thus a figure like Simon Magus, a rite such as baptism, or the preaching of Jesus with regard to the Sabbath regulations can be better understood in relation – even in contrast – to the aforementioned religious movements. It may seem at first glance that the expressions of Mohammedan, Persian, Hindu or Buddhist religiosity could not possibly offer much that would facilitate the work of Old and New Testament interpreters. Yet the potential significance of classical forms of alien religions quite generally speaking is very great, and it would be a grave error for the Christian theologian or philosopher or even the interested layman to neglect them. The layman has been singled out for mention in this connection with good reason, there being a notion abroad that the layman should be expected to be conversant with all foreign religions as with everything else that may be worth knowing. One of the most acute critics of the educational ideals of the nineteenth century, Nietzsche, attacked, in a rightly famous pamphlet on the advantages and disadvantages of historical knowledge for living, the indiscriminate amassing of information in service to a misconstrued ideal of education. The great danger of an *indiscriminate* appropriation of information regarding remote and exotic phenomena is its threat to our creative powers *(plastische Kraft)*. In the realm of religion this power has been greatly endangered throughout modern times, but especially in the nineteenth and twentieth centuries. To deal with the history of religions has come to mean for many, and not without reason, a limitless and hence hopeless relativism or scepticism. This conviction seems to justify the position into which we see those withdraw who believe that it is possible to revert to conditions as they prevailed before the 'fall', in other words to reject as superfluous and harmful all study of religions except that of one's own faith. Now the influence of which we spoke of foreign religions on our life, which has to be understood in a wide sense, has to be *filtered*. Not all and everything which we may come to know of facts, ideas, usages and institutions connected with alien faiths can or should be significant for and meaningful to us. We shall have in the study of religion, as in other disciplines, to stress the pedagogical viewpoint and to distinguish clearly between what may be *interesting* and what is *essential*. Every phenomenon is potentially interesting, and hence worthy of our attention, our study and our appreciation. Universality of comprehension will ever remain the ideal of this, as of all other scholarly disciplines. But the preservation and cultivation of the creative power, which is in danger of becoming paralysed as an effect of the increase in factual information which the historical age has brought, demands *concentration* upon the essential and the necessary.

We find ourselves to-day in the field of religious studies in a situation like that of the classical philologists who, under the impact of the immense widening of the horizon in the last century, at first ceased to regard as the *classical* the characteristically humanistic concept of the fifth century but are now reconsidering their position *(cf.* the *Lectures on the Problem of the Classical and Antiquity,* ed. W. Jaeger, 1931). We who have become acquainted with the manifold and variegated forms and figures of the non-Christian world have to develop a new feeling for the specific quality, the value and the significance of classical phenomena in the history of religions. The experience of satisfaction and elation at the successful inclusion of the figures of the world of the Old and New Testaments into the general history of religions, which in turn replaced the desire to defend their absolute value and uniqueness, is yielding to a new attitude in which acquaintance with the variety of historical expression of religious forms is blended with the desire to do justice to the classical among them.

[. . .]

'THE MEANING AND TASK OF THE HISTORY OF RELIGIONS
(*RELIGIONSWISSENSCHAFT*)'

On special occasions [...] a discipline has the right and the duty to look
about and to examine the correctness of its path, to ask about the well-
being of its method, and to ascertain what shall be the purpose of its task.
What is the meaning of *Religionswissenschaft*? There is an old traditional
discipline already concerned with religion, namely, theology. Why need
there be a *Religionswissenschaft* at its side? When this discipline took shape
during the nineteenth century in a very fascinating process of development,
there were many – and they still may be found now and then – who thought
that *Religionswissenschaft* was called to supplant theology. Recent *Religionswissenschaft*, insofar as it need be taken seriously, has definitely departed
from this error. At this point it is widely separated from the work of a meritorious scholar such as Ernst Troeltsch. Theology has its own task in identifying its own confessional norms, and none may take this task from it.
Theology is concerned with understanding and confirming its own faith.
Foreign religions, to a certain and not inconsequential degree, belong to its
realm of study; namely, as they exhibit close or distant relationships in
their respective histories or in their concerns. But this can never be the
reason for ascribing to theology the immense task of studying and describing the foreign religions in their manifold fulness. At the same time, the
development of religious studies tells us that the proposition 'he who knows
one religion knows all' is false. Thus, theology has every reason to show and
to cultivate a lively interest in the results of studying other religions. It
nevertheless leaves the study itself to the discipline which has come into
existence especially for this purpose. Quantitatively and qualitatively
Religionswissenschaft thus has a field of study distinct from that of theology:
not our own religion but the foreign religions in all their manifoldness are
its subject matter. It does not ask the question 'what must I believe?'
but 'what is there that is believed?' According to this definition, it may now
seem that the question raised by *Religionswissenschaft* is a superfluous, idle,
even harmful curiosity – for the satisfaction of which we can waste neither
time, nor energy, nor motivation today – especially at this juncture when
we ought to concentrate on what is absolutely necessary. It is good that
difficult times now and then compel people to recognize the superfluous for
what it is and to throw it overboard and then to limit themselves to what is
essential. For us this means that if *Religionswissenschaft* is only an aesthetically interesting or purely academic matter, then, indeed, it has no right
to exist today.
   The religions of exotic or primitive peoples have often, as has their art,
been regarded as curiosities. This is an insufficient, as well as an improper,

motive for occupying oneself with them. But even the pure, academic study of foreign religions, which ethically can be fully justified inasmuch as it rests on a broad desire for truth, must today be prepared to defend its right to exist. It cannot be denied that many a recent attempt in *Religionswissenschaft* is more or less exposed to the threefold criticism of lifelessness, intellectualism, and historicism. This accusation is often brought against the scientific disciplines in our own time. But it is an empirical, not a basic, shortcoming. *Religionswissenschaft* can as little do without learned research as can any other discipline. Nevertheless, this purely learned pursuit stands in the servitude of a higher purpose. Where research in religions, as a consequence of individual inability or from a basically false attitude, appears in the guise of a herbarium – a collection of and for linguists, ethnologists, and historiographers of religions – and where it appears as an occupation with theoretical and abstract formations of thought which dissolve values in unlikely comparisons, there it misses the purpose of *Religionswissenschaft*.

Religionswissenschaft, as we think of it, is alive; moreover, it is positive and practical. It is a living concern to the extent that it remains aware that the religion with which it deals is the deepest and the noblest in the realm of spiritual and intellectual existence, although, to be sure, it is difficult to see into the dark depth of that inwardness. *Religionswissenschaft* is alive, further, in that it recognizes the dynamic nature of religion, in that it knows that its goal will never be reached, and in that it can never sufficiently express that which it hopes to express. For the study of religious expressions, this means a never-ending task. *Religionswissenschaft* is also positive. A rather justified suspicion to the contrary has repeatedly been expressed – and not on the part of insignificant people. This suspicion has been nourished by the sounding from within our own realm of negative, overly critical, destructive, and nihilistic opinions. These tendencies could not help but produce justified defensive reactions since the enemies of religion disguised themselves as scholars.

However, *Religionswissenschaft* in its true intention does not dissolve values but seeks for values. The sense for the numinous is not extinguished by it, but on the contrary, is awakened, strengthened, shaped, and enriched by it. And as research in religions discloses religious feeling, desire, and action, it helps to reveal more fully the depth and breadth to which religiosity may radiate. A history of religions *(Religionsgeschichte)* which is inwardly connected with the history of cultures can accomplish much in this respect. When we have at last stated that *Religionswissenschaft* has a practical aspect, we must however protect this assertion against a possible misunderstanding. The practical benefit which justifiably is to some degree also demanded of all scientific disciplines must not be seen and sought too directly – which happens now as ever and which is supported by the spokesmen of contemporary need. How far-reaching in its often broad and indirect effects has been what appeared at first to be a very abstract philosophical investigation! The practical aspect must not be understood too narrowly. *Religionswissenschaft* cannot and must not serve the current moment in this bad sense.

What than is the practical significance of *Religionswissenschaft?* It broadens and deepens the *sensus numinis,* the religious feeling and understanding; it prepares one for a deeper conception of one's own faith; it allows a new and comprehensive experience of what religion is and means. This is as true of the religious experience as such as it is of the doctrinal and dogmatic aspect of religion, of its practice in the cult, and of the organization of the congregation. The effectiveness of the religious genius, the power and the formation of the religious community, the shaping of culture by religion – all these are experienced in new and manifold ways which do not paralyze but rather strengthen and fortify religious impulses.

Let us here remember the comparative approach; it has been much too overworked in the past, and too great expectations have been held concerning it. Now, in turn, it is easily underestimated. To observe the multiplicity of religious life and of religious expression, to discover similarities and relationships, need not, as some fear, have a sobering or paralyzing effect on one's own religiosity. On the contrary, it could become a support and an aid in the battle against the godless and estranged powers; it ought to lead to the examination and preservation of one's own religious faith. The value and significance of this may be recognized more clearly through that which is related but not identical. As Christians we have no reason at all to shy away from comparison – at any rate, not insofar as the idea and the impulse of our religion is concerned, although more, perhaps, in regard to practice. But there, precisely, the results of *Religionswissenschaft* could have very enlivening and encouraging effects. Precisely because the young person of our time has often very little living knowledge of the final and decisive religious experiences, the detour through examples and analogies from other religions may serve many a purpose.

Personally, I have many times seen young and open-minded students, in the study of the great subjects of *Religionswissenschaft,* attain, to their own surprise, a new understanding of the essentials of their own faith. The study of our various creeds – not as the dry enumeration of various doctrinal opinions, but as actual introductions into the piety of particular Christian movements – may accomplish something new. For example, in understanding the meaning of the cultic expressions of Catholicism, we may effect a richer and more forceful unfolding of our own religious life. As an instance from the general history of religions, the understanding of the immense role which the ethical aspect plays in the life of Buddhists will in theory and in practice lead increasing[y to a more intensive unfolding of the motives contained in the imperative of the Christian ethic. *Out of life and for life* – even though it is to be understood in the above-described sense – is the motto of every scientific discipline and consequently also of *Religionswissenschaft.*

It is of course especially clear that the discipline concerned with religion must be inwardly alive (more, perhaps than the disciplines concerned with economics, law, language, and art), that it can proceed finally only with the austerity and sacred depth appropriate to its great subject matter, with an ever renewing openness, with enthusiasm and thoroughness. It is an exaggeration, but nevertheless understandable, when some people in principle and because of the depth and delicacy of religious matters question the possibility of a *Religionswissenschaft* or of 'understanding' religion. Perhaps there is here a greater justification than there is for those who seek to interpret the documents of religious life no differently from documents of a business nature or than there is for those who cast judgment from the ivory tower of a modern intellectual enlightenment upon the customs and beliefs of the primitives. In any case, *Religionswissenschaft* would choose to assert rather less than too much. Happily, at least among us, it has freed itself from the pathos of optimistic positivism.

However much the work of *Religionswissenschaft*, as research, will always be careful about particulars – for here the meditation on the insignificant, of which Jakob Grimm spoke, cannot be thorough enough – the goal of *Religionswissenschaft* remains to understand and to present as living totalities the religions studied. After they have been disclosed and studied, its desire will always be to place the individual beliefs and ideas, the customs and communal modes, into that context in which alone they live; to connect them and to show them together with the spirit of the entire religion, with the basic intention that animates them, and with the creative religious intuition at their source.

Schleiermacher has said that every religion represents one aspect of the divine and develops a certain attitude toward it, an attitude which unfolds within the major spheres of religious expression, in doctrine, and in community. It is the task of *Religionswissenschaft* to show how strong, how weak, how enduring, the spirit *(Geist)* of a religion is, or how, in ever new beginnings it manifests itself externally. In this the hermeneutic circularity need not frighten us. This spirit must be understood by means of its dogmatic, cultic, and sociological expressions so that it may then be presupposed in the interpretation of these same manifestations. Religious language in the broader sense of 'expression' *(Ausdruck)* is always a code which points beyond itself. This is the truth of the hermeneutic of depth-exegesis, which we encounter in all great religious complexes and which – however arbitrary and unprovable its interpretation of the particulars may seem – has an eternal right over against all rationalism in the understanding of religious expressions.

In a religious doctrine, or in a cultic act, there is always more intended than can be recognized (because expressions in word, pitch, and gesture always limit that which is to be expressed). And then again in excess of what is intended, there is also something in an expression of the religious totality which is represented by it and hinted at by it. The demand to do justice always to all these relationships is put on the student of religions. It is exactly the decisive trend, the central motivation of a given religiosity, which is often very difficult to grasp, to trace, and to describe. And still, this apparently theoretical and abstract undertaking is of special practical significance. It is significant for missions; they are just as much entitled to make use of the work of *Religionswissenschaft* as the latter will always thankfully accept for study – and this does not exclude criticism – the results of missionary reports about other religions. For the sake of contact *(Anknüpfung)*, it will be very important to recognize the primary motivating forces of the religiosity which one confronts. These forces are definitely not always expressed in the ideas and beliefs of the primary official doctrine. It is important to identify them, to determine where and to what extent a religion is alive and has power to live. It is important to determine where the negative and sensitive spots are that require considerate care and to determine where positive values appear, the admiration of which is required for contact and communication to occur.

From what has been discussed, it should be clear that the central concern of *Religionswissenschaft* must be the understanding of other religions. Before we speak about this understanding proper, we shall venture yet a few words toward the further clarification of what has been said. Today, especially, the study of religions which are not our own is obliged to defend its ambitions. First, it has to defend itself against the theological objection that 'he who knows one religion knows them all'. Then, further, it must defend itself not only with respect to external opportunity (Can one afford to occupy oneself beyond the present concerns of our nation and our hemisphere with the religions of distant lands and times?) but also against skepticism that knowledge is possible about that which transcends one's own vital and spiritual life, feeling, thought, and will. To the point respecting opportunity, we may add that *Religionswissenschaft* in its presentations and in its research has to distinguish between what is important and what is less important, what is interesting and what is peripheral, what is necessary to know and what is worthy of knowing. But this is essentially a didactic matter. It is understandable that today in lectures and in courses it is primarily the religions which appeal to the wider public that must be discussed:

those which stand prior historically to our Christianity — as for example, the Germanic religion as the early faith of our people — or, in another way, the high religions with which our own struggles today at so many places. In this, *Religionswissenschaft* will have to claim the totality of religious phenomena as the task of its research — to study them and to understand them — but it will also have to claim penetration into most distant realms. A discussion of the final reasons for this would lead us deeply into the systematic problems of philosophy of religion, on the one hand, and into the methodology of the intellectual disciplines, on the other. Therefore, in the present context we must omit such a discussion. But since again and again in the course of time the possibility of understanding other religions has been doubted, *Religionswissenschaft* has a fundamental interest in this question.

The student of religions must be clear about the difficulties to which critics have rightly pointed. We refer here to the difficulties contained in the very naïve assumption that religious phenomena, if only sufficient materials were available, could readily be understood through the scientific approach. This assumption still plays a great role among the various types of positivism, as well as in that study of religions which is determined by it. Of course, a radical skepticism as a consequence of either religious indifference or of agnosticism or as a result of historical skepticism (where the history of religions, as all history, is a *fable convenue*) must be rejected just as must be any naïve optimism concerning phenomenological imagery.

The difficulties in our understanding are of various types. *First*, they are quantitative in nature: for example, the often considerable distance in time and space, especially serious with respect to the 'dead', the exotic, and the primitive religions. With the consequent lack of information, with the discontinuities and transformations among the traditions or source materials, may one still hope at all to attain a more or less true picture of the religions from the distant past and from distant realms? One need only think for instance of the religions of Egypt, Babylonia, China, and Mexico. *Second*, there are the qualitative difficulties that hinder our understanding: the uniqueness of foreign inwardness, which is likewise inherent in its expressions. Spengler, to name only one widely known thinker, has recently pointed especially to the uniqueness of ancient thought, feeling, and perceptivity. Who is there who has not felt the unfathomable depths that inhabit the religious representations of the Far East or the demonic so typical of African religions?

However, not only *Religionswissenschaft* is burdened with both of these types of difficulties; rather, all intellectual disciplines concerned with cultures, especially the historical disciplines, share them. In long and toilsome work they have sought to develop methods and criteria which would allow to some degree the mastery of these difficulties. If one looks to the results of these labors, one will have to admit how astonishingly and how extensively they have been crowned with success. We actually have a body of knowledge about the religions of peoples long since past as well as of distant places. This knowledge can withstand the most exacting tests and controls; it completes, broadens, and extends itself continuously, and it constitutes more than a subjective picture of particulars. Moreover, we are even able to test against the certain results of research the false pictures which are based on insufficient and one-sided information; here the error of poor subjectivity appears to be eliminated to a very great extent. Nevertheless, nobody will therefore underestimate the difficulties that have been mentioned.

We continuously have reasons to examine within an ever-extending problematic the possibilities, the chances, and the limits in understanding other religions. How difficult it is even to obtain a clear picture of the religiosity of a person near to us – still within the realm of common faith and familiarity! How difficult it is to comprehend the piety of our predecessors of perhaps only a few decades, of the faiths of neighboring lands, of the faith of Islamic peoples who still have certain religious influences in common with Europe, and finally of the people of India and China.

With this we actually have arrived at the *third* major difficulty with which the understanding of other religions must struggle. This difficulty is unique in that it concerns the nature of the religious. It will certainly be less difficult to obtain a picture of the legal customs and of the linguistic and artistic expressions of a people than of their religion. The last is above everything else kept in high esteem. It may even be fearfully hidden from foreign eyes and guarded as an arcanum. And even when it is possible to look into it, it is really not easy to grasp its meaning. A simple example will point this out: a Roman Catholic mass, in which so much is interrelated and unfamiliar, even foreign, to the Protestant who attends. If it is a church service according to the Greek, the Coptic, or the Armenian rite, the strangeness is immediately greater. This foreignness grows again as we encounter no longer a Christian but, for example, a Jewish, or an Islamic, or even a Buddhist worship service. How difficult for consequent understanding are the religious root-conceptions and root-customs of taboo, totem, nagual, and others. How different the baroque mythology of Japanese Shinto, the orgiastic cults of certain Indian Shiva sects, the fanaticism of the Islamic Shi'ah, appear to us. Here our discussion closes in on a great and serious problem: the secret of plurality among religious experiences. We can only lead up to this problem, for its consideration is a concern for philosophy of religion and for theology. Here we shall deal only with the question whether and how it is possible for *Religionswissenschaft* to understand other religions. We have already seen that many practical proofs of its possibility are available. Hermeneutically, on what does this possibility rest?

We have spoken above of what is generally representative of spiritual, and therefore also of religious, expressions. The expression then becomes transparent; it allows something to shine through of the specific and perhaps unique spirit *(Geist)* of a certain religious context. Thus it is that views into the depths *(Tiefenblicke)* become possible. Not always and not to everybody do they open themselves. But it is amazing how much a small and peripheral aspect, taken from the conceptions and customs of a faith, can disclose to a gifted and trained mind. Actual intuition *(Divination)* here, as always, is the exception. Synthesis *(Kombination)* stands in the foreground of all intellectual endeavors, as it does in *Religionswissenschaft*. If then, perhaps, in a happy and fruitful interplay of both avenues to knowledge, some decisive characteristics of a foreign religiosity have emerged for the researcher, he may then dare to grasp and describe its basic intention. In this it is a great help for the human understanding that in the structure of spiritual expressions (of such great and deep experiences as are the productively religious ones) there is inherent an amazing continuity *(Folgerichtigkeit)*. Nor is this continuity absent in the structures of the historical religious systems.

It is not very difficult for one who has really comprehended the central intuition of Islam, its experience of the deity, as this is expressed in the original revelation to the prophet Muhammed, to discover it again in the doctrine, theology, cosmology, anthropology, soteriology, and cult. In spite of all other influences, this central intuition develops within the framework of these expressions. The experience of suffering within a world of change, fundamental for Buddhism, is displayed with such a continuity in its doctrine, is presented in its symbols, and is shaped within its ethic, so that the understanding of this may, like a great key, unlock an otherwise strange-appearing world of expressions.

Such considerations certainly ought not minimize the difficulties; they ought not delude us about the levels and degrees of understanding, about the differences involved among its various risks. But by considering and by honoring differences, an old truth must not be forgotten. As Goethe and Wilhelm have formulated it, in every man there dwell all the forms of humanity. Novalis asked at one time: How can a man have an understanding of something of which he does not have the seed within himself? This insight in no way implies the lack or the weakness of him who does the understanding; rather, it implies the conviction that in all of us is contained more than becomes manifest in the co-operation of circumstances and fate.

Only very recently Eduard Spranger in his illustrative investigation of the primary levels of reality-consciousness *(Abhandlungen der Akademie der*

Wissenschaften [Berlin], 1934) has proven that in all of us there are latently present certain more primeval structures of consciousness. What is called 'mind' has the ability to activate these and to understand, so to speak, the atavistic and distant expressions of our soul, the expressions which are alien to our present consciousness. Novalis again says: We stand in relationship with all parts of the universe, with the future and with the past. What relationship we shall primarily develop and what relationship for us shall become primarily effective and important depend only on the direction and duration of our attentiveness. This means that in principle there could resound in each of us something of the ecstatic, the spectral, the unusual – something of that which to us, the children of another age, of another race, and of other customs, appears strange among the religious expressions of distant lands. Where this natural disposition is developed through training, there also the prerequisite for an actual understanding of foreign religiosity exists.

This can be illustrated through the example of myth. In myth, religious experience is expressed in unique categories. As recent ethnological and psychological research has shown, our logical norms are not necessarily valid for these categories. Thus the myths of primitive peoples with their identifications, their theriomorphisms, and so on, at first seem abstruse to the uninformed, contemporary reader or listener. And still, it does not seem impossible to sense something of the intended reality of the myth. Such immersions into archaic modes of consciousness are generally more easily attained by young people. Such modes of consciousness are almost self-evident and present for them. I am reminded of our youth associations and their experience, their symbolism and their customs; in them the world of primitive man *(Naturmensch)* is not only imitated externally but actually felt in participation, and it becomes clear that their experience of it is not a purely intellectual affair.

In the human understanding, as the excellent hermeneutics of Wilhelm Dilthey has shown, the totality of mind and soul *(Totalität des Gemüts)* is effective. Concretely stated, the religious content of myth cannot be found alone in a careful and thorough, though necessary, analysis of its ideological elements and motives; rather, the entire personality of him who studies and understands is spoken to. If he wishes to understand the attitude from which the mythological faith and custom have issued, he must respond. An inner aliveness and broadness is necessary if we actually wish to understand other religions. In this connection it should be stated explicitly that the one-sided advancement of a particular point of view is bad for the understanding. As justified and fruitful as may be the co-operative approaches of psychology, sociology, and typology, pure psychological, pure socio-logical, and pure typological answers do not help us to understand foreign

religiosity. Unfortunately, our discipline is rich in one-sided attempts that
have been based on false, narrow, and oblique conceptions of the nature of
religion.

It appears to be a truism to say that hermeneutics demands that he who
wishes to understand other religions must have a sense *(Organ)* for religion
and in addition the most extensive knowledge and training possible. Many
still think that one of these two prerequisites is sufficient. While all sorts of
dilettantes (a famous example is the interpretation of Laotse's *Tao te King)*
err in one of these directions, often philologists, ethnologists, and other
specialists go amiss in the other. The first demand is stated by some in a
still more strict and narrow sense. Well aware of the above-mentioned difficulties in understanding other religions, they think that one must actually
belong to a community of believers if one wishes to grasp its actual concern.
This is a significant assertion, and it must be seriously examined. If it proves
to be fully correct, the ground on which *Religionswissenschaft* builds will
have been withdrawn. Here, too, a glance at the results of a century rich
in religious studies of the most varied kinds will reveal in fact that even those
who have not studied another religion as a member of that particular religious community may be successful. The same can likewise hardly be denied
of knowledge concerning the entire realm of expressions, that is, of the doctrine, cult, and constitution of the religious community concerned.

But the matter gets more difficult when we are dealing with the inner
experience, the understanding and intention to which such expressions bear
witness. There can be no question that growing up within a tradition,
belonging to the community of faith, can be a favorable precondition. However, the effect of habit, the absence of distance, and so on, may certainly
also be negative influences. Standing within a tradition is nevertheless
important. It could perhaps be an advantage in certain situations for the
convert over the outsider. It could enable him to grasp the conscious ambition of the community which he joins. But one would want to ask, with
respect to understanding Buddhism, for example, whether he who through
conversion has been accepted into the community actually has a greater
insight than the outsider, perhaps a Westerner, who for a long time has
immersed himself in Buddhist studies. We may admit without reservation
that standing in a tradition is something that is difficult to replace and that
– provided the other prerequisites which we have found necessary are also
present – the chances for understanding the actual intention of a religious
community are increased. But in practical confrontation with the multiplicity of phenomena, with which the student of religions must deal, such
a participation will not be possible. Thus, the demand that one belong to
the religious community which one wishes to understand cannot be made a
prerequisite – not to speak of the new errors which could arise under these

circumstances. The problem of knowledge and faith, of faith and understanding, cannot be discussed here. Only this much must be summarized: being rooted in a personal faith — a faith which may well blind one to other things but which, in contrast to the opinion of many, need not do so – does not necessarily mean a disadvantage for him who seeks to understand. The demand of a *tabula rasa* has long been recognized as utopian; and even though such objectivity might be desirable, it is actually impossible. Schleiermacher has seen that we must learn from our personal religious life in order to encounter the foreign. We need not a blank sheet but an impregnated one, one that will preserve the pictures projected onto it.

[...]

NOTES

1. *Cf.* Niebuhr, *The Social Sources of Denominationalism*, pp. 26 ff., speaking for a balance of views.

2. Weber, *G. A.*, I, 240.

3. Louis Finkelstein, *The Pharisees: The Sociological Background of Their Faith* (Philadelphia: Jewish Publication Society of America, 1938).

4. *Soziallehren*, Introduction. *Cf.* also William Christie MacLeod, *The Origin and History of Politics* (New York, John Wiley; London, Chapman and Hall, 1931), chap. 10: 'Economic Determinism'; and Samuel Morison in his studies on Puritanism [. . .]. Even Ernest Sutherland Bates, *American Faith* (New York, W. W. Norton, 1940), protests (p. 12, but *cf.* p. 34)

5. Rudolf Otto, *The Idea of the Holy*, trans. J. W. Harvey (London and New York, Oxford University Press [Humphrey Milford], 1925). For some, we would think, justified criticism cf. Archibald Allan Bowman, *Studies in the Philosophy of Religion* (London, Macmillan 1938), Vol. I, chap. 7. (point of disagreement: psychological emphasis and relation of the numinous to the holy). Also David Mial Edwards, *Christianity and Philosophy* (Edinburgh, T. and T. Clark 1932), esp. chap. 2; John Morrison Moore, 'The *a priori* in Rudolf Otto's Theory of Religious Experience,' *RR*, II (1937), 128, and the same author's excellent study, *Theories of Religious Experience (with Special Reference to James, Otto, Bergson)* (New York, Round Table Press, 1938), esp. pp. 75 ff.

6. Brightman, *Philosophy of Religion*, chaps. 1, 14, well defines religious experience as 'any experience of any person taken in its relation to his God' (p. 415). *Cf.* there, pp. 85 ff., his theory of religious values.

7. In one of the recent books by Radin, *Primitive Religion* (1937), the above-criticized concept of religion is formulated anew (*cf.* chap. 1: 'The Nature and Substance of Religion'). *Cf.* also Wach, 'Das religiöse Gefühl' ('Vorträge des Instituts für Geschichte der Medizin [Univ. Leipzig]'), No. 4 (1931), a critical discussion of Freud's theory of religion.

8. John MacMurray, *The Structure of Religious Experience* ('Terry Lectures', New Haven, Yale University Press, 1936), pp. 4, 23.

9. *Cf.* below, chap. 2, n. 10.

10. The methodological problem of this 'circle' has been exhaustively studied by the translator of William James into German, Georg Wobbermin, *Systematische Theologie* (2nd. ed.; Tübingen, J. C. B. Mohr, 1925 ff.), esp. Vol. II.

11. In the systematic chapter of his study of theories of religious experience (cf. above, n. 5) J. M. Moore reviews various emotional, intellectual, and volitional theories of religion (chap. iv). We disagree with his criticism of the assumption of a definite quality or structure of religious experience. We can determine not only its function but also its nature in general terms (objective quality, etc.), notwithstanding the variety of its particular forms (pp. 226 ff.). *Cf. ibid.*, pp. 187 ff., for Moore's classification of types of religious experience.

12. A similar program is outlined by Max Ferdinand Scheler, *Vom Ewigen im Menschen* (Berlin: Der Neue Geist Verlag, 1933), pp. 227 ff., and partly anticipated in George Herbert Mead's theory of gestures *(Mind, Self, and Society: From the Standpoint of a Social Behaviorist*, ed. Charles W. Morris (Chicago, University of Chicago Press, 1937), Part II).

13. Georg Wilhelm Friedrich Hegel, *Lectures on the Philosophy of Religion*, trans. E. B. Speirs (London; K. Paul, Trench, Trubner and Co., 1895). [. . .].

14. Unfortunately, Dilthey's writings are not translated *(Gesammelte Schriften*, (Leipzig, B. G. Teubner, Vols. I, V, pp. 371 ff., and VII). *Cf.* John Laird, *Recent Philosophies* (London, T. Butterworth, 1936), pp. 68 ff.; Wach, *Die Typenlehre Trendelenburgs und ihr Einfluss auf Dilthey* (Tübingen, J. C. B. Mohr, 1926). Rightly, modern anthropology refers to these concepts (Benedict, *Patterns of Culture*, chap. 3: 'Integration of Culture'; Goldenweiser, in *Contemporary Social Theory*, (1940), pp. 93 ff.). *Cf.* also below, n. 16.

15. *Cf.* Wach, *Das Verstehen*, Vol. II, chap. 3: 'Die Hermeneutik Steinthals.'

16. Baillie, *Interpretation of Religion*, esp. p. 30; Edwards, *Christianity and Philosophy*, p. 55.

17. *Cf.*, e.g., Malinowski's instance at this point, in his article on 'Culture' in *ESS*, IV, 621 ff., and 'The Group and the Individual in Functional Analysis', *AJS*, XLIV (1938), 938 ff.

18. R. Benedict, *Patterns of Culture;* W. I. Thomas, *Primitive Behavior.*

19. Ruth Benedict, *The Concept of the Guardian Spirit in North America (Mem. AAA*, Vol. XXIX, 1923), esp. p. 24; *cf.* Alfred Vierkandt, *Die Stetigkeit im Kulturwandel* (Leipzig, Duncker Humblot, 1908).

20. This aspect is greatly stressed – and overemphasized – with regard to higher religion by some psychologists, as by Floyd Allport, *Institutional Behavior: Essays toward a Re-interpreting of Contemporary Social Organization* (Chapel Hill, University of North Carolina Press, 1933), chap. XX.

21. Schleiermacher's 'Discourses' are centered around this thought, especially the Fifth Discourse. *Cf.* now Richard B. Brandt, *The Philosophy of Schleiermacher* (New York and London, Harper, 1940); see also Julius Seelye Bixler, 'The Spirit and the Life: A Dialogue', *RR*, I (1937), 113 ff.

22. R. Otto, *The Idea of the Holy.* See Heiler, 'Die Bedeutung R. Ottos für die vergleichende Religionsgeschichte', in *Religionswissenschaft in Neuer Sicht*, pp. 13 ff.; R. F. Davidson, *Rudolf Otto's Interpretation of Religion;* Wach, *Types of Religious Experience*, Chap. 10.

23. F. von Hügel, *Essays and Adresses on the Philosophy of Religion*, I, 2; II, 5. See Nédoncelle, *Baron Friederich von Hügel.*

24. Webb, *Religious Experience.* There is no monograph on his work.

25. The development of our studies in this second period (and in the third) has been traced by Puech, 'Bibliographie générale', in series "Mana" vol. I. (pp. XVII—LXIII), and for Scandinavia by Widengren, 'Die religionswissenschaftliche Forschung in Skandinavien', *Zeitschrift für Religions- und Geistesge. schichte*, V (1953), 193 ff., 320 ff. MassonOursel, 'La connaissance de l'Asie en

France depuis 1900, *Revue Philosophique*, Nos. 7—9 (1953), pp. 342 ff.; Pado-
vani, 'La Storia delle religioni in Italia', *Semaine Internationale d'ethnologie
religieuse*, IV (1925), 47 ff.

26. See the symposium by Miller *et al.*, *Religion and Freedom of Thought*,
contributions of Miller, Calhoun, Pusey, and Reinhold Niebuhr.

27. For a historical orientation, see Davies, *The Problem of Authority in the
Continental Reformers*. For a balanced systematic treatment, see Temple,
Nature, Man and God, Chap. 13; Kruger, 'Das Problem der Autorität', in
Offener Horizont, pp. 44 ff. Anti-authoritarian is Zaehner, 'Dogma', *Hibbert
Journal*, III (1954), 9 ff.

28. H. W. Schneider, *Religion in Twentieth Century America*, p. 33.

29. Farnell, *The Attributes of God*, p. 10, wrote correctly that the intellectual
student of the science of religion 'may be merely devoted to truth and indifferent
to the possibly far-reaching practical results of his work.' He adds that it is
clear that such results, direct or indirect, are inevitable.

30. Troeltsch, *Die Absolutheit des Christentums und die Religionsgeschichte*, p.51.

31. *Types of Experience*, Chap. 1.

32. Richardson, *Christian Apologetics*, Chap. 5.

33. The author has frequently addressed himself to this question. See 'Zur
Methodologie der Religionswissenschaft', ZMR (1923); 'Zum Problem der exter-
nen Würdigung der Religion', ZMR (1923); *Religionswissenschaft;* 'Sinn und
Aufgabe der Religionswissenschaft', ZMR (1935); *Das Verstehen*, Vols. I–III.
See also Bollnow, *Das Verstehen*.

34. 'Comprendre et rendre compréhensible la modalité du sacré' is the task,
according to Eliade, *Traité d'histoire des religions*, p. 19.

35. See Pinard de la Boullaye, *L'Etude comparée*, I, 30 ff.

36. Webb, *God and Personality*, p. 84.

37. This was the postulate of some of the authors treated in our history of
nineteenth-century hermeneutics and is strongly stressed by Bultmann in 'Das
Problem der Hermeneutik', in *Glauben und Verstehen*, II, 211 ff. See Dinkler,
'Existentialist Interpretation of the New Testament', *Journal of Religion*,
XXXII (1952), 87 ff. See also Bollnow, *Das Verstehen*, pp. 37 ff.

38. Pinard de la Boullaye, *L'Etude comparée*, pp. 31 ff.

39. Wach, *Sociology of Religion*, Chap. VI.

40. Allport, *The Individual and His Religion;* Grensted, *Psychology of Religion*.

41. 'The real weight of the 'evidence' which is accepted as sufficient ground for
assurance can only be judged by a mind of the right kind and with the right
kind of training'. Taylor, 'The Vindication of Religion', *Essays Catholic and Critical*, Selwyn, ed., p. 39.

42. The excellent article by Earle, 'The 'Standard Observer' in the Sciences of
Man', *Ethics*, LXIII (1953), 293 ff., stresses that 'man' in distinction from the
data of the sciences proper is not a 'public datum', that he is objective only for
the 'total nature of man'. Accordingly the wise man, the lover, the poet, the
saint is the true observer (296 f.).

43. William James, *The Varieties of Religious Experience* (New York and London, Longmans-Green, 1902).

44. Paul Tillich, 'The Problem of Theological Method', *Journal of Religion*,
XXVII (1947), 23.

45. W. James, *op. cit.*, p. 58.

46. Paul E. Johnson, *Psychology of Religion* (New York, Abingdon-Cokesbury
Press), p. 36.

47. Émile Durkheim agrees with W. James that 'religious beliefs rest upon a specific experience whose demonstrative value is, in one sense, not one bit inferior to that of scientific experiments, though different from them'. *(The Elementary Forms of the Religious Life*, trans. J. W. Swain (1915), (Glencoe (Ill.), Free Press, 1947), p. 417.) He adds, and rightly, that it does not follow from the fact that a 'religious experience exists and has a certain foundation, that the reality which is its foundation conforms objectively to the idea which believers have of it'.

48. Johnson, *Psychology*, p. 47, and John M. Moore, *Theories of Religious Experience* (New York, Round Table Press, 1938), who criticizes Rudolf Otto's assumption of the cognitive nature of the numinous feeling (pp. 86 ff., 95 ff.). We distinguish between apprehension and intellectual expression.

49. This point is well brought out by Canon B. H. Streeter, *The Buddha and the Christ* (London, Macmillan, 1932), pp. 157 ff.

50. Bronislaw Malinowski, *Magic, Science, and Religion, and other Essays* (Glencoe (Ill.), Free Press, 1948), p. 1.

51. *Cf.* the methodological prolegomena in J. Wach, *Sociology of Religion* (London, Kegan Paul, 1947); Part I. *Cf.* there many references and bibliography for statements in the text above.

52. *Cf.* Aldous Huxley, *The Perennial Philosophy* (London: Chatto and Windus, 1945), chap. 12.: 'Time and Eternity'.

53. There is the *analogy* of the senses (sight, hearing, smell, touch; what is experienced is described as 'light', voices are heard, sweet odours are smelt), then the analogy of physical phenomena (procreating, eating), that of the various activities of man [warfare, peaceful pursuits (agriculture; pastoral life; other professions), travelling (pilgrimage)] and of human relationships (kin, social, marital relations). Professor Bevan has especially studied the symbolic use of time and space notions. Urban again has stressed the analogies of the *sun* – 'the Sun with its powerful rays, its warmth and light, its life-giving qualities, becomes a natural symbol for the creating and eliciting power' (Urban, *Language*, p. 589) – and *sex* – 'sex love, its heights and its depths, its horrible darkness and its blinding light is never wholly alien to the creative love of which Plato, no less than Christian theologians and philosophers, discourse' (Urban, loc. cit., p. 591). M. A. Ewer *(A Survey of Mystical Symbolism* (London, S. P. C. K., 1933)) analysed the analogies of the senses in mystical symbolic language. E. Underhill has concentrated upon the symbolic notions of pilgrimage (for divine transcendence), of love and of transmutation *(Mysticism* (London, Methuen, 12th ed., 1930), chap. 6).

54. Gerardus van der Leeuw, *Religion in Essence and Manifestation* (London, Allen and Unwin, 1938), pp. 655-7. Mircea Eliade, *Traité d'histoire des religions* (Paris: Payot, 1949), chaps. 10, 11.

55. Otto Franke, 'Der Kosmische Gedanke in der Philosophie und dem Staat der Chinesen', *Vorträge der Bibliothek Warburg* (Leipzig, Teubner, 1928); Wach *Sociology of Religion*, pp. 49 ff.; T. W. Rhys Davids, 'Cosmic Law in Ancient Thought' *(Proceedings of Brit. Academy* (Oxford: University Press, 1917), pp. 18, 279 ff.). Roger Caillois, *L'homme et le sacré*, series "Mythes et religions" (Paris, Leroux, 1939), pp. 9 ff; Eliade, *Traité*, chaps. 10, 11.

56. 'The symbolism of the World Quarters, of the Above, and of the Below, is nowhere more elaborately developed among American Indians than with the *Pueblos*. Analogies are drawn not merely with colours, with plants and animals, and with cult objects and religious ideas, but with human society in all the rami-

fications of its organization, making of mankind not only the theatric centre of the cosmos, but a kind of elaborate image of its form' (Hartley Alexander, 'North American Mythology', in *The Mythology of All Races* (Archaeological Institute of America, 1936), Vol. X., 185.

57. 'He [the savage] encounters the divine stimulus here, there and anywhere within the contents of an experience in which percepts play a far more important part than concepts' (Marett, *Faith, Hope and Charity in Primitive Religion* (Oxford, Clarendon Press, 1932), p. 144). *Cf.* also Frankfort, etc., *The Intellectual Adventure of Ancient Man* (Chicago, University Press, 1946), 130 ff.

58. *Cf.* J. Wach, *Types of Religious Experience* (1951), Chap. 10.

59. Thus the criticism which J. M. Moore *(Theories*, pp. 91 ff., 103 ff.) levels rightly at Rudolf Otto's concept of 'feeling' does not apply to our theory.

60. Van der Leeuw, *op. cit.*, Part I; Eliade, *op. cit.*

61. Martin P. Nilsson, 'Letter to Professor A. D. Nock' *(Harvard Theological Review*, XLII (1949), 91).

62. *Cf.* the excellent chapter 'Curiosity' in Marett, *Faith, Hope and Charity in Primitive Religion* (1932), chap. 8. *Cf.* also: V. Gordon Childe, *Magic, Craftsmanship and Science* (Liverpool, University Press, 1950).

63. Malinowski, 'Myth in Primitive Society' *(op. cit.*, pp. 72 ff., 76, 93 f.). Malinowski's solution – the sociological theory of myth, in his own words – does not satisfy because of his preoccupation with the *pragmatic* aspect of both religious and magical activities. He neglects the problems of meaning, structure and motivation. A more promising approach seems to be Ernesto de Martino's *Il Mondo Magico* (Firenze, Giulio Einaudi, 1948) who is concerned with the nature of the *reality* to which magic thought and acts refer (p. 11).

64. *Cf.* for the general framework: Wach, *Sociology of Religion*, Part I, chap. 2.

PART FOUR

Later Contributions
from Other Disciplines

Carl Gustav Jung

Carl Gustav Jung was born in 1875 in Kesswil, Switzerland. He received his primary school education at Klein-Huningen near Schaffhausen, and his secondary school education in Basel. In 1895 he enrolled in the University of Basel, and after attending courses in the natural sciences for a while, he decided to continue with medicine. He finished his studies in 1900 and wanted to specialize in psychiatry. Jung took up an assistantship at the Burghölzli Hospital of the University of Zürich, where he worked under Eugen Bleuler. In 1902 he obtained his doctorate with a dissertation on 'The Psychology and Pathology of So-Called Occult Phenomena'. In the same year he worked one semester in Paris with Pierre Janet and then continued his work and research at the Burghölzli Hospital. In 1905 Jung became *Privatdozent* for Psychiatry at the University of Zürich and chief medical doctor at the Hospital. In 1907 Jung visited Freud in Vienna, and they were on close terms. In 1909, after having given up his post at the hospital, Jung went on a trip to America with Freud and S. Ferenczi, where they gave lectures at Clark University, Worcester, Massachusetts. After a period of collaboration, Jung departed from Freud's views in his 'Transformations and Symbols of the Libido' in 1912 and it came to a break between them in 1913. In that year Jung abandoned his teaching post at the University of Zürich in order to devote himself to his research and psychiatric practice. In the early twenties he traveled through Africa and America, in connection with his psychological interest in African and Indian ways of thought and life. In 1933 Jung started to teach at the Federal Higher Technical School at Zürich, where he became full professor in 1935. In 1942 he had to renounce this post for reasons of health. Again, after having occupied the new chair of Medical Psychology at the University of Basel in 1944, he had to abandon this for the same reasons in 1945. Jung participated actively in the annual Eranos meetings at Ascona. In 1948 the 'C. G. Jung Institute Zürich' was founded, where further research and teaching of Analytical Psychology could be carried out. Jung died at Küsnacht, Switzerland, in 1961.

The most important books by C. G. Jung on the study of religion which have been translated into English are the following: 1931 *The Secret of the Golden Flower* (Commentary on the translation and explanation by Richard Wilhelm); 1938 *Psychology and Religion;* 1951 *Introduction to a Science of Mythology. The Myth of the Divine Child and the Mysteries of Eleusis* (In collaboration with Karl Kerényi); 1953 *Psychology and Alchemy* (Coll. Works, vol. 12); 1956 *Answer to Job;* 1956 *The Trickster. A Study in American Indian Mythology* (Commentary by Karl Kerényi and C. G. Jung on a text translated by Paul Radin); 1958 *Psychology and Religion: West and East* (Coll. Works, vol. 11); 1959 *The Archetypes and the Collective Unconscious* and *Aion: Researches into the Phenomenology of the Self* (Coll. Works, vol. 9, Parts I and II). C. G. Jung's *Collected Works* had started to appear in English already before his death.

As an analytical psychologist Jung developed a new approach to the study of religion on the level of depth psychology. Departing from what he called 'psychic reality', and in particular from his hypothesis of a collective unconscious proper to mankind, he gave a psychological interpretation of mythology, religious symbolism, religious speculation and parapsychological phenomena. He was much concerned with the religious needs expressed by his patients and developed his thought on the realization of the 'Self' as a religious process. He worked out a theory on archetypes which is of interest to the study of religion and mythology.

The following texts have been taken from Jung's *Psychology of Religion*, where he speaks of his principles of research, and from his *Introduction to a Science of Mythology*, where he speaks of his approach to ancient myth materials.

ON 'PSYCHOLOGY OF RELIGION'

As it seems to be the intention of the founder of the Terry Lectures to enable representatives of science, as well as of philosophy and of other spheres of human knowledge, to contribute to the discussion of the eternal problem of religion, and since Yale University has bestowed upon me the great honor of delivering the Terry Lectures of 1937, I assume that it will be my task to show what psychology, or rather that special branch of medical psychology which I represent, has to do with or to say about religion. Since religion is incontestably one of the earliest and most universal activities of the human mind, it is self-evident that any kind of psychology which touches upon the psychological structure of human personality cannot avoid at least observing the fact that religion is not only a sociological or historical phenomenon, but also something of considerable personal concern to a great number of individuals.

Notwithstanding the fact that I have often been called a philosopher, I am an empiricist and adhere to the phenomenological standpoint. I trust that it does not collide with the principles of scientific empiricism if one occasionally makes certain reflections which go beyond a mere accumulation and classification of experience. As a matter of fact I believe that an experience is not even possible without reflection, because 'experience' is a process of assimilation, without which there could be no understanding. As this statement indicates, I approach psychological matters from a scientific and not from a philosophical standpoint. In as much as religion has a very important psychological aspect, I am dealing with it from a purely empirical point of view, that is, I restrict myself to the observation of phenomena and I refrain from any application of metaphysical or philosophical considerations. I do not deny the validity of other considerations, but I cannot claim to be competent to apply them correctly. I am aware that most people believe they know all there is to be known about psychology, because they think that psychology is nothing but what they know of themselves. But I am afraid psychology is a good deal more than that. While having little to do with philosophy, it has much to do with empirical facts, many of which are not easily accessible to the average experience. It is my intention in this book to give a few glimpses, at least, of the way in which practical psychology becomes confronted with the problem of religion. It is self-evident that the vastness of the problem requires far more than three lectures, as the necessary demonstration of concrete detail needs a great deal of time as well as of explanation. My first chapter will be a sort of introduction to the problem of practical psychology and religion. The second is concerned with facts which bear out the existence of an authentic religious function in the unconscious mind. The third deals with religious symbolism by unconscious processes.

Since I am going to present a rather unusual argument, I cannot assume that my audience is completely aware of the methodological standpoint of that kind of psychology which I represent. This standpoint is exclusively phenomenological, that is, it is concerned with occurrences, events, experiences, in a word, with facts. Its truth is a fact and not a judgment. Speaking for instance of the motive of the virgin birth, psychology is only concerned with the fact that there is such an idea, but it is not concerned with the question whether such an idea is true or false in any other sense. It is psychologically true in as much as it exists. Psychological existence is subjective in so far as an idea occurs in only one individual. But it is objective in so far as it is established by a society – by a consensus gentium.

This point of view is the same as that of natural science. Psychology deals with ideas and other mental contents as zoology for instance deals with different species of animals. An elephant is true because it exists. The elephant, moreover, is neither a conclusion nor a statement nor a subjective judgment of a creator. It is a phenomenon. But we are so used to the idea that psychical events are wilful and arbitrary products, even inventions of the human creator, that we can hardly liberate ourselves from the prejudiced view that the psyche and its contents are nothing but our own arbitrary invention or the more or less illusory product of assumption and judgment. The fact is that certain ideas exist almost everywhere and at all times and they can even spontaneously create themselves quite apart from migration and tradition. They are not made by the individual, but they rather happen – they even force themselves upon the individual's consciousness. This is not platonic philosophy but empirical psychology.

In speaking of religion I must make clear from the start what I mean by that term. Religion, as the Latin word denotes, is a careful and scrupulous observation of what Rudolf Otto[1] aptly termed the 'numinosum', that is, a dynamic existence or effect, not caused by an arbitrary act of will. On the contrary, it seizes and controls the human subject, which is always rather its victim than its creator. The numinosum is an involuntary condition of the subject, whatever its cause may be. At all events, religious teaching as well as the consensus gentium always and everywhere explains this condition as being due to a cause external to the individual. The numinosum is either a quality of a visible object or the influence of an invisible presence causing a peculiar alteration of consciousness. This is, at least, the general rule.

There are, however, certain exceptions when it comes to the question of practice or ritual. A great many ritualistic performances are carried out for the sole purpose of producing at will the effect of the numinosum by certain devices of a magic nature, such as invocation, incantation, sacrifice, meditation and other yoga practices, self-inflicted tortures of various descriptions and so forth. But a religious belief in an external and objective divine cause always precedes any such performance. The Catholic church, for instance, administers the sacraments with the purpose of bestowing their spiritual blessings upon the believer; but since this act would amount to enforcing the presence of divine grace by an indubitably magic procedure, it is logically argued that nobody is able to compel divine grace to be present in the sacramental act, but that it is nevertheless inevitably present, the sacrament being a divine institution which God would not have caused to be if he had not had it in mind to support it.*

Religion appears to me to be a peculiar attitude of the human mind, which could be formulated in accordance with the original use of the term 'religio', that is, a careful consideration and observation of certain dynamic factors, understood to be 'powers', spirits, demons, gods, laws, ideas, ideals or whatever name man has given to such factors as he has found in his world powerful, dangerous or helpful enough to be taken into careful consideration, or grand, beautiful and meaningful enough to be devoutly adored and loved. In colloquial language one often says of somebody who is enthusiastically interested in a certain pursuit, that he is almost 'religiously devoted' to his cause; William James, for instance, remarks that a scientist often has no creed, but 'his temper is devout'.[2]

I want to make clear that by the term 'religion'[3] I do not mean a creed. It is, however, true that on the one hand every confession is originally based upon the experience of the numinosum and on the other hand upon Πίστις,

---

* The gratia adiuvans and the gratia sanctificans are the effects of the sacramentum ex opere operato. The sacrament owes its efficiency to the fact that it is immediately instituted by Christ himself. The church is unable to connect the rite with grace, so that the actus sacramentalis would produce the presence and the effect of grace, i.e., res et sacramentum. Thus the ritual carried out by the priest is not causa instrumentalis but merely causa ministerialis.

the loyalty, trust, and confidence toward a definitely experienced numinous effect and the subsequent alteration of consciousness: the conversion of Paul is a striking example of this. 'Religion', it might be said, is the term that designates the attitude peculiar to a consciousness which has been altered by the experience of the numinosum.

Creeds are codified and dogmatized forms of original religious experience.[4] The contents of the experience have become sanctified and usually congealed in a rigid, often elaborate, structure. The practice and the reproduction of the original experience have become a ritual and an unchangeable institution. This does not necessarily mean a lifeless petrification. On the contrary it can become the form of religious experience for ages of time and for millions of people without there being any vital necessity for alterations. Although the Catholic church has often been blamed for a particular rigidity, it admits nevertheless that the dogma has its life and hence is capable of undergoing change and development. Even the number of dogmas is unlimited and can be augmented in the course of time. The same holds true of the ritual. Yet all changes and developments are confined within the frame of the originally experienced facts, thereby involving a particular kind of dogmatic content and emotional value. Even Protestantism – which has surrendered apparently to an almost unlimited liberation from dogmatic tradition and from codified ritual and has thus split into more than four hundred denominations – even Protestantism is bound at least to be Christian and to express itself within the frame of the conviction that God has revealed himself in Christ, who suffered for mankind. This is a definite frame, with definite contents, which cannot be coupled with or amplified by Buddhistic or Islamic ideas and emotions. Yet it is unquestionable that not only Buddha or Mohammed or Confucius or Zarathustra represents religious phenomena, but that Mithras, Attis, Kybele, Mani, Hermes and many exotic cults do so as well. The psychologist, in as much as he assumes a scientific attitude, has to disregard the claim of every creed to be the unique and eternal truth. He must keep his eye on the human side of the religious problem, in that he is concerned with the original religious experience quite apart from what the creeds have made of it.

Being a doctor and a specialist in nervous and mental diseases my point of departure is not any creed, but the psychology of the homo religiosus, the man who takes into account and carefully observes certain factors which influence him and, through him, his general condition. It is easy to denominate and define those factors according to historical tradition or anthropological knowledge, but to do the same thing from the standpoint of psychology is an uncommonly difficult task. What I can contribute to the question of religion is derived entirely from my practical experience, both with my patients and with so-called normal beings. As our experience with people depends considerably upon what we do with them, I can see no other way of proceeding than to give you at least a general idea of the line I take in my professional work.

[. . .]

Although the four is an age-old, presumably prehistoric symbol,* always associated with the idea of a world-creating deity, it is, however – curiously enough – rarely understood as such by those modern people to whom it occurs. I have always been particularly interested to see how people, if left to their own devices and not informed about the history of the symbol, would interpret it to themselves. I was careful, therefore, not to disturb them with my own opinions and as a rule I discovered that people took it to symbolize themselves or rather something in themselves. They felt it as belonging intimately to themselves as a sort of creative background, a life-producing sun in the depths of the uncounscious mind. Though it was easy to see that it was often almost a replica of Ezekiel's vision, it was very rare that people recognized the analogy, even when they knew the vision – which knowledge, by the way, is pretty rare nowadays. What one could almost call a systematic blindness is simply the effect of the prejudice that the deity is *outside* man. Although this prejudice is not solely Christian, there are certain religions which do not share it at all. On the contrary they insist, as do certain Christian mystics, upon the essential identity of God and man, either in the form of an a priori identity, or of a goal to be attained by certain practices or initiations, as we know them, for instance, from the metamorphoses of Apuleius, not to speak of certain yoga methods.

The application of the comparative method indubitably shows the quaternity as being a more or less direct representation of the God manifested in his creation. We might, therefore, conclude that the symbol, spontaneously produced in the dreams of modern people, means the same thing – *the God within*. Although the majority of cases do not recognize this analogy, the interpretation might nevertheless be true. If we take into consideration the fact that the idea of God is an 'unscientific' hypothesis, we can easily explain why people have forgotten to think along such lines. And even if they cherish a certain belief in God they would be deterred from the idea of God within by their religious education, which always depreciated this idea as 'mystical.' Yet it is precisely this 'mystical' idea which is enforced by the natural tendencies of the unconscious mind. I myself, as well as my colleagues, have seen so many cases developing the same kind of symbolism that we cannot doubt its existence any longer. My observations, moreover, date back as far as 1914 and I waited fourteen years before I alluded publicly to them.

---

* *Cf.* the palaeolithic 'Sun Wheels' of Rhodesia.

It would be a regrettable mistake if anybody should understand my observations to be a kind of proof of the existence of God. They prove only the existence of an archetypal image of the Deity, which to my mind is the most we can assert psychologically about God. But as it is a very important and influential archetype, its relatively frequent occurrence seems to be a noteworthy fact for any theologia naturalis. Since the experience of it has the quality of numinosity, often to a high degree, it ranks among religious experiences.

I cannot omit calling attention to the interesting fact that whereas the central Christian symbolism is a Trinity, the formula of the unconscious mind is a quaternity. As a matter of fact even the orthodox Christian formula is not quite complete, because the dogmatic aspect of the evil principle is absent from the Trinity, the former leading a more or less awkward existence as devil. Since a God identical with man is a heretical assumption,* the 'God within' is also dogmatically difficult. But the quaternity as understood by the modern mind directly suggests not only the God within, but also the identity of God and man. Contrary to the dogma there are not three, but four aspects. It could easily be inferred that the fourth represents the devil. Though we have the logion: 'I myself and the Father are one. Who seeth me seeth the Father,' it would be considered as blasphemy or as madness to stress Christ's dogmatic humanity to such a degree that man could identify himself with Christ and his homoousia. But this is precisely the inference. From an orthodox standpoint, therefore, the natural quaternity could be declared to be 'diabolica fraus' and the capital piece of evidence would be the assimilation of the fourth aspect which represents the reprehensible part of the Christian cosmos. The church, I assume, has to invalidate any attempt at taking such results seriously. She must even condemn any approach to these experiences, since she cannot admit that nature unites what she has separated. The voice of nature is clearly audible in all the events that are connected with the quaternity, and this arouses all the old suspicions against anything connected with the unconscious mind. Scientific exploration of dreams is old oneiromancy and as objectionable as alchemy. Close parallels to the psychology of dreams are to be found among Latin alchemical tracts and are, like these, full of heresy.[5] There, it seems, was once reason enough for secrecy and protective metaphors.[6] The symbolic statements of old alchemy issue from the same unconscious mind as modern dreams and are just as much the voice of nature.

If we were still living in a medieval setting where there was not much doubt about the ultimate things and where every history of the world began with Genesis, we could easily brush aside dreams and the like. Unfortuna-

* I do not refer to the dogma of the human nature of Christ.

tely we live in a modern setting, where the ultimate things are doubtful, where there is a prehistory of enormous extension, and where people are fully aware of the fact that if there is any numinous experience at all, it is the experience of the psyche. We can no longer imagine an empyrean world revolving round the throne of God, and we would not dream of seeking for Him somewhere behind the galactic systems. But the human soul seems to harbor mysteries, since to an empiricist all religious experience boils down to a peculiar condition of the mind. If we want to know anything of what religious experience means to those who have it, we have every chance nowadays of studying every imaginable form of it. And if it means anything, it means everything to those who have it. This is at least the inevitable conclusion one reaches by a careful study of the evidence. One could even define religious experience as that kind of experience which is characterized by the highest appreciation, no matter what its contents are. Modern mentality, in as much as it is formulated by the verdict 'extra ecclesiam nulla salus', will turn to the soul as to a last hope. Where else could one obtain experience? The answer will be more or less of the kind which I have described. The voice of nature will answer and all those concerned with the spiritual problem of man will be confronted with new baffling problems. Through the spiritual need of my patients I have been forced to make a serious attempt at least to understand some of the extraordinary implications of the symbolism produced by the unconscious mind. As it would lead much too far to go into a discussion of the intellectual as well as the ethical consequences, I have to content myself with a mere allusion.

The main symbolic figures of a religion are always expressive of the particular moral and mental attitude involved. I mention, for instance, the cross and its various religious meanings. Another main symbol is the Trinity. It is of an exclusively masculine character. The unconscious mind, however, transforms it into a quaternity, being a unity at the same time, just as the three persons of the Trinity are one and the same God. The old philosophers of nature represented the Trinity, in as much as it was 'imaginata in natura', as the three ἀσώματα or 'spiritus', or 'volatilia', viz., water, air and fire. The fourth constituent on the other hand was τὸ σώματον, the earth or the body. They symbolized the latter by the Virgin.[7] In this way they added the feminine element to their physical Trinity, producing thereby the quaternity or the circulus quadratus, the symbol of which was the hermaphroditic Rebis, the filius sapientiae. The medieval philosophers of nature undoubtedly meant earth and woman by the fourth element. The principle of evil was not openly mentioned, but it appears in the poisonous quality of the prima materia and in other allusions. The quaternity in modern dreams is a product of the unconscious. As I explained in the first chapter, the unconscious is often personified by the anima, a female figure. Apparently the symbol of the quaternity issues from her. She would be the matrix of the quaternity, a θεοτόκος or Mater Dei, just as the earth was understood to be the Mother of God. But since the woman, as well as evil, is excluded from the Deity in the dogma of the Trinity, the element of evil would also form a part of the religious symbol, if the latter should be a quaternity. It needs no particular effort of imagination to guess the far-reaching spiritual consequence of such a development.

ON MYTHS AND ARCHETYPES

[...] The customary treatment of mythological motifs so far in separate departments of science, such as philology, ethnology, history of civilization and comparative religion, was not exactly a help to the recognition of their universality; and the psychological problems raised by this universality could easily be shelved by hypotheses of migration. Consequently Adolf Bastian's ideas met with little success in their day. Even then there was sufficient empirical evidence available to permit far-reaching psychological conclusions, but the necessary premises were lacking. Although the psychological knowledge of that time included the formation of myths in its province – witness W. Wundt's *Psychology of Nations* – it was not in a position to demonstrate this same process as a living function actually present in the psyche of civilized man, any more than it could understand mythological motifs as structural elements of the psyche. True to its history, where psychology was first of all metaphysics, then the study of the senses and their functions, then of the conscious mind and *its* functions, psychology identified its proper subject with the conscious psyche and its contents and thus completely overlooked the existence of an unconscious psyche. Although various philosophers, among them Leibnitz, Kant, and Schelling, had already pointed very clearly to the problem of the dark side of the psyche, it was a physician who felt impelled, from his scientific and medical experience, to point to the *unconscious* as the essential basis of the psyche. This was C. G. Carus, the authority whom Eduard von Hartmann followed. In recent times it was, once again, medical psychology that approached the problem of the unconscious without philosophical preconceptions. It became clear from many separate investigations that the psychopathology of the *neuroses* and of many *psychoses* cannot dispense with the hypothesis of a dark side of the psyche, i.e. the unconscious. It is the same with the psychology of *dreams*, which is really the *terra intermedia* between normal and pathological psychology. In the dream, as in the products of psychoses, there are numberless combinations to which one can find parallels only in mythological associations of ideas (or perhaps in certain poetic creations which are often characterized by a borrowing, not always conscious, from myths). Had thorough investigation shown that in the majority of such cases it was simply a matter of forgotten knowledge, the physician would not have gone to the trouble of making extensive researches into individual and collective parallels. But, in point of fact, typical mythologems were observed among individuals to whom all knowledge of this kind was absolutely out of the question, and where indirect derivation from religious ideas that might have been known to them, or from popular figures of speech, was impossible.[8] Such conclusions forced us to assume that we must be dealing with 'autochthonous' revivals independent of all tradition, and, consequently, that 'myth-forming' structural elements must be present in the unconscious psyche.[9]

These products are never (or at least very seldom) myths with a definite form, but rather mythological components which, because of their typical nature, we can call 'motifs', 'primordial images', types or – as I have named them – *archetypes*. The child archetype is an excellent example. Today we can hazard the formula that *the archetypes appear in myths and fairy-tales just as they do in dreams and in the products of psychotic fantasy*. The medium in which they are embedded is, in the former case, an ordered and for the most part immediately understandable context, but in the latter case a generally unintelligible, irrational, not to say delirious sequence of images which nonetheless does not lack a certain hidden coherence. In the individual, the archetypes occur as involuntary manifestations of unconscious processes whose existence and meaning can only be inferred, whereas the myth deals with traditional forms of incalculable age. They hark back to a prehistoric world whose spiritual preconceptions and general conditions we can still observe today among existing primitives. The myths on this plane are as a rule *tribal history* handed down from generation to generation by word of mouth. Primitive mentality differs from the civilized chiefly in that the conscious mind is far less developed in extent and intensity. Functions such as thinking, willing, etc. are not yet differentiated; they are pre-conscious, a fact which in the case of thinking, for instance, shows itself in the circumstance that the primitive does not think *consciously*, but that thoughts *appear*. The primitive cannot assert that he thinks; it is rather that 'something thinks in him'. The spontaneity of the act of thinking does not lie, causally, in his conscious mind, but in his unconscious. Moreover, he is incapable of any conscious effort of will; he must put himself beforehand into the 'mood of willing', or let himself be put – hence his *rites d'entrée et de sortie*. His conscious mind is menaced by an almighty unconscious: hence his fear of magical influences which may cross his path at any moment; and for this reason, too, he is surrounded by unknown forces and must adjust himself to them as best he can. Owing to the chronic twilight state of his consciousness, it is often next to impossible to find out whether he merely dreamed something or whether he really experienced it. The spontaneous manifestation of the unconscious and its archetypes intrudes everywhere into his conscious mind, and the mythical world of his ancestors – for instance, the *aljira* or *bugari* of the Australian aborigines–is a reality equal if not superior to the material world.[10] It is not the world as we know it that speaks out of his unconscious, but the unknown world of the psyche, of which we know that it mirrors our empirical world only in part, and that, for the other part, it moulds this empirical world in accordance with its own psychic assumptions. The archetype does not proceed from physical facts; it describes how the psyche experiences the physical fact, and in so doing the psyche often behaves so autocratically that it denies tangible reality or makes statements that fly in the face of it.[11]

The primitive mentality does not invent *myths*, it *experiences* them. Myths as original revelations of the pre-conscious psyche, involuntary statements about unconscious psychic happenings, and anything but allegories of physical processes.[12] Such allegories would be an idle amusement for an unscientific intellect. Myths, on the contrary, have a vital meaning. Not merely do they represent, they *are* the mental life of the primitive tribe, which immediately falls to pieces and decays when it loses its mythological heritage, like a man who has lost his soul. A tribe's mythology is its living religion, whose loss is always and everywhere, even among the civilized, a moral catastrophe. But religion is a vital link with psychic processes independent of and beyond consciousness, in the dark hinterland of the psyche. Many of these unconscious processes may be indirectly occasioned by consciousness, but never by conscious choice. Others appear to arise spontaneously, that is to say, from no discernible or demonstrable conscious cause.

Modern psychology treats the products of unconscious imagination as self-portraits of what is going on in the unconscious, or as statements of the unconscious psyche about itself. They fall into two categories. Firstly, fantasies (including dreams) of a personal character, which go back unquestionably to personal experiences, things forgotten or repressed, and can thus be completely explained by individual anamnesis. Secondly, fantasies (including dreams) of an impersonal character, which cannot be reduced to experiences in the individual's past, and thus cannot be explained as something individually acquired. These fantasy-pictures undoubtedly have their closest analogues in mythological types. We must therefore assume that they correspond to certain *collective* (and not personal) structural elements of the human psyche in general, and, like the morphological elements of the human body, are *inherited*. Although tradition and transmission by migration certainly play a part there are, as we have said, very many cases that cannot be accounted for in this way and drive us to the hypothesis of 'autochthonous revival'. These cases are so numerous that we cannot but assume the existence of a collective psychic substratum. I have called this the *collective unconscious*.

The products of this second category resemble the types of structures to be met with in myth and fairy-tale so much that we must regard them as related. It is therefore wholly within the realm of possibility that both, the mythological types as well as the individual types, arise under quite similar conditions. As already mentioned, the fantasy-products of the second category (as also those of the first) arise in a state of reduced intensity on the part of consciousness (in dreams, delirium, reveries, visions, etc.). In all these states the check put on the unconscious contents by the concentration of the conscious mind ceases, so that the hitherto unconscious material streams, as though from opened side-sluices, into the field of consciousness. This mode of origination is the general rule.*

Reduced intensity of consciousness and absence of concentration and attention, Janet's *abaissement du niveau mental*, correspond pretty exactly to the primitive state of consciousness in which, we must suppose, myths were originally formed. It is therefore exceedingly probable that the mythological archetypes, too, made their appearance in much the same manner as the manifestations of archetypal structures among individuals today.

The methodological principle in accordance with which psychology treats the products of the unconscious is this: *Contents of an archetypal character are manifestations of processes in the collective unconscious*. Hence they do not refer to anything that is or has been conscious, but to something *essentially unconscious*. In the last analysis, therefore, *it is impossible to say what they refer to*. Every interpretation necessarily remains an 'as-if'. The ultimate core of meaning may be circumscribed, but not described. Even so, the bare circumscription denotes an essential step forward in our knowledge of the pre-conscious structure of the psyche, which was already in existence when there was as yet no unity of personality (even today the primitive is not securely possessed of it) and no consciousness at all. We can also observe this pre-conscious state in early childhood, and as a matter of fact it is the dreams of this early period that not infrequently bring extremely remarkable archetypal contents to light.[13]

If, then, we proceed in accordance with the above principle, there is no longer any question of whether a myth refers to the sun or the moon, the father or the mother, sexuality or fire or water; all we can do is to circumscribe and give an approximate description of an *unconscious core of meaning*.

---

* Except for certain cases of spontaneous vision, *automatismes téléologiques* (Flournoy), and the processes in the method of 'active imagination', which I have described.

The ultimate meaning of this nucleus was never conscious and never will be. It was, and still is, only interpreted, and every interpretation that more or less approximates to the hidden sense (or, from the point of view of the scientific intellect, nonsense, which comes to the same thing) has always, right from the beginning, laid claim not only to absolute truth and validity but to instant reverence and religious devotion. Archetypes were, and still are, psychic forces that demand to be taken seriously, and they have a strange way of making sure of their effect. Always they were the bringers of protection and salvation, and their violation has as its consequence the 'perils of the soul' known to us from the psychology of primitives. Moreover, they are the infallible causes of neurotic and even psychotic disorders, behaving exactly like neglected or maltreated physical organs or organic functional systems.

What an archetypal content is always expressing is first and foremost a *figure of speech*. If it speaks of the sun and identifies with it the lion, the king, the hoard of gold guarded by the dragon, or the force that makes for the life and health of man, it is neither the one thing nor the other, but the unknown third thing that finds more or less adequate expression in all these similes, yet – to the perpetual vexation of the intellect – remains unknown and not to be fitted into a formula. For this reason the scientific intellect is always inclined to put on airs of enlightenment in the hope of banishing the spectre once and for all. Whether its endeavours were called euhemerism, or Christian apologetics, or Enlightenment in the narrow sense, or Positivism, there was always a myth hiding behind it, in new and disconcerting garb, which then, following the ancient and venerable pattern, gave itself out as ultimate truth. In reality we can never legitimately cut loose from our archetypal foundations unless we are prepared to pay the price of a neurosis, any more than we can rid ourselves of our body and its organs without committing suicide. If we cannot deny the archetypes or otherwise neutralize them, we are confronted, at every new stage in the differentiation of consciousness to which civilization attains, with the task of finding a new *interpretation* appropriate to this stage, in order to connect the life of the past that still exists in us with the life of the present, which threatens to slip away from it. If this link-up does not take place, a kind of rootless consciousness comes into being no longer orientated to the past, a consciousness which succumbs helplessly to all manner of suggestions and, practically speaking, is susceptible to psychic epidemics. With the loss of the past, now become 'insignificant', devalued, and incapable of revaluation, the saviour is lost too, for *the saviour is either the insignificant thing itself or else rises out of it*. Over and over again in the *Gestaltwandel der Götter* (Ziegler), he rises up as the prophet or first-born of a new generation and appears unexpectedly in the most unlikely places (sprung from a stone, tree, furrow, water, etc.) and in ambiguous form (Tom Thumb, dwarf, child, animal, and so on).

This archetype of the 'child-god' is extremely wide-spread and intimately bound up with all the other mythological aspects of the child-motif.

[. . .]

The child-motif not infrequently occurs in the field of psychopathology. The 'imaginary' child is common among women with mental disorders and is usually interpreted in a Christian sense. Homunculi also appear, as in the famous Schreber case,[14] where they come in swarms and plague the sufferer. But the clearest and most significant manifestation of the child-motif in the therapy of neuroses is in the maturation process of personality induced by the analysis of the unconscious, which I have termed the process of *individuation*.[15] In it, we are confronted with pre-conscious processes which, in the form of more or less concretely shaped fantasies, gradually pass over into the conscious mind, or become conscious as dreams, or, lastly, are made conscious through the method of *active imagination*.[16] These materials are rich in archetypal motifs, among them frequently that of the child. Often the child is formed after the Christian model; more often, though, it develops from earlier, altogether non-Christian levels – that is to say, out of chthonic animals such as crocodiles, dragons, serpents, or monkeys. Sometimes the child appears in the cup of a flower, or out of an egg, or as the centre of a *mandala*. In dreams it often occurs as the dreamer's son or daughter, as a boy, youth, or young girl; occasionally it seems to be of exotic origin, Indian or Chinese, with a dusky skin, or, appearing more cosmically, surrounded by stars or with a starry coronet; as the king's son or the witch's child with daemonic attributes. Seen as a special instance of 'the treasure hard to attain' motif,[17] the child-motif is extremely protean and assumes all manner of shapes, such as the jewel, the pearl, the flower, the chalice, the golden egg, the quaternity, the golden ball, and so on. It can be interchanged with these and similar images almost without limit.

As to the *psychology* of our theme I must point out that every statement going beyond the purely phenomenal aspects of an archetype lays itself open to the criticism we have expressed above. Not for a moment dare we succumb to the illusion that an archetype can be finally explained and disposed of. Even the best attempts at explanation are only more or less successful translations into another metaphorical language. (Indeed, language itself is only a metaphor). The most we can do is to *dream the myth onwards* and give it a modern dress. And whatever explanation or interpretation does to it, we do to our own souls as well, with corresponding results for our own well-being. The archetype – let us never forget this – is a psychic organ present in all of us. A bad explanation means a correspondingly bad attitude to this organ, which may thus be injured. But the ultimate sufferer is the bad interpreter himself. Hence the 'explanation' should always be such that the functional significance of the archetype remains unimpaired, i.e. that an adequate and appropriate relationship between the conscious mind and the archetypes is insured. For the archetype is an element of our psychic structure and thus a vital and necessary component in our psychic economy. It represents or personifies certain instinctive premises in the dark, primitive psyche, in the real but invisible *roots of consciousness*. Of what elementary importance the connexion with these roots is, we see from the preoccupation of the primitive mentality with certain 'magic' factors, which are nothing less than what we call archetypes. This primary form of *religio* ('linking up') is the essence, the working basis of all religious life even today, and always will be, whatever future form this life may take.

There is no 'rational' substitute for the archetype any more than there is for the cerebellum or the kidneys. We can examine the physical organs anatomically, histologically, and embryologically. This would correspond to an outline of archetypal phenomenology and its presentation in historical and comparative terms. But we only arrive at the *meaning* of a physical organ when we begin to ask teleological questions. Hence the query arises: What is the biological purpose of the archetype? Just as physiology answers such a question for the body, so it is the business of psychology to answer it for the archetype.

Statements like 'the child-motif is a vestigal memory of one's own childhood' and similar explanations merely beg the question. But if, giving this proposition a slight twist, we were to say: 'The child-motif is a picture of certain *forgotten* things in our childhood', we are getting closer to the truth. Since, however, the archetype has always to do with a picture belonging to the whole human race and not merely to the individual, we might put it better this way: *'The child-motif represents the pre-conscious, childhood aspect of the collective psyche.'**

[. . .]

---

* It may not be superfluous to point out that lay prejudice is always inclined to identify the child-motif with the concrete experience 'child', as though the real child were the cause and pre-condition of the existence of the child-motif. In psychological reality, however, the empirical idea 'child' is only the means (and not the only one) to express a psychic fact that cannot be formulated more exactly. Hence by the same token the mythological idea of the child is emphatically not a copy of the empirical child, but a *symbol* clearly recognizable as such: it is a wonder-child, a divine child, begotten, born, and brought up in quite extraordinary circumstances, and not – this is the point – a human child. Its deeds are as miraculous or monstrous as its nature and physical make-up. Simply

The psychologist has to contend with the same difficulties as the mythologist when an exact definition or clear and concise information is demanded of him. The picture is concrete, clear, and subject to no misunderstandings only when it is seen in its habitual context. In this form it tells us everything it contains. But as soon as one tries to abstract the 'real essence' of the picture, the whole thing becomes cloudy and indistinct. In order to understand its living function, we must let it remain an organic thing in all its complexity and not try to examine the anatomy of its corpse in the manner of the scientist, or the archaeology of its ruins in the manner of the historian. Naturally this is not to deny the justification of such methods when applied in their proper place.

In view of the enormous complexity of psychic phenomena, a purely phenomenological point of view is, and will be for a long time, the only possible one and the only one with any prospect of success. 'Whence' things come and 'what' they are, these, particularly in the field of psychology, are questions which are apt to call forth untimely attempts at explanation. Such speculations are moreover based far more on unconscious philosophical premises than on the nature of the phenomena themselves. Psychic phenomena occasioned by unconscious processes are so rich and so multifarious that I prefer to *describe* my findings and observations and, where possible, to classify them, that is, to arrange them *under certain definite types*. That is the method of natural science, and it is applied wherever we have to do with multifarious and still disorganized material. One may question the utility or the appropriateness of the categories or types used in the arrangement, but not the correctness of the method itself.

Since I have been observing and investigating the products of the unconscious in the widest sense of the word, namely dreams, fantasies, visions, and delusions of the insane, for years, I have not been able to avoid recognizing certain regularities, that is, *types*. There are types of *situations* and types of *figures* that repeat themselves frequently and have a corresponding meaning. I therefore employ the term 'motif' to designate these repetitions. Thus there are not only typical dreams but typical motifs in the dreams. These may, as we have said, be situations or figures. Among the latter there are human figures that can be arranged under a series of types, the chief of them being, according to my proposal*, the *shadow*, the *Wise Old Man*, the

---

and solely on account of these highly unempirical properties is it necessary to speak of a 'child-motif' at all. Moreover, the mythological 'child' has various forms: now a god, giant, Tom Thumb, animal, etc., and this points to a causality that is anything but rational or concretely human. The same is true of the 'father' and 'mother' archetypes which, mythologically speaking, are likewise irrational symbols.

child (including the child-hero), the *mother* ('Primordial Mother' and 'Earth Mother') as a superordinate personality ('daemonic' because superordinate), and her counterpart the *maiden*, and lastly the *anima* in man and the *animus* in woman.

[. . .]

NOTES

1. Rudolf Otto, *Das Heilige* (1917).
2. 'But our esteem for facts has not neutralized in us all religiousness. It is itself almost religious. Our scientific temper is devout'. (William James, *Pragmatism* (1911), pp. 14 ff).
3. 'Religio est, quae superioris cuiusdam naturae (quam divinam vocant) curam caerimoniamque affert'. (Cicero, *De invent. Rhetor.*, Lib. II); 'Religiose testimonium dicere ex jurisjurandi fide'. (Cicero, *Pro Coel.*, 55).
4. Heinrich Scholz *(Religionsphilosophie*, 1921) insists upon a similar point of view; see also H. R. Pearcy, *A Vindication of Paul* (1936).
5. I refer chiefly to works containing alchemistic legends (Lehrerzählungen). A good example is M. Majer, *Symbola aureae mensae duodecim nationum* (1617), containing the symbolic peregrinatio, pp. 569 ff.
6. As far as I know there are no complaints in alchemistic literature of persecution by the church. The authors allude usually to the tremendous secret of the magisterium as a reason for secrecy.
7. See *Pandora* (The glorification of the body in the form of an assumption of Mary), 1588. St. Augustine has also symbolized the Virgin by the earth: 'Veritas de terra orta est, quia Christus de virgine natus est' *(Sermones*, 188, I, 5, p. 890). The same Tertullian, 'Illa terra virgo nondum pluviis rigata nec imbribus foecundata . . .' *(Adv. Iud.*, 13, p. 199 A).
8. A working example in *Seelenprobleme der Gegenwart* (1931), pp. 161 ff.
9. Freud, in his *Interpretation of Dreams*, paralleled certain aspects of infantile psychology with the Oedipus legend and observed that its 'universal validity' was to be explained in terms of a similar infantile preconception ! The real working out of mythological material was then taken up by my pupils (A. Maeder, *Arch. der Psychologie*, T. VI, 1907, *Psych.-Neurol. Wochenschrift*, X; F. Riklin, *Psych.-Neurol. Wochenschrift*, IX, *Schriften zur angewandten Seelenkunde*, 2, 1908; C. Abraham, *Schriften zur angewandten Seelenkunde*, 4, 1909). They were succeeded by Otto Rank of the Viennese school *(Schriften zur angewandten Seelenkunde*, 5, 1909). In the *Psychology of the Unconscious* (1911),

---

* To the best of my knowledge no other proposals have been made so far. Critics have contented themselves with asserting that no such archetypes exist. Certainly they do not exist, any more than a botanical system exists in nature ! But will anyone deny the existence of natural plant-families on that account ? Or will anyone deny the occurrence and continual repetition of certain morphological and functional similarities ? It is much the same thing in principle with the typical figures of the unconscious. They are forms existing *a priori*, or biological norms of psychic activity.

I presented a somewhat more comprehensive examination of psychic and mythological parallels. Cf. also my essay 'Über den Archetypus', *Zentralblatt für Psychotherapie*, IX (1936).

10. The fact is well known, and the relevant ethnological literature is too great to be mentioned here.

11. *Cf.* note 10 *supra*.

12. *Cf. Seelenprobleme der Gegenwart* (1931), pp. 167 ff.

13. The relevant material can only be found in the unprinted reports of the Psychological Seminar at the Federal Polytechnic in Zürich, 1936–39, and in Dr. Michael Fordham's recent book *The Life of Childhood* (London, Kegan Paul, 1944).

14. Schreber, *Denkwürdigkeiten eines Nervenkranken* (1903).

15. For a general presentation see *The Integration of Personality* (Kegan Paul, 1933), chap. 1. Specific phenomena in the following chapters, also in 'Traumsymbole des Individuationsprozesses', *Eranos-Jahrbuch* 1935.

16. *Die Beziehungen zwischen dem Ich und dem Unbewussten* (1928), chap. 3.

17. *The Psychology of the Unconsious*, p. 103 and *passim*.

Bronisław Malinowski

Bronislaw Kaspar Malinowski was born in 1884 in Cracow, Poland, where he received his primary and secondary school education. He was a student at the University of Cracow and obtained his Ph. D. degree in physics and mathematics in 1908. After having worked on physical chemistry in Leipzig between 1908 and 1910, Malinowski decided to devote his life to anthropology. He went to England, where he studied from 1910 to 1914 at the London School of Economics with C. G. Seligmann, E. Westermarck and W. H. R. Rivers, and where, on many occasions, he met J. G. Frazer. In 1916 he obtained the D. Sc. in Anthropology at the University of London. In 1914 he went to Australia, where he was interned as an enemy alien because of his Austrian nationality. However, he was allowed to make three large field trips for anthropological research, one of which to New Guinea and two of which to Boyawa, one of the Trobriand Islands, where he lived among the native population (1915—16 and 1917—18). Thereupon he spent a year at the Canary Islands and two years in Cavoise, Australia. In 1923 he moved to Northern Italy where later he used to spend his summers. Then Malinowski became a Reader in Social Anthropology at the University of London, and Professor of Anthropology in 1927. In 1929 he settled down definitely in London. In 1938 Malinowski went to the United States for his work, and took up a post at Yale University in 1939; in 1940 and 1941 he did fieldwork in Mexico. He died at New Haven in 1942.

The main books by Malinowski of direct interest to the study of religion are: 1922 *Argonauts of the Western Pacific;* 1935 *Coral Gardens and their Magic* (2 vols.); 1936 *The Foundations of Faith and Morals;* 1944 *A Scientific Theory of Culture and Other Essays;* 1954 *Magic, Science and Religion, and Other Essays;* 1962 *Sex, Culture and Myth.*

Malinowski's work is of interest to the study of religion in the first place because of his fieldwork methodology, whereby he prescribed that the anthropologist has to be a participant observer in the society studied. In his interpretations he stressed the general problems of cultures which should be seen in terms of fundamental human situations. His concern was with the actual function which the real elements of a culture perform within that culture, and he opposed himself to the attempt to reconstruct a past of such a culture with the help of a relatively small number of survivals. For Malinowski, religion, just as other social institutions, is a basically emotional response to the needs of cultural survival. Although magic and religion are both a function of culture, the latter distinguishes itself by its non-utilitarian purpose.

The following fragment has been taken from *Magic, Science and Religion* and clearly shows, after a survey of some existing theories, Malinowski's functional approach in his study of religion and magic.

THE STUDY OF 'PRIMITIVE MAN' AND HIS RELIGION

Studies on primitive religion

There are no peoples however primitive without religion and magic. Nor
are there, it must be added at once, any savage races lacking either in the
scientific attitude or in science, though this lack has been frequently attributed to them. In every primitive community, studied by trustworthy and
competent observers, there have been found two clearly distinguishable
domains, the Sacred and the Profane; in other words, the domain of Magic
and Religion and that of Science.

On the one hand there are the traditional acts and observances, regarded
by the natives as sacred, carried out with reverence and awe, hedged around
with prohibitions and special rules of behavior. Such acts and observances
are always associated with beliefs in supernatural forces, especially those
of magic, or with ideas about beings, spirits, ghosts, dead ancestors, or
gods. On the other hand, a moment's reflection is sufficient to show that
no art or craft however primitive could have been invented or maintained,
no organized form of hunting, fishing, tilling, or search for food could be
carried out without the careful observation of natural process and a firm
belief in its regularity, without the power of reasoning and without confidence in the power of reason; that is, without the rudiments of science.

The credit of having laid the foundations of an anthropological study of
religion belongs to Edward B. Tylor. In his well-known theory he maintains
that the essence of primitive religion is animism, the belief in spiritual
beings, and he shows how this belief has originated in a mistaken but
consistent interpretation of dreams, visions, hallucinations, cataleptic
states, and similar phenomena. Reflecting on these, the savage philosopher
or theologian was led to distinguish the human soul from the body. Now the
soul obviously continues to lead an existence after death, for it appears in
dreams, haunts the survivors in memories and in visions and apparently
influences human destinies. Thus originated the belief in ghosts and the
spirits of the dead, in immortality and in a nether world. But man in
general, and primitive man in particular, has a tendency to imagine the
outer world in his own image. And since animals, plants, and objects move,
act, behave, help man or hinder him, they must also be endowed with souls
or spirits. Thus animism, the philosophy and the religion of primitive man,
has been built up from observations and by inferences, mistaken but
comprehensible in a crude and untutored mind.

Tylor's view of primitive religion, important as it was, was based on too
narrow a range of facts, and it made early man too contemplative and
rational. Recent field work, done by specialists, shows us the savage interested rather in his fishing and gardens, in tribal events and festivities than

brooding over dreams and visions, or explaining 'doubles' and cataleptic fits, and it reveals also a great many aspects of early religion which cannot be possibly placed in Tylor's scheme of animism.

The extended and deepened outlook of modern anthropology finds its most adequate expression in the learned and inspiring writings of Sir James Frazer. In these he has set forth the three main problems of primitive religion with which present-day anthropology is busy; magic and its relation to religion and science; totemism and the sociological aspect of early faith; the cults of fertility and vegetation. It will be best to discuss these subjects in turn.

Frazer's *Golden Bough*, the great codex of primitive magic, shows clearly that animism is not the only, nor even the dominating belief in primitive culture. Early man seeks above all to control the course of nature for practical ends, and he does it directly, by rite and spell, compelling wind and weather, animals and crops to obey his will. Only much later, finding the limitations of his magical might, does he in fear or hope, in supplication or defiance, appeal to higher beings; that is, to demons, ancestor-spirits or gods. It is in this distinction between direct control on the one hand and propitiation of superior powers on the other that Sir James Frazer sees the difference between religion and magic. Magic, based on man's confidence that he can dominate nature directly, if only he knows the laws which govern it magically, is in this akin to science. Religion, the confession of human impotence in certain matters, lifts man above the magical level, and later on maintains its independence side by side with science, to which magic has to succumb.

This theory of magic and religion has been the starting point of most modern studies of the twin subjects. Professor Preuss in Germany, Dr. Marett in England, and MM. Hubert and Mauss in France have independently set forth certain views, partly in criticism of Frazer, partly following up the lines of his inquiry. These writers point out that similar as they appear, science and magic differ yet radically. Science is born of experience, magic made by tradition. Science is guided by reason and corrected by observation, magic, impervious to both, lives in an atmosphere of mysticism. Science is open to all, a common good of the whole community, magic is occult, taught through mysterious initiations, handed on in a hereditary or at least in very exclusive filiation. While science is based on the conception of natural forces, magic springs from the idea of a certain mystic, impersonal power, which is believed in by most primitive peoples. This power, called *mana* by some Melanesians, *arungquiltha* by certain Australian tribes, *wakan, orenda, manitu* by various American Indians, and nameless elsewhere, is stated to be a well-nigh universal idea found wherever magic flourishes. According to the writers just mentioned we can find among the most primitive peoples and throughout the lower savagery a belief in a supernatural, impersonal force, moving all those agencies which are relevant to the savage and causing all the really important events in the domain of the sacred. Thus *mana*, not animism, is the essence of 'pre-animistic religion', and it is also the essence of magic, which is thus radically different from science.

There remains the question, however, what is *mana*, this impersonal force of magic supposed to dominate all forms of early belief? Is it a fundamental idea, an innate category of the primitive mind, or can it be explained by still simpler and more fundamental elements of human psychology or of the reality in which primitive man lives? The most original and important contribution to these problems is given by the late Professor Durkheim, and it touches the other subject, opened up by Sir James Frazer: that of totemism and of the sociological aspect of religion.

Totemism, to quote Frazer's classical definition, 'is an intimate relation which is supposed to exist between a group of kindred people on the one side and a species of natural or artificial objects on the other side, which objects are called the totems of the human group'. Totemism thus has two sides: it is a mode of social grouping and a religious system of beliefs and practices. As religion, it expresses primitive man's interest in his surroundings, the desire to claim an affinity and to control the most important objects: above all, animal or vegetable species, more rarely useful inanimate objects, very seldom man-made things. As a rule species of animals and plants used for staple food or at any rate edible or useful or ornamental animals are held in a special form of 'totemic reverence' and are tabooed to the members of the clan which is associated with the species and which sometimes performs rites and ceremonies for its multiplication. The social aspect of totemism consists in the subdivision of the tribe into minor units, called in anthropology *clans, gentes, sibs,* or *phratries.*

In totemism we see therefore not the result of early man's speculations about mysterious phenomena, but a blend of a utilitarian anxiety about the most necessary objects of his surroundings, with some preoccupation in those which strike his imagination and attract his attention, such as beautiful birds, reptiles and dangerous animals. With our knowledge of what could be called the totemic attitude of mind, primitive religion is seen to be nearer to reality and to the immediate practical life interests of the savage, than it appeared in its 'animistic' aspect emphasized by Tylor and the earlier anthropologists.

By its apparently strange association with a problematic form of social division, I mean the clan system, totemism has taught anthropology yet another lesson: it has revealed the importance of the sociological aspect in all the early forms of cult. The savage depends upon the group with whom he is in direct contact both for practical co-operation and mental solidarity to a far larger extent than does civilized man. Since – as can be seen in totemism, magic, and many other practices – early cult and ritual are closely associated with practical concerns as well as with mental needs, there must exist an intimate connection between social organization and religious belief. This was understood already by that pioneer of religious anthropology, Robertson Smith, whose principle that primitive religion 'was essentially an affair of the community rather than of individuals' has become a *Leitmotiv* of modern research. According to Professor Durkheim, who has put these views most forcibly, 'the religious' is identical with 'the social'. For 'in a general way . . . a society has all that is necessary to arouse the sensation of the Divine in minds, merely by the power that it has over them; for to its members it is what a God is to its worshippers'.[1] Professor Durkheim arrives at this conclusion by the study of totemism, which he believes to be the most primitive form of religion. In this the 'totemic principle' which is identical with *mana* and with 'the God of the clan . . . can be nothing else than the clan itself'.[2]

These strange and somewhat obscure conclusions will be criticized later, and it will be shown in what consists the grain of truth they undoubtedly contain and how fruitful it can be. It has borne fruit, in fact, in influencing some of the most important writing of mixed classical scholarship and anthropology, to mention only the works of Miss Jane Harrison and Mr. Cornford.

The third great subject introduced into the Science of Religion by Sir James Frazer is that of the cults of vegetation and fertility. In *The Golden Bough*, starting from the awful and mysterious ritual of the wood divinities at Nemi, we are led through an amazing variety of magical and religious cults, devised by man to stimulate and control the fertilizing work of skies and earth and of sun and rain, and we are left with the impression that early religion is teeming with the forces of savage life, with its young beauty and crudity, with its exuberance and strength so violent that it leads now and again to suicidal acts of self-immolation. The study of *The Golden Bough* shows us that for primitive man death has meaning mainly as a step to resurrection, decay as a stage of rebirth, the plenty of autumn and the decline of winter as preludes to the revival of spring. Inspired by these passages of *The Golden Bough* a number of writers have developed, often with greater precision and with a fuller analysis than by Frazer himself, what could be called the *vitalistic* view of religion. Thus Mr. Crawley in his *Tree of Life*, M. van Gennep in his *Rites de Passage*, and Miss Jane Harrison in several works, have given evidence that faith and cult spring from the crises of human existence, 'the great events of life, birth, adolescence, marriage, death . . . it is about these events that religion largely focuses.[3]

The tension of instinctive need, strong emotional experiences, lead in some way or other to cult and belief. 'Art and Religion alike spring from unsatisfied desire.'[4] How much truth there is in this somewhat vague statement and how much exaggeration we shall be able to assess later on.

There are two important contributions to the theory of primitive religion which I mention here only, for they have somehow remained outside the main current of anthropological interest. They treat of the primitive idea of one God and of the place of morals in primitive religion respectively. It is remarkable that they have been and still are neglected, for are not these two questions first and foremost in the mind of anyone who studies religion, however crude and rudimentary it may be? Perhaps the explanation is in the preconceived idea that 'origins' must be very crude and simple and different from the 'developed forms', or else in the notion that the 'savage' or 'primitive' is really savage and primitive!

The late Andrew Lang indicated the existence among some Australian natives of the belief in a tribal All-Father, and the Rev. Pater Wilhelm Schmidt has adduced much evidence proving that this belief is universal among all the peoples of the simplest cultures and that it cannot be discarded as an irrelevant fragment of mythology, still less as an echo of missionary teaching. It looks, according to Pater Schmidt, very much like an indication of a simple and pure form of early monotheism.

The problem of morals as an early religious function was also left on one side, until it received an exhaustive treatment, not only in the writings of Pater Schmidt but also and notably in two works of outstanding importance: the *Origin and Development of Moral Ideas* of Professor E. Westermarck, and *Morals in Evolution* of Professor L. T. Hobhouse.

It is not easy to summarize concisely the trend of anthropological studies in our subject. On the whole it has been towards an increasingly elastic and comprehensive view of religion. Tylor had still to refute the fallacy that there are primitive peoples without religion. Today we are somewhat perplexed by the discovery that to a savage all is religion, that he perpetually lives in a world of mysticism and ritualism. If religion is co-extensive with 'life' and with 'death' into the bargain, if it arises from all 'collective' acts and from all 'crises in the individual's existence', if it comprises all savage 'theory' and covers all his 'practical concerns' – we are led to ask, not without dismay: What remains outside it, what is the world of the 'profane' in primitive life? Here is a first problem into which modern anthropology, by the number of contradictory views, has thrown some confusion, as can be seen even from the above short sketch. We shall be able to contribute towards its solution in the next section.

Primitive religion, as fashioned by modern anthropology, has been made to harbor all sorts of heterogeneous things. At first reserved in animism for the solemn figures of ancestral spirits, ghosts and souls, besides a few fetishes, it had gradually to admit the thin, fluid, ubiquitous *mana;* then, like Noah's Ark, it was with the introduction of totemism loaded with beasts, not in pairs but in shoals and species, joined by plants, objects, and even manufactured articles; then came human activities and concerns and the gigantic ghost of the Collective Soul, Society Divinized. Can there be any order or system put into this medley of apparently unrelated objects and principles? This question will occupy us in the third section.

One achievement of modern anthropology we shall not question: the recognition that magic and religion are not merely a doctrine or a philosophy, not merely an intellectual body of opinion, but a special mode of behavior, a pragmatic attitude built up of reason, feeling, and will alike. It is a mode of action as well as a system of belief, and a sociological phenomenon as well as a personal experience. But with all this, the exact relation between the social and the individual contributions to religion is not clear, as we have seen from the exaggerations committed on either side. Nor is it clear what are the respective shares of emotion and reason. All these questions will have to be dealt with by future anthropology, and it will be possible only to suggest solutions and indicate lines of argument in this short essay.

'Rational mastery by man of his surroundings'

The problem of primitive knowledge has been singularly neglected by anthropology. Studies on savage psychology were exclusively confined to early religion, magic and mythology. Only recently the work of several English, German, and French writers, notably the daring and brilliant speculations of Professor Lévy-Bruhl, gave an impetus to the student's interest in what the savage does in his more sober moods. The results were startling indeed: Professor Lévy-Bruhl tells us, to put it in a nutshell, that primitive man has no sober moods at all, that he is hopelessly and completely immersed in a mystical frame of mind. Incapable of dispassionate and consistent observation, devoid of the power of abstraction, hampered by 'a decided aversion towards reasoning', he is unable to draw any benefit from experience, to construct or comprehend even the most elementary laws of nature. 'For minds thus orientated there is no fact purely physical.' Nor can there exist for them any clear idea of substance and attribute, cause and effect, identity and contradiction. Their outlook is that of confused superstition, 'prelogical', made of mystic 'participations' and 'exclusions'. I have here summarized a body of opinion, of which the brilliant French sociologist is the most decided and competent spokesman, but which numbers besides, many anthropologists and philosophers of renown.

But there are also dissenting voices. When a scholar and anthropologist
of the measure of Professor J. L. Myres entitles an article in *Notes and
Queries* 'Natural Science', and when we read there that the savage's
'knowledge based on observation is distinct and accurate', we must surely
pause before accepting primitive man's irrationality as a dogma. Another
highly competent writer, Dr. A. A. Goldenweiser, speaking about primitive
'discoveries, inventions and improvements' – which could hardly be attributed to any pre-empirical or prelogical mind – affirms that 'it would be
unwise to ascribe to the primitive mechanic merely a passive part in the
origination of inventions. Many a happy thought must have crossed his
mind, nor was he wholly unfamiliar with the thrill that comes from an idea
effective in action.' Here we see the savage endowed with an attitude of
mind wholly akin to that of a modern man of science!

To bridge over the wide gap between the two extreme opinions current
on the subject of primitive man's reason, it will be best to resolve the
problem into two questions.

First, has the savage any rational outlook, any rational mastery of his surroundings, or is he, as M. Lévy-Bruhl and his school maintain, entirely 'mystical'? The answer will be that every primitive community is in possession of a
considerable store of knowledge, based on experience and fashioned by reason.

The second question then opens: Can this primitive knowledge be regarded
as a rudimentary form of science or is it, on the contrary, radically different,
a crude empiry, a body of practical and technical abilities, rules of thumb
and rules of art having no theoretical value? This second question, epistemological rather than belonging to the study of man, will be barely touched
upon at the end of this section and a tentative answer only will be given.

[. . .]

'Life, death, and destiny in early faith and cult'

We pass now to the domain of the *sacred*, to religious and magical creeds
and rites. Our historical survey of theories has left us somewhat bewildered
with the chaos of opinions and with the jumble of phenomena. While it was
difficult not to admit into the enclosure of religion one after the other,
spirits and ghosts, totems and social events, death and life, yet in the
process religion seemed to become a thing more and more confused, both
an all and a nothing. It certainly cannot be defined by its subject matter
in a narrow sense, as 'spirit worship', or as 'ancestor cult', or as the 'cult of
nature'. It includes animism, animatism, totemism, and festishism, but it
is not any one of them exclusively. The *ism* definition of religion in its
origins must be given up, for religion does not cling to any one object or

class of objects, though incidentally it can touch and hallow all. Nor, as we have seen, is religion identical with Society or the Social, nor can we remain satisfied by a vague hint that it clings to life only, for death opens perhaps the vastest view on to the other world. As an 'appeal to higher powers', religion can only be distinguished from magic and not defined in general, but even this view will have to be slightly modified and supplemented.

The problem before us is, then, to try to put some order into the facts. This will allow us to determine somewhat more precisely the character of the domain of the *Sacred* and mark it off from that of the *Profane*. It will also give us an opportunity to state the relation between magic and religion.

The creative acts of religion. It will be best to face the facts first and, in order not to narrow down the scope of the survey, to take as our watchword the vaguest and most general of indices: 'Life.' As a matter of fact, even a slight acquaintance with ethnological literature is enough to convince anyone that in reality the physiological phases of human life, and, above all, its crises, such as conception, pregnancy, birth, puberty, marriage, and death, form the nuclei of numerous rites and beliefs. Thus beliefs about conception, such as that in reincarnation, spirit-entry, magical impregnation, exist in one form or another in almost every tribe, and they are often associated with rites and observances. During pregnancy the expectant mother has to keep certain taboos and undergo ceremonies, and her husband shares at times in both. At birth, before and after, there are various magical rites to prevent dangers and undo sorcery, ceremonies of purification, communal rejoicings and acts of presentation of the newborn to higher powers or to the community. Later on in life the boys and, much less frequently, the girls have to undergo the often protracted rites of initiation, as a rule shrouded in mystery and marred by cruel and obscene ordeals.

Without going any further, we can see that even the very beginnings of human life are surrounded by an inextricably mixed-up medley of beliefs and rites. They seem to be strongly attracted by any important event in life, to crystallize around it, surround it with a rigid crust of formalism and ritualism – but to what purpose? Since we cannot define cult and creed by their objects, perhaps it will be possible to perceive their function.

A closer scrutiny of the facts allows us to make from the outset a preliminary classification into two main groups. Compare a rite carried out to prevent death in childbed with another typical custom, a ceremony in celebration of a birth. The first rite is carried out as a means to an end, it has a definite practical purpose which is known to all who practice it and can be easily elicited from any native informant. The post-natal ceremony, say a presentation of a newborn or a feast of rejoicing in the event, has no purpose: it is not a means to an end but an end in itself. It expresses the feelings of the mother, the father, the relatives, the whole community, but there is no future event which this ceremony foreshadows, which it is meant to bring about or to prevent. This difference will serve us as a *prima facie* distinction between magic and religion. While in the magical act the underlying idea and aim is always clear, straightforward, and definite, in the religious ceremony there is no purpose directed toward a subsequent event. It is only possible for the sociologist to establish the function, the sociological *raison d'être* of the act. The native can always state the end of the magical rite, but he will say, of a religious ceremony that it is done because such is the usage, or because it has been ordained, or he will narrate an explanatory myth.

In order to grasp better the nature of primitive religious ceremonies and their function, let us analyze the ceremonies of initiation. They present right through the vast range of their occurrence certain striking similarities. Thus the novices have to undergo a more or less protracted period of seclusion and preparation. Then comes initiation proper, in which the youth, passing through a series of ordeals, is finally submitted to an act of bodily mutilation: at the mildest, a slight incision or the knocking out of a tooth; or, more severe, circumcision; or, really cruel and dangerous, an operation such as the subincision practiced in some Australian tribes. The ordeal is usually associated with the idea of the death and rebirth of the initiated one, which is sometimes enacted in a mimetic performance. But besides the ordeal, less conspicuous and dramatic, but in reality more important, is the second main aspect of initiation: the systematic instruction of the youth in sacred myth and tradition, the gradual unveiling of tribal mysteries and the exhibition of sacred objects.

The ordeal and the unveiling of tribal mysteries are usually believed to have been instituted by one or more legendary ancestors or culture heroes, or by a Superior Being of superhuman character. Sometimes he is said to swallow the youths, or to kill them, and then to restore them again as fully initiated men. His voice is imitated by the hum of the bull-roarer to inspire awe in the uninitiated women and children. Through these ideas initiation brings the novice into relationship with higher powers and personalities, such as the Guardian Spirits and Tutelary Divinities of the North American Indians, the Tribal All-Father of some Australian Aborigines, the Mythological Heroes of Melanesia and other parts of the world. This is the third fundamental element, besides ordeal and the teaching of tradition, in the rites of passing into manhood.

Now what is the sociological function of these customs, what part do they play in the maintenance and development of civilization? As we have seen, the youth is taught in them the sacred traditions under most impressive conditions of preparation and ordeal and under the sanction of Supernatural

Beings – the light of tribal revelation bursts upon him from out of the shadows of fear, privation, and bodily pain.

Let us realize that in primitive conditions tradition is of supreme value for the community and nothing matters as much as the conformity and conservatism of its members. Order and civilization can be maintained only by strict adhesion to the lore and knowledge received from previous generations. Any laxity in this weakens the cohesion of the group and imperils its cultural outfit to the point of threatening its very existence. Man has not yet devised the extremely complex apparatus of modern science which enables him nowadays to fix the results of experience into imperishable molds, to test it ever anew, gradually to shape it into more adequate forms and enrich it constantly by new additions. The primitive man's share of knowledge, his social fabric, his customs and beliefs, are the invaluable yield of devious experience of his forefathers, bought at an extravagant price and to be maintained at any cost. Thus, of all his qualities, truth to tradition is the most important, and a society which makes its tradition sacred has gained by it an inestimable advantage of power and permanence. Such beliefs and practices, therefore, which put a halo of sanctity round tradition and a supernatural stamp upon it, will have a 'survival value' for the type of civilization in which they have been evolved.

We may, therefore, lay down the main function of initiation ceremonies: they are a ritual and dramatic expression of the supreme power and value of tradition in primitive societies; they also serve to impress this power and value upon the minds of each generation, and they are at the same time an extremely efficient means of transmitting tribal lore, of insuring continuity in tradition and of maintaining tribal cohesion.

We still have to ask: What is the relation between the purely physiological fact of bodily maturity which these ceremonies mark, and their social and religious aspect? We see at once that religion does something more, infinitely more, than the mere 'sacralizing of a crisis of life'. From a natural event it makes a social transition, to the fact of bodily maturity it adds the vast conception of entry into manhood with its duties, privileges, responsibilities, above all with its knowledge of tradition and the communion with sacred things and beings. There is thus a creative element in the rites of religious nature. The act establishes not only a social event in the life of the individual but also a spiritual metamorphosis, both associated with the biological event but transcending it in importance and significance.

Initiation is a typically religious act, and we can see clearly here how the ceremony and its purpose are one, how the end is realized in the very consummation of the act. At the same time we can see the function of such acts in society in that they create mental habits and social usages of inestimable value to the group and its civilization.

Another type of religious ceremony, the rite of marriage, is also an end in itself that it creates a supernaturally sanctioned bond, superadded to the primarily biological fact: the union of man and woman for lifelong partnership in affection, economic community, the procreation and rearing of children. This union, monogamous marriage, has always existed in human societies – so modern anthropology teaches in the face of the older fantastic hypotheses of 'promiscuity' and 'group marriage'. By giving monogamous marriage an imprint of value and sanctity, religion offers another gift to human culture. And that brings us to the consideration of the two great human needs of propagation and nutrition.

[. . .]

The function of magic

Magic and science. [. . .]

We are now in a position to state more fully the relation between magic and science already outlined above. Magic is akin to science in that it always has a definite aim intimately associated with human instincts, needs, and pursuits. The magic art is directed towards the attainment of practical aims. Like the other arts and crafts, it is also governed by a theory, by a system of principles which dictate the manner in which the act has to be performed in order to be effective. In analyzing magical spells, rites, and substances we have found that there are a number of general principles which govern them. Both science and magic develop a special technique. In magic, as in the other arts, man can undo what he has done or mend the damage which he has wrought. In fact, in magic the quantitative equivalents of black and white seem to be much more exact and the effects of witchcraft much more completely eradicated by counter-witchchraft than is possible in any practical art or craft. Thus both magic and science show certain similarities, and, with Sir James Frazer, we can appropriately call magic a pseudo-science.

And the spurious character of this pseudo-science is not hard to detect. Science, even as represented by the primitive knowledge of savage man, is based on the normal universal experience of everyday life, experience won in man's struggle with nature for his subsistence and safety, founded on observation, fixed by reason. Magic is based on specific experience of emotional states in which man observes not nature but himself, in which the truth is revealed not by reason but by the play of emotions upon the human organism. Science is founded on the conviction that experience, effort, and reason are valid; magic on the belief that hope cannot fail nor desire deceive. The theories of knowledge are dictated by logic, those of magic by the association of ideas under the influence of desire. As a matter of empirical fact the body of rational knowledge and the body of magical lore are incorporated each in a different tradition, in a different social setting and in a different type of activity, and all these differences are clearly recognized by the savages. The one constitutes the domain of the profane; the other, hedged round by observances, mysteries, and taboos, makes up half of the domain of the sacred.

Magic and religion. Both magic and religion arise and function in situations of emotional stress: crises of life, lacunae in important pursuits, death and initiation into tribal mysteries, unhappy love and unsatisfied hate. Both magic and religion open up escapes from such situations and such impasses as offer no empirical way out except by ritual and belief into the domain of the supernatural. This domain embraces, in religion, beliefs in ghosts, spirits, the primitive forebodings of providence, the guardians of tribal mysteries; in magic, the primeval force and virtue of magic. Both magic and religion are based strictly on mythological tradition, and they also both exist in the atmosphere of the miraculous, in a constant revelation of their wonderworking power. They both are surrounded by taboos and observances which mark off their acts from those of the profane world.

Now what distinguishes magic from religion? We have taken for our starting-point a most definite and tangible distinction: we have defined, within the domain of the sacred, magic as a practical art consisting of acts which are only means to a definite end expected to follow later on; religion as a body of self-contained acts being themselves the fulfillment of their purpose. We can now follow up this difference into its deeper layers. The practical art of magic has its limited, circumscribed technique: spell, rite, and the condition of the performer form always its trite trinity. Religion, with its complex aspects and purposes, has no such simple technique, and its unity can be seen neither in the form of its acts nor even in the uniformity of its subject matter, but rather in the function which it fulfills and in the value of its belief and ritual. Again, the belief in magic, corresponding to its plain practical nature, is extremely simple. It is always the affirmation of man's power to cause certain definite effects by a definite spell and rite. In religion, on the other hand, we have a whole supernatural world of faith: the pantheon of spirits and demons, the benevolent powers of totem, guardian spirit, tribal all-father, the vision of the future life, create a second supernatural reality for primitive man. The mythology of religion is also more varied and complex as well as more creative. It usually centers round the various tenets of belief, and it develops them into cosmogonies, tales of culture heroes, accounts of the doings of gods and demigods. In magic, important as it is, mythology is an ever-recurrent boasting about man's primeval achievements.

Magic, the specific art for specific ends, has in every one of its forms come once into the possession of man, and it had to be handed over in direct filiation from generation to generation. Hence it remains from the earliest times in the hands of specialists, and the first profession of mankind is that of a wizard or witch. Religion, on the other hand, in primitive conditions is an affair of all, in which everyone takes an active and equivalent part. Every member of the tribe has to go through initiation, and then himself initiates others. Everyone wails, mourns, digs the grave and commemorates, and in due time everyone has his turn in being mourned and commemorated. Spirits are for all, and everyone becomes a spirit. The only specialization in religion – that is, early spiritualistic mediumism – is not a profession but a personal gift. One more difference between magic and religion is the play of black and white in witchcraft, while religion in its primitive stages has but little of the contrast between good and evil, between the beneficent and malevolent powers. This is due also to the practical character of magic, which aims at direct quantitative results, while early religion, though essentially moral, has to deal with fateful, irremediable happenings and supernatural forces and beings, so that the undoing of things done by man does not enter into it. The maxim that fear first made gods in the universe is certainly not true in the light of anthropology.

In order to grasp the difference between religion and magic and to gain a clear vision of the three-cornered constellation of magic, religion, and science, let us briefly realize the cultural function of each. The function of primitive knowledge and its value have been assessed already and indeed are not difficult to grasp. By acquainting man with his surroundings, by allowing him to use the forces of nature, science, primitive knowledge, bestows on man an immense biological advantage, setting him far above all the rest of creation. The function of religion and its value we have learned to understand in the survey of savage creeds and cults given above. We have shown there that religious faith establishes, fixes, and enhances all valuable mental attitudes, such as reverence for tradition, harmony with environment, courage and confidence in the struggle with difficulties and at the prospect of death. This belief, embodied and maintained by cult and ceremonial, has an immense biological value, and so reveals to primitive man truth in the wider, pragmatic sense of the word.

What is the cultural function of magic? We have seen that all the instincts and emotions, all practical activities, lead man into impasses where gaps in his knowledge and the limitations of his early power of observation and reason betray him at a crucial moment. Human organism reacts to this in spontaneous outbursts, in which rudimentary modes of behavior and rudimentary beliefs in their efficiency are engendered. Magic fixes upon these beliefs and rudimentary rites and standardizes them into permanent traditional forms. Thus magic supplies primitive man with a number of ready-made ritual acts and beliefs, with a definite mental and practical technique which serves to bridge over the dangerous gaps in every important pursuit or critical situation. It enables man to carry out with confidence his important tasks, to maintain his poise and his mental integrity in fits of anger, in the throes of hate, of unrequited love, of despair and anxiety. The function of magic is to ritualize man's optimism, to enhance his faith in the victory of hope over fear. Magic expresses the greater value for man of confidence over doubt, of steadfastness over vacillation, of optimism over pessimism.

Looking from far and above, from our high places of safety in developed civilization, it is easy to see all the crudity and irrelevance of magic. But without its power and guidance early man could not have mastered his practical difficulties as he has done, nor could man have advanced to the higher stages of culture. Hence the universal occurrence of magic in primitive societies and its enormous sway. Hence do we find magic an invariable adjunct of all important activities. I think we must see in it the embodiment of the sublime folly of hope, which has yet been the best school of man's character.

NOTES

1. E. Durkheim, *The Elementary Forms of the Religious Life*, p. 206.
2. E. Durkheim, *loc. cit.*
3. J. Harrison, *Themis*, p. 42.
4. J. Harrison, *op. cit.*, p. 44.

Robert H. Lowie

Robert Harry Lowie was born in 1883 in Vienna, where he received part of his primary school education. In 1893 his family moved to the United States where he received his secondary school education. He studied at New York City College, where he received his A. B. in 1901, and he did his graduate work in anthropology at Columbia University under Franz Boas. In 1908 he obtained his Ph. D. degree. Between 1908 and 1921 he worked at the American Museum for Natural History in New York, first as an assistant in the Department of Anthropology (1908—1909), then as an assistant curator (1909–1913) and finally as an associate curator (1913—1921). He was a lecturer at Columbia University in 1920-21. Lowie was Associate Professor of Anthropology at the University of California at Berkeley in 1917–18 and from 1921 until 1925, and Professor of Anthropology from 1925 until 1950, when he retired. He died at Berkeley in 1957.

His main publications dealing with the study of religion are: 1918 *Myths and Traditions of the Crow Indians;* 1920 *Primitive Society;* 1924 *Primitive Religion;* 1934 *An Introduction to Cultural Anthropology;* 1935 *The Crow Indians;* 1937 *The History of Ethnological Theory;* 1954 *Indians of the Plains;* in 1960 were published *Lowie's Selected Papers in Anthropology.*

Lowie's anthropological studies are of interest to the study of religion, before everything else, because his comparative studies among North American Indian tribes put an end to a number of current theories on religion as well as on marriage. Psychological interpretations of religious and other data could not be isolated from cultural constellations or from the history of the group studied. Lowie showed certain psychological qualities to be requisite to leadership in religion. He is counted among the adherents of the diffusionist school, but did not adopt a firm theory, always keeping to accurate factual research.

The following fragment has been taken from the Introduction to *Primitive Religion* and shows Lowie's strictly empirical approach, also in his terminology.

ON THE TERM 'RELIGION'

A work on 'Primitive Religion' may well begin with a definition of the terms in its title, for neither unfortunately is unambiguous. Th e word 'primitive' by its etymology suggests 'primeval', but when the an thropologist speaks descriptively of 'primitive peoples' he means no mo re – at least, he has no right to mean more – than peoples of a relatively simple culture; or, to be more specific, the illiterate peoples of the world. To be sure, it is impossible to suppress the inference that what is shared by the illiterate peoples of rudest culture in contrast to those possessing a more complex civilization dates back to a relatively great antiquity; but this *is* an inference, not an immediate datum of experience. Moreover, it is certain that, no matter how simple a particular culture may be, it has had a long history. Human civilization may be roughly said to be 100,000 years old. It is inconceivable that any distinct subdivision of mankind, even if separated from others for only one-tenth of that immense span of time, should have remained in an absolutely static condition. There are two cogent reasons to the contrary. First, isolation has never been more than relative when very great periods are considered. In other words, influences from without have everywhere produced *some* changes in custom, belief, and the material arts of life. Secondly, such alterations occur, though more slowly, even in the absence of extraneous stimulation because of the social results of individual variation, that is, of innovations successfully impressed on each generation by some able individuals of sufficiently powerful personality. Both determinants of change can be detected in so isolated and so simple a people as the Andaman Islanders of the Bay of Bengal. Their remoteness did not prevent them from borrowing the device of the outrigger canoe, presumably from some Malaysian tribe; and the local variations found within their islands, both in language and social heritage, prove the occurrence of novel ideas even in a population ignorant of metals and every form of husbandry, nay, lacking even the dog and the art of fire-making. In other words, the Andamanese culture of fifty years ago is not the culture of their ancestors five hundred years ago, or in still earlier periods; and, so far as direct observation goes, we cannot select any one feature of their social life as of hoary antiquity. 'Primitive', then, for our purposes shall be devoid of chronological import.

It is far more difficult to explain what shall be designated by the word 'religion'. Of course, a formal definition of religion would be as futile at the outset as a corresponding definition of consciousness in a textbook of psychology, or of electricity in a treatise on physics. The rich content of these comprehensive concepts can be appreciated only *after* a survey of the relevant data is completed. Yet some circumscription of what is to be included is not only possible but necessary, and it will be convenient to begin by illustrating the wrong approach to a definition by two extreme instances gleaned from Fielding's novels. Says Parson Thwackum in *Tom Jones*:

'When I mention religion, I mean the Christian religion; and not only the Christian religion but the Protestant religion; and not only the Protestant religion, but the Church of England.'

And Parson Adams, in *Joseph Andrews,* is equally explicit:

'The first care I always take is of a boy's morals; I had rather he should be a blockhead than an atheist or a Presbyterian.'

Why do utterances such as these strike us as ineffably parochial? From one angle it might seem that a man has the right to define his terms as he will, provided only he adhere to the usage once established; and if to embrace the Anglican Church means salvation, while Calvinism spells perdition, then from that particular point of view there is nothing to choose between being a Presbyterian and being an atheist. This position is indeed inexpugnable so long as it is avowedly no more than a personal evaluation; it is shattered as soon as it pretends to give an objective classification of the pertinent data. In this second role it recalls that comical classification of some aboriginal language by which male adult members of the tribe are of one gender, while all other persons are lumped in a vast complementary category together with animals, plants, and objects. We require no proof that a boy or a woman or a foreigner is nearer to a tribesman than to a tree or a rock; and so we see at once that it is arbitrary to dichotomize the religious universe after the manner of Fielding's persons, that such division wrests the phenomena out of their true context and does violence to their true inwardness.

But when once committed to this moderately tolerant attitude, we are still without guidance as to where the line shall be drawn. Working our way backwards from a particular branch of Christianity, we are still able to recognize some kinship between our faith and that of other monotheistic creeds. When we come to Buddhism, with its theoretical atheism, many of us will be inclined to deny that any doctrine dispensing with the notion of a personal deity can fairly be brought under the same heading with familiar religions. Yet William James, our greatest psychologist, has espoused the view that Buddhism, like Emersonian transcendentalism, makes to the individual votary an appeal and evokes a response 'in fact indistinguishable from, and in many respects identical with, the best Christian appeal and response'.[1] James may conceivably err in this particular judgment, but anthropologically speaking, there can be no doubt of the correctness of his test: *if* Buddhism satisfies that part of the Buddhist's nature which corresponds to the devout Christian's longing for acceptance by the deity, then it is a veritable religion, just as polygyny is anthropologically no less a form of marriage than monogamy, and an oral tradition must be reckoned, despite etymology, a specimen of literature. What we should determine is wherein such satisfaction essentially lies. Confronted with beliefs and practices divorced from an organized priesthood, lacking congregational worship and a standardized cosmogony, we must ask not whether this or that objective feature shall be counted as essential but whether the subjective condition of the believers and worshipers corresponds to that of an unequivocally religious frame of mind.

That the mere presence of some objective feature is wholly irrelevant may be illustrated by citing the opening paragraphs of Leibniz's *Metaphysics*:

'The conception of God which is the most common and the most full of meaning is expressed well enough in the words: *God is an absolutely perfect being*. The implications, however, of these words fail to receive sufficient consideration. For instance, there are many different kinds of perfection, all of which God possesses, and each one of them pertains to him in the highest degree.

·We must also know what perfection is. One thing which can surely be affirmed about it is that those forms or natures which are not susceptible of it to the highest degree, say the nature of numbers or of figures, do not permit of perfection. This is because the number which is the greatest of all (that is, the sum of all the numbers), and likewise the greatest of all figures, imply contradictions. The greatest knowledge, however, and omnipotence contain no impossibility. Consequently power and knowledge do admit of perfection, and in so far as they pertain to God they have no limits.

'Whence it follows that God, who possesses supreme and infinite wisdom, acts in the most perfect manner not only metaphysically, but also from the moral standpoint. And with respect to ourselves it can be said that the more we are enlightened and informed in regard to the works of God the more will we be disposed to find them excellent and conforming entirely to that which we might desire.'

Is this passage an expression of religious sentiment? Of course it is in thorough harmony with traditional religion, yet it belongs to a different compartment. It shares with monotheistic religion its subject-matter as an artist and a scientist may share a bit of landscape, the one for depiction, the other for a study of the flora. In Leibnitz the religious flavor is singularly absent, because his abstract propositions leave the *religious* consciousness cold. Whatever disagreement may exist on the subject, the dominance of the emotional side of consciousness in religion is universally accepted, and where that phase of mental life is in relative abeyance religion must be considered wanting.

It is the insufficient consideration given to the emotional factor of religion that makes it necessary to qualify and revise the views enunciated by the greatest of comparative students in this field. When, in 1871, Edward B. Tylor published the first edition of his *Primitive Culture*, he was above all interested in the problem of evolution. Darwin's *Origin of Species* had begun to stimulate historical thinking in other than biological lines, and the investigator of culture naturally sought to parallel the paleontologist's and embryologist's record by corresponding sequences in industrial arts, social organization and belief. As to the last-mentioned branch of culture, it was clear that if evolution were accepted at all there must have been some stage in the development of man, whether corresponding to a human or prehuman level, at which religion had not yet evolved. Then there inevitably arose the query, whether that stage was represented by any people still living. It was this problem, among others, that Tylor set out to solve. But in order to solve it he was obliged to frame a 'minimum definition' of religion. Rejecting as too exclusive, as expressing rather special developments than the basic nature of religion, various current definitions, he found its essence to lie in animism, that is, in 'the belief in Spiritual Beings'; and because such a belief had been reported from all adequately described tribes on the face of the globe, Tylor inferred the universality of religion.[2]

What more recent scholars reject is not this conclusion itself, which stands practically unchallenged, but its motivation. In Tylor's discussion the belief in spiritual beings, that is, religion in his sense, is made to arise in response to an *intellectual* need, – the desire of an explanation for the physiological phenomena of life, sleep, dream and death. This rationalistic bias appears clearly from the very phrases used in referring to primitive animism, which is again and again alluded to as a philosophy, a doctrine, 'the theory of dreams', 'a perfectly rational and intelligible product of early science', 'the theory of souls'.[3] It is conceivable that the craving for a causal explanation might lead to the notion of spirits as suggested by Tylor without the slightest consequent or associated emotional reaction essential to religion; indeed, not a few examples might be cited of spiritual beings postulated by primitive tribes for, so far as one can see, an exclusive satisfaction of their metaphysical demands.

In this way, then, Tylor's formulation is not exacting enough for it omits an essential determinant of the phenomenon to be defined. Yet in another sense, meager as it may appear at first sight, it demands more than is required. For we have already seen that even a system of belief devoid of animistic conceptions, like Buddhism, may function as the psychological equivalent of Christianity or any other of the faiths of Western civilization. What, then, is the bond that unites beliefs which on the surface are so divergent? The essentially correct answer seems to me to have been given by Dr. R. R. Marrett and Dr. N. Söderblom, the Archbishop of Upsala, and I will try to set forth in a few words the most significant points involved. In every society, no matter how simple it may be, there is a spontaneous division of the sphere of experience into the ordinary and the extraordinary. Some writers, notably Lévy-Bruhl, impressed with the fantastic theoretical

notions obtaining among unlettered peoples in regard to the constitution
and origin of the universe, have broached the view that such odd fancies
must be rooted in a mental condition radically different from our own. Yet
closer attention to the usages of savage life demonstrates beyond the possibility of doubt that in grappling with the problems of everyday life primitive
man often employs precisely the same psychological processes of association,
observation, and inference as our own farmers, engineers, or craftsmen.
When a Hopi Indian in Arizona raises corn where a white tiller fails, when
a Papuan boatwright constructs elaborate buildings without nails or metal
implements, when a Polynesian carves the most esthetic patterns with a
shark's tooth, he is solving his everyday problems not only competently
but with elegance. All these activities, however, though sometimes curiously
associated with (to our mind) irrelevant considerations, belong in the main
to what Dr. Marett would call the *workaday* world, i.e., the domain of
reason, of normal experience, of an empirical correspondence of cause and
effect. But everywhere there is, in addition to such practical rationalism,
a sense of something transcending the expected or natural, a sense of the
Extraordinary, Mysterious, or Supernatural. Certainly that sense is very
frequently, and conceivably might be always, linked with the recognition
of spiritual beings; but to what extent such a correlation obtains is a matter
for empirical inquiry and should not be prejudged. But even were this
association of spirit-belief with a sense of mystery an invariable phenomenon, it would still be legitimate to argue that it is the latter which is indispensable to religion, that the belief in spirits derives its religious value
solely from this association instead of being religious in its own right. The
fact that subjective states indistinguishable from religious ones are indifferently found with and without animistic notions definitely settles the
matter. We shall therefore recognize as the differentia of religion what Drs.
Marett and Goldenweiser have called 'supernaturalism'.[4]

Reverting to the problem that engaged Tylor's attention, we shall say:
Religion is verily a universal feature of human culture, not because all
societies foster a belief in spirits, but because all recognize in some form or
other awe-inspiring, extraordinary manifestations of reality. The present
treatise is accordingly dedicated to the discussion of those cultural phenomena of the simpler societies which center about or are somehow connected
with the sense of mystery or weirdness. Owing to the many ramifications
of such supernaturalism, this definition leads not to a rigid exclusion but
merely to a somewhat different appraisal of features commonly treated
under the head of religion.

For the colorless terms employed above Dr. Söderblom substitutes the
concept of the Holy or the Sacred. It is undoubtedly true that in a great
many instances that which is set over in contrast to everyday experience

is invested with a halo of sanctity that justifies the use of the terms cited. However, if I correctly interpret the data, the Supernatural is Janus-headed, and its more sinister aspect is not adequately rendered by our word 'holy' with its traditional connotations. I therefore prefer to use noncommittal expressions when groping for a *minimum* definition of religion, though I am the last to deny the great frequency with which the Extraordinary or Supernatural assumes the aspect of the Holy.

In studying alien religions the same precaution must be observed as in the study of comparative linguistics. Pioneer investigators of primitive languages were wont to pattern their descriptions on the Latin grammar. Indeed, many of us were taught English grammar on the same plan, – obliged to recite the non-existent datives and accusatives of nouns and the equally chimerical imperfect subjunctives of verbs. Gradually, however, philologists came to realize that Latin grammar, thus used, was a Procrustean bed and that each tongue must be viewed according to its own genius. The application is obvious. When we approach an alien faith, we have no right to impose our received categories. Because *our* sacred Book contains an account of cosmogony, it does not follow that a given primitive cosmogony comes within the scope of religion. Though immortality has played an enormous part in the history of Christianity, it need not occupy the center of the stage in other forms of belief.

The only legitimate mode of approach will then correspond to the modern linguist's: considering each religion from the point of view of its votaries, let us ascertain what are their concepts of the Supernatural, how they are interrelated and weighted with reference to one another. [. . .]

NOTES

1. William James, *The Varieties of Religious Experience* (1902), p. 34.
2. E. B. Tylor, *Primitive Culture* (1913), Vol. I, p. 424.
3. E. B. Tylor, *op. cit.*, Vol. I, pp. 440, 447. Idem, *Anthropology* (1881), p. 371.
4 R. R. Marett, *The Threshold of Religion* (1914, 2nd edition), pp. 101–121.
A. A. Golden weiser, *Early Civilization* (1922), p. 231.

Paul Radin

Paul Radin was born in 1883 in Lodz, Poland, and brought to the United States as an infant. He received his primary and secondary school education in New York and received his A. B. in 1902 from New York City College. Subsequently he studied at the universities of Berlin and Munich, and worked at the Berlin Museum of Ethnology. On his return to America he studied biology, history, and anthropology under Franz Boas at Columbia University, and obtained his Ph. D. degree in 1911. Radin was ethnologist at the Bureau of American Ethnology from 1910 until 1912, and, since 1912, field ethnologist for the Geological Survey of Canada in Ottawa. Radin taught at a number of American universities, the last of which Brandeis University from 1957 onwards. He died in 1959.

His main publications dealing with the study of religion are: 1911 'The Ritual and Significance of the Winnebago Medicine Dance'; 1914 Some Myths and Tales of the Ojibwa of South-Eastern Ontario; 1920 'The Autobiography of a Winnebago Indian'; 1924 Monotheism among Primitive Peoples; 1927 Primitive Man as Philosopher; 1932 Social Anthropology; 1933 The Method and Theory of Ethnology: an Essay in Criticism; 1937 Primitive Religion: its Nature and Origin; 1945 The Plot of Life and Death. A Ritual Drama of the American Indians; 1949 Winnebago Culture as Described by Themselves; 1953 The World of Primitive Man; 1956 The Trickster: a Study in American Indian Mythology. (With commentary by Karl Kerényi and C. G. Jung).

As an anthropologist Radin investigated the religious-mindedness of the people belonging to the communities studied. He found, among other things, that there is a clear difference between those who are more religious minded, of the philosopher-artist type and constituting a potential religious leadership as religious formulators, and those who are less religious minded and are only occasionally interested in religious explanations and meanings. Radin considered fear due to a lack of economic security as the psychological origin of religion; consequently religion is a compensation phantasy and a religious elite shows neurotic features. Establishing that a great variety of religious thought, imagination and morality exists within the communities studied, Radin contended that there is no specific religious behavior or thought and that there is no reason to deny rational thought to primitive people. In fact the religious elite deals quite rationally with the problems of life for which they try to find solutions very much in the same way as theologians do in the Western world.

The following fragments have been taken from Primitive Religion, Primitive Man as Philosopher, and The World of Primitive Man. They show Radin's depth psychological approach in his analysis of religious feeling, the methodological carefulness and the distinction made between religious and non-religious man as two psychological types.

'THE NATURE AND SUBSTANCE OF RELIGION'

To describe the nature of religion is extremely difficult. Obviously it means different things to different people. We may safely insist, however, that it consists of two parts: the first an easily definable, if not precisely specific feeling; and the second certain specific acts, customs, beliefs, and conceptions associated with this feeling. The belief most inextricably connected with the specific feeling is a belief in spirits outside of man, conceived of as more powerful than man and as controlling all those elements in life upon which he lays most stress. On the one hand these two components may be regarded as always having been associated and thus as forming an inseparable and indissoluble whole; on the other, one of them may be regarded as having preceded the other in time.

The customs and beliefs play an important role among all individuals. The specific feeling, on the contrary, varies in degree with each person. The less intense it is, the greater the relief with which the customs and beliefs stand out and the stricter the punctilious adherence to them. The converse is not true, however, for the greatest intensity of feeling may accompany the observance of the customs without any decrease in their importance.

Yet beliefs and customs do not as such contain any religious ingredient. They belong to that large body of strictly folkloristic elements toward which the individual and the group assume an attitude of passive acceptance. They are embedded in a mechanism devised by man for determining and evaluating the interrelationship between him and the external world. What makes certain of them part of the religious unit is their connexion with the specific feeling. The degree in which this feeling exists does not matter nor does it matter whether this feeling is held by every member of the group.

This feeling itself is not a simple unit. Its physiological indications are specific acts which we are accustomed to regard as the external signs of mental and emotional concentration, such as folding the hands, reclining the head, kneeling, and closing the eyes. Psychologically, on the other hand, it is characterized by a far more than normal sensitiveness to specific beliefs, customs, and conceptions, manifesting itself in a thrill, a feeling of exhilaration, exaltation, awe and in a marked tendency to become absorbed in internal sensations. Negatively one finds an abeyance of interest in external impressions. The condition itself, we may surmise, differs little from such states as intense aesthetic enjoyment or even the joy of living, for example. What distinguishes it from them is the nature of the subject matter calling it forth.

Naturally enough, the specific feeling is not often encountered in a pure form among primitive peoples. It is rare enough among ourselves. From the nature of the folkloristic background with which it has been always specifically associated among primitive men, it has become assimilated to their other emotions as well. This composite feeling may, in the case of certain individuals, frequently dwarf other feelings. With the vast majority of men and women, however, it is only one among others, rising at times to a predominant position yet more frequently becoming almost completely obliterated. Often indeed it is artificial, in the extreme, to attempt a separation.

The other component we have already described. It is the belief, invariably found associated with the specific feeling, in spirits outside of man, to whom are ascribed powers greater than his and who are depicted as in control of everything on which man lays most stress. This, from now on, we shall call the religious feeling. The spirits thus predicated have at all times been identified with the physical and the social-economic background. The specific quality of the religious feeling is thus conditioned by that background. It is the emotional correlate of the struggle for existence in an insecure physical and social environment.

This struggle for existence must not be interpreted too narrowly. It had, particularly in the early phases of man's history, a spiritual as well as a biological side. The spiritual side was concerned with the battle of that reflective consciousness which is the especial earmark of the human as opposed to the animal mind, with the physical make-up he has in common with his animal ancestors. This mentality has expressed itself most clearly in what might be called the social precipitates of fear. Among all peoples these have clustered around three things: first, the physiological facts of birth, puberty, disease, and death; second, the contact of man with the external world and the forces of nature; and third, the collision of man with man.

The manifold customs and beliefs connected with these three elemental forces represent what I have called the social precipitates of fear. Those associated with birth, puberty, disease, and death have conceivably maintained their original form most tenaciously. Physiological facts do, after all, remain unchanged.

It is not surprising then that religion has, at all times, been overwhelmed with such specific precipitates. By themselves, they in no sense partake of the religious, nor would they ever have led to the development of religion as such. And this holds not only for these particular beliefs but for the other elements in religion as well. None of them, as such, contain a religious element and yet they are always found associated with religious feeling. How is this to be explained?

There is, broadly speaking, only one possible explanation, and that is to regard religion as one of the most important and distinctive means for maintaining life-values. As these vary, so will the religious unit vary. Religion is thus not a phenomenon apart and distinct from mundane life nor is it a philosophical inquiry into the nature of being and becoming. It only emphasizes and preserves those values accepted by the majority of a group at a given time. It is this close connexion with the whole life of man that we find so characteristically developed among all primitive cultures and in the early phases of our own civilization. Only when other means of emphasizing and maintaining the life-values are in the ascendant, does religion become divorced from the whole corporate life of the community. 'The history of humanity' is, as M. Reinach has very correctly observed, 'the history of a progressive laicization'.

In the midst of the multiplicity of life-values three stand out most prominently and tenaciously – the desire for success, for happiness, and for long life. Similarly, from among the heterogeneous mass of beliefs, the one which stands out most definitely is the belief in spirits who bestow on man success, and long life. At the basis of primitive religion there thus lies a specific problem: the nature of the relation of these spirits to the life-values of man. It is well to bear this clearly in mind, for most theorists and theologians have assumed just the reverse. And it is also well to remember that this association is secondary, that it does not flow from the nature of the spirits as originally conceived.

Yet all we have just said does not help us to answer the one question in religion which so many regard as paramount. What is it that originally led man to postulate the supernatural? The reader will, I hope, pardon me if, in answering it, I digress somewhat from my main theme.

To understand the beginnings of religion we must try to visualize as accurately as we can the conditions under which man lived at the dawn of civilization. Manifestly he lived in a variable and essentially inimical physical environment and possessed a most inadequate technological preparation for defending himself against this environment. His mentality was still overwhelmingly dominated by definitely animal characteristics although the life-values themselves – the desire for success, for happiness, and for long life – were naturally already present. His methods of food production were of the simplest kind – the gathering of grubs and berries and the most elementary type of fishing and hunting. He had no fixed dwellings, living in caves or natural shelters. No economic security could have existed, and we cannot go far wrong in assuming that, where economic security does not exist, emotional insecurity and its correlates, the sense of powerlessness and the feeling of insignificance, are bound to develop.

With fear man was born. Of that there can be little doubt. But this fear did not exist in a vacuum. Rather it was the fear inspired by a specific economic situation. All this naturally led to a disorientation and disintegration of the ego. The mental correlate for such a condition is subjectivism, and subjectivism means the dominance of magic and of the most elementary forms of coercive rites. If the psychoanalysts wish to call this narcissism, there can be no legitimate objection.

Expressed in strictly psychological terms the original postulation of the supernatural was thus simply one aspect of the learning process, one stage of man's attempt to adjust the perceiving ego to the things outside himself, that is, to the external world. This attempt did not begin with man. It is clearly rooted in his animal nature and has, from the very beginning, been expressed in three generalized formulae. According to the first one, the ego and the objective world interact coercively: according to the second, man coerces the objective world, and according to the third, the objective world coerces man. With the coming of man there appeared for the first time a differential evaluation of the ego and the external world. That evaluation which ascribed the coercive power to man alone or to the coercive interaction of the ego and the object found its characteristic expression in magic and compulsive rites and observances; that which ascribed this coercive power to the object found its characteristic expression in the religious activity.

We can arrange this hypothetical evolution, from magic to religion, in four stages:

1) The completely coercive and unmediated. Here the relation between the ego and the objective world is almost in the nature of a tropism.
2) The incompletely coercive and unmediated. Here a measure of volition is imputed to the object.
3) The reciprocally coercive. Here volition is imputed to both the ego and the object.
4) The non-coercive. Here the ego is regarded as being in conscious subjection to the object.

In other words, we are dealing here with a progressive disentanglement of the ego from an infantile subjectivism; the freeing of man, as Freud has correctly observed, from the compulsive power of thought. But this freeing of man from his compulsive irrational anchorage did not take place in that intellectual vacuum with which psychologists so frequently operate, but in a material world where man was engaged in a strenuous struggle for existence. From the very first appearance of man, consequently, there must have begun that economic utilization of religion which has always remained its fundamental characteristic. In fact it is the never-ceasing impact of this doubly real social-economic struggle which has specifically brought about the freeing of man's activities from the compulsive power of thought.

But we have digressed far from our original question. Let us return to it now and, from our new vantage point, ask again: Why did man originally postulate the supernatural?

The correlate of economic insecurity, we have seen, is psychical insecurity and disorientation with all its attendant fears, with all its full feeling of helplessness, of powerlessness, and of insignificance. It is but natural for the psyche, under such circumstances, to take refuge in compensation fantasies. And since the only subject matter existing in that primal dawn of civilization was the conscious struggle of man against his physical and economic environment, and his unconscious struggle against his animal-mental equipment as stimulated by his reflective consciousness, the main goal and objective of all his strivings was the canalization of his fears and feelings and the validation of his compensation dreams. Thus they became immediately transfigured, and there emerged those strictly religious concepts so suggestively discussed by the well-known German theologian Rudolf Otto in his work called *Das Heilige*. Being a theologian and a mystic he naturally misunderstood the true nature of these concepts and of their genesis.

From fear, according to Otto, came awe, the terrible, the feeling of being overpowered and overwhelmed, crystallizing into what he calls the *tremendum* and the *majestas;* out of the sense of helplessness, of powerlessness, of insignificance, came that *creature-feeling* so well described in the Old Testament, and out of the compensation fantasies arose, finally, the concept of that *completely other* which is rooted in the familiar and which is yet entirely new. From the compulsion implied in coercion there developed eventually that willing sense of subjection which is implied in *fascination*. All the ingredients are here from which the supernatural arose. Merged and interpenetrated with what is always primary, the implications of living and the economic struggle for existence in an inimical physical environment, they gave us primitive religion.

Man thus postulated the supernatural in order primarily to validate his workaday reality. But not every man felt the need for it to the same degree, a fact that can be easily demonstrated by examining the differences in the definitions of the supernatural and the formulations of the relationship between the ego and the supernatural postulated as existing. It is of fundamental importance to understand this if we wish correctly or fruitfully to analyse primitive religion.

If religious feeling is to be characterized as a far more than normal sensitiveness to certain customs, beliefs, and superstitions, it is fairly clear that no individual can remain in this state continuously. In some individuals, however, it can be called up easily. These are the truly religious people. They have always been few in number. From these to the essentially unreligious individual the gradations are numerous. If these gradations are arranged in the order of their religious intensity, we have three types: the truly religious, the intermittently religious, and the indifferently religious.

The intermittently religious really fall into two groups – those who may be weakly religious at almost any moment; and those who may be strongly religious at certain moments, such as at temperamental upheavals and crises.

In the intermittently and indifferently religious groups are included by far the large majority of people, but since so many extra-religious factors enter into their religious consciousness, they are actually the most poorly adapted for the study of religion. To understand religion and its developments we must study those individuals who possess the religious feeling in a marked degree. Much of the confusion that exists in so many analyses of primitive religion is due to the fact that, in so far as these analyses were based on the study of distinct individuals, the individuals selected belonged to the class of intermittently religious or, at best, the abnormally religious. The only way of avoiding confusion is to start with the markedly religious individual and then study the expressions of religion among the intermittently and indifferently religious with reference to him.

Yet it is not enough to postulate this division of people into three religious groups; we must also try to discover when the religious feeling is called forth. Now quite apart from the degree of religious susceptibility a given person may possess, it may legitimately be asserted that the members of all three groups show a pronounced religious feeling at certain crises of life, and that these crises are intimately connected with all the important social-economic life-values of the tribe – puberty, sickness, death, famine, etc. The frequent appearance, on such occasions, of temperamental disturbances is unquestionably a great aid in heightening this religious feeling. Whatever be the cause, however, it is during individual and tribal crises that the majority of man and women are possessed of what, in spite of other ingredients, must be designated as a true religious feeling'i

It is at crises that the majority of men obtain their purest reli g ous thrill, because it is only at such times that they are prone to permit inward feelings to dominate. Yet more than that: it is only at crises that the majority of men obtain a religious feeling at all. In the case of the markedly religious man the situation is quite different. His specific susceptibility permits him to obtain a religious thrill on innumerable occasions, and since with each thrill are associated certain beliefs and attitudes, he sees the entire content of life from a religious viewpoint. For him the function of religion is always that of emphasizing and maintaining the life-values of man, life-values which are determined by his traditional background and which are always primary. Such is his formulation. And this formulation is taught to the intermittently and indifferently religious, who accept it unhesitatingly as far as they comprehend it. Assuredly they rarely see life entirely from a religious standpoint. There are occasions, however, in the corporate life of a community – such as at a ceremony or a ritual – where a religious feeling is, at times, diffused over the whole content of life. Certainly even the intermittently and indifferently religious who participate in these activities must partake somehow of this feeling. At a ceremony many of the conditions favourable to the calling forth of a religious thrill are given – the presence of truly religious people, acts and customs associated with religious feeling, a conscious detachment from the outer world, and, lastly, the important fact that an individual has been taught to expect a religious feeling at such times.

Summing up, it may be said that all people are spontaneously religious at crises, that the markedly religious people are spontaneously religious on numerous other occasions as well, and that the intermittently and indifferently religious are secondarily religious on occasions not connected with crises at all.

With this difference in religious intensity has always gone a marked difference in the interest manifested in strictly religious phenomena and theories. The non-religious man is simply not articulate in such matters and leaves their definition and formulation entirely to the religiously articulate members of his group.

The failure to recognize this has led many ethnological theorists unwittingly into numerous misrepresentations of primitive thought and religion. It lies at the basis of the fundamental error running through one of the major theoretical discussions of primitive mentality written in the last fifty years, the well-known work of M. Lévy-Bruhl, *Les Fonctions mentales dans les sociétés inférieures.* Had M. Lévy-Bruhl recognized the presence of these different types of individuals, I feel confident that he would never have postulated either a *prelogical mentality* or *mystical participation* as the outstanding traits of all primitive thinking and that he would never have been led into the strange error of denying the existence, among primitive groups, of individuals who think as logically as do some of us and who are found alongside of others as irrational as are so many of us. For M. Lévy-Bruhl all primitive thought is really a form of experience lying somewhere between magic and the earliest appearance of religion. What he has really done is to identify all primitive thinking with what is really the very earliest stage of thought, one in which the ego and the external world are regarded as continually constraining each other and where the individual is, in the most unrelieved Freudian fashion, regarded as still completely under the domination of the compulsive power of thought. But such a condition can have applied, at best, only to the very earliest period of man's history. Among no primitive peoples of today is such thinking found, and where certain approximations to it are encountered, they are found among individuals who represent the characteristically non-religious attitude of mind which we have just discussed.

Let me give an illustration. This will show better than any general psychological discussion how these two contrasting types of mind, the religious and the essentially non-religious, approach the concept of the supernatural, particularly the concept of supernatural power which, under the general name of *mana*, has played such a great role in all recent theories of primitive religion. Codrington defined *mana* as 'a force altogether distinct from physical power which acts in all kinds of ways for good and evil and which it is of the greatest advantage to possess and control'.[2] Subsequent European students of the subject described it differently. Indeed there were certain contradictions in Codrington's own account. The differences between these various authors are of two kinds, one group emphasizing the essentially impersonal aspect of the *mana* concept, the other the personal; one stressing the idealistic-mystical, the other the materialistic-magical side.

We cannot simply dismiss this conflict of opinion as due to a difference in the approach and temperament of the investigators. Manifestly there must have been something in the data themselves that led to this division of opinion.

In all discussions concerning primitive religion it is always best to begin the inquiry with the actual statements of natives and not with the generalizations and syntheses of European observers no matter how correct they may seem. The moment we observe this elementary caution we discover that the informants themselves fall into two groups. An old Maori interviewed in 1921 by Beattie[3] manifestly regarded *mana* as, in no sense, supernatural power *per se*, but rather as something localized in a specific object or at best as personal magnetism. He apparently could not conceive of it in any other manner. The gods differ from man only in the fact that their *mana* can never be overwhelmed or destroyed. Man's can. This particular Maori is thus an excellent example of the religious thinker and formulator, to be contrasted with those Maori who could conceive of *mana* only as supernatural power and who stressed its predominantly magical side, thus representing the non-religious and matter-of-fact individuals. To such a class also belonged the Fiji Islander who told an investigator that 'a thing has *mana* when it works; it has no *mana* when it does not work'.

Occasionally one is fortunate enough to have a native himself present the two viewpoints. To a Dakota priest we are indebted for the following statement of the priest-thinker's interpretation:

'*Ton* is the power to do supernatural things. All the gods have *ton*. When the people say *ton*, they mean something that comes from a living thing, such as the birth of anything or the discharge from a wound or a sore or the growth from a seed.'[4]

And surely it was no religious man who, among the Maori, insisted that gods die unless there are priests to keep them alive, or who permitted one Maori deity to say to another: 'When men no longer believe in us, we are dead.' But is was a Maori religious thinker and formulator of no low order who described the god *Io-te-pukenga* as 'the source of all thought, reflection, memories; of all things planned by him to possess form, growth, life, thought, strength. There is nothing outside his jurisdiction. All things are his'. Similarly it was only the religious thinker among the Dakota who could say that:

'The *sicun* is an immaterial god whose substance is never visible. It is the potency of mankind and the emitted potency of the gods. Considered relative to mankind, it is many, but apart from mankind it is one.'

No further evidence then is needed to demonstrate the existence of two general types of temperament among primitive peoples, that of the priest-thinker and that of the layman; the one only secondarily identified with action, the other primarily so; the one interested in the analysis of the religious phenomena, the other in their effect. To the former *mana* was the generalized essence of a deity residing in an object or in man; to the latter it was magical potency, that which worked, had activity, was an effect.

PRIMITIVE MAN AS PHILOSOPHER'

'Preface'

When a modern historian desires to study the civilization of any people, he regards it as a necessary preliminary that he divest himself, so far as possible, of all prejudice and bias. He realizes that differences between cultures exist, but he does not feel that it is necessarily a sign of inferiority that a people differs in customs from his own. There seems, however, to be a limit to what an historian treats as legitimate difference, a limit not always easy to determine. On the whole it may be said that he very naturally passes the same judgments that the majority of his fellow countrymen do. Hence, if some of the differences between admittedly civilized peoples often call forth unfavorable judgment or even provoke outbursts of horror, how much more must we expect this to be the case where the differences are of so fundamental a nature as those separating us from people whom we have been accustomed to call uncivilized.

The term 'uncivilized' is a very vague one, and it is spread over a vast medley of peoples, some of whom have comparatively simple customs and others extremely complex ones. Indeed, there can be said to be but two characteristics possessed in common by all these peoples, the absence of a written language and the fact of original possession of the soil when the various civilized European and Asiatic nations came into contact with them. But among all aboriginal races appeared a number of customs which undoubtedly seemed exceedingly strange to their European and Asiatic conquerors. Some of these customs they had never heard of; others they recognized as similar to observances and beliefs existing among the more backward members of their own communities.

Yet the judgments civilized peoples have passed on the aborigines, we may be sure, were not initially based on any calm evaluation of facts. If the aborigines were regarded as innately inferior, this was due in part to the tremendous gulf in custom and belief separating them from the conquerors, in part to the apparent simplicity of their ways, and in no small degree to the fact that they were unable to offer any effective resistance.

Romance soon threw its distorting screen over the whole primitive picture. Within one hundred years of the discovery of America it had already become an ineradicably established tradition that all the aborigines encountered by Europeans were simple, untutored savages from whom little more could be expected than from uncontrolled children, individuals who were at all times the slaves of their passions, of which the dominant one was hatred. Much of this tradition, in various forms, disguised and otherwise, has persisted to the present day.

The evolutionary theory, during its heyday in the 1870's and '80's, still further complicated and misrepresented the situation, and from the great classic that created modern ethnology – Tylor's *Primitive Culture*, published in 1870– future ethnologists were to imbibe the cardinal and fundamentally misleading doctrine that primitive peoples represent an early stage in the history of the evolution of culture. What was, perhaps, even more dangerous was the strange and uncritical manner in which all primitive peoples were lumped together in ethnological discussion – simple Fuegians with the highly advanced Aztecs and Mayans, Bushmen with the peoples of the Nigerian coast, Australians with Polynesians, and so on.

For a number of years scholars were apparently content with the picture drawn by Tylor and his successors. The rebellion against it came in large measure from the American ethnologists, chiefly under the influence of Prof. Franz Boas. Through methods of work foreshadowed by some of Boas' immediate predecessors but more penetratingly and systematically developed by him, a large body of authentic information has been gathered on the American Indians. Add to this the great monographs produced by European ethnologists for other parts of the world, and we have, for the first time in the history of the science, a moderately favorable opportunity for examining anew the nature of primitive man's mentality.

That it is important to the ethnologist, the historian, the sociologist, and the psychologist to understand the true nature of the mentality of primitive man is, of course, self-evident. But practical questions of far more general import are also involved. In Asia, Africa, the islands of the Pacific, Mexico, and South America there exist to-day millions of so-called primitive peoples whose relation to their white and Mongolian conquerors is of vital importance both to the conquerors and to the conquered, or semi-conquered, aborigines. Up to the present all attempts that have been made to understand them, or to come to any reasonable adjustment with them, have met with signal failure, and this failure is in most instances due to the scientifically accredited theories of the innate inferiority of primitive man in mentality and capacity for civilization quite as much as to prejudice and bias. Some governments, notably those of Great Britain and France, have already begun to recognize this fact. But how can we expect public officials to take an unbiased view of primitive mentality when the dominant tradition among ethnologists, among those who ostensibly devote their lives to the subject, is still largely based on an unjustified, or at least undemonstrated, assumption?

The most pressing need in ethnology, then, is to examine anew the older assumptions which, wittingly or unwittingly, ethnologists themselves have harbored for two generations and which threaten to become fixed traditions among psychologists, sociologists, and historians. Among the more important of these assumptions is the notion that there is a dead level of intelligence among primitive peoples, that the individual is completely swamped by and submerged in the group, that thinkers and philosopheres as such do not exist – in short, that there is nothing even remotely comparable to an intellectual class among them.

These conceptions of primitive mentality the writer regards as wholly unjustified, and it is with the object of contraverting them that the following pages have been written. Since the contrary view still holds the field among most scholars, including not a few ethnologists, I have been at considerable pains to collect my material in as irreproachable a manner as possible.

The first requisite of all proof is, of course, that data be accurate and subject to control. To meet this requirement I have, in almost all cases, used only data that have been obtained at first hand and have been published in the original with a translation that could be vouched for. This, perhaps, may appear unduly pedantic, and it may possibly entail the omission of valuable material; but it cannot be too strongly emphasized that if the ethnologist wishes to obtain credence among the more skeptically inclined public, he must be willing to adopt a method of presentation that commends itself to them as meeting every critical test.

A good deal of the data presented in the following chapters were obtained by the author himself. Perhaps I should ask indulgence for using my own published and unpublished material so extensively. This is not due to any over-evaluation of either its accuracy or its importance, but simply to the fact that I happened to be interested specifically in a question which other ethnologists had touched only in passing. In the interests of greater accuracy, and in order to substantiate statements that unsupported might seem incredible to the reader accustomed to obtaining his descriptions of primitive culture from secondary works, native sources have been voluminously quoted. If certain tribes have been stressed more than others, it is simply because we happen to have for them better specific data of the kind desired. Yet it is my firm conviction that the conclusions arrived at on the basis of the study of a necessarily limited number of tribes will hold for practically every tribe.

Perhaps it is not necessary to emphasize the dangers besetting the path of anyone venturing to describe and characterize the ideas and mental workings of others, particularly those of races so different ostensibly from ourselves as are primitive peoples. Added to the ordinary risk of misunderstanding, ethnologists often find it necessary to give what are simply their own impressions and interpretations. But to this there can hardly be objection provided the ethnologist is fully aware of all pitfalls, for, surely, the impressions and interpretations of a person who has spent many years among primitive peoples must possess a value in a high degree. Yet the layman, on the other hand, is right in demanding that the investigator prove that he is not confusing facts with impressions. I must confess myself to have had frequent recourse to impressions and interpretations, which I have then sought to illustrate by appropriate examples. But I realize quite clearly how easy it is to obtain appropriate examples, and mine, I hope, have been chosen judiciously.

'Introduction'

The study of primitive peoples is a comparatively recent discipline. It can be said to have been first definitely and adequately formulated by Edward B. Tylor. To-day, after more than two generations of development, compared with such older disciplines as history it is still barely out of its swaddling clothes. There are comparatively few places where its principles are taught and as a result it is still, to an appreciable extent, the happy hunting ground of well-meaning amateurs. It would be a gross injustice to minimize the services these amateurs have rendered. But amateurs are enthusiasts and, as a class, likely to be both sentimental and uncritical; and while the academic intolerance of them is often unfair and ridiculous, it is nevertheless true that no science can be said to have attained its full majority until the number of amateurs engaged in it, as compared with those specially qualified, is reasonably negligible.

Judged by this criterion, ethnology to-day is still in its adolescent stage. Yet adolescence has its charms, and among these charms is optimism and faith. Optimism is, in fact, the keynote of present-day ethnology. How else can we explain the nonchalance with which an ethnologist embarks on the task of describing, single-handed, the language, mythology, religion, material culture, art, music, and social organization of a people whose language he very rarely can speak and whose mode of thought and life is far more remote from his own than is that of an Illinois farmer from the mode of life and thought of a Hindu?

The keepers of the older disciplines, where specialization often reaches its apotheosis of aridity and futility, sit back in half-contemptuous bewilderment at the boyish pranks of the adventurer-ethnologist who sets out to conquer a new world. Perhaps in the end the laugh will be on the critics. For the present, however, it must be admitted that their bewilderment and incredulity are amply justified. Every statement, for example, that an historian makes is expected to be controlled by a large body of corroborative material. Surely, it is contended, the ethnologist does not expect us to take his uncorroborated word for everything. Unfortunately he does, and there are practical reasons why, dangerous as this situation avowedly is, it must be accepted and made the best of.

With very few exceptions, the descriptions of primitive peoples cannot be controlled in the manner that is customary in subjects like history. The observer not only collects the facts, but to him belongs the power to fix, often for all time, what precisely those facts shall be. It is clearly dangerous to entrust such power to any man, yet for practical reasons attendant upon the collection of ethnological data, it is somewhat difficult to avoid this fundamentally undesirable and unreasonable condition. Since, however, his work is so conditioned, the observer's emotional and intellectual approach, his expressed and his unexpressed assumptions, the many intangible trifles that influence even the most careful and critical, all these naturally assume a greater significance for the ethnologist than for the historian.

It cannot be said that the majority of ethnologists are fully aware of the ways in which certain tacit or conscious attitudes make themselves felt, and how definitely such attitudes are likely to color their records. There is only one way of avoiding this danger, and that is the old way, the one in vogue in history for centuries – to obtain the facts in the original and to attempt no manipulations and no rearrangements of them whatsoever. Whatever interpretations are necessary must be completely separated from the original data. This rather obvious procedure is only now becoming at all common in ethnology. Some of the most famous monographs written by Europeans and Americans, for instance, sin most egregiously against this elementary rule.

But if the historian to-day differs markedly from the ethnologist in the degree of trust he is willing to place in the uncontrolled reports of a single man, no matter how qualified he may be, he differs equally in another even more important regard, namely, the selection of the aspect of culture most to be emphasized. In all recent treatments history has come to be the history of the intellectual class, and at all times it has been the history of the exceptional man. In ethnology, on the contrary, partly owing to its genesis, partly to paucity of material, the emphasis has been quite otherwise, and it is the group beliefs as such that are described. Ethnologists have not always been conscious of this fact, yet even when they are well aware of marked individual differences among primitive men, these are dismissed with the summary comment that they do not represent the general consensus of opinion.

On the whole, it can justifiably be claimed that the prevalent descriptions of primitive peoples represent the beliefs and customs of the non-intellectual class among them, or at best a hopeless mixture of the viewpoint of the intellectual and the non-intellectual class which no lay reader can possibly disentangle. This defect would be in no way mitigated even if it should eventually be shown that ninety-nine per cent of all primitive peoples belong to the non-intellectual class. There would still be one per cent of the aboriginal population to be accounted for, and for this one per cent our present descriptions would be just as distorted and inadequate as if we were to accept Frazer's *The Golden Bough* as a true picture of the beliefs and customs of the intellectual class of Western Europe.

Throughout this book I am making one assumption, namely, that among primitive peoples there exists the same distribution of temperament and ability as among us. This I hold to be true in spite of all the manifest differences in the configuration and orientation of their cultures. In justice to myself I should add that the predication of an identical distribution of ability and temperament for civilized and primitive peoples is not the result of any general theory that I happen to hold; it represents a conviction that has been slowly forced upon me from my observations and contact with a number of aboriginal tribes.

To repeat, then, my object here is to describe primitive cultures in terms of their intellectual class, from the viewpoint of their thinkers. Thinkers, however, are not, and can not be, isolated from life among primitive peoples in the same way as this has repeatedly been done among us, nor do they probably exercise the same degree of influence on their fellows. To attempt, therefore, to envisage primitive culture from their standpoint is equivalent to looking at it through a very restricted lens. I am fully aware of this. The result will give only a partial picture, one which will necessarily hold true for only a very small number of individuals in each group, and it must not be mistaken for anything else. That would be as great an error as the one committed by those who assume that there is no intellectual class in primitive culture.

The following book is grouped into two parts, the first dealing with the relation of man to society and to his fellow men, and the second with what I have called the higher aspects of primitive thought. In this way, it is hoped, it will be possible to indicate to what extent each thinker shared and participated in the ideas of the average man of his group and in what way he transcended them.

Throughout it has been my endeavor to allow the natives to talk for themselves, interpreting their thoughts only in those cases where explanation seemed necessary and of value. Perhaps I shall be criticized for quoting too much and for giving the book more the appearance of an anthology of the thoughts of primitive people than a discussion of them. But, in a sense, what I have really tried to do is to be a commentator. I need not say that this role has at times been changed into that of an interpreter.

Had it been possible, I should have much preferred to gather all the sources available to-day into a separate volume and to restrict the present one simply to discussion. But the time for such a procedure has not yet arrived, although it is clearly not far off. It is perhaps better at the present stage, considering the ignorance, incredulity, and prejudice still prevalent even among otherwise well-informed laymen on the whole subject of primitive culture, to carry our proof along with us and to substantiate every unusual statement as soon as it is made.

Let me repeat, before we begin our study, that in the present condition of our knowledge any attempt to describe the intellectual view of life of primitive peoples is destined to be tentative, provocative of further investigation and interpretation rather than permanent and final. I can only say with an unknown Hawaiian poet:

> *The day of revealing shall see what it sees:*
> *A seeing of facts, a sifting of rumors.*

THE RELIGIOUS AND THE NON-RELIGIOUS MAN

Just as we find two contrasting psychological types among aboriginal peoples, one oriented toward action and the other toward thinking and contemplation, so we encounter a division there of individuals into groups based on their inward relation to religious phenomena. By and large we can predicate two basic types, the inherently and continuously religious, and the essentially non-religious man. But such a classification has little meaning unless we first are quite clear as to what we understand by religion,

By religion is here meant the fusion of a particular feeling and attitude with an interconnected series of specific acts and beliefs. Both the feeling, the acts and the beliefs are merged and interpenetrated by the material and spiritual implications of living in a clearly-defined cultural framework. Let us, for the moment, not raise the question as to which of these elements is most important or whether one preceded the other in the formation of what I am here calling religion. At all times, moreover, religion has had a primary social function namely, the validation of the life-values of man.

Feeling or attitude is admittedly not too adequate a term However, what I intend by this term will emerge in the course of my .discussion. Primary of course, are the physical environment, the psycho-physical make-up of man and his cultural framework.

From the beginning of man's existence they have been inextricably interwoven. That man brought with him into the world 600,000 years ago psychical traits belonging to his animal-psychical ancestry we can safely assume. That, in the early period of his adjustment to the world around him and to the struggle for existence, the specific animal-psychical inheritance played an important role, this stands to reason. Yet, we must not overstress the animal inheritance even for that early period and regard man as a purely instinctual animal. Pekin man knew how to make fire and I suspect that for more than a hundred thousand years man has not regarded the objective world as simply the projection of his emotions and phantasies. What I am suggesting, then, is this, that from the very beginning of man's emergence there have existed individuals who were capable of discursive thinking, that man from the beginning has been not only *homo faber*, but also *homo oeconomicus-politicus* and *homo religiosus*.

However, I am not dealing here with the religion of prehistoric man but with that of living aborigines, the direct inheritors of a human experience that has now lasted more than half a million years. Throughout this long period man has been faced with the problem of adjusting himself to the natural world around him, of developing methods for assuring his food supply and elaborating mechanisms for living harmoniously with his fellow-men and with himself. During the greater part of this time it is not too daring to assume that religions have existed. I would even hazard the guess that the feeling, attitude, actions and beliefs connected with it have not changed essentially throughout this long period of time.

Now the belief most inextricably connected with the specific feeling is that in a *something* outside of man, more powerful than man and influencing or exercising control over those elements in life upon which he lays most emphasis. I see no objection to calling this *something* a spirit as long as it is not thought of in too definite a form. For the present, that is immaterial. The important thing to remember is that this *something* is individualized.

Let us forget, for the moment, all questions as to the nature of the connection of the belief in this *something* with the other elements in our definition and focus our attention upon one point, namely, that a number of things are, from the start, predicated about it. It is outside of man; it is more powerful than man; it exercises control over man's life values. Let us also remember that the three things here predicated are always bound together and form a single, indissoluble whole.

However, this positing of a *something*, of a being outside of man, is not the only thing involved here. Many miscellaneous beliefs are also included. These belong strictly to the folkloristic background which varies from group to group. Of these, two seem to be constant, the belief in a soul or souls and the belief in immortality.

It is when we attempt to characterize specifically the nature of the feeling and attitude that our difficulties begin. We must be careful to distinguish them clearly and adequately from other related feelings and attitudes and not predicate the existence of the latter for all human beings or, for that matter, assume that they are found with the same intensity in any person all the time.

This feeling and attitude possesses both a physiological and a psychological side. The physiological side is expressed in acts which are always associated with the external preparations for mental and emotional concentration – the closing of the eyes, reclining of the head, fasting, some form of washing, etc.

The psychological side is expressed in a far more than normal sensitiveness when in the presence of certain external objects. This manifests itself, positively, in a sensation of exhilaration, mild euphoria, etc., and, negatively, in one of terror, fear, helplessness, bewilderment, self-rejection, etc. This more than normal sensitiveness is always accompanied by a marked tendency to become absorbed in internal sensations, stirrings and feelings, and by an equally marked tendency for interest in external impressions to be suspended.

The primary question then becomes: how shall we account for this more than normal sensitiveness in the presence of this *something?*

It goes without saying that no mature individual, in a given group, is not thoroughly familiar with the religious notions of his tribe. It likewise goes without saying or, at least should, that, such being the case, an individual is so to say prepared beforehand both for the normal indications of this *something* – let us call it the supernatural – and for the sensations and emotions he has been taught to expect as being associated with it. Consequently, we must assume that this more than normal sensitiveness arises when an object or a situation is completely outside those with which a man is acquainted. On such occasions there arises, at least, among primitive peoples, the awareness of an unbalance in the order of the external world which is accompanied by a psychical unbalance or a crisis of varying intensity within oneself.

I do not think that one can overestimate the importance attached by aboriginal peoples to the external world's maintaining its balance, maintaining its proper and fixed order. That order is assumed to have existed either from beginning of time or to have been established at some particular time in the dim past. Its characteristics are fixed. It can be interfered with in only two ways, either by supernatural beings or by man.

In the second of our unbalances, that within man himself, we are dealing with a psychical crisis which the individual cannot solve and for which he needs help. So they, the spirits he has predicated, they, upon whom man must lean in order to live, they, who are eternal and omnipresent, also become his helpers and healers. It is because they have now and have always had this double relationship to him that they have become truly supernatural or better, super-natural.

I am using the term *psychical unbalance, psychical crises*, in a very broad sense so that it can include a wide range of mental conditions, varying from a slight unbalance to a true psycho-neurosis.

My postulation that man needs help from supernatural beings because of the existence of an unbalance within his own psyche brings us to what I regard as one of the fundamental problems in all religion, namely, how many individuals possess such a psychical unbalance? What are its characteristics, what are the signs by which it can be recognized? How continuous is it? What factors have brought it about?

Let me attempt to answer the last question first and begin where one must always begin, *with man in the midst of life*. It is best in such a discussion, I feel, to start with concrete examples, and I shall, therefore, select two from a tribe that has been better and more fully described than any other in the world, the Eskimo.

[. . .]

Just as the non-religious and intermittently religious man is primarily a man of action and a pragmatist for whom an effect precedes a cause, so is the truly religious man primarily a 'subjective idealist'. In aboriginal societies, however, he, too, must be a man of action or, at least, behave like one. We have seen that he is constrained and impelled by his whole nature to concern himself with his subjective states, to ponder upon them, to analyze them, and to attempt to synthesize them. He attaches great importance both to the influence of his subjective states upon his actions and to the explanations he has developed. He insists on a description in terms of a cause-and-effect relation, never, however, in terms of an effect-and-cause one.

The sharpness with which this cause-and-effect relation is brought out differs markedly from the two basic types of truly religious temperament. Both clearly are thinkers. However, where we are dealing with individuals whose psychical unbalances are acute, where compulsion plays so large a part, whether more or less permanent or transient, where feeling is as important as thinking, there it might perhaps be best to say such men are prone to analyze causes as such and effects as such and leave the interaction between them blurred, although they are keenly aware that a nexus exists. It is exceedingly important to remember this fact.

On the other hand, where we are dealing with the second of our truly religious types, a causal nexus is specifically predicated. At times there is indeed a tendency to treat the object toward which the feeling is directed as if it were the cause of the feeling itself, that is, of the subjective condition. In the first type the object, the divine, the supernatural, is regarded as secondary. It is the feeling that individualizes it, that so-to-speak deifies it. In the second, we have just the reverse, and the divine is primary.

It will be seen at once that the intermittently religious individual, the pragmatist, actually wavers between these two contrasting attitudes and philosophies. This follows naturally from his whole orientation toward life.
[. . .]
Assuredly I do not have to emphasize what the clash of the two temperaments, the truly religious and the intermittently and non-religious, has meant in the history of religion; how the coordinating formulations of the first have permeated the activities and thinking of the latter; and how the activities of the second have continually disrupted these formulations. In fact, this disruption of the formulations of the truly religious man, expressed and implied, constitutes one of the main functions of our man of action. However, although, it is true that we frequently cannot understand many aspects of the formulations of the articulate religious thinker without due and proper regard for the activities of the non-religious individual, we cannot understand religion and religious experience at all except by studying and analyzing the ideas and the behavior of the truly religious man. To understand primitive religions we must begin with his description and with his analysis of the religious experience.

Having now pointed out the presence and importance of certain psychological types in aboriginal societies, we can proceed to a description of the economic framework within which the man of action, the thinker, the religious and the non-religious man must function. It cannot be too strongly stressed that it is this framework which, in the last analysis, determines how these individuals are to function and which interpenetrates all their creations, giving them body, meaning and direction.

NOTES

1. Rudolf Otto, *Das Heilige*. Gotha, 1926.
2. R. H. Codrington, *The Melanesians*. Oxford, 1891, pp. 118—119.
3. Beattie in *Journal of the Polynesian Society* (New Plymouth, N. Z.), Vol. 30, 1921.
4. J. Walker, *The Sun Dance of the Oglala Division of the Dakota*. Anthropological Papers of the American Museum of Natural History, XVI, Part II. New York, pp. 152 ff.

Alfred R. Radcliffe-Brown

Alfred Reginald Radcliffe-Brown was born in 1881 in Wales, where he received his primary school education. He received his secondary school education in Birmingham, and became a student at Cambridge in 1901. From 1901 until 1906 he studied here at Trinity College, concentrating on 'mental and moral science' as a student of W. H. R. Rivers. He made a travel to South Africa in 1905, and received a 'studentship in ethnology' enabling him to do fieldwork on the Andaman Islands from 1906 until 1908. On his return to England Radcliffe-Browne became in 1908 a fellow of Trinity College, where he taught comparative sociology, and a lecturer at the London School of Economics, where he taught ethnology. He also became a honorary professor of social anthropology at the University of Liverpool. From 1910 until 1912 he did fieldwork in Western Australia; in 1913–14 he gave, besides his other teaching duties, lectures at the University of Birmingham. In 1914 he went to Australia, where he stayed during the First World War: from 1915 until 1917 in Sydney, and becoming in 1917 Director of Education in the kingdom of Tonga, on the Friendship Islands. Subsequently he went to South Africa, where he was for a short time lecturer in Psychology at the University of Witwatersrand, then ethnologist at the Transvaal Museum in Pretoria, and finally professor of Social Anthropology at the University of Cape Town, where he organized the School of African Life and Languages. From 1926 until 1931 Radcliffe-Brown was professor of Anthropology at the University of Sydney, where his courses were taken by administrators and missionaries to New Guinea and other dependent territories; here he founded the journal *Oceania* in 1930. Thereupon, Radcliffe-Brown was a visiting professor of anthropology at the University of Chicago from 1931 until 1935 and again in 1936–37. In 1935–36 he was a visiting professor at the University of Yenching, China. In 1937 he was called to the newly created chair of social anthropology at Oxford. During his English period he was President of the Royal Anthropological Institute for two years (1940 and 1941), and also for two years during the war visiting professor at the University of São Paulo, Brazil (1942–44). After his retirement from Oxford in 1946, Radcliffe-Brown taught for some years sociology at the University Farouk I at Alexandria, and social anthropology at Grahamstown, South Africa. He returned to England in 1955 and died in London in that year.

Of Radcliffe-Brown's publications the following may be mentioned here: 1913 *Three Tribes of Western Australia;* 1922 *The Andaman Islanders. A Study in Social Anthropology;* 1931 *The Social Organisation of Australian Tribes;* 1952 *Structure and Function in Primitive Society. Essays and Addresses;* 1957 *A Natural Science of Society;* 1958 *Method in Social Anthropology. Selected Essays.*

Radcliffe-Brown's methodological concern was to come to a rational division of the different subjects of anthropology. One of his basic distinctions is that between ethnology on the one hand, reconstructing the growth of social institutions, and social anthropology on the other hand, investigating the function of social institutions in their social systems and exploring by means of 'comparative sociology' the universal laws which govern human social behavior. Radcliffe-Brown's researches all concentrated on the problem of social structures to be studied by a systematic and scientific method. Consequently, his work stresses the importance of theory, and he may be called one of the creators of modern social anthropology.

The following text has been taken from the article 'Religion and Society' (1945), in which the author approaches religion from this social anthropology.

'RELIGION AND SOCIETY'

The Royal Anthropological Institute has honoured me with an invitation to deliver the Henry Myers Lecture on the rôle of religion in the development of human society. That is an important and complex subject, about which it is not possible to say very much in a single lecture, but as it is hoped that this may be only the first of a continuing series of lectures, in which different lecturers will each offer some contribution, I think that the most useful thing I can do is to indicate certain lines along which I believe that an enquiry into this problem can be profitably pursued.

The usual way of looking at religions is to regard all of them, or all except one, as bodies of erroneous beliefs and illusory practices. There is no doubt that the history of religions has been in great part a history of error and illusion. In all ages men have hoped that by the proper performance of religious actions or observances they would obtain some specific benefit: health and long life, children to carry on their line, material well-being, success in hunting, rain, the growth of crops and the multiplication of cattle, victory in war, admission of their souls after death to a paradise, or inversely, release by the extinction of personality from the round of reincarnation. We do not believe that the rainmaking rites of savage tribes really produce rain. Nor do we believe that the initiates of the ancient mysteries did actually attain through their initiation an immortality denied to other men.

When we regard the religions of other peoples, or at least those of what are called primitive peoples, as systems of erroneous and illusory beliefs, we are confronted with the problem of how these beliefs came to be formulated and accepted. It is to this problem that anthropologists have given most attention. My personal opinion is that this method of approach, even though it may seem the most direct, is not the one most likely to lead to a real understanding of the nature of religions.

There is another way in which we may approach the study of religions We may entertain as at least a possibility the theory that any religion is an important or even essential part of the social machinery, as are morality and law, part of the complex system by which human beings are enabled to live together in an orderly arrangement of social relations. From this point of view we deal not with the origins but with the social functions of religions, *i.e.* the contribution that they make to the formation and maintenance of a social order. There are many persons who would say that it is only *true* religion *(i.e.,* one's own) that can provide the foundation of an orderly social life. The hypothesis we are considering is that the social function of a religion is independent of its truth or falsity, that religions which we think to be erroneous or even absurd and repulsive, such as those of some savage tribes, may be important and effective parts of the social machinery, and that without these 'false' religions social evolution and the development of modern civilization would have been impossible.

The hypothesis, therefore, is that in what we regard as false religions, though the performance of religious rites does not actually produce the effects that are expected or hoped for by those who perform or take part in them, they have other effects, some at least of which may be socially valuable.

How are we to set to work to test this hypothesis? It is of no use thinking in terms of religion in general, in the abstract, and society in the abstract. Nor is it adequate to consider some one religion, particularly if it is the one in which we have been brought up and about which we are likely to be prejudiced one way or another. The only method is the experimental method of social anthropology, and that means that we must study in the light of our hypothesis a sufficient number of diverse particular religions or religious cults in their relation to the particular societies in which they are found. This is a task not for one person but for a number.

Anthropologists and others have discussed at length the question of the proper definition of religion. I do not intend to deal with that controversial subject on this occasion. But there are some points that must be considered. I shall assume that any religion or any religious cult normally involves certain ideas or beliefs on the one hand, and on the other certain observances. These observances, positive and negative, *i.e.*, actions and abstentions, I shall speak of as rites.

In European countries, and more particularly since the Reformation, religion has come to be considered as primarily a matter of belief. This is itself a phenomenon which needs to be explained, I think, in terms of social development. We are concerned here only with its effects on the thinking of anthropologists. Among many of them there is a tendency to treat belief as primary: rites are considered as the results of beliefs. They therefore concentrate their attention on trying to explain the beliefs by hypotheses as to how they may have been formed and adopted.

To my mind this is the product of a false psychology. For example, it is sometimes held that funeral and mourning rites are the result of a belief in a soul surviving death. If we must talk in terms of cause and effect, I would rather hold the view that the belief in a surviving soul is not the cause but the effect of the rites. Actually the cause-effect analysis is misleading. What really happens is that the rites and the justifying or rationalizing beliefs develop together as parts of a coherent whole. But in this development it is action or the need of action that controls or determines belief rather than the other way about. The actions themselves are symbolic expressions of sentiments.

My suggestion is that in attempting to understand a religion it is on the rites rather than on the beliefs that we should first concentrate our attention. Much the same view is taken by Loisy, who justifies his selection of sacrificial rites as the subject of his analysis of religion by saying that rites are in all religions the most stable and lasting element, and consequently that in which we can best discover the spirit of ancient cults.[1]

That great pioneer of the science of religion, Robertson Smith, took this view.[2]

[. . .]

The relative stability of rites and the variability of doctrines can be illustrated from the Christian religions. The two essential rites of all Christian religions are baptism and the eucharist, and we know that the latter solemn sacrament is interpreted differently in the Orthodox Church, the Roman Church and the Anglican Church. The modern emphasis on the exact formulation of beliefs connected with the rites rather than on the rites themselves is demonstrated in the way in which Christians have fought with and killed one another over differences of doctrine.

Thirty-seven years ago (1908), in a fellowship thesis on the Andaman Islanders (which did not appear in print till 1922), I formulated briefly a general theory of the social function of rites and ceremonies. It is the same theory that underlies the remarks I shall offer on this occasion. Stated in the simplest possible terms the theory is that an orderly social life amongst human beings depends upon the presence in the minds of the members of a society of certain sentiments, which control the behaviour of the individual in his relation to others. Rites can be seen to be the regulated symbolic expressions of certain sentiments. Rites can therefore be shown to have a specific social function when, and to the extent that, they have for their effect to regulate, maintain and transmit from one generation to another sentiments on which the constitution of the society depends. I ventured to suggest as a general formula that religion is everywhere an expression in one form or another of a sense of dependence on a power outside ourselves, a power which we may speak of as a spiritual or moral power.

This theory is by no means new. It is to be found in the writings of the philosophers of ancient China.

[. . .]

The view taken by this school of ancient philosophers was that religious rites have important social functions which are independent of any beliefs that may be held as to the efficacy of the rites. The rites gave regulated expression to certain human feelings and sentiments and so kept these sentiments alive and active. In turn it was these sentiments which, by their control of or influence on the conduct of individuals, made possible the existence and continuance of an orderly social life.

It is this theory that I propose for your consideration. Applied, not to a single society such as ancient China, but to all human societies, it points to the correlation and co-variation of different characteristics or elements of social systems. Societies differ from one another in their structure and constitution and therefore in the customary rules of behaviour of persons one to another. The system of sentiments on which the social constitution depends must therefore vary in correspondence with the difference of constitution. In so far as religion has the kind of social function that the theory suggests, religion must also vary in correspondence with the manner in which the society is constituted. In a social system constituted on the basis of nations which make war on one another, or stand ready to do so, a well-developed sentiment of patriotism in its members is essential to maintain a strong nation. In such circumstances patriotism or national feeling may be given support by religion. Thus the Children of Israel, when they invaded the land of Canaan under the leadership of Joshua, were inspired by the religion that had been taught to them by Moses and was centred upon the Holy Tabernacle and its rites.

War or the envisaged possibility of war is an essential element in the constitution of great numbers of human societies, though the war-like spirit varies very much from one to another. It is thus in accordance with our theory that one of the social functions of religion is in connection with war. It can give men faith and confidence and devotion when they go out to do battle, whether they are the aggressors or are resisting aggression. In the recent conflict the German people seem to have prayed to God for victory not less fervently than the people of the Allied Nations.

It will be evident that to test our theory we must examine many societies to see if there is a demonstrable correspondence of the religion or religions of any one of them and the manner in which that society is constituted. If such a correspondence can be made out, we must then try to discover and as far as possible define the major sentiments that find their expression in the religion and at the same time contribute to the maintenance of stability in the society as constituted.

An important contribution to our study is to be found in a book that is undeservedly neglected by anthropologists, *La Cité antique*, by the historian Fustel de Coulanges. It is true that it was written some time ago (1864) and that in some matters it may need correction in the light of later historical research, but it remains a valuable contribution to the theory of the social function of religion.

The purpose of the book is to show the point-by-point correspondence between religion and the constitution of society in ancient Greece and Rome, and how in the course of history the two changed together. It is true that the author, in conformity with the ideas of the nineteenth century, conceived this correlation between two sets of social features in terms of cause and effect, those of one set being thought of as the cause producing those of the other set. The men of the ancient world, so the argument runs, came to hold certain beliefs about the souls of the dead. As the result of their beliefs they made offerings at their tombs.

'Since the dead had need of food and drink it appeared to be a duty of the living to satisfy this need. The care of supplying the dead with sustenance was not left to the caprice or to the variable sentiments of men; it was obligatory. Thus a complete religion of the dead was established, whose dogmas might soon be effaced, but whose rites endured until the triumph of Christianity.'[3]

It was a result of this religion that ancient society came to be constituted on the basis of the family, the agnatic lineage and the *gens*, with its laws of succession, property, authority and marriage.

'A comparison of beliefs and laws shows that a primitive religion constituted the Greek and Roman family, established marriage and paternal authority, fixed the order of relationship, and consecrated the right of property and the right of inheritance. This same religion, after having enlarged and extended the family, formed a still larger association, the city, and reigned in that as it had reigned in the family. From it came all the institutions, as well as all the private law, of the ancients. It was from this that the city received all its principles, its rules, its usages and its magistracies. But, in the course of time, this ancient religion became modified or effaced, and private law and political institutions were modified with it. Then came a series of revolutions, and social changes regularly followed the development of knowledge.'[4]

In his final paragraph the author writes:

'We have written the history of a belief. It was established and human society was constituted. It was modified, and society underwent a series of revolutions. It disappeared and society changed its character.'[5]

This idea of the primacy of belief and of a causal relation in which the religion is the cause and the other institutions are the effect is in accordance with a mode of thought that was common in the middle of the nineteenth century. We can, as I indeed do, completely reject this theory and yet retain as a valuable and permanent contribution to our subject a great deal of what Fustel de Coulanges wrote. We can say that he has produced evidence that in ancient Greece and Rome the religion on the one side and the many important institutions on the other are closely united as interdependent parts of a coherent and unified system. The religion was an essential part of the constitution of the society. The form of the religion and the form of the social structure correspond one with the other. We cannot, as Fustel de Coulanges says, understand the social, juridical and political institutions of the ancient societies unless we take the religion into account. But it is equally true that we cannot understand the religion except by an examination of its relation to the institutions.

A most important part of the religion of ancient Greece and Rome was the worship of ancestors. We may regard this as one instance of a certain kind of religion. A religious cult of the same general kind has existed in China from ancient times to the present day. Cults of the same kind exist to-day and can be studied in many parts of Africa and Asia. It is therefore possible to make a wide comparative study of this type of religion. In my own experience it is in ancestor-worship that we can most easily discover and demonstrate the social function of a religious cult.

The term 'ancestor-worship' is sometimes used in a wide, loose sense to refer to any sort of rites referring to dead persons. I propose to use it in a more limited, and more precisely defined sense. The cult group in this religion consists solely of persons related to one another by descent in one line from the same ancestor or ancestors. In most instances descent is patrilineal, through males. But in some societies, such as the Bakongo, descent is matrilineal, and the cult group consists of descendants of a single ancestress. The rites in which the members of the group, and only they, participate have reference to their own ancestors, and normally they include the making of offerings or sacrifices to them.

A particular lineage consists of three or more generations. A lineage of four or five generations will normally be included as a part in one of six or seven generations. In a well-developed system related lineages are united into a body, such as the Roman *gens*, or what may be called the clan in China. In parts of China we can find a large body of persons, numbering in some instances as much as a thousand, all having the same name and tracing their descent in the male line from a single ancestor, the founder of the clan. The clan itself is divided into lineages.

A lineage, if it is of more than three or four generations, includes both living persons and dead persons. What is called ancestor-worship consists of rites carried out by members of a larger or smaller lineage (*i.e.*, one consisting of more or fewer generations) with reference to the deceased members of the lineage. Such rites include the making of offerings, usually of food and drink, and such offerings are sometimes interpreted as the sharing of a meal by the dead and the living.

In such a society, what gives stability to the social structure is the solidarity and continuity of the lineage, and of the wider group (the clan) composed of related lineages. For the individual, his primary duties are those to his lineage. These include duties to the members now living, but also to those who have died and to those who are not yet born. In the carrying out of these duties he is controlled and inspired by the complex system of sentiments of which we may say that the object on which they are centred is the lineage itself, past, present and future. It is primarily this system of sentiments that is expressed in the rites of the cult of the ancestors. The social function of the rites is obvious: by giving solemn and collective expression to them the rites reaffirm, renew and strengthen those sentiments on which the social solidarity depends.

We have no means of studying how an ancestor-worshipping society comes into existence, but we can study the decay of this type of system in the past and in the present. Fustel de Coulanges deals with this in ancient Greece and Rome. It can be observed at the present time in various parts of the world. The scanty information I have been able to gather suggests that the lineage and joint-family organization of some parts of India is losing something of its former strength and solidarity and that what we should expect as the inevitable accompaniment of this, a weakening of the cult of ancestors, is also taking place. I can speak with more assurance about some African societies, particularly those of South Africa. The effect of the impact of European culture, including the teaching of the Christian missionaries, is to weaken in some individuals the sentiments that attach them to their lineage. The disintegration of the social structure and the decay of the ancestral cult proceed together.

Thus for one particular type of religion I am ready to affirm that the general theory of the social function of religions can be fully demonstrated

A most important contribution to our subject is a work of EmileDurkheim published in 1912. The title is *Les formes élémentaires de la vie religieuse,* but the sub-title reads: *Le système totémique en Australie.* It is worth while mentioning that Durkheim was a pupil of Fustel de Coulanges at the École Normale Supérieure and that he himself said that the most important influence on the development of his ideas about religion was that of Robertson Smith.

Durkheim's aim was to establish a general theory of the nature of religion. Instead of a wide comparative study of many religions, he preferred to take a s imple type of society and carry out an intensive and detailed analysis, and for this purpose he selected the aboriginal tribes of Australia.

He held the view that these tribes represent the simplest type of society surviving to our own times, but the value of his analysis is in no way affected if we refuse to accept this view.

The value of Durkheim's book is as an exposition of a general theory of religion which had been developed with the collaboration of Henri Hubert and Marcel Mauss, starting from the foundations provided by Robertson Smith. Durkheim's exposition of this theory has often been very much misunderstood. A clear, though very brief, statement of it is to be found in the Introduction written by Henry Hubert in 1904 for the French trans- lation of the *Manuel d'Histoire des Religions* of Chantepie de la Saussaye. But it is not possible on this occasion to discuss this general theory. I wish only to deal with one part of Durkheim's work, namely his theory that religious ritual is an expression of the unity of society and that its function is to 're-create' the society or the social order by reaffirming and strengthen- ing the sentiments on which the social solidarity and therefore the social order itself depend.[6] This theory he tests by an examination of the totemic ritual of the Australians. For while Frazer regarded the totemic rites of the Australian tribes as being a matter of magic, Durkheim treats them as re- ligious because the rites themselves are sacred and have reference to sacred beings, sacred places and sacred objects.

In 1912 very much less was known about the Australian aborigines than is known at present. Some of the sources used by Durkheim have proved to be unreliable. The one tribe that was well known, through the writings of Spencer and Gillen and Strehlow — the Aranda — is in some respects atypical. The information that Durkheim could use was therefore decidedly imperfect. Moreover, it cannot be said that his handling of this material was all that it might have been. Consequently there are many points in his exposition which I find unacceptable. Nevertheless, I think that Durk- heim's major thesis as to the social function of the totemic rites is valid and only requires revision and correction in the light of the more extensive and more exact knowledge we now have.[7]

The beings to which the Australian cult refers are commonly spoken of as 'totemic ancestors', and I have myself used the term. But it is somewhat misleading, since they are mythical beings and not ancestors in the same sense as the dead persons commemorated in ancestor-worship. In the cos- mology of the Australian natives the cosmos, the ordered universe, including both the order of nature and the social order, came into existence at a time in the past which I propose to speak of as the World-Dawn, for this name corresponds to certain ideas that I have found amongst the aborigines of some tribes. This order (of nature and of society) resulted from the doings and adventures of certain sacred beings. These beings, whom I shall call the Dawn Beings, are the totemic ancestors of ethnological literature. The ex-

planations of topographical features, of natural species and their characteristics, and of social laws, customs and usages are given in the form of
myths about the happenings of the World-Dawn.

The cosmos is ruled by law. But whereas we think of the laws of nature
as statements of what invariably does happen (except, of course, in miracles),
and of moral or social laws as what ought to be observed but are sometimes
broken, the Australian does not make this distinction. For him men and
women ought to observe the rules of behaviour that were fixed for all
times by the events of the World-Dawn, and similarly the rain ought to
fall in its proper season, plants should grow and produce fruit or seed, and
animals should bear young. But there are irregularities in human society
and in nature.

In what I shall venture to call the totemic religion of the Australian aborigines, there are two main types of ritual. One of these consists of rites
carried out at certain spots which are commonly referred to as 'totem
centres'. A totem centre is a spot that is specially connected with some
species of object, most commonly with a particular species of animal or
plant, or with an aspect of nature such as rain or hot weather. Each centre
is associated with one (or occasionally more than one) of the Dawn Beings.
Frequently the Being is said to have gone into the ground at this spot. For
each totem centre there is a myth connecting it with the events of the
World-Dawn. The totem centre, the myth connected with it and the rites
that are performed there, belong to the local group that owns the territory
within which the totem centre lies. Each totem centre is thought of as
containing, in a rock or a tree or a pool of water or a heap of stones, what
we may perhaps call the life-spirit or life-force of the totem species.

The rites performed at the totem centre by the members of the local
group to which it belongs, or under their leadership and direction, are
thought to renew the vitality of this life-spirit of the species. In eastern
Australia the totem centre is spoken of as the 'home' or 'dwelling-place' of
the species, and the rites are called 'stirring up'. Thus, the rite at a rain
totem centre brings the rain in its due season, that at a kangaroo centre
ensures the supply of kangaroos, and that at the baby totem centre provides for the birth of children in the tribe.

These rites imply a certain conception, which I think we can call specifically a religious conception, of the place of man in the universe. Man is
dependent upon what we call nature: on the regular successions of the
seasons, on the rain falling when it should, on the growth of plants and the
continuance of animal life. But, as I have already said, while for us the
order of nature is one thing and the social order another, for the Australian
they are two parts of a single order. Well-being, for the individual or for the
society, depends on the continuance of this order free from serious dis-

turbance. The Australians believe that they can ensure this continuance or at least contribute to it, by their actions, including the regular performance of the totemic rites.

In the rites that have been described, each group takes care (if we may so express it) of only a small part of nature, of those few species for which it owns totem centres. The preservation of the natural order as a whole therefore depends on the actions of many different groups.

The social structure of the Australian natives is based on two things: a system of local groups, and a system of kinship based on the family. Each small local group is a closed patrilineal descent group, that is, a man is born into the group of his father and his sons belong to his group. Each group is independent and autonomous. The stability and continuity of the social structure depend on the strong solidarity of the local group.

Where there existed the totemic cult which I have just described (and it existed over a very large part of Australia), each local group was a cult group. The totemic ritual served to express the unity and solidarity of the group and its individuality and separation from other groups by the special relation of the group to its *sacra:* the totem centre or centres, the Dawn Beings associated with them, the myths and songs referring to those Beings, and the totems or species connected with the centres. This aspect of the social function of totemism was emphasized, and I think somewhat over-emphasized, by Durkheim.

There is, however, another aspect, for while the local totemic groups are separate individual and continuing social entities, they are also part of a wider social structure. This wider structure is provided by the kinship system. For an individual in Australian native society, every person with whom he has any social contact is related to him by some bond of kinship, near or distant, and the regulation of social life consists essentially of rules concerning behaviour towards different kinds of kin. For example, a man stands in very close relation to his mother's local group and, in many tribes, in a very close relation to its *sacra:* its totems, totem centres and totemic rites.

While Australian totemism separates the local groups and gives each an individuality of its own, it also links the groups together. For while each group is specially connected with certain parts of the natural order *(e.g.,* with rain, or with kangaroo) and with certain of the Beings of the World-Dawn, the society as a whole is related through the totemic religion to the whole order of nature and to the World-Dawn as a whole. This is best seen in another kind of totemic cult, part of which consists of sacred dramas in which the performers impersonate various Dawn Beings. Such dramatic dances are only performed at those religious meetings at which a number of local groups come together, and it is on these occasions that young men are initiated into manhood and into the religious life of the society.

Australian society is not merely a collection of separate local groups; it is also a body of persons linked together in the kinship system. Australian totemism is a cosmological system by which the phenomena of nature are incorporated in the kinship organization. When I was beginning my work in Australia in 1910, a native said to me, '*Bungurdi* (kangaroo) (is) my *kadja* (elder brother).' This simple sentence of three words gives the clue to an understanding of Australian totemism. The speaker did not mean that individuals of the kangaroo species are his brothers. He meant that to the kangaroo species, conceived as an entity, he stood in a social relation analogous to that in which a man stands to his older brother in the kinship system. I am sorry that there is not time on this occasion to expound this thesis more fully.

The account I have just given of Australian totemism differs considerably from that given by Durkheim. But far from contradicting, it confirms Durkheim's fundamental general theory as to the social function of the totemic religion of Australia and its rites. The two kinds of totemic cult are the demonstration, in symbolic action, of the structure of Australian society and its foundations in a mythical and sacred past. In maintaining the social cohesion and equilibrium, the religion plays a most important part. The religion is an intrinsic part of the constitution of society.

I have dwelt, if only cursorily, with two types of religion: ancestor-worship and Australian totemism. In both of them it is possible to demonstrate the close correspondence of the form of religion and the form of the social structure. In both it is possible to see how the religious rites re-affirm and strengthen the sentiments on which the social order depends. Here then are results of some significance for our problem. They point to a certain line of investigation. We can and should examine other religions in the light of the results already reached. But to do this we must study religions *in action;* we must try to discover the effects of active participation in a particular cult, first the direct effects on the individual and then the further effects on the society of which these individuals are members. When we have a sufficient number of such studies, it will be possible to establish a general theory of the nature of religions and their role in social development.

In elaborating such a general theory it will be necessary to determine by means of comparative studies the relations between religion and law and between religion and morality. There is only time to refer very briefly here to the question of religion and morality. As representing a theory that seems to be widely held, I quote the following passages from Tylor:

'One great element of religion, that moral element which among the higher nations forms its most vital part, is indeed little represented in the religion of the lower races.'[8]

'The comparison of savage and civilized religions brings into view, by the side of a deep-lying resemblance in their philosophy, a deep-lying contrast in their practical action on human life. So far as savage religion can stand as representing natural religion, the popular idea that the moral government of the universe is an essential tenet of natural religion simply falls to the ground. Savage animism is almost devoid of that ethical element which to the educated modern mind is the very mainspring of practical religion. Not, as I have said, that morality is absent from the life of the lower races. Without a code of morals, the very existence of the rudest tribe would be impossible; and indeed the moral standards of even savage races are to no small extent well-defined and praiseworthy. But these ethical laws stand on their own ground of tradition and public opinion, comparatively independent of the animistic beliefs and rites which exist beside them. The lower animism is not immoral, it is unmoral. . . . The general problem of the relation of morality to religion is difficult, intricate, and requiring immense array of evidence.'[9]

I agree with Tylor that the problem of the relation of morality to religion is difficult and intricate. But I wish to question the validity of the distinction he makes between the religions of savages and those of civilized peoples, and of his statement that the moral element 'is little represented in the religion of the lower races'. I suspect that when this view is held it often means only that in the 'lower races' the religion is not associated with the kind of morality which exists in contemporary Western societies. But societies differ in their systems of morals as in other aspects of the social system, and what we have to examine in any given society is the relation of the religion or religions of that society to their particular system of morality.

Dr. R. F. Fortune, in his book on Manus religion, has challanged the dictum of Tylor.[10] The religion of Manus is what may be called a kind of spiritualism, but it is not ancestor-worship in the sense in which I have used the term in this lecture. The Manus code of morals rigidly forbids sexual intercourse except between husband and wife, condemns dishonesty and insists on the conscientious fulfilment of obligations, including economic obligations, towards one's relatives and others. Offences against the moral code bring down on the offender, or on his household, punishment from the spirits, and the remedy is to be found in confession and reparation for wrong.

Let us now reconsider the case of ancestor-worship. In the societies which practise it, the most important part of the moral code is that which concerns the conduct of the individual in relation to his lineage and clan and the individual members thereof. In the more usual form of ancestor-worship, infractions of this code fall under religious or supernatural sanctions, for they are offences against the ancestors, who are believed to send punishment.

Again we may take as an example of the lower races the aborigines of Australia. Since the fundamental social structure is a complex system of widely extended recognition of relations of kinship, the most important part of the moral code consists of the rules of behaviour towards kin of different categories. A most immoral action is having sexual relations with any woman who does not belong to that category of his kinsfolk into which he may legally marry.

The moral law of the tribe is taught to young men in the very sacred ceremonies known as initiation ceremonies. I will deal only with the Bora ceremonies, as they are called, of some of the tribes of New South Wales. These ceremonies were instituted in the time of the World-Dawn by Baiame, who killed his own son Daramulun (sometimes identified with the sacred bull-roarer) and on the third day brought him back to life. As the ceremony is conducted, the initiates all 'die' and are brought back to life on the third day.[11]

On the sacred ceremonial ground where these initiations take place there is usually an image of Baiame made of earth, and sometimes one of Baiame's wife. Beside these images sacred rites are shown to the initiates, and sacred myths about Baiame are recounted.

Now Baiame instituted not only the initiation ceremonies, which are, amongst other things, schools of morals for young men, but also the kinship system with its rules about marriage, and behaviour towards different categories of kin. To the question, 'Why do you observe these complex rules about marriage?' the usual answer is, 'Because Baiame established them.' Thus Baiame is the divine law-giver, or, by an alternative mode of expresson, he is the personification of the tribal laws of morality.

I agree with Andrew Lang and Father Schmidt that Baiame thus closely resembles one aspect of the God of the Hebrews. But Baiame gives no assistance in war as Jehovah did for the children of Israel, nor is Baiame the ruler or controller of nature, of storms and seasons. That position is held by another deity, the Rainbow-Serpent, whose image in earth also appears on the sacred ceremonial ground. The position held by Baiame is that of the Divine Being who established the most important rules of morality and the sacred ceremonies of initiation.

These few examples will perhaps suffice to show that the idea that it is only the higher religions that are specially concerned with morality, and that the moral element is little represented in the religions of the lower races, is decidedly open to question. If there were time I could provide instances from other parts of the world.

What makes these problems complex is the fact that law, morality and religion are three ways of controlling human conduct which in different types of society supplement one another, and are combined, in different ways. For the law there are legal sanctions, for morality there are the sanctions of public opinion and of conscience, for religion there are religious sanctions. A single wrongful deed may fall under two or three sanctions. Blasphemy and sacrilege are sins and so subject to religious sanctions; but they may also sometimes be punishment by law as crimes. In our own society murder is immoral; it is also a crime punishable by death; and it is also a sin against God, so that the murderer, after his sudden exit from this life at the hands of the executioner, must face an eternity of torment in the fires of Hell.

[. . .]

To return to our main topic, a writer who has dealt with the social function of religions on the basis of a comparative study is Loisy, who devotes to the subject a few pages of the concluding chapter of his valuable *Essai historique sur le Sacrifice*.[12] Although he differs from Durkheim in some matters, his fundamental theory is, if not identical, at any rate very similar to that of the earlier writer. Speaking of what he calls the sacred action *(l'action sacrée)*, of which the most characteristic form is the rite of sacrifice, he writes:

'We have seen its role in human societies, of which it has maintained and strengthened the social bonds, if indeed it has not contributed in a large measure to creating them. It was, in certain respects, the expression of them; but man is so made that he becomes more firmly fixed in his sentiments by expressing them. The sacred action was the expression of social life, of social aspirations, it has necessarily been a factor of society . . .

'Before we condemn out of hand the mirage of religion and the apparatus of sacrifie as a simple waste of social resources and forces, it is proper to observe that, religion having been the form of the social conscience, and sacrifice the expression of this conscience, the loss was compensated by a gain, and that, so far as purely material losses are concerned, there is really no occasion to dwell on them. Moreover the kind of sacred contribution that was required, without real utility as to the effect that was expected from it, was an intrinsic part of the system of renunciations, of contributions which, in every human society, are the condition of its equilibrium and its conservation.'[13]

But besides this definition of the social function in terms of social cohesion and continuity, Loisy seeks for what he calls a general formula *(formule générale)* in which to sum up the part that religion has played in human life. Such a formula is useful so long as we remember that it is only a formula. The one that Loisy offers is that magic and religion have served to give men confidence.

In the most primitive societies it is magic that gives men confidence in face of the difficulties and uncertainties, the real and imaginary dangers with which he is surrounded.

"A la merci des éléments, des saisons, de ce que la terre lui donne ou lu refuse, des bonnes ou des mauvaises chances de sa chasse ou de sa pêche, auss. du hasard de ses combats avec ses semblables, il croit trouver le moyen de régu.

lariser par des simulacres d'action ces chances plus ou moins incertaines. Ce qu'il fait ne sert à rien par rapport au but qu'il se propose, mais il prend confiance en ses entreprises et en lui-même, il ose, et c'est en osant que réellement il obtient plus ou moins ce qu'il veut. Confiance rudimentaire, et pour une humble vie; mais c'est le commencement du courage moral.'[14]

This is the same theory that was later developed by Malinowski in reference to the magical practices of the Trobriand Islanders.

At a somewhat higher stage of development,

'when the social organism has been perfected, when the tribe has become a people, and this people has its gods, its religion, it is by this religion itself that the strength of the national conscience is measured, and it is in the service of national gods that men find a pledge of security in the present, of prosperity in the future. The gods are as it were the expression of the confidence that the people has in itself; but it is in the cult of the gods that this confidence is nourished.'[15]

At a still higher stage of social development, the religions which give man a promise of immortality give him thereby an assurance which permits him to bear courageously the burden of his present life and face the most onerous obligations. 'It is a higher and more moral form of confidence in life.'[16]

To me this formula seems unsatisfactory in that it lays stress on what is only one side of the religious (or magical) attitude. I offer as an alternative the formula that religion develops in mankind what may be called a sense of dependence. What I mean by this can be best explained by an example. In an ancestor-worshipping tribe of South Africa, a man feels that he is dependent on his ancestors. From them he has received his life and the cattle that are his by inheritance. To them he looks to send him children and to multiply his cattle and in other ways to care for his well-being. This is one side of the matter; on his ancestors he *can* depend. The other side is the belief that the ancestors watch over his conduct, and that if he fails in his duties they will not only cease to send him blessings, but will visit him with sickness or some other misfortune. He cannot stand alone and depend only on his own efforts; on his ancestors he *must* depend.

We may say that the beliefs of the African ancestor-worshipper are illusory and his offerings to his gods really useless; that the dead of his lineage do not really send him either blessings or punishments. But the Confucians have shown us that a religion like ancestor-worship can be rationalized and freed from those illusory beliefs that we call superstition. For in the rites of commemoration of the ancestors it is sufficient that the participants should express their reverential gratitude to those from whom they have received their life, and their sense of duty towards those not yet born, to whom they in due course will stand in the position of revered ancestors. There still remains the sense of dependence. The living depend on those of the past; they have duties to those living in the present and to those of the future who will depend on them.

I suggest to you that what makes and keeps man a social animal is not some herd instinct, but the sense of dependence in the innumerable forms that it takes. The process of socialization begins on the first day of an infant's life and it has to learn that it both *can* and *must* depend on its parents. From them it has comfort and succour; but it must submit also to their control. What I am calling the sense of dependence always has these two sides. We can face life and its changes and difficulties with confidence when we know that there are powers, forces and events on which we can rely, but we must submit to the control of our conduct by rules which are imposed. The entirely asocial individual would be one who thought that he could be completely independent, relying only on himself, asking for no help and recognizing no duties.

I have tried to present to you a theory of the social function of religion. This theory has been developed by the work of such men as Robertson Smith, Fustel de Coulanges, Durkheim, Loisy. It is the theory that has guided my own studies for nearly forty years. I have thought it worth while to indicate that it existed in embryo in the writings of Chinese philosophers more than twenty centuries ago.

Like any other scientific theory it is provisional, subject to revision and modification in the light of future research. It is offered as providing what seems likely to be a profitable method of investigation. What is needed to test and further elaborate the theory is a number of systematic studies of various types of religion in relation to the social systems in which they occur.

I will summarize the suggestions I have made:

1) To understand a particular religion we must study its effects. The religion must therefore be studied *in action*.

2) Since human conduct is in large part controlled or directed by what have been called sentiments, conceived as mental dispositions, it is necessary to discover as far as possible what are the sentiments that are developed in the individual as the result of his participation in a particular religious cult.

3) In the study of any religion we must first of all examine the specifically religious actions, the ceremonies and the collective or individual rites.

4) The emphasis on belief in specific doctrines which characterizes some modern religions seems to be the result of certain social developments in societies of complex structure.

5) In some societies there is a direct and immediate relation between the religion and the social structure. This has been illustrated by ancestor-

worship and Australian totemism. It is also true of what we may call national religions, such as that of the Hebrews or those of the city states of Greece and Rome.[17] But where there comes into existence a separate, independent religious structure by the formation of different churches or sects or cult-groups within a people, the relation of religion to the total social structure is in many respects indirect and not always easy to trace.

6) As a general formula (for whatever such a formula may be worth) it is suggested that what is expressed in all religions is what I have called the sense of dependence in its double aspect, and that it is by constantly maintaining this sense of dependence that religions perform their social function.

NOTES

1. 'Les rites étant dans toutes les religions l'élément le plus consistant et le plus durable, celui, par conséquent, où se découvre le mieux l'esprit des cultes anciens. Loisy, *Essai historique sur le Sacrifice*, Paris, 1920, p. 1.

2. W. Robertson Smith, *Lectures on the Religion of the Semites*, 1907, pp. 16–17 and 20.

3. Fustel de Coulanges, *The Ancient City* (translation of *La Cité antique*, 1864, by Willard Small), p. 23.

4. *Ibid.*, p. 12.

5. *Ibid.*, p. 529.

6. Emile Durkheim, *Les formes élémentaires de la vie religieuse; le système totémique en Australie*, 1912, pp. 323, 497 and elsewhere.

7. For a criticism of some points in Durkheim's work, see A. R. Radcliffe-Brown, 'The sociological theory of Totemism,' *Proceedings of the Fourth Pacific Science Congress*, Java, 1929, Vol. II, pp. 295–309.

8. E. B. Tylor, *Primitive Culture*, 3rd ed., 1891, Vol. I, p. 427.

9. *Ibid.*, Vol. II, p. 360.

10. R. F. Fortune, *Manus Religion*, Philadelphia, 1935, pp. 5 and 356. This book is a useful contribution to the study of the social function of religion and deals with a religion of a very unusual type.

11. The suggestion has been made that we have here the influence of Christianity, but that opinion can be dismissed. The idea of ritual death and rebirth is very widespread in religion, and the three-day period is exemplified every month in every part of the world by the death and resurrection of the moon.

12. A. Loisy, *Essai historique sur le Sacrifice*, 1920, pp. 531–540.

13. *Ibid.*, pp. 535–537.

14. *Ibid.*, p. 533.

15. *Ibid.*, p. 533.

16. *Ibid.*, p. 534.

17. '. . . among the ancients what formed the bond of every society was a worship. Just as a domestic altar held the members of a family grouped about it, so the city was the collective group of those who had the protecting deities, and who performed the religious ceremony at the same altar.' Fustel de Coulanges, *op. cit.*, p. 193.

Martin P. Nilsson

Martin Ph. Nilsson was born in 1874 in Ballingslöv, Sweden, where he received his primary school education. He received his secondary school education in Kristianstad, and in 1892 entered the University of Lund to study Classics. In 1900 he obtained his Ph. D. degree with a thesis on the Attic festivals of Dionysus. He then became 'docent' in Greek Language and Literature at the same university, teaching archeology as well and showing an interest in ethnography and ethnology. He took part in the Danish excavations at Lindos, Rhodes, between 1905 and 1907. In 1909 Nilsson occupied the new chair of Classical Archeology and Ancient History at the University of Lund. Besides his publications on Greek religion and folklore, he also published a number of studies on Swedish folklore. In the 1930's he taught at Berkeley for a year and at other universities in the United States. Nilsson retired in 1939. He died in 1967.

Nilsson's main books on Greek and Roman religion in English are the following: 1925 *A History of Greek Religion*; 1926 *Imperial Rome. 1: Men and Events. 2: The Empire and its Inhabitants*; 1927 *The Minoan-Mycenaean Religion and its Survival in Greek Religion*; 1932 *The Mycenaean Origin of Greek Mythology*; 1933 *Homer and Mycenae*; 1940 *Greek Popular Religion* (1961 *Greek Folk Religion*); 1948 *Greek Piety*; 1951 *Cults, Myths, Oracles, and Politics in Ancient Greece. With two Appendices: The Ionian Phylae, The Phratries*; 1951–60 *Opuscula Selecta Linguis Anglica, Francogallica, Germanica Conscripta*, 3 vols.; 1957 *The Dionysiac Mysteries of the Hellenistic and Roman Age*.

Two fragments have been chosen from Nilsson's two 'Letters to Professor Arthur D. Nock' (1949 and 1951). Nilsson's friend and colleague Arthur D. Nock was Professor of the History of Religions at Harvard University, and asked Nilsson to write him on the progress of the study of Greek religion. These letters by Nilsson have been published. A third fragment has been taken from his essay 'Religion as Man's Protest against the Meaninglessness of Events' (1954). In the first two fragments the scholar speaks about the advancement of historical research on Greek religion, and in the third about the problem of meaning and religion as he saw it.

ON METHOD AND THEORY

[. . .] During my long life I have seen so many theories of the science of religion accepted as a solution of the problems, dominate and even dominate tyrannically, contested, and brought down to their proper proportions, that I have learned the necessity of criticising *le dernier cri* too. I am not inclined to fall down and pay respect exclusively to the idols of the day. Only the poor ruins are left of the proud chateau of nature mythology, animism was ousted by preanimism, the claims of totemism to unlock all locks were shown to be an illusion, the mechanical causality of the doctrine of power and of magic was rejected and the importance of emotion emphasized. However, if one is not the prisoner of preconceived opinions, one must acknowledge, justly, that none of these idols of a day has been vain. All of them have taught us to understand better the problem of religion and its origin, after criticism has reduced them to their true importance. This is true too in regard to the belief in the High God. It was put in the shadow by other dominating opinions and was pushed to one side. It does not give the answer to the last question, if one does not trust in the *Uroffenbarung*, but it renders an important contribution to the understanding of religious development, I purposely use the anathematized word evolution. We have to distinguish the two figures discussed above. In later religions the gods are often not the creators of the world, nor in the religions of primitive peoples is the god of the heavens. This god is a simple personification of the kind which has been discussed above. It is possible, perhaps likely, that he belonged to certain peoples, e.g., the Indo-Europeans, from the beginning, has developed and has become a very important factor in their religion. But I cannot believe and there is nothing to prove that the other gods of a polytheistic religion were created by splitting off from him. At best it may be possible that he has been 'so to speak' a midwife helping other gods to spring off from the animatism which endowed natural objects with a soul, so that they got a shape and were seen by phantasy, personifications in the sense in which the word is taken here.

Phenomenology. Finally something must be said of phenomenology, a recent method of the science of religion, because it is at the back of the new opinions. It classifies religious phenomena according to their similarity or kinship. The question may be asked whether phenomenology has any further purpose than putting the phenomena into their respective boxes, whether it tries to find a connection between them. It cannot be the historical connection, development, and cross-influences. For phenomenology puts together phenomena from different peoples, differing as to age and development. In principle it cares neither for time nor for history. Consequently, if any connection is sought for, it must consist in a quality of thought which is common to mankind and acts originating from these thoughts. If it be so phenomenology comes very near to the old comparative science of religion against which it opposes. The difference is that while the latter is occupied with simple phenomena, the former is occupied with complicated ideas and rites. The risk is that the phenomena may be oversimplified and adapted according to the scheme into which they are put. In spite of all the tendency to find development, evolutionism, to use this bad word, is apparent. For a development to higher forms cannot be denied. Just as the faculty of thought is developed, so that, e.g., a Greek philosopher thinks more clearly than, say, an Australian native or a farmer of olden times, so religious ideas are developed to higher forms. There is a difference between the Baiame of the Australians, the Zeus of the Greek, and Jahwe in the later Jewish religion.

ON THE ADVANCEMENTS MADE IN THE STUDY OF GREEK RELIGION

You ask me to list the *positive* gains in the science of Greek and Roman religion during my lifetime. As I was born in 1874 this time covers three-quarters of a century, or if you count from my first publication on Greek religion in 1900, half a century.

Your question is very difficult. It is easier to write a survey of research in my time, such as that to be found in the beginning of each of the volumes of my *Geschichte der griechischen Religion*, although such a survey must imply a large subjective element, a judgment of values. To answer your question with regard to positive gains, gains which will persist throughout the changing years, – in Saecula Saeculorum –, is indeed beyond human power, for no human being can make such a forecast.

I shall begin with the comparison of Greek religion to the religions of primitive peoples and to popular customs and beliefs, for the study of these analogies was of paramount importance in the decades when my study of Greek religion began.

Greek religion is in its beginning intimately linked up with primitive religion and these links persisted, at least there are traces of them even in the classical age; but Greek religion is the religion not of a primitive people, but of a people with a very highly developed and glorious culture. Those who have searched eagerly for primitive ideas in Greek religion often seem to have forgotten the latter truth, which has indeed become a truism. That is so even in regard to popular customs and beliefs. Similarities and analogies are undeniable. Apart from the objections made above, a comparison of the religion of the Greeks with those of primitive peoples and with primitive customs and beliefs enlarges our understanding of Greek religion, in general, but only in general, for it is a mistake to think that such a comparison can help to reconstruct phenomena in Greek religion in detail, as at times has been attempted. The positive gain is not to be found in the various hypotheses and the attempted solutions of the problems envisaged but in the putting of the question and the expanding of our horizon.

This intimate relation of Greek religion to primitive religions and to rustic customs and beliefs is a great gain and at the same time a great problem for the study of religion in general. Greek religion, if it does not begin in primitive religious ideas and rites, has its roots therein – reaching up with the works of Plato and other philosophies and ideas which came to the fore in late antiquity, to the highest religious spheres. Greek religion was never systematized, nor subjected to a thoroughgoing reform until the age of the Neoplatonists. Other philosophical schools had no great importance for religious life; they prepared building materials but did not create from them a structure of living religion. To realize the importance of this fact let us glance at the religions of the Near East known to us through a multitude of texts. All these texts were composed and written by priests. They are an outcome of priestly wisdom, of priestly expounding and systematizing of ritual and beliefs. Look at Egypt or at Babylonia or Persia. What do we know of the beliefs, the ideas, and the customs current among the people? They are hidden from our eyes by the iron curtain of priestly wisdom, through which we can but dimly perceive a little, a very little, such as animal cult and magical practices in Egypt, and the daemons and incantations popular in Babylonia. Greek religion was never elaborated nor systematized by priestly wisdom; until the age of syncretism it had no holy books, no ritual texts, unless you count the Orphic writings as such, but they were restricted to narrow circles. To realize this fact is a positive gain.

I return to the relation of Greek religion to primitive religion. The general ideas and theories advanced from time to time and prevailing successively in our views of primitive religion have been the foundations upon which scholars built when grappling with the problems of the beginnings of Greek religion and trying to apprehend them. These attempts were the children of their age, bore its marks, and were full of errors.

I sing no dirge over the bier of natural mythology, for in that case I should have to sing dirges over other theories too, such as totemism, and, as Thetis over Achilles, I should have to wail over the living too. Greek religion supplies only extremely few examples on forced interpretations which can be used to illustrate the belief in the universal High God or the 'ritual-mythical pattern'. Theories which once upon a time ruled and dominated, have been subject to criticism, have been supplanted by others, have faded into insignificance and been reduced to their proper proportions. Nobody can deny the part played by spirits, power, magic, taboo. They too are undeniable ingredients in the religion of the Greeks and of other people. The mistake was that the importance of the factors was overemphasized, and they were thought to unlock all doors and to solve all problems.

The statement of general laws depends on induction and the value of the induction depends on the greater or lesser completeness of the materials. As regards the religions of primitive peoples the materials are on one hand extremely numerous, on the other insufficient. What in anthropological research would seem to be an induction is something much less. It is the taking as proofs of examples illustrating a theory when it would be just as easy to find examples illustrating a diametrically opposite theory. I read long ago two works of anthropological research. In one the savage was pictured as atrocious and ferocious, given to bloodshed, in the other he is peaceful and cowardly and if it comes to blows the combatants disperse at the first sight of blood. Both adduce good examples for their views. The error is of course generalization on the basis of too few, deliberately selected instances, the wish to prove a preconceived theory, the neglect of differences between different peoples, customs, and different ages. From such errors which vitiate many anthropological works Greek religion is, at least in some measure, protected. The materials refer to one people, to definite times, and are numerous. But the above remarks may not be out of place, because there was a time when general theories deduced from anthropology played a great part in research on Greek religion.

There are writings on Greek religion whose authors proceed in a somewhat similar manner searching, as they say, for 'the lasting values of Greek religion'. We ought to remember that religious values change from time to time. They were different in the early Christian church than in the Middle Ages, different to Catholics than to Protestants, different to the Greeks of the Classical Age than to the contemporaries of Nonnos and the Emperor Julian.

Another great advantage in the study of Greek religion which too is really a truism is this: we can follow its development and evolution, as far as the texts are concerned, through a millennium from Homer to Proklos. This fact which cannot be denied is a sure gain in respect to the anti-evolutionism which nowadays is preached so confidently and with high-sounding words. Its supporters cannot deny evolution in Greek as well as in some other religions known to us through written documents. Their field is primitive religions, but even these religions are subject to changes, say an evolution in the length of times, although we know them only for a brief space of time. I leave anti-evolution at its value. I have said what it implies elsewhere in the *Harvard Theological Review* (XLII, 1949, 73 ff.). In Greek religion we are happily not concerned with it.

Up to now I have spoken as much of primitive religion as of Greek religion, because in the beginning of our century research in the latter was closely linked up with theories concerning primitive religion. The gain may seem to be negative rather than positive when exaggerated, or hasty theories have been reduced to their proper proportions. Yet it is a positive gain that our views of Greek religion have been enlarged and enriched, and have become more many-sided and varied.

The same may be said of some out-standing books, dealing especially with Greek religion, Sir Arthur Evans' *Tree and Pillar Cult*, Usener's *Götternamen*, Rohde's *Psyche*, Miss Harrison's *Prolegomena to the Study of Greek Religion*, not to speak of some less important ones. The theories advanced by these prominent scholars have been reduced to their proper proportions. This is not meant to deny the high value and the stimulating influence of these books, it is simply stating a fact. No one can now subscribe wholesale to their views.

You ask for the positive gains in our knowledge of Greek religion. Well, look at the discovery of the Minoan and Mycenaean culture. It has added a millennium to the history of the religions of Greece. The Minoan religion has come down to us as a picture book without a text. When we try to write such an interpretative text a great diversity of opinions ensues. The interpretation may be uncertain and contested, but the monuments and their relation to religion are hard facts. The consequences of this are most important. The Minoans were a non Indo-European people whose culture had attained to full bloom when the Greeks immigrated to the country which was to be theirs. The religion of historical Greece proceeded from a fusion of what was Minoan with Indo-European elements which the Greeks brought with them, perhaps in forms already developed specifically. Opinions may vary and do vary in regard to the important problem of how this fusion came about and just what the proportions of the two different ingredients are. The monuments give no reply. Unfortunately the religion of the immigrating Greeks is much less known than that of the Minoans and it is difficult, almost impossible to discern any appreciable element of it in the religion of the Mycenaean Greeks who were thoroughly Minoized in the exterior aspects of their civilization. It may be that the wholly Minoized representations found on the Mycenaean sites cover very different religious ideas. It is demonstrable that Homer contains elements which have come down from the Mycenaean age. The question arises if this is so even in religion. The problem is there but can only be answered by subjective hypotheses.

The gain is greater when we come to the myths: Certain myths can with some probability be traced down from the Minoan and with still more certainty from the Mycenaean age. The great cycles of heroic myth were, at least for a great part, developed in this age. In detail much is of course uncertain and opinions may vary but the principle is evident. The decisive proof is the close correlation, even in regard to their respective importance, of the centres of the mythological cycles to the centres of Mycenaean civilization. This fact is relevant also for the question of historical elements in the heroic myths, which has been variously judged. We are sure that they exist, although we are unable to discern them with certainty. To this end a control from known historical facts is needed, such as is possible say for the *Nibelungenlied*, but in Greece this control is wanting.

We come to the historical age of Greece. I do not think that any book produced during my lifetime will last so long as Lobeck's *Aglaophamus*, printed in 1829, which is still consulted with profit. It destroyed old phantasies and collected recondite materials. The negative gain of research seems to be more lasting than the positive. It is perhaps understandable because of the bias of scholars to produce new and startling but fragile theories. But look at the increase of the materials at our disposal, texts, inscriptions, and monuments of the arts. Many inscriptions were known earlier, we had the *Corpus Inscriptionum Graecarum*, but the increase has been tremendous. I might mention some inscriptions especially important in religious respects: the hymn of Palaikastro whose religious importance far surpasses the many other hymns found, the old-fashioned *lex sacra* from Cyrene, the more recent, closely regulated sacral laws from Cos, the inscriptions concerning the mysteries at Andania and Lycosura, from the beginning of syncretism the Isis aretalogies, the sacral law of a private cult at Philadelphia, the statutes of the Iobacchoi from Athens. Still more important are the masses of inscriptions from the great sanctuaries: Eleusis, Epidaurus, Delphi, Delos. It is characteristic that Olympia has yielded but little of religious significance. (It was chiefly a place for the Games. In the intervals between the great festivals few people lived there save priests and temple servants, or went there, save sometimes athletes in training. Monuments of victors and champions are numerous but votive offerings are seldom found except in the very earliest layers.) Further there are the inscriptions from various cities of which the most important are Athens, Sparta from the end of the Hellenistic age onwards, Pergamon, Miletus, etc. At Delos the inscriptions give a vivid picture of the mixture of people from various countries and the administration of the temples. The inscriptions teach us the fate of the public cults, their regulation, the attempts at maintaining and restoring them, and their final decline.

The monuments, sculptures, vase paintings, coins, are single pieces, but I may mention here a large group of sculptures and vase paintings pertaining to the Eleusinian cult and myth, which teach us something of the cults and beliefs on which the mysteries, the secrets of which were jealously guarded, were founded. Monuments teach us also something of the little known house cult and of the small rustic shrines and cave sanctuaries, the objects here found show the piety of simple people. I need not call to mind the great temples in Athens, Epidaurus, Pergamon, and the like. In regard to the Roman age I mention only the monumental work of Cumont on the texts and monuments relating to the mysteries of Mithras and the subsequent discoveries at Dura-Europos.

When I mentioned texts, you may have thought of new texts recently discovered, especially papyri. Of these but a few are relevant for Greek religion, in the Hellenistic age, for example the edict of Ptolemy Philopator enjoining worshipers to submit to him the books of the Dionysiac mysteries; and the badly mutilated fragment of an Orphic text edited by Smyly, whose recent death we all regret. Most of the papyri are later and do not contain much of interest to the student of Greek religion proper.

However, one ought to think not only of new texts but also of known texts the importance of which had been neglected earlier but which now has been recognized. Some of the magic papyri had been edited already in an inadequate manner. In the nineties Dieterich called attention to them, recognizing their value. Since then they have been vigorously studied but more in their relation to magic and foreign religions than in their bearing upon the Greek religion of their age. In 1904 Reitzenstein called attention to the Hermetic tracts which had been much read in the Renaissance but later were almost forgotten. They constitute a most important contribution to the mystic aspect of late paganism and are nowadays duly appreciated. Nock and Festugière have recently published an excellent edition and new texts have appeared in a find of Coptic papyri. Another book of the utmost importance for the latest phase of paganism, Jamblichos, *De mysteriis,* is unduly neglected because a good edition is wanting; the last one is nearly a hundred years old and not to be had.

The study of syncretism which is of as much importance for late paganism as for early Christianity belongs wholly to the period of which we are speaking. A pioneer work was Hatch's Hibbert lectures on the influence of Greek ideas upon the Christian church, delivered in 1888. Then, this study was taken up eagerly by classical scholars, first by Usener, later the foremost ones were Cumont and Reitzenstein. Their initiative was very stimulating and far-reaching; they brought forth a mass of texts and passages from various sources, Christian and Oriental writings, but the light thrown upon them was one-sided. One is reminded of what was once said with reference to art: Rome suffocated in the grasp of the Orient. This has proved not to be true and the same is valid of religion. Greek authors and sources must be ransacked not only to find evidence for Oriental influence but also to find evidence for Greek influence, the part which Greek thought and Greek science had in building up the complex structure of syncretism. It is not small but has been unduly put to one side. Some reaction is in process.

These critical remarks are not intended to diminish the merits of the great scholars mentioned. They have taken the initiative and they have done a stimulating work which can hardly be too highly appreciated; they have brought forth hitherto unnoticed materials; their work is of fundamental mportance, although their theories may be criticized and may prove in part fallacious.

In the last years classical scholars and theologians seem to have parted company to a certain extent. This is to be regretted, for both strive after the same end, a history of syncretism, the preliminaries of the most important revolution of the religions of the peoples of Europe, which led to the victory of Christianity. The synthesis of these studies, which are not so old as the writer of these lines, must needs comprise the paganism of the ancient world, including the Orient, as well as Christianity. These studies are in their infancy; the time is not yet ripe for such a synthesis, it must be left to our descendants. But it is a positive gain of our time to have advanced and seriously to have called attention to this unsurpassingly great problem in the history of Greek, Roman, and European religion.

Some attention has been paid to the non-literary and social aspect of Greek religion which was neglected earlier. Religion is not a complex of beliefs and ideas, cults and practices, separated from other aspects of human life, it is bound to change with historical and social changes; it is subject to the influence of the separation or the fusion of peoples and classes. Religion may in a simple society be collective, determined by the family and the state in which man is born; if social conditions change these bonds may be slackened and man may choose his religion. One who has a certain belief tends always to associate himself with those who have the same belief for mutual edification and help. They tend to develop certain acts or practices, however simple, special to them, the beginning of a cult. Religion is not only an individualistic but to a very great extent also a social phenomenon.

When you have read these lines you may feel disappointed. You had asked for 'an article listing the chief positive gains in our knowledge of Greek and Roman religion in your lifetime'. I have not entered upon Roman religion, for the increase of materials for its native form is not considerable and the problems are in suspense; it was early fused with Greek religion and shared its fate. I think you meant research work, and I have found the positive gains in the increase of materials, not in the theories of learned scholars. I really do not underestimate theories and hypotheses; they are stimulating, they are necessary to bring order in and to throw light upon the mass of accumulated materials. They are the steam which drives the engine of research; the materials may be said to be fuel; without fuel no steam. But theories and hypotheses are children of their age; they are commonly one-sided and because of this innate quality frail, subject not only to criticism from other points of view but also to be upset by newly discovered or neglected materials. We need them absolutely and we must take them as they are and be cautious not to hail a new attractive theory as the last word of science. νᾶφε καὶ μέμνασ᾽ ἀπιστεῖν. Scholars will have something to say in a coming age also. It has been said that history must be rewritten in every generation to be understandable to the people of that generation. The like is true of the history of religion. Every synthesis, all views depend on the spiritual horizon of the writers and the readers and is conceived and elaborated accordingly.

Finally, even with these restrictions the positive gains in our knowledge of ancient religion in my lifetime are immense.

ON RELIGION

On the next to the last page of the second volume of my History of Greek Religion I said bluntly that religion is a protest against the meaninglessness of events, without making any comment. I added only that this view is akin to Høffding's definition of religion as a belief in the permanence of values.[1] It may be worth while to expound this point of view further and to try and see whether it is fruitful.

It has rightly been objected to Høffding's definition of religion that he does not say which is the value that religion maintains. In the following pages I shall try and give a reply to this query. The value which religion maintains is that life and events have a meaning, and if they are or seem to be meaningless religion protests against the meaninglessness and tries to find a meaning in them, viz. to interpret them as having meaning. This is the positive protest, but we shall see that in some religions there is a negative protest too: the meaninglessness of life and events is acknowledged, and man seeks his salvation in being freed, released from them.

In Professor Nock's address to Dom Casel on March 28, 1948, of which through the author's kindness I possess a typewritten copy, I find the following sentence: 'R. R. Marett has spoken of the "birth of humility" as the differentia of genuine religion. To put it in another way, we may define religion as man's refusal to accept helplessness or to think that help comes from men alone.' This definition seems to come near the sentence which I put forward at the beginning. The man who is struck by an accident encounters it helplessly; what he does afterwards, if he is not killed, to help himself is another thing. Still more apparent is his helplessness when subject to mechanical causation. In both cases he is objectively helpless when struck by an event, and subjectively it is meaningless to him. Relying solely upon human power and skill he is helpless when struck by disastrous events in human life, and he is helpless when death carries him away.

To begin with I must make some preliminary statements which I ask the reader to bear carefully in mind as he reads the following pages; otherwise my exposition will be thoroughly misunderstood.

First of all, I deprecate any suspicion that by these words I am aiming to give a definition of religion. Many definitions of religion have been proposed, none has been generally accepted. There is no need to recount or to discuss them. Religion is much too complex and varied a phenomenon to be compressed within the narrow limits of a definition. The business of the science and history of religion is research into the various phenomena of religion; but this science is not simply phenomenology — it also strives to discover the psychological foundation and the historical developments and interrelations of religious phenomena. In saying that religion is a protest against the meaninglessness of events I wish only to emphasize one side of the various aspects of religion and to try and see what its importance is.

Secondly, when I speak of 'meaning', this word is to be understood solely in a subjective sense, i.e. the meaning of a man, an individual or a group of men, the meaning which he or they may or may not find in an event which is of interest to him and his life or to them and their life. The protest is that he or they try to find a meaning in a seemingly meaningless event. There is absolutely no question about the meaning or reason which, afterwards, considering an event or a series of events, we (or others) may find in them or attribute to them. Accordingly I avoid the word 'irrationalism' which introduces such an idea. I take 'meaning' as purely subjective, the meaning which a certain man or certain men who form a group find or do not find in a certain event in its relation to him or to them.

Meaninglessness is of two kinds. The one of which we think first is the pure incident, as when an icicle falls from a roof and perhaps kills a passer-by, or when someone slips on a banana-peel left lying in the street, falls, and breaks his neck. There is no need to say anything about the meaninglessness of such accidents to the man who experiences them, and they are fairly common. The second kind of meaninglessness is due to mechanical causation. Here it appears why the word 'irrational' must be avoided. Mechanical causation is rational, but it is meaningless to man. It excludes his free will; and that man has a free will is a conviction deeply ingrained in his mind, whatever may be said of it by philosophers. He feels mechanical causation as something beyond him, outside of him; he is a prey to it, objectively, but subjectively it is not related to him. This feeling is expressed by the simile that man is caught between the wheels of events. This type of meaninglessness appears only when thought and religion have reached a higher level, but it then becomes all the more important.

I do not wish to enter into the philosophical discussion of causality. Hume has said: 'Causation is known as an habitual antecedent and a tendency on our part to look for something definite to come. Apart from this practical meaning it has no significance.' Modern physicists seem to agree with him, for to them causation is rather a statistical verity than a law without exception. The elaboration of the concept of causality given by ancient philosophers is sufficient for me. They called it *heimarmene*, in Latin *fatum*, and defined it as an interconnected cause of that what exists, or more explicitly as the order and series of causes by which one cause joined with another produces an event. I shall come back to this below. This suffices for my purpose; for as we shall see the principal clash between the idea of causality and religion took place in ancient times, namely in astrology. Astrology in what we may call its scientific form was the strictest example of mechanical causation which antiquity knew. It is of course false, a pseudo-science; but, as is usual also with many modern hypotheses, the falsity lies in the premises – the identification of the celestial bodies and their qualities with certain gods and their qualities – not in the logic by which the system is constructed. Ancient man felt himself bound in iron fetters by the merciless, senseless mechanical causation of the stars. He tried to escape from it. He hit upon the idea that it was valid only for the body, not for the soul which belongs to another and transcendent world. Or he adopted the view that the planets are gods, and gods can of course be either moved by prayers and sacrifices or compelled by magical rites. So he offered cultus to the stars, or used incantations and magical arts to deflect their workings. Thus astrology had a powerful influence in driving men to the bosom of religion. Here they found their shelter from the mercilessness and meaning-lessness of mechanical causation.

The idea of the free will of man is opposed to the idea of causality, for if man has a free will he may by his interference break the chain of causes. We shall see what power this idea has, which is as deeply ingrained in human mind as that of causality. Nor is it possible to enter upon a philosophical discussion of this controversial subject. I quote only what a prominent Swedish mathematician has said from his point of view.[2] Having stated a problem of mathematical physics in which it is impossible to predict what the result of a movement will be, he concludes: 'As far as I see the direction of the future evolution of science can be foreseen with such a satisfactory perspicuity that it can with certainty be asserted that it will never contra-dict the belief in the freedom of the will.' The freedom of man's will is the principal argument against mechanical causation. It is curious that in recent years an almost fanatical belief in causation is found, not among natural scientists but among certain historians, e.g. K.J. Beloch and G. Ferrero. To them the free will of man is of no importance. The will of a man, however outstanding, cannot influence the course of history. Thus it happens that when an idea has begun to be undermined in the centre it persists in the periphery.

Philosophy has not been able to overcome the clash between the two principles which are equally essential to man, causation and free will.

Future generations may see if natural science is able to do so, following the line of Epicurus of which I shall speak below. This lies on the knees of the gods. To religion the problem has been non-existent, for it always insisted on the free will of gods and men. Philosophical thinking obtruded the problem upon it.

[. . .]

Death is meaningless. Life is full of meaningless events. Man protests through beliefs and acts, trying to find a meaning relevant to him. He believes in the Nether World or in metempsychosis, he performs certain acts to avert meaningless interruptions in the orderly course of Life and Nature, he ascribes them to the wrath of gods or of God because of certain trespasses. Another form of meaninglessness is mechanical causation. Springing forth from fatalism it was worked out by astrology and drove men to the bosom of religion. Materialism accepts the meaninglessness of events. So does Indian religious thought too but strikes a note of deep pessimism. The crowning end is Buddhism: Life is a chain of evils and the evils are continued, each existence producing new existences by causal necessity. The only escape is Nirvana.

NOTES

1. *Geschichte der griechischen Religion*, Vol. II, 1950, p. 700: 'Religion ist der Protest gegen die Sinnlosigkeit des Geschehens, oder, um mit Höffding zu reden, der Glaube an das Bestehen des Wertes, muss aber, um Volksreligion zu werden, eine Form annehmen, welche die Vielen, nicht nur die Erlesenen verstehen.'

2. C.W. Oseen in an inaugural lecture delivered before the University of Uppsala 1909 on the problem of the freedom of the will viewed from the standpoint of the natural sciences (in Swedish).

Walter F. Otto

Walter Friedrich Otto was born in 1874 in Heckingen, Germany. He received his primary and secondary school education in Stuttgart. In 1892 he enrolled at the University of Tübingen, first to study theology, then in 1893 transferring to classical studies under Otto Crusius, Ludwig Schwabe and Wilhelm Schmidt. He pursued these studies at the University of Bonn with Hermann Usener and Franz Bücheler. In 1897 W.F. Otto obtained his Ph.D. degree with a dissertation on Roman proper names. After having passed a teacher's examination, he became assistant to the 'Thesaurus Linguae Latinae' in 1898, and he was editor of the 'Onomasticum Latinum' in Munich until 1911. In 1905 Otto passed his *Habilitation* for classical studies with Otto Crusius at the University of Tübingen. He became *Extraordinarius* at the University of Vienna in 1911, professor at the University of Basel in 1913, and thereupon at the University of Frankfurt am Main in 1914. In 1934 he was obliged to transfer to Königsberg, from where he had to leave in 1944. In 1945 Otto taught Greek language and literature at the University of Munich, in 1946 for a while at the University of Göttingen and in the same year he became professor of Greek at the University of Tübingen. He died at Tübingen in 1958.

The only book of W.F. Otto which is available in English translation is: 1954 *The Homeric Gods: the Spiritual Significance of Greek Religion*.

The following fragments have been chosen from *The Homeric Gods*, and from *Theophania*, published in German in 1956. They show the way in which W.F. Otto strove after an understanding of Greek religion in its religious apprehensions, and this in opposition to current views on religion and to psychological explanations.

ON THE STUDY OF GREEK RELIGION: 'THE HOMERIC GODS'

'Introduction'

I. For modern man it is no easy task to attain a true understanding of ancient Greek religion. Before the images of the gods from the great period he is filled with awe and admiration, and he feels that the majesty of these figures is incomparable and can never be equalled. Their presence may indeed thrill him with a sense of the eternal, but what he hears of these gods and of their relations with mankind evokes no response in his soul. The somber religious reverberation, that melody of ineffable exaltation and consecration familiar and revered from childhood, seems to be wanting. If we examine this impression further we perceive what it is we miss. This religion is so natural that holiness seems to have no place in it. Such stirring of the soul, of the world itself, as is proclaimed by the words 'Holy, holy, holy, Lord God of Hosts' or *'Sanctus Dominus Deus Sabaoth'* the presence of no Greek god can provoke. In these gods too, as in the temper of their votaries, we miss the moral earnestness which we regard as the inseparable concomitant of true religion: we cannot call them amoral, but they are much too natural and joyous to reckon morality as the supreme value. And finally, we can only be estranged by the realization that no cordial intimacy can subsist between man and these gods. That he loves and honors them there can be no doubt: but where can we find soulful devotion, sacrifice of what is most precious, even of self, communion of heart with heart, the bliss of oneness? Always the interval between man and deity remains, even when deity loves man and favors him. Indeed the delimitations are purposefully accentuated. The gods retain their own existence, from which man is by his nature forever kept apart. The effect is almost cruel when at a feast of the gods the poet represents the Muses as delighting the immortals by singing of their majesty and of the sorrows and afflictions of mankind.[1] We must not infer that the gods delighted in mischief or were consciously indifferent, but of this there can be no doubt: that such gods could have no thought of redeeming man from the world and raising him to themselves. And if religion does not hold out this promise, what meaning can it have for us?

To be sure, this remoteness does not apply equally to all periods of Greek civilization. The mysteries and Orphism are in many respects a closer approach to our own sensibilities. And if we descend to the post-classical centuries, traits which strike us as familiar multiply. It is for this reason that religious scholarship bestows particular attention on these movements and eras. Yet in essentials it must be acknowledged that the impression of strangeness persists. It is most striking for the observer who looks not at the centuries of waning creativity but rather at the early age of genius whose first and greatest monument is the body of Homeric poems. This is the period where belief in the gods was maintained with the liveliest conviction; and it is precisely here that conceptions of the divine have so little capacity to touch the heart of modern man directly that many critics have denied them any religious content whatever.

This is understandable, and yet most extraordinary. Consider Homer, who is the prime object of the charge. We admire not only the art of his poems but also the richness and depth and grandeur of his thought. Who could think of attributing superficial views on cosmic issues to a work which can still thrill us after nearly three thousand years? And yet upon his belief in gods we bestow an indulgent smile at best, or we explain him as a primitive — as if in a world so spiritually mature a primitive belief would not be the greatest paradox of all. Is not the fault to be found in the prejudices of the critics themselves? One may truly wonder at the assurance with which judgment is passed upon a nation's most inspired ideas on matters of supreme import without testing whether the position assumed produces valid insights into an alien realm of thought.

II. The properties which we miss in ancient Greek religion are the specific attributes of Christianity and kindred religions which derive from Asia. It is by the gauge of these religions that the Greek has regularly been assayed, usually, to be sure, unconsciously, but therefore with all the greater assurance. Wherever religion has been defined in a higher sense, it is these religions, and they alone, that have furnished the paradigm. Hence in the Greek realm of belief men unconsciously searched for oriental religiosity under the illusion that they were seeking religiosity in general. But since astonishingly little could be discovered, especially in the centuries of Greek culture freshest in vitality and spirit, the conclusion that no truly religious content was present seemed inescapable. The early Christian explanation that heathen beliefs were a work of the devil could no longer apply. And yet the early Christians were more competent judges. They did not take paganism lightly, as if it were puerile or superficial, but recognized it with horror as the opposite pole to the Christian viewpoint. A man's soul was not to grow and mature when he accepted the Christian faith, but must be renewed from its very roots. Such was the impression evoked by paganism in its decline; how much stronger would it have been in the presence of the ancient Greek religion, still genuine and unadulterated! But if Greek religion stands diametrically opposed to that which has to this day constituted the gauge for religion in general, we can realize that a true understanding was impossible. Where shall we find a new and better viewpoint?

Where else than in Hellenism itself? Religion is not a possession added on to a people's other belongings which might just as well be different or lacking altogether. In religion what is most venerable to man finds expression. Love and existence are rooted in the same ground and are in spirit one. Everything truly essential is being confronted with the vital ideas of its contents, its power, and its goal, and these ideas are regarded as divine entities. It is therefore inevitable that the eternal should have been revealed to the ancient Greek in a form quite different from that of the Hebrew, the Persian, or the Hindu. And in his religion the eternal could only be reflected in the measure that this creative and discerning race was capable of seeking, beholding, and revering it.

III. The worldliness and naturalness with which the religion of the Greeks is reproached is encountered in their plastic art also. Here too the difference from the oriental is immeasurable. Organic structure takes the place of monstrosity; instead of symbolism and denotation we have what we have learned – through the Greeks – to understand as forms of nature. And yet all of these works breathe a loftiness and nobility which lifts us above the transitory and earthbound world of facts. Before our eyes a miracle takes place: the natural has become one with the spiritual and eternal, without surrendering a whit of its abundance, warmth, and immediacy in the amalgam. Should not the spirit for which exact observance of the natural led to the vision of the eternal and infinite have made the religion of the Greeks the very thing it was?

There has never been a religion in which the miraculous, in the literal sense of transcending the natural order, has played so slight a rôle as in the ancient Greek. The reader of Homer must find it remarkable that despite frequent reference to the gods and their power the narrative contains virtually no miracles. To appreciate how remarkable this circumstance is, we may draw a comparison with the Old Testament. Here Yahweh fights for his people, and without making any defense they are delivered from the pursuing Egyptians. The sea divides so that the children of Israel can pass dry-shod, but the waves close over the Egyptians so that none escapes. Or God permits his people to conquer a city whose walls collapse of themselves at the trumpet blasts and shouts of the Israelites who parade around it, so that they need only to march in. In Homer, of course, nothing happens without the god concerned manifesting himself. But despite this remarkable proximity of the divine, everything takes its natural course. We hear, indeed we see in lifelike imagery, how a god whispers a saving device to a baffled warrior at the right instant, we hear that he rouses spirit and kindles courage, that he makes limbs supple and nimble and gives a right arm accuracy and strength. But if we look more closely at the occasions when these divine interventions take place, we find that they always come at the critical moment when human powers suddenly converge, as if charged by electric contact, on some insight, some resolution, some deed. These decisive turns which, as every attentive observer knows, are regularly experienced in an active life, the Greeks regarded as manifestations of the gods. Not only the flow of events with its critical moments, however, but also duration itself indicated the divine. In all larger forms and conditions of life and existence the Greek perceived the eternal visage of divinity. Taken all together these essences constitued the holiness of the world. Hence the Homeric poems are filled with divine proximity and presence as are those of no other people or age. In their world the divine is not superimposed as a sovereign power over natural events; it is revealed in the forms of the natural, as their very essence and being. For other peoples miracles take place; but a greater miracle takes place in the spirit of the Greek, for he is capable of so regarding the objects of daily experience that they can display the awesome lineaments of the divine without losing a whit of their natural reality.

Here we perceive the spiritual tendency of the people destined to teach mankind to investigate nature, – both within and around man; the Greek approach, that is to say, first gave mankind the idea of nature which is so familiar to modern man.

IV. From experience, history, and anthropology we learn that the world may present itself to man's mind and emotion in manifold guises. Among possible modes of perceiving and thinking, two in particular stand out and claim our attention because neither is wholly wanting in any place or age, diverse as their apparent significance may be. The one we may call the objective or – if the word be not limited to the sense of the calculating intellect – the rational. Its object is the reality of nature, and its aim is to apprehend the substance of nature in all directions and to regard its forms and laws with reverence.

The other mode of thought is the magical. It always has to do with the dynamic; power and action are its basic categories, and therefore it seeks and reveres the extraordinary. Certain primitive peoples have special names for the wonder-working aspect in man himself or in objects in the world. This feeling for the miraculous derives from a peculiar composition of human emotions, which in some indescribable manner become aware of a power out of which limitless, which is to say supernatural, effects may emanate. Hence we are justified in speaking of a magical mode of thought. To the human consciousness of power significant phenomena of the outer world present themselves as events and manifestations of power. Natural experience of the regular or normal obviously takes place here also, but passionate interest in the extraordinary denotes a very narrow conception of what is natural. The domain of nature is interrupted by the intervention of the tremendous, at which point the sphere of limitless powers and effects, the domain of quivering dread or joy, takes its inception. The matter which is here offered for admiration and worship is unintelligible and formless. It is completely sovereign in its opposition to the world of experience, and its only correspondence lies in the magic power of human emotions. From this point of view nothing in the natural world is firmly fixed. The properties of things undergo limitless change; anything may turn into anything.

This mode of thought seems to be associated with primitive civilizations; but in itself it is by no means primitive. It is capable of attaining grandeur and sublimity. It is so deeply rooted in human nature that no people and no age can wholly deny it, though differences in its effects are very considerable. In higher religions it gives rise to belief in a deity who faces the natural world with infinite power and whom it is impossible to comprehend. The

greatest expansion of this power is to be observed in the spiritual development of ancient India. Here the mysterious omnipotent, the 'truth of the
truth' (Brahman), is made positively equal to the psychic power within
man (Atman); and it was inevitable that the world of experience should be
relegated from the rank of a lesser reality to the nothingness of mere
appearance.[2]

The thing here designated and characterized as magical thought was
naturally not wholly alien to the Greeks. But anyone with an eye for the
basic traits of various conceptions of the world must realize that the Greek
attitude was hostile to magical thought to a quite marked degree. Its
position is at the opposite pole, and is the most magnificent objectivation
of the rational mode of thought. Instead of a narrow concept of the natural,
here we have the broadest possible. Indeed, when we today utter the word
nature in the large and vital sense in which Goethe used it, we are in the
debt of the Greek spirit. The natural can therefore of itself stand in the
glory of the sublime and divine. To be sure, upon the intervention of Greek
gods also, extraordinary and thrilling events took place. This does not,
however, mean the appearance of a force with limitless power; it does mean
that existence manifests itself in infinitely various living expressions as
the essence of our world. First and highest is not the power that acts, but
the being that is manifested in the form of the act. And the holiest shudder
comes not from the tremendous and infinitely powerful, but rather from the
depths of natural experience.

This concept of the world which we call specifically Greek found its first
and greatest expression in the age whose monuments are the Homeric
poems. It is recognizable at once by the almost complete absence of the
magical element. Goethe represents Faust as uttering a wish at the end of
his life:

> *All magic – from my path if I could spurn it,*
> *All incantation – once for all unlearn it,*
> *To face you, Nature, as one man of men –*
> *It would be worth it to be human then.*[3]

Nowhere but in the Greek world is this wish fulfilled; it is in the Greek
spirit that nature, before which Faust wished to stand with nothing foreign
interposed, was transformed into idea.

The Greek genius must have received the figures of its religion and its
worship in pre-Homeric times, for in Homer they are fixed, and this book
proposes to show that they remained basically what they were for Homer.
To find one's world is tantamount – whether for a people or an individual –
to finding one's self, to attaining realization of one's own character. The
period whose concept of the world we learn from Homer is therefore the

period of genius in Hellenism. Whatever notions earlier generations may have associated with the names of the Homeric gods are of slight significance in comparison. The specifically Greek idea which made them what they were was originated in and belonged to the age for which Homer is our witness.

It is often said that it is the needs of human nature, and their growth and change that are expressed in the formulation of the gods. True enough, but surely among these needs are the requirements of thought and perception. The most significant event in the life of a people – whether or not we detect a connection with external vicissitudes – is the emergence of the mode of thought that is peculiar to it, as if designed for it from the beginning of time, by which it is henceforward distinguishable in the world's history. This process took place when the prehistoric view was transformed into the view which we first find in Homer and which we never thereafter encounter with comparable clarity and grandeur. However much we may ascribe to the poet's own rich thought and taste in his presentation of divine manifestations, the natural idealism or ideal naturalism which astonishes and enchants us in these manifestations remains the basic character of this new and in a true sense Greek religion.

V. The ancient Greek religion comprehended the things of this world with the most powerful sense of reality possible, and nevertheless – nay, for that very reason – recognized in them the marvellous delineations of the divine. It does not revolve upon the anxieties, longings, and spiritual broodings of the human soul: its temple is the world, from whose vitality and movement emanates its knowledge of the divine. It alone has no need to seclude itself from the evidence of experiences, for only by all the rich gamut of their tints, light and dark, do they crystallize on the large images of the divinities.

We shall not let ourselves be deterred by the officious judgments of zealots and pedants who charge Homeric religion with immorality or primitive crudeness because its gods are partial and at odds and sometimes indulge in conduct that is outlawed in bourgeois ethics. To be sure, Greek philosophers also engaged in this kind of criticism, but the fact that the pious sense of nature could fade even in Hellenism does not justify such criticism. For pious naturalism many things are true and important which may seem foolish and wicked to theorists and moralizers. But once we have apprehended what it is that this piety reveres we shall no longer venture to condemn the things it tolerates and condones.

In ancient Greek worship there is revealed to us one of humanity's greatest religious ideas – we make bold to say *the religious idea of the European spirit*. It is very different from the religious idea of other civilizations, and particularly of those which customarily supply our religious scholarship and philosophy with examples for the origin of religion. But it is essentially related to all genuine thoughts and creations of Hellenism, and is conceived in the same spirit. Like other eternal achievements of the Greeks it stands before humanity large and imperishable. The faculty which in other religions is constantly being thwarted and inhibited here flowers forth with the admirable assurance of genius – the faculty of seeing the world in the light of the divine, not a world yearned for, aspired to, or mystically present in rare ecstatic experiences, but the world into which we were born, part of which we are, interwoven with it through our senses and, through our minds, obligated to it for all its abundance and vitality. And the figures in which this world was divinely revealed to the Greeks – do they not demonstrate their truth by the fact that they are still alive today, that we still encounter them when we raise ourselves out of petty constraints to an enlarged vision? Zeus, Apollo, Athena, Artemis, Dionysus, Aphrodite – wherever the ideas of the Greek spirit are honored, there we must never forget that these were its greatest ideas, indeed in a sense the totality of its ideas in general; and they will endure as long as the European spirit, which in them has attained its most significant objectivation, is not wholly subjugated to the spirit of the Orient or to that of utilitarian rationality.

Note. The birth of the spirit, of which we have here spoken in anticipation, is premised in the Homeric poems in which it finds its most definitive as well as its earliest expression. Our account is therefore based upon Homeric evidence. Evidence adduced from other sources is intended as complement and commentary for the picture of Homeric beliefs.

We can disregard wholly any difference of date between the *Iliad* and the *Odyssey* and also any diversity between individual portions of the epic, because in all essentials the religious outlook is consistent throughout.

Objections should not be taken to such expressions as 'Homeric Age', which are not infrequently used for the sake of convenience. They mean nothing more than the time during which the views of the world documented by Homer were matured and established. There is no intention to delimit the scope of their validity and force either in spatial or in societal sense.

It is an unfortunate superstition of our age that thoughts concerning the world arise out of the necessities of the many, only to attain solitary heights in the minds of the few. It is rather among rare and spiritually gifted men – whether in groups or individuals – that they are born, only to be abased and to sink to the point where they become meager, dull, and crude, and are finally rigidified. Only an age spiritually poor could believe that popular religious usages and ideas have never had meaning beyond the capacities of a simple man's thought and experience. To find their living source one must ascend into the higher regions.

Every religion and every world view is entitled to be judged not by the levels where it is flattened, coarsened, and, for want of character, is like any other, but by the clear and large contours of its heights. It is only there that it is what it truly is and what others are not.

'Conclusion'

We have reached the end, and glance backward once more.

Much that is important has doubtless been passed over and must await some future interpreter to place it in its proper light. But very soon we come to a barrier at which we must acknowledge that there is a great deal which cannot be spoken. The Greek conception of the divine is as broad as the world and therefore, like the world itself, in the last analysis ineffable. It presents itself to us candidly, without obfuscation and without pathos. In it mystery does not occupy the foreground, and hence it requires no creed or confession of faith: it abides serene in the depths and allows all thoughts upon it to issue in the inexpressible. Out of it we recognize a cosmic feeling of unexampled strength and abundance which, as unerringly as nature, always finds the right images. What possesses substance must be consistent, and so it comes about that despite the absence of creed we find agreement and unity; indeed we can discover a system of ideas which has never been conceptually apprehended. But behind the clarity of view stands the enigma of being, and here all is inexplicable.

Despite its admirable transparency the enigma is greater and weightier than in any other religion. Greek thought overwhelms us by its uniqueness. Other religions cannot help us here, because the Greek cannot be compared with any of them. Hence it has seldom been appreciated and almost always it has been misunderstood; indeed it has not even been noticed, for we have learned to seek the holy in other religions, from which the Greek stands isolated in solitary grandeur.

Thus the belief of the most perceptive of all peoples has remained unheeded and unpraised – this wonderful and admirable belief which arose out of the riches and depths of life, not out of its anxieties and yearnings – this meteor of a religion which could not only see the brilliance of life with an eye more luminous than the rest of mankind but is also unique in that its lucid gaze confronted the insoluble conflict of life with candor and out of its most terrifying darkness conceived the majestic achievement of tragedy.

ON THE GREEK GODS AND ON MYTH

Are the Ancient Greek Gods no longer of concern to us? We admire the great achievements of the ancient Greeks, their architecture, their sculpture, their poetry, philosophy and contributions to science. We are well aware that they have laid the foundations of European thought. So many generations have always turned to them again in more or less decisive revivals. We realize that the Greeks have created values in practically every field that are unsurpassed and perhaps even infinitely valid and exemplary. Homer, Pindar, Aeschylus and Sophocles, Phidias and Praxiteles, to mention only a few, are still names of first importance to us. We read Homer as if he had written precisely for us; we stand deeply impressed before statues of Greek deities and Greek temples; we follow, deeply moved, the mighty unfolding of dramatic events in a Greek tragedy.

But the gods themselves to whose existence the statues and temples bear witness, the gods whose spirit permeates the entire Homeric epic, the gods whom Pindar glorifies in his hymns and who in the tragedies of Aeschylus and Sophocles hold human existence in check and control it – are they really no longer of any concern to us? And if so, to whose failure should this be attributed? To the Greeks or to us?

Should we not confess that these eternal works of art would never have become what they are without the influence of the gods, and even specifically without those Greek gods who seem no longer of any concern to us? Has it not been their spirit, and none else, that awakened creative powers, which produced fruits which continue to edify the human mind and which even today may engender a religious mood?

How, therefore, can we remain indifferent to them! How can we acquiesce in the prevalent view that they were the product of a primitive delusion and that they are of interest only when they seem to coincide with our own religious conceptions, but are incapable of awakening any creative powers in us as they did in the past?

This, actually, has been the attitude of classical scholarship up to the present day. Doctrines of Salvation, ideas of immortality, initiation mysteries and similar phenomena which strongly appeal to the modern religious mind, are being studied with supreme interest, though it cannot be denied that they were alien to the representatives of ancient Greek religion from Homer to Pindar and the Greek dramatists. But prejudice is so strong that the absence of religious ideas is regarded as a regrettable defect, whereas that which is characteristic of the religious attitude of these authors is considered to be an expression of immature thought, the errors of which must be explained from the history of the development of the human mind.

So it happens that the admirer of Greek poetry and art deprives himself of an experience that is not less valuable, but perhaps even the most valuable element of aesthetic enjoyment. He sees the figures created by man, but is not at all aware of the lofty figure that stood behind them and called them into being: divine inspiration!

The Divine can be understood by experience only. In this essay we intend to travel by the opposite road.

The merits of scholarly research of the past generations are unquestionable. By the industrious collection and sifting of facts they have amassed material that was unprecedented in previous periods. Yet, despite all efforts of scholarship and acumen, the results are extremely insignificant. We have not learnt more of the essence of ancient Greek religious thought than what we knew already before, namely what it was *not*. It was not akin to Jewish-Christian religiosity, but was rather abhorred by the latter, which considered it to be polytheist, anthropomorphic, close to nature, not exactly ethical, or in one word 'pagan'. Yet, in contrast to all other pagan religions it was *Greek*. What this means has hardly ever been seriously asked. On account of the outstanding beauty of the divine statues it was believed permissible to regard Greek religion as a 'religion of art', therefore a religion which actually was no religion at all. And a sense of astonishment was felt that such great ages as the Homeric age and those following it could be satisfied with a faith that so completely failed the human soul in its deepest needs and yearnings. For, what could these deities mean, as none of them was God in the true sense of the word?

We on our part wish to oppose to this current prejudice another and less superficial theory, viz. that deities cannot be invented or thought out or imagined, but can only be experienced.

To every human tribe the divine presents itself in its own way, giving shape to its existence and giving form to the purpose for which it was made. This is the way in which the Greeks must have conceived their own experience of the divine. And if we value their works, it is all the more incumbent on us to ask how the divine presented itself to them in particular.

The affairs of Heaven and earth, Goethe writes to Jacobi, constitute such a vast realm, that only the organs of all beings together may comprehend it. How, therefore, could in the great choir of humanity the voice of the most spiritual and most productive of all nations fail to be heard? It can be perceived very well if we are only prepared to hear what the great witnesses from Homer onwards have to say.

Before we start, one other observation on the current bias must be made. We must give a brief analysis of the attitudes and theories that still always stand in the way of a real understanding of Greek religion.

What is the cause of this disdain for the world of the Greek Gods? Why is it that the pantheon of the ancient Greeks is held in such disregard that, though it is studied as an object of antiquarian interest with scholarly zeal, nobody realizes that above and beyond this it has a meaning and a value of its own and, like all important achievements of the past, may also have some relevance to us?

The first reason is of course the victory of a faith which — in contrast to the tolerance of all previous religions — claims to represent universal and exclusive truth. Consequently, all other religions and in particular Greek and Roman religion which had been prevalent in Europe before the advent of Christianity could be nothing but untrue and reprehensible. Moreover, the eloquent champions of the Christian faith have always been in the habit of judging the religions of Antiquity on the basis of their most objectionable manifestations.

We have already pointed to the incomparable creative power of Greek religious thought. In this context we may observe, contrary to the Christian damnatory judgment of ancient religion, that the great periods of Greek, and also Roman, paganism were undoubtedly more deeply religious than in the Christian era. In other words: the idea of the divine, and what man owes to it and what is due to it, was far more closely interwoven with human existence. The sacred and the profane were not so much separated that only certain days or hours were given to religion, whereas secular affairs could lead a life of their own, according to their own laws.

The interpretation of myths and psychoanalysis. In conclusion some observations may be made on the modern fashion of interpreting myths by psychoanalytical methods — the methods of depth psychology. Its name already implies that here the alleged depth of the human soul must take the place of the depth of the reality of the world. This is a most dangerous aberration. The psychoanalytical method answers the suicidal tendency towards self-contemplation of modern man in a most seducing manner.

Psychoanalysis is no longer interested in different patterns of thought, but in psychological experiences and visions, which might not have existed among prehistoric man, but which can be observed at present in great detail. Thus psychoanalysis teaches its adherents to turn their eyes from the world around them and to direct them towards their own soul where, according to this school, all mythical events really occur. In this way psychoanalysis contributes piteously to the spiritual impoverishment of modern man who, because of his scientific and technical achievements is on the way to losing the world completely and becoming concerned with his own self exclusively.

Psychoanalysis alleges that, by analyzing dreams and dreamlike situations of persons who are of unsound mind or ill, it arrives at real mythical concepts which may therefore inform us about the origin and essence of Myth. Moreover, these dreamlike visions, according to the psychoanalysts, are so similar to the mythical concepts that have come down to us from remote Antiquity, that one must unescapably conclude that they have mysteriously returned. They are therefore called *archetypes*, i.e. original images, and are assumed to have preserved themselves, without the awareness of the waking mind, in the so-called unconscious soul throughout the millennia, only to emerge in dreams at moments when the soul is in need of them. In order to make us understand this strange process we are asked to assume the existence of a 'collective soul', capable of preserving with astonishing faithfulness all that has been thought or seen from times immemorial.

If this is true, then even at the first appearance of myths they must have been somewhat akin to the active consciousness, but later they sank into the unconscious where they have been resting until now. The modern psychotherapist sees them emerging in dreams and he then makes them conscious to his patients.

Let us assume for the moment that these dreamlike visions are so akin to the original conception of the gods, that the conclusion of a direct connection is unavoidable. Even so the hypothesis of an unconscious mind in which concepts of a primeval age have been preserved should be the very last conclusion to be drawn. Apart from the demands which such a hypothesis in itself makes on logical thinking, it is based on the silent supposition that original myth does not contain any existential reality. If it did, the possibility should have to be taken into account that its truth, in certain circumstances, might be experienced even today as objective reality being still the same as it presented itself in the original myth. But it would be highly improbable that this would happen in the dreams of any ordinary individual.

For real myth – to state this right from the start – is always highly spiritual, i.e. it takes its origin not in any dream of the soul but in the clear observation of the spiritual eye to which the essence of things has been disclosed. Therefore, it is not only unrelated to dreamlike visions, but is their exact opposite. True, there are people who have the faculty of being 'of a clear mind' (ἔμφρονες) also in their dreams. But, in general, man when sleeping or dreaming is only open to what happens within him or is of his personal concern, but not to essential truths. The Greek philosopher Heraclitus has said:

'In sleep, when the channels of observation are closed, reason in us is severed from the link with its surroundings ... but when awakening it looks out once again through the channels of observation, as if through window openings, and when meeting with its surroundings, reassumes its spiritual faculties.'[4]

But now the main point. It is not true at all that the dreamlike visions here discussed are comparable to or even identical with the figures of mythology. The psychoanalytical interpretation of myths moves around in a circle: it presupposes what it means to prove. It starts from a preconceived idea of the mythical in order to find it confirmed in the dreamlike visions. And this concept of the mythical is based on a misunderstanding.

It is possible that someone in great psychological distress may feel reassured when his dreams comfort him with a mother image and the security it seems to offer. But this mother image has nothing in common with the ancient divine concept of a 'Great Mother'.

In any original myth a god reveals himself within his immediate living surroundings. This god, by whatever name he may be called and distinguished from his equals, is never a single power, but always the whole essence of the world in his own characteristic manifestation. We call those powers demons or spirits, whose area of operation is restricted. But it is a gratuitous assertion of the theory of evolution that ever any of them should have developed into a god.

Thus also the Mother Goddess – to keep to this example – is as a deity a living original divine figure, in whom the unmeasurable inexpressible essence of the world manifests itself. How could she otherwise have taken such possession of human beings and have dragged them out of their own insignificant being, body and soul into the awesomeness of divinity, as we are able to watch in the partly horrifying and cruel cults dedicated to her? Only the original ground of all existence, become visible, has been able to do this to man, when, with full conscious senses and completely prepared for what Goethe calls 'the breadth of the Deity', he directs himself to it.

Compare the images found by the psychotherapist in the dreams of his patients with the primeval divine figures, and the similarities which even at a first glance seemed questionable will dissolve themselves in nothingness. However illuminating dreams may be as to the individual psychological conditions and situations of those dreaming, they say nothing of the 'common divine Logos' (κοινος και θείος).[5] Any reference to them will therefore only serve to obscure the essence of myth.

The primeval manifestation of myth. Even though many still expect psychoanalysis to deliver the decisive word on the concept of myth, its entire system of reasoning is incompatible to the very thing it attempts to define. It throws man back onto himself and bars him from being receptive to the divine element looming large in the visible world. In this, psychoanalysis is entirely a child of the present era of 'demythologization', which speaks of 'nature' when it means logical ideas and experiments, and of 'being' when analyzing psychological attitudes. Thus the terms 'myth' and 'the eternal return of the primeval images' are used for situations in which the diseased human mind, severed from the light and secluded, dreams its own dreams.

But the time has arrived to speak of myth not only in negative terms, but to interrogate it about its own essence. We have become accustomed to conceive myth as a report that cannot be literally true, but which probably contains a deeper meaning. In this sense the word μῦθος was already used by the Greeks themselves. Socrates, according to Platon, composed such 'myths' about the Hereafter and about the adventures of the human soul, and stated explicitly that it would be unwise to assume that everything had occurred exactly as told by these myths. However, he dared to assert that matters transcending our own understanding had happened more or less as told by these myths.

However, the men during the era of the great myths must have thought in a very different manner. Apart from any other consideration, the term μῦθος – which means nothing but 'word' – denoted originally not a word, a report, on what was imagined, but on what existed. But these ancient myths must have seemed so untrustworthy to later generations, that they could only chose either to declare them absurd or, as was done by certain philosophers, to regard them as the product of imagination with a deeper meaning.

This is the way in which we ourselves are likewise accustomed to think. We call any narrative which is seriously meant but which runs counter to our own knowledge of natural processes – including therefore any belief in miracles –, 'mythical'. When in the Old Testament the sun stands still at the request of Joshua, or when the walls of Jericho collapse at the blowing of the trumpets of the Israelites, when the Gospels mention the resurrection of dead people and the expulsion of demons, then all this is today called 'mythical', because 'we know' that there are no demons, as was recently stated by the main representative of the school of demythologization.

But the belief in miracles in itself is not mythical. A quite different element distinguishes mythical concepts from those that are considered correct by us. The problem of whether all statements said to be mythical are of the same order has been neglected. Much confusion has already arisen from the proposition that one should distinguish only one group with specific, essential qualities as being 'mythical' in the true sense of the word, the other so-called myths being only superficially similar.

Ancient civilizations, like primitive cultures of today, distinguish among their fabulous narratives a special category to which supreme awe is due not because they are miraculous in the highest degree but because they possess the character of *holiness*. This distinction is not based on mere tradition or on the apparent value of an archaic pattern of thought. This myth in the proper sense of the word has an incomparable character indeed: it is dynamic, it has acting power, it intervenes in life. This is a quite different matter than when, according to experience, superstitious ideas exercise a certain influence. Here is real productivity, here non-transitory figures are formed, here man is created anew.

Original and true myth cannot be conceived without its connection with cult, i.e. a solemn attitude and action lifting man into a higher sphere. The relation between *myth* and *cult* has been seen in a different light in different periods. At first it was thought a matter of course that myth had come first, and that cult had associated itself with it at a later stage as a kind of visualization. In the era of rational and technical methods of interpretation the order was reversed. Cult was believed to have preceded myth because of its archaic rites whereas myth is often only found in a more recent tradition. It was believed that cult could be explained from magic, and myth was then regarded as a fictional interpretation of the various rites of the cult whose original meaning was no longer understood. But when, some decades ago, more painstaking research led to the conviction that there is not and has never been any cult without myth, the problem had to be posed again.

It was impossible to return to the earlier concept of cult as a mere visualization of myth. Cult, as cult acts that are preserved to this day show, is by no means a visual reflection of mythical events but these events themselves, in the full meaning of the word. Otherwise it would hardly be possible to expect salvational effects from it. The error must be sought in the manner in which the problem is posed, in the question as to their mutual dependence. Not only is no real cult possible without myth, but conversely real myth is impossible without cult. Both are in the last instance one and the same. This is of decisive importance for the correct understanding of both concepts.

That they are in the last instance one is easily understood as soon as one frees oneself from the erroneous presupposition that myth is only capable of bringing something to light which can be expressed in words and not, perhaps in an even more original way, through the attitudes and activities of man in a living and productive creative process. Just remember the highly impressive solemnity of cultic gestures, of attitudes, of movements, the majestic language of the temples and of the statues of deities. These are manifestations of the divine truth of myth that are no less direct than the literal proclamations which alone are often regarded as Revelations.

We are here confronted with a primeval phenomenon of the religious attitude. This itself – whether as a gesture, an act or a word – is *the manifestation of the sacred character of the deity*.

In verbal myths it appears as a figure – and with an unfathomable sense of mystery as a human-like figure –. In this way it is in the center of any real myth. It is an element that cannot be arrived at by reasoning, but only by experience. Therefore, with all its paraphernalia in myth, it is not miraculous or the miracle par excellence because it is not in keeping with the laws of nature. But it belongs to another existential area than what is part of the products of thought and logic.

We may distinguish three different stages in the self-manifestation of the divine which, however, does not imply a chronological order:

a) The attitude of man, which is upright, directed towards heaven, and which is proper to man alone. This is the first evidence of the myth of Heavens, the Sun and the Stars, which here manifests itself not in words, but in the upright attitude of the body. We are no longer aware of its religious meaning, but we are still conscious of this religious meaning in other attitudes that have been familiar to us from time immemorial. For example the pious or ecstatic standing still (Latin *superstitio*), the lifting of arms and hands, or conversely the bowing down or even kneeling down, the folding of hands, etc. These attitudes are originally not the expression of a belief: they are the revelation of the divine to man, in themselves they are revealed myth.

b) The manifestation of myth as an element in the movements and actions of man. Solemn procession, rhythm and the harmony of dancing, etc., are all self-manifestations of a mythical truth that wants to come to light.

The same applies to man-made objects. A stone is placed, a column erected, a temple built, a statue sculpted. It is left to the unilluminated to brand the veneration of these objects as 'fetishism'. Nor are they monuments of something that has to be brought to mind, felt or remembered. They are myth itself, i.e. the obvious manifestation of truth, which in its divine nature wants to dwell in a visible form.

More easily understandable to us are cultic acts. The myth of salvationist experience is less susceptible to misunderstanding, when appearing as an act in solemn practices than when announced in the form of a proclamation. In the latter case it may seem as if reference is made only to a specific event of the past. Nothing is a greater adulteration of myth than this view. The real meaning of such myths has been understood far better by the bright-minded friend of the Emperor Julian when he said: 'This has never happened, but *is* forever'. Our church rites have likewise preserved the awareness that they are not merely commemorative ceremonies. They are divine action itself, regularly repeated. And finally:

c) Myth as the Word, as its original name indicates. That the divine is willing to reveal itself in the word is the most important achievement of myth. And just like cultic attitudes, activities and shapes are themselves myth, so also the holy word itself is the direct manifestation of the divine presence and its actions.

Objection to the fact that this Divine Presence assumes a human form was made already in Antiquity by those misunderstanding myth, and their objection is even greater today. They object to the lack of transparency of myth and do not realize at all that their own premises are anything but transparent. If they consider it necessary that the divine itself must be without any corporality, is it then not necessary for it to assume a human form when wanting to reveal itself to man ? It is really no superstition but rather the earmark of true Revelation when the Deity approaches Man with a human face.

Summarizing this section we can conclude that the primeval manifestations of Myth, that what has been done and that what has been said, cult and myth in a narrower sense, are related in such a way that in cult man lifts himself up to the divine sphere and lives and acts together with the gods, but that in myth the Divine descends and becomes human.

NOTES

1. *Homeric Hymn to Apollo*, pp. 189 ff.
2. *Cf.* H. Oldenberg, *Die Lehre der Upanishaden und die Anfänge des Buddhismus.* Göttingen 1915.
3. Goethe, *Faust.* Translated by L. MacNeice.
4. Heraclitus, *Vorsokratiker.* 6th edition, I, p. 148.
5. *Ibid.*, pp. 147 ff.

PART FIVE

Perspectives of a Phenomenological
Study of Religion

Raffaele Pettazzoni

Raffaele Pettazzoni was born in 1883 at San Giovanni Persiceto, Italy. Having received his primary and secondary school education, he studied at the University of Bologna where he obtained his doctorate in 1905. In 1909 he became inspector at the Royal Prehistorical and Ethnographical Museum in Rome. In 1913 he became *libero docente* for the History of Religions at the University of Rome. In 1914 Pettazzoni was appointed to the chair of the History of Religions at the University of Bologna, and occupied this chair at the University of Rome in 1923. Pettazzoni was President of the International Association for the History of Religions from 1954 onwards, and presided the International Congress for the History of Religions held in Rome in 1955. He developed the interest for the study of religion in his country in a number of ways. He died at Rome in 1959.

The following two books of Pettazzoni are available in English: 1954 *Essays on the History of Religion;* 1956 *The All-Knowing God. Researches into Early Religion and Culture.*

Pettazzoni is known in particular because of his research on monotheism, which he wanted to distinguish in its historical forms from the high god belief on the one hand, and from the hypothetical primeval monotheism on the other hand.

The following text is that of an article in which Pettazzoni pleads for a closer relationship between the phenomenology and the history of religion, as two forms of a science of religion which is one.

"HISTORY' AND 'PHENOMENOLOGY' IN THE SCIENCE OF RELIGION'

There are today several different ways of attacking the study of religions. One of them consists in analysing individual religious facts from a purely external point of view. The philologist striving for the most correct interpretation of a text dealing with religious matters, the archaeologist aiming at a reconstruction of the plan of an ancient sanctuary or at explaining the subject of a mythological or other scene, the ethnologist giving a detailed report of certain ritual practices of an uncivilised tribe, the sociologist endeavouring to form an idea of the organisation and structure of a religious community and of its relations with the world of the profane, the psychologist analysing the religious experience of this or that person, – all these various scholars study religious facts without quitting the bounds of their special sciences. They therefore study religious data in the very spirit of each of these sciences, as if they had to deal in the first place with philological, archaeological, ethnological or other facts, setting aside their specific and essential nature, which is religious.

These researches have a very considerable value for our studies, and their results are sometimes imposingly important. It is to these investigations that we often owe a widening and a deepening of our knowledge. On the other hand, it is clear that they cannot wholly satisfy the demands of the scientific spirit. The peculiar nature, the very character, of religious facts as such give them the right to form the subject of a special science. That science is the science of religion in the proper sense of the words; the essential character of religious facts is the necessary and sufficient reason for its existence. This science cannot be philological nor archaeological nor anything else. Nor can it be the sum total of the particular religious facts studied by philology, archaeology, ethnology and so on. Its definition in contrast to these various sciences is not a matter of quantity but of quality, being connected with the special nature of the data which constitute its subject-matter.

The science of religion is constructive. It does not confine itself to the verification and the analytical explanation of single data such as are studied separately by the various specialised disciplines. It seeks to coordinate religious data with one another, to establish relations and to group the facts according to those relations. If it is a matter of formal relations, it classifies religious data under types; if the relations are chronological, it makes them into series. In the former case the science of religion is merely descriptive; in the second, when the relationships in question are not merely chronological, when, in other words, the succession of the events in time corresponds to an internal development, the science of religion becomes a historical science, the history of religion.

The history of religion aims first of all at settling the history of the various religions. Each separate religion is studied by the historian of religion in its own environment, in its development within that environment, and in its relations with the other cultural values belonging to the same environment, such as poetry, art, speculative thought, social structure and so on. The history of religion therefore studies religious data in their historical connections not only with other religious data but also with those which are not religious, whether literary, artistic, social or what not.

At this point a reflexion comes quite naturally into our minds. Does not this perspective which discovers regions of a different kind, which looks out upon other spheres than religion, run the risk of turning the history of religion away from its proper object, which is religion in itself? Is there not a certain lack of systematic strictness in this manner of studying religious data in connection with other data which are not religious? Is it not probable that a more concentrated study of the religious data in their relations to other data of the same kind, apart from any contact with the non-religious world, would have a better chance of reaching a complete understanding of religion?

This theoretical postulate has been given a concrete answer in practice. We have told ourselves that it is not enough to know precisely what happened and how the facts came to be; what we want above all to know is the meaning of what happened. This deeper understanding cannot be asked for from the history of religion; it springs from another religious science, phenomenology.

Religious phenomenology has nothing to do with the historical development of religion: 'von einer historischen 'Entwicklung' der Religion weisz die Phänomenologie nichts', says van der Leeuw. It sets itself above all to separate out the different structures from the multiplicity of religious phenomena. The structure, and it alone, can help us to find out the meaning of religious phenomena, independently of their position in time and space and of their attachment to a given cultural environment. Thus the phenomenology of religion reaches a universality which of necessity escapes a history of religion devoted to the study of particular religions, and for that very reason liable to the inevitable splitting up of specialisations. Phenomenology does not hesitate to stand forth as a science *sui generis*, essentially different from the history of religion: 'die Religionsphänomenologie ist nicht Religionsgeschichte', to quote van der Leeuw again.

Is there no more to be said? No doubt phenomenology represents the most important innovation which has come about in the realm of our studies during the last half-century (apart from certain anticipatory antecedents of it). However, we feel a certain perplexity at accepting as a final systematisation the division of the science of religion into two different sciences, one historical the other phenomenological. We are tempted to ask if it is absolutely necessary to sacrifice the unity of the science of religion, founded on the unity of its subject, to this dualistic system. Certainly, as contrasted with a history of religion given up exclusively to specialised philological research (the word 'philological' is used here in its widest sense), too interested in the 'cultural' manifestations of religion and too little in the essential values of religious life and experience, phenomenology represents a reaction as legitimate as it is laudable. And yet it is allowed to ask if that is really the most justifiable point of view and if it is not rather a diminution of the history of religion to restrict it to the study of individual religions and their development.

From a general point of view it is the very idea of history which is at stake here. The conception of a history which is merely a knowledge of the past, a past totally unconnected with the present, the idea in fact of history separated from life, is rejected by many historians who draw their inspiration from a philosophical thought other than that which lies at the base of phenomenology. And as regards the history of religion in particular, is it allowable to declare that it has nothing to tell us about the meaning of religious phenomena, and that historical development is fundamentally indifferent and totally negligible to phenomenological interpretation? Religious phenomena do not cease to be realities historically conditioned merely because they are grouped under this or that structure. Does not phenomenological judgement *(Verstehen)* run a risk on occasion of ascribing a like meaning to phenomena whose likeness is nothing but the illusory reflexion from a convergence of developments different in their essence; or, on the contrary, of not grasping the similar meaning of certain phenomena whose real likeness in kind is hidden under an apparent and purely external dissimilarity?

The only way of escape from these dangers is to apply constantly to history. Phenomenology knows it and admits it, declaring that it depends upon history and that its own conclusions always remain susceptible of revision in view of the progress of historical research. Then what are the real systematic relations between these two sciences, which have but one object and collaborate so closely? Have we really to do with two different sciences? Are they not rather in reality simply two interdependent instruments of the same science, two forms of the science of religion, whose composite unity corresponds to that of its subject, that is to say of religion, in its two distinct components, interior experience and exterior manifestations?

Far from achieving the final systematisation of our studies therefore, the cleaving of the science of religion into phenomenology and history would represent merely a stage on the road towards the foundation of a single science of religion on its essential bases and in its undivided form. There is even some reason to ask if at bottom this dualistic system does not connect somehow with another and much older dualism, which goes back to the very beginnings of the science of religion and has never ceased to exert its influence, a negative one, in the sphere of our studies. I mean the dualism of its sources, one from theology and the other from the humanist sciences, of which we cannot say that their waters have quite overflowed the various obstacles which prevent them from mingling entirely in the great stream of religious history. To realise the empirical unity, beyond all traditional separation between Biblical and profane religions; to realise the unity of system beyond all tendency to dualism or pluralism; those are two conditions which are called upon to play a leading part in the future of the science of religion.

Hendrik Kraemer

Hendrik Kraemer was born in 1888 in Amsterdam. He received his primary and part of the secondary school education in Deventer and Amsterdam. Between 1905 and 1909 he was at a missionary school in Rotterdam, where he obtained a diploma allowing him to be sent out as a missionary teacher to the Dutch East Indies. However, he accepted a proposal to be trained as a language expert in the service of the Dutch Bible Society, in view of its Bible translations. Kraemer completed his secondary education between 1909 and 1911, and enrolled in the University of Leiden, Faculty of Arts, in 1911. There he studied Arabic, Javanese, Malay languages and literatures and showed a broad interest in oriental religions and civilizations. For his future task, the scholar and missionary Dr. N. Adriani who had stimulated Kraemer to pursue his studies in this direction, gave advice and suggestions to Kraemer. After having obtained his Ph. D. degree in 1921 with a dissertation on a Javanese mystical text, and after having spent some months working in Paris, Kraemer was sent to Java as a missionary expert and adviser in the service of the Dutch Bible Society. His first stay lasted from 1922 until 1928. Kraemer participated actively in the International Missionary Conference in Jerusalem in 1928. His second stay in the Dutch Indies was from 1930 until 1935. On his return he was asked by the International Missionary Council to write a study which would be presented to the International Missionary Conference in Tambaram, India, in 1938: 'The Christian Message in a Non-Christian World'. In 1936–37 Kraemer spent some six months in the United States. In 1937 he occupied the chair of the history and phenomenology of religion at the University of Leiden, Faculty of Theology. In 1938 he was one of the leading figures at the Tambaram conference, after which he again visited the Dutch Indies. During World War II Kraemer stimulated an internal revival and reorganization of the Dutch Reformed Church. In 1947 he resigned from his professorship and became the Director of the Ecumenical Institute of the World Council of Churches, at Château de Bossey, Switzerland, in 1948. He held this post until 1955, taught for some time in the United States and retired in Holland. He died at Driebergen in 1965.

The following books of Kraemer are relevant to the study of religion: 1938 *The Christian Message in a Non-Christian World;* 1956 *Religion and the Christian Faith;* 1960 *World Cultures and World Religions.*

Besides his activities with regard to Christian missions and ecumenism, Kraemer had broad scholarly interests. The following fragment has been taken from his *Religion and the Christian Faith,* where he speaks of the presuppositions and limits of the scholarly study of religion.

ON THE PRESUPPOSITIONS AND LIMITS OF THE SCIENCE OF RELIGION

In the preceding chapter we explained that in recent decades it has been realized that the aim of modern scientific study of Religion and Religions should be not so much to *explain* religion as to understand, to 'comprehend' it, and to define what every concrete religion represents as an entity in itself. More often we are presented with a mixture of explanation and understanding, and it must steadily be kept in mind that to maintain systematically a clear delimitation of two approaches is very difficult. Explanation is easily thought of as the best way of understanding. It is, as we say, especially Phenomenology of Religion and the so-called *verstehende Psychologie* (understanding psychology) in which some of the leading names are Spranger and Jaspers,[1] that have emphasized the necessity of understanding religion in its various manifestations from within, and not from without. The latter is often the case with explanations of religion. We have, however, seen in the previous chapter that the so-called phenomenological approach implies in a new form the permanent problem of the tension of the pure observer and the appreciator of values, who are always present in the same man.

'The natural explanation of religion'

In the nineteenth century particularly, but also in our own days, however, the object of most research and interpretation was and is to find a so-called *natural explanation* of religion. By natural explanation is meant an immanent explanation; one which finds the generating factors of religion in some region of man's consciousness, a certain psychological attitude or social necessity, a lack of adequate knowledge of the world. A clear expression of this approach is to be found, for instance, in Comte's famous division of the mental history of mankind into an 'état théologique ou fictif', an 'état métaphysique ou abstrait' and an 'état scientifique ou positif', thus explaining thought in terms of evolution, the last period becoming the present and definite one. It does not concern us here that in later life, as an appendix to his *Système de politique positive*, he conceives a 'Religion de l'Humanité' with a fully-fledged hierarchical structure.[2]

The logical consequence of the method of natural explanation is, of course, to regard religion as a stage in the development of human self-consciousness, and therefore as seen from the standpoint now attained, in principle, as atavism. The argument is not always carried to this its logical conclusion, because the attempts at a natural explanation are often combined with a recognition of the great significance, of the abiding place, of religion in human life. And so the modern scientific study of religion has produced a host of theories about the origin and evolution of religion, from the so-called 'primitive' to the 'highest' stages, Christianity included. To mention the main theories, which have brought to light an overwhelming amount of data about the bewildering variety of religious experience and attitude:

The Animistic theory of Tylor, which sought the origin of religion in ancestor-worship and a primitive attempt to explain the phenomena of Nature;

Durkheim's attempt to make Totemism the matrix of all religion and Society as the real object of religious cult;

The theories of Lévy-Bruhl and his school on the pre-logical mentality (in later life Lévy-Bruhl has dropped this assumption) of 'primitive' peoples, and their conception of the world and of life as *participation mystique;*

The Dynamist or Prae-animistic School, as represented by Marett for instance, being a result of Codrington's discovery of the great significance of *Mana* or *Macht* (dynamis);

Frazer's theory that religion was adopted as a means of mastering life when men had passed through the stage of magic and found out that magic did not deliver the goods;

The 'high gods' theory of Andrew Lang, which tried to explain the significance of the so-called *dei otiosi* (gods aloof from man), so conspicuous in many religious traditions, and which was set by Söderblom in a more fruitful context in his thesis about the *Urheber-Religion;*

Freud's theory that religion originated from an oedipus complex in the primitive horde; religion as the projection of fears or wishful thinking, thus personified in gods and demons – a theory most aptly condensed in Feuerbach's well-known phrase that man created god(s) after his image, and that *Theologie ist Anthropologie,* the explanation of 'depth-psychology'; and so on.

The well-known theories of William James in his *Varieties of Religious Experience* that the core of religion is the experience of the Divine Presence, whatever definition one may give of 'divine', and of Rudolf Otto, who derives religion from the experience of the 'holy', of the 'numinous', try to transcend the field of the naturalist-psychological or sociological explanation.

It would take too much space to enter here into a discussion of all these theories, their merits and demerits, their errors, their distortions and their truth, or of the fruitful mutual criticism that has resulted from scientific discussion about them. Nor do we have space to estimate the abiding value of the discoveries, and the contribution thus made by creators of these theories to a more open-minded and acute understanding of Religion. Emil Brunner in *Offenbarung und Vernunft*[3] is quite right when he says: 'The naturalistic-psychological explanation of religion is partly right. A number of religious facts can be explained as products of fear, wishful thinking, need for happiness, mythological phantasy, projection of the unconscious'. Religion is conditioned by historical, psychological and sociological causes.

In all ages common sense knew this, but the modern systematic study of religions has elevated this notion to the level of well-established irrefutable knowledge and acute relevance. Nobody will deny that through Marett's *mana-tabu* formula as minimum definition of religion, through the 'numinous' as characterized by Otto, through Durkheim's distinction of *sacré-profane*, through Lang's 'high gods' or *Urheber*, through Söderblom's insistence on *Heilig, das erste Wort der Religion* (holy, sacred, the first religious word), we have learned things of great importance. Their weakness, apart from errors of observation, description and evaluation (which occur in all fields of science) appears when they pretend to *explain* religion in this way, whereas what they really do is uncover hidden aspects or partial truths. These endeavours to bring religion in its rich manifestations and motivations under a common denominator do not do justice to the Science of Religion itself.

In mentioning William James and Rudolf Otto we said that they tried to transcend the realm of naturalistic-psychological and sociological explanation of religion. Their efforts point to a different kind of explanation; that is to say, the transcendental-philosophical. They regard religion as a necessary expression of the human *spirit*, and as the realm where the human spirit encounters the Ultimate, the Absolute, and transcends nature. According to these and other a-prioristic explanations, the Transcendent, the Divine, that which brings about a meeting of the spirit of man with the ultimate basic realities, is to be found either in his moral consciousness, the domain of the will, or in his aesthetic consciousness, i.e., feeling, or else in Reason *(Vernunft)*. So Kant defined religion as 'die Erfassung aller Pflichten als göttliche Gebote' (the conceiving of all duties as divine commands), without, however, indicating what he meant by 'God'; for Schleiermacher the core of religion was 'das Gefühl der Einheit mit dem Unendlichen, das Gefühl der schlechthinnigen Abhängigkeit' (the feeling of oneness with the Infinite; the feeling of absolute dependency); Hegel defined it in the words: 'Religion ist Beziehung des Geistes auf den absoluten Geist' (Religion is the relatedness of the human spirit with the absolute spirit), or 'das Wissen des göttlichen Geistes' (the knowledge which the Divine Spirit has of itself by the intermediary of the finite spirit). In these three cases which we take as examples, Christianity is always conceived as being the highest realization of religion in general.

'Comparative religion'

This last remark leads us to another point of great importance. One of the current names for the Science of Religion is 'Comparative Religion' *(religion comparée, vergleichende Religionswissenschaft)*. This name, so easily used, contains in itself a number of philosophical problems. We only mention the chief one. The name implies that the scholar 'compares', that is to say, that he constructs for the religions a hierarchical scale, according to their content and truth-value, from 'lower' to 'higher' and even 'highest' *(Höchst-religionen)* religions. Various scales have been proposed. This activity, however, necessarily implies that one has a criterion, a standard of reference by which one is able to grade and compare. Where does this come from? On what grounds is it held to be the true criterion? Those who would explain Religion naturalistically have not bothered much about this crucial question, because they erroneously considered themselves 'neutral, objective' observers and onlookers and, wholly unphilosophically, left out of account the fact that their approach, their emphasis, their selection of facts etc. were determined by their ultimate attitude towards the world and life (their *Weltan-schauung)* and their – mostly undefined – understanding of man. This uncritical attitude makes them, however, rather self-confident about what they take to be pure induction, and in no sense arbitrary deduction. In regard to the thinkers of the transcendental-philosophical school, the situation is different. They give account of the how and why of their understanding and of their grading of the truth-value in the religions. They acknowledge the God-consciousness of man *(Gottesbewusstsein)* as a fact because they acknowledge a transcendental reality and therefore express partial truths; as, for instance, that it is undeniable that religion is organically related to the moral, aesthetic and noetic consciousness of man. In the light of their consequences for the interpretation of religion, the transcendental explanations of religious life are therefore constantly to be scrutinized as to their merits and demerits.

Yet the philosophically innocent representatives of Comparative Religion and the transcendentalists agree on one central point. The important concept by which they aimed at arranging and classifying the material in different grades is that of the Essence of Religion *(das Wesen der Religion)*, an all-embracing and all-explaining formula. Either one hopes to discover it by persevering research, and formulates provisional working definitions, or more precise ones, of what religion *is*, or one starts from a philosophical concept of the Essence of Religion, making it the criterion of judgment and explanation. In either case it is considered to be derived from the religions which are crude or sublime expressions of it. This is conceived as the real business of the philosophy of religion and is as old as philosophy itself, with an illustrious pedigree (Plato, Aristotle, the Stoics, Neo-Platonism etc.).

Originally the idea meant (in distinction from theology) a philosophical treatment of ultimates, not based on revelation but on philosophical thinking. In the eighteenth century, however, because the movement of emanci-

pation from the authority of ecclesiastical dogma and of revelation arose at
that moment with peculiar force, the Philosophy of Religion became the
rival and, often, the declared enemy of Theology. It claimed to develop the
right doctrine of the Essence of Religion which is present in all religions.
These religions can then be demonstrated as more or less imperfect embodiments of it. Inevitably the idea of progressive evolution and realization of
the Essence of Religion played a distinguished role in this thinking. This
concept of the Essence of Religion as its secret and ultimate standard of
reference was often consciously opposed to revelation. The religions of revelation were also explained and evaluated in the light of some concept of the
'Essence of Religion'. It is extremely interesting to see how the great Adolf
Harnack[5] rejected a special chair for the History of Religions by the argument 'The study of the Christian Religion is almost a substitute for the study
of the other religions. Whosoever does not know this religion, knows none,
and who knows it, knows all religions.'[6] But yet on the other hand he remained in the camp of the philosophers of the Essence of Religion by saying:
'Christianity is by an enormous reduction, which unveils the kernel of all
religions, the summit of all religions'.

The patent fact, however, is that there is no unanimity as to what the
Essence of Religion is. As we explained in the preceding chapters, there can
be none, because every philosophical approach rests ultimately on an attitude and a decision as to what to think about man and his attitude in relation
to the Beyond, *which cannot be cogently and universally demonstrated.* Hence
a universally and compellingly valid concept of the 'Essence of Religion'
is not to be expected. Here again we have to accept our human condition,
which requires that the search for scientific and metaphysical truth will go
on as a spiritual contest – full of risks and precious results, to be sure – and
not as a march towards intellectual unanimity.

[...]

'Religion: not singular but universal'

There is no such thing as Religion in the singular, but there is something
which exists universally; namely, religious consciousness. It embodies and
expresses itself in concrete forms of religion, as we see in the empirical religions in the past and in the present; or as a specific quality found in certain
individuals, in their way of apprehending life and the world, but which is
not crystallized into a definite pattern of religion as a social phenomenon.
Many instances of the last category are given in William James's *Varieties
of Religious Experience.* This *religious consciousness* is an empirical reality,
which testifies to man's specific condition and quality. It expresses itself
in two ways.

First, in a 'subjective' way: that is, the special type of religiosity and piety or inner religious life, according to the particular religion as part of which this 'subjective' religiosity functions. Under this 'subjective' one must also include the religiosity of individuals (often very important ones) who detach themselves from any positive religion, but possess a strong religious consciousness. A good name would be *unbeheimatete Religion* (homeless religion).

The second way is the so-called 'objective' religion, that is the peculiar body of doctrine, myth, rite, cult and worship, which constitute the 'established' religions as we treat them in the handbooks of the History of Religion.

It is more profitable to observe and analyse as accurately as possible these various concrete manifestations of religious consciousness, individual as well as collective, than to seek for an abstract Idea of Religion, either as the common denominator or as the universal essence of all religions. The scholars in Schleiermacher's lineage, as for instance Gustav Mensching, tread this way. He lays a strong stress, too strong, on the irrational character of religion, which he calls a peculiar quality of life and experience determined by the 'Category of the Holy'. It is, he says, impossible to seize and understand this peculiar reality by theoretical analyses of the Idea of God or the rational explanation of rites. He therefore criticizes both rationalistic Liberalism and rationalistic Orthodoxy. He warns against overestimating 'parallels' and the tendency to find the right explanation in historical dependence of identical phenomena elsewhere (the *Homologe* is not necessarily identical with the *Analoge*). These parallels are often converging expressions of a type of life, and the main concern should be to find out: what does it mean?

A Dutch professor of Missions, J. H. Bavinck, has published a very interesting study on the matter of religious consciousness under the title *Religieus besef en Christelijk geloof* (Religious Consciousness and Christian Faith). He starts from the fact of the existence of religious consciousness. In technical language his approach would be called a phenomenology or morphology of the religious consciousness. He comes to the following conclusions:

a) There are religions, and types of religious experience, dominated by a genuine experience of the totality of existence. That is to say, man is primarily experiencing himself as part of a coherent, cosmic whole. The so-called primitive religions, and Chinese, Japanese, Indian religions – Schleiermacher's 'Sinn und Geschmack für das Unendliche' (aptitude and taste for the Infinite) – are conspicuous examples. In India *the* great vice is therefore *ahamkāra* (egotism). The great, cosmic Whole is conceived as a numinous, divine 'It', and man is part of 'It'. I myself, in my book *The Christian Message in a Non-Christian World,* have called religions of this type embodiments of Naturalistic Monism.

b) In other religions, the focus is the consciousness of being related to a Norm, a moral world-order, which is in us and above us. It is in the discourse with this normative world that the religious experience occurs *(cf.* Indian *Rta,* Chinese *Tao,* the ordered cosmos of the Stoa). The experience of the 'ought' is determinative in this kind of religious consciousness. These two types, *(a)* and *(b),* often intermingle.

c) In all religions, experience of a relationship with a higher power, vaguely or more clearly understood as personal, is one of the basic utterances of religious consciousness.

d) Again, other religions are strongly characterized by the elementary feeling that life is a contest between human action and super-human fate: cf. the ancient religions of the Near East with their astrological beliefs; the preponderant role of *tyché* in Hellenism; the Greek tragedians in a quite different grandiose way; Islam in its struggle about free will and divine predestination. In short, in the great systems of life there is present in varying degrees the awareness of a Mysterious Other, a Partner Divine.

These are excellent observations. It is possible to offer as a result of disinterested observations other examples of dominant trends in the religious consciousness; such, for instance, as the deep feeling of the mystery of life, hidden in the mystery of death, that is prominent in the ancient Mediterranean religions. Moreover, no great religion is characterized only by one emphasis. There is always a dominant emphasis and a gamut of subsidiary emphases combined. But, be this as it may, Dr. Bavinck is right when he concludes that, in *looking* at religions in this way, one does not discover Religion in the singular, as the matrix or ideal pattern of all the different religions, but that one does discover certain crossing-points *(Knooppunten)* or 'magnetic fields', around which, in many converging and deeply diverging ways (though every way, by the peculiar combination of emphases, is a way in its own right) human thinking has crystallized. In them, it seems, man tries to express a kind of answer to the primary concerns and divinations which impose themselves upon him and compel him somehow to *believe,* however fantastic or sublime the forms may be in which he expresses it (myth, rite, magic, behaviour).

'The underivable fact of religion'

The conclusion forces itself upon us that man can only reach out to the reality of life and the world through a religious apprehension. This religious consciousness seems underivable; it is given with the fact of human existence.

For many decades one of the preoccupations of the scientists of religion has been to find the origin of religion. A search for *religionslose Völker* (religion-less peoples) was organized. This search revealed that there were none, and at the present moment the interest in this quest, from which the theories about Animism, Pre-animism, etc., originated, has died out amongst scholars. The origin of religion is not a historical problem, nor a psychological or sociological one, because it lies outside our possibilities of empirical knowledge. One can only make more or less interesting speculative guesses about it, which reveal more about the peculiar bias of the proposer than about the origin of religion. This question of the origin of religion has meaning and significance only if it is wittingly philosophical or theological. One can confidently assert that it is true to say that all religions, all possible types of expression of the religious consciousness, still exist and will continue to exist, whether their most representative, concrete, historic embodiments still exist or are existing now in more concealed ways, or assimilated into existing religions.

Rudolf Otto has formulated this underivable fact of the religious consciousness and of religion in the words: 'Religion fängt mit sich selber an' (Religion begins with itself). This is, perhaps, the wisest thing that can be said. Dostoievski, who with his visionary and prophetic mind had certainly more feeling for the mystery of religion than most philosophers and psychologists, says in one of the many revelatory passages in *The Idiot*: 'The essence of the religious sentiment escapes all reasoning. . . . There is always in it something intangible and inaccessible to any atheistic argument.'

Still the question remains: 'Where does this religious consciousness come from?' for it points to something beyond man. 'L'homme surpasse l'homme.' The Transcendent looms up out of man's life-situation in whatever way the Transcendent may be defined. In other words, if there is an answer, it cannot but be a philosophical or theological one. We shall have to deal with this crucial point in one of the subsequent chapters, and then make clear that for us a theological answer can only mean a Christian theological answer. The English philosopher H. A. Hodges[8] cogently shows that underlying every standpoint and attitude or *Weltanschauung* there is 'belief as a responsible act', which cannot be explained further. In the field of basic attitudes the intellect is always dependent on the will, and this dominates our intractable human situation. Hodges himself is of the opinion that the view of Christian theology is singularly to the point: 'Sin to account for our intellectual situation, salvation and divine restoration as solution of the problem.'

Another point has to be made as a result of the systematic study of religions. It is this. The Christian religion in its many historical manifestations shows the same disturbing combination of sublime, abject and tolerable elements as the non-Christian religions. Seen from this angle, Christianity as a phenomenon in history has to be considered as *a* form of religion just like the others, although, also like them, it has, of course its peculiar empha-

ses and concerns. This thesis must constantly be repeated in order to avoid
the frequently occurring identification or partial identification of Christianity, one of the religions, with the Revelation of God in Christ.

'Fairness in the intercourse of religions'

If this is kept in mind by all parties it can result in a greater fairness in the
intercourse between religions. Even tendencies to assert the superiority of
one's own religion can then to a great extent be checked. Not out of relativism, but out of a sense of fairness and humility, out of the sense of realistic
self-knowledge, which sees the obvious point that self-praise at others' cost
seldom commends itself and that hurtful criticism of others deservedly calls
forth the same sort of criticism on one's own religion. Both ways cause
nothing but alienation and bitterness, and are, certainly in their effect and
most often in their motive, contrary to true religion.

There is however a still more weighty consideration for discounting attitudes of superiority. As long as there is no universally acknowledged norm
of religious Truth – and it is evident that there is not, indeed there cannot
be one – it is, logically speaking, useless to talk about the superiority of one
religion over another. It always amounts to the confident assertion of one's
own religious Ego as the standard. In the light of the Biblical revelation,
which is in no way identical with the Christian religion as a historical phenomenon, one must go even further and assert that a feeling of superiority has
its roots in a definite consciousness of *achievement*. In the light of the revelation of the divine Grace as the sole basis of existence, thinking in terms of
achievement, ethical or religious, is self-contradictory.

Boasting about one's own religion, its excellency and superiority, coupled
with delight in condemnation of other religions, is, as everybody knows,
one of the most frequent sins of men everywhere. It is, in the field of religion,
a universal human trait to combine conviction of the superiority of one's
own opinions with a low estimate of others' ideas. The polemics between
people of various branches of secular knowledge indeed often prove that.
It is striking that in regard to religion it is most deeply resented as a scandal.

'Value and truth in all religions'

To become more deeply aware of the stupendous richness and depth of religious life in *all* religions has made the question of value and truth in the non-
Christian religions more, not less, acute. For many, it has made the question
an agonizing one, as it is rightly felt that it has become impossible and utterly
objectionable to dispose lightly of these religions in regard to their value
and truth. [...]

NOTES

1. *Cf.* his *Psychologie der Weltanschauungen* [Psychology of World-Views].

2. Charles de Rouve in his *Auguste Comte et le Catholicisme* (1928) attempts to explain it as a conscious endeavour of Comte's to create a positivistic counterpart to and rival of Roman Catholicism.

3. English translation: E. Brunner, *Revelation and Reason* [Offenbarung und Vernunft]. London, S. C. M. Press.

4. E. Brunner, *Offenbarung und Vernunft*, p. 255.

5. *Cf.* his address on *Die Aufgaben der Theologie und die allgemeine Religionswissenschaft* [The task of Theology and the Science of Religion.], 1901.

6. 'Das Studium der Christlichen Religion ersetzt nahezu das der übrigen Religionen. Wer diese Religion nicht kennt, kennt keine, und wer sie kennt kennt alle.'

7. In a booklet called *Language, Standpoints and Attitudes*, p. 68.

Max Scheler

Max Scheler was born in 1874 at Munich, Germany, where he received his pri
mary and secondary school education. In 1891 he enrolled in the University of
Munich to study philosophy and the natural sciences, and continued these studies
at the University of Berlin where he studied under Wilhelm Dilthey, Carl Stumpf
and Georg Simmel. After a short stay in Heidelberg, he went to the University
of Jena where he worked with Rudolf Eucken, and obtained his doctorate in 1897
with a dissertation on 'The Determination of the Relations between Logical and
Ethical Principles'. In 1899 he passed his *Habilitation* at the University of Jena
with a thesis on 'Transcendental and Psychological Methods'. Scheler then became *Privatdozent* at the University of Jena where he continued teaching until
1907. Between 1907 and 1910 he taught at the University of Munich, and lived
then as a private scholar working along phenomenological lines. In 1919 Scheler
was appointed to the chair of Philosophy and Sociology at the University of
Cologne and became Director of the Institute of Social Studies there. Shortly
after having accepted a position at the University of Frankfort on the Main, he
died at Cologne in 1928.

The following books of Scheler appeared in English translation: 1954 *The
Nature of Sympathy;* 1958 *Philosophical Perspectives;* 1960 *On the Eternal in
Man;* 1961 *Ressentiment;* 1961 *Man's Place in Nature.*

Scheler is known as a philosopher inspired by Husserl's phenomenology. The
following fragments have been taken from *On the Eternal in Man* (First German
edition 1921) and show how Scheler conceived besides an essential a concrete
phenomenology, how the latter distinguishes itself from psychology, and what
tasks he assigns to the essential phenomenology of religion.

PSYCHOLOGY, 'CONCRETE' AND 'ESSENTIAL' PHENOMENOLOGY OF
RELIGION

Nevertheless, the psychology of religion, which is so favoured and overrated
today, needs to be methodologically redirected within its proper boundaries.

The modern psychology of religion, in its essentials, originated historically in the spirit of positivism. (Among the moderns David Hume was its
progenitor.) This is of course no accident. For inasmuch as religion's claim
to truth was meeting a *rebuff* of one kind or another, it was to be expected
that the religion of the positivists should decline to nothing more than a
collection of psychic phenomena, which required to be described, causally
explained, and at best conceived teleologically (from the biological aspect)
as a particular stage in man's adaptation to his environment. But apart

from the historical origin of modern religious psychology it is a misrepresentation to argue according to the following favourite method of outlining its sense and purpose:

'Whatever one thinks of religion's truth, affirming or denying, whatever the religion to whose milieu one belongs, *in any case* religion is a collection of psychic phenomena and experiences, and as such is indubitably an object for psychology. The appropriate branch of psychology is called the psychology of religion, and this psychology of religion is a science which can be practised just as well by Christians as by Muslims, by atheists as by believers, etc., etc. It is thus entirely *free of preconceptions* and *interconfessional'.*

This argument is purely specious and of no account. No one who makes use of it can have clearly grasped the question of what the conditions are under which *anything whatsoever* becomes the object of psychological elucidation, and what the objective premises (or preconceptions) from which every branch of explanatory psychology must operate.

To the nature of psychology, or rather to the type of perception and perceptual state in which a datum of the type 'psychic' can enter a cognitive consciousness, two things belong: always the psychic is *primarily* the object of a perception of *otherness*, not a perception of a thing proper to the subject; secondly, it is invariably the case that the psychic is primarily something which is held to be error, delusion or in some way *abnormal*. Now, while it is true that reflexive perception of things proper to the subject together with all kinds of 'self-observation', need not necessarily have been genetically formed under the influence of an already exercised perception of extraneous things, such perception is nevertheless in essence (as a *type* of act and mental disposition) simply extra-perception to which – by chance – the object assigned is not that which is adequate to perception of that kind *(i.e.* some instance of the 'alien' and 'other'), but the modifications of the reflexive self. Or we may thus express it: to adopt a 'psychological' attitude to oneself is to behave towards oneself *as if one were a stranger or 'someone else'.*

Again: it is impossible to adopt a psychological attitude toward the 'other' until one has by some method relinquished the natural relationships subsisting between spiritual subjects *(shared experience* of the same objects, values, etc., the relationship of *understanding).* Not until the personal quality of the other has vanished or appears to have done so (madness is the clearest instance), or until we exercise an artificial abstraction upon his being, upon the significant content of his intentions, thus upon the intentions themselves, does the other yield a potential object of psychology. By strict analogy, I must also abstract my own free person and its mental intentions – must feign to remove them – if I wish to adopt an attitude of self-perception toward myself.

Finally: if a person judges that twice two are four, it is absurd to demand a psychological explanation of the fact. The only meaningful question to ask in these circumstances is why he so judges now, in this connection and not in that one. But if a person judges that twice two make five, then the content of his judgment, not only the occasion of his judging, is a possible object of psychological elucidation.

Psychology, then, is primarily always psychology of the *other, divested of spirit and personality,* and psychology of that which is held to be false or nonsensical at its intentional face-value.

But this noetic origin of explanatory psychology (in the modern sense of the word) is also of some importance for the so-called psychology of religion. Religion simply is not, as that argument would have it, 'in any case' a psychic phenomenon. It is *that* only on occasions when – and to the extent that – it rests on delusion and error, or is perhaps already seen as delusion. So anyone investigating religion as an object of psychology has already emptied it of meaning and intention – even if only in a feigned and tentative manner, for the purposes of research. But if anyone deprive religion of all possible truth, he should not claim that he can still practise the psychology of religion. He should rather say: 'There is nothing left of what men called religion. There is only a collection of psychic phenomena, which as 'religion' used mistakenly to be considered the essential embodiment of certain acts directed to a common object, and these morbid phenomena of the *psyche I* will investigate.' This is a sensible way of talking, whereas the other is senseless.

If the modern explanatory psychology of religion is obviously preoccupied with the abnormal, *pathological* phenomena of religious life, it is clear that this is no accidental penchant but derives from its very nature and origin.

Methodologically it is no less erroneous to believe that a psychology of religion *free* of religious or confessional premises is possible – other than one merely descriptive.

For explanatory psychology, in *all* its branches, presupposes the reality of the objective field whose action and reaction on the *psyche* it is investigating. Thus all explanatory sensual psychology postulates the concept of attraction, *i.e.* a real causal relation between the organism and physical bodies or kinds of energy. On the other hand all descriptive sensual psychology postulates a bare minimum of definite objective phenomena, such as colours or sounds. If we apply this principle to our present field of inquiry we ascertain that specific real, religious objects must be postulated before the attempt can be made to investigate their effect on the human *psyche*.

But on what basis are they to be postulated? It is the answer to *this* question which decisively precludes an interconfessional psychology of religion. For this is the answer: Since it is of the *essence* of a religious object that it can attest its possible reality only through and in an act of *faith*, all those who do not possess the appropriate belief in a religious reality fail to satisfy the *precondition* for empirically knowing and observing the action of the religious object on the *psyche*.

To give an example, it is clear that nobody who does not possess *belief* in the Real Presence of Christ in the Sacrament can seek even to *describe* the psychic experiences induced by a Catholic's pious assistance at the holy Mass. He is as little able to do so as a person totally blind is able to describe the sensation and mood produced by colours vivid to unimpaired perception. Therefore, a psychological investigation of this religious object is only possible among those who believe the relevant dogma – not, then, among a group of people some of whom believe it and some of whom do not. The psychology of religion is confronted by this wholly peculiar situation, that the reality of the object whose reaction on the psyche it seeks to examine can only be received in the state of faith. Even the much-bruited 'empathy', by which one may enter the religious act of another, is no kind of substitute for the real performance of the act. For it is only the *reality* of the religious object and material, a reality experienced in real and genuine faith but necessarily wanting in the object of merely empathetic faith, which can faithfully reproduce the psychic condition that is required for inspection.

Thus it is that merely descriptive religious psychology, as distinct from the explanatory—which can only be practised from premises of unbelief— is upheld in its well-defined and limited rights. But even this type of religious psychology is only meaningful and possible within a single religious community and not among different communities or their individual members – at least, not as applied to the psychic action of objects affected by the disparity of religious viewpoints. There are therefore as many psychologies of religion as there are *separate confessions*. For the psychic condition which is here to be 'psychologically' explored, the psychic experiences induced by the conceptual possession of religious objects, *arise* in the first place under the influence of different metaphysical and dogmatic systems.

There is to be sure another quite separate line of inquiry, in addition to the spurious, atheistic, explanatory religious psychology and the kind of psychology which is conditional on the unity of the religious community. It is best described as the *concrete* phenomenology of religious objects and acts. There is naturally a fundamental difference between this and all types of eidological or *essential* phenomenology of religion, such as envisage the 'essence' of the act or object. This because it seeks to understand as fully as possible the meaning of one or a number of religious constructs, and attempts an intelligent reconstruction of the acts through which their meanings were or are transmitted. Thus I can describe the polytheistic world corresponding to a particular phase of Greek religion and can give a *direct* account of its material content, *i.e.* not merely a description of the Greeks' own representations of that world. I can investigate its hierarchic system, demonstrate its relation to the world and the life of man. In the same manner I can treat of acts of worship – their forms and types – in which the Greek of that era turned to his gods, in homage, in supplication, etc. But of psychology here there is no question, since all I am doing is lifting the concrete material of intentions and acts, in its intentional relation to its objects' positive meaning, out of the context of the 'spiritual world' existing among the Greeks of those days – and in this the reality of the objects stands disregarded. There is here no question of psychologically describing the internal repercussion of the gods (felt as their spontaneous action) upon the psychic life of the Greeks, and it goes without saying that there is also no question of any objectively real action of the gods, since (according to our own religious notions) they did not really exist.

This concrete phenomenology of religions is a basic discipline for the positive, systematic study of religion and at the same time a *sine qua non* for all religious history concerned with the *evolution* of religions; this latter study may be as strictly distinguished from the systematic science of religions, which *itself* descriptively and comparatively investigates the structure and ramification of mankind's religious object-world, as the jurist has long been wont to distinguish (for example) an inquiry into the doctrine and system of Roman law – at a particular moment in Roman history – from legal *history*, whose business it is to trace legal concepts in their evolution from the collective influences of earlier civilization.[1]

Now, *fundamentally* different from all the above religious disciplines is the *essential phenomenology of religion*.[2]

It is not metaphysics, neither is it natural theology, nor epistemology, nor explanatory and descriptive psychology, nor the concrete phenomenology of religion, but it is the ultimate *philosophical foundation* of *all and every* other philosophical and scientific study of religion. It must be perfected before we may clearly know the declared *independence of religion*, as much in its *ontological* and *objective* aspect as in that of *active* religion. But in process of demonstrating this independence it also performs a second valuable function: by concentrating on the essence of religion it disengages from the religious objects found as items of faith in religions, as positively studied, the essences, the essential correlative principles and structures, which are realized in all the religious realities we have before us in positive religions. Thus it uncovers what we would call the logic of religious acts, *i.e.* the active principles of *religious* reason. These are not in themselves 'norms' but essentially principles of construction and logical development by which religious acts themselves combine or evolve one from another. But they *become* norms for the empirical subject 'man'. However, since all religious knowledge has its final source in some kind of revelation (in that sense of the word which is defined on an earlier page), the whole of religious logic has simply the one significance: it shows the manner and principles whereby religious reason leads man to readiness to receive the light of revelation – light from all the basically different gradations of revelation. Thus, even if we follow these 'norms' they lead us only to the threshold of obtaining revelation, whose substance must then be grasped in the act of faith, grasped as evident in evident faith; they do not lead to any spontaneous cognition of God or (as many seem to think) to any *ex*cogitation or construction of religious objects.

Branches of study. The essential phenomenology of religion has three ends: 1) the essential nature of the divine; 2) the study of the forms of revelation in which the divine intimates and manifests itself to man; 3) the study of the religious act through which man prepares himself to receive the content of revelation, and through which he takes it to himself in faith.

In so far as the divine presents and manifests itself in things, events and orders which belong to the natural reality accessible in principle to all, to the reality of the mind, to the social reality of history, we shall refer to *natural revelation,* whose subjective correlate is *natural religion.* In so far as the divine on the other hand presents or announces itself through the medium of the word and through persons *(homines religiosi* in the most eminent sense), let us speak of *positive* revelation. In so far as the divine – the 'godly' – is a being taking the form of *personality,* it can *only* reveal itself in the second, positive form of revelation; and only while it does *not* contain the idea of a person as ontological form – *e.g.* while it is defined only as *ens a se,* infinite being, eternal reason, spirit, etc. – can it also present itself to man in the form of natural revelation.

Furthermore, there is one essential study of the stages of natural revelation and another of the stages of positive revelation. For if the divine reveals itself in some way at all levels of being, it reveals different characteristics of its essence on different levels, and reveals itself with different degrees of adequacy. The way of its revelation also varies as between different *general* forms of contingent existence – inanimate nature, living nature, the soul of man, society, history. And its various outward forms of revelation are grasped by various kinds of religious acts. The fact remains that in so far as the divine is a person and manifests itself to us in persons, its only possible medium of revelation is the *word.* But the positive forms of revelation also have their essential stages, according to whether the divine reveals merely a limited something of itself – a particle of knowledge, thought, will, as offered to the intelligence – or its whole personal essence and being: thus there is functional revelation and self–revelation.

Again, there correspond to the different forms in which the divine communicates itself in and through persons the different *essential types of 'homines religiosi'*, the recognition of which offers another very important field of research to the essential phenomenology of religion. They begin with the lowest forms and rise to the highest imaginable. The wizard, the magician, the seer, the sage, the prophet, the lawgiver and judge, the king and hero, the priest, the saviour, the redeemer, the mediator, the messiah, and finally the idea of the highest conceivable form, the *essential idea of the person* to whom God has imparted his own personal essence and being: these are examples whose nature and gradation must be thoroughly examined. We must therefore first establish the essential difference between the *homo religiosus* or 'holy man' and other value-types of person, such as the genius, the hero, etc., and so a thoroughgoing investigation of these types must form the basis of our inquiry. Furthermore, the difference between the so-called founder of religion (the original holy man) and the merely derivative *homines religiosi* must also be clearly established. (Among the 'derivative' I include the apostle, the patriarch, the dogmatist, the 'reformer', the 'witness', and the saint within the established fold.)

In view of the essentially *social* nature of all religion, another discipline which must be accepted into the essential phenomenology of religion is the study of the *essential forms of sociological structure* taken by communities to whom revelation is proclaimed as collective revelation (as opposed to grace and individual illumination) by the medium of a 'representative'. Directly relevant to this field of study is what is predicated of the nature of God as lord, protector, head, lawgiver, judge and king of communities (including the nation, the family, the professions and kindred vocational groups, the Church, etc.), as are collective acts of worship and liturgy, communal prayer, forms of homage and devotion.

Finally, the essential phenomenology of religion must submit to scrutiny the *historical* order of succession of the natural and positive revealed forms of the divine. This study must form the basis of any historical philosophy of religion, just as the preceding one must underlie the theory of religious communities (Church, sect, school, monastic order and the rest).

It is not, however, our present intention to construct the entire phenomenology of religion. We will confine ourselves in general to examining the *religious act* in more elaborate detail. For it is from that act and its internal logic that we may most plainly see how there may come into being a religious self-evidence which, residing in faith, resides in itself, and how religion proceeds to unfold and throw out new and higher structures in conformity with its own autonomous laws. [. . .]

*Appendix**

[…] The descriptive method, *not* aiming at essential philosophical insights, of reducing given religious and metaphysical systems *(e.g.* Buddhism, Augustinism, the philosophies of Plato, Aristotle, Schopenhauer) to their *original empirical contents, i.e.* of *reconstructing* and re-intuiting the basis of what appears in them as matured, developed, rationalized, ossified, – thereby revitalizing its *original meaning* and restoring its perceptual validity for today – *this,* as the method used in the descriptive study of Weltanschauungen, is in fact a 'common whore'. It is in the very fact that it *is* a 'common whore' that its outstanding, positive value lies. But it goes without saying that this reconstructive phenomenology cannot be *productive:* proceeding as it does from *given* 'ideas', it can only rediscover, therefore produce nothing new, for one cannot *re*discover what no one has ever observed. It is likewise unable to determine the positive cognitive value of the system under investigation: it cannot, that is to say, determine the degree of adequacy or inadequacy of the underlying perceptual intuitions to the full objective content of the object; nor the degree to which, if at all, the existence of the objects of the given knowledge is dependent on, or a function of, the existence and mode of being of the subject; nor the truth or falsity, or formal correctness (logical consequence), of the corresponding judgments, inferences and organized propositions. Hence reconstructive phenomenology must and *should* be *unlimitedly* 'relativistic'. But it is no less clear that *essential* phenomenology – including of course the essential phenomenology of religion – is able to go much further. Although, like reconstructive phenomenology, it on *no* occasion enables one to assert the *reality* of a given object (for the simple reason that one begins with a conscious renunciation of one's competence to deal with the existential coefficient of the objects under review), one yet knows *a priori* that the 'essential correlations' which it discovers, since they are true of the *essence* of this or that object, are also true of all possible contingent objects of the same 'nature' or essence, whence it follows that it can make true judgments about those objects. But reality itself can only be established, 'in accordance with' these essential co-relations, by some kind of *contingent* experience (taking into account its subsequent thinking over, development, supplementation), and for supersensual objects this implies either *metaphysics* or God's *positive self-communication, i.e.* 'revelation', whose assumption thereupon is enacted solely in receptive acts of faith. It may be contended, however, that in the course of argument the author has not always kept apart these four cognitive forms or procedures – descriptive phenomenology, essential phenomenology, metaphysical dis-

---

* From the Preface to the second German edition.

course and whatever he may have affirmed subjectively here and there as articles of faith (though in the last instance he has always expressly made this affirmation known as applying to an act of *faith*). Against any such contention the author would invoke the fact that it is quite impossible, in the course of investigating any given object to set down, step by step, the underlying epistemology of the investigation. But, in fact, the author believes that he has even distinguished more clearly than has been done before what he considers metaphysically (not phenomenologically) demonstrable in the idea of God, what (secondly) can rest solely on the basis of the essential elementary phenomena, accessible to all men, of *all* religion ('natural revelation') — and what finally can rest, in his theory, *only* on judgment from faith and positive revelation. Only one who knows nothing but 'causal' and other 'inferences' from empirical data to supersensual things or, conversely, positive revelation and its dogmatic formulation — only one therefore who does not acknowledge any *primordial* religious phenomena or, alternatively, any special, specifically religious experience in specifically *'religious acts'* — can from *his* standpoint, which our book precisely refutes and replaces, find 'confusion' where he is in fact in presence of a new and deeper *clarification* of the different sources of knowledge of God. [. . .]

NOTES

1. Similarly Utitz is right to distinguish the systematic study of art from the history of art.
2. The German *'philosophische Wesenserkenntnis der Religion'* has been translated as *'the essential philosophy of religion'*. This 'philosophy' is for Scheler actually 'Phenomenology' *(Editor)*. In his Preface to the second German edition, Max Scheler stresses the crucial distinction between essential phenomenology and descriptive or reconstructive phenomenology. *(Translator)*. See 'Appendix'.

Gaston Berger

Gaston Berger was born in 1896 in St. Louis, Senegal. He received his primary and part of his secondary school education in Perpignan, France, and had to take up a position in an industrial firm. After having performed his military duties in World War I, he became an associate of the owner of the firm. Berger decided to continue his studies. He worked with René Le Senne and passed his *baccalauréat*. He then enrolled in the University of Aix-en-Provence where he studied philosophy under Maurice Blondel. Having passed his *licence*, he obtained a *diplôme d'Etudes Supérieures* with a thesis on the 'Relations between the conditions of intelligibility on the one hand and the problem of contingency on the other hand.' In 1926 Berger founded with some friends the *Société de Philosophie du Sud-Est* and its periodical *Les Etudes Philosophiques*. In 1938 he organized the first Congress of French Language Societies of Philosophy. During these years he regularly went to see Edmund Husserl in Freiburg, Germany. In 1941 Berger submitted his two *thèses de doctorat d'Etat*, the first entitled 'Investigations on the Conditions of Knowledge. Essay of Pure Knowledge', the second 'The 'Cogito' in Husserl's philosophy'. Berger then left his industrial firm and became first a *Chargé de Cours*, then a *Maître de Conférences* for Philosophy at the University of Aix-en Provence. In 1944 he became full professor. In 1949 be became secretary general of the Fulbright Commission, in charge of the cultural relations between France and the United States. In 1953 Berger was appointed Director of Higher Education at the Ministry of Education, Paris. He became Director of the International Institute of Philosophy, and President of the Committee of the *Encyclopédie Française*. Together with Dr. Gras he founded the *Centre de Prospective*, with its periodical *Prospective*. He died in 1960.

One of the few texts of Berger available in English is his paper 'Experience and Transcendence' in: Marvin Farber, ed., *Philosophic Thought in France and the United States*. Buffalo, 1950.

Berger is known as a phenomenological thinker and as the one who has coined the term *prospective* as a category of thought and action in the time process. His broad interest also covered Eastern philosophies, mysticism and parapsychology. The following text is his Preface to the section 'Religion' in the *Encyclopédie Française* (Vol. XIX, 1957, in French). It shows how Berger conceived phenomenological research in the field of religion.

ON PHENOMENOLOGICAL RESEARCH IN THE FIELD OF RELIGION

When one opens a book on religion, everything seems to be settled from the very start: one either believes in God, and one condemns the atheist and the heathen – or one does not believe in Him, and all manifestations of religious life appear to be absurd gestures.

Will the spirit of this Encyclopedia, which does its best to understand everything, fail when entering this new area? Understanding something means knowing how it works, but does understanding a doctrine not imply approval? Are we allowed to take sides in advance, by accepting or rejecting? But if we, in order to remain impartial, limit ourselves to objectively describing the observable phenomena or to recording accounts of personal experiences, do we not miss the essence? Can an indifferent person understand a sentiment in which he does not take part at all? And if he does take part in it, can his account be relied upon?

The alternatives are so sharply defined only if we presume to *give a judgment,* that is to say, if we allow the value of truth to impose on us its demands of 'all or nothing'. An exact proposition is either true or false, without any reservations, but understanding a state of mind and soul necessitates qualifications one way or the other. Moreover, the half-heartedness or indifference of so many self-styled believers, and the intolerant attitude of so many atheists, make us suspect that matters are not all that simple, and that the option, if it imposes itself at all, does not occur at those points where we at first think we perceive it.

It is legitimate, but not sufficient, to ask psychology and sociology to provide some enlightenment. Those disciplines are very useful for assembling a large number of facts and details and for indicating the regular way in which they follow one after the other. But they do not give us any insight into the facts of religion. If we want to make any use of their contributions, we need first of all to have acquired a certain understanding of what spiritual life is, and that understanding can be acquired only by participating in it. We can, from the outside, grasp the relations between atoms and molecules. But if we press on with our analysis and want to discover what takes place *inside* the atom, we are forced to distinguish between its components. If we fail in doing that, we will at least have gained something, and that is the knowledge that in nature every explanation exteriorizes: it 'unfolds'.

But it is not self-evident that the soul is part of nature. Religion assumes, without any exceptions, that nature is not the same as reality and that there is something supernatural. That belief may be illegitimate – this is not the place for such a judgment –, at least its existence ought to be understood. That understanding, in turn, presupposes two things: firstly, that it is possible to perceive a fundamental intention in the multitude of experiences, rites, and beliefs; secondly, that this intention can branch out into special intentions giving birth to just as many deep structures.

By means of the title of this Part ['Religion' of the *Encyclopédie Française*], we wished to underline that unity, and show how seriously we take the object of our studies. 'Religion' is not the same as 'religions'. The plural could have given the impression that it was our main object to draw up an exhaustive inventory of all doctrines. It is no doubt important to stress both the analogies and the differences. But that cannot be done until the essence of whatever is in question has been grasped. Even the table in the third section of this entry has been drawn to make apparent the spirit of some of the principal religions, rather than to summarize their theologies.

The phenomenological method may be able to help us, it seems, to take the right attitude and to understand religious life. It reminds us, first of all, that all meaning is based on a conscious intention and that thought and acts are in fact incomprehensible when they are isolated from the movement that constitutes them. It also teaches us that if we find it impossible to suppress our own beliefs and our own personal feelings when studying human material, we can at least put them into parentheses, so that they become suspended without our having to become unfaithful to them, and we can sympathize with other people's deepest emotions, without having to approve all acts into which those are translated. The phenomenologist thus stops confusing truth and meaning. He does not necessarily regard everything he describes as true or good, but through various examples, he applies himself to the task of discovering deep-lying structures, the meaning of which becomes clear to him. He is like a faithful translator who is prepared to respect the thought of his author, also when he is aware that he does not approve him. Later, perhaps, he will be his judge, but for the time being, he only wants to be his friend.

A considerable effort has to be made, and it is a difficult undertaking, and particularly when we pass from human facts in general to religious facts. Here the indifferent do not understand anything, and the intolerant do not want to understand anything they do not approve. Beyond the former's poverty and the latter's fanaticism there is room for a comprehensive sympathy, generous enough to be able to take part in other people's spiritual emotions, before presuming to change them. Any dialogue, religious or not, tends towards conversion, but presupposes understanding.

That is the kind of attempt at intentional description, that we asked the contributors to our first group of articles to make. We did not invite them to write about a particular 'part' of the problem. We did not even see fit to reserve a particular 'area' for each of them. All we asked them to do was to describe spiritual life from a certain point of view and in a certain perspective. They simply had to tell what they saw. This method, which respects the authors' freedom and guarantees the authenticity of their accounts, sometimes causes certain themes to be regarded from various points of view, which, to us, appears to be essential in order to convey simultaneously the unity and the variety of spiritual life. This results in a religious structure that corresponds to a sensible piece of architecture: the way it is organized is understood better as it is viewed from different angles.

Our illustrations also try to apply the same suggestive procedures by means of examples. The reason we selected the theme of pilgrimage was not because it provided a good excuse for reproducing picturesque documents. It was because that theme helps us to understand the tension between the spiritual and historical elements which is inherent in all religion. It also points to an essential characteristic of all spiritual life, namely that it is a force, a march, a movement towards being, towards light, towards salvation. It is only interesting to get to know the details of the itineraries, of the customs, of the ceremonies, if one has first conceived a longing for the great adventure.

Sources and Acknowledgments

The author wishes to give due credit here for the kind permissions granted to reproduce in his anthology material from the publications listed below. Except if stated otherwise, permission has been granted by the publishers of the sources.

BACHOFEN, JOHANN J.
'Symbol and myth' and 'Matriarchy and religion' from *Myth, Religion and Mother Right. Selected Writings of J. J. Bachofen*. Translated by Ralph Manheim. Preface by George Boas. Introduction by Joseph Campbell. Princeton (N. J.), Princeton University Press (Bollingen Series), 1967, pp. 48–50, 84–92.

BERGER, GASTON
'On phenomenological research in the field of religion' (new translation) from the Preface to the section 'Religion', *Encyclopédie Française*, Paris, Vol. XIX, *Philosophie et Religion*, 1957, pp. 1932.1–1932.4.

CHANTEPIE DE LA SAUSSAYE, PIERRE D.
'The science of religion' and 'Phenomenology of religion' from *Manual of the Science of Religion*. London–New York, Longmans, Green & Co., 1891, pp. 3–10, 67–73.

DELITZSCH, FRIEDRICH C. G.
'Babel and Bible' from *Babel and Bible. Two Lectures delivered before the Members of the Deutsche Orient-Gesellschaft in the Presence of the German Emperor*. Edited, with an Introduction by C. H. W. Johns. New York, Putnam–London, Williams & Norgate, 1903, pp. 34–56, 67–72, 171–173, 175–178, 209–211, 216–221.

DURKHEIM, EMILE
'The elementary forms of the religious life' from *The Elementary Forms of the Religious Life*. New York, Collier Book edition, 1961, pp. 13–21, 37–39, 51–57, 62–65, 106–107, 112–117. © 1915 by George Allen & Unwin, London. New York, first Free Press Paperback edition, Macmillan 1963.

FRAZER, JAMES GEORGE
'"The golden bough" and the study of religion' from *The Golden Bough, A Study in Magic and Religion*, 3rd. ed., Part I, *The magic art and the evolution of kings*, repr. Vol. I, London, Macmillan, 1951, pp. VII–XXVII. By permission of the Estate of Sir James Frazer.

FREUD, SIGMUND
'Religion as illusion' from *The Standard Edition of the Complete Psychological Works of Sigmund Freund*. Revised and edited by James Strachey. London, Sigmund Freud Copyrights Ltd., The Institute of Psycho-Analysis, and The Hogarth Press, 1953, Vol. 21, *The Future of an Illusion*, pp. 30–33. Also by permission of Liveright Publishing Corp., Copyright © 1955, New York.
'The question of a Weltanschauung' from *Ibid.*, Vol. 22, *New Introductory Lectures on Psycho-analysis*, pp. 158–160, 166–171, 174, 181–182. Also by permission of W. W. Norton, New York.
'The story of religion' from *Ibid.*, Vol. 23, *Moses and Monotheism*, pp. 130–137. Also by permission of Alfred A. Knopf, New York, publishers with Random House of a Vintage Books edition.

FRICK, HEINRICH
'The aim of the comparative study of religions (typology)' (new translation) from *Vergleichende Religionswissenschaft* [The Comparative Study of Religions]. Berlin–Leipzig, Walter de Gruyter (Sammlung Göschen), 1928, pp. 10–19.

FUSTEL DE COULANGES, NUMA D.
'The necessity of studying the earliest beliefs of the ancients in order to understand their institutions' from *The Ancient City: A Study on the Religion, Laws, and Institutions of Greece and Rome*. New York, Doubleday Anchor Book, pp. 11–14.

GENNEP, ARNOLD VAN
'On the method to be followed in the study of rites and myths' (new translation) from 'De la méthode à suivre dans l'étude des rites et des mythes', *Revue de l'Université Libre de Bruxelles*, Vol. 16 (1910), pp. 503–523.

HEILER, FRIEDRICH
'Prayer' from *Prayer: A Study in the History and Psychology of Religion*. Translated by Samuel McComb. © 1932 by Oxford University Press and © 1959 by Arthur K. McComb. New York, Oxford University Press, 1958, pp. III–IV, XIII–XVIII.
The par. 'The object of the study of religion' (new translation) from *Das Gebet. Eine religionsgeschichtliche und religionspsychologische Untersuchung*. Unveränderter Nachdruck der 5. Auflage mit Literaturergänzungen. München–Basel, Ernst Reinhardt Verlag, 1969, pp. 16–22.
'The scholarly study of religion' (new translation) from *Erscheinungsformen und Wesen der Religion* [The Manifestations and Essence of Religion]. Stuttgart, W. Kohlhammer, 1961, pp. 14–21.

JAMES, WILLIAM
'The study of religious experience' from *The Varieties of Religious Experience: A Study in Human Nature. The Gifford Lectures 1901–1902*. New York, New American Library, 1958, pp. IX, 22–25, 39–41, 52–57.

JUNG, CARL GUSTAV
'On psychology of religion' from *Psychology and Religion*. © 1938 by Yale University Press, New Haven (Conn.), pp. 1–8, 71–77.
'On myths and archetypes' from C. G. Jung and C. Kerényi, *Introduction to*

a Science of Mythology: The Myth of the Divine Child and the Mysteries of Eleusis. London, Routledge & Kegan Paul, 1951, pp. 97–106, 108–111, 217–219. Also by permission of Princeton University Press, Princeton (N. J.).

KRAEMER, HENDRIK
'On the presuppositions and limits of the science of religion' from *Religion and the Christian Faith.* London, Lutterworth Press, 1956, pp. 54–60, 78–83.

KRISTENSEN, WILLIAM BREDE
'On the study of religious phenomena' from *The Meaning of Religion.* With an Introduction by Hendrik Kraemer. The Hague, Martinus Nijhoff, 1960, and 1968, pp. 6–15.

LANG, ANDREW
'The making of religion' from *The Making of Religion.* London–New York–Bombay, Longmans, Green & Co., 1898, pp. 1–3, 43–71, 326–331.

LEEUW, GERARDUS VAN DER
'Some recent achievements of psychological research and their application to history, in particular the history of religion' (new translation) from 'Über einige neuere Ergebnisse der psychologischen Forschung und ihre Anwendung auf die Geschichte, insonderheit die Religionsgeschichte', *Studi e Materiali di Storia delle Religioni,* Vol. 2 (1926), pp. 1–12. By permission of the Istituto di Studi Storico-Religiosi, Rome.
'On phenomenology and its relation to theology' (new translation) from 'Strukturpsychologie und Theologie', *Zeitschrift für Theologie und Kirche,* N. F. IX (1928), pp. 322–324. By permission of Drs. J. R. van der Leeuws Amsterdam.
'On "understanding" ' (new translation) from *Inleiding tot de theologie* [Introduction to Theology]. Amsterdam, H. J. Paris, 1948², pp. 66–71.
'Religion in essence and manifestation' from *Religion in Essence and Manifestation: A Study in Phenomenology.* 2 Vols., New York, Harper Torchbooks, 1963, pp. 671–679, 683–689. Also by permission of George Allen & Unwin, London.
'Beauty and holiness' from *Sacred and Profane Beauty: The Holy in Art.* Preface by Mircea Eliade. Translated by David E. Green. New York, © Holt, Rinehart & Winston, 1963, pp. 3–7. Also Weidenfeld & Nicholson, London.

LÉVY-BRUHL, LUCIEN
' "Primitive mentality" and religion' from *How natives think.* Introduction by Dr. Ruth L. Bunzel. New York, Alfred A. Knopf, and Washington Square Press, 1966, pp. 49–54, 108–117, 330–335.

LOWIE, ROBERT H.
'On the term "Religion" ' from *Primitive Religion.* New York, © Liveright Publ. Corp., 1970, pp. IX–XVIII.

MALINOWSKI, BRONISŁAW
'The study of "Primitive man" and his religion' from *Magic, Science and Religion, and Other Essays.* Introduction by Robert Redfield. New York, Doubleday Anchor Book, 1954, pp. 17–26, 36–41, 86–90. By permission of the Society for Promoting Christian Knowledge, Holy Trinity Church, London.

MARETT, ROBERT R.
'The Tabu-Mana formula as a minimum definition of religion' from *Archiv für Religionswissenschaft*, Vol. 12 (1909), pp. 186–194. By permission of BSB B. G. Teubner Verlagsgesellschaft, Leipzig.

MAUSS, MARCEL
'Classification systems and religion' from Emile Durkheim and Marcel Mauss, *Primitive Classification*. Translated by Rodney Needham. Chicago, University of Chicago Press, 1963, pp. 76–88. Also by permission of Routledge & Kegan Paul.

MÜLLER, F. MAX
'Plea for a science of religion' from *Chips from a German Workshop*, Vol. I, *Essays on the Science of Religion*. London, Longmans, Green & Co., 1867, pp. XVIII–XXV, XXVII–XXVIII.
'The comparative study of religions' from *Introduction to the Science of Religion. Four Lectures delivered at the Royal Institution, with two Essays on False Analogies, and the Philosophy of Mythology*. London, Longmans, Green & Co., 1873, pp. 4–17, 24–35.

NILSSON, MARTIN P.
'On method and theory' from 'Letter to Professor Arthur D. Nock on some fundamental concepts in the science of religion', *Harvard Theological Review* (Cambridge, Mass.), Vol. 42 (1949), No. 2, pp. 106–107.
'On the advancements made in the study of Greek religion' from 'Second letter to Professor Nock on the positive gains in the science of Greek religion', *Harvard Theological Review* (Cambridge, Mass.), Vol. 44 (1951), No. 4, pp. 143–151.
'On religion' from 'Religion as man's protest agains the meaninglessness of events', *Kungl. Human Vetenskapssamfundets Lund Årsberättelse*, 1953–1954, pp. 25–29, 92.

OTTO, RUDOLF
'The idea of the holy' from *The Idea of the Holy: An Inquiry into the Non-rational Factor in the Idea of the Divine and its Relation to the Rational*. Translated by John W. Harvey. London–New York, Oxford University Press, 1964[4], pp. 1–7, 112–116, 136–145.
'Religious history' from *Religious Essays: A Supplement to The Idea of the Holy*. Translated by Brian Lunn. London, Oxford University Press, 1931, pp. 88–89, 95–109.

OTTO, WALTER F.
'On the study of Greek religion: "The Homeric Gods" 'from *The Homeric Gods: The Spiritual Significance of Greek Religion*. New York, Pantheon Books, 1954, pp. 3–12, 287. By permission of Verlag Gerhard Schulte-Bulmke, Frankfurt am Main.
'On the Greek Gods and on myth' (new translation) from *Theophania: Der Geist der altgriechischen Religion*. [Theophania: The Spirit of Ancient Greek Religion]. Hamburg. Rowohlt Taschenbuch Verlag (Rowohlts Deutsche Enzyklopädie 15) 1956, pp. 7–10, 19–27.

PETTAZZONI, RAFFAELE
' "History" and "phenomenology" in the science of religion' from *Essays on the History of Religion*. Leiden, E. J. Brill, 1954 and 1967, pp. 215–219.

RADCLIFFE-BROWN, ALFRED R.
'Religion and society' from *The Journal of the Royal Anthropological Institute of Great Britain and Ireland* (London), Vol. 75 (1945), pp. 33–43.

RADIN, PAUL
'The nature and substance of religion' from *Primitive Religion: Its Nature and Origin*. New York, Dover Publications, 1957, pp. 3–14.
'Primitive man as philosopher' from *Primitive Man as Philosopher*. With a foreword by John Dewey. New York–London, Appleton, 1927, pp. VII–XI, 1–7.
'The religious and the non-religious man' from *The World of Primitive Man*. New York, H. Schuman, 1953, pp. 68–73, 102–104. By permission of Murnat Publications, New York.

RENAN, ERNEST
'Vindication of a critical mind' from *Studies of Religious History*. London, William Heinemann, 1893, pp. XI–XVIII, XXV–XXVII, XXIX–XXXI.

ROBERTSON SMITH, WILLIAM
'The study of the religion of the Semites' from *Lectures on the Religion of the Semites. First Series: Fundamental Institutions*. New edition revised throughout by the author. London, Adam & Charles Black, 1894, pp. VI–VII, 1–5, 8, 15–17, 21–26.

SCHELER, MAX
'Psychology, "concrete" and "essential" phenomenology of religion' from *On the Eternal in Man*. Translated by Bernard Noble. London, © SCM Press 1960, pp. 18–19, 156–162. Also by permission of Harper & Row, New York.

SCHMIDT, WILHELM
'The origin and growth of religion' from *The Origin and Growth of Religion: Facts and Theories*. London, Methuen, 1931, pp. 1–3, 8–16.
'The quest of the Supreme Being' from *High Gods in North America. Upton Lectures in Religion, Manchester College, Oxford 1933*. Oxford, Clarendon Press, 1933, pp. 1–14.

SCHWEITZER, ALBERT
'The quest of the historical Jesus' from *The Quest of the Historical Jesus: A Critical Study of its Progress from Reimarus to Wrede*. London, Adam & Charles Black, 1926², pp. 1–12.

SÖDERBLOM, NATHAN
'The origin of the belief in God' (new translation) from *Das Werden des Gottesglaubens: Untersuchungen über die Anfänge der Religion* [The Origin of the Belief in God]. Leipzig, J. C. Hinrichs'sche Buchhandlung, 1926², pp. 340–345. By permission of Mr. Jon Olof Söderblom, Uppsala. (Checked with the Swedish original text).
'The living God' from *The Living God: Basal Forms of Personal Religion. The Gifford Lectures delivered in the University of Edinburgh in the Year 1931*. London, Oxford University Press and Humphrey Milford, 1933, pp. 1–2, 384–386. By permission of Mr. Jon Olof Söderblom, Uppsala.

SPENCER, HERBERT
'Ancestor-worship' from *The Principles of Sociology*. London–Edinburgh–Oxford, Williams & Norgate, Vol. I, 1876, from pp. 280–299.

TIELE, CORNELIS P.
'Elements of the science of religion' from *Elements of the Science of Religion. Gifford Lectures 1896 and 1898*. Edinburgh–London, William Blackwood & Sons, 1897, Vol. I: Part I, *Morphological*, pp. 4–6, 8–11, 15–19, 25; and 1899, Vol. II: Part II, *Ontological*, pp. 1–3, 22–24.

TYLOR, EDWARD B.
'Animism' from *Primitive Culture: Researches into the Development of Mythology, Philosophy, Religion, Language, Art, and Custom*. London, John Murray (Publishers), 1891, Vol. I, 3rd ed., revised, pp. 417–428, 499–501.

WACH, JOACHIM
'Religion and society' from *Sociology of Religion*. Chicago, University of Chicago Press (Phoenix Paperback), 1962⁹, pp. 12–17.
'On comparative studies in religion' from *The Comparative Study of Religions*. New York, Columbia University Press, 1958, pp. 6–15.
'Universals in religion' and 'The concept of the "classical" in the study of religions' from *Types of Religious Experience: Christian and Non-Christian*. London, Routledge & Kegan Paul, 1951, pp. 30–37, 48–53. By permission of The University of Chicago Press, Chicago.
'The meaning and task of the history of religions (Religionswissenschaft)' from Joseph M. Kitagawa (ed.) with the collaboration of Mircea Eliade and Charles H. Long, *The History of Religions. Essays on the Problem of Understanding*. Chicago, University of Chicago Press, 1967, pp. 1–15.

WEBER, MAX
'Symbolic meaning and religion' from *The Sociology of Religion*. © 1922 by J. C. B. Mohr (Paul Siebeck), Tübingen; English translation (from 4th ed.): Boston (Mass.), © Beacon Press, 1967³, pp. 1–9. Also by permission of Methuen, London.

WELLHAUSEN, JULIUS
'Historical research on the Pentateuch' from *Prolegomena to the History of Ancient Israel*. Edinburgh, Adam & Charles Black, 1885, pp. 1–13.

Indexes

Introductory Note

Since the present book can be considered to be a source-book on methodology with reference to persons and to subjects of research, three specific indexes have been devised instead of one general index. They contain, respectively, personal names, scholarly concepts and concrete subjects, and they refer to the introduction (pp. 1–78) as well as to the texts of the anthology (pp. 85–666).

The *Index of Personal Names* contains all names of scholars and other persons which figure in this book, with the exception of the names of Buddha and Jesus which are to be found in the Index of Concrete Subjects, and, in the case of the latter, also in the Index of Scholarly Concepts. The names printed in italics *(Adriani)* are those of scholars treated in the introduction; those printed in small capitals (Bachofen) are names of scholars represented in the texts of the anthology. In the case of the latter, the following bold figure **(117)** refers to the page with the bio-bibliographical introduction of the scholar in question, while the figures in italics *(117–125)* refer to his text which has been reproduced in the anthology.

The *Index of Scholarly Concepts* contains those terms which may be considered to be part of the methodological and theoretical terminology which is used in the study of concrete materials. Unless such concepts occur in the introduction, they are given with the immediate context in which the concept is used; in such cases the name of the scholar using the concept in the given sense is added.

There are two possibilities then. In those cases in which the concept is of such a general nature or interest that different scholars have given different interpretations of it, the names of these scholars precede the references in alphabetical order. In this way it is easy to find what the different scholars have written here about a general item like 'religion'. In other cases, where a concept appears to be important because of its specific quality or meaning and where only one or two scholars have used this particular concept, the reference precedes the name of the scholar which is then added between brackets.

The references to the different uses which one scholar makes of a particular concept follow each other not in alphabetical order but in the order of the relevant page numbers, so as to suggest the broad line of reasoning. A number of cross-references and duplications have been used to guarantee the coherence of this index. Page numbers which are printed in italics *(85–95)* indicate that these pages as such deal with the concept or item in question, e.g. that it is the subject of the text which was reproduced.

The *Index of Concrete Subjects* contains the terms which refer to the subject matter itself and distinguishes itself thereby from the Index of Scholarly Concepts, which indicates the intellectual tools of that study. All items in question, including the names of Buddha and Jesus, have been subject of investigation or reference in the pages indicated. In exceptional cases, like in that of the item 'religion' or 'Jesus', one item may occur both in the Index of Concrete Subjects and in that of Scholarly Concepts. Proper names of places, like 'el-Amarna', are to be found in this index.

By distinguishing these three indexes, an attempt has been made to assist the reader who may be consulting the index from different angles of interest. He may be anxious to know if the name of a particular person occurs in this book, whether and how a specific scholarly concept has been used, or whether a particular subject of scholarly research can be located in this book. To those using the book as a source book on methodology, the Index of Scholarly Concepts will provide the necessary keys for further location, analysis and investigation.

Index of Personal Names*

* For an explanation of the organization of this Index, see pp. 675-676.

Index of Scholarly Concepts*

Absolute
    numinous background of the 'wholly other' is antecedent and fundamental to the idea of the — 447–448 (R. OTTO)
Absolutist pretensions
    historical research and comparative studies indirectly used against — of one religion 52
Analogous and homologous 649 (KRAEMER)
Analogy
    distinct from homology 484–486 (FRICK); expression and understanding by means of — from what is known and ¦familiar 501–502, 522 n. 53 (WACH); significance in 'mythological thinking' 359 (WEBER)
Anamnesis 446 (R. OTTO)
Ancestral cult
    disintegration of the social structure and decay of the — proceed together 595 (RADCLIFFE-BROWN)
Ancestor-worship
    RADCLIFFE-BROWN: — and moral code 600
    SCHMIDT: theory of — 269
    SPENCER: rise of — as origin of religion 29, *199–208*
Ancients
    the earliest beliefs of the — to be studied in order to understand their institutions and laws *134–137* (FUSTEL DE COULANGES)
Animatism
    — as Herbert Spencer's theory 260, 263 (MARETT); — as used by Söderblom 383
Animism
    application of hypothesis of — in anthropological research 32
    DURKHEIM: theories of — and naturism submitted to criticism and refuted 317–318
    VAN GENNEP: 304
    LANG: refutation of — 32–33, 226–239; — as theory about the earliest faith 227–228; — as theory on the origin of religion criticized by experimental psychology 235–238; — and ghost theory 242 n. 7
    MALINOWSKI: 546–547
    MARETT: Tabu-mana formula and theory of — as ultimate categories for rudimentary religion *260–263:* — and the problem of a more impersonal conception of the supernatural 263
    RADCLIFFE-BROWN: — and the ethical element 600

* For an explanation of the organization of this Index, see pp. 675–676.

OTTO, W. F.: myths not understood by theory of — 631
Areas of civilization, *see under;* culture cycles
Art and religion
    FRAZER: 550
    VAN DER LEEUW: 57, *425–428*; art as holy act 427–428
    RENAN: 127, 129
Atheism
    unjust attribution of — by theologians 30, 211 (TYLOR)
Atheistic
    argument and religious sentiment 651 (KRAEMER)
Attitude(s)
    FREUD: psychological knowledge leads to a change in one's — to the
        problem of religion 364
    SCHMIDT: successive — in the history of religion 272–273
Awareness and experience
    — opposed to belief and ideas 445 (R. OTTO)
Awe
    FRICK: notion of — as essential psychological moment of all religious
        attitudes 482
    MARETT: feeling of — 37–38
    OTTO, R.: arising from fear 572 (ref. RADIN)

Beautiful
    relation between the — and the holy 58, *425–428* (VAN DER LEEUW)
Being
    enigma of — 627 (W. F. OTTO)
Belief(s)
    CHANTEPIE DE LA SAUSSAYE: close relationship between — and worship
        and between these and their objects 113
    DURKHEIM: — and rites two fundamental categories of religious phenomena
        311, 314
    FREUD: believing and disbelieving in religious assertions 363
    JUNG: — and ritual 530
    KRISTENSEN: — of the believers as subject and norm of scholarly research
        55, 396
    LANG: — of primitives in vision, hallucinations, 'clairvoyance' and the
        acquisition of knowledge to be compared with records of similar
        experiences among living civilized men 222, 225–226
    LÉVY-BRUHL: experience does not necessarily change — 335–339
    RADCLIFFE-BROWN: emphasis on — in doctrines of some modern religions
        to be seen as the result of certain social developments in complex
        societies 604
    RADIN: — and customs are in themselves not necessarily religious 568
    ROBERTSON SMITH: primacy of ritual over — 21
    SÖDERBLOM: origin and types of the — in God *382–386*
    TYLOR: — of the heathen hated and despised by the religious ¡world
        211
Bible
    higher criticism of the — and theory of revelation-value 138–139 (JAMES);
        studies 20–27, *138–185*
    See also under; New Testament, Old Testament

Biology
  bio-anthropological perspective on the religious venture of mankind 52;
    science of religion owes its existence to — 288–289 (VAN GENNEP)

Calvinism and early capitalism 49
Categories
  formal — needed for a classification of religious phenomena 62; concern
    with — as classificatory terms 37, *258–263* (MARETT)
Categorization
  role of — in established frameworks for the interpretation of facts 295
    (VAN GENNEP)
Change
  — in man thanks to a movement of intelligence 135 (FUSTEL DE COULAN-
    GES); — also among 'primitives' 561 (LOWIE)
Charisma
  two types of — as concept for extraordinary powers 49, 353–354 (WEBER)
Child-motif
  as an archetype 540–542 (JUNG)
Christianity
  study of Christian religion separated from that of non-Christian reli-
    gions 31
  FREUD: psychological development of — as founded by Paul 375–376
  KRAEMER: — as a form of religion like the others 651–652
  OTTO, R.: superiority of — 433, 445
  OTTO, W. F.: — as a handicap for understanding other religions 621, 630
Chthonian religion and mystery 121–122 (BACHOFEN)
Classical
  the — as a category and principle of classification in the study of religions
    64, *504–508;* definition of the — 507 (WACH); — scholars and theo-
    logians are parting company 613–614 (NILSSON)
Classification
  — of religious data and phenomena 52, 62
  DURKHEIM: — of religions is not possible 303
  FRICK: — of religions 481–482
  VAN GENNEP: — of religious facts 43, 288
  LÉVY-BRUHL: mystical participation as basis of — systems 47, 339–341
  MARETT: concern with categories as classificatory terms 37, *258–263*
  MAUSS/DURKHEIM: divisions of society as basis of divisions for — systems
    46, 329; relation between — and divination, — and myth, — and
    the evolution of religious thought 325–327; — systems and religion
    325–333; the same essential characteristics can be found in primitive
    and scientific — s 328; philosophical — s 327–328; technological — s 333
  TIELE: scientific — of religions 98
  WACH: — according to a structural order of the elements of historical
    religion 505; — of religious materials according to different views
    and — according to the 'classical' 64, 504–508
Coercive systems
  law, morality and religion as — 601–602 (RADCLIFFE-BROWN)
Cognitive
  — act renders meaning to the object 411; three spheres in the — methods to
    be distinguished 412; hierarchy of — processes 412 (VAN DER LEEUW)

Comparative research 23
  KRISTENSEN: necessary but not ideal 390; — leads to generaliza-
    tions which play as fictitious realities a role in directing re-
    search and in understanding 391–392; evolutionary type of — 394–
    395
Comparative study of language
  CHANTEPIE DE LA SAUSSAYE: 107
  MÜLLER: — compared with the comparative study of religion 91–92
Comparative study of religions 52, 63–64
  CHANTEPIE DE LA SAUSSAYE: — leads to a better understanding of Chris-
    tianity 109
  FREUD: influence of the — on religious belief 366
  FRICK: *480–486*
  LOWIE: — compared with comparative linguistics 566
  MÜLLER: 86–87, *88–95;* place of Christianity in — 86; — and the Christian
    faith 86–87; — and the religious problems of mankind 87; — and
    one's own religion 88–89, 90–91; — compared with the comparative
    study of languages 91–92; — important for missionaries 87; utility
    of — to be recognized by theologians 91; — changes views commonly
    held about religions 93; — demands knowledge of the most primitive
    form of every religion 94
  WACH: history of — 492; method of — 497–498; nature and task of —
    63–64, *491–498;* results and potentialities of the — 494; — to be
    based on critical historical and philological studies 491
  See also under: Comparative history of religions, Comparative reli-
    gion
Comparison
  FRICK: technique of — has to be developed into an exact method for the
    — of religions 62, 485
  KRAEMER: problem of a criterion for the comparison of content and truth-
    value 647
  MÜLLER: — as basis for all higher knowledge 91; gains of — for the study
    of language and of religion 91–93
  OTTO, R.: — of content and value of religions 458–459
  ROBERTSON SMITH: — of religion of the Hebrews with those of other
    Semitic people 151
  WACH: — and comparative approach 511–512
  WEBER: — as a form of analogy 359
Conceptualization and definition 37
Confession
  every — originally based upon the experience of the *numinosum* and
    upon '*pistis*' 530 (JUNG)
Consciousness
  collective — 631 (W. F. OTTO); reflective — 569 (RADIN); rootless — 539;
    roots of — 541 (JUNG)
Consensus gentium 529–530 (JUNG)
Creeds 531 (JUNG)
Criticism
  RENAN: conflict between religions and — 128; critical scholar of religion
    in conflict with habitual doctrines 128; principles of — to be applied
    to Jewish and Christian religion 130

CHANTEPIE DE LA SAUSSAYE: — of outward forms of religion from inward processes 109–110

KRAEMER: — and understanding 644; naturalistic-pyschological and sociological — of religion 645–647; transcendental-philosophical — of religion 646–647

VAN DER LEEUW: — and understanding in the study of religion 53–54, 404

OTTO, R.: — in the domain of spirit only out of spirit 439–440

Expression(s)

MAUSS: indissoluble link underneath all — of a society 45

WACH: adequate interpretation of objective — is dependent on insight into inner experience 490; individual experience and forms of traditional — in religion 491; motives and modes of — 503–504; universals in the forms of — of religious experience 503–504

Facts

study of reality in terms of objective — 29

DURKHEIM: refutation of the idea that — have an interest only in proportion to their generality 319; value of — is more important than their number 320

FRAZER: function of hypotheses with regard to — 248, 256

JUNG: — opposed to judgment 65, 529

Faith

FREUD: — in reason 51

KRISTENSEN: absolute character of all — 390–391

LANG: connection of — in God and — in the immortality of the soul with the problem of the origin of religion 226–232

VAN DER LEEUW: — and epochè 420; relation between — of comprehension and — of religion 421

MÜLLER: faculty of — 93

SCHELER: act of — 657; difference between empathetic and genuine — 657

WACH: personal — is not necessarily a disadvantage for understanding 519

Fantasies

of a personal and of an impersonal character as products of unconscious imagination 537 (JUNG)

Fear

— giving rise to religion 569–572; social precipitates of — 68–69, 569 (RADIN)

Fetish-worship or festishism 8, 269

Fieldwork

methodical — 38–39; methodology of — 66

Folklore 12–13

DURKHEIM: importance of — as survivals 310–311, 315

FRAZER: — as evidence 34; use of — in comparative religion 245–246

VAN GENNEP: study of — 42–43, 294–295, 300; in the study of — there is a possibility to investigate the rise of legends 294–295

Folk psychology 40, 490, 505 (WACH)

See also under: Ethno-psychology, Psychology of nations

Free will and causality 616–618 (NILSSON)

Function

understanding of the living — of a mythological picture 542 (JUNG)

Functional
approach 49, 70; — interpretation of religion 66
Fundus animae 438 (R. OTTO)

Generalization(s)
VAN GENNEP: — actual process of work leads to scholarly — 292–293
KRISTENSEN: — as fictitious realities which play a role in directing research and in understanding 391–392
Ghost(s)
LANG: — theory and animism 242 n.7
SCHMIDT: — theory 269
SPENCER: — the first traceable conception of a supernatural being 199, 208; propitiation of the — 199–200
TYLOR: problem of objective reality of — or apparitional souls 217
God(s)
discovery of a new type of — 42
FREUD: emergence of the idea of a single great — and its compulsive character 371–372; murder of — 375–376; rise of the idea of — from totem animal 373–374
HEILER: search of — by mankind and search of mankind by — 461
JUNG: identity of — and man 65
KRAEMER: — consciousness of man 647
KRISTENSEN: understanding of the essence of — makes the alien element disappear 392
LANG: conception of — need not to be evolved out of reflections on dreams and 'ghosts' 221
VAN DER LEEUW: horizontal and vertical line to — 424; — for phenomenology neither subject nor object, nor phenomenon 424
MALINOWSKI: primitive idea of one — 550
OTTO, R.: the rational and the non-rational in the idea of — 59, 432–435, 443; rational attributes of — 433–434; *a priori* knowledge of the interdependence of the rational and the non-rational elements in the idea of — 443
SCHELER: different sources of knowledge of — 662
SÖDERBLOM: origin and types of the belief in — *382–386;* rise of experiences and thoughts of — 385; *The living* — *386–389,* 474 (ref. HEILER)
WEBER: rise and development of — and demons 355–356
See also under: High Gods
Goddess
great — or mother — 42
Group
identity of the — expresses itself religiously 45 (DURKHEIM)
Guilt
sense of — leading to religions of Judaism and Christianity and integrated into the religious system 51, 374–376 (FREUD)

Habitus in religion 62, 483, 486 (FRICK)
Henotheism 327
Hermeneutic(al)
theories 53

VAN DER LEEUW: — circle 57, 430
WACH: — circularity 512; — exegesis 512-513
Hermeneutics
VAN DER LEEUW: 417-418, 422, 430 n.45; science as — 417; philological
    and phenomenological — 418
WACH: 63, 517-518, 521 n.37
Hierography, hierology, hierosophy 15 (GOBLET D'ALVIELLA)
High Gods
    LANG: accounts of — and creative beings believed in by the most backward
        races 221, 645-646
    NILSSON: theory of — 607
    SCHMIDT: theory of the existence of true — or Supreme Beings among
        primitive peoples and of — as the oldest element of religion 41, 271-272;
        historical survey of study of — 274-276; investigators of Supreme
        Beings and — *274-286;* research on — and Supreme Beings in North
        America 281-283
    SÖDERBLOM: theory of belief in — 54, 382-383
Higher criticism in the study of the Bible 188-189
Historian of religions
    KRISTENSEN: aim of — and phenomenologist of religion 56, 391; — and
        phenomenologist of religion must be able to surrender themselves
        to others 396
    WACH: — is concerned with what is characteristic, individual, historical
        and typical 506
    See also under: Scholar of religion
Historical analysis the only means of explanation of recent religions 303
    (DURKHEIM)
Historical and comparative study of religion relatively autonomous 72
    (KRAEMER)
Historical borrowing
    hypothesis of — opposed to other explanatory hypotheses 23
Historical consideration of religion
    transition from a religious to a — 19
Historical—critical school 20
Historical development
    no — of religions recognized 56
Historical research
    KRISTENSEN: limited validity of — 390; mutual relation and fruition of
        — and phenomenological research 56, 392-393
    VAN DER LEEUW: — implies application of an ideal typology 406
    SCHMIDT: possibility of — among primitive peoples by some scholars
        denied 278
    WELLHAUSEN: — on the Pentateuch *139-149;* history of this research 141-149
Historical study of religion and theology 48
Historicism 48, 56, 505
Historicity and the concept of history 25
History
    CHANTEPIE DE LA SAUSSAYE: — of civilization essential to the science
        of religion 106-107
    VAN DER LEEUW: difference study of — and psychology is methodologically
        small 400

MÜLLER: — of Christianity treated in a historical spirit 86; profane and sacred — 89

PETTAZZONI: idea of — and — of religion in particular 641–642; — and phenomenology in the science of religion *639–642*

RENAN: difference of opinion upon the — of a religion between the partisans of that religion and disinterested science 130–131

SCHMIDT: idea of — 41, 266–267; pragmatic — as an inward understanding of the outward course of events 266

History of religion(s) 54–64, 70–72

establishment of the — as an autonomous discipline 13–17

CHANTEPIE DE LA SAUSSAYE: ethnographical and historical division of — 108; — not excluding Judaism and Christianity 108–109

FREUD: — as history of a collective neurosis 50, 367, 372–377

HEILER: object of — is always an individual structure 465–466

LANG: conclusions of the — is not beyond doubt and its whole theory is to be reconsidered 220–221

MARETT: 262–263; — eventually to be dealt with genetically 262

MÜLLER: 93

NILSSON: — must be rewritten in every generation 615

PETTAZZONI: 640

RENAN: view of — 127

ROBERTSON SMITH, W.: peculiar interest of the Semites for the student of the — 152

SCHMIDT: definition of — 265–267; history of research in the — 41, 267–273; nineteenth century not favorable to — 265; — as a real science 268

SÖDERBLOM: — for Christian theology as the field of Divine Self-communication 55, 387–388; — as a proof that God lives (ref. HEILER) 474

WACH: field of — is ever broadening 504–505; reactions on the — 508; the meaning and task of the — *509–519;* — and cultural history 510

History of religion and philosophy of religion

KRISTENSEN: — equally autonomous in their own territories 395

TIELE: 100

History of religion and theology 26

Holiness

OTTO, W. F.: quality of — as a creative quality 633–634

SÖDERBLOM: quality of — 54, 646

Holy

KRAEMER: category of the — 649

VAN DER LEEUW: the — as the 'wholly other' 426; the — and religious consciousness 426; relations, paths and boundaries between the — and the beautiful as experienced by man 58, *425–428*

LOWIE: the — 565–566

OTTO, R.: the — a complex category combining rational and non-rational components as *a priori* elements 437, 441; the — as a purely *a priori* category 59, 437–445; the — as an autonomous category of meaning and value 59–60, 435; the — contains a specific 'moment' not to be apprehended in terms of concepts 435; genuine as opposed to false recognitions of the — 446; the idea of the 54, 59–60, *432–447;* overplus of meaning above moral significance in the — 436–437; rational elements of the category of the — are contained in the 'pure reason', and non-rational elements of the — are contained in the *fundus*

Intentional description of religious life 73, 665 (BERGER)
International cooperation of scholars
    WACH: 492
Interpretation
    —, explanation and understanding in the study of religion 77; no absolute
    validity to be given to one system of —, principle or method 399
    (VAN DER LEEUW)
Inventions, possibility or impossibility of repeated — 40
Introspection
    — needed for religious psychological understanding, all psychology includ-
    ing psychology of religion is based on — 61, 470–471 (HEILER)
Intuition
    FREUD: — an illusion 365
    KRISTENSEN: 393–394
    VAN DER LEEUW: 405

Jesus of Nazareth
    problem of historicity 25; consequence of the doctrine of Christ for the
    interest in the historical — 176–177; contradiction between Messianic self-
    consciousness and the conduct of — as a problem of historical research
    180–182, 184; difference between the historic — and the — Christ of the
    doctrine of the two Natures 177; difficulties in the sources for the study of
    the historical life of — 179–181; historical research on the person of —
    174–185; and the history of this research 174–179, 182–185; long indiffer-
    ence of Christianity towards the life of the historical — 176–177; metho-
    dological difficulties in the study of the historical person of — 25, 179–184;
    rise of historical interest in the historical person of — 25, 177; study of
    the — of history emerged as an ally in the struggle against the tyranny
    of dogma 177–179; theology and the critical study of the life of — 176–179
    (SCHWEITZER)
    See also: INDEX OF CONCRETE SUBJECTS, *under:* Jesus
Judaism
    psychological development of — 373–375 (FREUD); study of — *see under:*
    Wissenschaft des Judentums
Judgment
    BERGER: — in the study of religion 664
    JAMES: distinction between existential — and value — 27, 188

Knowledge
    FREUD: — is separate from illusions and from outcomes of emotional
        demands 365
    LANG: supernatural acquisition of — in trance 33
    SPENCER: — as a factor in the proces of evolution 29
    WACH: — is one 497

Laicization, progressive — 570 (RADIN)
Language
    study of — and its relation to religion and mythology 13–14
    LÉVY-BRUHL: disease of — 347
    MÜLLER: disease of — substitutes *numina* for *nomina* 13
Layers of culture, *see under:* Cultural layers

Laws
   general — in the history of religion and in religions of primitive peoples
   to be based on induction 609–610 (Nilsson)
Liberalism
   positive results of the age of — in terms of scholarship and knowledge
   492 (Wach)
Liberation
   emergence of search for — in religion 454–455 (R. Otto)
Life
   — experience of religion 19
   Lang: early man conceiving of — 230–231
   van der Leeuw: approach to — as an aporia — 413; man's situation
   in — 419
   Malinowski: rites and beliefs in connection with — -crises 553–556
   Radin: social function of religion is that of emphasizing and maintaining
   the — of man 569–570, 573, 583
Linguistics 39
Literature
   role of written — in changing thought 245 (Frazer)
Living tradition
   as source on early religion 245–246 (Frazer)
Locus de Religione 109
Logical categories
   the first — were social categories, the first logical relations were domestic
   relations 329–330 (Mauss/Durkheim)
Logical hierarchy
   — is another aspect of social hierarchy 329 (Mauss/Durkheim)
Logical operations
   sociology throws light on the genesis and functioning of — 332 (Mauss/
   Durkheim)

Magic
   — as one of the sources of religion 36
   Frazer: — as a primitive science and as the result of a wrong use of
   reason 35; principle of — 254
   Malinowski: — as a pseudo-science 556–557; function of — 556–559
   Schmidt: — as fore-runner of religion 270
   Weber: — and magical art 353–357; development of — from a direct
   manipulation of forces into a symbolic activity 356–358
Magic and religion
   scholarly discussion of the relation between — 36
   Beth: 38
   Frazer: 34–36, 249, 547, 645
   Malinowski: 67, 557–559, 547–548, 551
   Marett: 38, 260–261
   Radcliffe-Brown: 602–603
   Radin: 69
   Wach: 503
Magic and science
   Frazer: 35, 547
   Malinowski: 556–557

Magic and subjectivism
    RADIN: 570–571
Magical or religious behaviour
    — is relatively rational 353; — not to be set apart from everyday purposive
    conduct 353 (WEBER)
Magico-religious
    concept of — criticized 260 (MARETT)
Man
    as product, epitome of all earlier epochs 137 (FUSTEL DE COULANGES)
Mana
    MALINOWSKI: 547–548
    MARETT: 36–38, 259, 260–261; — and tabu as the positive and negative
        modes of the Supernatural 258–260
    RADIN: 575–576
    SÖDERBLOM: 383, 384–385
    WACH: 503, 506
    WEBER: 353
Manism 29, 269
    See also under: Ancestor-cult, Ancestor-worship
Marxian doctrine 63, 488
Materialism 63, 488
Materialistic system
    protest against — 33, 221 (SCHMIDT)
Matriarchy
    and religion *119–124* (BACHOFEN)
Meaning
    problem of religious — 9–10; layers of — 52; — beyond the opposition
        of subject and object 53; problem of religion as a problem of — 71;
        problem of the — of religious phenomena is central in a phenomeno-
        logical study of religion 82
    BERGER: — based on a conscious intention 665; — not to be confused
        with truth 665
    FRICK: equivalence of — as a morphological equivalence 485
    VAN GENNEP: the — of a rite or myth is only clear if seen as part of a
        ceremony 299
    JUNG: archetype has an unconscious core of — 66, 538–539; religious
        experience means everything to those who have it 534
    VAN DER LEEUW: psychological technique of re-experiencing religious —
        57; experience of understanding as experience of a unity of — 405;
        — and structure like a net cast by the observer over reality 411–412;
        — is situated between subject and object 411, 414; — as entrance
        gate to the reality of primal experience 414; man's search for — in
        life 419
    NILSSON: — in a subjective as opposed to an objective sense 616,
        618
    OTTO, W. F.: — manifesting itself 72
    TYLOR: scholarly search for — as reasonable thought in strange doctrines
        and observances 212
    WEBER: symbolic — and religion *353–359*
Meaninglessness
    two kinds of — 616, 618 (NILSSON)

Mediators 24,42
Mentality
    prelogical — 574 (RADIN)
Method(s)
    — of active imagination 540 (JUNG); — of approach not dealing with the origins but with the social function of religion 589–590 (RADCLIFFE-BROWN); — of the fact coming-into-being 43, 293–296 (VAN GENNEP); — of study of religion should be unified and adequate for the subject matter 64, 497–498 (WACH); adequacy of — demands recognition of individuality, value and freedom 497–498 (WACH); *a priori* — rejected 158 (ROBERTSON SMITH); deductive — based on the results of the inductive, empirical, historical and comparative methods 101 (TIELE); depth psychological — does not do justice to the meaning of myths 630–632 (W. F. OTTO); dilemma of a 'scientific' and a — *sui generis* 497–498 (WACH); empirical — culminating in positivism 101 (TIELE); ethnographical — 43, 289–293 (VAN GENNEP); ethnological — or — of the natural environment 43, 296–297 (VAN GENNEP); evolutionistic — 271, 275 (SCHMIDT); experimental — of social anthropology implies study of religions and cults in their relation to their societies 590 (RADCLIFFE-BROWN); genetic-speculative — 101 (TIELE); historical — 43, 289 (VAN GENNEP); historical — against evolutionism 271, 276–279, application of the historical — on the origin of sacrifice 279–281, results of the historical — 283–284 (SCHMIDT); historical — yielding exclusively historical results 100–101 (TIELE); philosophical — is deductive by discerning how the phenomena develop from the essence 395 (KRISTENSEN); psychoanalytic — disclosing the dimension of the soul 51; plurality of scientific — 411; questionnaire — 471 (HEILER); sequential — studies a fact in relation to what precedes and what follows it 43, 297–300 (VAN GENNEP); sociological — different from the anthropological method (of Tylor) 319–322 (DURKHEIM); speculative — 101 (TIELE); successive — of the history of religion 271–272 (SCHMIDT); three — (procedures) to study rites and myths *287–300* (VAN GENNEP); typological — 54 (SÖDERBLOM)
Methodology
    — in the study of religion V–VI; methodological questions arise 4–5; — of fieldwork 38–39, 66
    VAN DER LEEUW: — for the understanding of religious phenomena 57, 412, 427
    OTTO, R.: — to analyze religious experiences 59
    WACH: methodological and epistemological problems to be raised and answered 493
Migrations
    early — and their dating 40–42, 279 (SCHMIDT); hypotheses of — 535, 537 (JUNG)
Mind
    moralistic and religious state of — 193–194 (JAMES)
Modes
    — of perceiving and thinking, rational and magical 623–624 (W. F. OTTO); — of thought, logical and pre-logical 48, 339–345 (LÉVY-BRUHL)
Monotheism 388
    — in the Bible 384 (SÖDERBLOM); Primeval —,
    see under: Primeval

Morality
  MALINOWSKI: place of — in religion 67, 550
  RADCLIFFE-BROWN: comparative studies on the relations between — and
    religion 599–600
  See also under: Ethical
Morphological
  — equivalence as equivalence of meaning 485; — structure 486
  (FRICK)
Morphology
  — of the religious consciousness 649–650 (KRAEMER)
Motifs
  as repetitions 542 (JUNG)
Mysterious
  BACHOFEN: sense of the — cultivated by woman 121
  OTTO, R.: the — 444–445
  WACH: quality of — 503
Mystery
  BACHOFEN: element of — is the true essence of all religion 17–18, 121;
    — religion, chthonian religion and matriarchy *121–124*
  DURKHEIM: sentiment of — important in Christianity but not in all
    religions 310
  KRISTENSEN: — religion and its significance 10, 55, 391
  LOWIE: supernaturalism as sense of — as the differentia of religion 565–566
Mystic
  reality and communion with it 47, 335–336, 339, 347–348 (LÉVY-BRUHL)
Mysticism
  — as God-mysticism and as Saviour-mysticism 455–457 (R. OTTO)
Myth(s)
  — and ritual 23, 67; nature of — 24; parallel motifs in — 65
  BACHOFEN: — and symbol: the former as exegesis of the latter 17, *117–119*
  VAN GENNEP: — and rites: methods to study *287–300*
  JUNG: — and archetypes have a relationship *535–543;* — formation as
    a function in psychic life 66, 535–536; reference of a — 538; — to
    be dreamt onwards 540
  LÉVY-BRUHL: 346–350; — appeals through the mystic element which
    surrounds the positive content of the story and is expression of group
    solidarity 47, 347–348; 'explanatory' hypotheses of the genesis of —
    to be distrusted 349; — in their relation to the mentality of the group
    where they originate 346; increasing complexity of — makes their
    interpretation more difficult 349–350; transformation of — and the
    problem of their dating 350; — as substitutes for a real participation
    47, 346
  OTTO, W. F.: *628–636,* — based on spiritual vision 631; in any original
    — a god reveals himself 632; — and cult have a connection 634–636;
    depth psychological method does not do justice to the meaning of
    — 630–632
  SCHMIDT: interpretation of nature — 268–269
Mythical concepts and statements
  and dreamlike visions are different 631–633 (W. F. OTTO)
Mythologems
  recurr independently 536 (JUNG)

tivity 418; sole desire of — is to testify to what has been manifested 418-419

NILSSON: — as classification, looking for connections in a universal quality of thought 607

SCHELER: concrete — of religious objects and acts as a basic discipline for the positive study of religion 657-658

Phenomenology of the expression of religious experience
  need for a — 490 (WACH)

Phenomenology of religion
  classical — 52-64, 82, *379-524*

CHANTEPIE DE LA SAUSSAYE: — as a discipline of classification of the most important ethnographic and historical material connected with the phenomena of religion, and discussing the meaning of the most important classes of religious phenomena 16, 110; — intermediary between history and philosophy of religion 16, 105; — closely connected with psychology studying facts of human consciousness 16, 109-110; — as a special branch of the study of religion 105, *109-113*; richest material for the — in religious acts, cult and custom 111; — begins with considering the objects of belief and worship 112

HEILER: tension between *deus ipse* or absconditus and *deus revelatus* as focus of — 61, 477; — along theological lines 61, 477-478; — intends to penetrate to the essence of religion 473-475; — based on the *analogia entis* 61, 477-478

KRISTENSEN: — as descriptive comparative religion 56; principal ideas of — are borrowed from philosophy of religion 392; task of — is to give the illustration of man's religious disposition 392; way of working of — is the grouping of characteristic data 392; search of the essence of religion requires knowledge of material provided by — 393; place of — is between history and philosophy as systematic history of religion and applied philosophy or religion 393; — works with presumptions and anticipations 393; — makes use of comparative methods 394

VAN DER LEEUW: — intermediary between history and theology 16; — leading to anthropology and to theology 57; Van der Leeuw's — as experiential liturgy 58; delimitation of — 58, *422-425;* — studies religion in essence and manifestation *412-425;* possibility of a — 419-421; — has to free itself constantly from every non-phenomenological standpoint 424; other names of — 430 n.49

PETTAZZONI: rise of — 640-641, — is a science *sui generis* with a quest for meaning and universality 641

SCHELER: concrete reconstructive descriptive — is not productive and is relativistic 661; essential — 658-662; difference between concrete and essential — 73, 657-662; essential — envisages the 'essence' of the act or object 657; essential — is the ultimate philosophical foundation of all study of religion 658; three ends of the essential — 659; limit of the essential — 659; essential — is able to make true judgments based on metaphysics or revelation 661

TIELE: — as the first stage of the philosophical science of religion 15, 102
See also under: Typology of religion

Phenomenology of religion and history of religions
  VAN DER LEEUW: 422-423

Psychologist
    — assumes scientific attitude 531; — is concerned with the original religious
    experience apart from what the creeds have made of it 531 (JUNG)
Psychology
    27–28; — as an instrument of understanding 56–58; analytical — 65;
    depth —, *see under:* Depth psychology; medical — 528 (JUNG); practical
    — and religion 529 (JUNG)
    CHANTEPIE DE LA SAUSSAYE: phenomenology of religion closely connected
        with — studying facts of human consciousness 16, 109–110
    JAMES: *187–197*
    JUNG: — works with empirical facts and has little to do with philosophy
        529, change of the proper subject of — in last century 535
    VAN DER LEEUW: objectivism and subjective school in — are complementary
        to each other 399–401; indispensability of subjectivity in — 400–401;
        — concerned both with actual and with historical experiences 431
        n.83
    SCHELER: conditions and premisses of any explanatory — 655; noetic
        origin of explanatory — 655–656
Psychology and history
    VAN DER LEEUW: difference study of — is methodologically small
        400
Psychology and science of religion
    VAN DER LEEUW: parallel developments in — 57, 399
Psychology and sociology
    BERGER: do not give insight in the facts of religion 664
Psychology of nations
    CHANTEPIE DE LA SAUSSAYE: 106
    JUNG: 535
    WACH: 505
    See also under: Folk psychology, Ethno-psychology
Psychology of religion 27–28, 56–57
    HEILER: task and methods of — 469–471
    JAMES: *187–197*
    JUNG: 65–66, *528–535*
    VAN DER LEEUW: — and phenomenology of religion 423
    OTTO, R.: task of — is to explain the phenomena of religion 439–440
    SCHELER: — and phenomenology of religion 73, *654–662;* positivism in
        — sees religion as a collection of psychic phenomena 654–655; rise
        of modern — 654–657
    SCHMIDT: 266–267, protestant students of the — assume that a mixture
        of religion and magic has been the first stage in man's religious
        development 270
    See also under: Religious psychology
Pure and impure, concepts of — 259 (MARETT)

Quality of religious life
    peculiar — to be grasped in prayer 463 (HEILER)
Quaternity
    interpretation of — as an archetypal image of the deity 532 (JUNG)
Questions
    nature of the — to be put to religious data 53

Rational elements in religion
connection or union between the — and the non-rational elements is
a priori 59, 441–444 (R. OTTO)
Rationalism
contrast between — and profounder religion 434 (R. OTTO)
Rationalistic approaches to religion 53
Rationality and superstition
opposition between — 34 (FRAZER)
Rationalization
increasing — in the course of history, as a process of abstraction also in
religious representations 50, 354–356 (WEBER)
Reason
faith in — 51
FREUD: unifying power of — 370
MALINOWSKI: — of primitive man 552
SCHELER: religious — 658–659
Reconstruction
of reality on the side of the scholar 413 (VAN DER LEEUW)
Recurrence
LANG: test of — criticized 224
TYLOR: theory of — and survival 30
Reduction and scientism 496 (WACH)
Reflective consciousness
battle of — 569 (RADIN)
Religio naturalis 7
See also under: Natural religion
Religion(s)
as a special subject of research, and motivations for taking it so 52–64,
379–524; as a reality in itself 54; as a value category 53–54; as the first
stage of man's mental development 29; basic — 486 (FRICK); concept
of — is part of us 3–4; critique of — 18; definition of —, *see under:*
Definition of religion; essence of —, *see under:* Essence of religion; historical
existence of — 9; new approaches to — VII; occurrence of certain elements
in certain — 39; origin of —, *see under:* Origin of religion; plurality of
— 29; scholar's notion of — 4; scholarly image of — or religion in the
West 74; survivals of ancient — 13; widening perspective on — related
to changing attitudes toward — 76
BACHOFEN: profound influence of — on the life of nations and lever of
all civilization 119–120; — debased by wrong interpretations of students
of antiquity 121
BERGER: permanent tension between the spiritual and the historical
elements in — 73, 666; — assumes that nature is not the same as
reality and that there is something supernatural 664; — and religions
665; unity of — 665; phenomenological research in the field of —
664–666
CHANTEPIE DE LA SAUSSAYE: science of religion presupposes unity of — in
its various forms 16, 109; — as an inward relation to something
absolute 16, 110; many objects of — but the only real object of — is
God 16, 112–113; subjective and objective side of — 108; outward
forms of — to be explained from inward processes 109–110; man's
desire to attain certain benefits in his — through representative acts

Scholarly study of religion
 demands on the — 61, *471–478* (HEILER); philosophical problems of
 approach in the — 77
Scholarship
 MñLLER: rules of critical — 93
 WACH: — should now concentrate upon the essential and the necessary 508
Science
 DELITZSCH: traditional religion and modern — 24
 FREUD: — not to be limited by religion and philosophy 365–366; — works
  slowly but is solid 370–371
 HEILER: each — has presuppositions 471
 VAN DER LEEUW: eschatology of — 410; — as hermeneutics 417
 RENAN: — does not imply anti-religious proselytism 130; — should not
  be under the censure of a power which has nothing scientific about it 131
 TIELE: characteristics constituting a — 97; genuine — 99; — has the
  right to investigate religion 99
Science of language
 MÜLLER: — compared with the science of religion 86–87, 89, 91, 92–93
 TIELE: 97
Science of religion
 CHANTEPIE DE LA SAUSSAYE: *23–31, 105–113;* three conditions of the
  foundation of a true — realized *since 1850* 16, 106–108, difference
  between — and theology 16, 109; — different from science of the
  Christian religion 109; — assumes an independent existence 105–106;
  — is possible thanks to discoveries made by empirical disciplines 107;
  foundation of chairs for the — 108; object of the — is the essence
  and manifestations of religion 16, 108; — consist of philosophy and
  history of religion, which are closely connected 108; — presupposes
  unity of religion in its various forms 16, 109; history of civilization
  essential to the — 106–107; — useful for missionaries 109; — implies
  study of the relationship between religious ritual, doctrine, and
  feeling in past and present 110–111
 DURKHEIM: — starts with concrete reality but needs hypothesis for interpretation 304
 FREUD: consequences of the — for one's attitude to the problem of religion
  50, 363–364
 FRICK: is — as typology beyond the dilemma of either historical-philological research or philosophical deduction 486
 VAN GENNEP: aims of the — 43, 300; — characterized by the systematic
  comparison of facts of a religious nature and by their classification
  288; — threatened by a movement wanting to deflect the — to a
  kind of endless road, in order to appropriate it 288; — uses the general
  comparative method adapted to its own needs as the ethnographical
  method 289–293; takes part in the universal battle of theories and
  ideas 289–290; — attempts general syntheses on the basis of well-
  defined similarities and differences 290; — in the past seperate investigations with tendencies towards over-simplification conducted
  without previous organization of work 291–292; — did not yet transpose study methods from other areas of science 295–296; — is more
  than history of religion 300
 KRAEMER: presuppositions and limits of the — 73, *644–653*

47*

Theologia naturalis 533 (JUNG)
 See also under: Natural theology
Theological apparatus and machinery
 similarity of the forms of — in East and West 457 (R. OTTO)
Theological Encyclopedia
 place of the general science of religion in the — 109 (CHANTEPIE DE LA
 SAUSSAYE)
Theological phenomenology as science of religion 57, 407–408 (VAN DER LEEUW)
Theology
 KRAEMER: — and philosophy of religion 648
 VAN DER LEEUW: phenomenological — between historical — and systematic
 — 407–408; — and phenomenology 407–408, 421, 423–424
 MÜLLER: conservative character of — 93
 OTTO, R.: — superseding the mythical 450–452
 SCHWEITZER: — and the critical study of the life of Jesus 176–179
 SÖDERBLOM: difference between Christian — and religious research 55, 387
 TROELTSCH: — and the historical study of religion 48
 WACH: — and comparative study of religion 493–494; — and study of
 religion 509
Theories
 CHANTEPIE DE LA SAUSSAYE: — as preliminary classifications 15, 105
 NILSSON: — and hypotheses as children of their age 614–615
 SCHMIDT: successive — of the history of religion 267–271
Thinking
 CHANTEPIE DE LA SAUSSAYE: relationship between religious — and acting
 110–111
 OTTO, W. F.: rational and magical modes of — and perceiving 623–624;
 thoughts concerning the world born among rare and spiritually gifted
 men 626–627
 RADIN: man from the beginning capable of discursive — 583
Thought
 damage done by religious inhibition of — 370 (FREUD)
Total social phenomena
 study of religious as — 45–46 (MAUSS)
Totemism
 DURKHEIM: 45, 318–322, 596–599, 645; — a cult more fundamental and
 more primitive than animism and naturism 318; advantages of the
 study of Australian — 320–321
 FRAZER: 34–36, 250–252, 548
 VAN GENNEP: 43
 GOLDENWEISER: 39
 MACLENNAN: — as a form of religion 28
 MALINOWSKI: — and the sociological aspect of early faith 548–549
 SCHMIDT: theory of — 269–270
 RADCLIFFE-BROWN (DURKHEIM): social function of totemic rites 596–599
 ROBERTSON SMITH: theory of — and sacrifice 21
Traditional religion
 radical reinterpretation of the — of the West 76
Transcendent (The) 646, 651 (KRAEMER)
Transcendentalism (Emersonian) 562 (LOWIE)
Travel reports, value of — 7–8, 294

Index of Concrete Subjects*

* For an explanation of the organization of this Index, see pp. 675–676.

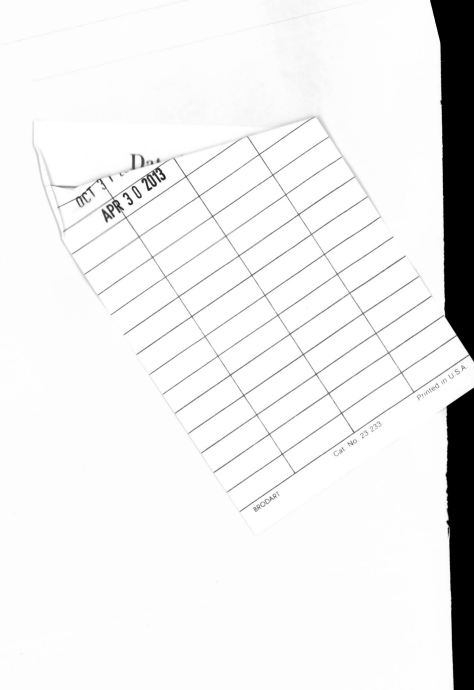